DISPOSED OF
BY LIBRARY
HOUSE OF LORDS

Foundations of the Planning Enterprise

Foundations of the Planning Enterprise

Critical Essays in Planning Theory: Volume 1

Edited by

Jean Hillier and Patsy Healey

University of Newcastle upon Tyne, UK

ASHGATE

© Jean Hillier and Patsy Healey 2008. For copyright of individual articles please refer to the Acknowledgements.

All rights reserved. No part of this publication may be reproduced, stored in a retrieval system or transmitted in any form or by any means, electronic, mechanical, photocopying, recording or otherwise without the prior permission of the publisher.

Wherever possible, these reprints are made from a copy of the original printing, but these can themselves be of very variable quality. Whilst the publisher has made every effort to ensure the quality of the reprint, some variability may inevitably remain.

Published by
Ashgate Publishing Limited
Gower House
Croft Road
Aldershot
Hampshire GU11 3HR
England

Ashgate Publishing Company
Suite 420
101 Cherry Street
Burlington, VT 05401-4405
USA

Ashgate website: http://www.ashgate.com

British Library Cataloguing in Publication Data
Critical essays in planning theory
    vol. 1: Foundations of the planning enterprise
    1. City planning 2. Regional planning
    I. Hillier, Jean II. Healey, Patsy
    307.1'2

Library of Congress Cataloging-in-Publication Date
Critical essays in planning theory / edited by Jean Hillier and Patsy Healey.
    p. cm.
 Includes bibliographical references and index.
 ISBN 13: 978-0-7546-2719-7 (alk. paper)
 1. City planning. 2. Regional planning. 3. Community development, Urban.
 I. Hillier Jean. II. Healey, Patsy.
HT166.C75 2008
307.1'216–dc22

                                                                        2007037444

ISBN: 978–0–7546–2719–7

Printed in Great Britain by TJ International Ltd, Padstow, Cornwall

Contents

PART III PLANNING AS RATIONAL SCIENTIFIC MANAGEMENT

Acknowledgements

The editors and publishers wish to thank the following for permission to use copyright material.

Copyright Clearance Center for the essays: Philip Selznick (1949), 'Introduction: TVA and Democratic Planning', in R.L. Beals, Franklin Fearing and W.S. Robinson (eds), *TVA and the Grass Roots*, Berkeley: University of California Press, pp. 3–16; Barclay M. Hudson with comments by Thomas D. Galloway and Jerome L. Kaufman (1979), 'Comparison of Current Planning Theories: Counterparts and Contradictions', *Journal of the American Planning Association*, **45**, pp. 387–98; Paul Davidoff (1965), 'Advocacy and Pluralism in Planning', *Journal of the American Institute of Planners*, **31**, pp. 331–38; John W. Dyckman (1966), 'Social Planning, Social Planners, and Planned Societies', *Journal of the American Institute of Planners*, **32**, pp. 66–76; Robert A. Beauregard (1991), 'Without a Net: Modernist Planning and the Postmodern Abyss', *Journal of Planning Education and Research*, **10**, pp. 189–94; Sherry R. Arnstein (1969), 'A Ladder of Citizen Participation', *Journal of the American Institute of Planners*, **35**, pp. 216–24.

Elsevier for the essays: Patsy Healey, Glen McDougall and Michael J. Thomas (1982), 'Theoretical Debates in Planning: Towards a Coherent Dialogue', *Planning Theory Prospects for the 1980s*, Oxford: Pergamon Press, pp. 5–22; Paul Davidoff and Thomas A. Reiner (1973), 'A Choice Theory of Planning', in Andreas Faludi (ed.), *A Reader in Planning Theory*, Oxford: Pergamon Press, pp. 11–39. Copyright © 1973 Elsevier; John Friend and Allen Hickling (1987), 'Foundations', in John Friend and Allen Hickling, *Planning Under Pressure: The Strategic Choice Approach*, Oxford: Butterworth-Heinmann, pp. 1–26. Copyright © 1987 Elsevier; Andreas Faludi (1973), 'What is Planning Theory?', in Andreas Faludi , *A Reader in Planning Theory*, Oxford: Pergamon Press, pp. 1–10. Copyright © 1973 Elsevier.

Faber and Faber Limited for the essay: J. Brian McLoughlin (1969), 'The Guidance and Control of Change: Physical Planning as the Control of Complex Systems', in J. Brian McLoughlin, *Urban and Regional Planning: A Systems Approach*, London: Faber and Faber, pp. 75–91.

Andreas Faludi (1973), 'The Rationale of Planning Theory', in Andreas Faludi, *Planning Theory*, Oxford: Pergamon Press, pp. 35–53. Copyright © 1973 Andreas Faludi.

Pion Limited for the essay: O. Yiftachel (1989), 'Towards a New Typology of Urban Planning Theories', *Environment and Planning B: Planning and Design*, **16**, pp. 23–39.

Princeton University Press for the essay: John Friedmann (1996), 'Two Centuries of Planning Theory: An Overview', in Seymour J. Mandelbaum, Luigi Mazza and Robert W. Burchell (eds), *Explorations in Planning Theory*, New Brunswick, NJ: Centre for Urban Policy Research, pp. 10–29.

Sage Publications, Inc. for the essay: Susan S. Fainstein (2000), 'New Directions in Planning Theory', *Urban Affairs Review*, **34**, pp. 451–78. Copyright © 2000 Sage Publications, Inc.

Springer for the essays: Aaron Wildavsky (1973), 'If Planning is Everything, Maybe it's Nothing', *Policy Sciences*, **4**, pp. 127–53; Horst W.J. Rittel and Melvin M. Webber (1973), 'Dilemmas in a General Theory of Planning', *Policy Sciences*, **4**, pp. 155–69.

Taylor and Francis Publishing for the essays: F.A. Hayek (1944), 'Planning and Democracy', in F.A Hayek, *The Road to Serfdom*, London: Routledge & Kegan Paul, pp. 42–53; Stephen V. Ward (2003), 'Re-examining the International Diffusion of Planning', in Robert Freestone (ed.), *Urban Planning in a Changing World: The Twentieth Century Experience*, London: E and FN Spon, pp. 40–60.

Every effort has been made to trace all the copyright holders, but if any have been inadvertently overlooked the publishers will be pleased to make the necessary arrangement at the first opportunity.

Introduction

Powerful theories re-direct us toward problems and issues we might otherwise have ignored – or from which we have been ideologically or methodologically distracted. (Forester, 1993, pp. 1–2)

The Aim of this Collection

Those who are involved in, or encounter, the planning field talk routinely about the challenge of relating 'theory' to 'practice', or ask questions about the concepts which have influenced the development of the ideas and practices of planning. However, despite influential reviews of planning debates over the years, it is not so easy to access the material which those discussing issues in planning theory refer to, or to position them in relation to the development of ideas in the field. The traditions of debate in planning are discussed in different ways in planning programmes. Not all programmes include required modules in planning theory and not all those interested in the planning field have studied on a planning education programme. So, even those with a formal planning education are not necessarily aware of the debates within planning theory. In this three-volume collection, we seek to provide, in an accessible form, important and influential essays from the twentieth-century debates and to help readers 'position' the debates being undertaken in and between these essays. Some essays also give an idea of current inspirations, which give a flavour of how ideas about the nature, purpose and practices of planning may evolve in the future. The collection is organized on a broadly chronological basis, with each volume containing three strands of discussion. In Part I of this volume, we introduce the field with essays that review its development and suggest 'navigation devices' through its various strands and debates. In this overall Introduction, we present our own overview, not as a review of different strands but of issues which repeatedly arise in the field as a whole.

Planning Theory as an Intellectual Field

The field of 'planning theory' centres around debates and 'conversations' (Rorty, 1980) among those interested in the ideas and concepts which inform, could and/or should inform, the practical activity of planning. It emerged as a recognizable academic focus, in the sense of contributions which built on or cross-referred to each other, in the mid-twentieth century (Friedmann, 1987; Reade, 1987). Prior to this, planning 'theories' existed primarily as proposals for how societies and cities should develop, or could be developed, as part of political programmes or professional practices rather than through well-argued academic debate. Some have argued that the failures of planning as practised have arisen due to the lack of adequate theorization (Reade, 1987). However, although some have understood 'planning theory' as a type of general practice model or set of rules by which practice should be performed, or as some kind of linear process whereby a planning theory is first articulated by academics and then put into practice, the relation between how people have imagined and debated the idea of planning and its various forms as practices has always been a complex, interactive one. Debates about the nature, purpose and practice of planning – the core of the planning theory field – are more like a kind of philosophical grounding, infused with conceptions of the nature of societies, cities, regions and places, of what governments should do to shape futures and how they should act.

In these debates, two dimensions through which the focus of the field has been articulated have been in continual dialectical tension. One concerns the substantive content of the field and the other concerns what planning consists of as a process. The substantive dimension has focused variously on the organization of societies, on the development of cities, regions and places, on the promotion of particular qualities in societies and cities, and sometimes on all three. The process dimension has also varied in focus, from a narrow preoccupation with technical management to the encouragement of intelligent, deliberative communities of inquiry. Critical debate in the planning field has sometimes asserted the primacy of one dimension over the other, or of one focus over another. Yet these polarizing debates are regularly drawn back into arguments about the interaction between content and process, between appreciation of place dynamics and qualities, and the governance dynamics in which places are situated.

A further dimension also generates continual tensions in the field. For many, planning is a practical project for improving conditions in societies and cities. In this view, planning theory and practice is deeply committed to normative agendas about how societies and cities should be. But others have criticized such commitment for its naïve idealism and potentially dangerous consequences. Instead, such critics argue, much more attention should be paid to analysing the dynamics through which societies and cities evolve, to identifying where planning activity might be positioned in these dynamics and to anticipating the effects such activity might have. Once again, the relation between these normative commitments and analytical emphases in planning theory debates has been a complex one, with many participants recognizing the significance of both.

There have been several attempts to produce chronologies of the evolution of the field of planning theory. Such chronologies are themselves structured by the position that authors take with respect to the above dimensions. Ideas about the physical planning of towns and regions were vigorously promoted as industrialization processes in the nineteenth century spurred massive urbanization worldwide. Ideas about planning societies and about appropriate governance processes for such endeavours emerged in the first part of the twentieth century, as the complexity of governance for complex urbanizing societies became ever more evident. The chronologies themselves have been structured by how authors have positioned themselves in relation to the dimensions mentioned above. The essays in Part I of this volume provide chronologies and/or 'maps' of the field. In Part II we provide examples of ideas being promoted in the first half of the twentieth century.

Initially, as with other knowledge 'disciplines', those authors advocating or engaging in planning as an activity drew on all kinds of inspiration – from utopias to analyses of particular conditions, from ideologies to the practices of urban development and management. By the mid-twentieth century, however, several strands of debate began to intertwine in various 'nodes' in intellectual networks, such as particular university departments, or through conference events, edited collections and academic journals. A key nodal meeting-point in the 1940s was the University of Chicago, where ideas about societal management, drawing on US 'New Deal' social and regional development programmes, encountered conceptions of 'management science' and its application to public and private administration (Friedmann, 1973; Faludi, 1987). These ideas were strongly shaped by a Keynesian conception of the role of the state in developing the conditions for a mixed, capitalistic economy in a democratic society, paralleling European strategies for developing 'welfare states'. Planning, in this conception, was understood as a key mechanism for articulating future development trajectories, for nations, regions and cities. Later, this approach was to be characterized by geographer David Harvey (1989) as 'managerialist'.

This focus, however, evolved tangentially to, and sometimes confrontationally with, two other strands of debate about the nature and role of planning. One paralleled the Chicago School ideas, but had its home in primarily European socialist politics and analyses. It built on the critique of capitalist society as crisis-riven, founded on an exploitative relation between capitalist entrepreneurs and the labouring classes. This conception developed from the powerful analyses by Marx, Engels and others of the inhumane industrial conditions which developed in Europe in the nineteenth and early twentieth centuries. It was given political force by the experiences of repeated economic depressions which made people's lives even more difficult and precarious. Instead of the Keynesian idea of managing markets to reduce crisis potentialities and the development of welfare provision to avoid the sufferings of those most at risk from 'market failures', the socialist agenda recommended the replacement of the economics of capitalism by state-run economic processes. The idea of planning was promoted as the mechanism by which resources could be allocated between and within spheres of state activity, in relation to development objectives. The legitimacy of 'planned societies' was derived from the assumption that the 'state' was 'of' the people and therefore would provide 'for' the people, in ways which 'the market' did not. Although we now know more about how the politics and practices of states can subvert that idea, it remained an important reference point in the mid-twentieth century for those authors who criticized the way in which 'mixed' economy states (combining 'state' and 'market' processes in some form) actually developed (see Volume 2,(Hillier and Healey 2008a), Part I).

A further strand centred on the practices of 'building cities', of physical urban development. This strand had its nodal home in the networks of architects, engineers and surveyors who exchanged ideas, techniques and exemplars on an international basis. Such exchanges were enabled in part by the opportunities provided by the networks of the imperial states of the early twentieth century, but also by both professionals and activists who recognized the particular challenges facing the rapid urbanization being experienced in many parts of the world as industrialization took hold. Ideas about clean, healthy, aesthetically-pleasing and habitable cities emerged in these debates, in opposition to the 'city of dreadful night'– of pollution, poverty and uncontrollable polities – as many described the emerging urban complexes (Hall, 1988). The professional networks of city builders became increasingly consolidated into the planning dimension of the 'modern' movement, producing what became the CIAM (Charter of Athens) declaration (Gold, 1997).[1] But challenging these debates were

---

[1]   CIAM, the *Congrès Internationale d'Architecture Moderne*, was founded in 1928 and was a major advocate for modernist ideas in architecture and planning.

always alternatives, relevant to how people actually lived and moved through places, from the anarchist search for smaller-scale, self-regulating communities to practical ideas about new town management (Hall, 1988; Ward, 1994, 2002). Issues of the relative importance of 'state' and 'market' provision were of less importance in these debates, which instead focused, if in often determinist ways, on the relation between the physical environment and how people could, and should, live.

Debates about the forms of societal development and their relation to urban development were not entirely new, however. The general revival of knowledge about the ancient 'classical' Greek and Roman world in European Renaissance and Enlightenment thought allowed proponents of the planning idea in the early twentieth century to look back into history for their inspiration.[2] But the twentieth-century development of the planning idea has been different, partly because of the scale of scientific, technological and industrial innovation which has changed both how economies operate and how cities develop, partly because of the huge increases and spatial shifts in population and wealth produced by these developments, and partly because of the steady global shift from primarily rural to primarily urban societies.[3] The idea of planning, whether of societal development or of urban development, was closely linked in the first part of the twentieth century to the search for ways of imposing some kind of order, or stabilizing force, in rapidly changing conditions (Boyer, 1983; Huxley, 2007).

Thus, as with the practices of planning, debates about planning ideas and concepts are not conducted among a closed enclave of dedicated scholars, although sometimes it might seem like this. Instead, 'planning theory' discussions are situated in the currents of prevailing intellectual environments and in relation to lived experiences, political projects and particular practices. This 'situatedness' of planning ideas and concepts has itself been an important issue of debate among planning theorists, especially in more recent years. Once considered as somehow 'outside' the messy flow of the world, advising political leaders how best to stride forward and create futures, planners are now much more likely to be presented as within the flow of processes through which the future is emerging (see below, and the essays presented in Volume 3 (Hillier and Healey, 2008b)). In addition, the increasing internationalization of knowledge about planning ideas and experiences has brought about a more acute realization of the way in which the particularities of context shape how planning is understood, how it is practised and what its effects have been and might be.

This recognition of the situatedness of planning theory debates also combines with an openness to influences from other fields of intellectual inquiry. Those making contributions to these debates have been inspired by ideas from the fields of economics, political science and management, from geography, sociology and anthropology, from philosophy and the humanities, and from architecture, engineering, operations research and systems science. As a result, the field of planning theory, while having the qualities of a 'disciplinary conversation' in itself, is also multidisciplinary in many of its inspirations, referents and styles of argumentation. Moreover, perhaps even more pronounced than this multidisciplinary character has been the field's openness to the intellectual waves and political movements

---

[2]   In the Greek 'polis', the idea of city, society and politics was combined into an integrated concept, for free males at least! This is reflected in the family of words we now use – polity, politics, policy, and 'polis'.

[3]   Fifty per cent of the world's population are reported to live in urban areas as of 2007.

which have swept across the social sciences since the mid-twentieth century, from systems thinking in the 1960s, to structuralist political economy in the 1970s, to the postmodernist and other 'posts' of the 1980s and 1990s, the 'cultural turn' and post-structuralism in the 1990s and the interest in 'complexity' in the 2000s. This openness creates huge challenges in 'reading' planning theory contributions, as authors rarely have space to explain adequately how their ideas and vocabularies derive from these 'waves', and there are all kinds of time-lag effects, as foundational ideas of one group of authors are rediscovered and given a different colouring by a later group.[4] Terms rarely have stable meanings and continually need to be located in the 'thought-world' from which their authors are writing. Yet the 'porosity' of the field – its very openness – gives planning theory a capaciousness[5] which helps to create sensitivity to the multiple dimensions of the manifestations of planning as a practised activity.

These qualities of porosity and capaciousness are especially important at the present time, when planning concepts and debates are diffusing widely across the world. This increasingly highlights the extent to which ideas, such as those about how cities and societies should develop, and about what constitutes good governance, are located in particular institutional contexts and intellectual traditions. The planning idea, and planning theory, is primarily Western in its origins and formulations, though infused in many other parts of the world, since the nineteenth century, with practice experiences primarily associated with the colonial activities of imperial states (al-Sayyad, 1992; Driver, 1992; Gunder Frank, 1967; Legg, 2007; Perera, 2002a, 2005; Rabinow, 1989). It has also had other biases which have been underlined in recent years as Western democracies have struggled to overcome their own paternalist, bourgeois traditions of politics and government, in which the management of society was seen as the preserve of well-educated men (Perera, 2002b). These biases have rendered invisible many potential contributions to planning thought by making it hard for women, those from lower classes and those from groups marginalized by race, ethnicity or particular histories from having a voice in public affairs (Stoler, 1995) and in academic literature. We try to correct these biases to an extent in the selections we have made, but cannot counteract them entirely, although there are some significant shifts underway (see the selections on the theme of diversity in Volume 2, Part II and on recent post-structuralist work in Volume 3, Part III (Hillier and Healey 2008 a and b)).

These shifts reflect the increasing attention being paid over the past 20 years, in public policy in many Western countries and in debates within planning theory, to bringing these marginalized voices from the background to the foreground. In turn, the notion of a society of a plurality of interest groups, as promoted in accounts of the United States in the mid-twentieth century, has been expanded into a much more complex conception of plurality and multiplicity. Increasing acceptance of multiple ways of seeing and understanding the world – that is, a cultural pluralism – offers potential for the recognition of tension and conflicts not just between groups over the distribution of resources and opportunities within a polity,

---

[4]   For example, French social thinker Michel Foucault had a considerable influence in continental European thinking on planning in the 1970s and 1980s before it was taken up in Anglo-American discussion, and ideas about 'complexity' were being actively discussed in relation to planning work in the 1980s (notably at the 1986 Planning Theory Conference at Torino, Italy), before surfacing vigorously again in the 2000s.

[5]   This idea was suggested to us by Niraj Verma, in a comment on the Introduction to Volume 2, Part III (Hillier and Healey, 2008a).

but also between conceptions of the qualities of a place and a polity. This opens up questions about what counts as valid 'knowledge' and what grounds judgements about the legitimacy of planning actions. Such appreciation of multicultural diversity has had a major impact, not merely on contemporary discussions in the fields of political science and public policy (Benhabib, 1992; Connolly, 2005; Young, 1990), but also in the planning field, with a particular emphasis on what is involved in plural coexistence in the shared spaces of daily life (Healey, 2006; Hillier, 2006; Sandercock, 2003). Thus the 'grand themes' of politics – who has power over whom, how rights and responsibilities are distributed, how governments are legitimated, whose 'voices' count – are re-examined in the planning field in the practices of urban place management and in strategy-making processes (see Volume 3 (Hillier and Healey, 2008b)).

Planning Theory and the 'Planning Idea'

Debates in planning theory thus range across a wide spectrum, from considerations of the micro-management of urban neighbourhoods to philosophical questions about what people are like (our subjectivities and identities), what and whose arguments are 'legitimate' and how we should live in collectivities/polities (how we relate to and recognize 'others'). What holds these issues together in the development of planning ideas is a commitment to focus on the relation between theory and practice. Those involved in practices which claim to realize planning as an 'activity' are called on to articulate and to justify what the nature of the activity is and should be. Those developing ideas about the nature of the activity are pressed to consider the implication of such ideas for the practice of the activity of 'planning'. We discuss this below as a major theme flowing through planning theory debates.

The commitment to an interactive relation between theory and practice is continually under challenge for two reasons. First, it often seems as if the gap between the 'theory' people and 'practitioners' is unbridgeably large, especially when some theorists move towards the seemingly more abstract issues raised in some other domain of the social sciences and the humanities, and all are rebuked for paying too little attention to each other. Second, what constitutes 'planning activity' is itself an unclear and continually shifting concept. Is it the planning of societal development, or the development and delivery of any public policy programme, or is it the planning of places, of cities and regions? And, whatever the focus, what is the contribution carried by the planning 'idea'? Does it lie in the approach to government – a process idea of good governance in general, or, more specifically, of open, transparent, policy-driven government? Or does it lie in the values about society which it promotes – in considerations of social justice or cohesion, of environmental quality and sustainability, of economic vitality and 'competitiveness'?[6] Or does the heart of the planning idea lie in how these sets of values are combined? And what happens when the planning idea is promoted in situations where such values are themselves marginalized? How then does, could and should 'planning as an activity' proceed? Are there any particular 'instruments and techniques' of the craft of planning, which can carry the planning idea forward, whatever its specific content, to challenge practices which show little attention to the values of the planning idea? Is a 'plan'

---

[6]   Many analyses of contemporary planning practices focus on the struggle between a prevailing 'neo-liberal' ideology which stresses the promotion of 'economic competitiveness' and other policy discourses which give more attention to social justice and/or environmental sustainability.

one such instrument? Are evaluation and assessment techniques another? Or does the heart of planning lie in the adoption of a particular process, whether a set of rational steps to decision-making or an interactive, collaborative process? And where does the legitimacy for promoting such instruments, techniques and processes come from?

These difficult questions are the subject of continual debate in the planning theory field, as the essays in these volumes richly illustrate. How they are treated and the conclusions arrived at are in part related to the disciplinary backgrounds of the proponents, each providing different vocabularies and reference points. But what seems to be diffuse is held together by a concern for the 'governance of place' or, as described by Friedmann (1987), the guidance of societal development, whether of small communities or large national and transnational polities. The planning idea as practised thus involves the attempt to manage societal development in places in ways which promote the 'betterment', however understood, of the human condition as experienced through time and as lived in a wider world of human and non-human relations and forces.

From the perspective of the twenty-first century, planning theorists and historians tend to provide accounts of the history of planning ideas which emphasize major shifts in understanding. The ambition of planning societal development in an integrated way at all levels of the nation-state has, in the face of recognition of the complexity of governance processes and transformative initiatives,[7] given way to a more humble ambition of contributing to shaping emergent urban and regional dynamics and place qualities. The idea that the 'planner', as some kind of trusted technocrat above and apart from the messy bustle of the world, could articulate programmes and plans which could 'order' what would otherwise be the chaos of unfettered and unjust market processes has given way, first, to the idea of planning as more of a 'guiding hand' or a corrective 'steering' mechanism, and, second, to conceptions of how to recognize, 'shape' and manage non-linear, unpredictable emergent processes. The conception of 'planning practice' – planning as an activity – has shifted from that of a government activity pursued through formally constituted administrative structures and legally authoritative, enforceable plans and standards to a recognition of practice as actively constituted by groups of people in interaction with each other: of planners continually faced with complex, ethically-freighted judgements about who to listen to, what knowledge to draw on, what roles to enact and how to perform them in specific situations. We chart these shifts in these three volumes of essays and show how they relate to wider intellectual and political debates.

In the next section, we develop our introduction to the debates and questions that flow through the volumes by looking in more detail at some of the recurrent, overlapping themes with which the essays engage. Some of these debates have been introduced already. Most connect to broader intellectual debates but have been developed within the planning field with particular specificities. There are some which have emerged from within the field itself. But they all provide insight into what it means to promote planning as an idea, what it means as an activity and the complex ethical and performative dilemmas of what is involved in being 'a planner' and doing 'planning work'.

---

[7]   These days, also, there are major questions about the nature and role of the 'nation-state form' as a form of government organization.

Recurrent Themes

Theory and Practice

One of the significant contributions of the planning field to knowledge generally is its continual engagement with the interaction between theory and practice. At one level, this interaction is very specific. Practitioners involved in designing and regulating major development projects may look for principles to justify claims – for example, that providing such and such a design or mix of facilities is 'a public benefit' or that demanding this or that contribution from a developer is for 'the public interest'. Such claims open up questions about the meaning of 'public', 'benefit', 'interest' and to whom. This leads towards an engagement in planning theory with debates in law and philosophy. Planning theorists may also engage in critical debate about why the practice of development projects is constructed so that such claims arise. What is the justification for a 'negotiated' approach to designing development projects? Could other practices be imagined, what would such practices look like, and with what implications for whom?

What, then, is 'planning theory' for? It may be thought of in the metaphor of a 'template' for action, as an *a priori* source of principles and criteria for practice. Or it may be seen as some kind of abstract ideal, of a good planning process or a well-designed city, or as a basis for evaluating the messy worlds of actualities. Such abstract principles have been heavily criticized for failing to connect with the social forces through which actual societal and urban change happens, thereby unthinkingly promoting particular agendas (see the essays in Volume 2, Parts I and II and Volume 3, Part III (Hillier and Healey, 2008a and b) in particular). Such critical arguments call attention to the ways in which social groups may harness abstract planning theory ideas to justify and legitimize particular, tangible programmes. Concepts of planning as a rational process (see Part III of this volume) and as a collaborative process (see Volume 3, Part I (Hillier and Healey 2008b) have both been used in this way.

A different argument locates the role of planning theory firmly within the challenges of practices. Hoch summarizes a pragmatic conception of theory, conceiving 'planning theory ... as a kind of practical reasoning rather than a kind of template or primal rationale (2007, p. 279). Forester (1989) argues that planners look to theories for help in expanding their understanding of particular situations. They learn especially from the way in which other practitioners have 'theorized' about their practices. This emphasizes that theory may come from practice, as well as being available as a resource for practice (see also Throgmorton, 1996). Such an approach grounds the enterprise of 'planning theory' firmly in the world of planning practitioners and others involved in the enterprise of societal guidance or place governance. Its justification lies in the inspirations and instrumentalities offered to the flow of practice. Its consolidation into propositions, inspirational narratives and vocabularies which give coherence to a practice, and into techniques to use in specific situations, enables flows of learning to expand from a particular site to encourage and inform others elsewhere.

The above arguments reflect different philosophical orientations. The first, often associated with logical positivism, grounds the planning enterprise in 'objective' science or in general philosophical principles which transcend the particularities of specific practices. In this conception, practice is, or should be, the application of philosophically and scientifically grounded general principles to specific situations. The relation between theory and practice is conceived in a linear way, moving from theory to practice. This positivist conception dominated the development of planning theory in the mid-twentieth century, emphasizing abstract ideals of city form and policy processes, grounded either in unifying transcendent principles to which human societies should seek to conform and/or in the existence of scientific laws which could be discovered to guide human behaviour. Planning theorists were encouraged to discover ideal forms and to develop logically deductive processes for arriving at strategies to achieve pre-set goals. The role of planning activity, in this view, was to correct 'pathologies' which could develop when societal development or urbanization processes moved away from the trajectories indicated by such principles and laws. Such a perspective provided legitimacy for a planning project of 'ordering' society and cities according to pre-existing goals and criteria.

But, as the essays in Parts II and III of this volume show, such a conception was not the only inspiration for the ideas being debated about the 'good city' and the 'rational planning process'. Many proponents were also influenced by a more pragmatist and social constructivist conception of the relation of knowledge to action. In this conception, principles to guide action are not developed *a priori*, but rather in the flow of action relevant to the particularities of circumstances. Understandings, values and 'goals' are not to be derived from 'pure forms', analytical logic or scientific 'law', but from continuous socially situated activity in probing inquiry, collective sense-making and the testing out of ideas to see if they 'work' and mobilize attention. Planning theorists are encouraged to enhance the critical sensibilities of those involved in planning as a practical activity, suggesting exploratory questions with which to probe understandings and sense-making processes, and offering 'alerts' to issues that may lie behind the visible and noisy flow of present action, or which may be looming over the horizon. It is this view of the theory–practice relation which increasingly came to the fore in the later part of the twentieth century. The shift in conception can be seen in a revival of interest in the pragmatist tradition, through the work of John Forester and others (see Volume 2 (Hillier and Healey 2008a), Part III) and in the opening up of a range new ideas presented in Volume 3 (Hillier and Healey 2008b).

Knowing about Places

What, then, is distinctive about the knowledge which is mobilized in planning activity and where does this come from? What, specifically, is the 'substance' of a planner's knowledge and skill? There are two dimensions to this question. One relates to content – what those involved in planning activity need to know in order to guide societal development and place development. This content draws on the knowledge available in the social science disciplines which analyse societal development processes and urban and regional dynamics, as well as on the sciences of natural and physical processes as these affect environmental qualities and dynamics. Within these discussions there are critical debates about how to understand place qualities and spatiality and about what constitutes 'development'. However, those who view planning as an activity within the flow of practice also stress other sources of knowledge and insight, particularly those generated by experience and by interactive creativity. This highlights the second dimension of the challenge of 'knowing about places', which relates to what counts as 'knowledge'. What does it mean to 'know about' something? Whose 'knowledge' counts?

Debates in both dimensions once again link back to broad philosophical questions about ontology (about existence, 'being' and identity) and about epistemology (about knowledge). Is identity to be associated with the image of the 'atomistic' individual, with pre-formed values and preferences, celebrated in the neoclassical economics tradition? Or is identity always forged in social contexts which shape values and commitments? When 'social groups' are recognized in debates about place qualities or societal direction, is this a 'pluriverse' of groups of individuals who acknowledge similarities in their preferences? Or does it mean recognition of a diversity of social contexts in which a sense of self and values is forged – recognition of multidimensional diversity? Is the knowledge which counts that created by the search for 'scientifically objective' laws or does it centre on the search for meanings, metaphors, analogies and similarities?

Such questions about ontology and epistemology, subjectivity, identity and knowledge forms have recurred in debates about understanding places and mobilizing knowledge. Are places to be understood as physical objects, which can be described as discrete entities side-by-side as on a map? Or are they places of social dwelling and flow? Is space just an inactive surface on which objects are arranged? Or is it an active force, which shapes what evolves? Is a 'place' an inert thing, or can it 'act'? What constitutes 'development' which attends to the spatiality of relations and the qualities of places? How far can 'places' be made? To what spatialities should those involved in planning activity pay attention? It is generally assumed that, through professional experience and education, those who act in an expert capacity as planners should have some awareness of the debates about these questions. The early twentieth-century architects, engineers and others who promoted planning as city development were particularly interested in regional development (see Part II of this volume). The issue of place quality recurs in the work of the critical political economists (see Volume 2 (Hillier and Healey, 2008b), Part I) and in the discussions of networks and place-as-flow in Volume 3 (Hillier and Healey, 2008b). How planning theorists and advocates have understood place quality, spatiality and development has had a considerable impact on whether planners are seen as master-builders, regulators or strategic shapers of the ongoing flow of place development activity.

John Friedmann (1987) describes planning as the application of knowledge to public problems. One dimension he has in mind is analytical capability, which emphasizes that assertions about 'what is' should be grounded in evidence and logic, and validated by some social process of knowledge confirmation. This provides a critical angle, reinforcing Reade's (1987) general critique of the theoretical deficiency of the planning enterprise, which generates practice techniques with little grounding in analysis and testing. The movement to provide indicators of policy performance, for example, has been described as a 'practice myth' in search of a theory (Sawicki, 2002). But what actually provides the grounding and 'evidence' for such analysis and testing? Is it 'data' gathered by scientifically validated methods? Or is it experiential knowledge, collected by opinion surveys, or by getting 'stakeholders' to tell their stories? How far are systematized and analytical knowledges able to bring to light the issues and values which come to count in an episode of planning activity? How much is hidden below the surface in 'taken-for-granted' assumptions and beliefs? How and when should these 'tacit' knowledges and understandings be brought to the surface? When might such 'excavation' of a range of stakeholders' knowledges be therapeutic, and when dangerous and destructive? Issues such as these underline the power dynamics which lie in the mobilization of knowledge in the course of planning activity and in the ways in which claims about knowledge perform in challenges to the legitimacy of planning arguments and policies.

Contextualizing Planning Activity

The philosophical shift towards attention to 'practices' raises important questions about the contextual contingency of planning activity. Is it still possible to consider 'planning activity' and 'the planner' as having some kind of *a priori* meaning? Or can the meaning of both the activity and the role of specific actors within it only be grasped in specific actualizations? Is there some way of classifying contingencies and contexts, so that 'best-practice' strategies can be applied appropriately? Or should each context be treated as a unique conjunction, to be grasped through the skills of anthropological sensitivity or the techniques of Foucauldian genealogy, 'contemporary history' or novelistic narrative?

Mid-twentieth-century planners were much criticized for their assumptions that particular solutions were generally applicable. For instance, New Towns were designed using general principles, while ways of preparing comprehensive development plans were circulated around nations and around the world. In the UK, legislation in 1968 introduced the tool of a 'structure plan' (or general strategic plan) which had the same basic format for an inner district of the London metropolis and for the highlands of Scotland. Such an instrument was then 'applied' in different contexts – fitted onto the specifics of situations – leading to a practice in which the analysis of that context became 'formulaic', conducted in standard categories and modes of analysis. This approach tended, in particular, to miss the power dynamics of specific contexts. Local 'realities' would continually break in, disrupting processes and procedures towards the 'smooth' adoption of a plan, not only undermining the legitimacy of the plan itself but also leading to knowledge failures and potentially damaging consequences resulting from the planning activity.

This instrumental approach was a derivative of the 'external' perspective described above. Its justification was that the planning 'ideal' should lead the 'reality', legitimated formally by the adoption of the planning tool in legislation. However, if planning activity, including the formation of the legislation itself, is positioned inside, rather than outside, the flow of events, then a different approach to context is needed. What becomes acutely important in day-to-day planning activity is to discover the context, what matters, and to whom, what power struggles are underway, how a planning intervention might affect these, and how to behave ethically where choices are being – or should be – made over the allocation of resources, over the calling up of identities and over the types of knowledge that are validated. Such recognition has been emphasized in particular by the work of John Forester (1989, 1993, 1999) since the late 1970s (see Volume 2 (Hillier and Healey, 2008a), Part III and Volume 3 (Hillier and Healey, 2008b), Part I). But it is also unfolding in other contributions (see, for example, Campbell, 2006; Hillier, 2007).

This perspective emphasizes that planning activity involves making judgements about the appropriateness of proposed interventions in the flow of action. It suggests that all those involved are 'inside' politics and governance processes, not outside and apart from this messy business. Their activity is inherently 'political', in the sense that planning activity involves conscious action to affirm or transform established ways of organizing societies and cities. Some critics worry, however, that such a focus on the 'agency' of planning activity leads to a failure to grasp the broader forces which may be shaping contexts. An 'agency' may miss the structural forces which embed inequalities, or institutionalize prejudices and injustices. As a result, it may end up being too conservative and too little attentive to wider political forces and embedded power dynamics. This criticism has led some authors to give more attention to analysing the institutional dimensions of the contexts in which planning work is undertaken (see Volume 3 (Hillier and Healey, 2008b), Part II). Other authors have paid renewed attention to the ideals which could, or should, inform planning work, such as 'justice' (Fainstein, Chapter 9, this volume; Campbell, 2006) or 'sustainability principles' (Beatley, 1989; Owens and Cowell, 2002). Such contributions sometimes seem to return to a philosophical search for transcendent principles. Yet those who see planning activity as located in the ongoing flow of practices of various kinds, and who imagine futures as created through complex conjunctions with indeterminate trajectories and outcomes, also explore how collective action now can affect the flow of events in the future and how agents can act as mobilizers and catalysts for transformative action (see Volume 3 (Hillier and Healey, 2008b), Part III). These different viewpoints relate to differences in understanding the sources of 'theory'. Those seeking a stance 'outside' the flow of events look to principles of natural laws and transcendent values or ideal forms to provide a logic of what it is 'right' to do in a particular situation. Those who situate planning ideas and theories in the flow of action argue for the cultivation of the capacity for judgement about what might be 'appropriate' in a particular instance.

Planning, Governance and Power

In the last quarter of the twentieth century, analyses of planning activity, concerns about what it takes to 'implement' a planning policy and intellectual shifts in philosophy and the social sciences were all leading to much more attention being paid in planning theory to 'practices' and the power dynamics with which they are entangled. Planning is an inherently political project, in that it is concerned with shaping futures for collective benefits. This beams the 'practice' lens into the worlds of government, public policy-making and the relations between the state and the wider society. Three major themes emerged from this focus.

The first theme concerned the relation between planners and politicians. The essays in Part III of this volume present a neat distinction between the technocratic planner and the politicians who articulate the goals of the society. This conception was subsequently much criticized, with some authors arguing that it represented planners as mere lackeys of political programmes, while others thought that planners themselves were acting politically because their goals were inherently political, despite being wrapped up in technical values. Paul Davidoff (Chapter 20, this volume) famously argued that planners could not be free of values and therefore should align themselves with groups in society which held similar values, promoting a politics of pluralist interest-group argumentation. Others subsequently stressed that planning is inherently a value-laden and ideological project. Many authors, inspired by critical urban political economy in the 1970s, claimed that the social motivations linked to the planning project were merely a legitimating rhetoric for the promotion of the interests of capitalist market appropriations of land and property value (see Castells, 1977 and the essays in Volume 2 (Hillier and Healey, 2008a), Part I). These critics argued that planning activity should be informed by a more radical promotion of social justice (see Scott and Roweis, 1977; Fainstein and Fainstein, 1979; Harvey, 1985). In recent years, planning activity has still been critiqued by some for facilitating, rather than shaping and restricting, the free exploitation of land and property market value, although the critical standpoint now includes an argument to safeguard environmental sustainability or sustainable development, as well as social justice (Luke, 1999; Swyngedouw, Moulaert and Rodriguez, 2003).

The above ideological critique of the planning project undermines the separation of planners and politicians. The promotion and justification of planning activity can arise from many positions in a polity. The activity of planning, rather than being a technical exercise carried out for politicians by specially trained experts in defined 'offices', becomes an arena of struggle between competing forces and itself a force within that struggle. Contributions to planning theory are often criticized for failing to consider 'power' or for 'bracketing power' into the background of attention (Yiftachel, 1999; Yiftachel and Huxley, 2000). Such critiques leave open the question of what the mobilization of power means. Some see power in terms of the struggle between classes for control over the production and distribution of material resources. Others see power as embedded in the flow of action, in the micro-politics of the daily life of governance. Some contrast the planning idea of 'rationality' with the 'real rationality' of the power-play of politicians, or with projects to 'rationalize' or order social formations (Flyvbjerg, 1998). Still others see that rationalities are potentially multiple and are themselves expressions of, and carriers of, the power to shape emergent futures and highlight the struggles between different 'rationalities' for dominance in public policy arenas (Healey, 2006; Sandercock, 2003; Watson, 2003, Hillier, 2007). While some planning theorists have sought to work out ways of situating the work of planners in the micro-politics of specific practices, others have given more attention to how the institutional designs of planning systems, playing out in different contexts, have helped to construct practices with particular power dynamics embedded in them. In both, the limitation of conceptions of power to that of dominance, 'power over', is challenged by a parallel conception of power as energy, 'power to'. This leads some planning theorists to explore how prevailing power dynamics can be challenged and changed by the mobilization of transformative energies through building greater awareness of the dynamics shaping the futures of particular places (see, for example, Friedmann, 1987; Throgmorton, 1996; Flyvbjerg, 1998; Hillier, 2000; Healey, 2007).

These two broad themes are enriched by the third, which centres on giving much greater attention to the constitution and power of agency to mobilize action. Accounts of planning activity, such as those cited above, provide rich narratives of diverse actors, often called stakeholders, situated in complex social networks and interacting in various arenas in struggles over the future of places and over how to use the tools provided for government planning systems. In these accounts, generalized distinctions of roles and identities (for example, the planner, the politician, the resident, the developer) and generalized hypotheses about what 'planning' is and does dissolve in the face of the many different configurations which appear in practice. In this messy world of 'real-life' governance activity, issues about the legitimacy and accountability of planning activity and of those contributing to governance through their role as planners become extremely complex.

The Identity, Expertise and Ethics of 'the Planner'

Who, then, is 'the planner'? Is everyone involved in planning activity a planner, or does the term refer to those with particular positions which give defined roles and responsibilities? Or does it refer to those with particular professional training and experiences? In the past 100 years, the creation of planning systems to formalize planning activity, the formation of professional institutions to legitimate planning expertise and the provision of educational programmes to train planners have all tended to conflate planning activity with the performance of planning systems and the contribution of those trained as planning experts. The 'planner' has become a character in the cast list of contemporary societies, like doctors, architects, lawyers and social workers. However, as underlined in the discussion of the previous themes, planning activity draws in many 'characters' and involves all kinds of people in one way or another.

In the early twentieth century, the 'planner' was often presented as a 'leader', showing the way forward to politicians and administrators towards a progressive, enlightened world. Planners saw themselves as leaders of the 'modern movement' through their society-building and city-building ideas. Their legitimacy lay in their view of themselves as carriers of a society's best values, as technically translated into the work of building futures. By the mid-twentieth century, this evangelistic confidence had largely given way to a concept of the 'planner' as standing apart from the messy world of politics, yet constrained within the legitimacy of representative democracy via the role of politicians in setting goals. In this model it was possible to 'bracket off' power dynamics to create an 'action space' (Faludi, 1973) in which the technocratic work of planners could proceed. This view presented planners as technical translators of society's values and goals, legitimated by their expertise, combined with their accountability to politicians.

Since the 1980s planners are much more likely to be presented as playing all kinds of roles, depending on circumstances – mediators, regulators, facilitators, catalysts, mobilizers of attention, co-designers, analysts, advocates, experimenters (see, for example, Forester, 1999; Albrechts, 1999). In this view, their expertise lies partly in their knowledge of the multiple dimensions which affect societal and place development, but the breadth of such knowledge is such that no single expert could encompass it. This has led some to centre the expertise of the planner around skills in mobilizing all kinds of expertise and forms of knowledge in encounters through which strategies about how places could, and should, develop may be produced. However, without some grasp of the dynamics of place development in the context of societal development and of the institutional dynamics of specific situations, such process skills have difficulty in getting leverage. Arguments about the formation of specialist expertise in planning have thus formed a key arena in which the tension introduced at the start of this Introduction – between substantive content and process content – has been played out. The identity of the planner cannot be taken for granted. The 'characters' of planners, their relation to others involved in planning activity, the nature of their particular skills, values and ethical qualities will depend on both the actuality of the particular context in which planning activity is performed and the images and perceptions which others have of what a planner is and should be.

Those who believe in the possibility of a stance outside the flow of practical life emphasize that the values and legitimacy of the planner are derived externally to specific 'applications' of the planning idea. Those emphasizing a stance always situated in the flow of practices stress the active construction of legitimacy in practice contexts. Those seeking to 'stand outside', emphasize attention to generalized values abstracted from particular situations. Those 'moving from within' underline attention to ethical behaviour in a messy, unpredictable world. Those 'standing outside' imagine a planner with a 'kitbag' full of alternative plan ideas, or possible planning processes, of standard techniques for assessment and evaluation. Those who see planners as positioned within the flow of action imagine a planner's 'kitbag' full of practical wisdom, of sensibilities to feelings and cultural resonances; they envision the planner as intuitively perceptive, as well as analytically competent, with capacities for catalysing and mobilizing attention in some situations and critically facilitating the enterprise of collectivities where they already have momentum. These sensibilities require capabilities in critical reflexivity or what Schon (1983) called 'double-loop learning'. Such a stance demands acute sensitivity to the particularities of context, yet legitimates the planner's own experience as a contribution to what is debated and devised in specific situations.

In recent years it is this 'inside' view which has come to prominence in the planning theory literature (see Volume 3 (Hillier and Healey, 2008b)). In this view, planners are rarely leading (though they may do so), frequently unable to control (though they sometimes can), but yet have the capacity to shape futures. As a result, they carry ethical responsibilities for how they 'perform' in practice contexts. The images of the powerful planner as a leader or the expert planner as a technocrat nevertheless remain strongly present in popular conceptions of 'the planner', fed by experiences of governmental planning systems dominated by land-use regulation. Those trained as planners, in Western societies at least, tend to describe themselves in much more modest terms these days. But does this modest role deny the promise of planning, with its emphasis on the possibility of guiding societies and places towards better futures?

Shaping Futures and Promoting Hope

The planning idea is oriented towards shaping futures in which better conditions for human life and planetary survival can be achieved. Inherently, it connects to how societies and communities think about what 'futures' can be imagined and what might be 'better'. But, in the more modest role for planning ideas and practices which have been inherited from the late twentieth century, what can such a planning idea really offer? The capacity to imagine and evaluate possible futures can be found in many places – film, art and literature, in media debate, in all kinds of academic disciplines, and not just in the worlds of politics and planning technique. Moreover, in several societies, ideas of 'progress' and 'hope' for an 'enlightened' future have become tarnished by real-world experiences of political projects undertaken in the name of 'progress'.

In the 1980s the so-called 'postmodern' critique of the hopes of modernist progress led to a kind of hedonist enjoyment of the moment – a celebration of 'being' (Baudrillard, 2007; Cooke, 1990; Hassan, 1987). In this project, the role of planning as an idea had little leverage. Instead, what was encouraged was individual expression (Ward, 1994). But, since then, there have been many voices arguing for a revival of a perspective on future 'becoming' (Harvey, 2000; Hillier, 2007; Murdoch, 2006; Grosz, 2001). This is partly sustained by those who recognize that postmodern 'play' could increase the segregation of those marginalized and excluded from opportunity, hence enhancing inequalities and injustices. The focus of environmental arguments on threats to the future sustainability of the conditions for life has also rekindled attention to efforts to shape futures, while the demands of non-Western states for more affirmative terms of trade and recognition in global arenas also creates a politics of futures. In this context, the 'mobilization of hope' has now become a growing theme in planning theory debate (see Volume 3 (Hillier and Healey, 2008b), Part III). Compared to a century ago (see Part III of this volume), however, such efforts reflect an appreciation of the complexity of the relations through which futures emerge and the unpredictability attached to any intervention with future-shaping intent. Planning activity, with this sensibility, becomes an effort in knowledgeable experimentation coupled with situated judgement, underpinned by an ethics of attention to multiple considerations, identities and values and by a practical wisdom which combines awareness of constraints with a refusal to be limited by them.

The Collection of *Critical Essays in Planning Theory*

In this collection of essays we have aimed to illustrate the range and richness of the planning theory field. We have to acknowledge that our own work has been much more in line with the idea of planning activity as unfolding in the flow of governance practices, yet with the potential to become an active force as one of the many influences and dynamics shaping futures (see the essays in Volume 3 (Hillier and Healey, 2008b)). But we have tried not to emphasize our own positions. Instead, our objective has been to present positions and debates at different periods in the development of the 'planning theory conversation'.

Every field and practice has its 'history' of ideas and experiences, as well as its 'trajectories' of debates. Without an anchor in such a history, the 'planning project' (or 'place management project') risks being grounded in whatever is the latest wave of popular policy ideas without any 'cautionary tales' from previous debates and practice experiences. The history also shows that current ideas and practice models are often grounded in contexts very different from those in which they are now used, but nevertheless continue to shape the debates about new ideas. Some 'excavation' of the context in which older ideas developed is therefore useful. Reading the original works is very helpful for this. Looking back also highlights the way in which particular themes recur in planning theory debate, as we have illustrated above.

Making a selection has been extraordinarily difficult. We have had to leave out many essays which we believe should have had more influence than they did. And we are very conscious that some important voices were never heard by our predecessors because they were academically missing or invisible (see above). We have sought to include essays which have been influential in establishing new directions or key reference points for later discussions. In terms of selection, the contemporary period has been the most difficult. Several intellectual waves came across the field in the 1990s, in the 'postmodernist'/'post-positivist', post-structural upheaval in social sciences in general. Some waves have ebbed away, some remain strong, and some are edging in, but are difficult to identify. In Volume 3 (Hillier and Healey, 2008b), we try to give a flavour of these intellectual waves, their impact on the 'field' and their possible future trajectories.

We have arranged the essays in a broadly chronological order, but in a way that emphasizes streams of thought rather than the treatment of particular topics. For each Part, we have provided a short introduction which aims to review and situate the debates in the essays, as well as introducing their content. Although we recognize that readers may well only wish to look at one particular essay, we suggest that it would be helpful to read the introductory sections.

Overall, we hope that readers will find these essays inspirational as well as informative. The work of earlier planning theorists can refresh our thinking, as they confronted issues which we now confront. The 'new' does not always come from thinking into the future. It can also come as a (re)discovery from the past. We, too, have been 'refreshed' (and often humbled) by reading and rereading essays from previous decades. The world is, and always has been, full of 'ideas' about how to think and what to do. Looking back enhances the capacity to dream and make futures. What makes for the 'new' is the relation of ideas to new contextual configurations, as new imaginations and potentialities emerge from our struggles with our current dilemmas.

Acknowledgements

We are deeply indebted to the following who have acted as advisers and commentators on our selection of essays and on the introductions to each part of the volumes. Their contribution has greatly improved our selection and our work, but omissions and errors in coverage and interpretation are, of course, our own! The advisers were: Heather Campbell, Angelique Chettiparamb, Michael Gunder, Charles Hoch, Beth Moore Milroy, Niraj Verma and Vanessa Watson. In addition, some people have made very helpful comments on individual section introductions. These are acknowledged separately. Our thanks also to Bernie Williams for her help in preparing the final text.

PATSY HEALEY AND JEAN HILLIER

References

al-Sayyad, N. (ed.) (1992), *Forms of Dominance: On the Architecture and Urbanism of the Colonial Enterprise*, Aldershot: Avebury.

Albrechts, L. (1999), 'Planners as Catalysts and Initiators of Change', *European Planning Studies*, **7**, pp. 587–603.

Baudrillard, J. (2007), 'The Indifference of Space', *International Journal of Baudrillard Studies*, **4**, at: http://www.ubishops.ca/BaudrillardStudies/vol4_1/protopf.htm. Accessed 21 July 2007.

Beatley, T. (1989), 'Environmental Ethics and Planning Theory', *Journal of Planning Literature*, **4**, pp. 1–32.

Benhabib, S. (1992), *Situating the Self: Gender, Community and Postmodernism in Contemporary Ethics*, London: Routledge.

Boyer, C. (1983), *Dreaming the Rational City*, Cambridge, MA: MIT Press.

Campbell, H. (2006), 'Just Planning: The Art of Situated Ethical Judgement', *Journal of Planning Education and Research*, **26**, pp. 92–106.

Castells, M. (1977), *The Urban Question*, London: Edward Arnold.

Connolly, W.E. (2005), *Pluralism*, Durham, NC: Duke University Press.

Cooke, P. (1990), 'Modern Urban Theory in Question', *Transactions of the Institute of British Geographers*, NS **15**, pp. 331–43.

Davidoff, P. (1965), 'Advocacy and Pluralism in Planning', *Journal of the American Institute of Planners* **31**, pp. 331–8.

Driver, F. (1992), 'Geography's Empire – Histories of Geographical Knowledge', *Environment and Planning D: Society and Space*, **10**, pp. 23–40.

Fainstein, S.S. and Fainstein, N. (1979), 'New Debates in Urban Planning: The Impact of Marxist Theory in the United States', *International Journal of Urban and Regional Research*, **3**, pp. 381–403. Also published as Chapter 3 in Hillier and Healey (2008a).

Faludi, A. (1973), *Planning Theory*, Oxford: Pergamon Press.

Faludi, A. (1987), *A Decision-Centred View of Environmental Planning*, Oxford: Pergamon Press.

Flyvbjerg, B. (1998), *Rationality and Power*, Chicago: University of Chicago Press.

Forester, J. (1989), *Planning in the Face of Power*, Berkeley: University of California Press.

Forester, J. (1993), *Critical Theory, Public Policy and Planning Practice: Toward a Critical Pragmatism*, Albany, NY: State University of New York Press.

Forester, J. (1999), *The Deliberative Practitioner: Encouraging Participatory Planning Processes*, London: MIT Press.

Friedmann, J. (1973), *Re-tracking America: A Theory of Transactive Planning*, New York: Anchor Press.

Friedmann, J. (1987), *Planning in the Public Domain*, Princeton, NJ: Princeton University Press.

Gold, J. (1997), *The Experience of Modernism: Modern Architects and the Future City: 1928–1953*, London: E. & F.N. Spon.

Grosz, E. (2001), *Architecture from the Outside*, Cambridge, MA: MIT Press.

Gunder Frank, A. (1967), *Capitalism and Underdevelopment in Latin America: Historical Studies in Chile and Brazil*, London: Monthly Review Press.

Hall, P. (1988), *Cities of Tomorrow*, Oxford: Blackwell.

Harvey, D. (1985), *The Urbanisation of Capital*, Oxford: Blackwell.

Harvey, D. (1989), 'From Managerialism to Entrepreneurialism: The Formation of Urban Governance in Late Capitalism', *Geografisker Annaler*, **71B**, pp. 3–17.

Harvey, D. (2000), *Spaces of Hope*, Edinburgh: Edinburgh University Press.

Hassan, I. (1987), *The Postmodern Turn: Essays in Postmodern Theory and Culture*, Columbus, OH: Ohio State University Press.

Healey, P. (2006), *Collaborative Planning: Shaping Places in Fragmented Societies* (2nd edn), London: Macmillan.

Healey, P. (2007), *Urban Complexity and Spatial Strategies: Towards a Relational Planning for our Times*, London: Routledge.

Hillier, J. (2000), 'Going Round the Back: Complex Networks and Informal Action in Local Planning Processes', *Environment and Planning A*, **32**, pp. 33–54. Also published as Chapter 14 in Hillier and Healey (2008a).

Hillier, J. (2006), 'Multiethnicity and the Negotiation of Place', in W. Neill and H-U. Schwedler (eds), *Migration and Cultural Inclusion in the European City*, Basingstoke: Palgrave Macmillan, pp. 74–87.

Hillier, J. (2007), *Stretching Beyond the Horizon: A Multiplanar Theory of Spatial Planning and Governance*, Aldershot: Ashgate.

Hillier, J. and Healey, P. (2008a), *Political Economy, Diversity and Pragmatism: Critical Essays in Planning Theory, Volume 2*, Aldershot: Ashgate.

Hillier, J. and Healey, P. (2008b), *Contemporary Movements in Planning Theory: Critical Essays in Planning Theory, Volume 3*, Aldershot: Ashgate.

Hoch, C. (2007), 'Pragmatic Communicative Action Theory', *Journal of Planning Education and Research*, **26**, pp. 272–83.

Huxley, M. (2007), 'Geographies of Governmentality', in J. Crampton and S. Elden (eds), *Space, Knowledge and Power*, Aldershot: Ashgate, pp. 185–204.

Legg, S. (2007), 'Beyond the European Province: Foucault and Postcolonialism', in J. Crampton. and S. Elden (eds), *Space, Knowledge and Power*, Aldershot: Ashgate, pp. 265–89.

Luke, T. (1999), *Capitalism, Democracy and Ecology: Departing from Marx*, Urbana, IL: University of Illinois Press.

Murdoch, J. (2006), *Post-structuralist Geography*, London: Sage.

Owens, S. and Cowell, R. (2002), *Land and Limits: Interpreting Sustainability in the Planning Process*, London: Routledge.

Perera, N. (2002a), 'Indigenising the Colonial City: Late Nineteenth Century Colombo and its Landscape', *Urban Studies*, **39**, pp. 1703–21.

Perera, N. (2002b), 'Feminising the City: Gender and Space in Colonial Colombo', in S. Sarker and E.N. De (eds), *Trans-Status Subjects: Gender in the Globalization of South and South East Asia*, Durham, NC: Duke University Press, pp. 67–87.

Perera, N. (2005), 'Importing Problems: The Impact of a Housing Ordinance on Colombo, Sri Lanka', *The Arab World Geographer*, **8**, pp. 61–76.

Rabinow, P. (1989), *French Modern*, Chicago: University of Chicago Press.

Reade, E. (1987), *British Town and Country Planning*, Milton Keynes: Open University Press.

Rorty, R. (1980), *Philosophy and the Mirror of Nature*, Oxford: Blackwell.

Sandercock, L. (2003), *Mongrel Cities: Cosmopolis 11*, London: Continuum.

Sawicki, D. (2002), 'Improving Community Indicators: Injecting More Social Science into a Folk Movement', *Planning Theory and Practice*, **3**, pp. 13–32.

Schon, D. (1983), *The Reflective Practitioner*, New York: Basic Books.

Scott, A.J. and Roweis, S.T. (1977), 'Urban Planning in Theory and Practice: A Reappraisal', *Environment and Planning A*, **9**, pp. 1097–119. Also published as Chapter 1 in Hillier and Healey (2008a).

Stoler, A.L. (1995), *Race and the Education of Desire: Foucault's History of Sexuality and the Colonial Order of Things*, Durham, NC: Duke University Press.

Swyngedouw, E., Moulaert, F. and Rodriguez, A. (eds) (2003), *The Globalized City: Economic Restructuring and Social Polarisation in European Cities*, Oxford: Oxford University Press.

Throgmorton, J. (1996), *Planning as Persuasive Story-telling*, Chicago: University of Chicago Press.

Ward, S.V. (1994), *Planning and Urban Change*, London: Paul Chapman Publishing.

Ward, S.V. (2002), *Planning in the Twentieth Century: The Advanced Capitalist World*, London: Wiley.

Watson, V. (2003), 'Conflicting Rationalities: Implications for Planning Theory and Practice', *Planning Theory and Practice*, **4**, pp. 395–407. Also published as Chapter 10 in Hillier and Healey (2008b).

Yiftachel, O. (1999), 'Planning Theory at the Crossroads', *Journal of Planning Education and Research*, **18**, pp. 67–69.

Yiftachel, O. and Huxley, M. (2000), 'Debating Dominance and Relevance: Notes on the "Communicative Turn" in Planning Theory', *International Journal of Urban and Regional Research*, **24**, pp. 907–13.

Young, I.M. (1990), *Justice and the Politics of Difference*, Princeton, NJ: Princeton University Press.

Part I
The 'Project' of
Planning Theory

Introduction to Part I

Planning is not merely concerned with the efficient instrumentation of objectives; it is also a process by which society may discover its future. (Friedmann, 1973, p. 4)

In Part I of this volume of essays on critical planning theory, we have collected together essays which overview the field. The explicit enterprise of 'planning theory', understood as a social science with an applied orientation, originated in the University of Chicago's Program of Education and Research in Planning in the 1940s (Friedmann, 1973; Faludi, 1987). This deliberately focused on planning as the practice of societal guidance. It drew on the concepts of the eighteenth-century European Enlightenment and the hopefulness of the 'American Dream' of the early twentieth century (Friedmann, 1987). This hope centred on the idea that, through the application of knowledge, understood with a capacious sensibility to the method of scientific inquiry, societies could develop towards greater justice, prosperity and democracy. Such ideas had informed the great 1930s regional planning experiment of the Tennessee Valley Authority (TVA) (Selznick, 1949) and influenced US aid programmes to Latin American and other governments during the 1950s. Chicago planning theorists such as Edward Banfield (1968) and Harvey Perloff (1957) produced critical analyses and practical guidance which permeated US planning literature through texts and the pages of the *Journal of the Institute of American Planners* (later the *Journal of the American Planning Association*)[1]. However, this was not the only understanding of the planning project. In Europe, utopian and architectural traditions have also had an important influence on planning thought and practice in the twentieth century, and socialist conceptions of alternatives to capitalist forms of development have been more prevalent. Material representing these traditions is provided in Part II of this volume and in Part I of Volume 2, (Hillier and Healey, 2008a).

By the 1960s the ideas about planning as a knowledgeable societal guidance process were flowing across the Atlantic into European debates, where such social scientific conceptualizations had to struggle with a much more strongly developed architectural tradition surrounding the practice of urban planning. In 1973 Andreas Faludi, then based at the Oxford Polytechnic in the UK, was able to produce a book and a reader on 'planning theory' which brought together the US debates and concepts of planning as the rational scientific management of public policy programmes (Faludi, 1973a, 1973b). Faludi was particularly inspired by these ideas as a safeguard against the violence and disruption of the evil and chaos of war, of which he had personal experience. Yet, from the 1950s, the debates about approaches to societal guidance and the planning of cities were conducted against a background of a prevailing 'Cold War' climate, in which managing capitalism to spread the benefits of growth in a democratic context, inspired by Keynesian economics, was to be a bulwark against the infiltration of socialist concepts of a state-owned economy, run in the interests of the masses.

---

[1]   Charles Hoch has reminded us that the closing down of the Chicago School planning 'program' led to a 'diaspora' of planning faculty which helped to fuel the growth of the planning academy in other US Schools, notably MIT, UC Berkeley, UCLA and Pennsylvania State University.

Planning theory debates have been regularly reinvigorated by developments in other social sciences and philosophy, and by practice experiences. In the 1960s the Chicago model of societal guidance, imbued with the kind of rational scientific principles associated especially with the contribution of Herbert Simon (1945), came under increasing critical scrutiny. European critics drew on the much stronger influence of Marxist sociology and ideology to emphasize the tension between achieving inclusive social justice and the inherently exploitive relations between capitalists and workers which, in Marxist analysis, underpinned capitalist economic relations (see Hillier and Healey, 2008a, Part I). Also, during this same decade, inequality and injustice continued to persist in US cities, leading to the critical questioning of policies and programmes (Davidoff, Chapter 20, this volume; Gans, 1969; Marris and Rein, 1967). Meanwhile, Edward Banfield (under the influence of monetarist economist Milton Friedman) began to question the whole enterprise of planning (Banfield, 1968; Friedmann, 1987). In parallel, practice experiences were filtering back into planning theory debate, through famous cases of the difficulties encountered by attempts at rational comprehensive planning (Meyerson and Banfield, 1955; Altshuler 1965), and through the experiences of those involved in Latin American economic and urban development (Dyckman, Chapter 21, this volume; Friedmann, 1973; Peattie, 1987).

Two influential essays which appeared in the early 1970s, contemporaneously with Faludi's books, raised serious challenges to the project of planning as societal guidance. One came from planning economists Horst Rittel and Mel Webber (see Chapter 4), the other from policy scientist Aaron Wildavsky (see Chapter 3). These authors questioned the societal value of the planning project, at least as presented in the dominant rationalist perspective. Such critiques helped create intellectual space for other perspectives which jostled for attention during the 1970s. By then, with the political radicalization of a generation of students in the '1968' period, and the increasing evidence of the damage of unthinking environmental exploitation, the planning theory field was dividing into multiple strands and positions aimed at redefining the nature and conceptual underpinnings of the planning project. In these strands, different ideologies, epistemologies and practical commentaries coexisted in confused encounters.

It is in this context that attempts were made to impose some intellectual organization on the diversity of planning theory debate. In an influential 1979 essay (reproduced as Chapter 5 in this volume), Hudson was able to identify five strands of planning theory – synoptic (or rational comprehensive), incremental, transactive, advocacy and radical – which he referred to with the acronym SITAR. He also developed criteria for evaluating them, identifying strengths in articulating the public interest, but weaknesses in relating to specific content, or phenomena to be 'planned', and in critical reflexivity. A related attempt was made a few years later by one of the present authors (Healey), who, with colleagues at the then Oxford Polytechnic in the early 1980s, organized a conference on 'Planning Theory' (Healey *et al.*, 1982) which attempted a more European-centred review of debate. This gave more prominence to both critical urban political economy and the vigorous critiques of planning from a structural Marxist position, which had been developing energetically in Europe in the 1970s.[2] The authors also argued strongly for more emphasis, first, on the interaction between planning procedures and the 'substance', or

---

[2]   This conference was followed in 1986 by the Turin Conference on planning theory, which drew academics together across continents, creating networks which helped to give birth later to the journal, *Planning Theory*, initially edited by Italian planning academic and practitioner, Luigi Mazza.

content, of what the process was directed at and, second, on the relation of planning activity to specific political–institutional contexts. These issues of context and content were reiterated in Yiftachel's contribution seven years later, reproduced in this volume as Chapter 7. Yiftachel, with a background in Australia and Israel, developed his typology in order to bring broad debates about policy processes away from general principles and towards a closer link with the actual practices with which 'planning' was associated. He reviewed the debates in relation to three questions: what urban planning is taken to be; what is understood as a good urban plan; and what is understood as a good planning process.

But the most significant and influential review of the planning theory field was the magisterial work of John Friedmann (1987). A student in the Chicago Program in the late 1940s, with experience in TVA and in economic development programmes in Latin America, Friedmann maintained his focus on the radical, transformative potential of the planning project, but revised substantially his conception of how society might be guided. Instead of understanding planning as practised through the efforts of elite corps of experts, advising national governments, Friedmann, by the 1970s, had come to advocate a more bottom-up view of development, centred on the energies of people trying to improve the quality of their own social worlds. His account of the emergence of ideas about societal guidance provided the foundation for his grouping of contemporary strands of planning debate into a focus on social reform, on policy analysis, on social learning and social mobilization. By this time, Friedmann's own work had come to focus on the possibilities of bottom-up forms of 'territorial development', underpinned by a normative idea of the transformative energies and possibilities of civil society initiatives. This reiterated the nature of the planning project as a political activity and highlighted the struggles in both planning thought and planning practice between system-maintaining directions and system-transforming ones. This located the planning project within the context of governance practices and their various modes, governance referring to collective action initiatives, whether by governments or originating in civil society or the economy.

By the 1990s the 'Cold War' backcloth to debates about forms of governance had faded away with the fall of the Berlin Wall. By this time, the whole project of governance based on informed expertise was under pressure from the 'postmodernist' turn across the social sciences. As Beauregard argued (1989; also Chapter 8, this volume), this turn embodied new perspectives on cities and their governance. It drew inspiration from the feminist movement, the environmental movement, European post-structural social philosophy and from the increasingly strident critique of Western planning ideas as imposed in very different cultural contexts. What, then, can 'modernist' modes of planning mean, Beauregard asks, 'to those whose lives take on meaning in multi-valent, multivocal and intentional narratives' (p. 135). How planning theorists have struggled to address this question is illustrated in the contributions in Volume 3 of this collection (Hillier and Healey, 2008b). The field of planning theory debate seemed to fragment into multiple discourses. Yet in 1995, a paper by Judith Innes articulated a strand of ideas which had been developing through the 1980s, under the heading of the 'communicative turn'. This strand attracted so much attention that soon there were complaints about its overdominance. By the early 2000s, however, the planning theory field once again seemed to have a 'diverse and fragmented landscape' (Allmendinger, 2002, p. 96). In an influential essay, Susan Fainstein (Chapter 9), writing in the United States, assessed the field as being dominated by three perspectives: the communicative approach, a new enthusiasm for urban design (the 'new urbanism') and a continuing preoccupation with achieving social justice through urban policies.

The nine essays included in Part I present reviews of the planning theory field as it unfolded in the second part of the twentieth century, and particularly from the 1970s onwards. The collection starts with Friedmann's synthesis of the arguments of his 1987 book. This is followed by a brief statement by Faludi, which summarizes the predominant perspective in the United States in the 1960s, and which influenced a generation of planning students across the world who were educated with Faludi's reader (Faludi, 1973b). This is followed by the powerful critiques of this body of thought from Wildavsky and from Rittel and Webber. Wildavsky targets the idea that the future can be controlled by informed planning effort; Rittel and Webber demand a more pluralistic approach in order to address the 'wicked problems' of any attempt at societal or urban and regional guidance. The next three essays present typologies of the fragmenting field, from Hudson, from Healey, McDougall and Thomas, and from Yiftachel. Part I concludes with a statement from Beauregard introducing the postmodern unravelling of the twentieth century modernist dream of progress through science and efficient public management and Fainstein's review of what she understands as the dominant strands of debate at the start of the twenty-first century.

The themes raised in these essays unfold in more detail in Parts II and III and in Volumes 2 and 3 of this collection (Hillier and Healey, 2008a and b). Reading them today with hindsight, they combine a sense of particular times and contexts, as well as considerable prescience as to what might evolve in the future. Echoing through the various debates about the nature, purpose and method of planning which these essays attempt to chart are concerns which continue to preoccupy the field. Is planning some kind of societal guidance process, or is it just a specific practice focused on cities or on place development? At its core, is it an endeavour focused on means, methods and governance processes, or is it about shaping the way in which cities and regions develop, or about pursuing social and environmental justice goals in different situations? Can these issues of context, substance and process be separated into different spheres or are they always co-evolving, co-constituting each other? Are there universal principles which can be articulated to guide the endeavour of planning or is it an enterprise inherently situated in particular times and places? And how does the work of analysis and 'scientific' inquiry coexist with normative ideas about how the world could, and should, become? What do the answers to such questions mean for the ethics of planning actors and of planning systems? We have not, in the overall collection of essays, attempted a 'typology' of planning theory of our own. Instead, we hope readers will want to go back and forth between contributions as the authors debate questions such as these in different contexts and from different perspectives.

PATSY HEALEY AND JEAN HILLIER

References

Allmendinger, P. (2002), 'Towards a Post-positivist Typology of Planning Theory', *Planning Theory*, **1**, pp. 77–99.

Altshuler, A. (1965), *The City Planning Process: A Political Analysis*, Ithaca, NY: Cornell University Press.

Banfield, E. (1968), *Unheavenly City*, Boston, MA: Little Brown.

Beauregard, R.A. (1989), 'Between Modernity and Postmodernity: The Ambiguous Position of US Planning', *Environment and Planning D: Society and Space*, **7**, pp. 381–95. Also published as Chapter 10 in Hillier and Healey (2008b).

Faludi, A. (1973a), *Planning Theory*, Oxford: Pergamon Press.

Faludi, A. (ed.) (1973b), *A Reader in Planning Theory*, Oxford: Pergamon Press.

Faludi, A. (1987), *A Decision-Centred View of Environmental Planning*, Oxford: Pergamon Press.

Friedmann, J. (1973), *Re-tracking America: A Theory of Transactive Planning*, New York: Anchor Press.

Friedmann, J. (1987), *Planning in the Public Domain*, Princeton, NJ: Princeton University Press.

Gans, H. (1969), 'Planning for People not Buildings', *Environment and Planning A*, **1**, pp. 33–46.

Healey, P., McDougall, G. and Thomas, M. (eds) (1982), *Planning Theory: Prospects for the 1980s*, Oxford: Pergamon Press.

Hillier, J. and Healey, P. (2008a), *Political Diversity and Pragmatism: Critical Essays in Planning Theory, Volume 2*, Aldershot: Ashgate.

Hillier, J. and Healey, P. (2008b), *Contemporary Movements in Planning Theory: Critical Essays in Planning Theory, Volume 3*, Aldershot: Ashgate.

Innes, J. (1995), 'Planning Theory's Emerging Paradigm: Communicative Action and Interactive Practice', *Journal of Planning Education and Research*, **14**, pp. 183–89. Also published as Chapter 5 in Hillier and Healey (2008b).

Marris, P. and Rein, M. (1967), *Dilemmas of Social Reform: Poverty and Community in the United States*, London: Routledge and Kegan Paul.

Meyerson, M. and Banfield, E. (1955), *Politics, Planning and the Public Interest*, New York: Free Press.

Peattie, L. (1987), *Planning: Rethinking Cuidad Guyana*, Ann Arbor: University of Michigan Press.

Perloff, H.S. (1957), *Education for Planning: City, State and Regional*, Baltimore, MD: Johns Hopkins Press.

Selznick, P. (1949), *TVA and the Grass Roots*, Berkeley: University of California Press.

Simon, H. (1945), *Administrative Behavior*, Free Press, New York.

[1]

Two Centuries of Planning Theory: An Overview

John Friedmann

The idea that scientifically based knowledge about society could be applied to society's improvement first arose during the eighteenth century. Figure 1.1 describes the forms of that idea over the last two hundred years, mapping the intellectual influences that have shaped contemporary planning theory in the United States. Schools of thought and individual authors are placed along a continuum of social values, from conservative ideology on the left-hand side of the figure to utopianism and anarchism on the right. To simplify exposition, we may divide this continuum into three parts. On the extreme left of the diagram are shown those authors who look to the confirmation and reproduction of existing relationships of power in society. Expressing predominantly technical concerns, they proclaim a carefully nurtured stance of political neutrality. In reality, they address their work to those who are in power and see their primary mission as serving the state.

Systems Analysis derives from a cluster of theories that may be loosely grouped under the heading of *Systems Engineering* (cybernetics, game theory, information theory, computer science, robotics, and so on). Scientists in this tradition work chiefly with large-scale quantitative models. In specific planning applications, they may use optimizing techniques such as

This chapter is adapted from John Friedmann, *Planning in the Public Domain: From Knowledge to Action* (Princeton, NJ: Princeton University Press, 1987), chapter 3, with permission of the publisher.

An earlier version of this chapter appeared in *Society* 26, 1 (November/December 1988), Transaction Publishers, New Brunswick, New Jersey.

Operations Research; alternatively, they may construct long-range fore-casting models. Most futures research leans heavily on systems-analytic languages.

More closely allied to public administration than to systems analysis, *Policy Science* subjects specific issues in public policy to socioeconomic analysis. Stock-in-trade concepts include the analysis of costs and benefits, zero-base budgeting, cost effectiveness, and program evaluation. Theorists of this school generally prefer problems that are well-bounded and goal statements that are unambiguous. Note, too, that policy science is heir to a long intellectual tradition. Such logic as it has derives largely from neoclassical economics with its several offshoots of welfare economics and social choice theory. An amalgam with the institutional approach of public administration, however, is its very own.

Public Administration, finally, has been more generally concerned with the functions of central planning, the conditions for its success, and the relationship of planning to politics. In recent decades, a special area of concern has been the implementation of public policies and programs. A central contribution to planning theory from the traditions of public administration was made by Herbert Simon, whose early work, *Administrative Behavior* (Simon 1976 [1945]), approached the bureaucratic process from a behavioral perspective that stressed conditions limiting rationality in large organizations.

On the opposite side of the spectrum (extreme right of Figure 1.1) are authors who look to the transformation and transcendence of existing relationships of power within civil society. Here it is no longer the state that is addressed but the people as a whole, particularly those of working class origins who, it is believed, are fundamentally opposed to the bureaucratic state and, more generally, to every form of alienated power. The mode of discourse adopted by these authors is frankly political.

Most extreme in their rejection of power are the *utopians* and *social anarchists*, who deny all claims of higher authority in their search for a world of non-hierarchical relations. Parallel to this tradition is *Historical Materialism* and, more recently, *Neo-Marxism*. Writers in this vein tend to espouse the revolutionary transformation of the prevailing "mode of production." In contrast to utopians, they accept the state as a necessity. Class relations constitute a central analytical preoccupation of historical materialists. It is through relentless class conflict, they argue, that existing relations of power will eventually be "smashed" and replaced with a socialist state that will reflect the organized power and material interests of the working class as a whole.

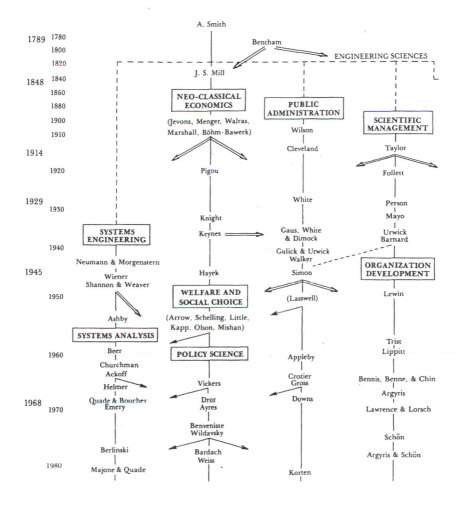

FIGURE 1.1

Intellectual influences on American planning theory

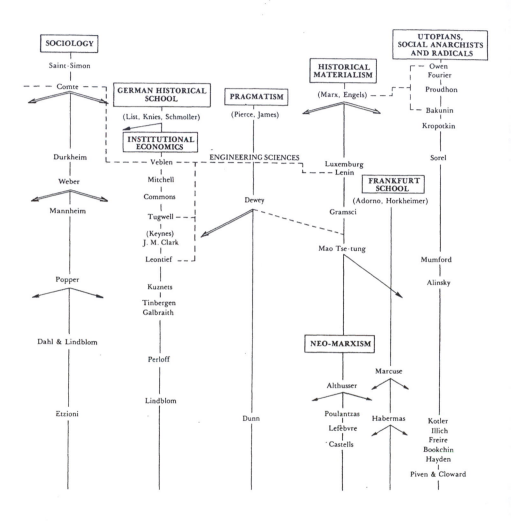

FIGURE 1.1 (continued)

Midway between utopian anarchism and historical materialism, I have located a secondary tradition, particularly important to planning theorists, in the "Frankfurt School of Critical Sociology" (Jay 1973). This school's radical critique of the cultural manifestations of capitalism (including the deification of technical reason itself) is grounded in Hegelian and Marxist thought.

Moving toward the central portions of Figure 1.1, we enter the gray area of overlap between the conservative pole of "ideology" where present relations of power remain largely unquestioned and the radical pole of "utopia," with its transcendent moral vision. Here we encounter the reformist traditions of planning and the related fields of *Public Administration* and *Scientific Management* and the seminal work of Frederick Winslow Taylor (1919 [1911]). Taylor's notion that management could be rationalized through the application of science enjoyed remarkable success in its time. Though he directed his attention to capitalist firms, his doctrines were attractive to radical thinkers such as Veblen and Lenin, who conceived of society as a large workshop or factory and of planning as a form of social engineering. For all of them, conservatives and radicals alike, the watchword was efficiency. In an age of industrialism, they thought, its invocation would magically unlock the gateway to the future.

After 1945, work on scientific management spawned the new field of *Organization Development*. Its principal client was the large, private corporation, to which it tendered a message steeped in humanistic rhetoric. With works by Eric Trist, Chris Argyris, Donald Schön, Charles Hampden-Turner and others, the field produced a literature that gradually moved away from profit as the sole criterion of management, bringing psychological values of self-development to the foreground.

Along more conventional liberal lines is *Institutional Economics*. An American branch of the nineteenth century "German Historical School," but by no means rigorously defined, it emphasizes the study of existing economic and social institutions over abstract theorizing in the style of neoclassical economics. Institutionalists prefer to examine the failings of specific institutional arrangements in relation to social purpose, and to identify reforms. They have contributed major ideas for planning full employment, economic growth, regional resources development, New Towns policies, public housing schemes, and social welfare. In the 1930s, the institutionalization of a central planning function was one of their major concerns.

Institutionalists tend to regard the state as a benign and rational actor, responsive to political pressure. In this sense, they stand very much in the tradition of Auguste Comte, who thought that social scientists should offer their knowledge to the rulers of nations. Like the father of positive philosophy himself, they believe in the powers of technical reason to determine what is correct, to persuade the ignorant and doubtful, and to forge the consensus needed for public action. Suspicious of free-wheeling democratic politics, they place their faith in a technocracy of the meritorious. Located between the traditions of institutionalism and historical materialism, we find the philosophical school of *Pragmatism*. For present purposes, this is an important tradition primarily because of John Dewey's exceptional influence on the intellectual history of planning. His influence is especially notable among institutional economists, many of whom came to accept Dewey's championship of a "scientific politics" in which learning from social experiments was regarded as fundamental to the development of a healthy democracy. A more recent exponent of a Dewey-like pragmatic philosophy is Edgar Dunn.

The center line of Figure 1.1 is labeled *Sociology*, for want of a better term. Here we meet the great synthesizers of social knowledge. Without exception, the great sociologists of the past stressed the importance of technical reason in human affairs. The classic European masters of this tradition include Emile Durkheim, Max Weber, Karl Mannheim, and Karl Popper. Durkheim stressed the importance of consensual values in social organization and the "organic solidarity" of the division of labor, while Weber emphasized the dominant role of bureaucratic structures in an industrial society devoted to the worship of functional order. Mannheim, the most distinguished continental sociologist of his time, was a critic of mass society and an advocate of "rational planning" as a way of overcoming the evils of unreason that had overtaken inter-war Europe. In contrast, Popper, an Austrian emigré scholar living in England, inveighed against the image of a totally planned society and defended the intellectual and moral credibility of piecemeal social engineering.

This classic tradition has been carried forward in the United States by Robert Dahl and Charles Lindblom whose *Politics, Economics and Welfare* (1957) was the first major American theoretical statement on planning, and by Amitai Etzioni, whose *The Active Society* (1968) may be read as a worthy successor to Mannheim's *Man and Society in an Age of Reconstruction*, written during a period of general crisis a generation earlier (1949b [1940]).

A dashed line, labeled *Engineering Sciences*, runs across the top of Figure 1.1, connecting Saint-Simon and Auguste Comte in the center with *Scientific Management, Public Administration, Systems Engineering*, and *Institutional Economics*. (An influence on Lenin is also shown.) A case can be made that the methods of engineering inform major sectors of the planning theory tradition down to this day. At his celebrated Paris dinners during which his basic ideas took shape, Saint-Simon played host to some of the leading professors of the new "École Polytechnique" (established in 1794); later, he surrounded himself, by preference, with young polytechnicians who were both his audience and inspiration. Among them was Auguste Comte, who was expelled from the École for disciplinary reasons only months before he was to graduate.

The École Polytechnique may be seen as the prototypical institution of the new Industrial Age and the source of its managerial ideology. Engineering applied the knowledge of natural sciences to the construction of bridges, tunnels, and canals. By the same logic, why should not a new breed of "social engineers" apply their knowledge to the task of reconstructing society? In a brilliant essay on the École tradition, Friedrich von Hayek tells us how the new institution, born in revolutionary times, shaped the character and outlook of its pupils.

> The very type of the engineer with his characteristic outlook, ambitions, and limitation was here created. That synthetic spirit which would not recognize sense in anything that had not been deliberately constructed, that love of organization that springs from the twin sources of military and engineering practices, the aesthetic predilection for everything that had been consciously constructed over anything that had "just grown," was a strong element which was added to—and in the course of time even began to replace—the revolutionary ardor of the young polytechnicians. . . . It was in this atmosphere that Saint-Simon conceived some of the earliest and most fantastic plans for the reorganization of society, and . . . it was at the École Polytechnique where, during the first twenty years of its existence, Auguste Comte, Prosper Enfantin, Victor Considerant, and some hundreds of later Saint-Simonians and Fourierists received their training, followed by a succession of social reformers throughout the century down to Georges Sorel. (Hayek 1955, 113 [1941–44])

The engineer's sense of certainty (and his ignorance of history) informed some of the most prominent of later planning theorists, among them Thorstein Veblen, Rexford Tugwell, and Herbert Simon, all of whom were enthralled by the idea of "designing society."

Even Simon, who was certainly aware of the difficulties inherent in the project, could not resist discussing social planning as the task of "designing the evolving artifact," as though society were merely a complex piece of machinery (Simon 1982 [1969]). It is precisely when we turn from designing genuine artifacts to society, however, that the design model breaks down. Simon seems to be conscious of the contradiction:

> Making complex designs that are implemented over a long period of time
> and continually modified in the course of implementation has much in
> common with painting in oil. In oil painting, every new spot of pigment
> laid on the canvas creates some kind of pattern that provides a continuing
> source of ideas to the painter. The painting process is a process of cyclical
> interaction between painter and canvas in which current goals lead to
> new applications of paint, while the gradually changing patterns suggest
> new goals. (Simon 1982 [1969], 187)

An oil painting is not a machine, and urban designers do not paint in oils. What is more, and to confuse the metaphor, society is not a canvas to be painted by an inspired artist. Engineers can build bridges and automata; it is an illusion to think that they can "build" society. There was a moment in time when aeronautic and space engineers thought that, having reached the moon, they could now turn their energies to solving the problem of growing violence in cities along with other urban "crises." But the two types of problems—how to conquer space and how to eliminate urban violence—were of an essentially different nature, and their discovery that urban violence would not yield to engineering solutions was not long in coming (Rittel and Webber 1973).

This "quick read" across the horizontal axis of Figure 1.1 needs to be complemented now with a more detailed discussion of the time dimension in the evolution of planning thought. Certain key dates are marked in bold type on the left-hand margin.

FOUR TRADITIONS OF PLANNING THOUGHT

A slightly different approach to essentially the same intellectual history appears in Figure 1.2. I have placed key figures in the history of planning thought within four major traditions, each addressing the links between knowledge and action. To be grouped into a common "tradition," authors had to meet three requirements:

1. They had to speak in the "languages" (such as economics or mathematics) of the tradition;

2. They had to share a certain philosophical outlook; and

3. They needed to address a small number of central questions that defined the particular intellectual tradition.

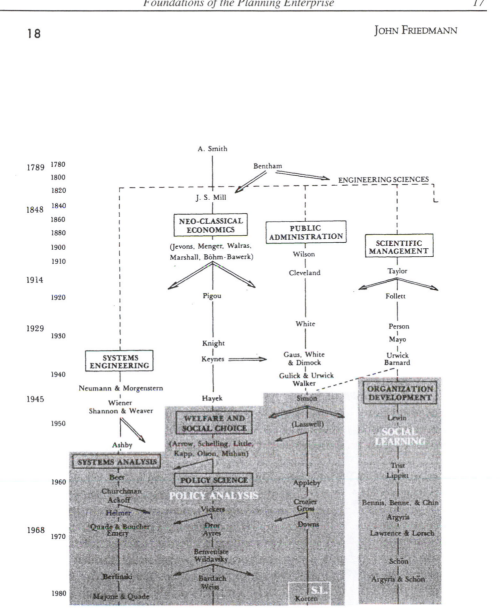

FIGURE 1.2
Major traditions of planning theory

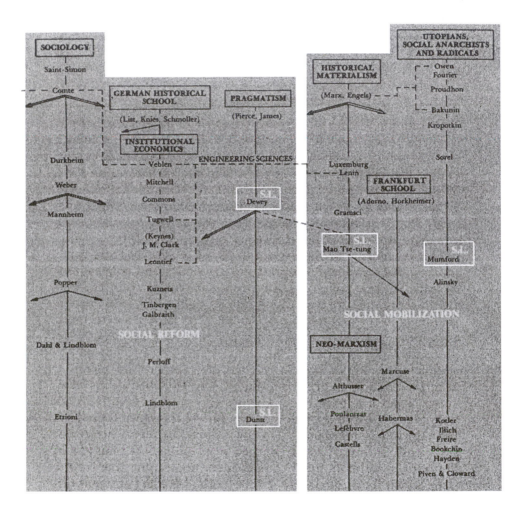

FIGURE 1.2 (continued)

The traditions extend across the entire ideological spectrum, from support for the state and affirmation of its authority to the abolition of every form of authority, including that of the state. The two older traditions, *Social Reform* and *Social Mobilization*, reach back to the first half of the nineteenth century. The other two, *Policy Analysis* and *Social Learning*, have their origins in the period between the Great Depression and World War II.

Social Reform

This tradition focuses on the role of the state in societal guidance. It is chiefly concerned with finding ways to institutionalize planning practice and make action by the state more effective. Those writing in this tradition regard planning as a "scientific endeavor"; one of their main preoccupations is with using the scientific paradigm to inform and to limit politics to what are deemed to be its proper concerns. *Policy Science*—Karl Mannheim's *wissenschaftliche Politik*—is one of its products (Mannheim 1949a [1929]).

The vocabulary of social reform derives primarily from three sources: macrosociology, institutional economics, and political philosophy. In their political convictions, the authors in this tradition affirm liberal democracy, human rights, and social justice. Within limits, they are tolerant of positive social change. They believe that through progressive reforms, both capitalism and the bourgeois state can be perfected.

Philosophically, authors in this tradition understand planning to be the application of scientific knowledge to public affairs; they also consider it a professional responsibility and an executive function. Many fields in the planning terrain are, therefore, fenced off from the intrusions of politicians and ordinary citizens who, it is argued, are not sufficiently informed to be seriously engaged in planning. As planners in the reform tradition, these authors advocate a strong role for the state, which they understand to have both mediating and authoritative roles. Since the publication of Keynes's *General Theory* in 1936 (Keynes 1964), they have argued for three areas of scientifically based and legitimate state intervention: the promotion of economic growth, the maintenance of full employment, and the redistribution of income.

The central questions addressed by planners in this tradition tend to be of a broad philosophical nature:

1. What is the proper relation of planning to politics?

2. What is the nature of the public interest, and should planners have the power (and the obligation) to articulate and promote their version of it?

3. In the context of planning, what should be the role of the state in a market economy? To what extent would "social rationality" be served through market interventions by the state? Under what conditions would such interventions be considered legitimate?

4. If planning is a "scientific endeavor," what is meant by science? Is it Karl Popper's (1974 [1945]) view that scientific knowledge is the residue of hypotheses that have successfully resisted all efforts at "falsification" through contradictory evidence? Is it Thomas S. Kuhn's celebrated theory of science as the dynamic interplay of "normal paradigms" and "scientific revolutions" (Kuhn 1970 [1962])? Or is it John Dewey's (1927) pragmatic epistemology, in which knowledge exists only in the act of knowing, and the validity of any statement is derived from its usefulness in application? Which of these views is most appropriate for planning, and what implications follow from adopting it?

5. There is great debate within the social reform tradition over the institutionalization of planning. Should planning be used comprehensively as an instrument of central guidance, coordination, and control by the state? Should it be divided among a large number of relatively autonomous actors working on more narrowly defined problems, who can, therefore, adapt their calculations more precisely to a constantly changing environment for decision making? Or does the "correct" organization for planning lie somewhere in between synoptic central planning and a decentralized planning that involves "mutual partisan adjustments" among actors?

In addition to debating these philosophical questions, social reform theorists, and particularly the economists among them, have fashioned the tools needed by a state that is increasingly determined to manage the economy "in the general interest." These instruments, so important to mainstream planning, include business cycle analysis (Mitchell), social accounting (Kuznets), input–output analysis (Leontief), economic policy models (Tinbergen), urban and regional economics (Perloff), and development economics (Hirschman). Major specialized fields of study have evolved out of these pioneering efforts, and several of the inventors of planning tools have been honored with the Nobel Prize in economics.

Policy Analysis

This tradition was strongly influenced by the early work of Herbert Simon, whose revolutionary study of 1945, *Administrative Behavior*, focused on the behavior of large organizations and particularly on how they might improve their ability to make decisions. Simon had absorbed several intellectual traditions into his own thinking, among them Weberian sociology and neoclassical economics, and his approach stressed synoptic analysis and decision making as the means of identifying the best possible courses of action. What was "best," of course, would inevitably be limited by the normal constraints on rationality, which include the resources, information, and time that are available for making decisions. Simon's was a model of "bounded" rationality.

The ideal-typical decision model applied by authors in the policy analysis tradition has the following identifiable "stages":

1. Formulation of *goals and objectives*.

2. Identification and design of *major alternatives* for reaching the goals identified within the given decision-making situation.

3. Prediction of major sets of *consequences* that would be expected to follow upon adoption of each alternative.

4. *Evaluation* of consequences in relation to desired objectives and other important values.

5. *Decision* based on information provided in the preceding steps.

6. *Implementation* of this decision through appropriate institutions.

7. *Feedback* of actual program results and their *assessment* in light of the new decision-situation.

For the most part, policy analysis has concentrated on stages 2, 3, and 4. In recent years, some excitement has also been generated about the implementation problems of policies and programs (stage 6). This has led to a modification of the original decision model, in which implementation concerns are now incorporated as early as stage 2—the design of alternative courses of action. The vocabulary of policy analysis tends to be specialized. Most analysts are versed in neoclassical economics, statistics, and mathematics. Beyond this, they tend to cluster into specialized subdisciplines such as systems analysis (with its emphasis on mathematical modeling), policy science (with its combined emphasis on neoclassical economics and political science), operations research (that tends to focus on problems having determinate outcomes), and "futures research," which is still a rather eclectic field. In addition, much of the language of policy analysis derives from work with specific analytical techniques such as gaming, simulation, evaluation research, linear and nonlinear programming, and the like.

Policy analysis has, strictly speaking, no distinctive philosophical position. On larger issues of society and justice, its practitioners are typically conventional in their thinking. They tend to think of themselves as technicians or, more flatteringly, as "technocrats" serving the existing centers of power—large private corporations and the state. On closer inspection, some of their views are remarkably similar to those of Saint-Simon and Auguste Comte. They believe that by using appropriate scientific theories and mathematical techniques, they can, at least in principle, identify and precisely calculate "best solutions." They are social engineers. If challenged on epistemological grounds, policy analysts are likely to reply that it is better to arrive at decisions through an imperfect (but perfectible) science than through a process of unmediated politics that is subject to personal whim, fickle passion, and special interest. The reliance of policy analysts on the tools of neoclassical economics implies that the value premises of that discipline are built into their work; chief among these values are individualism, the supremacy of the market in the allocation of resources, and the inherent conservatism of the equilibrium paradigm. Because market outcomes are regarded as "rational" for the actors involved, deviations from them are normally thought to require special justification and are admitted only reluctantly.

The central questions informing this tradition, in keeping with its basic ethos, are of an essentially technical nature:

1. What are the relative advantages of comprehensive and incremental policy analysis? Comprehensive models provide an extensive overview of a given terrain but they are subject to huge, if indeterminate, error. Incremental analysis is parsimonious in its demands for information, concentrates on the consequences of limited change, and can be modeled to yield determinate solutions. Which model is to be preferred, and under what conditions?

2. Different models yield different types of solutions. Some are structured to allow for the maximization of "payoff" variables such as profits, employment, or savings in travel time. Others are essentially "optimizing" models that yield "best combinations" of results over a variety of objective variables. Still others yield only second-best solutions (in Herbert Simon's neologism, they are merely "satisficed"). The choice of a model for evaluating consequences and recommending technically correct solutions to political decision makers matters a great deal in policy analysis. And how should decision makers be informed? Should

they be given, for example, the one "best" solution? Should they be given the results of various "simulations" together with the assumptions that were used to obtain them? Or should they be asked to take part in "gaming situations" where they simulate the group dynamics of strategic choices, much as the Army General Staff might simulate war games or conduct field maneuvers?

3. How might market prices be modified to express social criteria of valuation? Should cost–benefit studies, for example, use current market rates of interest or some "shadow" price of money that reflects social preference? If so, and in the absence of political guidance, how might shadow prices be calculated? Or, in the case of goods for which there is no ready form of market valuation, what conventions of "social accounting" might permit them to be included in the overall policy calculus? Should women's household work, for instance, be assigned a shadow price and, if so, what should it be?

4. Policy analysts make forecasts about economic variables, expected changes in reproductive behavior, environmental impacts, technological innovations, changes in settlement patterns and land use, and many other things. What are the most reliable methods for mid- and long-range forecasting?

5. Most policy analyses contain huge areas of uncertainty about the future and even greater areas of ignorance. ("What is the probability of global warming within the next fifty years?") How should these great unknowns be treated, and what advice should be given to those responsible for decisions? Are there ways of controlling for uncertainty, and what mathematical values should be assigned to express different degrees of subjective uncertainty? Should alternative courses of action be designed to be compatible with the known areas of ignorance ("planning without facts"), especially when the consequences of a "wrong" decision might be politically, environmentally, or in some other way disastrous?

Social Learning

This tradition focuses on overcoming the contradictions between theory and practice, or knowing and acting. Its theory derives from two streams.

The first is the pragmatism of John Dewey and, more specifically, his epistemology that put so much stress on "learning by doing." A second stream, evolved within Marxism, has its origins in Marx's "Theses on Feuerbach" (1978 [1844]) that ends with the famous declaration, "The philosophers have only *interpreted* the world, in various ways; the point, however, is to *change* it." From this immortal sentence derives the basic Marxist proposition concerning the essential unity of revolutionary theory and practice, that found its fullest expression in Mao Tse-Tung's 1937 essay "On Practice" (1968).

Social learning may be regarded as a major departure from the planning paradigms of Saint-Simon and Comte. Whereas these early founders of the planning tradition had treated scientifically based knowledge as a set of "building blocks" for the reconstruction of society, theorists in the social learning tradition have claimed that knowledge is derived from experience and validated in practice, and is therefore integrally a part of action. Knowledge, in this view, emerges from an ongoing dialectical process in which the main emphasis is on practical undertakings: Existing understanding (theory) is enriched with lessons drawn from experience, and this "new" understanding is then applied in the continuing process of action and change. Whereas Comte and his fellow positivists believed that the social world behaved according to immutable "social laws," social learning theorists assert that social behavior can be changed and that the scientifically correct way to do this is through social experimentation, the careful observation of the results, and a willingness to admit to error and to learn from it.

Not surprisingly, then, the central questions of the social learning tradition are primarily instrumental:

1. How can the normal processes of social learning, which are found in all cases of successful and extended action, be used to spread social learning techniques to all forms of social undertaking?

2. Since human beings are reluctant to alter their habitual ways and are prone to believe that their own opinion or ideology is the only correct one, and since there is an evident connection between ideology and power, how can change be accomplished? How might people be motivated to participate in a form of social learning that depends on openness, dialogue, a willingness to risk social experiments, and a preparedness to let these experiments affect their personal development as human beings?

3. How might formal and informal ways of knowing be linked to each other in a process of change-oriented action that involves mutual learning between those who possess theoretical knowledge and those whose knowledge is primarily practical, concrete, and unarticulated?

4. The social learning paradigm involves, among other things, frequent face-to-face transactions that require a relation of dialogue between the participating parties (Friedmann 1979, 1981). But under conditions where specific tasks must be performed, dialogic relations are difficult to bring about and maintain. What techniques might facilitate relations of trust and dialogue, especially between "planners" and "client-actors?"

5. What is the relationship of the social learning paradigm—with its emphasis on dialogic, non-hierarchical relations and its commitments to experimentation, tolerance for difference, and openness in communication—to democratic political theory? And what is its relationship to the growth and development of the autonomous, self-actualizing personality?

Social Mobilization

This departs from all other planning traditions by asserting the primacy of direct collective action "from below." It stands in stark contrast to the traditions of social reform and policy analysis, which address the role of the state and look toward a "scientific politics." In the social mobilization tradition, planning appears as a form of politics, conducted without the mediations of "science." Nevertheless, scientific analysis, particularly in the form of social learning, plays an important role in the transformative processes sought by social mobilization.

The vocabulary of social mobilization comes in part from the long tradition of mutually antagonistic social movements on the left: Marxists on the one hand, and utopians and social anarchists on the other. Only Marxism developed a full-fledged ideology, but the mutual attractions and repulsions of various factions and groupings on the left provide much of the rhetoric in which many popular struggles are expressed. A good deal of this rhetoric also stems from the collective memory of two centuries of conflict and communitarian effort. It is a history of oppression and triumphant revolutionary movements, from the Paris Commune to the Spanish Civil War, with its own pantheon of heroes and heroines, its own moments of glory in defeat. The language of social mobilization draws on this history as much as it does on the more abstract discourse of its philosophers, theoreticians, and gurus.

Philosophically, this tradition embraces utopian communitarianism, anarchist terrorism, Marxist class struggle, and the neo-Marxist advocacy of emancipatory social movements. These divisions are chiefly historical, however, and reflect disagreements over strategy and tactics more than basic differences in ideology. One might reasonably claim, for example, that the various proponents of social mobilization are of one mind in their condemnation of the pervasive oppression and alienation of human beings under the institutions of capitalism and the bourgeois state. Social mobilization is an ideology of the dispossessed whose strength derives from social solidarity, from the seriousness of their political analysis, and from their unflinching determination to change existing relations of power.

Two kinds of emancipatory politics may be involved in social mobilization. For utopians and anarchists, there is a "politics of disengagement" carried on by "alternative communities" that demonstrate to others new ways of living. For Marxists and neo-Marxists, there is a "confrontational politics" that emphasizes political struggle as necessary to transform existing relations of power and to create a new order that is not based on the exploitation of labor and the alienation of man from what is distinctly human.

Among the central questions faced by adherents to this tradition are the following:

1. What is the proper role of "vanguards," community organizers, and the leaders of movements for social mobilization? If emancipation from various forms of social oppression is the ideological goal, does it not require leadership elites to abide by thoroughly democratic procedures, including the full participation of movement members in collective decisions, a tolerance for open dissent, and non-manipulative methods of organizing group action?

2. How can the disinherited and those who have never had effective power suddenly gain confidence in their ability to "change the world"? How can the poor empower themselves to gain their freedom from oppression?

3. How can the commitment to a new life in community (utopians and anarchists) or a new life in struggle (Marxists and neo-Marxists) be maintained when only an occasional and partial

victory is gained in the seemingly interminable struggle against oppression?

4. What should be the basic components of a strategy? What role should be given to violence, to the choice of arena, to the timing of actions and their duration ("long march" or Armageddon), and what kinds of specific actions should be undertaken (strikes, demonstrations, street theater, terrorism, noncooperation with the state, formation of political alliances, establishment of alternative communities)?

5. What should be the characteristics of the "good society," the social ideal to be realized in practice, now or in the future? What importance should be given to such goals as a non-hierarchical and inclusive social order, the practice of self-reliance, voluntary cooperation, dialogic processes, and a radical leveling of social hierarchies?

New chapters in the history of planning thought are still being written. Specific modalities and styles of planning may become obsolete, but the linkage between knowledge and action will remain a lively concern, both ideologically and in practice. We cannot wish *not* to know, and we cannot escape the need to act. As social conditions and human understanding change, the actual and theoretical links between knowledge and action will surely undergo changes as well. If we wish to ensure the continued vitality of planning in the public domain, we would do well to examine, carefully and in a critical spirit, the traditions we now have.

REFERENCES

Dahl, R. A., and C. E. Lindblom. 1957. *Politics, economics, and welfare.* New York: Harper & Bros.

Dewey, J. 1927. *The public and its problems.* New York: Henry Holt.

Etzioni, A. 1968. *The active society: a theory of societal and political processes.* New York: Free Press.

Friedmann, J. 1979. *The good society.* Cambridge, MA: MIT Press.

_____. 1981. *Retracking America.* Emmaus, PA: Rodale Press. (Original edition 1973. Garden City, NY: Anchor Books.)

Hayek, F. A. 1955 [original editions 1941–44]. *The counterrevolution of science: studies on the abuse of reason.* New York: Free Press.

Jay, M. 1973. *The dialectical imagination: a history of the Frankfurt School and the Institute of Social Research, 1923–1950.* Boston: Little, Brown & Co.

Keynes, J. M. 1964 [1936]. *The general theory of employment, interest, and money.* New York: Harcourt, Brace, Jovanovich.

Kuhn, T. S. 1970 [1962]. *The structure of scientific revolutions.* 2d ed., enlarged. Chicago: University of Chicago Press.

Mannheim, K. 1949a [1929]. *Ideology and utopia.* New York: Harcourt-Brace.

———. 1949b [original edition 1940. London: Kegan Paul]. *Man and society in an age of reconstruction.* New York: Harcourt-Brace.

Mao Tse-Tung. 1968 [1937]. "On practice," in *Four essays on philosophy.* Peking: Foreign Language Press.

Marx, K. 1978 [1844]. Theses on Feuerbach, in R. C. Tucker, ed., *The Marx-Engels reader.* 2d ed. New York: W.W. Norton.

Padilla, S. M. 1975. *Tugwell's thoughts on planning.* San Juan: University of Puerto Rico Press.

Popper, K. R. 1974 [1945]. *The open society and its enemies.* 2 vols. London: Routledge & Kegan Paul.

Rittel, H. W. J., and M. M. Webber. 1973. Dilemmas in a general theory of planning. *Policy Sciences* 4, 2 (March): 155–69.

Simon, H. A. 1976 [1945]. *Administrative behavior.* 3rd ed. New York: Free Press.

———. 1982 [1969]. *The sciences of the artificial.* 2d ed. Cambridge, MA: MIT Press.

Taylor, F. W. 1919 [1911]. *The principles of scientific management.* New York: Harper & Bros.

[2]

WHAT IS PLANNING THEORY?

Andreas Faludi

Introduction

IN THIS introductory section, I shall set out to demonstrate that there is a useful distinction to be drawn between theory *in* planning and theory *of* planning, and why this reader concentrates on the latter. Also, I make a further distinction between *normative* and *positive* or behavioural theory of planning, and how this affects the material included. Finally, as an introduction to an important paper devoted to this topic, I shall review essays considering the question of what is planning theory.

THEORY IN PLANNING VERSUS THEORY OF PLANNING

Planning is the application of scientific method—however crude—to policy-making.[1] What this means is that conscious efforts are made to increase the validity of policies in terms of the present and anticipated future of the environment. What it does not mean is that planners take over in the field of politics.

Validity is an attribute of the process by which decisions are made. This process involves advisers, as the suppliers of scientific intelligence, and decision-makers. Advisers and decision-makers interact, thus forming a planning agency. Planning is what planning agencies do, i.e. bring scien-

[1] Definitions given for systems analysis (Quade, 1968) and operational research (Beer, 1966) are the same as that of planning given above. This underlines one of the points to be made about planning theory, i.e. the generality of the phenomenon planning, and hence its wide applicability.

2   *A Reader in Planning Theory*

tific advice to bear on decisions concerning policies during an interactive process involving the roles of advisers and decision-makers.

The relationship between decision-makers and their advisers is often presented as that between master and servant: managers employ operational researchers (Beer, 1966), military staffs employ systems analysts (Quade, 1968), planning committees employ planners. The assumption, each time, is quite clearly that of the adviser coming into the game *at the pleasure* of the decision-maker.

There is nothing inherently wrong with being employed to help. The question for the adviser is only whether the process by which he and his decision-making master arrive at decisions is valid, or whether their relationship distorts this process. He might ask questions like: Does he pay regard to the evidence which I submit? Does the decision-maker provide me with adequate guidance on the problems which he wants solved? Are the reasons for his making a decision valid in their own terms? These are reasonable questions to ask for somebody concerned with the validity of the process which he is engaged in.

The point is that decision-makers, like other people, do not like their actions and their motives being questioned, and certainly not by their advisers, who are supposed to help *them*. Advisers in many fields have therefore had occasion to complain about their masters. Having trained minds, they have gone beyond grumbling and asked that simple question which is at the heart of all scientific investigation: *Why?* Upon which they have concluded that their own relationship with their masters (in short, the planning agency) must become the object of reflection, theoretical understanding and, ultimately, transformation so that planning shall become more valid. They have moved from considering the role of their own type of scientific theory *in* planning to the theory *of* planning.

Rather than talking specifically about planners and politicians, I have couched this argument in general terms. This is because there is evidence for the generality of this phenomenon of advisers becoming interested in the way in which their advice reaches fruition. That town planners are concerning themselves with the theory of planning in these terms will be documented in this reader. But social workers are doing the same, especially now that they are reorganizing their departments (Kogan and Terry, 1971; Foren and Brown, 1971). Similarly, operational researchers have taken a look at planning in private enterprise (e.g. Beer, 1966; Ackoff, 1969) and in public authorities (Friend and Jessop, 1969). The extent to which their findings and prescriptions are similar, and the degree to which the different fields of planning begin to influence each other, suggest that planning is a general approach to decision-making and is not tied to the activities of any profession or department of government.

There are other reasons for making the distinction between theory of planning and theory in planning. One lies in the differences between *form* and *content*. A theory on which a policy is based may be perfectly valid in itself, and the policy still be invalid. Thus, some models may be a perfect way of allocating residential activities. Yet policies based on them sometimes run into difficulties because a local amenity group puts up a successful fight against expansion of their village. The conclusion which the model builder must draw from this is that the way in which what he should do has been determined in the first instance has been invalid, or that the politician is not really representative of his constituency. These are questions concerning precisely the form of the planning process, and not the content of planning policies.

The second reason why the distinction between theory in planning and theory of planning ought to be made is that there are unfortunate consequences in *not* making it. J. Brian McLoughlin (1969), in his book on the "systems approach" to urban and regional planning, advances a view of planning theory based in location theory, i.e. what I call theory *in* planning. But, quite clearly, he also makes pronouncements as regards the theory *of* planning. For instance, he suggests that the planning process must have a "shape" which is isomorphic to the process by which human beings transform their environment. In this way, the whole theory of planning becomes a corollary to theory in planning. The attention given to it is thereby reduced so that McLoughlin has been criticized—quite rightly as I think—for putting forward a simplistic view of the actual processes by which decisions are made (Silvester, 1971, 1972).

I hasten to say that I hope the distinction which I propose will not result in separation. There are hopeful signs that both sides are drawing closer together. Recent views of urban systems picture them as socio-technical complexes with their institutional part including planning agencies. Proponents of theory of planning, on the other hand, begin to take into account what Bolan, in the last paper included in this selection (see pp. 371–94), calls the "issue attributes". These reflect our knowledge con-

4   *A Reader in Planning Theory*

cerning the environment and hence the state of theory *in* planning, for example whether this leads to reliable predictions or whether there is a great element of uncertainty in predictions derived from it. It is perfectly conceivable, therefore, to envisage one type of planning theory forming an envelope to the other, and there is no *a priori* way of saying which would contain which. It is only that, currently, urban and regional planners still neglect the theory of planning, seeing it as somewhat ephemeral instead of the basis of what they are doing. It is this neglect which this reader should rectify.

NORMATIVE VERSUS POSITIVE THEORIES OF PLANNING

As regards theory of planning, the distinction has been drawn between normative and behavioural approaches, first of all to the study of decision-making in management (Cyert and March, 1959; Dyckman, 1961). It is a distinction made in the planning study by Daland and Parker (1962), and recently also in the study of "policy formation" by Bauer (1968). The distinction is analogous to that between (normative) political theory and (positive) political science: normative theory is concerned with how planners ought to proceed rationally. Behavioural approaches focus more on the limitations which they are up against in trying to fulfil their programme of rational action. (See Bolan's paper, in particular p. 373.)

Obviously, normative and positive theory of planning have some bearing on each other. In the first instance one might say that empirical findings modify prescriptions. Thus, Lindblom and his collaborators maintain that since in actual fact planning never proceeds rationally, rational-comprehensive planning is not a suitable normative concept (Dahl and Lindblom, 1953; Braybrooke and Lindblom, 1963; Lindblom, 1965, see also pp. 151–69).

But Banfield (see p. 149) draws the opposite conclusion from finding that organizations do not engage in rational planning. For him, what remains is precisely the validity of rationality as a normative ideal! Yet, surely this must mean that some form of progress towards this ideal is conceivable. It is precisely in the analysis of the conditions under which such progress may take place that behavioural approaches to the study of planning may help.

Closely related to this idea is that of turning the opposing ideals of rational-comprehensive and piecemeal planning into empirical concepts. Thus, Madge (1968) suggests: ". . . 'total' and 'piecemeal' theories are the poles between which actual ideologies of social planning vary."

Similarly, Kahn (1969), in a recent collection of *Studies in Social Policy and Planning*, observes: "In the United States . . . the distinction between the incremental and the comprehensive is quantitative and not qualitative."

I have myself moved into this direction in some of my own writing, devising "dimensions of planning behaviour", one of them being precisely that of the rational versus the piecemeal mode of planning (Faludi, 1970, 1971).

Generally, the existence of concepts and instruments for relating theory to empirical reality, i.e. of a positive theory of planning, is seen as a sign of *maturity* of an area of intellectual pursuit. Admitting that most of the material included remains on the level of normative theory therefore means admitting to lack of sophistication of the theory of planning. Thus, most of the papers in Parts II and III are more prescriptive than descriptive. Even where Banfield and Lindblom draw on the empirical study of planning, all that they provide are generalizations which, furthermore, relate primarily to what they have to say about the rational planning process as an ideal. The most clearly empirical study in these sections is Altshuler's essay (see pp. 193–209).

Part IV of this reader is somewhere between a normative and a descriptive orientation. It is full of empirical references, though mostly at the level of tentative observations. Use is made of the body of literature which is available in organizational behaviour, though interest is still with what planning ought to be.

It is only in Part V that the positive theory of planning dominates. Here, the poverty of this field becomes evident in the extremely narrow range of literature on which one can draw. Besides, what is presented are frameworks for empirical research, not results. The great amount of effort that would be needed to obtain such results makes it questionable whether a behavioural approach would really be the answer to that most pressing problem of theory of planning: to provide a basis for improvements to planning procedures and planning agencies, or what has been called *meta-planning* (Wilson, 1969).

Clearly for a long time to come such meta-planning will have to rely on

6   *A Reader in Planning Theory*

a theory of planning devoid of adequate empirical backing. Besides, assuming even all the requisite research effort being spent, the significance of a positive theory may simply be that of elucidating what the obstacles in the way of achieving *alternative* ideals are, not which ideal to choose. Thus, finding interdependencies between what many individuals in society do may be construed as supporting the idea of common action, or as a regrettable limitation on individual freedom to be reckoned with, depending on one's normative assumptions. The world-as-it-is does simply not provide a final clue as to how we should wish to see it!

FRAMEWORKS FOR THE STUDY OF THEORY OF PLANNING

There has been surprisingly little written on what planning theory is or ought to be. Even in the *Journal of the American Institute of Planners* papers considering its nature and scope are far and few between. Significantly, most of them have arisen out of the effort of academics to present to their students reasonably coherent frameworks for understanding planning. Having a corps of academics reflecting upon the nature of its activity, and thereby going beyond practice, is an asset for a profession like planning, a fact which is sometimes forgotten by its practitioners. All too often, the latter tend to see the planning schools as training camps for professionals in their own image. However, as Kaplan (1964) says, theorizing has novel responses as its behavioural correlate. The academic study of planning thus provides stimuli for innovation, an observation which can certainly be made of American planning.

Theory has already loomed large in Perloff's essay on planning education published after the closure of the famous Chicago School (Perloff, 1957). Benjamin A. Handler's seminar report "What is planning theory?" (1957) is another example of the concern of academics for developing this field. In recent years, Henry C. Hightower's (1970) review of the teaching of planning theory is highly instructive of the level of sophistication which has apparently been reached during the sixties, though he still reports lack of consensus on the subject-matter and the approaches to be taken.

Throughout the years, one or the other framework for "theory of planning" has been offered such as Lawrence L. Haworth's "An institutional theory of the city and planning" published during the same year (1957) as

Handler's report on that seminar at the University of Michigan. Handler's own contribution appended to that report, arguing for basing planning theory in economic theory, is another example. But of the papers building on the academic teaching of planning theory, Paul Davidoff and Thomas A. Reiner's "A choice theory of planning" has gained the highest reputation of all.

This is a normative theory of planning. On the basis of a series of postulates derived from economic analysis, and of philosophical assumptions concerning the purpose of planning, they suggest how the planner ought to proceed. Particularly noteworthy is their treatment of facts and values in goal-setting.

Davidoff and Reiner were subsequently challenged by John Dakin (1963). Points of contention were whether a theory of choice coming from economic theory was adequate to cover all aspects of planning, whether planning should aim at proceeding in a fully rational manner, whether the time was ripe for developing a general theory of planning such as the two authors had demanded, and whether theory ought to be so general as to explain planning under whichever political ideology.

Dakin insisted, for instance, that the role of intuition and experience should be acknowledged and that too much explicitness had its dangers. Davidoff and Reiner (1963) retorted by saying that ". . . intuition or experience unsupported by reason are weak reeds on which to rest".

They linked this with their belief in the essentially democratic nature of scientific planning, thus also answering the point about planning under different ideologies: properly conceived, it is *not* the servant of whichever power cares to employ planning. Scientific planning requires democracy: ". . . because of the need for value determination in science (in regard, for example, to the criteria and measures to be employed), a scientific decision model must resemble a democratic decision model."

Davidoff and Reiner put forward an elegant argument. However, some comments are still needed. These concern basic assumptions and the conclusions which they draw from them. It is evident that they take the position of *methodological individualism*, i.e. the doctrine ". . . that facts about society and social phenomena are to be explained in terms of facts about individuals" (Lukes, 1970).

For instance, they answer Dakin's point: "The question of whether or not planning is to be regarded as effective is probably not a choice within

8   *A Reader in Planning Theory*

society, but only as between one society and another. The cultural pattern of our society decides for us that planning is an effective kind of behaviour" in a way which shows their methodological assumptions saying that a ". . . social decision emerges as human beings . . . decide . . ." (Davidoff and Reiner, 1963). Thus, they in effect deny theoretical status to such collective concepts as cultural pattern. One is reminded of Durkheim's argument concerning the existence of "social facts", and the split in the social sciences which this has caused ever since.

With their refusal to grant theoretical status to concepts like cultural pattern goes their distaste for anything like the public interest. They clearly build on a pluralist model of society. Indeed, in their paper they use the concept of advocacy, around which Davidoff would eventually write his seminal paper on "Advocacy and pluralism in planning" included later in this reader (see pp. 277–96).

Their assumptions lead them to conclusions with important consequences for planning theory. Their theory can only prescribe how planners ought to operate, it does not explain planning: "We did not intend to present a law of the way planning has, does, or will operate. We do not believe there can be such a law, any more than a single theory of health or justice" (Davidoff and Reiner, 1963).

Apparently, planning itself, when referring to what planners generally do, is suspect as a concept because of the methodological connotations which this has. It is not a foregone conclusion, however, that methodological individualism and pluralist models of society are the only acceptable assumptions on which to base planning theory. I subscribe to Kaplan's (1964) principle that each level of analysis should be granted autonomy of inquiry. Papers included under "positive theory of planning" in Part V show that other writers have thought it perfectly conceivable to make pronouncements concerning the way in which planning operates, thus taking a position opposed to Davidoff and Reiner's.

REFERENCES

Part I

ACKOFF, R. L. (1969) *Corporate Planning*, John Wiley, New York.
BAUER, R. A. (1968) The study of policy formation: an introduction, *The Study of Policy Formation* (edited by BAUER, R. A. and GERGEN, K. J.) Collier–Macmillan, London.

BEER, S. (1966) *Decision and Control*, John Wiley, New York.

BRAYBROOKE, D. and LINDBLOM, C. E. (1963) *A Strategy for Decision-Policy Evaluation as a Social Process*, The Free Press, Glencoe, Illinois.

CYERT, R. M. and MARCH, J. G. (1959) "A behavioural theory of organisational objectives", *Modern Organization Theory* (edited by HAIRE, M.), John Wiley, New York.

DAHL, A. and LINDBLOM, C. E. (1953) *Politics, Economics and Welfare*, Harper, New York.

DAKIN, J. (1963) "An evaluation of the 'choice' theory of planning", *Journal of the American Institute of Planners*, Vol. 29, pp. 19–27.

DALAND, R. T. and PARKER, J. A. (1962) "Roles of the planner in urban development, *Urban Growth Dynamics* (edited by CHAPIN, F. S. and WEISS, F. S.), John Wiley, New York.

DAVIDOFF, P. and REINER, T. A. (1963) "A reply to Dakin", *Journal of the American Institute of Planners*, Vol. 29, pp. 27–28.

DYCKMAN, J. W. (1961) "Planning and decision theory", *Journal of the American Institute of Planners*, Vol. 27, pp. 335–45.

FALUDI, A. (1970) "The planning environment and the meaning of 'planning' ", *Regional Studies*, Vol. 4, pp. 1–9.

FALUDI, A. (1971) "Towards a three-dimensional model of planning behaviour", *Environment and Planning*, Vol. 3, pp. 253–66.

FOREN, R. and BROWN, M. J. (1971) *Planning for Service*, Charles Knight, London.

FRIEND, J. K. and JESSOP, W. N. (1969) *Local Government and Strategic Choice*, Tavistock Publications, London.

HANDLER, B. A. (1957) "What is planning theory?", *Journal of the American Institute of Planners*, Vol. 23, pp. 144–50.

HIGHTOWER, H. C. (1970) "Planning theory in contemporary professional education", *Journal of the American Institute of Planners*, Vol. 35, pp. 326–9.

KAHN, A. J. (1969) *Studies in Social Policy and Planning*, Russell Sage Foundation, New York.

KAPLAN, A. (1964) *The Conduct of Inquiry: Methodology for Behavioural Science*, Chandler, Pennsylvania.

KOGAN, M. and TERRY, J. (1971) *The Organisation of a Social Service Department: A Blue-Print*, Bookstall Publications, London.

LINDBLOM, C. E. (1965) *The Intelligence of Democracy*, The Free Press, New York.

LUKES, S. (1970) "Methodological individualism reconsidered", *Sociological Theory and Philosophical Analysis* (edited by EMMET, D. and MACINTYRE, A.), Macmillan, London.

MADGE, C. (1968) "Planning, social", *International Encyclopedia of the Social Sciences*, Vol. 9, pp. 125–9.

MCLOUGHLIN, B. J. (1969) *Urban and Regional Planning A Systems Approach*, Faber & Faber, London.

PERLOFF, H. S. (1957) *Education for Planning—City State and Regional*, John Hopkins, Baltimore.

QUADE, E. S. (1968) Introduction, *Systems Analysis and Policy Planning* (edited by QUADE, E. S. and BOUCHER, W. I.), Elsevier, New York.

SILVESTER, M. (1971) "Zur Kritik des Systemansatzes bei der Planung", *Stadtbauwelt*, Heft 32, S. 296–300.

10 *A Reader in Planning Theory*

SILVESTER, M. (1972) "The contribution of the systems approach to planning", *The Systems View of Planning* (Authors: DIMITRIOU, B., FALUDI, A., McDOUGALL, G., SILVESTER, M.), Oxford Working Papers in Planning Education and Research, No. 9.

WILSON, A. G. (1969) *Forecasting Planning*, Centre for Environmental Studies, London.

[3]

If Planning is Everything, Maybe it's Nothing

AARON WILDAVSKY

Graduate School of Public Policy, University of California, Berkeley

ABSTRACT

Where planning does not measure up to expectations, which is almost everywhere, planners are handy targets. They have been too ambitious or they have not been ambitious enough. They have perverted their calling by entering into politics or they have been insensitive to the political dimensions of their task. They ignore national cultural mores at their peril or they capitulate to blind forces of irrationality. They pay too much attention to the relationship between one sector of the economy and another while ignoring analysis of individual projects, or they spend so much time on specific matters that they are unable to deal with movements of the economy as a whole. Planners can no longer define a role for themselves. From old American cities to British new towns, from the richest countries to the poorest, planners have difficulty in explaining who they are and what they should be expected to do. If they are supposed to doctor sick societies, the patient never seems to get well. Why can't the planners ever seem to do the right thing?

Introduction

The planner has become the victim of planning; his own creation has overwhelmed him. Planning has become so large that the planner cannot encompass its dimensions. Planning has become so complex planners cannot keep up with it. Planning protrudes in so many directions, the planner can no longer discern its shape. He may be economist, political scientist, sociologist, architect or scientist. Yet the essence of his calling—planning—escapes him. He finds it everywhere in general and nowhere in particular. Why is planning so elusive?

The concept of planning stands between actors and their societies. It conditions the way they perceive social problems and it guides their choice of solutions. Their understanding of planning helps them to choose the questions they ask and the answers they find. It leads them to evaluate their experience, including their attempt to plan, in certain ways rather than others. The difficulties they experience in society are related to their understanding of the mechanism—planning—they believe will help them solve its problems.

Men think through language. They can hardly conceive of phenomena their words cannot express. The ways in which men think about planning affect how they act just as their attempts to plan affect how they think about it. The problems they have with the word mirror their problems with the world.

Planners begin by attempting to transform their environment and end by being absorbed into it. This pattern of failure is most evident in the poor countries of the world where glittering promise has been replaced by discouraging performance.[1] Nor, despite the high economic growth, are the results different in rich countries; brief examination of two critical cases—France and Japan—will show they also do not follow their plans or make good on them when they do. Planning fails everywhere it has been tried.

How can this be? The reasonable man plans ahead. He seeks to avoid future evils by anticipating them. He tries to obtain a more desirable future by working toward it in the present. Nothing seems more reasonable than planning. And that is where the problem begins; for if planning is reason, then reasonable people must be for it. A reasonable author addressing a reasonable reader cannot be opposed to reason. Is it irrational to dissent from this position?

One good question deserves another: can it be rational to fail? Now anyone can do the best he can and still not succeed. Suppose, however, that the failures of planning are not peripheral or accidental but integral to its very nature. Suppose planning as presently constituted cannot work in the environment in which it is supposed to function. Is it irrational to entertain this hypothesis? If it is irrational to pursue any hypothesis that does not confirm the rational nature of planning, then you are about to read an irrational essay.

Planning as Future Control

Practitioners and students of planning have given the word countless interpretations. Every writer, it seems, feels compelled to redefine the concept. And I am no exception. For the confusion resulting from this semantic Tower of Babel impinges on the practice of planning. How does one evaluate a phenomenon when there is little agreement about what it is? How can one say that planning is good or bad or in between when there are no accepted criteria for determining degrees of success or failure? Judgement of the performance of planning rests upon the nature of the expectations it arouses; and these expectations naturally vary with the definition one adopts. If planning is designed to make goals consistent on paper, one would judge it quite differently than if its purpose is actually to achieve social goals in the future.

Planning is the attempt to control the consequences of our actions. The more consequences we control, the more we have succeeded in planning. To use somewhat different language, planning is the ability to control the future by current acts. Instead of discovering his fate in the future, man plans to make it in his own image. But the present may be reluctant to give birth to the future. Man can attempt to plan and he can fail. As St. Paul put it in his letter to the Romans, "I do not understand my own

---

[1] This essay is a revised and expanded version of material appearing in Naomi Caiden and Aaron Wildavsky. *A Constant Quantity of Tears: Planning and Budgeting in Poor Countries* (The Twentieth Century Fund, forthcoming).

actions. For I do not do what I want, but I do the very thing I hate. . . . I can will what is right, but I cannot do it. For I do not do the good I want, but the evil I do not want is what I do." While man has helped cause these unanticipated events, he has not consciously intended (that is, planned) to bring them about. We must distinguish, therefore, between attempts to plan and actual success in planning.

Attempts to plan are no more planning than the desire to be wise may be called wisdom or the wish to be rich entitles a man to be called wealthy. Promise must be dignified by performance. The determination of whether planning has taken place must rest on an assessment of whether and to what degree future control has been achieved.

Planning must not be confused with the existence of a formal plan, people called planners, or an institution (henceforth called the planning commission) with the word planning in its official title. Formal plans are only one possible manifestation of planning, since planning may take place outside of formal planning organizations. The distinction here is between a written and an unwritten plan. No one today would claim that the British do not have a constitution (rules specifying the procedures for exercising political power) merely because theirs is found in legislation and custom rather than in a single document like that of the United States. Perhaps the existence of a formal plan suggests a greater commitment to the objectives and the subordinate goals in the plan than one would expect in the absence of such a visible public document. This question should be resolved by observation rather than by definition. Certainly the absence of a Bill of Rights in the "unwritten" British constitution does not reveal a lesser commitment to due process or democratic procedure than America's formal statement in its Constitution. In like manner, it would be wrong to say that a government that consciously improved the conditions of its people and increased their ability to live productive lives was not planning because it lacked the formal apparatus, while another government whose people suffered in these respects was planning because it had a plan and planners.

It is tempting to identify planning with government ownership of industry. Then the government is directly making decisions for the entire economy, and that would appear to eliminate the difficulties of plan implementation caused by a recalcitrant private sector. The decisions that are made, however, may turn out to run counter to the plan. Planned decisions often have unplanned consequences. It would be more accurate to say that these governments attempt to plan but do not necessarily succeed, if success means controlling the future direction of their society through a pre-determined series of actions. Achievement and not the plan must be the final arbiter of planning. Otherwise, planning exists because there is a plan, no matter what fate has in store for it.

We want a definition of planning that will enable us to compare the efficacy of different ways of achieving control over the future. We want to be able to say that one process or strategy or social structure is better or worse in enabling society to move in the direction it chooses in the most expeditious manner. Central direction of the economy, reliance on a price mechanism, devotion to traditional culture, emphasis on agriculture and small industry, any and all bases for action may be judged by their consequences so long as none are identified as planning itself.

A definition based on attempts to plan—planning as a goal-directed behavior—leaves open the question of whether the actions involved have resulted in the kind of future control envisaged. By defining planning according to its inputs (different modes of trying to control the future) rather than its outputs (extent of future control) the element of direction is removed from planning. Such a definition might be appropriate for those interested in different styles of decision for their own sake but not for people concerned with appraising purposeful social action.

For if a definition covers all attempts to plan, whether they succeed or not, planning encompasses whatever men intend to do in the world. Since practically all actions with future consequences are planned actions, planning is everything, and nonplanning can hardly be said to exist. Nonplanning only exists when people have no objectives, when their actions are random and not goal-directed. If everybody plans (well, almost) it is not possible to distinguish planned from unplanned actions.

A definition of planning based on formal position—planning is whatever planners do—is useful if one wishes to examine the activities of people who occupy these places. But a formal definition rules out on *a priori* grounds the likelihood that ability to control the consequences of current actions may be more widely diffused in society. The question becomes not "who in society succeeds in planning?" but "how successful are formal planners in planning?" The planners are the active element, their society the passive beneficiary of their efforts.

Planning is often used (though this definition is rarely made explicit) as if it were equivalent to rationality. Once norms associated with rational action are identified—efficiency, consistency, coordination—any process of decision may be appraised according to the degree to which it conforms to them. The assumption is that following these norms leads to better decisions. Defining planning as applied rationality focuses attention on adherence to universal norms rather than on the consequences of acting one way instead of another. Attention is directed to the internal qualities of the decisions and not to their external effects.

The confusions surrounding the meaning of planning may have a social explanation. Unable to control the future, planners have resisted any other definition that would brand them as failures. After all, no one else is forced to make public predictions that rarely turn out right. Planners want credit for their aspirations, for a noble effort, so they grope toward a definition that stresses the activities in which they engage or the processes through which they work. Exhibition displaces power. The focus of meaning can then shift from events in the world to their own exemplary behavior.

These definitions are not merely different ways of looking at the same thing. They are not just words. They imply different standards for planning and they direct our attention to different phenomena. To define planning as future control, for instance, does away with the distinction between drawing up plans and implementing them, setting goals and achieving them. The objective and its fulfillment are part of the same series of actions.[2] Separating goals from achievements, as most definitions do by emphasizing intention over accomplishment, blurs the distinction between planning

---

[2] See Jeffrey L. Pressman and Aaron Wildavsky, *Implementation* (University of California Press, 1973, forthcoming).

and other purposeful behavior. Hence planning becomes a self-protecting hypothesis; so long as planners try to plan, it cannot be falsified.

In order to understand the implications of these rival definitions, let us consider what is involved in the statements about planning made by practitioner and theorist alike. Virtually everyone would agree that planning requires: (1) A specification of future objectives and (2) a series of related actions over time designed to achieve them. We can now try to discover in general terms what is entailed by national planning.

Planning as Cause

We can say (beginning with the implementing actions) that the first requisite of national planning is causal knowledge: the existence of theory with at least some evidence to support it specifying causal relationships. If X and Y are done, then Z will result. If the consequences of contemplated actions cannot accurately be appraised, specified objectives will be achieved only by accident. The necessity for causal knowledge is made more stringent in long-range planning because the consequences of each action become the basis for the succeeding steps. Each error in prediction is magnified because of its impact on future decisions.

It will help if we specify the kinds of causal knowledge planning requires: a knowledge of the relationships in each of dozens of areas of policy from fisheries to foreign exchange. These relationships may be further subdivided: (1) interaction among the elements of the policy itself, (2) incentives for the people involved to carry out the policy or mechanisms for insuring compliance, (3) sufficient resources at the time required. In agriculture, for example, knowledge of the elements of the policy itself—the technology of production, the mechanisms of distribution, the availability of markets—must be right if the policy is to work. If the farmers will not plant the crops called for or if the prices do not bring them sufficient remuneration, they will sabotage the policy, either overtly or through passive resistance. If there is insufficient money for seeds or fertilizer or if the farmer lacks the education or the motivation to employ the necessary techniques, the policy will fail.

Even if good theory exists somewhere in the world, people in a particular society must be able to apply it in the specific context of their own country. Yet knowledge of how to apply theory is often as weak as the theory itself. Social circumstances may make a mockery of general principles. There may be few men who are capable of utilizing existing theory for practical purposes. Where causal theory is absent or imperfect, where applications are poor or nonexistent, where personnel to carry out policies is lacking or badly trained, the preconditions of formal planning cannot be met.

Yet we have not begun to exhaust the requirements of causal knowledge. Not only is it required in each important area of policy (actually it is also necessary to know which areas are important), but among areas of policy as well. Energy policy, for example, cannot be pursued apart from transportation, industrial and agricultural policy. The major consequences of each set of policy decisions for other areas of policy must be known; if they are not, some objectives will be achieved at the expense of others or none of the objectives will be achieved. Scarce as causal theory is within specific areas

131

of policy, it is superabundant compared to the lack of knowledge of interaction effects. There are no useful models of economies as a whole; either they contain so few variables as to be too general, or they contain so many that one cannot understand what goes on inside them, let alone in the world to which they are supposed to refer. If economic theory is weak, theories of society involving human motivation and incentive are barely alive. The provision of information itself is dependent on cultural norms, political support and administrative practices that usually work in the opposite direction. Thus the lack of theory means that one often does not know what kind of information to collect, and, in any event, it would probably not be available.

Causal knowledge is also necessary to relate the policies of the nation over time to changes in the international economy and political systems. Low income countries are especially vulnerable to fluctuations in the price of imports and exports and in the willingness of previous donor nations to supply aid. Should the plan require a certain amount of foreign currency, it can easily disintegrate if commodity prices drop, imports rise, and foreign aid disappears. There are no good predictive models of international prices or of willingness to supply aid.

National planning provides a hard test of causal knowledge. Men, resources and institutions must be mobilized and related to one another at successive stages in time in order to obtain predicted results that lead to the achievement of objectives. Nothing less than control of the future is involved.

Any regime, whether it professes to love planning and enshrines *the plan* in its hall of fame, or whether it rejects formal planning entirely, plans to the extent that it can control its future. Planning takes place when people in a society are able to cause consequences they desire to occur. Planning is, therefore, a form of social causation. It requires causal knowledge and the ability to wield that knowledge effectively in society. Power and planning are different ways of looking at the same events.

Planning as Power

Power is the probability of changing the behavior of others against opposition.[3] As soon as the prevalence of disagreement over social goals or policies is admitted into the discussion, it becomes clear that there can be no planning without the ability to cause other people to act differently than they otherwise would. Planning assumes power. Planning is politics.

Power is a reciprocal relationship. It depends not only on what one actor can do but on how the other relevant actors respond in turn. A group may decide not to attempt to realize its intentions because doing so would use up resources that might be better employed elsewhere. Or its efforts may fail because others lack the ability to carry out their instructions. The wielders of power are restricted not only by the limits

---

[3] See Andrew McFarland, *Power and Leadership in Pluralist Systems* (Stanford, California: Stanford University Press, 1969); Herbert Simon, *Models of Man* (New York: Wiley, 1957); John Harsanyi, "Measurement of Social Power, Opportunity Costs, and the Theory of Two-Person Bargaining Games," *Behavioral Science*, Vol. VII (Jan. 1962), pp. 67–80; Robert Dahl, "Power," *International Encyclopedia of the Social Sciences* (New York: Macmillan and Free Press, 1968), Vol. XII, pp. 405–415; James March, "The Power of Power," in David Easton, ed., *Varieties of Political Theory* (Englewood Cliffs, N.J.: Prentice-Hall, 1966), pp. 39–70.

on their own resources but also by the capacities of the respondents. Power must be viewed in its social context.[4]

Planning requires the power to maintain the preeminence of future objectives in the present. The nation's rulers must be able to commit its existing resources to the accomplishment of future objectives. If new rulers arise who make drastic changes in objectives, the original plan is finished. The continuity of the regime, of course, is one of the more problematical features of the poor country. Its unity may crumble, its devotion to original objectives may be undermined from within, and its ability to command the nation's resources may be dissipated through disagreement. Either the rulers must stay in power long enough to accomplish their original purposes or their successors must be people who share the same commitments.

If planning is to be more than an academic exercise, it must actually guide the making of governmental decisions. Governmental actions (and the private activities they seek to influence) must in large measure conform to the plan if it is to have practical effect. Planning, then, at any point in time, involves governmental decisions on resource allocation. A theory of how planning should be done, therefore, would be a theory of governmental resource allocation over time. Planning theory becomes a theory of successive government budgets. If we substitute the words "what the government ought to do" for the words "ought to be in the plan," it becomes clear that a normative theory of planning would have to include a political theory detailing what the government's activities ought to be at a particular time.

To plan, therefore, is to govern. Planning thus becomes the process through which society makes its decisions. If one takes a narrow view of politics, only acts by official government bodies are planning acts. A broader view of politics would include all acts, whether ostensibly private or public, that have substantial future impact on society. To plan is to make decisions that affect others. Planners are presidents, ministers, bureaucrats, party leaders, scientists, entrepreneurs—anybody whose acts have large future consequences.

But the act of governing need not necessarily involve planning; intentions in actions may be unrealized. Political leaders, like planners, may find that they cannot control the future. All may try but none may succeed. Planners and politicians may compete for the right to attempt to plan but there may be no victor to claim the spoils.

Formal planners may be viewed as rivals for control of policy with other government agencies and private groups. Can planners dominate these competitors? They can be nothing if no one listens to them. They may be used by others but have no independent force of their own. Planners may also be everything. They may become the government and exert most of the public force in their nation. Although planning theory sometimes suggests that this is the position planners would need in order to carry out their purposes, and though planners in moments of frustration may wish they had this power, it would be fair to say they do not envisage total control. The vision they have of themselves is of a small but dedicated band that somehow enables the nation to meet goals by bringing it to its senses when necessary. They have in mind a regulator role of the type found in cybernetic systems: amidst a vast complex of machinery there is a small but sensitive device that returns the system to its true path whenever

---

[4] Harsanyi, *op. cit.*

it strays. By pushing in the right direction at critical times the sum of the corrections adds up to achievement of the original goals. France and Germany might well adopt this thermostatic view of planning. But poor countries require far more than occasional correction; they need large inputs of energy in order to build important components of their systems. Thus planners vacillate between the thermostatic view, which is more in accordance with their potential, and the assumption of total power, which is beyond their grasp, when the small changes they can cause are overwhelmed by the large ones over which they have little control.

The experience of formal planners has a universal tinge. Life is full of small corrections. Rarely is it possible to pursue objectives on a once-and-for-all basis. Relative success in meeting goals depends on new actions in response to changing circumstances. Learning, adjustment, adaptation are the keys to accomplishment. What happens to the original objectives when behavior changes in the light of new conditions?

Planning as Adaptation

Until now I have taken for granted the existence of future objectives, each one neatly labeled as if they came out of a great national sausage machine in the sky. They have been assumed to exist somehow "out there". The time has come to inquire into the setting of objectives.

One way to determine future objectives is to extrapolate present trends. The goal in the future is to go where the society was headed in any event. The very idea of planning, however, suggests that one is not letting things go any which way, but intervenes to make them move in a different direction or faster or slower in the same direction. You do not need a plan to get you where you were going to be. How, then, are new objectives created?

It turns out that there are no rules for determining objectives. The rules we do have for resource allocation—efficiency, productivity—assume that objectives are given. These rules specify: achieve a given objective at lowest cost or achieve as much of a given objective as possible from a fixed amount of resources. They posit relationships between inputs and outputs; they do not say what the outputs should be, other than getting the most out of the inputs related to them.

Suppose that governmental leaders simply pick any set that appeals to them. What validity should be accorded these objectives? The obvious answer is that they are authoritative if set out by leaders who will attempt to achieve them. This amounts to saying that they are valid because the government says so. Yet the idea of planning, with its connotations of reason and intelligence, resists the thought that objectives are just stuck out there. Presumably the planners must relate these objectives in some way to the capabilities of the nation as well as to the desires of its leaders.

An objective may be desirable but unobtainable. The result of seeking it may be a waste of resources. Fidel Castro publicly accepts blame for setting a quota of sugar cane so high that cutting went far past the time and use of resources that were economically justified.[5] But no one knows what the right level would be. If sights are

---

[5] *The New York Times*, January 25, 1971, p. 55.

set too low, less may be done than desirable. If too high, unnecessary effort may be devoted to the task. Like Goldilocks, the leaders would like to come out just right. But that is too complex a task. So they simplify by allowing experience to modify the goals they set.

The Soviet Union's response to this dilemma has been instructive. The goals stated in their plans are meant to be targets. If a particular sector of the economy achieves its production goal, the standard is raised next time. Should the goal remain unfulfilled, the people involved are driven harder. If they still cannot make it, the target is lowered through negotiation.[6] There may be an implicit Pavlovian theory of human behavior in this process, but there is nothing scientific about the setting of objectives. Essentially, an arbitrary objective goal is set and then is modified with experience or sometimes just abandoned.

Another approach is to think of objectives as distant rather than near targets. Leaders spell out their objectives and hope to achieve them sometime, even if not in the period specified in the plan. Some might call this utopian, but others would say it represents a society going in a predetermined direction, though the pace of that effort is subject to change. Although this approach may be reasonable, it subverts the basic element of control which is supposed to differentiate planning from just mucking about.

What is the point of saying that the seven-year plan has been achieved in 22 months or that a certain industry has exceeded its quota or that it will take $9\frac{1}{4}$ years to achieve some part of the five-year plan? Presumably the idea of planning is that you get where you are going when you say you will and in the manner specified. Can it mean that you get some other place faster or the same place slower and in a way you did not anticipate? This is not a quibble. It goes to the heart of the idea of planning.

What has happened is that the objectives and the means for obtaining them are no longer fixed but have become subject to modification. The original set of objectives and the plan that embodies them are considered merely starting points. They are altered on the basis of experience and necessity. A new regime, a change in commodity prices, discovery of a new theory, accumulation of changes in national cultural mores, may all signify the desirability of changing objectives and the policies to implement them. Adaptation to changing circumstances is certainly a virtue of the intelligent man. But it smacks of *ad hoc* decisionmaking.

When planning is placed in the context of continuous adjustment it becomes hard to distinguish from any other process of decision. By making planning reasonable it becomes inseparable from the processes of decision it was designed to supplant. One plans the way one governs; one does the best one can at the time and hopes that future information will enable one to do better as circumstances change. Some call this adaptive planning; others call it muddling through. Under the criteria of adaptation, almost any process for making decisions in a social context can be considered to be planning.

---

[6] Joseph Berliner, *Factory and Manager in the U.S.S.R.* (Cambridge: Harvard University Press, 1957); David Granick, *The Red Executive* (Garden City, N.Y.: Doubleday, 1961).

Planning as Process

One cannot, for instance, discuss democracy for long without using the terms—goals, alternatives, appraisals, objectives—which are at the heart of almost any contemporary definition of planning. This suggests that electoral democracy may be considered a mode of planning.

The United States does not seek to achieve goals stated in a national plan. Yet that does not mean that the United States has no goals its decisionmakers try to achieve. There are institutions—the Federal Reserve Board, the Council of Economic Advisers, the Office of Management and Budget, Congressional committees, and more—whose task is to find goals and policies that embody them. There are specific pieces of legislation that are dedicated to full employment, ending or mitigating the effects of pollution, building highways, expanding recreational opportunities, improving agricultural productivity, and on and on. When these goals conflict, new decisions must be made concerning how much of each to try to achieve. Even a single goal like full employment may not be capable of achievement because there is not enough knowledge to do it or because it entails other costs, such as inflation, that prohibit it. Moreover, these goals are related to ultimate objectives. The Preamble to the Constitution states national goals and the remainder presents an institutional plan for achieving them. The government of the United States seeks to achieve domestic prosperity and to protect its interests overseas. While these broad objectives remain constant the intermediate goals change in response to forces in society.

When he was a student in the City Planning Department of the University of California at Berkeley, Owen McShane wrote a paper making explicit the similarities between planning (as found in the model developed by West Churchman, in his book, *The Systems Approach*) and electoral democracy as a process of making decisions. Churchman postulates that planning is concerned with multi-stage decisionmaking and "hence it must study (1) a decisionmaker who (2) chooses among alternative courses of action in order to reach (3) certain first-stage goals, which lead to (4) other-stage objectives."[7] It is easy to parallel this model in terms of electoral democracy as the operation of (1) the electorate which (2) chooses from a group of candidates in order to reach (3) certain first-stage goals, which lead to (4) the implicit goals of the society at large.

Placing the steps in each system side by side, McShane found that the electoral process fitted Churchman's model with remarkable nicety. Every step has an operational equivalent in any electoral democracy.

Similar comparisons could be made between the process of planning and the process of legislation and administration. Consider, for instance, a recent description of how public policy is made: "Generically, one can identify at least six different steps in the process of making government policy—publicizing a problem, initiating a search for a solution, evaluating alternative solutions, choosing a solution or a combination of solutions, implementing the measures decided upon, and finally,

---

[7] West Churchman, *The Systems Approach* (New York: Delacorte Press, 1968), p. 150.

136

TABLE I

THE PLANNING SYSTEM	THE ELECTORAL DEMOCRATIC SYSTEM
Program 1: Legitimacy	**Program 1: Legitimacy**
Relationship between the planning system (P.S.) and the decisionmakers.	Relationship between the constitution, etc., and the electorate.
(a) Justification (why the P.S. should exist and its role).	(a) Justification (why democracy should exist and its role).
(b) Staffing the P.S. and establishing responsibility and authority.	(b) Designing the institutions of democracy and establishing responsibility and authority.
(c) The Communication Subsystem	(c) The Communication Subsystem
(i) Persuasion (selling the P.S.)	(i) Persuasion (e.g. the Federalist, etc.)
(ii) Mutual education.	(ii) Public schools and media.
(iii) Politics identifying and changing the power structure of the organization.	(iii) Politics (constitutional amendments, judiciary).
(d) Implementation (installing the plan).	(d) Implementation (setting up the institutions and operating them).
Program 2: Analysis	**Program 2: Analysis**
Measurement (Identification, classification, prediction, etc.)	Measurement (Identification, classification, prediction, etc.)
(a) Identifying the decisionmakers, and customers of the larger system.	(a) Identifying interest groups, setting the franchise, etc.
(b) Discovering and inventing the alternatives.	(b) Selecting candidates for office.
(c) Identifying the first stage goals.	(c) Identifying and lobbying for first stage goals and policies.
(d) Identifying the ultimate objectives.	(d) Identifying the ultimate aims of society (e.g., Goal for Americans, Bill of Rights, etc.)
(e) Measuring the effectiveness of each alternative for each first stage goal.	(e) Assessing the candidate and his policy platform.
(f) Measuring the effectiveness of each first stage goal for the ultimate objectives.	(f) Assessing the effectiveness of policies for ultimate objectives (e.g. the Vietnam war as protecting democracy).
(g) Estimating the optimal alternative.	(g) Voting for the candidates of one's choice.
Program 3: Testing (*Verifying the Plan*)	**Program 3: Testing** (*Does the democracy work?*)
(a) Simulation and parallel testing.	(a) Comparison with other nations, self-appraisal by the citizenry.
(b) Controlling the plan once implemented.	(b) Checks and balances, news media, public debate, the opposition.

evaluating the consequences of a measure."[8] At this level of description there appears to be no significant difference between the United States (and almost any other government, for that matter) and societies that engage in planning.

When planning is conceived of as goal-directed behavior, almost any decisionmaking process will be found to contain similar elements. How then can we evaluate planning? Asking what has been caused by goal-directed behavior is like requesting an explanation for all that has happened. If the process of planning cannot usefully be separated from other modes of choice, the observer will be unable to attribute consequences to

---

[8] Richard Rose, "The Variability of Party Government: A Theoretical and Empirical Critique," *Political Studies* (Dec. 1969) vol. XVII, no. 4, p. 415.

planning that do not also belong to other ways of making decisions; its merits cannot be challenged by future events because they all have their origin in someone's efforts to secure his aims.

If planning is to be judged by its consequences, by what it accomplishes, we must return to the problem of causality. What has planning caused? What has happened differently because of the presence of plans, planners and planning commissions than would have happened without them? What, in the economist's language, is the value added by planning?

Evaluation of planning is not possible so long as it refers to mere effort. The only sportsmanlike response to a runner who has given his all, is "good try," especially if he has fallen at the first turn. Only if planning is defined to mean completed action, achieving a set goal, can its relative degree of success be appraised.

If we are willing to equate national planning with a formal plan, it is possible to ask whether the interventions specified in it have been carried out, and whether they have come close to achieving the desired ends. Evaluation of formal planning depends on forging a valid link between intentions expressed in the plan and future performance of the nation.

Planning as Intention

I have grossly simplified the problem of deciding whether intentions have been carried out by placing them solely in the hands of planners and assuming that their intentions are manifested in the national plan. Judging plans and planners by their intentions nevertheless has strong attractions. The plan itself has the inestimable advantage of existing in time and space and being separable from other phenomena. The plan speaks of accomplishing certain things in specified ways and one can ask whether these future states of affairs have indeed come about. If the plan predicts a rate of economic growth, supported by the development of certain sectors of the economy, propelled by various key projects, one can ascertain whether that rate has been achieved, whether the sectors singled out for special attention have grown in the way specified and whether the projects have been built and are bringing in the returns that were claimed for them. To the extent that the planners are not impossibly vague about what they intend, and relevant information is available and accurate, the plan may be judged by the degree to which its intentions have been carried out.

Yet the criterion of intention may easily prove superficial. Let us suppose that a plan has failed the test of accomplishing the goals set down in it. How might one explain that failure? If the plan is viewed as a series of predictions, it is evident that they have not come true. Yet calling a bad prediction a failure in an uncertain world seems harsh. More to the point would be a statement that the planners were unable to move the nation in the directions they intended. The claim can still be made, however, that much progress occurred, even if it fell short of the initial aims. Imagine a situation in which under Plan I a 4% growth rate was postulated and only 3% achieved, while in Plan II a 10% rate was set out and one of 6% achieved. Plan I was more successful in the sense that the growth rate came closer to the target, but Plan II was more successful in that the overall rate of growth was greater. Assume for the moment that both levels of growth are attributable to the plan. Why should one set

138

of planners be criticized because of their higher level of aspirations if their actual accomplishments are greater? When the intentions in plans are not realized it is difficult to know whether this failure is due to poor performance or unreasonable expectations. Did the nation try to do too little or too much? Were its planners over-ambitious or underachievers?

Planners are vulnerable. Unless they take the precaution of making their goals too vague to be tested, their failure is evident for all to see. They must spend their time not in explaining how they have succeeded but in arguing away their evident failures. A great deal can be learned about fulfilling intentions by noting what happens when early optimism is replaced by later rationalization.

When a venture runs into trouble there are a number of classic ways of justifying it without showing that its performance is actually better. The usual tactic is to claim that the venture has not been tried hard enough, that doing more of the same would bring the results originally envisaged. If the bombing of North Vietnam does not weaken the will of that government to resist, the answer is evidently not to stop but to do more of it. When the poverty programs in the United States lead to disappointing results, then the answer must be that not enough money has been poured into them. It is always difficult to know whether the theory behind the policy is mistaken, so that additional effort would mean throwing good money after bad, or whether greater input of resources would reach the critical mass presumed necessary to make it successful. The same argument is made in regard to formal planning: if only there were more effort, more dedication, more commitment, things would be better. This argument, however, presumes on behalf of formal planning precisely what it is supposed to prove. If things were as they were supposed to be, planning would not be necessary to correct them. The argument is reminiscent of a practitioner's comment about planning around the world: in Russia it is imperative, in France it is indicative, and in poor countries it is subjunctive.

The usual way of justifying formal planning in the absence of (or contrary to the evidence about) accomplishment is to shift the focus of discussion from goals to process. The critic of planning, it is said, has evidently mistaken the nature of the enterprise: by focusing in his simple-minded way on the intentions of the planners he has missed the beneficial effects of the processes through which the plan is made. A similar argument is heard about the United States space program: it is not merely reaching the moon but all the wonderful things learned on the way up and down (cf. technological fallout) that justify the cost of the effort. Planning is good, therefore, not so much for what it does but for how it goes about not doing it.

The process of planning presumably inculcates habits of mind leading to more rational choice. Officials are sensitized to the doctrine of opportunity costs, to what must be given up in order to pursue certain alternatives, and to the notion of enterprise as a productive force in the nation's economy. Time horizons are expanded because the future is made part of present decisions. Because of the existence of the plans and the planners, data may have been collected that otherwise would not have been; men with economic skills have been introduced into government. Those who come in contact with these new men are said to benefit from their new ways of looking at the world. To ask how these spinoff benefits are made tangible would be to retreat to the fallacy—comparing the intentions of planners with their accomplishments—that the process argument was designed to subvert.

There is another way of getting around the problem of intention and its realization; instead of merely saying that the intentions specified in the plan are not the real ones, one can argue that the planners are not the people whose intentions count. An interest-group leader or a politician may have hidden agenda the plan is supposed to achieve. The plan thus becomes an instrument for the purposes of others; its provisions are to be judged by the degree to which it serves their needs. To determine whether planning was successful or not would, therefore, require specific knowledge of the real purposes for which it was used and no *a priori* judgements from afar would be appropriate.

Plans and planners in this context are simply one element in a repertoire of responses in the political arena that are available to those powerful and clever enough to use them. Plans may be weapons wielded by one political faction against another. The forces of logic, reason and rationality may be used by a president against a recalcitrant ministry or by one ministry or region versus another. The possibilities are endless. If national leaders wish to be thought modern, for instance, they have a document with which to dazzle their visitors. Charts, tables, graphs, regressions, are trotted out, but no one who matters attends to them. The plan need not be a means of surmounting the nation's difficulties, but rather may become a mode of covering them up.

By taking the argument one step further, the idea of plans as intentions can be dissolved entirely. One no longer asks whether the intentions in the plan are carried out, but which of many competing intentions is validated, if, indeed, any are. In this view there is no single set of intentions, any more than there is a general will that can be embodied in a single plan. There are different wills and various interests that compete for shares in planning. Some of these "wills" get adopted as government plans for a time and then are altered or revised. The great questions then become: whose intentions are realized? Are anyone's plans made good by the unfolding of events?

Once conflict over goals is admitted, intention evaporates as a useful criterion for judging the success of planning. The planners lose their hold over intention; it is no longer immutable but problematical, a subject for bargaining, a counter in the flux of events. The stage shifts from the intentions specified in the plan to a multitude of actors whose intentions are alleged to be the real ones. The success of planning depends entirely on whose plans one has in mind.

My discussion of intention may be rejected, not necessarily because it's misleading (though that may be the case), but because it's seen as irrelevant. Sophisticated people, critics might say, have long since abandoned both the idea of national planning and of national intentions. They may go along with it for its symbolic value but they know it does not work. "So why bother to spend all this time discussing it," one can hear them say. Planners have a much more modest conception—to reduce the scope of efforts by concentrating on individual sectors of the economy and move in the direction of dealing with relatively small and circumscribed problems. They seek to discover an actual opportunity for decision, to elaborate a few alternatives and to discuss their probable consequences in a limited way. They cut their costs of calculations by vastly reducing the magnitude of the tasks they set for themselves.

140

This approach is basically conservative. It takes for granted the existing distribution of wealth and power. It works with whatever price mechanism exists. It seeks not to influence many decisions at once but only a few. Now the ordinary men who would otherwise have made these decisions in the absence of planners also concentrate on a very narrow area of specialization; they also consider a few different ways of doing things; they also estimate the probable consequences in a limited way, and they also choose the alternative that seems best under the circumstances. By making planning manageable it appears we have made it indistinguishable from ordinary processes of decision. Planning has been rescued by diminishing, if not entirely obliterating, the difference between it and everyday decisionmaking. Of what, then, do the advantages of planning consist?

Maybe we have been looking at planning in the wrong way. The place to look for the virtues of planning, perhaps, is not in the world but in the word. Planning is good, it seems, because it is good to plan.

Planning is not really defended for what it does but for what it symbolizes. Planning, identified with reason, is conceived to be the way in which intelligence is applied to social problems. The efforts of planners are presumably better than other people's because they result in policy proposals that are systematic, efficient, coordinated, consistent, and rational. It is words like these that convey the superiority of planning. The virtue of planning is that it embodies universal norms of rational choice.

Planning as Rationality

Certain key terms appear over and over again: planning is good because it is *systematic* rather than random, *efficient* rather than wasteful, *coordinated* rather than helter-skelter, *consistent* rather than contradictory, and above all, *rational* rather than unreasonable. In the interest of achieving a deeper understanding of why planning is preferred, it will be helpful to consider these norms as instructions to decisionmakers. What would they do if they followed them?

Be systematic! What does it mean to say that decisions should be made in a systematic manner? A word like "careful" will not do because planners cannot be presumed to be more careful than other people. Perhaps "orderly" is better; it implies a checklist of items to be taken into account, but anyone can make a list. Being systematic implies further that one knows the right variables in the correct order to put into the list, and can specify the relationship among them. The essential meaning of systematic, therefore, is having qualities of a system, that is a series of variables whose interactions are known and whose outputs can be predicted from knowledge of their inputs. System, therefore, is another word for theory or model explaining and predicting events in the real world in a parsimonious way that permits manipulation.[9] To say that one is being systematic, consequently implies that one has causal knowledge.

Here we have part of the answer we have been seeking. Planning is good because inherent in the concept is the possession of knowledge that can be used to control the world. Knowledge is hard to obtain; the mind of man is small and simple while the

---

9 See David J. Berlinski, "Systems Analysis", *Urban Affairs Quarterly*, September 1970, 7, no. 1, pp. 104–126.

world is large and complex. Hence the temptation to imply by a cover word possession of the very thing, causal knowledge, that is missing.

Be efficient! There is in modern man a deeply-rooted belief that objectives should be obtained at the least cost. Who can quarrel with that? But technical efficiency should never be considered by itself. It does not tell you where to go but only that you should arrive there (or part way) by the least effort.

The great questions are: efficiency for whom and for what? There are some goals (destroying other nations in nuclear war, decreasing the living standards of the poverty-stricken in order to benefit the wealthy) that one does not wish achieved at all, let alone efficiently. Efficiency, therefore, raises once more the prior question of objectives.

One of the most notable characteristics of national objectives is that they tend to be vague, multiple and contradictory. Increasing national income is rarely the only social objective. It has to be traded off against more immediate consumption objectives, such as raising the living standards of rural people. Cultural objectives such as encouraging the spread of native languages and crafts, may have to be undertaken at a sacrifice of income. Political objectives, such as the desire to improve racial harmony or assert national independence, may lead to distribution of investment funds to economically unprofitable regions and to rejection of certain kinds of foreign aid. A great deal depends on which objectives enter into national priorities first, because there is seldom room for emphasis on more than a few.

Stress on efficiency assumes that objectives are agreed upon. Conflict is banished. The very national unity to which the plan is supposed to contribute turns out to be one of its major assumptions.

Coordinate! Coordination is one of the golden words of our time. I cannot offhand think of any way in which the word is used that implies disapproval. Policies should be coordinated; they should not run every which-way. No one wishes their children to be described as uncoordinated. Many of the world's ills are attributed to lack of coordination in government. Yet, so far as we know, there has never been a serious effort to analyze the term. It requires and deserves full discussion. All that can be done here, however, is barely to open up the subject.

Policies should be mutually supportive rather than contradictory. People should not work at cross purposes. The participants in any particular activity should contribute to a common purpose at the right time and in the right amount to achieve coordination. A should facilitate B in order to achieve C. From this intuitive sense of coordination four important (and possibly contradictory) meanings can be derived.

If there is a common objective, then efficiency requires that it be achieved with the least input of resources. When these resources are supplied by a number of different actors, hence the need for coordination, they must all contribute their proper share at the correct time. If their actions are efficient, that means they contributed just what they should and no more or less.

Coordination, then, equals efficiency, which is highly prized because achieving it means avoiding bad things: duplication, overlapping and redundancy. These are bad because they result in unnecessary effort, thereby expending resources that might be used more effectively for other purposes. But now we shall complicate matters by introducing another criterion that is (for good reason) much less heard in discussion of planning. I refer to reliability, the probability that a particular function will be performed. Heretofore we have assumed that reliability was taken care of in the definition of efficiency. It has been discussed as if the policy in mind had only to work once. Yet we all know that major problems of designing policies can center on the need to have them work at a certain level of reliability. For this reason, as Martin Landau has so brilliantly demonstrated, redundancy is built-in to most human enterprises.[10] We ensure against failure by having adequate reserves and by creating several mechanisms to perform a single task in case one should fail.

Coordination of complex activities requires redundancy. Telling us to avoid duplication gives us no useful instruction at all; it is just a recipe for failure. What we need to know is how much and what kind of redundancy to build-in to our programs. The larger the number of participants in an enterprise, the more difficult the problem of coordination, the greater the need for redundancy.

Participants in a common enterprise may act in a contradictory fashion because of ignorance; when informed of their place in the scheme of things, they may obediently be expected to behave properly. If we relax the assumption that a common purpose is involved, however, and admit the possibility (indeed the likelihood) of conflict over goals, then coordination becomes another term for coercion. Since actors A and B disagree with goal C, they can only be coordinated by being told what to do and doing it. The German word, *Gleichschaltung*, used by the Nazis in the sense of enforcing a rigid conformity, can give us some insight into this particular usage of coordination. To coordinate one must be able to get others to do things they do not want to do. Coordination thus becomes a form of coercive power.

When one bureaucrat tells another to coordinate a policy, he means that it should be cleared with other official participants who have some stake in the matter. This is a way of sharing the blame in case things go wrong (each initial on the documents being another hostage against retribution). Since they cannot be coerced, their consent must be obtained. Bargaining must take place to reconcile the differences with the result that the policy may be modified, even at the cost of compromising its original purposes. Coordination in this sense is another word for consent.

Coordination means achieving efficiency and reliability, consent and coercion. Telling another person to achieve coordination, therefore, does not tell him what to do. He does not know whether to coerce or bargain or what mixture of efficiency and reliability to attempt. Here we have another example of an apparently desirable trait of planning that covers up the central problems—conflict versus cooperation, coercion versus consent—that its invocation is supposed to resolve. Planning suffers from the same disability that Herbert Simon illustrated for proverbial wisdom in administration:[11] each apparently desirable trait may be countered by its opposite—look before you leap, but he who hesitates is lost. An apt illustration is the use of "consistency".

Be consistent! Do not run in all directions at once. Consistency may be conceived

---

[10] Martin Landau, "Redundancy, Rationality, and the Problem of Duplication and Overlap", *Public Administration Review* (July 1969) vol. XXIX, pp. 346–358.

[11] Herbert Simon, "The Proverbs of Administration," *Public Administration Review* (Winter 1946) vol. VI, pp. 53–67.

as horizontal (at a moment in time) or vertical (over a series of time periods extending into the future). Vertical consistency requires that the same policy be pursued, horizontal consistency that it mesh with others existing at the same time. The former requires continuity of a powerful regime able to enforce its preferences, the latter tremendous knowledge of how policies affect one another. These are demanding prerequisites. One requires extraordinary rigidity to ensure continuity, the other unusual flexibility to achieve accommodation with other policies. Be firm, be pliant, are hard directions to follow at one and the same time.

The divergent directions implied in the term suggest that the virtues of consistency should not be taken for granted. It may well be desirable to pursue a single tack with energy and devotion but it may also prove valuable to hedge one's bets. Consistency secures a higher payoff for success but also imposes a steeper penalty for failure. If several divergent policies are being pursued in the same area they may interfere with each other but there also may be a greater chance that one will succeed. The admonition "Be consistent" may be opposed by the proverb, "Don't put all your eggs in the same basket."

Consistency is not wholly compatible with adaptation. While it may be desirable to pursue a steady course, it is also commonsensical to adapt to changing circumstances. There is the model of the unchanging objective pursued by numerous detours and tactical retreats but never abandoned and ultimately achieved. There is also the model of learning in which experience leads men to alter their objectives as well as the means of obtaining them. They may come to believe the cost is too high or they may learn they prefer a different objective. Apparent inconsistency may turn out to be a change in objectives. If both means and ends, policies and objectives, are changing simultaneously, consistency may turn out to be a will o' the wisp that eludes one's grasp whenever one tries to capture it.[12] The resulting inconsistency may not matter so much, however, as long as alternative courses of action are thoroughly examined at each point of decision.

Consider alternatives! Which ones? How many? Answers to these questions depend on the inventiveness of the planners; the acknowledged constraints; (such as limited funds, social values), and the cost in terms of time, talent, and money, that can be

---

[12] It is, by the way, often difficult to know when inconsistent actions are taking place. Leaving aside obtaining accurate information, there are serious conceptual problems. Policies are often stated in general terms that leave ample scope for varying interpretations of their intent. Ambiguity sometimes performs a political function by enabling people (who might otherwise disagree if everything was made clear) to get together. There cannot then be a firm criterion against which to judge consistency. There is also the question of conflicting perspectives among actors and observers. The observer may note an apparent commitment to a certain level and type of investment and see it vitiated by diversion of funds to wage increases. To the observer this means inconsistency. The actor, however, may feel consistent in pursuing his goal of political support. Given any two policies that lead to conflicts among two values one can always find a third value by which they are reconciled. Investment seemd to bring support when it was announced and so does spending for other purposes when its turn comes. The actors' values may be rephrased as "the highest possible investment so long as it does not seriously affect immediate political support." In view of the pressures to meet the needs of different people variously situated in society, most decisions are undoubtedly made on such a contingent basis. This is what it means to adapt to changing circumstance. As the goals of the actors shift with the times, consistency becomes a moving target, difficult to hit at the best of times, impossible to locate at the worst.

spent on each. While it used to be popular to say that all alternatives should be systematically compared, it has become evident that this won't work; knowledge is lacking and the cost is too high. The number of alternatives considered could easily be infinite if the dimensions of the problem (such as time, money, skill and size) are continuous.

Let us suppose that only a small number of alternatives will be considered. Which of the many conceivable ones should receive attention? Presumably those will be selected that are believed most compatible with existing values and to work most efficiently. But this presupposes that the planner knows at the beginning how the analysis will turn out; otherwise he must reject some alternatives to come up with the preferred set. At the same time there are other matters up for decision and choices must be made about whether they are to be given analytical time and attention. The planner needs rules telling him when to intervene in regard to which possible decisions and how much time to devote to each one. His estimate of the ultimate importance of the decision undoubtedly matters, but also it requires predictive ability he may not have. He is likely to resort to simple rules such as the amount of money involved in the decision and an estimate of his opportunities for influencing it.

We have gone a long way from the simple advice to consider alternatives. Now we know that this command does not tell anyone which decisions should concern him, how many alternatives he should consider, how much time and attention to devote to them or whether he knows enough to make the enterprise worthwhile. To say that alternatives should be considered is to suggest that something better must exist without being able to say what it is.

Be rational! If rationality means achieving one's goals in the optimal way, it refers here to technical efficiency, the principle of least effort. As Paul Diesing argues,[13] however, one can conceive of several levels of rationality for different aspects of society. There is the rationality of legal norms and of social structures as well as political rationality, which speaks to the maintenance of structures for decision, and economic rationality which is devoted to increasing national wealth.

What is good for the political system may not be good for the economy and *vice versa*. The overweening emphasis upon economic growth in Pakistan may have contributed to the relative neglect of the question of governmental legitimacy in the eastern regions. Any analysis of public policy that does not consider incompatibilities among the different realms of rationality is bound to be partial and misleading.

Strict economic rationality means getting the most national income out of a given investment. The end is to increase real GNP, no matter who receives it, and the means is an investment expenditure, no matter who pays for it. To be economically rational is to increase growth to its maximum. Speaking of economic rationality is a way of smuggling in identification with the goal of economic development without saying so.

Rationality is also used in the broader sense of reason. The rational man has goals that he tries to achieve by being systematic, efficient, consistent and so on. Since rationality in the sense of reason has no independent meaning of its own it

[13] Paul Diesing, *Reason in Society* (Urbana: University of Illinois Press, 1962).

can only have such validity as is imparted by the norms that tell us about what reasonable action is.

The injunction to plan (!!) is empty. The key terms associated with it are proverbs or platitudes. Pursue goals! Consider alternatives! Obtain knowledge! Exercise power! Obtain consent! Or be flexible but do not alter your course. Planning stands for unresolved conflicts.

Yet planning has acquired a reputation for success in some rich countries. Perhaps a certain level of affluence is required before planning becomes effective. Instead of stacking the deck against planning by asking whether it works in poor nations, let us play its best cards by looking at the record under the most propitious circumstances.

Planning in Rich Countries

Although I have geared my remarks to conditions existing in poor countries, they apply to rich ones as well. Formal planning aside, they are better able than poor nations to control their future. Governments in rich nations have more resources on which to draw, more adequate machinery for mobilizing them, and more trained people to make use of them. They can afford more failures as well as capitalize on their successes. Their prosperity is not guaranteed but their chances to do well for themselves are much higher than in the poor countries. It is possible that the failure of formal economic planning in rich countries actually has been hidden by their wealth. Confrontation with experience in formal planning has been avoided by casting the debate in terms that avoid the central question.

The debate over national economic planning in the past four decades has been conducted largely in terms of dichotomies: the individual versus the state; freedom versus dictatorship; private enterprise versus state control; price systems versus hierarchical command; rational economic choice versus irrational political inter-ference. The great questions were: could state planning be reconciled with personal liberty? Was central administrative command a better or worse way to make decisions than dependence on prices determined in economic markets? Would rational modes of economic thought, designed to increase national income in the long run, be able to overcome irrational political forces seeking to accumulate power in the short run? All these questions assume that national economic planning—as distinct from mere arbitrary political intervention—is a real possibility. But—if it doesn't work—if the goals of the plan do not move from the paper on which they are written to the society to which they are supposed to refer, then why worry about it; it can neither crush nor liberate mankind.

Is there a single example of successful national economic planning? The Soviet Union has had central planning and has experienced economic growth. But the growth has not been exceptional and has not followed the plan. Is there a single country whose economic life over a period of years has been guided by an economic plan so that the targets set out in the plan bear a modest resemblance to events as they actually occur? No doubt each reader will be tempted to furnish the one he has heard about. Yet the very fact (as anyone can verify by posing the same query) that it is hard to name an example suggests that the record of planning has hardly been brilliant.

146

For all we know, the few apparent successes (if there are any) are no more than random occurrences.

When really pushed to show results, somewhere, some place, sometime, planning advocates are likely to cite the accomplishments of indicative planning on the French model as the modern success story of their trade. The French example is indeed a good one because it puts the least possible demands on the planning enterprise. Where many national plans are comprehensive, in the sense that they try to set targets for virtually all sectors of the economy, the French dealt only with the major ones. While planners in some countries have to set the entire range of prices, the modified market economy in France makes this burden unnecessary. France has not been afflicted by the rapid turnover of key personnel that has contributed to the discontinuities in planning elsewhere. France is rich in many ways besides money—information, personnel, communication—that should make it easier for her planners to guide future events. Where some plans hope to be authoritative, in that both government and private industry are required to follow the guidelines contained in them, the French plans have been indicative, that is, essentially voluntary. While efforts are made to reward those who cooperate, there are no sanctions for failure to comply. French plans indicate the directions wise and prudent men would take, if they were wise and prudent. If planning does not work in France, where conditions are so advantageous, it would be unlikely to do better in less favorable circumstances.[14]

But like it or not, formal planning in France is a failure. Economic growth has taken place but not according to instructions in the plan. Targets have not been met in the first four plans. Neither for individual sectors nor for the economy as a whole have growth rates been approximated. Governments have consistently ignored the plan or opposed it in order to meet immediate needs. In order to justify the idea of planning, Steven Cohen, author of the best book on the subject, *Modern Capitalist Planning: The French Experience*,[15] suggests that if there were a democratic majority agreed on its goals, if their purposes could be maintained over a period of years, if they had the knowledge and power necessary to make the world behave as they wish, if they could control the future, then central planning would work. If . . .!

What Cohen's book actually shows is that limited economic planning in a major industrial country with considerable financial resources and talent did not work. What hope would there be for poor nations whose accumulated wealth is definitely less, whose reservoir of human talent is so much smaller, whose whole life is surrounded by far greater uncertainties? How could planning help radically change Africa or Asia when it has failed to produce even limited changes in France?

Significant control of the future demands mobilizing knowledge, power, and resources throughout a society. It does no good to propose measures that require nonexistent information, missing resources, and unobtainable consent. The planner cannot create, at the moment he needs them, things his society does not possess. He can, however, assume them to be true in that artificial world created in the plan. But planning is not a policy. It is presumably a way to create policies related to one

---

[14] The following paragraphs on France are taken from Aaron Wildavsky, "Does Planning Work?" *Public Interest*, Summer 1971, no. 24, pp. 95–104.

[15] Harvard University Press, Cambridge, Mass., 1970.

another over time so as to achieve desired objectives. The immense presumption involved, the incredible demands, not merely on the financial, but on the intellectual resources of societal organization explain the most important thing about national planning—it does not work because no large and complex society can figure out what simple and unambiguous things it wants to do, or in what clear order of priority, or how to get them done.

Before admitting defeat the advocate of planning would at least gesture in the direction of Japan, whose extraordinary economic growth has taken place in a period during which "the government has established long-term economic plans as the guiding principle for economic policies."[16] Of the dozen or so economic plans formulated since the end of the Second World War, five were officially adopted by the government and four have advanced far enough to appraise the fit between intention and accomplishment. In his splendid account, Isamu Miyazaki notes that the Five-year Plan for Economic Self-Support for fiscal years 1955–60 called for a five per cent rate of growth in gross national product. But "the economic growth rate turned out to be twice as large as what had been projected in the plan, and the growth in mining and manufacturing production and exports proved far greater than that envisaged in the plan. Thus the targets in the plan were achieved in almost two years." A second effort, the New Long-Range Economic Plan for fiscal years 1958–62, set the desired growth rate at 6.5%. "However, in actual performance, the rate again exceeded the projection, reaching about 10% on the average during the plan period."[17] The Doubling National Income Plan for fiscal years 1961–70, the third effort, postulated a real growth rate of some 7 to 8%. Miyazaki states that "In actual performance, however, the rate reached 11% on the average from fiscal 1961–63. Particularly notable was the performance of private equipment investment, which grew by almost 40% in fiscal 1960, followed by an additional 29% increase in fiscal 1961. This meant that the level which was expected to be reached in the final year of the plan was achieved in the first year."[18] The fourth and last national economic effort for which the returns are in, the Economic and Social Development Plan for fiscal years 1967–71, resulted in even larger gaps between promise and fulfillment. According to Miyazaki, it was

> estimated that the real growth rate would reach nearly 13% on the average for fiscal 1967–70 against 8.2% in the plan. The rate of increase of private equipment investment (nominal) was twice as large as the 10.6% of the forecast. Since the economic growth rate and private equipment investment have gone far beyond the projection, the plan cannot any more fulfill the role of a guide to private economic activities.[19]

Evidently the economy has been growing faster than anyone thought. Yet the purpose of plans and planners must surely be to guide economic growth in the expected direction, not to gasp in amazement at how wonderfully the country has grown contrary to (or regardless of) what they indicated. If plans are not guides, they have lost any meaning they might have had.

Questioning the meaningfulness of planning is likely to lead to impatience on the grounds that it represents man's best hope. What have you got to offer in its place?

---

[16] Isamu Miyazaki, "Economic Planning in Postwar Japan", *The Journal of the Institute of Developing Economies* (December 1970), vol. VIII, no. 4, p. 369.

[17] *Ibid*, p. 373.   [18] *Ibid*, p. 374.   [19] *Ibid*, p. 378.

That is likely to be the response. Putting the question that way suggests that planning provides a solution to problems. But planning is not a solution to any problem. It is just a way of restating in other language the problems we do not know how to solve.

But where's the harm? If planning is not the epitome of reason, it appears innocuous enough. If some people feel better in the presence of formal planning why not let it go on?

Formal Planning: Costs and Benefits

Planning is like motherhood; everyone is for it because it seems so virtuous. Over-population on one side has not given birth to doubts on the other. If we leave out the old controversy over whether centrally directed economies are better or worse than reliance on the price mechanism, there has been virtually no discussion of possible adverse effects of formal planning. Although planners are often economists who profess to believe that there is a cost for everything, they have not applied this insight to their own activity. It may be instructive, therefore, to list a few of the possible costs of planning.

The plan may provide a substitute for action. Working on it may justify delay as the cry-word goes out, "Let's not act until the plan is ready." Delay may also be encouraged because the planning commission becomes another checkpoint in an already cumbersome administrative apparatus. If its consent or comments are required and its people overburdened, planners may discourage the speedy adaptation to emerging events that is so essential in the volatile environments of the poor countries.

Planning uses important human resources. In nations where talent is chronically scarce, men who might be contributing to important public and private decisions may be wading through huge bodies of data or constructing elaborate models whose applicability is doubtful at best. The planners not only take up their own time, they intrude on others. They call in people from the operating ministries who need to answer their questions and, if necessary, run around countering their advice. Time, attention and talent that might be spent improving the regular administration on which the nation depends, may have to be invested in internal hassling with the planners.

The direct financial cost of paying the planners and their consultants may be small, but the long-run financial costs to the nation may be high. Planners tend to be spenders. Their rationale is that they will help promote current investments that will lead to future increases in income. They, therefore, have a vested interest in increasing the total amount of investment. Frustrated at the efforts of the finance ministry to keep spending down, the planners have an incentive to get hold of their own sources of funds. They thereby contribute to one of the basic financial problems of poor countries—the fragmentation of national income. Then they become another independent entity able to resist whatever central authority exists.

Investments may come in large packages or small amounts, in humdrum improvement of human resources, or in spectacular projects. The tendency of planners is to seek the large and loud over the small and quiet. Their talents are better suited to the analysis of big projects that have a substantial impact on the economy and that, by their cost, justify expensive analytical attention. They have too few people to supervise the multitude of small projects whose total impact may nevertheless be more important to the nation than the few big projects. Their fame and fortune depend on identification with visible objects and these are not to be found in the rural classroom or the feeder road.

The stock in trade of the planner is the big model. Sometimes it appears the larger and more complex the model (though it may actually be nothing more than a long list of variables) the more important the planner. Only he can interpret it and he may gain a kind of status from being its guardian. Bad decisions may result because these models are taken beyond any merits they might have. A spurious specificity may ignore the fact that the data used is bad, that the relevant calculations cannot be performed or that the model does not apply to the case at hand. As bad decisions are dressed up in pseudo-analytical garb, ministerial officials may become unduly cynical about analysis. When the devil quotes scripture, holy writ becomes suspect.

The planner makes his way by talking about the need of considering the future in present decisions. Yet poor countries have great difficulty in knowing where they are (even where they have been) in terms of income, expenditure, manpower and the like. Retrodiction is as much their problem as prediction. Yet the planners may neglect efforts to bring knowledge up to date because they have little stake in the present. Indeed, they may work hard to create what turn out to be imaginary future problems, as a way of gaining additional influence over forthcoming decisions.

The optimism of the planners may be desirable in order to give the nation a sense of hope amidst crushing burdens. This optimism, however, may result in unreal expectations that cannot be met. Demands may be made in anticipation of future income that does not materialize. Subsequent disappointment may create political difficulty where none need have occurred.

Though their formal plans may be irrelevant, actions of planners as an interest group may have impact. There is no need for us to argue here that formal planners are necessarily wrong. It suffices to say that they have their own built-in biases, and that these sometimes lead to unfortunate consequences. Why, then, is the worth of formal planning so rarely questioned?

Despite intermittent disaffection with planning—the contrast between the plan and the nation mocked the planners—it was difficult for national elites to forgo sight of the promised land. They so wanted an easy way out of their troubles. Besides, they soon discovered that the nonoperational quality of planning could be helpful. If it did not commit them to anything, it might yet be made into a useful instrument.

Formal planning may be useful as an escape from the seemingly insurmountable problems of the day. If life is gloomy in the present then a plan can help offset that by creating a rosier vision of the future. If groups cannot be indulged in the present, they can be shown the larger places they occupy in future plans. Formal planning can also be a way of buying off the apostles of rationality by involving them in tasks that take them away from the real decisions.

The reputation of a nation's leaders may depend on their having a glowing plan. International elites may expect it as evidence of competence and dedication to determine control of the future rather than simply being overtaken by events. International prestige may rest to some degree on one of the few national products that are visible and transportable—a beautifully bound set of national plans.

A government may find uses for planners as a group apart from the regular bureaucratic apparatus. Planning machinery may be a way deliberately to introduce competitive elements into the administration, either as a means of provoking reform or of blocking departmental ambitions. Planners may be used as a source of ideas outside regular administrative channels (as a kind of general staff for the executive) bypassing the normal chain of command. All this, however, has little to do with their ostensible reason for being, namely, planning, but much to do with the fact that since planners do exist, they may as well serve the purposes of others.

Trivial functions aside, planning might have withered from disappointment and disuse had not new clients insisted on it. When the United States made foreign aid fashionable, a number of poor countries were in a position to secure sums of money that were large in comparison to their small budgets. This created a need for institutional mechanisms that could do two things: spend surpluses and obtain foreign aid. The United States would not, of course, do anything so simple as to give money just because a country said it needed it; capitalist America insisted upon a plan. Since an existing bureaucracy would have had no experience in putting together these documents, it was necessary to create a mechanism for preparing them. It did not matter whether the plan worked; what did count was the ability to produce a document which looked like a plan, and that meant using economists and other technical personnel. If these skills were not available within the country, they had to be imported in the form of planners and foreign aid advisors. A demand existed and an entirely new industry was created to fill the need. Thus national planning may be justified on a strict cash basis: planners may bring in more money from abroad than it costs to support them at home.

These uses for formal planning suggest that I have been looking at plans, planners and planning commissions in the wrong way. I have been assessing (in the language of the sociologist) their manifest functions, the purposes they are supposed to serve. Formal planning also has latent functions; it serves other purposes as well.

Planning as Faith

While there is every evidence that national plans are unsuccessful, there is virtually no evidence that they do good, however "good" might be described. Yet no one thinks of giving them up. When people continue to do things that do not help them the subject cries out for investigation. Neither the governments nor the people they rule are presumed to be masochists. Why, then, do they not change their behavior?

Planners are men of secular faith. The word "faith" is used advisedly because it is hardly possible to say that planning has been justified by works. Once the word is in them it leaps over the realm of experience. They are confirmed in their beliefs no matter what happens. Planning is good if it succeeds and society is bad if it fails. That is why planners so often fail to learn from experience. To learn one must make mistakes and planning cannot be one of them.

Planning concerns man's efforts to make the future in his own image. If he loses control of his own destiny, he fears being cast into the abyss. Alone and afraid, man is at the mercy of strange and unpredictable forces, so he takes whatever comfort he can by challenging the fates. He shouts his plans into the storm of life. Even if all he hears is the echo of his own voice, he is no longer alone. To abandon his faith in planning would unleash the terror locked in him. For if God is dead, only man can save himself.

The greater his need, the more man longs to believe in the reality of his vision. Since he can only create the future he desires on paper he transfers his loyalties to the plan. Since the end is never in sight he sanctifies the journey; the process of planning becomes holy. Since he is the end of his own striving, his reason becomes the object of his existence. Planning is reason and reason is embodied in the plan. Worshipping it, he glorifies himself. But a secular idolatry is no easier to maintain than a religious one.

Faith in planning has an intermittent hold on political leaders. Their ascension to power is full of everlasting hope. The end of despair, they tell their people, is within sight. The leaders too, are overwhelmed by the gap between the future they promise and the present they cannot change. Progress is slow and painful. By allying themselves with the forces of reason, by embracing the plan as a visible sign of salvation, they hope to overcome the past and create a new life for their nation. When plans fail governmental leaders are tempted to abandon the god of reason. Once they have lost faith in planning, it becomes difficult for them to believe that there is any place for reasoned analysis. So they manipulate the plan and its planners for tactical purposes. If planning is reason, then reason flees when planning is in flight. Misplaced faith in the norms of rationality is easily transmuted into normless use of power.

The task of relating processes of decision to the social conditions in which they must operate is hampered because rational planning is supposed to stand as universal truth not subject to alteration through experience. It thus becomes difficult to evaluate experience; departure from the norms of planning are suspect as contradicting reason. Discussion of what seems to work in a particular context is inhibited because it may be inconsistent with "good planning practice." Rather than face up to actual conditions, planners are tempted to wish them away. If planning is a universal tool, planners find it reasonable to ask why their countries cannot live up to the requirements of rational decisionmaking. If planning is valid, they feel, nations should adjust to its demands rather than the other way round.

To save planning, planners may actually accept the blame. For if better behavior on their part would make planning work, the solution is not to abandon plans but to hire more talented planners. Martyrdom may be appropriate to their profession, but I would argue against allowing them to make the ultimate sacrifice.

Planning requires the resources, knowledge, and power of an entire people. If commodity prices suddenly fall, leading to a precipitous drop in national income, the ensuing difficulties may be attributed to faulty predictions by planners, but the relationship of the nation to international markets would seem to be the proper realm in which to seek scapegoats. Should it turn out that political leadership is divided, that may be because the planners could not convince them all, but it is more likely the result of causes deeply rooted in the nation's political history. It seems odd to blame the planners because the political leaders who agreed on a particular set of priorities are suddenly replaced by another group of men with quite different preferences. If private citizens send their capital abroad rather than investing it at home, it is the values of economic elites rather than the investment plan that deserves priority investigation. When taxes are not collected because social mores prohibit direct personal confrontations, national culture, not the national plan, is the place to look. When planning is viewed as a function of the society's ability to control its future, we seem better able to explain difficulties than if we look at the alleged shortcomings of planners.

If formal planning fails not merely in one nation at one time but in virtually all nations most of the time, the defects are unlikely to be found in maladroit or untalented planners. Nor can a failure be argued successfully by saying that the countries in question are not prepared to behave rationally or to accept the advice of rational men called planners. That is only a way of saying that formal planning, after innumerable iterations, is still badly adapted to its surroundings. It cannot be rational to fail. To err is human; to sanctify the perpetuation of mistakes is something else. If governments perseverate in national planning, it must be because their will to believe triumphs over their experience. Planning is not so much a subject for the social scientist as for the theologian.

[4]

Dilemmas in a General Theory of Planning*

HORST W. J. RITTEL

Professor of the Science of Design, University of California, Berkeley

MELVIN M. WEBBER

Professor of City Planning, University of California, Berkeley

ABSTRACT

The search for scientific bases for confronting problems of social policy is bound to fail, because of the nature of these problems. They are "wicked" problems, whereas science has developed to deal with "tame" problems. Policy problems cannot be definitively described. Moreover, in a pluralistic society there is nothing like the undisputable public good; there is no objective definition of equity; policies that respond to social problems cannot be meaningfully correct or false; and it makes no sense to talk about "optimal solutions" to social problems unless severe qualifications are imposed first. Even worse, there are no "solutions" in the sense of definitive and objective answers.

George Bernard Shaw diagnosed the case several years ago; in more recent times popular protest may have already become a social movement. Shaw averred that "every profession is a conspiracy against the laity." The contemporary publics are responding as though they have made the same discovery.

Few of the modern professionals seem to be immune from the popular attack—whether they be social workers, educators, housers, public health officials, policemen, city planners, highway engineers or physicians. Our restive clients have been telling us that they don't like the educational programs that schoolmen have been offering, the redevelopment projects urban renewal agencies have been proposing, the law-enforcement styles of the police, the administrative behavior of the welfare agencies, the locations of the highways, and so on. In the courts, the streets, and the political campaigns, we've been hearing ever-louder public protests against the professions' diagnoses of the clients' problems, against professionally designed governmental programs, against professionally certified standards for the public services.

It does seem odd that this attack should be coming just when professionals in

* This is a modification of a paper presented to the Panel on Policy Sciences, American Association for the Advancement of Science, Boston, December 1969.

the social services are beginning to acquire professional competencies. It might seem that our publics are being perverse, having condoned professionalism when it was really only dressed-up amateurism and condemning professionalism when we finally seem to be getting good at our jobs. Perverse though the laity may be, surely the professionals themselves have been behind this attack as well.

Some of the generators of the confrontation have been intellectual in origin. The anti-professional movement stems in part from a reconceptualization of the professional's task. Others are more in the character of historical imperatives, i.e. conditions have been thrown up by the course of societal events that call for different modes of intervention.

The professional's job was once seen as solving an assortment of problems that appeared to be definable, understandable and consensual. He was hired to eliminate those conditions that predominant opinion judged undesirable. His record has been quite spectacular, of course; the contemporary city and contemporary urban society stand as clean evidences of professional prowess. The streets have been paved, and roads now connect all places; houses shelter virtually everyone; the dread diseases are virtually gone; clean water is piped into nearly every building; sanitary sewers carry wastes from them; schools and hospitals serve virtually every district; and so on. The accomplishments of the past century in these respects have been truly phenomenal, however short of some persons' aspirations they might have been.

But now that these relatively easy problems have been dealt with, we have been turning our attention to others that are much more stubborn. The tests for efficiency, that were once so useful as measures of accomplishment, are being challenged by a renewed preoccupation with consequences for equity. The seeming consensus, that might once have allowed distributional problems to be dealt with, is being eroded by the growing awareness of the nation's pluralism and of the differentiation of values that accompanies differentiation of publics. The professionalized cognitive and occupational styles that were refined in the first half of this century, based in Newtonian mechanistic physics, are not readily adapted to contemporary conceptions of interacting open systems and to contemporary concerns with equity. A growing sensitivity to the waves of repercussions that ripple through such systemic networks and to the value consequences of those repercussions has generated the recent re-examination of received values and the recent search for national goals. There seems to be a growing realization that a weak strut in the professional's support system lies at the juncture where goal-formulation, problem-definition and equity issues meet. We should like to address these matters in turn.

I. Goal Formulation

The search for explicit goals was initiated in force with the opening of the 1960s. In a 1960 RAND publication, Charles J. Hitch urged that "We must learn to look at *our objectives* as critically and as professionally as we look at our models and our other inputs." [1] The subsequent work in systems analysis reaffirmed that injunction.

---

[1] Charles J. Hitch, "On the Choice of Objectives in Systems Studies" (Santa Monica, California: The RAND Corporation, 1960; P-1955), p. 19.

156

Men in a wide array of fields were prompted to redefine the systems they dealt with in the syntax of verbs rather than nouns—to ask "What do the systems *do*?" rather than "What are they made of?"—and then to ask the most difficult question of all: "What *should* these systems do?" Also 1960 was inaugurated with the publication of *Goals for Americans*, the report of President Eisenhower's Commission on National Goals.[2] There followed then a wave of similar efforts. The Committee for Economic Development commissioned a follow-up re-examination. So did the Brookings Institution, the American Academy of Arts and Sciences, and then President Nixon through his National Goals Research Staff. But these may be only the most apparent attempts to clarify the nation's directions.[3]

Perhaps more symptomatic in the U.S. were the efforts to install PPBS, which requires explication of *desired outcomes*; and then the more recent attempts to build systems of social indicators, which are in effect surrogates for statements of desired conditions. As we all now know, it has turned out to be terribly difficult, if not impossible, to make either of these systems operational. Although there are some small success stories recounted in a few civilian agencies, successes are still rare. Goal-finding is turning out to be an extraordinarily obstinate task. Because goal-finding is one of the central functions of planning, we shall shortly want to ask why that must be so.

At the same time that these formalized attempts were being made to discover our latent aims, the nation was buffeted by the revolt of the blacks, then by the revolt of the students, then by the widespread revolt against the war, more recently with a new consumerism and conservationism. All these movements were striking out at the underlying systemic processes of contemporary American society. In a style rather different from those of the systems analysts and the Presidential commissioners, participants in these revolts were seeking to restructure the value and goal systems that affect the distribution of social product and shape the directions of national policy.

Systems analysis, goals commissions, PPBS, social indicators, the several revolts, the poverty program, model cities, the current concerns with environmental quality and with the qualities of urban life, the search for new religions among contemporary youth, and the increasing attractiveness of the planning idea—all seem to be driven by a common quest. Each in its peculiar way is asking for a clarification of purposes, for a redefinition of problems, for a re-ordering of priorities to match stated purposes, for the design of new kinds of goal-directed actions, for a reorientation of the professions to the outputs of professional activities rather than to the inputs into them, and then for a redistribution of the outputs of governmental programs among the competing publics.

A deep-running current of optimism in American thought seems to have been propelling these diverse searches for direction-finding instruments. But at the same time, the Americans' traditional faith in a guaranteed Progress is being eroded by the same waves that are wearing down old beliefs in the social order's inherent goodness and in history's intrinsic benevolence. Candide is dead. His place is being

---

[2] The report was published by Spectrum Books, Prentice-Hall, 1960.

[3] At the same time to be sure, counter voices—uncomfortable to many—were claiming that the "nation's direction" presents no meaningful reference system at all, owing to the worldwide character of the problems and the overspill of crises across national boundaries.

occupied by a new conception of future history that, rejecting historicism, is searching for ways of exploiting the intellectual and inventive capabilities of men.

This belief comes in two quite contradictory forms. On the one hand, there is the belief in the "makeability," or unrestricted malleability, of future history by means of the planning intellect—by reasoning, rational discourse, and civilized negotiation. At the same time, there are vocal proponents of the "feeling approach," of compassionate engagement and dramatic action, even of a revival of mysticism, aiming at overcoming The System which is seen as the evil source of misery and suffering.

The Enlightenment may be coming to full maturity in the late 20th century, or it may be on its deathbed. Many Americans seem to believe both that we can perfect future history—that we can deliberately shape future outcomes to accord with our wishes—and that there will be no future history. Some have arrived at deep pessimism and some at resignation. To them, planning for large social systems has proved to be impossible without loss of liberty and equity. Hence, for them the ultimate goal of planning should be anarchy, because it should aim at the elimination of government over others. Still another group has arrived at the conclusion that liberty and equity are luxuries which cannot be afforded by a modern society, and that they should be substituted by "cybernetically feasible" values.

Professionalism has been understood to be one of the major instruments for perfectability, an agent sustaining the traditional American optimism. Based in modern science, each of the professions has been conceived as the medium through which the knowledge of science is applied. In effect, each profession has been seen as a subset of engineering. Planning and the emerging policy sciences are among the more optimistic of those professions. Their representatives refuse to believe that planning for betterment is impossible, however grave their misgivings about the appropriateness of past and present modes of planning. They have not abandoned the hope that the instruments of perfectability can be perfected. It is that view that we want to examine, in an effort to ask whether the social professions are equipped to do what they are expected to do.

II. Problem Definition

During the industrial age, the idea of planning, in common with the idea of professionalism, was dominated by the pervasive idea of *efficiency*. Drawn from 18th century physics, classical economics and the principle of least-means, efficiency was seen as a condition in which a specified task could be performed with low inputs of resources. That has been a powerful idea. It has long been the guiding concept of civil engineering, the scientific management movement, much of contemporary operations research; and it still pervades modern government and industry. When attached to the idea of planning, it became dominating there too. Planning was then seen as a process of designing problem-solutions that might be installed and operated cheaply. Because it was fairly easy to get consensus on the nature of problems during the early industrial period, the task could be assigned to the technically skilled, who in turn could be trusted to accomplish the simplified end-in-view. Or, in the more work-a-day setting, we could rely upon the efficiency expert to diagnose a problem and then solve it, while simultaneously reducing the resource inputs into whatever it was we were doing.

We have come to think about the planning task in very different ways in recent years. We have been learning to ask whether what we are doing is the *right* thing to do. That is to say, we have been learning to ask questions about the *outputs* of actions and to pose problem statements in valuative frameworks. We have been learning to see social processes as the links tying open systems into large and interconnected networks of systems, such that outputs from one become inputs to others. In that structural framework it has become less apparent where problem centers lie, and less apparent *where* and *how* we should intervene even if we do happen to know what aims we seek. We are now sensitized to the waves of repercussions generated by a problem-solving action directed to any one node in the network, and we are no longer surprised to find it inducing problems of greater severity at some other node. And so we have been forced to expand the boundaries of the systems we deal with, trying to internalize those externalities.

This was the professional style of the systems analysts, who were commonly seen as forebearers of the universal problem-solvers. With arrogant confidence, the early systems analysts pronounced themselves ready to take on anyone's perceived problem, diagnostically to discover its hidden character, and then, having exposed its true nature, skillfully to excise its root causes. Two decades of experience have worn the self-assurances thin. These analysts are coming to realize how valid their model really is, for they themselves have been caught by the very same diagnostic difficulties that troubled their clients.

By now we are all beginning to realize that one of the most intractable problems is that of defining problems (of knowing what distinguishes an observed condition from a desired condition) and of locating problems (finding where in the complex causal networks the trouble really lies). In turn, and equally intractable, is the problem of identifying the actions that might effectively narrow the gap between what-is and what-ought-to-be. As we seek to improve the effectiveness of actions in pursuit of valued outcomes, as system boundaries get stretched, and as we become more sophisticated about the complex workings of open societal systems, it becomes ever more difficult to make the planning idea operational.

Many now have an image of *how* an *idealized* planning system would function. It is being seen as an on-going, cybernetic process of governance, incorporating systematic procedures for continuously searching out goals; identifying problems; forecasting uncontrollable contextual changes; inventing alternative strategies, tactics, and time-sequenced actions; stimulating alternative and plausible action sets and their con-sequences; evaluating alternatively forecasted outcomes; statistically monitoring those conditions of the publics and of systems that are judged to be germane; feeding back information to the simulation and decision channels so that errors can be corrected—all in a simultaneously functioning governing process. That set of steps is familiar to all of us, for it comprises what is by now the modern-classical model of planning. And yet we all know that such a planning system is unattainable, even as we seek more closely to approximate it. It is even questionable whether such a planning system is desirable.

III. Planning Problems are Wicked Problems

A great many barriers keep us from perfecting such a planning/governing system: theory is inadequate for decent forecasting; our intelligence is insufficient to our tasks; plurality of objectives held by pluralities of politics makes it impossible to pursue unitary aims; and so on. The difficulties attached to rationality are tenacious, and we have so far been unable to get untangled from their web. This is partly because the classical paradigm of science and engineering—the paradigm that has underlain modern professionalism—is not applicable to the problems of open societal systems. One reason the publics have been attacking the social professions, we believe, is that the cognitive and occupational styles of the professions—mimicking the cognitive style of science and the occupational style of engineering—have just not worked on a wide array of social problems. The lay customers are complaining because planners and other professionals have not succeeded in solving the problems they claimed they could solve. We shall want to suggest that the social professions were misled somewhere along the line into assuming they could be applied scientists— that they could solve problems in the ways scientists can solve their sorts of problems. The error has been a serious one.

The kinds of problems that planners deal with—societal problems—are inherently different from the problems that scientists and perhaps some classes of engineers deal with. Planning problems are inherently wicked.

As distinguished from problems in the natural sciences, which are definable and separable and may have solutions that are findable, the problems of governmental planning—and especially those of social or policy planning—are ill-defined; and they rely upon elusive political judgment for resolution. (Not "solution." Social problems are never solved. At best they are only re-solved—over and over again.) Permit us to draw a cartoon that will help clarify the distinction we intend.

The problems that scientists and engineers have usually focused upon are mostly "tame" or "benign" ones. As an example, consider a problem of mathematics, such as solving an equation; or the task of an organic chemist in analyzing the structure of some unknown compound; or that of the chessplayer attempting to accomplish checkmate in five moves. For each the mission is clear. It is clear, in turn, whether or not the problems have been solved.

Wicked problems, in contrast, have neither of these clarifying traits; and they include nearly all public policy issues—whether the question concerns the location of a freeway, the adjustment of a tax rate, the modification of school curricula, or the confrontation of crime.

There are at least ten distinguishing properties of planning-type problems, i.e. wicked ones, that planners had better be alert to and which we shall comment upon in turn. As you will see, we are calling them "wicked" not because these properties are themselves ethically deplorable. We use the term "wicked" in a meaning akin to that of "malignant" (in contrast to "benign") or "vicious" (like a circle) or "tricky" (like a leprechaun) or "aggressive" (like a lion, in contrast to the docility of a lamb). We do not mean to personify these properties of social systems by implying malicious intent. But then, you may agree that it becomes morally objectionable for the planner to treat a wicked problem as though it were a tame one, or to tame a wicked problem prematurely, or to refuse to recognize the inherent wickedness of social problems.

1. There is no definitive formulation of a wicked problem

For any given tame problem, an exhaustive formulation can be stated containing all the information the problem-solver needs for understanding and solving the problem —provided he knows his "art," of course.

This is not possible with wicked-problems. The information needed to *understand* the problem depends upon one's idea for *solving* it. That is to say: in order to *describe* a wicked-problem in sufficient detail, one has to develop an exhaustive inventory of all conceivable *solutions* ahead of time. The reason is that every question asking for additional information depends upon the understanding of the problem—and its resolution—at that time. Problem understanding and problem resolution are concomitant to each other. Therefore, in order to anticipate all questions (in order to anticipate all information required for resolution ahead of time), knowledge of all conceivable solutions is required.

Consider, for example, what would be necessary in identifying the nature of the poverty problem. Does poverty mean low income? Yes, in part. But what are the determinants of low income? Is it deficiency of the national and regional economies, or is it deficiencies of cognitive and occupational skills within the labor force? If the latter, the problem statement and the problem "solution" must encompass the educational processes. But, then, where within the educational system does the real problem lie? What then might it mean to "improve the educational system"? Or does the poverty problem reside in deficient physical and mental health? If so, we must add those etiologies to our information package, and search inside the health services for a plausible cause. Does it include cultural deprivation? spatial dislocation? problems of ego identity? deficient political and social skills?—and so on. If we can formulate the problem by tracing it to some sorts of sources—such that we can say, "Aha! That's the locus of the difficulty," i.e. those are the root causes of the differences between the "is" and the "ought to be" conditions—then we have thereby also formulated a solution. To find the problem is thus the same thing as finding the solution; the problem can't be defined until the solution has been found.

The formulation of a wicked problem *is* the problem! The process of formulating the problem and of conceiving a solution (or re-solution) are identical, since every specification of the problem is a specification of the direction in which a treatment is considered. Thus, if we recognize deficient mental health services as part of the problem, then—trivially enough—"improvement of mental health services" is a specification of solution. If, as the next step, we declare the lack of community centers one deficiency of the mental health services system, then "procurement of community centers" is the next specification of solution. If it is inadequate treatment within community centers, then improved therapy training of staff may be the locus of solution, and so on.

This property sheds some light on the usefulness of the famed "systems-approach"

161

for treating wicked problems. The classical systems-approach of the military and the space programs is based on the assumption that a planning project can be organized into distinct phases. Every textbook of systems engineering starts with an enumeration of these phases: "understand the problems or the mission," "gather information," "analyze information," "synthesize information and wait for the creative leap," "work out solution," or the like. For wicked problems, however, this type of scheme does not work. One cannot understand the problem without knowing about its context; one cannot meaningfully search for information without the orientation of a solution concept; one cannot first understand, then solve. The systems-approach "of the first generation" is inadequate for dealing with wicked-problems. Approaches of the "second generation" should be based on a model of planning as an argumentative process in the course of which an image of the problem and of the solution emerges gradually among the participants, as a product of incessant judgment, subjected to critical argument. The methods of Operations Research play a prominent role in the systems-approach of the first generation; they become operational, however, only *after* the most important decisions have already been made, i.e. after the problem has already been tamed.

Take an optimization model. Here the inputs needed include the definition of the solution space, the system of constraints, and the performance measure as a function of the planning and contextual variables. But setting up and constraining the solution space and constructing the measure of performance is the wicked part of the problem. Very likely it is more essential than the remaining steps of searching for a solution which is optimal relative to the measure of performance and the constraint system.

2. Wicked problems have no stopping rule

In solving a chess problem or a mathematical equation, the problem-solver knows when he has done his job. There are criteria that tell when *the* or *a* solution has been found.

Not so with planning problems. Because (according to Proposition 1) the process of solving the problem is identical with the process of understanding its nature, because there are no criteria for sufficient understanding and because there are no ends to the causal chains that link interacting open systems, the would-be planner can always try to do better. Some additional investment of effort might increase the chances of finding a better solution.

The planner terminates work on a wicked problem, not for reasons inherent in the "logic" of the problem. He stops for considerations that are external to the problem: he runs out of time, or money, or patience. He finally says, "That's good enough," or "This is the best I can do within the limitations of the project," or "I like this solution," etc.

3. Solutions to wicked problems are not true-or-false, but good-or-bad

There are conventionalized criteria for objectively deciding whether the offered solution to an equation or whether the proposed structural formula of a chemical compound is correct or false. They can be independently checked by other qualified persons who are familiar with the established criteria; and the answer will be normally unambiguous.

For wicked planning problems, there are no true or false answers. Normally, many parties are equally equipped, interested, and/or entitled to judge the solutions, although none has the power to set formal decision rules to determine correctness. Their judgments are likely to differ widely to accord with their group or personal interests, their special value-sets, and their ideological predilections. Their assessments of proposed solutions are expressed as "good" or "bad" or, more likely, as "better or worse" or "satisfying" or "good enough."

4. There is no immediate and no ultimate test of a solution to a wicked problem

For tame-problems one can determine on the spot how good a solution-attempt has been. More accurately, the test of a solution is entirely under the control of the few people who are involved and interested in the problem.

With wicked problems, on the other hand, any solution, after being implemented, will generate waves of consequences over an extended—virtually an unbounded—period of time. Moreover, the next day's consequences of the solution may yield utterly undesirable repercussions which outweigh the intended advantages or the advantages accomplished hitherto. In such cases, one would have been better off if the plan had never been carried out.

The full consequences cannot be appraised until the waves of repercussions have completely run out, and we have no way of tracing *all* the waves through *all* the affected lives ahead of time or within a limited time span.

5. Every solution to a wicked problem is a "one-shot operation"; because there is no opportunity to learn by trial-and-error, every attempt counts significantly

In the sciences and in fields like mathematics, chess, puzzle-solving or mechanical engineering design, the problem-solver can try various runs without penalty. Whatever his outcome on these individual experimental runs, it doesn't matter much to the subject-system or to the course of societal affairs. A lost chess game is seldom consequential for other chess games or for non-chess-players.

With wicked planning problems, however, *every* implemented solution is consequential. It leaves "traces" that cannot be undone. One cannot build a freeway to see how it works, and then easily correct it after unsatisfactory performance. Large public-works are effectively irreversible, and the consequences they generate have long half-lives. Many people's lives will have been irreversibly influenced, and large amounts of money will have been spent—another irreversible act. The same happens with most other large-scale public works and with virtually all public-service programs. The effects of an experimental curriculum will follow the pupils into their adult lives.

Whenever actions are effectively irreversible and whenever the half-lives of the consequences are long, *every trial counts*. And every attempt to reverse a decision or to correct for the undesired consequences poses another set of wicked problems, which are in turn subject to the same dilemmas.

163

6. Wicked problems do not have an enumerable (or an exhaustively describable) set of potential solutions, nor is there a well-described set of permissible operations that may be incorporated into the plan

There are no criteria which enable one to prove that all solutions to a wicked problem have been identified and considered.

It may happen that *no* solution is found, owing to logical inconsistencies in the "picture" of the problem. (For example, the problem-solver may arrive at a problem description requiring that both *A* and not-*A* should happen at the same time.) Or it might result from his failing to develop an idea for solution (which does not mean that someone else might be more successful). But normally, in the pursuit of a wicked planning problem, a host of potential solutions arises; and another host is never thought up. It is then a matter of *judgment* whether one should try to enlarge the available set or not. And it is, of course, a matter of judgment which of these solutions should be pursued and implemented.

Chess has a finite set of rules, accounting for all situations that can occur. In mathematics, the tool chest of operations is also explicit; so, too, although less rigorously, in chemistry.

But not so in the world of social policy. Which strategies-or-moves are permissible in dealing with crime in the streets, for example, have been enumerated nowhere. "Anything goes," or at least, any new idea for a planning measure may become a serious candidate for a re-solution: What should we do to reduce street crime? Should we disarm the police, as they do in England, since even criminals are less likely to shoot unarmed men? Or repeal the laws that define crime, such as those that make marijuana use a criminal act or those that make car theft a criminal act? That would reduce crime by changing definitions. Try moral rearmament and substitute ethical self-control for police and court control? Shoot all criminals and thus reduce the numbers who commit crime? Give away free loot to would-be-thieves, and so reduce the incentive to crime? And so on.

In such fields of ill-defined problems and hence ill-definable solutions, the set of feasible plans of action relies on realistic judgment, the capability to appraise "exotic" ideas and on the amount of trust and credibility between planner and clientele that will lead to the conclusion, "OK let's try that."

7. Every wicked problem is essentially unique

Of course, for any two problems at least one distinguishing property can be found (just as any number of properties can be found which they share in common), and each of them is therefore unique in a trivial sense. But by *"essentially* unique" we mean that, despite long lists of similarities between a current problem and a previous one, there always might be an additional distinguishing property that is of overriding importance. Part of the art of dealing with wicked problems is the art of not knowing too early which type of solution to apply.

There are no *classes* of wicked problems in the sense that principles of solution can be developed to fit *all* members of a class. In mathematics there are rules for classifying families of problems—say, of solving a class of equations—whenever a certain, quite-well-specified set of characteristics matches the problem. There are explicit characteristics of tame problems that define similarities among them, in such fashion that the same set of techniques is likely to be effective on all of them.

Despite seeming similarities among wicked problems, one can never be *certain* that the particulars of a problem do not override its commonalities with other problems already dealt with.

The conditions in a city constructing a subway may look similar to the conditions in San Francisco, say; but planners would be ill-advised to transfer the San Francisco solutions directly. Differences in commuter habits or residential patterns may far outweigh similarities in subway layout, downtown layout and the rest. In the more complex world of social policy planning, every situation is likely to be one-of-a-kind. If we are right about that, the direct transference of the physical-science and engineering thoughtways into social policy might be dysfunctional, i.e. positively harmful. "Solutions" might be applied to seemingly familiar problems which are quite incompatible with them.

8. Every wicked problem can be considered to be a symptom of another problem

Problems can be described as discrepancies between the state of affairs as it is and the state as it ought to be. The process of resolving the problem starts with the search for causal explanation of the discrepancy. Removal of that cause poses another problem of which the original problem is a "symptom." In turn, it can be considered the symptom of still another, "higher level" problem. Thus "crime in the streets" can be considered as a symptom of general moral decay, or permissiveness, or deficient opportunity, or wealth, or poverty, or whatever causal explanation you happen to like best. The level at which a problem is settled depends upon the self-confidence of the analyst and cannot be decided on logical grounds. There is nothing like a natural level of a wicked problem. Of course, the higher the level of a problem's formulation, the broader and more general it becomes: and the more difficult it becomes to do something about it. On the other hand, one should not try to cure symptoms: and therefore one should try to settle the problem on as high a level as possible.

Here lies a difficulty with incrementalism, as well. This doctrine advertises a policy of small steps, in the hope of contributing systematically to overall improvement. If, however, the problem is attacked on too low a level (an increment), then success of resolution may result in making things worse, because it may become more difficult to deal with the higher problems. Marginal improvement does not guarantee overall improvement. For example, computerization of an administrative process may result in reduced cost, ease of operation, etc. But at the same time it becomes more difficult to incur structural changes in the organization, because technical perfection reinforces organizational patterns and normally increases the cost of change. The newly acquired power of the controllers of information may then deter later modifications of their roles.

Under these circumstances it is not surprising that the members of an organization tend to see the problems on a level below their own level. If you ask a police chief what the problems of the police are, he is likely to demand better hardware.

9. The existence of a discrepancy representing a wicked problem can be explained in numerous ways. The choice of explanation determines the nature of the problem's resolution

"Crime in the streets" can be explained by not enough police, by too many criminals, by inadequate laws, too many police, cultural deprivation, deficient opportunity, too many guns, phrenologic aberrations, etc. Each of these offers a direction for attacking crime in the streets. Which one is right? There is no rule or procedure to determine the "correct" explanation or combination of them. The reason is that in dealing with wicked problems there are several more ways of refuting a hypothesis than there are permissible in the sciences.

The mode of dealing with conflicting evidence that is customary in science is as follows: "Under conditions C and assuming the validity of hypothesis H, effect E must occur. Now, given C, E does not occur. Consequently H is to be refuted." In the context of wicked problems, however, further modes are admissible: one can deny that the effect E has not occurred, or one can explain the nonoccurrence of E by intervening processes without having to abandon H. Here's an example: Assume that somebody chooses to explain crime in the streets by "not enough police." This is made the basis of a plan, and the size of the police force is increased. Assume further that in the subsequent years there is an increased number of arrests, but an increase of offenses at a rate slightly lower than the increase of GNP. Has the effect E occurred? Has crime in the streets been reduced by increasing the police force? If the answer is no, several nonscientific explanations may be tried in order to rescue the hypothesis H ("Increasing the police force reduces crime in the streets"): "If we had not increased the number of officers, the increase in crime would have been even greater;" "This case is an exception from rule H because there was an irregular influx of criminal elements;" "Time is too short to feel the effects yet;" etc. But also the answer "Yes, E has occurred" can be defended: "The number of arrests was increased," etc.

In dealing with wicked problems, the modes of reasoning used in the argument are much richer than those permissible in the scientific discourse. Because of the essential uniqueness of the problem (see Proposition 7) and lacking opportunity for rigorous experimentation (see Proposition 5), it is not possible to put H to a crucial test.

That is to say, the choice of explanation is arbitrary in the logical sense. In actuality, attitudinal criteria guide the choice. People choose those explanations which are most plausible to them. Somewhat but not much exaggerated, you might say that everybody picks that explanation of a discrepancy which fits his intentions best and which conforms to the action-prospects that are available to him. The analyst's "world view" is the strongest determining factor in explaining a discrepancy and, therefore, in resolving a wicked problem.

10. The planner has no right to be wrong

As Karl Popper argues in *The Logic of Scientific Discovery*,[4] it is a principle of science that solutions to problems are only hypotheses offered for refutation. This

---

[4] Science Editions, New York, 1961.

166

habit is based on the insight that there are no proofs to hypotheses, only potential refutations. The more a hypothesis withstands numerous attempts at refutation, the better its "corroboration" is considered to be. Consequently, the scientific community does not blame its members for postulating hypotheses that are later refuted—so long as the author abides by the rules of the game, of course.

In the world of planning and wicked problems no such immunity is tolerated. Here the aim is not to find the truth, but to improve some characteristics of the world where people live. Planners are liable for the consequences of the actions they generate; the effects can matter a great deal to those people that are touched by those actions.

We are thus led to conclude that the problems that planners must deal with are wicked and incorrigible ones, for they defy efforts to delineate their boundaries and to identify their causes, and thus to expose their problematic nature. The planner who works with open systems is caught up in the ambiguity of their causal webs. Moreover, his would-be solutions are confounded by a still further set of dilemmas posed by the growing pluralism of the contemporary publics, whose valuations of his proposals are judged against an array of different and contradicting scales. Let us turn to these dilemmas next.

IV. The Social Context

There was a time during the 'Fifties when the quasi-sociological literature was predicting a Mass Society—foreseen as a rather homogeneously shared culture in which most persons would share values and beliefs, would hold to common aims, would follow similar life-styles, and thus would behave in similar ways. (You will recall the popular literature on suburbia of ten years ago.) It is now apparent that those forecasts were wrong.

Instead, the high-scale societies of the Western world are becoming increasingly heterogeneous. They are becoming increasingly differentiated, comprising thousands of minority groups, *each* joined around common interests, common value systems, and shared stylistic preferences that differ from those of other groups. As the sheer volume of information and knowledge increases, as technological developments further expand the range of options, and as awareness of the liberty to deviate and differentiate spreads, more variations are *possible*. Rising affluence or, even more, growing desire for at least subcultural identity induces groups to exploit those options and to invent new ones. We almost dare say that irregular cultural permutations are becoming the rule. We have come to realize that the melting pot never worked for large numbers of immigrants to America,[5] and that the unitary conception of "*The American Way of Life*" is now giving way to a recognition that there are numerous ways of life that are also American.

It was *pre*-industrial society that was culturally homogeneous. The industrial age greatly expanded cultural diversity. Post-industrial society is likely to be far more differentiated than any in all of past history.

It is still too early to know whether the current politicization of subpublics is

---

[5] See an early sign of this growing realization in Nathan Glazer and Daniel Patrick Moynihan, *Beyond the Melting Pot* (Cambridge: Harvard and MIT Presses, 1963).

going to be a long-run phenomenon or not. One could write scenarios that would be equally plausible either way. But one thing is clear: large population size will mean that small minorities can comprise large numbers of people; and, as we have been seeing, even small minorities can swing large political influence.

In a setting in which a plurality of publics is politically pursuing a diversity of goals, how is the larger society to deal with its wicked problems in a planful way? How are goals to be set, when the valuative bases are so diverse? Surely a unitary conception of *a* unitary "public welfare" is an anachronistic one.

We do not even have a theory that tells us how to find out what might be considered a societally best state. We have no theory that tells us what distribution of the social product is best—whether those outputs are expressed in the coinage of money income, information income, cultural opportunities, or whatever. We have come to realize that the concept of *the* social product is not very meaningful; possibly there is no aggregate measure for the welfare of a highly diversified society, if this measure is claimed to be objective and non-partisan. Social science has simply been unable to uncover a social-welfare function that would suggest which decisions would contribute to a societally best state. Instead, we have had to rely upon the axioms of individualism that underlie economic and political theory, deducing, in effect, that the *larger-public* welfare derives from summation of individualistic choices. And yet, we know that *this* is not necessarily so, as our current experience with air pollution has dramatized.

We also know that many societal processes have the character of zero-sum games. As the population becomes increasingly pluralistic, inter-group differences are likely to be reflected as inter-group rivalries of the zero-sum sorts. If they do, the prospects for inventing positive non-zero-sum development strategies would become increasingly difficult.

Perhaps we can illustrate. A few years ago there was a nearly universal consensus in America that full-employment, high productivity, and widespread distribution of consumer durables fitted into a development strategy in which all would be winners. That consensus is now being eroded. Now, when substitutes for wages are being disbursed to the poor, the college student, and the retired, as well as to the more traditional recipient of nonwage incomes, our conceptions of "employment" and of a full-employment economy are having to be revised. Now, when it is recognized that raw materials that enter the economy end up as residuals polluting the air mantle and the rivers, many are becoming wary of rising manufacturing production. And, when some of the new middle-class religions are exorcising worldly goods in favor of less tangible communal "goods," the consumption-oriented society is being challenged—oddly enough, to be sure, by those who were reared in its affluence.

What was once a clear-cut win-win strategy, that had the status of a near-truism, has now become a source of contentious differences among subpublics.

Or, if these illustrations seem to be posed at too high a level of generality, consider the sorts of inter-group conflicts imbedded in urban renewal, roadway construction, or curriculum design in the public schools. Our observation is not only that values are changing. That is true enough, and the probabilities of parametric changes are large enough to humble even the most perceptive observer of contemporary norms.

Our point, rather, is that diverse values are held by different groups of individuals—that what satisfies one may be abhorrent to another, that what comprises problem-solution for one is problem-generation for another. Under such circumstances, and in the absence of an overriding social theory or an overriding social ethic, there is no gainsaying which group is right and which should have its ends served.

One traditional approach to the reconciliation of social values and individual choice is to entrust *de facto* decision-making to the wise and knowledgeable professional experts and politicians. But whether one finds that ethically tolerable or not, we hope we have made it clear that even such a tactic only begs the question, for there are no value-free, true-false answers to any of the wicked problems governments must deal with. To substitute expert professional judgment for those of contending political groups may make the rationales and the repercussions more explicit, but it would not necessarily make the outcomes better. The one-best answer is possible with tame problems, but not with wicked ones.

Another traditional approach to the reconciliation of social values and individual choice is to bias in favor of the latter. Accordingly, one would promote widened differentiation of goods, services, environments, and opportunities, such that individuals might more closely satisfy their individual preferences. Where large-system problems are generated, he would seek to ameliorate the effects that he judges most deleterious. Where latent opportunities become visible, he would seek to exploit them. Where positive non-zero-sum developmental strategies can be designed, he would of course work hard to install them.

Whichever the tactic, though, it should be clear that the expert is also the player in a political game, seeking to promote his private vision of goodness over others'. Planning is a component of politics. There is no escaping that truism.

We are also suggesting that none of these tactics will answer the difficult questions attached to the sorts of wicked problems planners must deal with. We have neither a theory that can locate societal goodness, nor one that might dispel wickedness, nor one that might resolve the problems of equity that rising pluralism is provoking. We are inclined to think that these theoretic dilemmas may be the most wicked conditions that confront us.

[5]

Comparison of Current Planning Theories: Counterparts and Contradictions

Barclay M. Hudson
with comments by Thomas D. Galloway and Jerome L. Kaufman

This article reviews shortcomings in the synoptic, or rational comprehensive planning tradition, as well as in other, countervailing theories that have attempted to fill specific deficiencies in the synoptic tradition. The chief problem of the synoptic approach appears to be its lopsided application due to the difficulties of simultaneously bringing to bear other counterpart planning traditions. Each tradition resists blending with others; each has its own internally consistent, mutually sustaining web of methods, social philosophies, professional standards, and personal styles. Yet real world problems are not so consistent or self-contained. Effective solutions require diverse perspectives and multiple levels of action, extending beyond the scope of any contemporary American planning theory.

A five-part classification of planning traditions is discussed under the heuristic rubric of SITAR, covering the Synoptic, Incremental, Transactive, Advocacy, and Radical schools of planning thought. Comparison is made of their relative strengths and weaknesses, revealing ways they are often complementary, but often strongly at odds. Contradictions among them are not seen to be deficiencies in the theories themselves, but reflections of homologous tensions and contradictions in society at large. Parallel application of more than one theory is usually necessary for arriving at valid, three-dimensional perspectives on social issues and appropriate action implications.

For sake of a place to start, planning can be defined as "foresight in formulating and implementing programs and policies." The overall purpose of this article is to replace this unitary definition by defining more specific categories of planning, some of them complementary, and some of them contradictory to a degree that scarcely permits an umbrella meaning of planning.

The first section of the article presents a simple classification of planning traditions. The second section provides a general set of descriptive criteria for planning theories and practices. No single tradition of planning can do everything, and the list of criteria serves as a framework to compare the relative strengths and limitations of different approaches. The criteria reflect some timeless debates in the field of planning: why to plan, and how; for whom, and by whom. Major issues of this type are briefly discussed in connection with the criteria proposed.

The concluding section suggests some implications for planning theory, practice, and further empirical research: the need for more systematic comparative study of different planning approaches; the relative validity of different traditions to different settings and problems; the internal cohesiveness of each paradigm with regard to methods, professional groupings, and social philosophies; the nature of resistances to parallel or mixed use of diverse theories in tandem; and the extent of harmony or basic antagonism among the various traditions, both in theory and practice.

Bases for a classification scheme

If planning consists of "foresight in formulating and implementing programs and policies," then planners were clearly in evidence 4000 years ago when King Hammurabi caused the laws of Babylonia to be carved on stone. Typical problems of twentieth century planning have had their counterparts throughout history, and professionals have been there to solve them—in urban design and public works programs; in regulation of coinage and trade; in foreign policy and military defense; in forecasting the future and preparing against calamity; in pushing back geo-

The author, formerly with the Urban Planning Program at UCLA, now heads Barclay Hudson & Associates in Santa Monica, California, specializing in compact policy assessment—the application of rapid, intensive procedures for collating data and judgments applied to decision making, proposal evaluation, and task force management.

graphical frontiers and laying down transportation networks; and in devising laws for prevention of disease and disorder.

To understand planning, one has to look for the few abiding principles that underlie all purposeful action. The apparent diversity is mainly a matter of labelling and packaging, with subtle differences that are often exaggerated to achieve what salespeople are always seeking—"product differentiation" that will help sell the particular product each planner has to offer. For example, what yesterday was PPBS today is MBO (management by objectives), or ZBB (zero-based budgeting), or GAA (goals-achievement analysis), or logframe (logical framework programming). PPBS (the Planning–Programming-Budgeting System) is often cited as originating during World War II as a means for allocating scarce resources for the war effort. Others claim it goes back to the auto industry in an earlier decade. Similarly, benefit-cost analysis came to prominence in public policy making during the sixties, yet it played an important role in planning the canal system in the American Northeast as early as the 1830s. Nor was that by any means the first time anyone had added up costs and benefits of acting on a proposal. Private businessmen and entrepreneurs were doing that long before Adam Smith. Almost any form of investment is a form of planning.

Clearly, then, planning covers too much territory to be mapped with clear boundaries. It overlaps far into the terrain of other professions, and its frontiers expand continually with the historical evolution of social problems to be solved. The way to grasp a layout of the planning field is not by reconnoitering from the periphery, but by drawing demarcation lines radiating out from the most familiar crossroads at the center. In other words, one needs a classification scheme that will highlight comparative distinctions among current planning traditions without necessarily pinning down their farther limits.

A number of classification schemes might serve: *procedural* theories versus *substantive* theories (Hightower 1969; Faludi 1973b[1], or *algorithms* versus *heuristics*—that is, standardized problem-solving versus exploratory search procedures.[2] Another way of categorizing the field reflects different *sources of academic and professional literature*, entailing four major areas of concern: the tradition of rationalism, organizational development theory, empirical studies of planning practice, and philosophical synthesis relating to broad theories of social structural change (Friedmann and Hudson 1974).[3] These four "literary traditions" receive fairly balanced attention at the level of planning theory, but in planning practice, some far outweigh the others. Planning efforts in the field rarely make overt reference to philosophical synthesis or organizational development theory, nor

is much attention given to lessons of historical experience based on case studies of past planning efforts. Instead, predominant concern has generally centered on the tradition of rational comprehensive planning, also known as the synoptic tradition.

Because of its pre-eminence, the synoptic tradition serves as the centerpiece in the classification scheme to be developed below. The synoptic approach has dominated both American planning practice and the planning of development assistance programs overseas. The approach is well suited to the kind of mandate bestowed on government agencies: a set of constrained objectives, a budget, and accountability for not allowing one to stray too far out of line from the other.

There are, however, several other counterpoint schools of planning, most of which take their point of departure from the limits of the synoptic approach. The most important of these other traditions include *incremental planning, transactive planning, advocacy planning,* and *radical planning.* These by no means exhaust the range of contemporary planning traditions, but they cover enough ground to illustrate the major developments in planning theory and practice since roughly 1960, developments which have grown up in response to recognized deficiencies in the synoptic approach.

Each of the five traditions to be considered has an internally consistent, self-reinforcing network of methods, data requirements, professional skills, and working styles. Each has its own epistemology for validating information and its own institutional setting for putting ideas into practice. Each perceives the public interest in its own way, reflecting its particular assessment of human nature and its own sense of the legitimate range of interventions in social, economic, and political processes. The five traditions will be reviewed briefly in turn. Principal similarities and differences will then be discussed in terms of several descriptive criteria which have been chosen to highlight their relative strengths and weaknesses, their areas of complementariness, and their points of fundamental antagonism.

Synoptic planning

Synoptic planning, or the rational comprehensive approach, is the dominant tradition, and the point of departure for most other planning approaches, which represent either modifications of synoptic rationality or reactions against it.

Synoptic planning has roughly four classical elements: (1) goal-setting, (2) identification of policy alternatives, (3) evaluation of means against ends, and (4) implementation of decisions. The process is not always undertaken in this sequence, and each stage permits multiple iterations, feedback loops, and elaboration of sub-processes. For example evaluation can consist of procedures such as benefit-cost analysis, operations research, systems analysis, and forecasting research. Looking closer at forecasting, one finds that it can be broken down into deterministic models (trend extrapolation, econometric modelling, curve-fitting through multiple regression analysis); or probabilistic models (Monte Carlo methods, Markov chains, simulation programs, Beyesian methods), or judgmental approaches (Delphi technique, scenario writing, cross-impact matrices).

Synoptic planning typically looks at problems from a systems viewpoint, using conceptual or mathematical models relating ends (objectives) to means (resources and constraints), with heavy reliance on numbers and quantitative analysis.

Despite its capacity for great methodological refinement and elaboration, the real power of the synoptic approach is its basic simplicity. The fundamental issues addressed—ends, means, trade-offs, action-taking—enter into virtually any planning endeavor. Alternative schools of planning can nitpick at the methodological shortcomings of the synoptic approach, or challenge its particular historical applications, or take issue with its circumscribed logic, yet the practical tasks it encompasses must be addressed in some form by even its most adamant critics. For this reason, there is a sustained dialectical tension between synoptic planning and each of the other counterpart theories; neither side of the debate feels comfortable with its opposite, yet they cannot do without each other. Each helps define the other by its own shortcomings; each sharpens the other's discriminatory edge of intentions and accomplishments.

Incremental planning

A chief spokesperson for the incremental planning approach is Charles Lindblom, who describes it as "partisan mutual adjustment" or "disjointed incrementalism." Criticizing the synoptic approach as unrealistic, he stresses that policy decisions are better understood, and better arrived at, in terms of the push and tug of established institutions that are adept at getting things done through decentralized bargaining processes best suited to a free market and a democratic political economy. A good illustration of incremental planning is the apocryphal interview of a Yugoslavian official who was asked to describe his country's most important planning instrument. After a pause for thought the official replied, "the telephone." Yugoslavia in fact represents a blend of synoptic and incremental approaches. It promulgates national plans through a Federal Planning Bureau, but the country's economic and planning systems are composed of autonomous, self-governing working organizations. Plans are constructed by a mixture of "intuition, experience, rules of thumb, various techniques (rarely sophisticated) known to individual planners, and an endless

series of consultations" (Horvat 1972, p. 200). This description might apply to planning anywhere else in the world as well. Lindblom calls it "the science of muddling through."

The case for incremental planning derives from a series of criticisms leveled at synoptic rationality: its insensitivity to existing institutional performances capabilities; its reductionist epistemology; its failure to appreciate the cognitive limits of decision-makers, who cannot "optimize" but only "satisfice" choices by successive approximations. Incrementalists also take issue with the synoptic tradition of expressing social values (a priori goal-setting; artificial separation of ends from means; presumption of a general public interest rather than pluralist interests). Finally, synoptic planning is criticized for its bias toward central control—in the definition of problems and solutions, in the evaluation of alternatives, and in the implementation of decisions.

These criticisms are reflected in the countervailing tendencies of incremental planning, but also in the thrust of other planning approaches discussed below.

Transactive planning

The transactive planning approach focuses on the intact experience of people's lives revealing policy issues to be addressed. Planning is not carried out with respect to an anonymous target community of beneficiaries, but in face-to-face contact with the people affected by decisions. Planning consists less of field surveys and data analyses, and more of interpersonal dialogue marked by a process of mutual learning.

Transactive planning also refers to the evolution of decentralized planning institutions that help people take increasing control over the social processes that govern their welfare. Planning is not seen as an operation separated from other forms of social action, but rather as a process embedded in continual evolution of ideas validated through action (Friedmann 1973.)

In contrast to incremental planning, more emphasis is given to processes of personal and organizational development, and not just the achievement of specific functional objectives. Plans are evaluated not merely in terms of what they do for people through delivery of goods and services, but in terms of the plans' effect *on* people—on their dignity and sense of effectiveness, their values and behavior, their capacity for growth through cooperation, their spirit of generosity. By contrast, incremental planning adheres more closely to the economic logic of individuals pursuing their own self-interest.

Advocacy planning

The advocacy planning movement grew up in the sixties, rooted in adversary procedures modelled upon the legal profession, and usually applied to defending the interests of weak against strong—community groups, environmental causes, the poor, and the disenfranchized against the established powers of business and government. (Alinsky 1971; Heskin 1977.) Advocacy planning has proven successful as a means of blocking insensitive plans and challenging traditional views of a unitary public interest. In theory, advocacy calls for development of plural plans rather than a unit plan (Davidoff 1965). In practice, however, advocacy planning has been criticized for posing stumbling blocks without being able to mobilize equally effective support for constructive alternatives (Peattie 1968).

One effect of the advocacy movement has been to shift formulation of social policy from backroom negotiations out into the open. Particularly in working through the courts, it has injected a stronger dose of normative principles into planning, and greater sensitivity to unintended side effects of decisions. A residue of this can be seen in the increasing requirements for environmental, social, and financial impact reports to accompany large scale project proposals, whether originating in the private or public sector. Another result has been the stronger linkage between social scientists and judiciary processes in policy decisions. In the field of education, this alliance has left a mark in areas such as integration and busing, sources of school finance, equal provision for women in sports, disclosure of records, teacher training requirements, unionization, and selection of teaching materials. Advocacy planning has both reflected and contributed to a general trend in planning away from neutral objectivity in definition of social problems, in favor of applying more explicit principles of social justice.

Radical planning

Radical planning is an ambiguous tradition, with two mainstreams of thinking that occasionally flow together. One version is associated with spontaneous activism, guided by an idealistic but pragmatic vision of self-reliance and mutual aid. Like transactive planning, it stresses the importance of personal growth, cooperative spirit, and freedom from manipulation by anonymous forces. More than other planning approaches, however, its point of departure consists of specific substantive ideas about collective actions that can achieve concrete results in the immediate future. It draws on varying sources of inspiration—economics and the ecological ethic (Schumacher 1973), social architecture (Goodman 1971), humanistic philosophy (Illich 1973), and historical precedents (Katz and Bender 1976, Hampden-Turner 1975).

This is radicalism in the literal sense of "going back to the roots," content to operate in the interstices of the Establishment rather than challenging the system head-on. The philosophy which underlies its social vision can also be found in the thinking of educational figures like John Dewey, Paul Goodman (*Communitas*), Ivan Illich (*Deschooling Society*), and others who share the view that education needs to draw on materials from everyday life of local communities, with minimum intervention from the state and maximum participation of people in defining, controlling, and experimenting with their own environment. Somewhat the same concerns find their way into conventional planning—for example, as reflected in the Bundy Report on decentralizing the New York City school system, and in the HEW-sponsored educational voucher experiments aimed at letting neighborhood committees take over planning functions usually vested in central bureaucracies.

The second stream of radical thought takes a more critical and holistic look at large-scale social processes: the effect of class structures and economic relationships; the control exercised by culture and media; the historical dynamics of social movements, confrontations, alliances, and struggles. The focus is less on ad hoc problem solving through resurrected community, and more on the theory of the state, which is seen to permeate the character of social and economic life at all levels, and in turn determines the structure and evolution of social problems (Gordon 1971. See also Ellul 1954). Radicals in this tradition view conventional planning as a form of Mandarinism, playing "handmaiden to conservative politics" (Kravitz 1970).

It is not the purpose of this paper to describe at length particular schools of planning thought. Any list of planning forms and styles could be extended almost indefinitely. Those discussed above are probably sufficient, however, to illustrate the variety of concerns that planners address and the range of conceptual tools they bring to their task.

The five approaches described above can be summed up in an acronym, SITAR, based on the first letters of Synoptic, Incremental, Transactive, Advocacy, and Radical planning. The *sitar* is a five-stringed musical instrument from India, a type of lute which can be played by performing on a single string at a time, or by weaving a blend of harmony and dissonance from all five. The same applies to SITAR as a taxonomy of planning theories; each can render a reasonable solo performance in good hands, but fuller possibilities can be created by use of each theory in conjunction with the others.

Criteria for comparative description and evaluation of planning theories

In judging the value of any particular planning tradition one can ask, how constrained are we to using one theory at a time? No single approach is perfect, but a particular theory can establish itself as "best" simply because there are no salient options kept in view. The SITAR package suggests some of these options, but comparative evaluation requires another step—the establishment of criteria for comparison of different traditions' strengths and weakness, along with their varying intentions and accomplishments.

Table 1 presents a simple list of basic criteria that one might use for assessing the scope, character, and adequacy of the various planning traditions. The six criteria have been distilled from three independent selection processes; each process is somewhat subjective, but they overlap considerably in their results. First, the criteria were generated in part by *internal features* of the various SITAR traditions themselves, as expressed in the planning literature. Some criteria, such as definition of the public interest, reflect a common concern of all the SITAR traditions (although they differ considerably in their treatment of it). Other criteria, such as the use of substantive theories of political action and models of social change, represent a central concern—even a raison d'etre— of some traditions but are glaringly absent from others.

The second source of criteria was an informal review of *historical outcomes* from past planning efforts. Most of these cases are described in the literature;[4] some have been suggested by anecdotal sources and personal experiences shared with colleagues in the profession. The third source of nominations for criteria has been an advanced seminar in urban planning at UCLA, where over the years several cohorts of students have been posed the questions, "How do you judge a good planning theory? What planning experience can you cite that has been most successful, and what constitutes that success?" Their collated answers reflect considerable planning experience as well as academic grounding in planning theory, including general principles of policy science, social philosophy, and political economy.

From these various sources, roughly fifty different criteria were suggested, often overlapping, sometimes contradictory, occasionally esoteric. Winnowing and synthesis to a manageable set of criteria necessarily involves personal choices, and probably reflects the author's own implicit philosophy of planning. It should be noted, though, that final choice of the six criteria shown in Tables 1 and 2 reflects, in part, a deliberate effort to balance strengths and weaknesses within and among the five SITAR traditions.

Table 2 is an attempt to evaluate the five SITAR traditions against the list of criteria described in Table 1. The purpose of this comparison is to suggest areas of similarity and difference among the various planning approaches, the relative strengths and weaknesses within each theory, and the overall pattern of emphasis and neglect found in the planning field taken as a whole.

The SITAR theories differ both in terms of their intentions and how well they have succeeded historically in fulfilling their chosen purposes. The table indicates for each theory at least one area in which it claims special strength, other areas in which it offers a partial or one-sided approach, and still other areas where clear shortcomings can be observed.

In any given area (for example, action potential) the theories provide different prescriptions for the

Table 1. Criteria for describing and evaluating planning traditions

Criteria	Characteristics and applications
Public interest	Explicit *theory of the public interest*, along with methods to articulate significant social problems, and pluralist interests in outcomes. May include principles of distributive justice, and procedures for dealing with conflict.
Human dimension	Attention to the *personal and spiritual domains* of policy impacts, including intangible outcomes beyond functional-instrumental objectives—for example, psycho-social development, enhancement of dignity, and capacity for self-help.
Feasibility	*Ease of learning and applying* the theory. Implies the theory is practical to translate into policy implications, and adaptable to varying types of problems, scales of action and social settings.
Action potential	Provision for carrying ideas into practice, building on experience underway and identifying new lines of effective solutions to problems.
Substantive theory	*Descriptive and normative theory* of social problems and processes of social change. Predictive capacity based on informal judgments, not just trend extrapolation; ability to trace long range and indirect policy consequences; historical perspectives on opportunities and constraints on action.
Self-reflective	Capacity for laying analytical assumptions open to criticism and counter-proposals; provision for learning from those being planned for; capacity for depicting concrete experience in everyday language, as well as conceptual models using aggregate data.

Table 2. Relative emphasis of SITAR theories based on selected criteria

Major criteria, or descriptive characteristics of planning theory	The SITAR traditions				
	Synoptic planning	Incremental planning	Transactive planning	Advocacy planning	Radical planning
Public interest	O	O	O	●	●
Human dimension			●		O
Feasibility	●	●			
Action potential	O	O	O	O	O
Substantive theory		O	O		O
Self-reflective			O	O	O

Explanation of Table:
Characteristics are taken from Table 1
● indicates major strength or area of concern
O indicates partial or one-sided treatment
blank cells indicate characteristic weaknesses

planner—different analytical methods, varying substantive definitions of problems, different forms of action to consider. Consequently each of the six criteria included in the list presents an arena for debate on certain classic issues of planning theory and practice. The true meaning of the criteria is that they represent areas of philosophical choice in which planners must turn to one or another planning tradition for answers. Each tradition constitutes a body of foregone conclusions about problem definition and problem solutions. Planners can exercise better critical judgment about the assumptions they buy into if they consider the possibilities offered by a range of alternative candidate theories. A matrix like Table 2 may be simplistic for this purpose, but it is a place to start.

To give fuller meaning to the six criteria listed in Tables 1 and 2, it is worth discussing them briefly, with special attention to the kinds of issues that each one raises.

Theory of the public interest. Definition of the public interest raises a fundamental planning issue: can goals be considered separately from specific options? Synoptic planning responds "yes," most other approaches, "no." Another key issue is: should conflicts that arise among groups in connection with planning be underplayed in favor of seeking a consensus? Or should they be focal points for defining communities of interest and promoting organized efforts to achieve a more just distribution of benefits? Radical and advocacy planning are based on conflict models of the public interest. Transactive and incremental planning are based on dialogue and bargaining among plural interests, although without an explicit treatment of power. Synoptic planning largely ignores or avoids issues of conflict by referring to a unitary concept of the public interest. For example, the synoptic tradition tends to rely on the Pareto optimum to deal with the problem of skewed incidence of benefits—a fairly lenient stand-

ard of social justice. Synoptic rationality also focusses primarily on technical relationships and objective realities, to the exclusion of subjective and emotional discussion sparked by divergent perceptions of problems being addressed. In addition, synoptic planning typically creates a division of labor between planners (experts) and politicians—a split which casts planners as technicians who can simply ignore political considerations of the public interest.

The human dimension. Major issue: should planning seek to provide a framework of objective decision rules (e.g., as benefit-cost analysis provides in synoptic planning)? Or should it aim at a more holistic context for judgment, referring not just to scientific and technical data but to subjective realities, including political concerns, cultural, aesthetic, psychological and ideological considerations, and controvertible theories of social, ecological, and historical processes? Transactive planning gives special attention to psychosocial and institutional processes which facilitate growth and mutual learning between the planner and his constituency. Radical planning emphasizes the role of human will and ideological cohesiveness which gives effective power to technical knowledge. Both radical and transactive planning raise explicit questions about the limitations of social science as an exclusive way of understanding social problems. Both give specific attention to alternative epistemologies, or bases for validating the uses and limits of knowledge. Both emphasize the role of personal knowledge, using concrete experience and direct participation as the point of departure for problem-solving and social struggle.

Feasibility. The world is complicated, but planning methods need to be simple enough to make understanding manageable. How does one translate complexity into simplicity without falling into the trap of mistaking the model for reality itself? Indeed, planners tend to forget too often that the map is not the territory. Synoptic planning has the virtue of being easily grasped: its analytical techniques are fairly standard applications of social science, and its intentions are straightforward. Incremental and advocacy planning refer to the more subtle and complex processes of bargaining, but they come closer to what skilled entrepreneurs and politicians and social mobilizers do anyway, so they score fairly well on the criterion of feasibility. The operating principles of transactive and radical planning are less well known among planning professionals. Furthermore, both of these approaches call for the fostering and strengthening of community-based institutions which are presently overshadowed by centralized and bureaucratically organized agencies of government and corporate enterprise.

Another issue of feasibility revolves around a basic paradox of planning pointed out by numerous observers (Lindblom 1965; Caiden and Wildavsky 1974; Friedmann 1973). Where planning for the future is *feasible* (based on good data and analytical skills, continuity in the trends being extrapolated, and effective means to control outcomes), then planning is unnecessary—it is simply redundant to what already goes on. Conversely, where planning is most *needed* (where there is absence of data and skills and controls in the presence of primitive or turbulent social conditions), planning is least feasible.

Action potential. Here the issue revolves around the meaning of "action." Synoptic planning addresses possibilities of large scale action and major departures from current strategies of problem-solving, based on fresh insight and thorough examination of goals and policy alternatives. By the same token, however, rational comprehensive planning is vulnerable to the criticism that its plans never reach the stage of implementation. Master Plans are written and filed away, except in rare cases when vast new sources of funding become available in lumps and allow the planner to design programs from scratch, thus putting real clout into Government-by-Master-Plan. Examples of this are the Tennessee Valley Authority (financed by the first surge of economic pump-priming under the New Deal); and large-scale projects undertaken in developing countries by OPEC governments or institutions like the World Bank.

Other planning traditions seek to reduce the gap between decision making and implementation by embedding planning processes in the common everyday practice of social management and experimentation. Only in synoptic planning is there major emphasis on producing "plans." Elsewhere, planning is more characteristically a process that consummates itself in direct action rather than production of documents.

The "structuralist" version of radical planning is similar to synoptic planning in presenting a major gap between analysis of problems and means for

implementing solutions. Radicals would respond by saying that they are looking for long run, not short run results. If their effectiveness is not very visible, it is because most people are not educated in recognizing the contradictions within the system and the manifestations of growing tensions that will eventually lead to decisive transformations. Radicals also argue that significant change involves real but unrecognized forms of social, economic, and historical relationships which are being ignored by conventional social science and by the liberal philosophy that currently dominates social planning. Finally, the radicals would argue that radical change, when it comes, is rarely foreseeable; rather, it is a matter of being prepared for unique historical turning points. Other planning theories, in contrast, tend to focus exclusively on futures that are predictable on the basis of continuity in existing social structures and processes.

Outside of military science there is little writing in planning theory directly addressed to a theory of action. An important exception is the literature on "non-violent alternatives," which explicitly takes on the problem of power and ways of realigning it toward practical, short-term objectives. Although the historical foundations of non-violent action have evolved mainly in situations of overt conflict and transient confrontation, this is not always the case. In many respects, this literature provides a missing link between theory and practice which other theories have not fully provided. In Table 2, all five SITAR theories are shown to address this problem, but without full success. This is not surprising because one definition of planning is that it is an activity "centrally concerned with the linkage between knowledge and organized action" (Friedmann and Hudson 1974, p. 2). All traditions of planning struggle with this relationship. If any had fully succeeded, there would scarcely be need for more than that one approach.

Substantive theory. Mainstream theories of planning are principally concerned with procedural techniques. Substantive content is usually left to secondary levels of specialization in sectorial areas such as education, housing, poverty, industrial development, or land use regulation. Exceptions are radical planning and, to a lesser extent, transactive planning. Both insist that planning styles and methods must adapt to correspond to the specific nature of social problems being addressed. If they do not, our understanding of problems will be dictated by the arbitrary strengths and limits of our methodology, and not by an a priori appreciation of the substantive phenomenon. For example, to understand what "poverty" means, it is not enough to simply look at census data, nor is it enough to simply experience it first hand. One needs a substantive theory of poverty, built up from comparative and historical study of its nature, as well as from principles of social justice and theories of transformation in economic structures. Otherwise, methodological bias or random availability of data or purely arbitrary perceptions from personal experience will dictate the way poverty is perceived. In this case one can easily become locked into a partial—hence erroneous—explanation of poverty, variously interpreted as the consequence of personal or genetic or cultural traits, or as a problem rooted in family structures, or in the physical infrastructure of communities, or in national policies of neglect, or in global dynamics of resource flows favoring industrialized economies at the expense of weaker peripheral areas. A planner who is primarily a methodologist will likely be stuck on one or another of these levels of explanation. A planner who is grounded in substantive theory, however, can press beyond the limits of particular methods to see problems in their entirety.

Most planning theories do not embody explicit world views on any particular subject. The issue thus raised is whether they are remiss in this respect or simply being open-minded and adaptable. A synoptic planner or incrementalist or advocate planner might argue that their methods serve equally well for most purposes—civilian as well as military applications, the needs of the poor as well as the rich, the problems of neighborhoods and the problems of the world. Radical and transactive planners would tend to argue, to the contrary, that no method is neutral, but that each has a characteristic bias toward one or another group's way of depicting reality. Objectivity itself is a biased frame of reference, excluding those qualities of experienced reality that can only be known subjectively, and must be validated on grounds where social science is reluctant to tread.

The issue manifests itself, for example, in the use of predictions. Forecasting can consist of purely descriptive analysis: extrapolation of trends, curve fitting, probability envelopes, contingency models to accommodate foreseeable variations in patterns. Alternatively, forecasting can incorporate a strongly normative element, designed to provoke corrective action on problems whose warning signs are feeble but urgent. This goes far beyond method, drawing on qualities of imagination, willingness to exercise moral interpretation of facts, and sensitivity to historical dynamics. Most planners would admit that their craft is one of art as well as science. Most are uncomfortable, however, with depicting the future in the full richness of subjective color and detail which they know gives meaning to the present. Works like the *Limits to Growth, California Tomorrow*, the *Crash of '79, The Year 2000, 1984, Looking Backwards*, or *The Shape of Things to Come* all address the same issues that planners deal with in the normal course of their profession. Yet planners are uncomfortable with the literary method, which may be a valid and accurate means

of discussing social problems and solutions, but lacks the reliability and objectivity found in the more familiar tools of social science. Different schools of planning come down on different sides of this issue, but in the dominant synoptic and incremental traditions, theories of substance tend to be subordinated to theories of procedure.

Self-reflective theory. The central issue here is whether a planning theory needs to be explicit about its own limitations, and if so, how can the theory make clear what has been left out? Incremental planning is least explicit in this respect. The "science of muddling through" is full of hidden agendas and bargaining processes which encourage participants to keep their motives and means to themselves. In synoptic planning, there is far more emphasis on laying everything out on the table, but the rules of the game require that one deal with technical decisions on the basis of objective data. Corrections to the bias of neutral objectivity can be found, not within the synoptic tradition itself, but in the parallel applications of other SITAR traditions.

Etzioni (1968) has suggested a composite approach called "mixed scanning" which alternates between the synoptic approach to "fundamental" decisions and the incrementalist manner of dealing with "bit" decisions (see also Faludi 1973a; Allison 1968).

Transactive, advocacy, and radical planning each have specific procedures for pressing inquiry beyond the initial statement of a planning problem. Transactive planning emphasizes dialogue and development of trusting interpersonal relationships. Advocacy planning relies on the test of mobilizing people to challenge established procedures and institutions in protecting their collective interests. Radical planning calls for ideas to be tested in actions aimed at permanent change in social institutions and values. In contrast, synoptic planning refers to a more limited test of its adequacy in addressing problems: it creates a series of feed-back channels to correct errors in calculations, but the scope and substance of feedback are highly constrained. Like survey questionnaires, feedback channels are narrowly focussed on the dimensions of outcomes defined a priori as important. Signals from unexpected quarters, carrying messages beyond the previous scope of understanding a problem, do not easily get through.

There exist certain procedures of critical analysis which might be included as optional components of the synoptic approach, that can be used to challenge the hidden assumptions of rational comprehensive planning. One example is Richard Mason's "dialectical approach to strategy planning" (1969). Another is the synectics procedure, a structured method of brainstorming that encourages divergent thinking in problem-solving.

Beyond this, there is a growing literature in the

area of "critical theory" dealing with ways of bringing to light the logic and psychology of thinking about social problems, with a view to correcting its natural limitations and biases. This literature spans the sociology of knowledge, the philosophy of science, the effects of linguistic and cultural structures, the influence of conceptual paradigms, and other matters relating to planning epistemology (Mannheim 1949; Miller, Galanter, and Pribam 1960; Friedmann 1978; Polanyi 1964; Churchman 1971; Bruyn 1970; Hudson 1977). The majority of this writing, however, falls well beyond the scope of the synoptic tradition.

Directions for future work

Beyond the SITAR package of planning traditions, one can identify additional schools of thought—indicative planning, bottom up planning, ethnographic planning methods, social learning theory, comparative epistemologies of planning, urban and regional planning, basic needs strategies, urban design, environmental planning, macroeconomic policy planning—the list goes on. A question this raises is whether SITAR depicts a fair sample of current thinking in planning theory. Readers can draw their own conclusions. For purposes of this article, the main function of SITAR is to pose key issues that emerge as points of contention among the various planning traditions. A different sample of comparative theories might bring other issues to surface.

Another question concerns the choice of evaluative criteria used to describe and compare different planning traditions. The choice depends on one's professional personality. The selection process is a kind of Rorschach test of one's own cognitive style, social philosophy, and methodological predilections. In this sense, one could probably devise an instrument to measure personal planning styles based on individuals' preference ranking for an extended list of possible criteria.

Particularly within the synoptic tradition, it is easy to overlook the importance of personal work style and theoretical orientation in determining the compatibility between individual professionals and their clients. Planning is not simply the exercise of a technical capacity involving objective requirements of data, skills, procedures, and institutional mechanisms. Just as important is the social philosophy shared by the planner, the sponsor, and the constituency they are addressing. For some purposes, it may be enough to assess objective needs and deliver solutions to a "target" community. In many cases, however, it is necessary to understand problems through face-to-face interaction with those affected. In such situations, the planner's effectiveness depends on sharing implicit grounds of communication with both colleagues and clients on the levels of information processing styles, value premises, political sensitivities, and other foundations of mutual understanding. Much planning effort is spent on building up this framework of communication and problem definition, but perhaps there is a short-cut. An instrument to test basic attitudes toward alternative planning styles might provide a way of matching clients with congruent professional modus operandi from the outset.

This raises a related issue: how well do clients perceive differences in planning traditions? Are they aware they have a choice? Do they understand the implications of their choice—for example, the relative strengths and weaknesses associated with different traditions? Could clients grasp the significance of evaluative criteria offered to compare traditions—for example, different treatments of the public interest?

One strategy for eliciting client preferences and testing their ability to perceive meaningful choices would be to initiate planning efforts with a "prelude" stage, consisting of a few days of intensive work exposing clients to alternative modes of approaching issues at hand. In a series of dry run exercises, representatives of different approaches could bring in hypothetical data, solutions, feasibility considerations, and unresolved issues bearing on decisions to be made. The clients would get more than a review of planning theory; the process would go a long way toward clarifying their own objectives and substantive policy options. At the same time, planners who participated would get a fast education in the client's own view of issues, based on reactions to the presentations.

It is not clear whether there exists a significant market for this kind of prelude analysis. Funding agencies tend to operate with their own particular style of planning, mainly the synoptic mode. Opening up choices would tend to confound standard operating procedures, reduce the predictability of outcomes, and weaken agency influence over determination of results.

On the other hand, the feasibility and usefulness of intensive short-term policy analysis—either as prelude or substitute for longterm planning efforts—is relatively well established. "Compact policy assessment" exists in the form of a wide variety of quick and dirty procedures for problem formulation, project evaluation, decision making, assumptions analysis, and feasibility testing of proposals. Both in community and organizational settings, there are various specialized methods for pooling judgment, fixing points of consensus, and isolating areas of uncertainty or disagreement for subsequent in-depth study (Hudson 1979). The problem is not so much availability of tools for compact policy assessment, but perception of the need for it. The SITAR package helps make explicit the possibilities of choice between alternative styles and methods of planning. Practical choices, however, will depend on effective procedures for concisely presenting different approaches within the specific problem-solving situations posed by individual clients.

Another question concerns the internal cohesiveness of each planning tradition, and the balance between each tradition and its counterparts. Some combinations appear fairly complementary; others may generate fruitful tension; a few might prove fundamentally incompatible. Defining conditions that facilitate the use of different modes in tandem will require further study.

One must also determine whether each tradition functions as a self-contained paradigm—not just a theory, but a tight and impenetrable mesh of conceptual models, language tools, methodologies, and problem applications, together with its own professional community of believers. It can be argued that a planning paradigm tends to create a determined set of procedures locked into a particular historical environment of problems and solutions (Galloway and Mahayni 1977). Yet there are reasons to think that people have a certain latitude for choice among analytical paradigms (Hudson 1975). Allison (1968) has shown that very different models of decision-making can be used to interpret a single scenario of crisis management. Etzioni (1973) has argued for a "mixed scanning" approach that incorporates both synoptic and incremental planning modes. Historically, advocacy, transactive, and radical planning practices have appeared on the scene as countervailing methods to ongoing processes of synoptic planning, not with the result of replacing the dominant paradigm, but of introducing a broader perspective on issues and another set of voices for articulating the public interest. Systematic evaluation of historical precedents like these would help create more realistic strategies for getting diverse traditions to work together. Such analysis would also help identify ways of encouraging clients to demand and exercise that option.

Summary

Planning has come a long way in the last half century. The Great Depression and World War II provided decisive boosts to synoptic planning—the mandate for large-scale intervention in public affairs, a new repertoire of methods, general acceptance of deficit budgeting, and a firm belief that we can solve enormous problems with a little application of foresight and coordination in the public sector. In the last three decades, that promise has not been entirely fulfilled—either in subsequent wars or in resolving major social problems on the domestic front.

This paper has tended to focus on shortcomings of the synoptic tradition, yet the central problem is a

more general one. The real issue is whether *any* planning style can be effective without parallel inputs from other complementary and countervailing traditions. The synoptic planning tradition is more robust than others in the scope of problems it addresses and the diversity of operating conditions it can tolerate. But the approach has serious blind spots, which can only be covered by recourse to other planning traditions. The world is not all that clear or consistent in presenting problems to be solved. Having planners with the ability to mix approaches is the only way to assure that they can respond with sensitivity to the diversity of problems and settings confronted, and to the complexity of any given situation.

The short list of planning theories just reviewed is more than anyone can feasibly apply in the course of daily professional practice. Nevertheless, it can provide a tool kit for many contingencies, and it can serve as a locator map to understand better where other people are coming from.

Author's note

Grateful acknowledgement is made to Drs. George Copa and Jerome Moss, who commissioned an earlier version of this paper for the Seminar on Planning and Vocational Education at the Minnesota Research and Development Center, Department of Vocational and Technical Education, University of Minnesota at Minneapolis, October 1978.

Notes

1. *Procedural* theories of planning refer to techniques and conceptual models that define the work of planners themselves. In contrast, *substantive* theories concern the nature of problems and social processes which lie outside the profession, to which planners address themselves. Procedural theories would include principles of management and organizational development, communications skills for interacting with clients and communities, methods of data acquisition and analysis, historical knowledge of planning, laws and local regulations defining professional practice, and conceptual tools of sociology, economics, and other social sciences. Substantive theories, on the other hand, refer to specific problems or public policy sectors—for example, the nature of educational systems and issues, rural development policies, theories of poverty, future studies on energy policy, the politics of industrialized housing.

   The main problem with this dichotomous classification is that the line between substantive and procedural theories is blurry; procedures are often specialized in their application to particular substantive problem areas. Typically, in fact, a new procedure is invented to deal with a particular problem. Nevertheless, planning evolves through the continual application of old methods to new problems, and the discovery of new methods to deal with old problems. One of the distinctive features of planning is this reciprocal feedback between theory and practice, knowledge and action, conceptual models and the real world.

2. Algorithms versus heuristics. An *algorithm* is a set procedure for solving a known class of problems. It generally involves quantitative methods, and by definition it is capable of arriving at an optimal solution, based on specification of an objective function, resources, and constraints. Examples are linear pro-

gramming and input-output analysis, operations research, and trend projections. Most algorithms are backed up by theories. For example, the S-shaped curve used in making growth forecasts reflects underlying premises about the nature of growth dynamics and the ceilings on expansion—a generalized pattern derived from statistics, general systems theory, and common sense. Algorithms also require characteristic skills, and professionals undertaking this kind of work can be clearly credentialled for degree of competence. *Heuristic* methods consist of more open-ended search procedures which apply to fuzzy problems, and which offer no optimal solutions but only approximations or judgmental trade-offs. Quantitative methods usually play a less central role although they can have important supporting functions, for example in gaming and simulation procedures to explore scenarios of the future policy situations. The result is not a specific solution, but better judgment about the sensitivity of outcomes to different action possibilities, or different environmental conditions.

Some organizational settings demand strict accountability to standard procedures, and thus rely on algorithms. (In some cases, the planner's role is to justify a particular project or policy dictated by prior reasons of ethics or politics, using selected algorithms that do not bring controversial issues into view.) Other organizations thrive on heuristics, for example those engaged in future studies or trouble shooting, where neither the problem nor the solution is well defined, and the client is more likely to be open-minded about surprise findings and unorthodox recommendations for action. Some planners feel that the really interesting problems are those being encountered for the first time and those which are too "wicked" to be reduced to a standard algorithm. (Rittel and Webber 1973; Friedmann 1978.)

Heuristics and algorithms each have their distinctive uses, but most planning methods can serve either purpose. It is important for planners to clarify with their clients whether the goal is to solve a problem that is clear in everybody's minds, using prescribed techniques and predictable types of answers or whether the task is to gain greater understanding of the problem itself, critically challenging the assumptions underlying past methods of problem-solving, keeping in play judgment and imagination, intuitive leaps and creative insights, to challenge the "givens" of a situation rather than accommodate them. The problem with algorithms and heuristics as a classification scheme is that they are very closely intertwined in specific planning procedures. Systems analysis, for example, has many elements of an algorithm, as in the use of statistical models to estimate input-output or cause-effect or cost-effectiveness relationships among the parts of a system. On the other hand, there are also heuristic versions of systems analysis—the kind of procedure involving boxes and arrows, or a matrix format to array policy objectives against a list of strategy options, to gain a general impression of how well action choices stack up against the goals being sought.

3. Traditional divisions in planning literature refer to sources found in university-based planning programs, and reflected in the *AIP Journal*. Friedmann and Hudson (1974) have distinguished four broad categories of writing in this field:

Philosophical Synthesis (Mannheim, Lindblom, Etzioni, Schon, Friedmann, and others) attempts to locate planning within a larger framework of social and historical processes including: epistemological issues (relating to theories of knowledge and its limits); theories of social action and evolution; ideological contexts of planning; the tensions/reinforcements between planning and democracy; psycho-social development of communities; and social learning theory, which refers to society as a whole taken as a learning system.

Rationalism (Synoptic Rationality) is mainly concerned with procedural (as opposed to substantive) theories. Policy making

is seen as a science, emphasizing econometric models and other algorithms for decision-making (Herbert Simon, Jan Tinbergen, C. West Churchman, Jay Forrester).

Organizational Development theory (Chester Barnard, Kurt Lewin, Warren Bennis, Chris Argyris, Lawrence and Lorsch) centers on management of institutions involved in planning and implementation of plans. Emphasis is on awareness, attitudes, behavior, and values that contribute to understanding, personal development, learning, and growth of effectiveness over time. Whereas the rationalist approach is addressed to allocative planning (efficient distribution of resources among possible uses), organizational theory has more to say about innovative planning—situations which call for mobilization of new resources, toward goals not strictly limited to considerations of economic efficiency, and requiring transformation of perceptions, values, and social structures to bring about needed change (Friedmann 1973).

Empirical studies of planning practice include literature on urban planning (Caro's study of Robert Moses, *The Powerbroker*, is a good example) and also on national planning, especially for lesser developed countries (works by Bertram Gross, Albert Waterston, Albert Hirshman, Guy Benveniste). Also included are some good analyses of regional planning efforts in the U.S., for example Selznick's study of the Tennessee Valley Authority, in which he coined the term "cooptation," or Mel Webber's evaluation of BART in the San Francisco Bay Area. Some of the best work has used the comparative case study approach, which captures enough richness of local detail to avoid the pitfalls of reductionist models and grand abstractions, but which also permits generalizations to be made, and lessons captured from past experience. Good examples of this are the studies of comparative strategies of non-formal education for rural development (Ahmed and Coombs 1975; see also Coombs and Ahmed 1974).

4. See references to empirical studies of planning practice cited in the preceding footnote, and the elaborated discussion in Friedmann and Hudson (1974).

References

Ahmed, Manzoor, and Coombs, Philip. 1975. *Education for rural development: case studies for planners*. New York: Praeger Publishers.

Alinsky, Saul D. 1972. *Rules for radicals*. New York: Vintage Books.

Allison, Graham T. 1968. *Conceptual models and the Cuban missile crisis: rational policy, organizational process, and bureaucratic politics*. Cambridge, Mass.: Harvard University Press.

Argyris, Chris. 1965. *Organization and innovation*. Homewood, Ill.: Irwin Dorsey.

Argyris, Chris, and Schon, Donald. 1975. *Theory in practice*. San Francisco: Jossey-Bass.

Barnard, Chester I. 1938. *The functions of the executive*. New York: The Free Press.

Bennis, Warren G. 1969. *Organization development: its nature, origins, and prospects*. Reading, Mass.: Addison-Wesley.

Bennis, Warren G.; Benne, K. D.; and Chin, R. eds. 1976. *The planning of change*, 3rd ed. New York: Holt, Rinehart and Winston.

Benveniste, Guy. 1972. *The politics of expertise*. Berkeley, California: The Glendessary Press.

Bruyn, Severyn T. 1970. The new empiricists: the participant observer and phenomenologist, and The methodology of participant observation, pp. 283–287 and 305–327. In *Qualitative methodology: firsthand involvement with the social world*, ed., William J. Filstead. Chicago: Markham Publishing Company.

Bundy Report. New York City Mayor's Advisory Panel on Decentralization of the New York City Schools. 1967. *Reconnection for learning: a community school system for New York City*. New York: City of New York.

Caiden, Naomi, and Wildavsky, Aaron. 1974. *Planning and budgeting in poor countries.* New York: Wiley-Interscience Publications.

Caro, Robert. 1975. *The power broker—Robert Moses and the fall of New York.* New York: Vintage Books.

Churchman, Charles West. 1968. *The systems approach.* New York: Dell Publishing Company.

Churchman, Charles West. 1971. *The design of inquiring systems: basic concepts of systems and organizations.* New York: Basic Books.

Coombs, Philip, with Manzoor, Ahmed. 1974. *Attacking rural poverty. How nonformal education can help.* World Bank/ICED. Baltimore: Johns Hopkins Press.

Davidoff, Paul. 1965. Advocacy and pluralism in planning. *Journal of the American Institute of Planners* 31, November: 331–38.

Ellul, Jacques. 1954. *The technological society.* New York: Vintage Books, pub. 1964.

Etzioni, Amitai. 1968. *The active society: a theory of society and political processes.* New York: The Free Press.

Etzioni, Amitai. 1973. Mixed scanning. In *A reader in planning theory,* ed. A. Faludi. New York: Pergamon Press.

Faber, Mike, and Seers, Dudley. eds. 1972. *The crisis in planning.* Vol. I: *The issues;* Vol. II: *The experience.* London: Chatto and Windus for the Sussex University Press.

Faludi, Andreas, ed. 1973a. *A reader in planning theory.* New York: Pergamon Press.

Faludi, Andreas. 1973b. *Planning theory.* New York: Pergamon Press.

Forrester, Jay W. 1969. *Urban dynamics.* Cambridge, Mass.: The MIT Press.

Friedmann, John. 1973. *Retracking America. A theory of transactive planning.* Garden City, N.Y.: Doubleday-Anchor.

Friedmann, John. 1978. The epistemology of social practice: a critique of objective knowledge. *Theory and Society* 6, 1: 75–92.

Friedmann, John, and Hudson, Barclay. 1974. Knowledge and action: a guide to planning theory. *Journal of the American Institute of Planners* 40, 1: 3–16.

Galloway, Thomas D., and Mahayni, Riad G. 1977. Planning theory in retrospect: the process of paradigm change. *Journal of the American Institute of Planners* 43, 1: 62–71.

Goodman, Paul, and Goodman, Percival. 1960. *Communitas. Means of livelihood and ways of life.* Second Edition. New York: Vintage Books.

Goodman, Robert. 1971. *After the planners.* New York: Touchstone Books.

Gordon, David M. ed. 1971. *Problems in political economy: an urban perspective.* Lexington, Mass.: D.C. Heath and Company.

Grabow, Stephen, and Heskin, Allan. 1973. Foundations for a radical concept of planning. *Journal of the American Institute of Planners* 39:2: 106–14. Also "Comments" in *JAIP* 39:4 and *JAIP* 40:2.

Gross, Bertram M. 1965. National planning: findings and fallacies. *Public Administration Review* 25:4: 263–273.

Hampden-Turner, Charles. 1975. *From poverty to dignity.* Garden City, New York: Anchor Books.

Heskin, Allan. 1977. Crisis and response: an historical perspective on advocacy planning. Urban Planning Program Working Paper, DP-80. Los Angeles: Universiy of California at Los Angeles.

Hightower, Henry C. 1969. Planning theory in contemporary professional education. *Journal of the American Institute of Planners* 35, 5: 326–329.

Hirschman, Albert O. 1967. *Development projects observed.* Washington, D.C.: The Brookings Institution.

Horvat, Branko. 1972. Planning in Yugoslavia. In *The crisis of planning,* Vol. II. ed., Faber and Seers. London: Chatto and Windus for the Sussex University Press.

Hudson, Barclay. 1975. Domains of evaluation. *Social Policy* 6, 3: 79–83.

Hudson, Barclay. 1977. Varieties of science: not by rationalism alone; and Dialectical science: epistemology for evolutionary systems. Los Angeles: UCLA Urban Planning Program (manuscript).

Hudson, Barclay. 1979. Compact policy assessment and the delphi method: practical application of dialectical theory to educational planning and forecasting. Paper prepared for the Center for Studies in Education and Development, Harvard University, Cambridge, Massachusetts (February).

Illich, Ivan. 1973. *Tools for conviviality.* New York: Harper & Row.

Jantsch, Erich, ed. 1969. *Perspectives of planning.* Paris: Organization for Economic Co-operation and Development.

Katz, Alfred, and Bender, Eugene. 1976. *The strength in us.* New York: New Viewpoints.

Kravitz, Alan S. 1970. Mandarinism: planning as a handmaiden to conservative politics. In *Planning for politics: uneasy partnership,* eds., T. L. Beyle and G. T. Lathrop. New York: Odyssey Press.

Lawrence, Paul R.,and Lorsch, Jay W. 1967. *Organization and environment: managing differentiation and integration.* Boston: Harvard University Graduate School of Business Administration.

Lewin, Kurt. 1948. *Resolving social conflicts: selected papers on group dynamics.* New York: Harper and Bros.

Lichfield, N. 1970. Evaluation methodology of urban and regional plans: a review, *Regional Studies* 4: 151–165.

Lindblom, Charles E. 1959. The science of muddling through. *Public Administration Review* 19: 79–88.

Lindblom, Charles E. 1965. *The intelligence of democracy. Decision making through mutual adjustment.* New York: The Free Press.

Mannheim, Karl. 1949. *Ideology and utopia.* New York: Harcourt, Brace and Co.

Mason, R. O. 1969. A dialectical approach to strategic planning. *Management Science* 15: B-403–414.

Meyerson, M., and Banfield, E. C. 1955. *Politics, planning, and the public interest.* Glencoe, N.Y.: Free Press.

Miller, George A.; Galanter, Eugene; and Pribam, Karl H. 1960. *Plans and the structure of behavior.* New York: Henry Holt.

Mills, C. Wright. 1959. *The sociological imagination.* London: Oxford.

Peattie, Lisa. 1968. Reflections on advocacy planning. *Journal of the American Institute of Planners* 34, 2: 80–87.

Polanyi, Michael. 1964. *Personal knowledge: towards a post-critical philosophy.* New York: Harper Torch Books (orig. pub. 1958).

Rittel, Horst, W. J., and Webber, Melvin M. 1973. Dilemmas in a general theory of planning. *Policy Sciences* 4: 155–169.

Schumacher, E. F. 1973. *Small is beautiful.* New York: Harper & Row.

Scott, A. J., and Roweis, S. T. 1977. Urban planning in theory and practice: a reappraisal. *Environment and Planning* 9, 1: 1097–1120.

Schon, Donald. 1971. *Beyond the stable state.* New York: Random House.

Selznick, Philip. 1949. *TVA and the grass roots.* Berkeley: University of California Press.

Simon, Herbert. 1957. *Administrative behavior,* 2nd ed. New York: The Free Press.

Tinbergen, Jan. 1964. *Economic policy: principles and design.* Amsterdam: North Holland.

Waterston, Albert. 1965. *Development planning: lessons of experience.* Baltimore: The Johns Hopkins Press.

Wilson, James Q. 1968. *City politics and public policy.* New York: John Wiley and Sons.

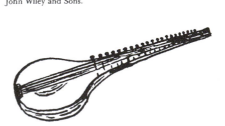

[6]

THEORETICAL DEBATES IN PLANNING:
TOWARDS A COHERENT DIALOGUE.

CONFERENCE POSITION PAPER

PATSY HEALEY, GLEN McDOUGALL & MICHAEL J. THOMAS

1. INTRODUCTION

This paper is concerned with reviewing and analysing the changes which have
occurred in planning theory in the last ten years and with establishing the
terms of common debate between the present plurality of theoretical positions.

From the war until the early '70's, the urban and regional planning theory
field was dominated by two 'paradigms' or theoretical positions. The first
was that which views planning as the three dimensional design of towns, in
shorthand, the urban design tradition. This dominated the field until the
1960's. The second which had a strong influence in the US in the 1950's and
entered British discussion in the 1960's through the work of McLoughlin,
Chadwick and others, was procedural planning theory, which views planning as
a general societal management process. (Galloway and Mahayni, 1977, describes the paradigm shift between the two in the US). This position rose to dominance in the 1960's.

However, in the 1970's we saw not only the collapse of the dominance of the
procedural planning theory position (see Hemmens and Stiftel, 1980, and
Hudson, 1979) but also the failure of any other theoretical position to establish dominance. In the 1970's we witnessed the rise of a number of competing theoretical positions in the urban and regional planning field with
little debate between the positions and with general ignorance on the part
of members of any one position of the concerns of any other position. This
theoretical pluralism and collective ignorance is one of the reasons for the
present conference and for this paper.

One important result of this pluralism and collective ignorance is that planning practice and the ideologies of planners have generally remained uninfor-
med by disciplined theoretical debate in the last decade. A distinctive
characteristic of the urban and regional planning tradition has always been
the readiness to adopt uncritically and often unwittingly the tenets of intellectual and ideological waves which sweep through the academic and para-
academic world. This has led to what may be described as the condition of
uncritical practice, in which not only do the practitioners have little basis
other than "hunch" and experience for determining and evaluating their actions, but there is no academic capacity for critical evaluation. (As an

6

indicator of this condition, most of the limited evaluative work on urban and regional planning has been done by academics (sociologists, geographers and political scientists) whose prime interest is not in planning). This condition of uncritical practice has been reinforced by the nature of much of the theorising in the urban and regional planning field in the last decade. Many of the recent theoretical positions have been unconcerned with the practical utility of theory and have frequently ignored (and often been ignorant of) the practice of planning. Ignoring practice on the part of planning theoreticians has encouraged practitioners to ignore theory: that is, many planning practitioners doubting the relevance of much existing planning theory have embraced a broader anti-theory position, denying the efficacy of any theory.

Consequently, one of the main objectives of this paper is to attempt to establish the terms of theoretical debate in the planning theory field once more and to demonstrate the practical necessity of theory. We wish to show how it may be possible to unify the field of theoretical discussion about the nature, purpose and method of planning in order to provide the basis for the critical evaluation and development of the various positions both in theoretical terms and in their relation to practice.

The area of debate we are concerned with is that of the nature, purpose and method of planning while the tradition to which we relate is the practice of urban and regional planning and the ideologies and methods of those who carry out this practice. In this concern we are not interested in constructing a discipline to which practitioners can relate, still less with providing them with an operational ideology. Our concern is with encouraging disciplined theoretical debate as the basis for the critical evaluation and development of explanation and prescription for planning activity. Furthermore, it is not our aim to unify the field theoretically. We anticipate the persistence of major oppositions. Our concern is to re-establish critical communication, as an aid to sharpening the theoretical focus of existing positions and encouraging theoretical development.

But before we turn to the task of proposing terms for unifying the debate it is necessary to both describe and explain the present theoretical pluralism in the urban and regional planning field. For the different theoretical positions are not just the product of the internal intellectual debates among academics and practitioners but more importantly are the product of wider societal forces which affect the practice of planning and the education of planners.

2. THE PRESENT PLURALITY OF THEORETICAL POSITIONS

Before developing an explanation of the present state of theory in the urban and regional planning field let us briefly review the various current theoretical positions and map their relationships to each other. In doing so we are, in some cases, formalizing into a position a collection of ideas whose proponents may not have been consciously associating themselves with one, most notably in the case of "implementation and policy".

We have identified the following seven distinctive theoretical positions:-

        1. Procedural planning theory
        2. Incrementalism and other decision-making methodologies
        3. Implementation and policy
        4. Social planning and advocacy planning
        5. Political economy approach
        6. The new humanism
        7. Pragmatism

These positions can be grouped in various ways. For instance, one could divide them into those which take a critical stance of the present structure and
values of advanced capitalist societies (e.g. political economy and the new
humanism) and those which generally accept the nature of existing society and
suggest adjustments to the way in which society operates (e.g. implementation
and policy, incrementalism). Or one could group them into those which adopt a
structural or holistic perspective on social organisation (e.g. procedural
planning theory, social planning, political economy approach) and those which
emphasise individual interaction or behaviour (e.g. the new humanism, incrementalism).

What we should like to emphasize is that all have either developed from or
in opposition to procedural planning theory. This is shown in Diagram 1
which not only provides a map of the relationships between various positions
but demonstrates their relationship to procedural planning theory. The
oppositional positions (the political economy approach and the new humanism)
are often termed 'radical' i.e. in terms of their critical stance towards
present society and towards procedural planning theory. Pragmatism is also
oppositional to procedural planning theory and to all theory being a direct
result of the failure of procedural planning theory and the other competing
positions to demonstrate their relevance to planning practice and planning

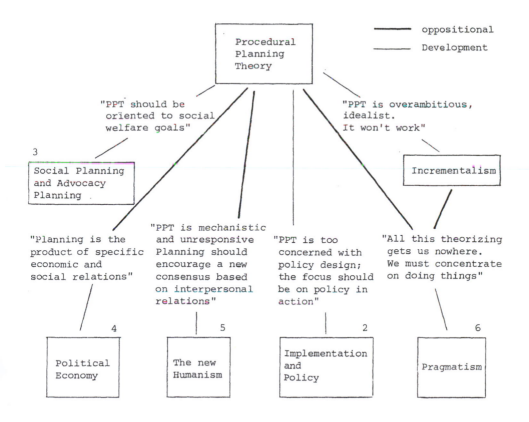

Diagram 1. A map of theoretical positions in planning theory in 1970's

8

practitioners. The other positions seek to modify procedural planning theory
to incorporate dimensions which they regard as particularly important. The
diagram shows how procedural planning theory, the dominant paradigm of the
early seventies, spawned the pluralism of the late seventies.

The following brief statements about each of the seven theoretical positions
are meant to describe the different positions for those who may not be familiar with them or who do not understand our terminology and to elaborate
the diagramatic map.

1. Procedural planning theory

This derives from a general systems model which ascribes to planning certain
societal tasks (notably self-regulation). These tasks are to be pursued
through a problem-solving technology based on rational procedures and methods
for decision-making. Characteristically these procedures and methods focus
on the clarification of policy goals, systematic analysis, logical generation of policy alternatives, systematic evaluation of these alternatives and
monitoring performance. This type of conceptualization rests on the assumption that there exists a distinctive type of planning thought and action
which occurs without reference to any particular object, and which can be
adopted within any societal context. Its central value is to promote the
"rationality" of societal action. It is thus not only "contentless" and
"contextless" (Thomas, M. 1979), but proposed that what is rational can be
demonstrated scientifically or logically. Its prescriptive emphasis is on
organizational structure and decision-making methods which will promote
rational decision-making. The most developed British exposition of this
approach can be found in Faludi (1973).

2. Incrementalism and other decision-making methodologies

The various attempts to construct alternative decision-making schemes are
best seen as developments of the procedural tradition. They address themselves to two critical issues, what is the most rational way of proceeding
and how to connect decision-making methodologies to the contexts in which
they are used, a necessary development once alternative methodologies are
proposed. The most concerted attack on both questions comes from the "incrementalists" (Lindblom, 1973, 1965; Braybrooke and Lindblom, 1963). These
argue that goal-directed, logically-deductive, comprehensive methodologies
are not rational in most public agencies because information requirements
cannot be met and political circumstances will inhibit them. They propose
the incrementalist method, modelled on market decision-making. Developing
from this, Etzioni proposed "mixed scanning" as an accommodation between the
two positions (Etzioni, 1973). Etzioni notes that the capacity for strategic
scanning relates to "the power positions of the planner", while Braybrooke
and Lindblom propose a matrix of positions (defined by degree of societal
change and degree of understanding) to which different methodologies can be
related (p.78). Some recent American work appears to be trying to relate the
various decision-making schemes that have been produced to typologies of
contexts, via contingency theory (Hudson, 1979; Galloway, 1979). This
focuses on finding the context to fit the method. Others have abandoned the
development of method technology for a focus on "organizational learning",
which emphasises the development of individual abilities to develop co-
ordination networks and devise relevant approaches to continuously redefined
situations. Thus Friend, Power and Yewlett, (1974) develop "connective
planning" based on networking skills, while Argyris and Schon (1974) emphasise the development of "theory-in-practice" (see also Bolan, 1980). This
work is explicitly interactional in orientation, and has close links with

the next position.

3. <u>From strategic choice to implementing strategies: implementation and</u>
    <u>policy</u>

These ideas attack the tendency in procedural planning theory to separate
policy from action/implementation (Friedman, 1969; Pressman and Wildavsky,
1973). Recent work in Britain has focused on policy implementation in multi-
organizational contexts, particularly in central-local relations. Analyses
draw on the literature in organization theory and local policies, and theoretical perspectives shift around the functionalism typical of procedural
planning theory, social exchange theories developed from the work of Blau
(1964), and socio-psychological/phenomenological explanations of organization behaviour (see Hill and others, 1979; also Rhodes, 1979a for US work).
Empirical studies have focused attention on micro-organizational behaviour
in explaining the way policies are defined and used, how resources are allocated, and the outcomes of such activities. A central theme in the work
recently sponsored by the SSRC (Rhodes, 1979b; and Hill and others, 1979)
is the exercise of discretion within work situations defined by rules,
organization cultures, professional cultures and the interplay of interests.
It focuses attention on the significance of bargaining over resources, the
negotiability of rules, directives and policy guidance, and the conflicting
demands placed on individuals and groups.

4. <u>Goal-directed planning: social planning and advocacy planning</u>

Here we have a different critique of procedural planning theory. While the
general method remains undisputed, it is attached to the promotion of specific values (the promotion of opportunities for all to achieve the conditions
of life they seek) and a model of interest which proposed that society is
composed of different groups with different interests. These various "clients'
of planning must therefore be identified and their interests made explicit.
For Gans, this must be done by careful research, and discussion with the
groups concerned (Gans, 1968). Davidoff (1965) challenges the ability of
government agencies to do this adequately, and proposes that all groups should
have access to independent planning expertise to "advocate" their interests.
Both Gans and Davidoff adopt a pluralist model of social organization, although the latter is more explicitly concerned with linking technical expertise
to a model of participatory democracy, and both recognise that pluralist competition is currently unequal. Consequently, compensatory action is important to help the disadvantaged. Gans' ideas on social planning came close to
those of Townsend and others in Britain who operate within the social democratic (Fabian) tradition which is based on a class-conflict model of society.
Social planning is thus about directing power and resources to the "have
nots" in order to reduce poverty and inequality (Townsend, 1975).

5. <u>Marx rediscovered: the new political economy</u>

The values underlying this fundamentally critical position are similar to
those of Townsend and others, namely the promotion of a fairer, more socially
just society. The difference lies in the analysis of capitalist societies
and the rejection of ameliorative policies as mechanisms for long term structural change. The unequal distribution of resources is presented as an inevitable product of the capitalist mode of production which creates two classes (the working class and the capitalist class) in fundamental opposition.
Government agencies are part of the state apparatuses which are determined,
structured or merely influenced (according to one's position in the debate)
by the interests of capital. These are capital accumulation in the short

10

and the long term. The state therefore plays a role in assisting capital to
collect profits (surplus value) now and ensure their production in the future.
It consequently only acts in the interests of the working class if these have
brought sufficient political pressure to bear to extract such concessions.
Many social welfare programmes are interpreted as either serving the reproduction needs of capitalists (e.g. key worker housing) or as maintaining support
for the system as a whole. There are of course major debates about the exact
nature of many of these relations (see E.O. Wright, 1978 for an excellent review). This very powerful theoretical tradition has lead to studies by sociologists (Castells and others, also Saunders and Newby), geographers and regional
scientists (Harvey especially, also Massey) and more recently political scientists (Dearlove and Dunleavy) (Castells, 1976, 1977; Saunders, 1980, Newby and
others, 1978; Harvey, 1973; Massey and Catalano, 1978; Dearlove, 1979;
Dunleavy, 1980) which have attempted to identify and explain the specific practices of planning as a state activity, intervening in land prices, land use
and development in relation to capitalist interests and to "social movements"
pressurising for concessions. We thus begin to have an approach which is able
to relate broad economic and political forces to the detailed operation of
government policy in the urban and regional field, a complete reversal of the
"contentless" and "contextless" character of procedural planning theory.

6. Retreat into idealism: the new humanism

This brand of radicalism, associated with the post-1970 work of John Friedmann,
and more generally with the ideas of Donald Schon and others (Freidmann, 1973;
Grabow and Heskin, 1973), is based on the search for a societal organization
based on individual interaction. The model proposed is of small scale communities within a cellular structure, self-organising and self-responsible
(and ecologically conscious) in which individuals will "learn" how to get on
with each other, identifying common interests but respecting individual ones.
The planner, somewhat curiously, becomes a radical change agent, educating
people in the principles of this new society. So far, these ideas appear to
have little allegience in this country.

7. "Getting things done": the relapse into pragmatism

Given the theoretical pluralism in planning, and the evident failings of most
of the positions discussed to get to grips with the specific practice of planning anti-theoretical reactions are no surprise. Many planners are now desperately concerned to demonstrate their "relevance" to local councils, to
central government and to a highly critical public. The emphasis is on
"getting things done", to quote the RTPI's 1980 Conference, producing visible
results. This is no doubt a commendable objective, but the creation of products in isolation from questions of purposes and values is ultimately a socially dangerous activity. It also makes planners more than usually vulnerable to the charge that they are nothing more than blind operators of the
systems within which they find themselves.

3. FACTORS UNDERLYING THE CHANGES IN THEORETICAL DEBATE

If, as we have claimed, these various theoretical positions do not arise
merely from the internal logic of intellectual development in the field, how
can we explain the fall of procedural planning theory and the development of
the present theoretical plurality? We would argue that planning theory is
not produced in a social vacuum. It is produced by individuals in concrete
social situations who are trying to explain, justify or change planning in
their particular social context. The theory and the theorist are intricately

bound to the practice of planning (i.e. planning as an activity of government
and as an occupation) and with the societal context of that practice. Consequently changes within planning practice and the context of planning are likely
to be reflected in changes in how the planning theorist conceptualises the
nature of planning, the nature and role of theory and the nature and processes
of society and social change. Therefore, in order to begin to understand the
changes in planning theory which have occurred in the last decade we must consider the political and economic forces which have affected the practice of
planning in the 1970's, the detailed changes in the practice itself and finally the problems faced by the planning profession, the occupational group
which carries out the practice.

Forces affecting the practice of planning

One of the most notable features of postwar Britain has been the expansion of
government activity, most notably in the 1960's, associated with the ideology
adopted by both Conservative and Labour administrations that a managed economy would produce substantial economic growth and widely distributed affluence. An increased proportion of this expanded government role was demanded
of local government, with local government's contribution to overall government expenditure increasing to a peak in 1974. Within this "managerial" concern, strong pressure was put on local government to reorganise not only its
boundaries but to become more efficient and more policy oriented (Dearlove,
1979). It was in the mid-sixties that planning practice was revised to improve its "planning" capacity (the new development plan system) accompanied
by changes which increased the numbers and improved the educational level of
planners. Similar changes, mechanisms for increasing policy orientation
and increasing educational levels for operatives, occurred in other policy
areas administered by central government, notably the social services. In
both urban planning and the social services, the management methods of procedural planning theory were seen as providing relevant guidance.

But it became clear during the 1970's, that under the guise of increasing
local autonomy, these new "policy vehicles" were as much to do with increasing central control of an increasing proportion of centrally provided expenditure. In effect, local government management was being encouraged to become more technocratic in order to provide greater efficiency and effectiveness for central government, reducing local control (Dearlove, 1979), and
confirming the view of those who have seen the sixties and seventies as characterised by a move towards corporatism (Winkler, 1977; Cawson, 1977).
Technocratic theories were therefore attractive as justification and methodological guides.

Public expenditure cuts, however, which helped to increase central control of
local authorities, made evident the political nature of this operation. This
was combined with increasing political opposition by many recipients of government policies (from claimants unions and community action groups to amenity
societies) to the products of these policies and to the processes by which
the policies were decided. Urban and regional planning found itself at the
forefront of this "revolt of the client", as it was called in the American
literature (Haug and Sussman, 1969), because planning decisions appeared to
affect adversely so many groups (industrialists seeking to expand, property
developers seeking to speculate, environmentalist groups seeking to conserve
their amenities, and those whose lives had been dislocated by urban redevelopment in the 1950's and 1960's).

There have thus been two contradictory tendencies affecting government programmes, and particularly planning, in the 1970's. On the one hand, has been

12

the tendency to centralism, to depoliticising decision-making and increasing
the role and power of technical experts, an essentially managerial tendency.
On the other, have been demands for more participation in decision-making,
more accountability on the part of local politicians and officials, and increasing criticism of technical expertise, in effect demands for increasing
politicization of decision-making. To use McAuslan's terminology, there has
been a clash between the "public interest" ideology used by government officials and the "participatory democracy" ideology of many outside government
(McAuslan, 1980).

Accompanying these contradictory tendencies in government, the economic performance of western capitalism has been increasingly shaky after the long
period of boom conditions after the war. This economic vulnerability has
been particularly evident in Britain one product of which has been academic
recognition of the persistence of inequality and pre-war class cleavages
(Westergaard and Resler, 1975) and its rediscovery by the growing numbers
suffering its consequences. Another has been the recognition of what O'Connor
(1973) has called the "fiscal crisis of the state". Both Marxists and mone-
tarists demonstrate the cost to capital accumulation of social expenditure
whether designed to reproduce capital in the long term, maintain social harmony or produce real gains in the living standard of the ordinary people.
Yet as Marxists note (O'Connor, 1973; Gough, 1975), total public expenditure
is not really being cut, merely transferred particularly towards various forms
of support for an ailing economy, and towards coping with the social consequences of unemployment. Thus the whole state enterprise is caught within an
increasingly overt contradiction - hence the current political debates on the
extent and form of public expenditure. With economic uncertainty and political exposure, technocrats, such as central and local government planners,
have difficulty in sustaining a role based on long term planned management in
the public interest. Thus we see among planners first a disillusionment with
the synoptic ideal and acceptance of the incrementalists,model (the "humdrum"
triumphing over the "heroic" as Haywood and Watson record in a general review
of planning exercises in Europe (Haywood and Watson, 1975)),followed by a
search for a different managerial style, linked on the one hand to negotiating
with and influencing different interests to achieve temporary agreements and
on the other to support for "partnership" - between central and local government (as in the inner city partnerships) and the public and private sectors.

Changes in planning practice

How has the organization of planning practice been affected by these contradictory tendencies affecting government as a whole? Urban planning led the
field in local government with the reorganization of development plans to
strengthen "the planning capacity" of town and country planning (Hebbert, 1977;
McKay and Cox, 1979). This development was closely linked (in the minds of
many planners at least) to the discussion of corporate planning in local government. Procedural planning theory was used to provide principles for constructing the earlier structure plans (Drake and others, 1975), the preparation of which has so far been a highly technocratic exercise. But the capacity
of structure plans to provide a long term strategic management framework for
a wide range of policy issues and for the detailed operation of land use planning has been undermined during the 1970's by (1) the traditional sectoralism
of both local and central governments, with major spending departments disinterested in giving up policy control for the goal of "co-ordination", and
the evolution of a variety of sectoral policy vehicles with different time
scales and organising principles (Stewart, 1977); (2) the resistance by many
local councillors to having policy control wrested from them (see Underwood,
1980; Darke, 1979); (3) economic uncertainty and public expenditure cuts

which have undermined the predictive capacity of long term plans; and (4)
the reorganization of local government (to which planners strongly objected)
which while providing larger ("more efficient") districts, broke any strategic
and co-ordinative capacity that remained in the statutory planning system.
This tendency has been continued in the proposals for "organic change" and the
weakening of links between strategic planning and development control in the
Local Government,Planning and Land Act, 1980.

Changes in planning practice, thus, have made it difficult to sustain a role
for planners as strategic policy directors and co-ordinators, which procedural
planning theory encouraged. To maintain a strategic role at all, they are
forced to develop capacities in the politics of influence (see Friend, Norris
and Carter, 1978). At the same time they are being encouraged into this at
the local level, with the increasing emphasis on entrepreneurial and promot-
ional activities, (e.g. small firm promotion in inner city programmes). It
is little wonder that the ideas we have called "implementation and policy"
are proving attractive as the basis for an alternative managerial style.
However, in addition to moving away from a synoptic planning mode (a similar
move occurred in the 1950's, Hebbert, 1977), the failure to make any co-
ordinative headway in intersectoral disputes has pushed planners back to the
"home ground" of development promotion and regulation. This has itself been
encouraged by government concern with land policy in the mid-seventies (reacting to the "unacceptable" land speculation of the early seventies and resulting in the now defunct Community Land Act) and by the emphasis in both inner
city programmes and more recent initiatives in encouraging economic investment by improving infrastructure and environmental appearance. Planning, and
regulating the private sector in the "public interest", have now given way to
promoting economic recovery (i.e. the private sector) in the "public interest".

Changes in the planning profession

In view of the way planning practice has been caught in the contradictory
tendencies in government, the chronic crisis of confidence from which the planning profession has suffered during the 1970's is to be expected. In the
1960's the profession was thrust into the wider arena of local government
policy planning which many planners welcomed with enthusiasm partly because
it opened up opportunities to exercise more power and influence, opportunities
which planners hoped to monopolise, and partly because it provided an alternative role to that of physical redevelopment, an activity in which the role
of planners was being increasingly criticised. Procedural planning theory
offered both a new position to replace the naive determinist assumptions of
the design tradition and a basis for enlarging professional status. But these
ambitions were stalled in the mid-seventies by the academic criticisms of the
concept of synoptic co-ordinated planning (particularly the incrementalists'
attack) and the practical problems of operationalizing the approach. Meanwhile, the assumption that planners were part of a practice which operated in
the general public interest, or as a defender of those interests not promoted
by the market was heavily dented by the "revolt of the client" as described
above, and by academic studies which demonstrated that planning had not necessarily promoted either the general interest, or the interests of those disadvantaged, but rural interests versus the urban poor (Hall, and others, 1973),
property developers versus local residents (Ambrose and Colenutt, 1975), administrative efficiency versus the local community (Dennis, 1970; Davies,
1972).

Planners had to take this criticism seriously partly because of the persistent
professional ideological tendency to see planning as "for people". Planners
have always believed they have a social conscience, if a vague one. The

14

client-oriented ideas of social planning and advocacy planning influenced the
thinking of many younger planners, particularly those working in areas of
social deprivation, such as the inner city. Planners also had to take academic criticism seriously because of the profession's concern to demonstrate
its comparative status by visibly improving the educational level of planners
(e.g. the promotion and expansion of degree courses in planning in the late
1960's and early 1970's). Procedural planning theory played a major role in
this academicization of the profession. Being based on the belief that the
methods of positivist social science could be applied to social, action social
scientists were drawn increasingly into planning, both to be trained as practitioners and as educators (Thomas, A.H., 1979). But it was these very same
social scientists in planning education and their colleagues in sociology,
geography and political science departments, who completed the academic dem-
olition of procedural planning theory already underway as a result of the
practical experience of attempts at application.

Where then could the profession look for a justifactory ideology? A review of
RTPI pronouncements during the 1970's is more indicative of divisions within
the profession reflecting the current theoretical pluralism than any clear
development. The old struggle of the 1960's between the traditional physical
planners and those aiming for a wider policy role, persisted into the 1970's
with the balance towards the former when the Institute settled for option 4A
(environmental planning) as the basis for membership. This did not prevent
the publication of Planning and the Future in 1976 which espouses procedural
planning theory. This was rapidly overtaken by the pressures described above
forcing planners back into a role defined by statute and institution (their
departments). Recent reports on development control, implementation, land
values and employment planning, though not necessarily consistent with each
other, illustrate the land and development/economic promotion base of much
of current practice.

The planning profession therefore finds itself in considerable difficulty.
Its claims to a wider role and higher status have been severely curtailed.
Even planners themselves doubt whether they have the developmental and financial training for the jobs they now see as relevant. Where their work
still involves policy issues, there are doubts about whether there is any
role for technical knowledge and skill. It is perhaps no wonder that there
is a strong undercurrent of criticism against planning education and academics
in the profession at present. The profession's increasingly desperate attempts to demonstrate "relevance" are hostile to the maintenance of a critical evaluative capacity, one reason for the relapse into "pragmatism".

4. EXPLAINING THE CHANGES IN THE THEORETICAL DEBATE

Having now charted the main changes which have affected the practice of planning and the planning profession in the last decade we can now return to the
question of why procedural planning theory lost its dominance and why a plurality of competing positions developed in planning theory. As we have seen,
ideologically procedural planning theory is based on a particular socio-
economic and political viewpoint which bears a strong resemblance to the
American "end of ideology" theorists (e.g. Bell). It rests upon a consensus
view of society where major conflicts over values and interests and consequently over social distribution are absent. Its operating values are technic-
ist and conservative and deny the political nature of planning practice.
Furthermore, procedural planning theory assumes that society will experience
economic growth and that this will ensure that political and social harmony
will be maintained.

15

Now it is not difficult to see why this view appealed to planners in the early seventies for it accorded very closely with some of the dominant tendencies of the time and provided an apparently appropriate operating ideology for the profession. We saw how there was a tendency in the early seventies to depoliticise decision-making and to increase the role and power of technical experts, how ideas about corporate management were in vogue in local government and how planning functions in local authorities were expanding. Furthermore we have seen that the profession was struggling to achieve credibility in both academic and professional terms.

Procedural planning theory provided a means of taking advantage of some of these developments whilst at the same time advancing the claims of the planning profession. It did this in three main ways. Firstly, procedural planning theory provided a guide for action which located planning activity within depoliticised technical structures stressing the superiority of the synoptic rational method of decision-making over day-to-day political conflicts. Secondly, it provided a rationale for the bid for power within local authorities on the part of professional planners by justifying their monopoly demands to all types of planning practice. Thirdly, it provided a basis for the planners' claim to professional distinctiveness and credibility which was independent of the outcomes of planning practice.

But the premises of procedural planning theory meant that it could not cope with any breakdown of political and social consensus, with economic stagnation, with challenges to the structure and processes of decision-making. Consequently as the seventies progressed, and the economic crisis and fiscal crisis of the state intensified, procedural planning theory could neither explain what was happening nor provide a suitable mode of operation for planning activity. Also procedural planning theory could not provide an adequate response to the increasing demands to justify the goals and outcomes of planning policy and to allow more participation and accountability in decision-making or to the growing challenges to the existing basis of planning expertise. Again, procedural planning theory seemed most inappropriate to the emphasis in local authorities from the mid-seventies on substantive issues in policy making and to the reawakened political interest in the land and its control and development. Neither did it provide a particularly resilient defence against central and local government cutbacks in expenditure and manpower.

Yet the search for alternatives which are value-less has persisted. The incrementalist critique of synoptic rational planning was adopted to demonstrate that planning had a "problem-orientation" and was "realistic" (Needham, 1971), in line with government advice to structure planners (the "key issues" circular DoE 94/74). "Mixed-scanning" was advocated as a suitable compromise between the synoptic ideal and practical reality. But since these alternative decision-making methods are merely alternative technologies, they resolve none of the political problems which undermine procedural planning theory. Focusing on the micro-politics of organizational behaviour, inter-personal interaction and the economic and cultural climate in which this occurs, the "implementation and policy" tradition, offers many attractions as a managerial alternative. Practioners find that its accounts describe their practices better than the ideal constructs of procedural planning theory and its prescriptive encouragement to negotiate, create networks, use discretion to manipulate the actions of others fits well with the entrepreneurial role in partnership with the private sector that many local authorities, actively encouraged by government, are currently seeking. The approach also allows consideration of political interest, with councillors and other interests as part of a perceived pluralist structure within which planners attempt to

16

implement policy. Yet as with procedural planning theory, these ideas espouse
no values (not even "rationality"), nor focus on any object in particular,
although detailed case studies of policy areas may be undertaken. Nor are
the political and economic forces structuring the practices which are described or prescribed treated as other than generalised and contextual. Thus,
this position does not provide an explanation of the changes which produce
changes in practice, and it cannot provide the basis for the profession's
claims to a distinctive role (in fact it tends to oppose such claims).

The client-centred and social welfare orientation of social planning and advocacy planning have been approached by planners with an ambiguity which reflects
the contradictory tendencies in government described above. On the one hand,
notions of participation and social justice accord well with the flabby social
conscience which the profession has retained from its early evangelist days
and with the pressures arising from the "revolt of the client". On the other,
practical attempts at pursuing such an approach impede "efficiency". They are
therefore typically undertaken in the technical terms of the planners (as the
whole experience of so-called public participation has shown) or undermined
by opposition elsewhere in local government (e.g. the failure of area management in Liverpool). Although many planners may still adhere to notions such
as Gans' version of social planning at an ideological level, its influence on
practice has been very limited. This is partly because it offers no explanation of specific practices nor of the changes occurring in the forces structuring practice, and very little guidance on how to change existing institutional
arrangements and operating procedures in order to implement the approach. In
any case, as Goodman (1972) and many involved in the CDPs discovered, small
scale compensatory programmes were either blocked by larger interests (often
embodied in local government organization) or by the way in which the distribution of wealth and opportunity was structured on a national scale. It is
this appreciation which has lead many of those involved towards the political
economy position.

The present appeal of the political economy approach lies only partly in its
criticism of the social distribution of advanced capitalist societies. Its
primary attraction lies in its explanatory power. It is the only position
which offers a coherent and relevant account of the way changes in the economy
are reflected in the dilemmas facing government, and how these in turn shape
the practices in which planners find themselves. The way in which industrial
and finance capital impact on local planning offices and the local community
are as much part of the current awareness of most planners today as· of
Marxist analysts. With the repoliticisation of government decision-making
as we have already described, older debates on social and economic change,
freedom and democracy have become manifest in the practice of government policy as well as in the wider political fields. The restatement of the radical
right position has gone hand-in-hand with the re-emergence of political economy. Furthermore, by identifying planning largely with state intervention in
the land market and development process, and the relations between the public
and private sectors, it provides planners with a clear substantive area of
concern, and one which relates to government procedures and institutional
arrangements. Planners are thus provided with a credible area of practical
expertise based on a wider theoretical knowledge of economic organization and
the role of the state (though not, of course, a professional ideology).

As yet, however, a great deal of detailed work needs to be done before the
potential of this approach is realised. Statements tend to be highly generalised and based on superficial evidence or case studies the typicality of which
is not specified. In addition, there has been very little work on prescriptions for practitioners. In part this is the product of the critical and

determinist nature of much of the discussion which adheres to the view that
the only valid social action is the promotion of major structural change.
Yet in other local government fields, such as public health, detailed prescriptions have been proposed and used, aimed at winning concessions for disadvantaged groups. Why has there been so little of this in planning?. One
explanation may be the dominance of contentless procedural planning theory
which deflected academic attention away from land and development issues.
Another must be the near monopoly of this approach in the planning field by
academics with little detailed knowledge of the operation of land use planning.

The appeal of the "new humanism" position is limited in Britain to a few
academics and reformist groups. In many ways it looks back to the community-
based reformist tradition which supported notions of town planning in the
late nineteenth and early twentieth centuries. It offers no explanation of
the present situation, but provides a model for individual action. It is
more radical than the previous position in two ways. Firstly, it offers a
philosophical basis for an individualist/interactionist mode of action and
secondly it challenges dominant notions of professionalism and expertise.
In this it accords with wider movements which we have commented on earlier
and which were particularly strong in the United States where this position
originated, which challenged the expertise of planners. It does not deny the
role of planning nor of the planner but the role of a planning profession
with monopoly claims over planning activity. It also seeks to deny the importance of political and economic forces and collective action by emphasising
the strength of the individual. The approach is exhortatory telling planners
what they should do in a different world but saying little about what to do
now. If economic and political conditions grow more difficult, this position
may attract more support in Britain being an essentially escapist ideal. A
more likely response is a relapse into pragmatism which we have already noted
and challenged.

By way of conclusion, it is possible to categorize theoretical debate about
the nature, purpose and method of planning into two tendencies, reflecting
the contradictory tendencies faced by all contemporary government efforts.
The first is the technocratic, managerial tendency displayed by procedural
planning theory, its developments into alternative decision methodologies,
and more recent work on implementation. The second is a social democratic
tendency focussed on resource redistribution and compensatory programmes,
with a nod in the direction of participatory democracy. Social planning and
advocacy planning reflect this tendency. To these two tendencies must be
added the "radical" position which cut across both sets of issues, one in an
idealist the other in a materialist way.

Yet debates about these positions have been conducted almost entirely by academics, many of whom have little contact with or knowledge of urban and regional planning practice. Ideas and issues do filter through to practitioners,
via planning education, planning literature and conferences, but in an undis-
ciplined way. Similarly, new problems in practice filter slowly into the
consciousness of academics, many of whom still write as if practitioners were
avid users of synoptic decision-making methodologies (e.g. Cawson 1977).
This brings us back to the central aim of this paper, after the somewhat
lengthy analysis. Do we have to leave the field of debate about planning
entirely at the mercy of the wider pressures which we have identified, or can
we unify it in such a way that we can inject theoretical discipline and practical relevance without compromising theoretical dispute. Without disciplined and relevant theoretical debate of this kind, the capacity for critical
evaluation in planning is to be lost.

18

5. THE BOUNDARIES AND TERMS OF DEBATE: "PLANNING" AND "THEORY"

In reviewing current theories about the nature, purpose and method of planning,
we have noted many failings. Some treat the practice within which planning
takes place in an implicit or superficial way (e.g. procedural planning theory). Many fail to specify the object to be planned or the values to be fur-
thered by planning it (e.g. incrementalism). Some approaches fail in explanation (e.g. new humanism), others in prescription (e.g. political economy
approach). Yet they nevertheless cover considerable common ground. All address themselves in one way or another to the nature and purpose of planning
(what and why questions), most have something to say about method (how questions), though few are very clear about the outcomes of planning. All consider the role of planners and of specialist expertise in relation to planning activity. All make some statement, even though implicit, about the societal situation in which planning occurs or is to occur and all have explanatory and normative elements if often unevenly developed.

Can we then formalise this common ground, bearing in mind the various critical
points we have raised in this paper, to provide a set of general procedural
rules to guide theory development and evaluation in our field? We argue that
you can and we shall attempt to provide such a set of rules relating to (a)
the boundaries and content of a planning theory, and (b) the construction of
adequate and valid theory. The first type of procedural rule is dependent on
the definition of planning which is used and the second type is dependent on
the definition of theory which is adopted. Therefore, we shall proceed to
define the two types of rules from the elaboration of the terms "planning"
and "theory".

"Planning"

The definition of planning, as we all know, is notoriously problematic. For
some, it is societal guidance, for others all government action. To some
again it is environmental regulation while others deny planning any objective existence. However, from looking at the range of definitions of planning, we would argue that the following four elements can be identified:-

(1) an activity of a particular type (such as rational procedures for the
     the identification and selection of policy alternatives);

(2) an activity undertaken by a particular type of institution, such as
     government (as opposed to the market);

(3) an activity involving the guidance/regulation of particular classes
     of events and objects (as in the regulation of land use);

(4) an activity undertaken by people who consider themselves to be
     planners or to be undertaking planning (the subjective "planning
     is what a planner does", and the objective "planning is what
     people I recognise as planners do").

Commonly, planning is defined as some combination of these. Thus "land use
planning" in Britain refers to the regulation of a set of objects, by government institutions, through the use (in theory) of rational principles reflecting policy directions, undertaken by operatives who consider themselves to be
planners.

Historically, however, within urban and regional planning we can see these
elements as developing from two distinctive, although related, traditions of
"planning". Firstly there is the idea of "planning society", using a plan or
planning process as a programme through which society controls and directs

itself — the notion of national (economic and/or social) planning, and secondly, "planning towns". in which the plan is a map used to control physical
development and related matters. Hebbert (1977) describes how the discussion of urban and regional planning has tended to oscillate between the two
and how the larger notion of planning society was attached, detached and
reattached to that of "planning towns" between the 1940's and 1970.

However, neither of these positions as they have been used is satisfactory.
The concept of "society" in the first is problematic as it is left unspecified in terms of object and goals (except in the social planning tradition).
Furthermore, assumptions are frequently made about the pursuit of collective
goals and interests without examination of the structure of interests and
power and how these are reflected in public policy. The idea of "planning
towns" can be seen as an object-specific subset of "planning society", i.e.
selected aspects of the built environment. Where the relationship of "planning towns" to "planning society" has been made explicitly (McLoughlin 1969),
it has been in general terms and to vaguely specified notions of society.
The result has tended to be the reification of environmental objects, isolated from a social and economic context (as in much of conservation literature
and practice).

In the fact of these definitional difficulties, procedural planning theory
defined planning by method (as a particular type of activity) and thus avoided the question of the social structures and processes within which the method
was exercised. This produced the "contentless" and "contextless" abstractions
to which we have already referred. We consider that it fails as a theory on
these grounds; in other words any theory about planning must make an adequate
relation to social structures and processes. All theories about planning rest
in any case on an explicit or implicit social theory of some kind, as we noted
above. But to leave this social theory implicit, or if explicit, unspecified
(for example as a generalised "context") robs theory about planning of a maj-
or analytical element. Planning, whether as a symbol or an activity, does
not exist in abstraction. It is part of a structured totality of relational
forces, economic, social and political, which give rise to the institutions
which attempt to regulate these forces and their relations. Put more simply,
planning is an activity of governments, and is structured by the characteristics of government activity and its relation to wider societal forces. Of
course in theorizing and researching, it is legitimate to focus attention on
planning activity. But it is not legitimate to ignore the way the specific
form of these wider forces structure that activity.

It should be clear by now that we are defining planning in terms of the first
two elements noted above. Planning is a distinctive activity, that of formally regulating and guiding sets of events, and it is undertaken by government institutions in specific programmes involving branches (sectors) and
levels of government. In this way it is possible to identify planning as a
concrete activity undertaken by identifiable actors and institutions, leading to outcomes which can be evaluated against objective criteria.

From this discussion, we are now able to specify the first three procedural
rules:-

(1) Any theory about planning must state what is meant by planning, why
     the activity is being undertaken, how it is or is to be undertaken
     and what results have occurred or are desired.

20

(2) More specifically, any theory about planning must specify the actual
     practices which it is seeking to explain and change; it must locate
     these within a specific socio-historical situation; it must specify
     the social theory on which its specification of the socio-historical
     situation rests.

(3) In particular, it must (a) articulate the relationship between:
     economic activities, social organization,processes of social change
     and the nature and role of government, and (b) articulate the
     relationship between these and government guidance and regulation
     programmes.

But these three rules still leave us with an enormous area of concern. If we
adapted only these then the result could be either a tendency to broad generalization unrelated to specific practices, a tendency we noted for example
in social planning, or a series of case studies, which it would be difficult
to generalise about (as in current tendencies within the "implementation and
policy" set). For practical purposes, and in order to develop adequate detailed understanding related to the broader issues about social structure and
the role of government, the field must be further specified.

Within the approaches we have discussed, we can identify four principal methods of subdivision. The first is by method, as in procedural planning theory
(see also the wider discussion of decision-making strategies and the behavioural analysis of the implementation approach). The second is by value, as
in the social welfare ideas of social planning. The third is by object as
in the concern with land, its use and development, and the fourth is by level
of government. These last two divisions are most commonly made by practitioners (since they are involved in the practice of local government land use
planning), but the implementation position emphasises local government programmes in particular and work in the political economy tradition focuses on
both local government and land.

We do not think there is any logical or theoretical necessity determining
which method of subdivision to adopt, although in our view questions of method and value i.e. how planners plan and why they plan are best treated as
research questions, within some other subdivision. We think it preferable
to begin with categories which can be derived from actual institutional arrangements and the actors and practices which constitute these in a specific
societal situation. Consequently we would argue that the subdivision would
be by object and level, as in our earlier definition of planning. But others
may offer different bases for subdivision. This is a question which must be
settled within the field and is not on a prior question defining the field.
From this we can arrive at our fourth procedural rule.

(4) Any theory about planning must specify and justify the way in which
     planning practices are subdivided for analytical purposes.

The four rules we have now elaborated are sufficient in our view to determine
and unify the boundaries and content of theoretical debate about planning.
But what sort of theory are we to be concerned with and how can the validity
of theories be established?

"Theory"

Present theories about planning perform three functions - to explain planning
activity, to justify present activity and to propose prescriptions for "good"
planning activity. Although it has been important in the search for profess-

ional identify and status, we reject the second function as a legitimate activity of theory building. We would argue that valid justifications can only
derive from valid explanation and prescription. Consequently justificatory
theories of planning are either derivative or lie in the sphere of ideology.
Nevertheless, our concern with planning is not merely as an explanation of
social phenomena but in evaluating it and proposing changes in how it is
done. This involves difficult methodological questions of prediction and
ethical questions about the values we use in evaluation and prescription.

Among the theories we have reviewed, there is a tendency for some to centre
on an explanatory mode, with the result that the products of this work are
criticised for "lack of practical relevance", (note the political economy position at present). Others, and more typically for theories about planning,
centre on prescription, often stepping easily into the justificatory mode
which we argue is untenable (e.g. new humanism and procedural planning theory).
Inevitably there are difficulties in linking the two modes of explanation and
prediction but these are problems faced by any "applied" field of study.
The distinctive quality we have as people interested in theorizing about planning is that we see the importance of linking these two modes and are not
content to be explanatory social scientists, or ideologists. We would not
wish to specify how any theory should make this explanatory/evaluative/pres-
criptive link; we merely demand that the link should be explicitly made,
hence we derive our fifth procedural rule:

(5)   Any theory about planning must explicitly formulate the relationship
      between its explanatory and normative elements, and between explan-
      ation, prediction, evaluation and prescription.   (If procedural rules
      1-4 are followed, it will of course relate theory to actual practices.)

This raises a further question, how can we judge the validity and efficicav
of a theoretical contribution which combines explanation and prescription.
This inevitably involves consideration of processes of change. In such cases
it will often not be possible to use forms of verification suitable for explanation theories. Nevertheless such forms of verification are useful in
judging the validity of explanation and the predicted and actual consequences
of prescription. Therefore it does not mean that we should reject methodological rules which help us to be clear, honest and inquiring investigators.
Ford (1975) provides four conceptions of "truth" in social science which can
help us here (as Saunders, 1980, points out). Theories should be honest, not
deliberately intending to deceive. They should be logically consistent, and
they should be testable against empirical evidence. Although such tests may
be formulated in a variety of ways (ethno-methodologists will differ from
historical materialists and positivist social sciences in the formulation of
such tests), nevertheless it is an important requirement of theory that it
should be capable of expression in testable form (see Wright, 1978, Chap.1;
Kitching, 1978).

How then are we to treat values? We would accept that no theory can be value-
free, but are some values more important than others? Are some inadmissable?
The adoption of one set of values as opposed to another is not capable of
empirical or logical verification, and is ultimately a question of belief and
commitment. One solution to this problem is to ignore the value dimension
since we may disagree. But this opens our work to the criticism of unthinking relativism which has characterised much of the justificatory theorising
about planning. We believe that it is fundamental to disciplined theoretical
discussion in the planning field, firstly that values underpinning theories
are clearly identified and their consequences for the form of the theory made
explicit, and secondly that we are prepared to discuss the value differences

22

between us and the differences between values. This therefore leads us to
our final procedural rules.

(6) Any theory about planning must be honestly produced (not concealing
     contrary evidence known to exist), be logically consistent, and
     capable of empirical verification.

(7) Any theory about planning must explicitly state the values which under-
     pin theory construction and identify how these affect the form of the
     theory and the practical consequences of adopting these values.

6. CONCLUDING COMMENTS

If we look at the theoretical positions we have in the urban and regional
planning field at present we can see that all fail against some of our procedural rules.

Procedural planning theory, despite its apparent scope, fails for its lack of
specificity and its consequent lack of testability, though strong on logical
consistency. Incrementalism is still abstracted from practices, though less
so, and focuses more on empirical tests (mainly because its proponents use
these to demolish procedural theory). The implementation position does relate to actual practices and seeks explanation, but like all these managerial
positions, is weak on links to wider aspects of societal structure and is not
explicit about values. The social planning position performs better on both
counts. We can therefore debate its model(s) of social relations. But it is
at too broad a level to relate clearly to actual practices or be subject to
empirical tests. The political economy tradition is much stronger on the
boundary and content rules, but is so far weak on the links between explanation and prescription and much is not readily subject to empirical tests.
Both new humanists and the pragmatists fail completely against our rules.
In general, the theories we have at present lack specificity, do not make
clear links between the detail of practices and the wider socio-historical
structure, and are weak on linking explanation and prescription.

We believe this condition need not persist if we are prepared to engage in
disciplined debate. Some may feel that our rules are so demanding that few
of us will engage in the business of theory building. We believe that it is
essential that we do for if we do not, the planning field will remain vulnerable to take over by the ideas and theories which "float" (and are often
actively pushed) into the conceptual world of planning academics and practitioners. We then became unconscious instruments of the wider forces which
structure planning practice.

In present circumstances, with all planning activity under threat and with
the town planning profession sensing its vulnerability it is not easy to
accept our call for maintaining a capacity for theoretically informed and
rigorous critical evaluation. However if we have any role as "planning
theorists", it must be to safeguard this capacity, for our contribution is
distinctive because of our concern to relate to specific practices and to
commit ourselves to prescription as well as evaluation. If we do not improve
the quality of our theory in our theoretical debates, we will be in no position to make this contribution.

BIBLIOGRAPHY

Bell, D. (1967). The End of Ideology. The Free Press, New York.
Braybrooke, D. and C.E. Lindblom (1963). A Strategy for Decision. Free
        Press, New York.
        Problems. John Wiley.
Castells, M. (1976). Theoretical propositions for an experimental study of
        urban social movements. In C.G. Pickvance (Ed.) Urban Sociology.
        Critical Essays, Tavistock, London.
Castells, M. (1977). "Towards a political urban sociology". In M. Harloe,
        (Ed.), Captive Cities: Studies in the Political Economy of Cities
        and Regions. Wiley, London.
Cawson, A. (1977). Environmental Planning and the Politics of Corporatism.
        University of Sussex, Urban and Regional Studies Working Paper No.7.
Darke, R. (1980). "Joint review of J. Bailey (1980). Ideas and Interventions
        and M. Camhis (1979), Planning theory and Philosophy". Int. J. Urb.
        and Reg. Res. 4 (3), 429-431.
Davidoff, P. (1965). "Advocacy and pluralism in planning". Jnl. Am. Inst.
        Plan. 31, November.
Davies, J.G. (1972). The Evangelistic Bureaucrat: A Study of a Planning
        Exercise in Newcastle upon Tyne. Tavistock, London.
Dearlove, J. (1979). The Reorganisation of British Local Government: Old
        Orthodoxies and a Political Perspective. Cambridge University Press.
Dennis, N. (1970). People and Planners. Faber and Faber, London.
Drake, M., B. McLoughlin, R.Thompson and J. Thornley (1975). Aspects of
        Structure Planning. CES Research Paper 20, Centre for Environ-
        mental Studies.
Faludi, A. (1973a). A Reader in Planning Theory. Pergamon, Oxford.
        the Dog Wag the Tail or the Tail Wag the Dog?". Urban Law and
        Policy, 3, No. 1, 41-58.
Friedmann, J. (1969). "Notes on societal action". Journal of the American
        Institute of Planners, 35, 311-318.
Friedmann, J. (1973). Retracking America: a theory of transactive planning.
        Anchor Press/Doubleday, New York.
Friend, J.K., M. Norris and K. Carter (1978). Regional Planning and Policy
        Change. Department of the Environment, London.
Friend, J.K., J.M. Power and C.J.L. Yewlett (1974). Public Planning: The
        Intercorporate Dimension. Tavistock, London.
Galloway, T.D., and R.G. Mahayni (1977). "Planning theory in retrospect:
        the process of paradigm change". Journal of the American Institute
        of Planners, 43, 1, 62-71.
Gans, H.J. (1968). People and Plans. New York, Basic Books, 1972.
        (Abridged edition - Penguin, Harmondsworth).
Goodman, R. (1971). After the Planners. Simon and Schuster, New York.
Gough, I. (1979). The Political Economy of the Welfare State. MacMillan,
        London.

22b

Grabow, S. and A. Heskin (1973). "Foundations for a radical concept of
     planning". Journal of the American Institute of Planners, 39, 2,
     106-114.
Hall, P., R. Thomas, H. Gracey and R. Drewett (1973). The Containment of
     Urban England. PEP, London.
Harvey, D. (1973). Social Justice and the City. Arnold, London.
Hebbert, M. (1977). The Evaluation of British Town and Country Planning.
     Unpublished Ph.D. thesis. University of Reading.
Hemmens, G.C. and B. Stiftel (1980). "Review essay: sources for the
     renewal of planning theory". Journal of the American Planning
     Association, 46, 3, 341-345.
     New York.
Hill, M.J. and others (1979). "Implementation and the Central-Local Relat-
     ionship". In Central-Local Government Relationships, SSRC.
Hudson, B.M. (1979). "Comparison of current planning theories: counterparts
     and contradictions. J. Amer. Plan. Assoc., 45 (4).
Lindblom, C.E. (1965). The Intelligence of Democracy. Free Press, New York.
Lindblom, C.E. (1973). "The science of muddling through". In A. Faludi (Ed.),
     A Reader in Planning Theory. Pergamon, Oxford. pp. 151-169.
McAuslan, P. (1980). The Ideologies of Planning Law. Pergamon, Oxford.
McKay, D.H., and A.W. Cox (1979). The Politics of Urban Change. Croom Helm,
     London.
McLoughlin, J.B. (1965). "The planning profession: new directions".
     Jnl. Town Plan. Inst., 51, 6, 258-61.
Massey, D., and A. Catalano (1978). Capital and Land: Landownership by
     Capital in Great Britain. Edward Arnold, London.
Newby, H., C. Bell, D. Rose, and P. Saunders (1978). Property, Paternalism
     and Power: Class and Control in Rural England. Hutchinson, London.
O'Connor, J. (1973). The Fiscal Crisis of the State. St. James' Press,
     New York.
Pressman, J.L., and A. Wildavsky (1973). Implementation: How Great Expect-
     ations in Washington are Dashed in Oakland: A Saga of the Economic
     Development Administration. University of California Press,
     Berkeley.
Rhodes, R.A.W. (1979). "Research into central-local relations: a framework
     for analysis". In G.W. Jones (Ed.), Central-Local Government
     Relationships. Social Science Research Council, London.
Rhodes, R.A.W. (1979a). Public Administration and Policy Analysis: Recent
     Developments in Britain and America. Saxon House, Farnborough.
Saunders, P. (1980). Urban Politics: A Sociological Interpretation.
     Penguin, Harmondsworth.
Thomas, M. (1979). "The procedural planning theory of A. Faludi". Planning
     Outlook, 22, (2), 72-77.
Underwood, J. (1980). Town Planners in Search of a Role. Occasional Paper
     No. 6, School for Advanced Urban Studies, Bristol.
Westergaard, J., and H. Resler (1975). Class in a Capitalist Society.
     Heinemann, London.
Wright, E.O. (1978). Class, Crisis and the State. New Left Books, London.

[7]

Towards a new typology of urban planning theories

O Yiftachel
Department of Geography, University of Western Australia, Nedlands, WA 6009, Australia
Received 16 April 1988; in revised form 25 August 1988

Abstract. Urban planning theory has been widely criticised by academics and practitioners as being confused and impractical. In this review paper a tentative first step to remedy the situation is proposed, outlining a new typology of urban planning theories with an aim to clarify the academic discourse and to provide a useful guide for practising planners. Three major 'debates' are identified as forming the main streams of thought in the development of urban planning. These are termed the 'analytical', 'urban form', and 'procedural' debates, which are shown to have developed in parallel. The three debates are also shown to focus on *different stages* of the planning process and to be mainly based on explanatory *or* prescriptive theories. Hence, it is argued that approaches which have often been described as irreconcilable can constructively coexist under the umbrella of urban planning theories without sacrificing their theoretical underpinnings. In this paper a general evolutionary trend from consensus to diversity is identified across the three streams of thought, and it is shown that, in the future, planning theories are likely to become more explicitly divided between openly politicised approaches and persisting technical-neutral orientations. The structure and evolution of the planning discipline outlined in this paper provide a framework for advancing towards a more clearly defined and coherent body of urban planning knowledge.

Introduction

The evolution, tasks, and properties of urban land-use planning theory in Western societies have been, in recent years, the subjects of an active debate. However, this debate appears, at least in part, to have complicated matters instead of clarifying previous problems and contradictions. Consequently, the theoretical foundations of land-use planning are still excessively eclectic, deeply divided, confused, and of little help to students and practitioners.

In this review paper I attempt to establish a framework within which formulation of a specific (rather than generic) theory of urban land-use planning can take place. A new typology of planning paradigms and concepts is proposed as a tool for influencing the development of planning theory and its more effective application. This typology identifies the activity of urban land-use planning as being composed of three major streams of thought, each addressing a different fundamental question of planning. These debates are termed 'analytical', 'urban form', and 'procedural'. I begin by demonstrating the need for a new approach to the study of planning theory. I then review previous classification attempts and introduce the proposed typology, demonstrating its academic, practical, and historical value. Later I review in brief the historical evolution of each of the three debates, concluding with a comment on the likely future development of planning theory.

The need for a new approach

A new approach to the study of planning theory is needed for three basic reasons. First, the procedural – substantive and explanatory – prescriptive divisions among planning theorists, although topics of lively debates (see Faludi, 1973a; 1982; 1987; Paris, 1982; Scott and Roweis, 1977; Simmie, 1987; Taylor, 1980; 1985) appear to have confused students and practitioners of planning. Second, an alarming gulf has been created between theory and practice. In this context it has been commented that planning theory is "in the doldrums" (de Neufville, 1983), that "the gulf between theory and practice is leading to a loss of credibility in both theory and policy" (Blowers, 1986, page 11) and that the few attempts to theorise land-use planning have been largely ignored by practising planners (Reade, 1987). Third, partially owing to the deficiencies mentioned above, planning as a discipline and as a profession has been increasingly challenged. This has been expressed by the now common practice of bypassing the urban statutory planning systems by the central governments in major Australian cities (Logan, 1986), the recent closure of established planning schools and agencies in Great Britain, and the fact that "planners now get blamed for everything" (Hall, 1988, page 418). In short, planning theory has simply failed to provide a backbone for the activity of land-use planning, as noted by Sorensen:

"Most professions concerned with the administration of human affairs ... are sustained by a conceptually powerful and widely accepted endogenous body of theory. Planning, it appears, is not. Planning-related theories abound but few originate within the profession ... planning may have no systematic theoretical base at all by which its goals and methods can be justified." (1982, page 184)

It therefore appears that, in order to ensure the survival of urban planning as a discipline and as a profession, its theoretical foundations must perform their necessary functions. Thus I presuppose that such urban planning theory needs to (a) describe and explain the planning of urban land-use planning, (b) provide knowledge for practising planners, and (c) enlighten planning students and stimulate research (Alexander, 1986; Bolan, 1982; Schon, 1982)[1]. In other words, planning theory should relate equally to 'what is planning?', 'what is good planning?', and 'what is a well-planned city?'. The typology proposed later, provides a first step in consolidating existing theories and concepts to construct a theoretical framework for the activity of land-use planning.

Previous classification attempts: contributions and deficiencies

A typology is a useful analytical tool with three basic functions: it corrects misconceptions and confusion by systematically classifying related concepts, it effectively organises knowledge by clearly defining the parameters of a given subject, and it facilitates theorising by delineating major subparts of distinct properties and foci for further research (Tiryakian, 1968). Such a tool is of particular value to urban planning, mostly owing to some intradisciplinary confusion and a lack of clearly defined theoretical parameters. A rich scholarly tradition exists in the field of planning theory. Many of these works are discussed later in the article, and the present section concentrates briefly on some notable examples of previous attempts to classify planning theories and on critical views expressed in subsequent scholarly debates.

Faludi (1973a) broke ground in his observation that a fundamental division exists between 'procedural' and 'substantive' planning theories, termed theories *of* planning and theories *in* planning, respectively. Procedural theories define and justify preferred methods of decisionmaking whereas substantive theories pertain to interdisciplinary knowledge relevant to the content of planning: that is, urban land-use. Faludi (1973a, page 7) went further to claim that "planners should view procedural theory as forming an envelope to substantive theory rather than vice versa".

---

[1] This extends beyond the narrower definitions of planning theory used by Faludi (1987), Healey et al (1983), and Scott and Roweis (1977). Unlike point (a), this paper argues that planning theory should explore the societal meaning of planning, and, contrary to (b) and (c), it is argued here that theory, inter alia, should help planners improve their performance.

In particular, the rational comprehensive model (first proposed by Meyerson and Banfield, 1955) was promoted by Faludi as the empirical, positive, and scientific course planners should take. Faludi's latter assumption of 'procedure over substance' has been subsequently attacked as being based on a consensus view of society, thereby promoting the depoliticisation of planning (Thomas, 1982) as concentrating on the uncontroversial (Christensen, 1985; Paris, 1982), and as fostering the narrow professional interpretations of planning as a technical and apolitical activity, thus rendering it irrelevant in the decisionmaking process (Friedman, 1973; Kiernan, 1983). In addition, the claim that planning procedures can be termed 'planning theory' at all has drawn sharp criticism from those advocating the development of a causal, explanatory form of theory (Cooke, 1983; Reade, 1974; 1985; 1987; Scott and Roweis, 1977).

In the face of this criticism Faludi (1982) attempted to refine his procedural–substantive dichotomy into a threefold typology, composed of 'the object-centred, control-centred, and decision-centred views of planning, which basically differ in their definition of planning. In the object-centred view planning is perceived as the comprehensive knowledge of an object from which prescriptive action flows directly. In the control-centred view (partial or total) planning is interpreted as a degree of control needed to affect environmental change, whereas the decision-centred paradigm revolves around preparing and evaluating alternative courses of action. This typology represented a more comprehensive attempt to classify planning theories, in particular (a) it accounted for the historical evolution of planning theory, noting that each of the three paradigms has developed in parallel, and (b) it placed planning in a broader societal context by including recent contributions to planning knowledge by the Marxist school of thought (termed the 'total control view'). Proponents of the typology, however, still failed to provide an adequate guide for research and action mainly because (1) they argued strongly in favour of the decision-centred paradigm, claiming that it renders the traditional object-centred view obsolete while 'tolerating', but not advocating, the control-centred view, and (2) they differentiated between the various types of planning theories entirely on the basis of the *procedural*, or plan-preparation, characteristics of these theories. These points were reiterated by Faludi (1987) who claimed that "tolerance is impossible ... as far as the object-centred view of planning is concerned" (page 84), and "planning methodology is the name of the game" (page 133).

Taylor (1980) departed from the procedural–substantive debate by observing that planning theories embody sociological and philosophical elements. The sociology of planning deals with its social impact, which can be studied empirically, whereas the philosophy of planning deals with the question of 'why plan?', which relates to the logic and ideology of state intervention in the marketplace. The philosophy of planning is in turn divided into philosophies regarding ethics (what is 'good'?) and knowledge (what is valid knowledge?). Taylor (1980) thus accounted for the normative-ideological component of planning and argued that "it must be distinguished from the strictly empirical study of planning which some [Faludi] describe as planning theory" (page 171). The main significance of Taylor's analysis is the attention it drew to the impossibility of separating process from substance, and to the critical (and by definition subjective) importance of the relationships between values, the nature of knowledge, and to land-use plans. The relevance of these observations to planning theory was further developed by Simmie (1987, page 304) who distinguished between two types of planning theory: 'explanatory' and 'action' (prescriptive) theories. In the first type an explanation of why certain phenomena occur is sought and how they may be empirically validated or falsified. Theories of the latter type draw on knowledge from explanatory theories but also add normative assumptions, which in

general cannot be tested empirically. Explanatory planning theories are dominated
by the sociological elements mentioned by Taylor, whereas the prescriptive theories
revolve around (part of) the philosophical dimension.

An important contribution to the debate was made by Cooke (1983) who attempted
to develop a broader theory of land-use planning by rejecting the substantive –
procedural distinction as a 'false dichotomy'. His classification included three types
of 'theories of planning and spatial relations': (a) theories of the development
process, (b) theories of the planning process, and (c) theories of the state. Cooke
therefore correctly stretched his classification to account for all aspects of 'what
planners do'—determine the character of development, pursue certain methodological
routes, and allocate resources. He also identified the parallel, and often independent,
development of each of these bodies of knowledge. Explicit in his analysis was
also the direct link between planning as an integral arm of public policy and theories
of the state. Cooke clearly dismissed the notion of a general and abstract procedural
theory of planning. He developed the early observations made by Taylor (1980)
on the inseparability of substance and process by exposing the links between the
nature of knowledge, the process of state intervention in the market place through
land-use planning, and the outcomes expressed as the spatial division of labour
(page 265).

In summary, these classifications have constructively exposed two prevailing
dichotomies among planning theories. These are 'enveloped' by theories of the state
to form five key elements which must be contained in an inclusive and constructive
typology of planning theories (figure 1). The most notably deficiencies evident in
most of the works reviewed above have been: (a) they did not attempt to deal
simultaneously with the procedural – substantive and explanatory – prescriptive axes
of planning theories, (b) they often inaccurately treated most theories as if they
were competing explanations for a common phenomenon, and (c) they did not
attempt to set clear boundaries to the field of planning inquiry. In the proposed
typology presented in the next section I attempt to build on the ideas raised in the
previous classifications, while avoiding the confusion and deficiencies outlined above.

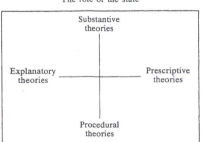

The role of the state

Substantive
theories

Explanatory   Prescriptive
theories   theories

Procedural
theories

Figure 1. Key elements and dichotomies in previous classifications of planning theories.

A proposed new typology of urban planning theories
The typology proposed in this paper identifies three main types of urban planning
theories. The three fundamental questions facing urban land-use planners are
addressed: 'what is planning?', 'what is a good urban plan?', and 'what is a good
planning process?'. These types of question give rise to *analytical*, *urban form*, and
procedural theories, respectively. Each of the above questions has been at the
centre of a distinct theoretical debate (figure 2).

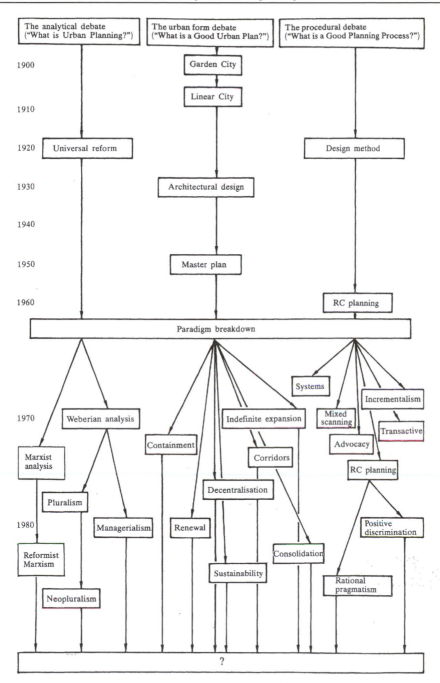

Figure 2. The evolution of the three debates of planning theory (simplified for graphical presentation).

The three categories reflect the importance of the main theoretical elements delineated in figure 1, by: (a) clearly separating explanatory (the analytical debate) and prescriptive (the urban form and procedural debates) theories[2], (b) distinguishing between substantive (the analytical and urban form debates) and procedural theories (figure 3), and (c) consolidating theories of the state as an integral part of the discipline. Although the three debates represent distinct areas of knowledge which have evolved in parallel (figure 2), it is useful to group them under the umbrella of 'planning theories' for three principal reasons: they mostly represent complementary rather than conflicting fields of inquiry, they directly relate to 'what planners do', and they place planning theories firmly within their historical context. In addition, the proposed classification clearly delineates the boundaries of the discipline, incorporating, inter alia, theories directly relevant to 'practical' areas in which urban planners operate. As such, the proposed typology may be useful for the full range of potential users of such theories—academics, students, and practitioners. The proposed framework also attempts to achieve better integration of planning knowledge derived from the USA and from theories developed elsewhere. That of the USA has mainly concentrated on the procedural–behavioural aspects of land-use planning, with many American planners being unaware of the development of a rich 'critical' planning analysis in the UK, Europe, and Australia (Hightower, 1984). In the following sections I will address several key aspects of the proposed typology in more detail.

A simple planning process	Level of analysis	Theoretical debate	Dominant theoretical characteristics
Formulation of goals	Broad societal/political	Analytical	Explanatory and substantive
Translation of goals into plan	Narrow professional	Procedural	Prescriptive and procedural
Analysis of plan	Broad professional	Urban form	Prescriptive and substantive

Figure 3. Operational levels and theoretical characteristics of the three debates of planning theory.

The compatibility of planning theories: a critical review
Despite frequent claims to the contrary (for example, Healey et al, 1983; Paris, 1982; Reade, 1987; Dear and Scott, 1981; Scott and Roweis, 1977) the three debates complement one another because, in the main, they operate on different levels of social processes and are related to largely different phenomena (figure 3). This will be demonstrated by critically reviewing some of the literature on this issue, and by exposing some scholarly misconceptions. As briefly noted, many

---

[2] Some exceptions to this general classification should be noted. Urban form and procedural debates have, no doubt, been dominated by a prescriptive approach, but the incremental theory of decisionmaking (Lindblom, 1959) and the corridor theory of urban expansion (Whebbell, 1969), for example, have been partially explanatory. Likewise, theories in the analytical debate, such as pluralism and Marxism, include implicit prescriptive elements.

analysts reject Faludi's claims on the centrality of methodology in the formulation of planning theory. For example:

> "To view planning theory as a separate ... set of procedural logics ... is to ignore what is crucial for any real understanding of planning. It could [represent] an attempt to focus on the uncontroversial and mundane at the expense of critical understanding" (Paris, 1982, page 7).

However, this criticsm has, to some extent, been misconceived. It attacks procedural planning theory for what it never endeavoured to be: explanatory or empirical theory. Therefore, "empirical planning theory is not an 'alternative' to procedural planning theory but rather a different *kind* of theory to be placed alongside the procedural theory" (Taylor, 1985, page 126, emphasis in original). Although it is accepted that procedural planning theories are inherently rooted in the real world, and are not, therefore, entirely generic or abstract (Cooke, 1983), it is still useful to separate between the two types, mainly because: (a) procedural theories are mostly prescriptive whereas analytical theories are explanatory, and (b) the two types do not, in the main, relate to the same phenomenon, as will be shown later.

The second contention, that "objective and rational procedure have been positioned over normative substance" (Faludi, 1973a) as the principal foci of planning theory, appears to have also been diffused recently. Faludi, the main exponent of this view, has now conceded that "there is no objectively rational planning ... therefore to talk about objective rationality is meaningless ..." (1987, page 20) and "my [1973a] attempt to develop positive procedural planning theory has been somewhat of a digression" (page 83). Hence, the rational concept is no longer defined as 'theory' but merely as a 'methodology' (page 117). This submission enables the treatment both of the procedural and of the substantive issues as integral components of knowledge required for land-use planning, with no one type of theory necessarily 'enveloping' the other.

Concerning the 'urban form' body of knowledge a more fundamental disagreement still exists, with most 'proceduralists' claiming 'conventional substantive theories' to be incompatible with the rational paradigms of planning (Faludi, 1987; Harris, 1978). It is not that empirical knowledge about the consequences of planning action is deemed useless, but it is claimed that such knowledge is only useful to planners when presented as part of the rational process of decisionmaking. However, as Schon (1982, page 351) notes: "planning knowledge [needs to be] embedded in what planners actually do ... knowledge *for* practice ought to be grounded in reflection on knowing *in* practice". Clearly, then, planning practitioners (and students) need theories about the object of their activity—the urban use and development of land. As Fainstein and Fainstein (1982, page 147) argue, there exists a need to develop "a theory of the planning process *and* a theory of urban structure and development" (my emphasis, see also Cooke, 1983, chapter 10). Knowledge on urban form is thus intrinsically important, not only in the context of selecting an optimal course of action.

Procedural theories should therefore continue to concentrate on debating the merits of competing decisionmaking and evaluation methods. While, as noted, some substantive knowledge is no doubt required to drive procedural theories, the advancement of knowledge about urban form phenomena cannot and should not be dependent on a need to decide between policy options. In other words, planners need to accumulate and advance knowledge about the social and physical repercussions of their urban strategies—be they urban consolidation, corridor-shaped metropolitan expansion or inner city renewal—not against other policy options, but as a worthy area of inquiry *in itself*. Importantly, it is also noted that relatively little empirical research has been carried out on this subject, with some of the few exceptions being the works of McLoughlin (1987) and Hall et al (1973). In this context it has been lately claimed that "(planners) never tried to check back and discover whether, or how far, they had in fact achieved anything; they were totally non-reflective (Hall, 1988, page 418).

The inclusion of urban form theories under the umbrella of planning theories is also important because, as Lindblom (1959) and Wildavski (1973) have shown, the planning process is by its very nature irrational. Planners, therefore, should be equipped with knowledge about land-use solutions, independent of considerations of decisionmaking procedures and/or of general social theories, even when external constraints seriously erode their ability to conduct a 'rational' study of planning alternatives.

Planning theories, stages of the planning process, and scholarly traditions
The compatibility of the three types of planning theories can also be demonstrated by constructing a simple model of planning processes (figure 3), which shows that much of the debate on 'which should be the dominant planning theory?' has been misconceived. Because the three types of theories focus mostly on *different* parts of the process, the inclusion of all three under the umbrella of 'planning theories' is possible without sacrificing the theoretical underpinning of each stream of thought. The analytical debate deals with the broad societal–political setting of planning, particulary its position within the state apparatus and its impact on social relations. It is there that the major goals and distributional effects of planning are determined. The translation of goals into plans is the domain of the procedural debate. Planning procedures and methodologies take the major goals of planning as largely predetermined (by politicians or 'the public') and thus exert little impact on the allocation of resources. The procedural debate operates on a narrow professional level: it is occupied with maximising the fit between ends and means, and is mainly controlled by planners. The urban form debate operates on a broader professional level, where the input of other professionals (such as economists, geographers, sociologists, and architects) is valuable. In order to be considered as a planning theory this input must, however, be synthesised by planners into knowledge specifically relevant to land control. Urban form theories may, for example, rely on theories on phenomena such as commercial decentralisation into subcentres, suburbanisation, urban renewal, and the like. These theories would not, however, be considered 'planning' theories unless they related to certain urban land-use plans. In short, the analytical debate examines the societal goals of urban planning, the procedural debate studies how best to achieve these given goals, and the urban form debate analyses the actual physical effects of planning goals and procedures.

It is also illuminating to note that the three debates originate from distinctly different disciplinary traditions which overlap to create the realm of urban planning theories (figure 4). This aspect of the proposed typology may be particularly useful

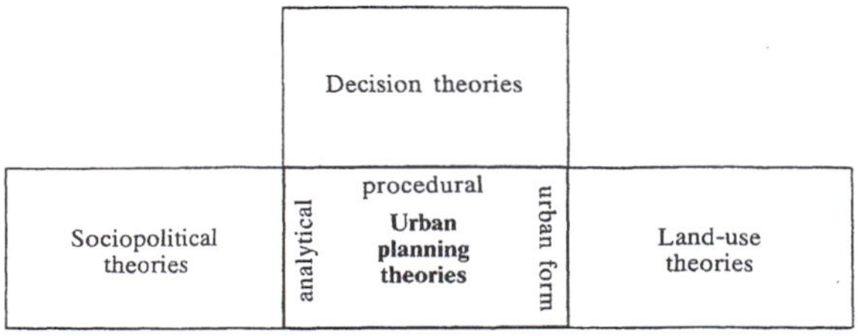

Figure 4. The interaction of knowledge that is relevant to urban planning theories.

for planning practitioners, providing them with a division of the hitherto confusing body of information known as 'planning theory' into three clearly understood areas of knowledge. These can be drawn upon whether a particular practical situation demands the application of specific knowledge.

The inconclusive influence of ideologies

An area in which the proposed typology provides a particularly new perspective is the understanding of the planning process as being 'vertical' as well as 'horizontal'. 'Horizontal' and 'vertical' refer here to the graphical dimensions of the typology depicted in figure 2. Horizontal connections describe a situation whereby ideologies exert strong influence across the three debates, and vertical connections are defined as the ones deriving from the historical evolution of knowledge within each debate.

Despite the somewhat harmonious picture portrayed in previous sections, it is recognised that areas of overlap between the three debates still exist, particularly regarding the common assertion that the ideologies of planners influence selected methodologies and proposed urban forms. Most notably, materialistic analysts have consistently claimed that owing to socioeconomic constraints, planning action would necessarily reflect the logic of capitalism, rendering planning procedures and urban land-use solutions as direct derivations of this mode of production (among others see, Dear and Scott, 1981; Fainstein and Fainstein, 1982; Hague, 1984; Pickvance, 1982).

In this paper, however, I contend that although ideological interlinks do exist between the three types of planning theories, these links are not necessarily unidimensional. Thus although the need to facilitate capital accumulation no doubt dominates the rationale for planning in Western societies, the translation of this need into procedures and actions may vary greatly between cases, which in turn may alter the formulation of societal goals. Likewise, social relations can be modified by changing spatial structures, but not necessarily in favour of dominant interests (Krumholtz, 1982). To further illustrate this point, both Marxist and Weberian analyses of planning may lead planners to espouse a 'positive discrimination' in procedures of decisionmaking (for the former see Fainstein and Fainstein, 1982, for the latter Hall, 1983; 1988). Likewise, similar solutions of urban form have been advocated in the name of rival ideological positions, as exemplified in Australia by the suburban self-containment strategy. The same concept was advocated on the grounds of social justice by the 1948 Cumberland Plan for Sydney, and was justified in the 1955 Plan for Perth for reasons of efficiency and market logic (Alexander, 1981; Yiftachel, 1988). Similarly, a satellite cities strategy was proposed for Perth in the mid-1970s by a Labor government for reasons of spatial equality. The same strategy has resurfaced in the late-1980s as the planning solution adopted by a right-wing Liberal opposition, argued in terms of greater efficiency in transport and land development (Yiftachel, 1988). The notion that ideology essentially predetermines methodology and urban form is therefore not necessarily accurate or constructive. It is argued here that concentrating on each stream of thought is a another constructive way to advance planning knowledge. This multidimensional pattern of ideological links between the three debates reinforces their existence as distinct—though not entirely independent—bodies of planning knowledge.

The importance of links and interactions between the three debates

Once the three debates on planning theories are clearly defined, other areas of research emerge as being central to planning knowledge, namely the links and interactions between the three debates. If planning theory is to become a useful foundation for the discipline, the interrelations between state intervention, policy formulation, and urban form must be thoroughly examined. The critical importance of researching the links between the three debates can be illustrated by briefly examining a case study. The 1970 Corridor Plan for metropolitan Perth (WA) was hastily conceived owing to pressures for urban expansion emanating from the growing mining activity in the northwest of the state. The plan advocated indefinite and rapid urban growth—a strategy directly influenced by the political economy of the time. This strategy was then translated by what was later described as a "rational-looking design method" (Yiftachel, 1987, page 71) into an urban plan which advocated growth along four transport corridors. The plan has since suffered major problems of implementation and rising infrastructure costs and is currently under revision. It is suggested here that part of the problems associated with the Corridor Plan for Perth resulted from a lack of knowledge on the links between politico-economic goals, decisionmaking processes, and physical prescriptions, thus demonstrating the need for a more thorough exploration of the connections between the analytical, procedural, and physical spheres of urban planning. Further research on the case of Perth could, for example, address the following questions: 'what part did the Western Australian Government expect urban planning to play in its overall push for rapid economic expansion?', 'how did these governmental expectations influence both the decisionmaking processes and the recommendations of the Corridor Plan?', 'what knowledge did Perth's planners have about the merits and problems of the proposed corridor urban form?', or 'what were the redistributional effects of these political and spatial processes?', and so on. Empirical answers to such questions, across a number of case studies, would constitute an important foundation to a consolidated theory of urban land-use planning.

Explaining the connections between the three debates would also link planning to currently active contemporary discourse in the social sciences: that of the relations between spatial structures and social relations (Cooke, 1983; Gregory and Urry, 1985). It is also noted that because much of the debate in planning theory has so far concentrated on the question 'what should planning theory be?', not much research has been devoted to exploring the links between the various types of theory (for a notable exception see Cooke, 1983). In summary, then, the three streams of thought identified here and the interrelations could form the theoretical basis for urban land-use planning and could provide a clear direction for research that would be useful for academics and practitioners alike.

The three debates of urban planning: evolutionary patterns
Another property of the proposed typology is that it allows students of land-use planning to trace the historical evolution of planning thought, a topic of intrinsic value. This evolution is illustrated in figure 2, and will be reviewed below. The following historical review is given as an example of the manner in which the proposed typology can be constructively employed to organise and analyse planning knowledge, making use of the vertical and horizontal dimensions mentioned earlier. Several general trends can be discerned in the historical evolution of the three debates. These include diversification, politicisation, an increasing orientation toward social science, ideological polarisation, and some recent convergence.[3]

---

[3] The following section gives a review of the 20th century only, and the theories discussed represent notable examples rather than a comprehensive description.

The analytical debate

The sociopolitical role of land-use planning is the centre of the analytical debate. It seeks "to discover the nature of planning as a concrete social phenomenon and practice" (Scott and Roweis, 1977, page 1098). Early planners perceived their activity as an act of universal reform. Planning was 'good for everyone', rescuing ailing industrial cities from chaos and decay. The faith in planning as an agent of reform is illustrated in the writings of Howard (1898, page 48) advocating his Garden City principles: "Town and country must be married and out of this joyous union will spring a new hope, a new life, a new civilisation". This belief in the ability of urban planning to affect social progress dominated the profession until the 1960s, reaching its peak during the immediate post-War period—the 'golden age' of planning—when it was "seen as an important element of the welfare state, the various components of which were linked by the common denominator of land" (Hague, 1984, page 62).

During the 1960s, however, with the general social and political evolution of Western societies, the conventional wisdom of land-use planning as 'working in the public interest' was being challenged, leading to a 'paradigm breakdown' (Schon, 1982, page 353). Planning was increasingly perceived as a integral arm of the capitalist state, to be analysed within the framework of theories of the state. Marxist and Weberian interpretations of the state have dominated this political–ideological debate. In short, Marxist analysts view the state as performing a dual role of facilitating capital accumulation and of legitimising the capitalist socioeconomic system (among many others, see Dear and Scott, 1981; Dunleavy and O'Leary, 1987; Hague, 1984; Harvey, 1973), whereas Weberian scholars claim the state serves a multiplicity of societal interests, increasingly controlled by a rational and independent bureaucracy (Weber, 1978). Substreams of Weberian-inspired thought have developed the pluralist theory of the state (Dahl, 1977) and the managerial thesis of urban politics (Pahl, 1974). In this context, Marxists interpret urban planning as an activity embedded in the logic of capitalism, a view typically expressed by Dear and Scott:

"... when the dislocations, irrationalities and conflicts of the urban system begin to subvert social relationships, urban planning makes its historical appearance as a means of collectively re-adjusting the spatial and temporal development of urban land use" (1981, page 12) ... "it is, in short, a mode of intervention that is only implemented when it serves the specific interests of capitalism." (1981, pages 14)

Although this explanation has gained prominence in some academic circles, it has never been fully accepted by practitioners, who have preferred to subscribe to the pluralist or managerialist interpretations of planning as a neutral mode of state intervention (Yiftachel, 1988). This has prompted Kiernan (1983, page 72) to observe that "the view that planners' work is primarily technical, professional and apolitical has been cherished and persistent throughout the relatively brief history of the planning profession".

During the last few years several developments have pointed to some mutual convergence in the debate, evidenced by the emergence of 'neopluralism' (Dunleavy and O'Leary, 1987; Simmie, 1987) and 'reformist-Marxism' (also termed 'realist-materialist', see Blowers, 1986; Cooke, 1983; Stilwell, 1983). Both views search for ways to redefine urban planning as a reformist activity within the constraints of the capitalist state, with a desire "to get away from the debilitating functionalism and reductionalism which previously plagued this debate" (Cooke, 1983, page 11). In general, though, the analytical debate continues to be divided along ideological lines, reflecting the broken consensus since the 'paradigm breakdown' of the 1960s.

The urban form debate
Land-use solutions to urban problems constituted the main area of planning inquiry until the 1960s. This is not the place to review the range of prescriptive theories of urban form which are extensively covered elsewhere (see Chapin, 1965; Gallion and Eisner, 1977; Hall, 1975; Lynch, 1981). Several pertinent examples should suffice to illustrate that, as in the analytical debate, consensus has given way to a wide diversity of competing concepts. Early formulations of urban form solutions to metropolitan problems, such as the concepts of Garden City (Howard, 1898) and Linear City (Garnier, 1901), advocated the separation of incompatible land-uses, easy access to country areas for the urban residents, and a relatively small urban size. In particular, the Garden City concept received universal acclaim and has been subsequently adopted and applied by urban and regional planners across the Western World until the present day (Hall, 1975). This consensus in the profession was still evident during the 1920s and 1930s, as urban planning was strongly influenced by exponents of the Modern Movement of architecture with its connotations of social reform, and also during the 1940–60 period when it was dominated by the 'master plan' approach (Gallion and Eisner, 1977; Hague, 1984; Lynch, 1981).

The assumption that planners were technical experts protected from social criticism was shattered during the 1960s. Since then, like the analytical debate on the role of urban planning, the urban form debate has been divided between competing theories. Unlike the analytical debate, however, these have not occurred along explicitly ideological lines, but reflect the succession of dominant paradigms and the impact of technological, academic, and professional circumstances. To illustrate, in Australia from the late-1960s to the early-1970s urban planning was characterised by a strong influence of transport engineers, under which all mainland capitals adopted metropolitan plans based on an extensive network of freeways and corridor-like urban expansion. This influence was guided by the advent of computers and the 'quantitative revolution' of the social sciences during that time. In contrast, during the mid-1980s to late-1980s the dominant paradigm has shifted to what is termed here 'urban sustainability' (Newman, 1986), with a strong emphasis on environmental protection, energy efficiency, and urban consolidation (see also Bunker, 1987; Yiftachel and Hedgcock, 1988). Other notable urban form contentions during the last two decades have been the clearance/redevelopment versus conservation/rehabilitation emphases of urban renewal, urban centralisation versus decentralisation, and metropolitan containment versus indefinite expansion.

The procedural debate
The procedural debate, which deals with the evolution of decisionmaking procedures, shows a somewhat different evolutionary pattern to the other two debates in that it currently faces a second 'paradigm breakdown'. As shown in figure 1, the first five decades of the century were dominated in what is termed here the 'design method', whereby substantial knowledge about a given object was translated into a plan via the intuition or inspiration of the planner. Geddes' (1915) 'survey before plan' approach provided the theoretical backbone for this method. During the 1960s, the increasing recognition that planning was a component of state policy prompted a wide acceptance of the rational comprehensive model, first advanced by Meyerson and Banfield (1955). Faludi (1973a) attempted, as noted, to develop this approach into a planning theory 'proper', indicating the popularity the method enjoyed among practitioners and academics alike. The pervasive approval of this method can also be linked to the 'quantitative revolution' in the social sciences, mentioned earlier, that found expression in the systems approach to planning (Chadwick, 1970;

McLoughlin, 1969). The prevailing rational model of planning was not, however, free of criticism. Its dominance was not supported by the kind of consensus evident during the early decades of the century. Notable competing concepts of planning procedures were the 'disjointed incrementalism' (Lindblom, 1959), the 'mixed scanning' (Etzioni, 1967), the 'advocacy' (Davidoff, 1965), and 'transactive' (Friedman, 1973) approaches, all drawing on weaknesses and problems embedded in the rational comprehensive method (comprehensive reviews of these approaches appear in Camhis, 1980; Faludi, 1973b; Hudson, 1979).

These challenges to the dominance of the rational method, although intellectually significant, remained marginal (Hoch, 1984; Hudson, 1979). It is only during the last few years, under the growing influence of the previously mentioned attack mounted by nonprocedural planning theorists (Christensen, 1985; Reade, 1974; 1987; Scott and Roweis, 1977; Thomas, 1982) and because of the worsening economic conditions which exposed the political and often particularistic nature of planning that the rational model has lost its ascendency. The procedural debate is currently in the stage of "a search for a new paradigm" (Hoch, 1984, page 62). Under this uncertainty two major competing approaches have emerged. The first— the 'positive discrimination' view—draws on the advocacy approach of the 1960s and on the materialistic theories of planning formulated in the 1970s (see, among others, Blowers, 1986; Fainstein and Fainstein, 1982; Hall, 1983; Krumholtz, 1982). It is contended that the only option open to progressive planners is based on the view of a just society (see Harvey, 1973; Rawls, 1971). Planning procedures are thus seen as potential instruments for affecting the outcome of political processes.

"As a fundamental principle for approaching issues, the positive discrimination paradigm offers the promise of an entirely new style of planning, one infinitely more politicised, committed, and relevant than that offered by the pseudo-professionalism of contemporary practice." (Kiernan, 1983, page 85)

The second emerging paradigm—the 'pragmatic rationalism' view—concedes that absolute rationality and comprehension are not only impracticable but also politically impossible in the increasingly politicised environment of governmental decisionmaking. Proponents of this approach contend, nonetheless, that planners should maintain a rational analytical process, while recognising that detailed problem solving methods are 'bounded' by external constraints (Christensen, 1985, page 68; Faludi, 1987, page 121). This view, which is observed to "help in tailoring strategies to [suit] the institutional and political situation in which the planner operates" (Faludi, 1987, page 121), has been termed elsewhere 'a contingency approach' (Alexander, 1984) or 'reconstructed pragmatism' (Hoch, 1984). The tenets of this approach are well summarised by Alexander

"... this approach seems to offer the best prospect for a new decision making paradigm to supplant the rational model. In principle it has the potential for synthesising research findings with normative prescriptions .... We will have to continue to make do with the rational model .... combined with the accumulating insights of empirical research and the pragmatic lessons of real-life experience" (1984, pages 67–68).

A comment on the future of urban planning theories

"The planning profession, like any other body of practising social scientists, is not single minded .... No consensus within the discipline appears to be emerging regarding its content, method or purpose. Instead, it is now expected that planners will operate according to their own explicit normative stand." (Logan, 1979, page 51)

This statement can now be reviewed with some hindsight. The evolutionary trends depicted in figure 2 indicate that despite the growing politicisation of the discipline, a certain apolitical and technical orientation has been preserved. Because of the mutual relations between theory and practice, urban planning theories can be expected to be divided in the future between ideological aims and enduring technical-neutral pursuits. In other words, the increasingly political orientations of most of the recent planning theories will gradually affect the behaviour of planners, and the political constraints of working for revolving political masters will have an impact on those attempting to theorise 'what planners do' (Schon, 1982). The politicisation of planning theories has become explicit following the 'paradigm breakdown' (figure 2). Recent advances in planning knowledge, which have demonstrated beyond doubt that urban planning affects unevenly the allocation of societal resources, are bound to gradually erode the myth according to which planners are portrayed as neutral and apolitical experts.

> "Planners regard themselves as experts on shaping our surroundings. But it may be that the use we make of our land and the design of our built environment are not matters of expertise but matters of opinion, of values rather than facts, in short, they are political." (Blowers, 1986, page 14)

The discipline is therefore likely, at least in part, to become more openly politicised. As shown by the previous discussion, this has already occurred in the academic field, evidenced by the pluralist–Marxist controversy in the 'analytical debate' and by the rationalist–advocacy rivalry in the procedural debate, both of these debates reflecting competing ideological positions. It is expected, nonetheless, that these divisions will gradually become manifest among practising planners, thus reflecting growing professional maturity. Just like lawyers or economists who are intimately involved in the formulation of public policy, planners, too, are expected to become associated with certain political ideologies. This is not only perceived here as a 'natural' process but also as a necessary and desired course of action which can ensure that planners will remain *relevant* in the decisionmaking process.

However, it can also be expected that some planners and planning theorists will prefer to remain in the cozy domain of 'neutrality' and rationality and serve loyally their ever-changing political masters. This appears to be a reemerging paradigm in the United Kingdom where it has been recently commented that planners should scale down their goals and accept the objectives and values set by politicians (Reade, 1987). By so doing, however, they would knowingly remove themselves from a meaningful influence on the formulation of public policy goals, opting to define planning as a technical activity positioned outside the arena of socially significant decisionmaking. In this context Cloke (1988, page 122) observes how planners and academics have quietly accepted the 'slide into ruthlessness' of the relationships between state and society in the United Kingdom of the 1980s. He goes on to comment that "Planning has been sucked into the slide and has in some ways made itself redundant in the process .... Impartial technical expertise seems unlikely to reverse the trend".[4]

Conclusion

The typology proposed in this paper shows that theories of urban planning can be organised usefully along three clearly defined debates, which should form a framework for a more coherent and consistent body of knowledge aimed at explaining the phenomenon of urban planning, advocating methods of decisionmaking, and at examining the merits of different solutions of urban form. More specifically, the

---

[4] For a detailed historical review of the 'slide' of British planning, see Ambrose (1986).

proposed classification:

(a) clearly delimits the parameters of planning inquiry;

(b) identifies avenues for research and areas for the development of expertise—namely knowledge about and within each debate and the links and interactions between them;

(c) helps to bridge the gap between theory and practice by partially basing the reorganisation of planning theory on 'what planners do', and by providing practitioners with a clear guide to theories relevant to various practical situations;

(d) clarifies existing confusions regarding the distinction between (1) explanatory and prescriptive theories, and (2) substantive and procedural theories; and

(e) illuminates major trends in the evolution of planning thought, particularly the shift from consensus to ideological competition among views within each of the three debates.

The proposed typology also demonstrates that much of the debate on which theory should prevail as planning theory 'proper' has been misconceived, by displaying that the three streams of planning thought operate on different societal levels, originate from different scholarly traditions, and historically have mostly developed in parallel rather than in competition. It is therefore time to 'bury the hatchet' and concentrate on advancing knowledge that is useful specifically for urban land-use planners. Further research is encouraged to follow the directions proposed here, developing and advancing planning theories that are both academically significant and practically useful.

Acknowledgements. I am thankful for helpful comments received from the anonymous reviewers of *Environment and Planning B*, and for the stimulating ideas raised through many discussions in the Graduate School of the Department of Urban and Regional Planning at Curtin University, Perth, particularly by Ian Alexander and Dave Hedgcock.

References

Alexander E R, 1984, "After rationality what?" *Journal of American Planning Association* **50** 62–69

Alexander E R, 1986 *Approaches to Planning* (Gordon and Breach, New York)

Alexander I C, 1981, "Post-war metropolitan planning: goals and realities", in *Equity in the City* Ed. P Troy (Allen and Unwin, Sydney) pp 145–171

Ambrose P, 1986 *Whatever Happened to Planning?* (Methuen, Andover, Hants)

Blowers A, 1986, "Town planning—paradoxes and prospects" *The Planner* April, 82–96

Bolan R S, 1982, "Do planning theory courses teach planning?" *Journal of Planning Education and Research* **1** 12–14

Bunker R, 1987, "Metropolitan planning in Adelaide and Melbourne" *Australian Planner* **25** 5–9

Camhis M, 1980 *Planning Theory and Philosophy* (Tavistock Publications, Andover, Hants)

Castells M, 1977 *The Urban Question* (Edward Arnold, London)

Chadwick G A, 1970 *A Systems View of Planning* (Pergamon Press, Oxford)

Chapin S F, 1965 *Urban Land Use Planning* (University of Illinois Press, Champaign, IL)

Christensen K S, 1985, "Coping with uncertainty in planning" *Journal of the American Planning Association* **51** 63–73

Cloke P, 1988, "Review essay: on reflection, role, revision, retreat and relationships in planning" *Environment and Planning B: Planning and Design* **15** 119–123

Cooke P, 1983 *Theories of Planning and Spatial Development* (Hutchinson, London)

Dahl R A, 1977 *Polyarchy: Participation and Opposition* (Yale University Press, New Haven, CT)

Davidoff P, 1965, "Advocacy and pluralism in planning" *Journal of the American Planning Institute* **31** 331–338

Dear M, Scott A J, 1981, "Towards a framework for analysis", in *Urbanization and Urban Planning in Capitalist Societies* Eds M Dear, A J Scott (Methuen, Andover, Hants) pp 3–18

de Neufville Innes J, 1983, "Planning a theory and practice: bridging the gap" *Journal of Planning Education and Research* **3** 35–43

Dunleavy P, O'Leary B, 1987 *Theories of the State: The Politics of Liberal Democracy* (Macmillan, London)

Etzioni A, 1967, "Mixed scanning: a third approach to decision making" *Public Administration Review* December, 217–242

Fainstein N I, Fainstein S S, 1982, "New debates in urban planning: the impact of Marxist theory within the United States", in *Critical Readings in Planning Theory* Ed. C Paris (Pergamon Press, Oxford) pp 147–176

Faludi A, 1973a *Planning Theory* (Pergamon Press, Oxford)

Faludi A, 1973b (Ed.) *A Reader in Planning Theory* (Pergamon Press, Oxford)

Faludi A, 1982, "Three paradigms of planning theory", in *Planning Theory: Prospects for the 1980s* Eds P Healey, G McDougall, M Thomas (Pergamon Press, Oxford) pp 81–101

Faludi A, 1987 *A Decision Centred View of Environmental Planning* (Pergamon Press, Oxford)

Friedman J, 1973 *Retracking America: A Theory of Transactive Planning* (Doubleday, New York)

Gallion B, Eisner S, 1977 *The Urban Pattern* (van Nostrand Reinhold, New York)

Garnier T, 1901, "The modern industrial city", quoted in Rowland K, 1966 *The Shape of Cities* (Ginn and Company, Aylesbury, Bucks) pp 102–105

Geddes P, 1915 *Cities in Evolution* (Williams and Norgate, London)

Gregory D, Urry J (Eds), 1985 *Social Relations and Spatial Structures* (Macmillan, London)

Hague C, 1984 *The Development of Planning Thought* (Hutchinson, London)

Hall P, 1975 *Urban and Regional Planning* (Penguin Books, Harmondsworth, Middx)

Hall P, 1983, "The Anglo–American connection: rival rationalities in planning theory and practice, 1955–1980" *Environment and Planning B: Planning and Design* **10** 41–46

Hall P, 1988, "The coming revival of town and country planning" *RSA Journal* **136** 417–430

Hall P, Thomas R, Gracey H, Drewett R (Eds), 1973 *The Containment of Urban England* (2 volumes) (Allen and Unwin, Hemel Hempstead, Herts)

Harris B, 1978, "A note on planning theory" *Environment and Planning A* **10** 221–224

Harvey D, 1973 *Social Justice and the City* (Edward Arnold, London)

Healey P, McDougall G, Thomas M (Eds), 1983, "Introduction", in *Planning Theory: Prospects for the 1980s* Eds P Healey, G McDougall, M Thomas (Pergamon Press, Oxford) pp 1–4

Hightower H C, 1984, "Book Review on C Paris (ed) Critical readings in planning theory" *Journal of the American Planning Association* **50** 85–86

Hoch C, 1984, "Doing good and being right—the pragmatic connection in planning theory" *Journal of American Planning Association* **50** 335–343

Howard E, 1898 *Garden Cities of Tomorrow* (Faber and Faber, London)

Hudson B, 1979, "Comparison of current planning theories: counterparts and contradictions" *Journal of the American Planning Association* **45** 387–398

Kiernan M J, 1983, "Ideology, politics, and planning: reflections on theory and practice of urban planning" *Environment and Planning B: Planning and Design* **10** 71–87

Krumholtz N, 1982, "A retrospective view of equity planning: Cleveland 1969–79" *Journal of the American Planning Association* **48** 163–178

Lindblom C E, 1959, "The science of 'muddling through'" *Public Administration Review* Spring, 151–169

Logan B, 1986, "The shape of Melbourne: a political geography of Melbourne's planning in the 1970s and 1980s", in *Urban Planning in Australia: Critical Readings* Eds B J McLoughlin, M Huxley (Longman Cheshire, Melbourne) pp 131–156

Logan W S, 1979, "Post convergence political geography—death or transfiguration?" Monash Publication in Geography number 18; available from Monash University, Wellington Road, Clayton, Vic 3168, Australia

Lynch K, 1981 *A Theory of Good City Form* (MIT Press, Cambridge, MA)

McLoughlin J B, 1969 *Urban and Regional Planning: A Systems Approach* (Faber and Faber, London)

McLoughlin B J, 1987, "Studying planning practice: an expedition to an academic outback" *Australian Planner* **25** 9–14

Meyerson M, Banfield E C, 1955 *Politics, Planning and the Public Interest* (The Free Press, New York)

Newman P, 1986, "Towards a more sustainable city" *Environment WA* **3** (1) and (2)

Pahl R, 1974, "Urban managerialism reconsidered", in *Whose City?* (second edition) Ed. R Pahl (Longman, Harlow, Essex) pp 187–195

Paris C, 1982, "Introduction by the editor", in *Critical Readings in Planning Theory* Ed. C Paris (Pergamon Press, Oxford) pp 1–8

Pickvance C, 1982, "Physical planning and market forces in urban development", in *Critical Readings in Planning Theory* Ed. C Paris (Pergamon Press, Oxford) pp 69–82

Rawls J, 1971 *A Theory of Justice* (Harvard University Press, Cambridge, MA)

Reade E J, 1974, "Review of 'Planning Theory'" *Town Planning Review* **45** 444–446

Reade E J, 1985, "An analysis of the use of the concept of rationality in the literature of planning", in *Rationality in Planning: Critical Essays on The Role of Rationality in Urban and Regional Planning* Eds M Breheny, A Hooper (Pion, London) pp 77–97

Reade E J, 1987 *British Town and Country Planning* (Open University Press, Milton Keynes)

Saunders P, 1983 *Social Theory and the Urban Question* (Hutchinson, London)

Schon D A, 1982, "Some of what a planner knows" *Journal of American Planning Association* **48** 351–364

Scott A J, 1984, "Letter to the editor: A comment on Taylor's procedural theory of planning" *Environment and Planning B: Planning and Design* **11** 127–129

Scott A J, Roweis S T, 1977, "Urban planning in theory and practice: a reappraisal" *Enviornment and Planning A* **9** 1097–1119

Simmie J, 1987, "Planning theory and planning practice: an analysis of the San Francisco downtown plan" *Cities* **5** 304–324

Sorensen A D, 1982, "Planning comes of age—a liberal perspective" *The Planner* November, 184–187

Stilwell F J B, 1983, "The role of the state in urban and regional development", in *State and the Australian Economy* Ed. B W Head (Oxford University Press, Melbourne, VIC) pp 25–36

Taylor N, 1980, "Planning theory and the philosophy of planning" *Urban Studies* **17** 159–172

Taylor N, 1984, "A critique of materialist critiques of procedural planning theory" *Environment and Planning B: Planning and Design* **11** 103–126

Taylor N, 1985, "Letters to the editor: The usefulness of a conceptual theory of rational planning: a reply to Scott's comment" *Environment and Planning B: Planning and Design* **12** 235–240

Thomas M J, 1982, "The procedural theory of A Faludi", in *Critical Readings in Planning Theory* Ed. C Paris (Pergamon Press, Oxford) pp 13–25

Tiryakian E A, 1968, "Typologies" *International Encyclopedia of the Social Sciences* 177–186

Weber M, 1978 *Economy and Society: volume 2* (University of California Press, Berkeley, CA)

Whebbell C F J, 1969, "Corridors: a theory of urban systems" *Annals of the Association of American Geographers* **59** 36–54

Wildavsky A, 1973, "If planning is everything, maybe it's nothing" *Policy Science* **4** 127–153

Yiftachel O, 1987, "The role of theory in urban planning: a study of metropolitan planning in Perth, Western Australia" *Geowest* **24** University of Western Australia occasional publication in Geography, available from author

Yiftachel O, 1988, "The role of the state in metropolitan planning: the case of Perth, Western Australia" *Urban Policy and Research* **6** 8–18

Yiftachel O, Hedgcock D, 1988, "The planning of Perth's changing urban form: invention or convention?" *Australian Planner* **26** December (forthcoming)

[8]

Without a Net:
Modernist Planning
and the Postmodern Abyss

Robert A. Beauregard

One of the story lines in Peter Marris's novel *The Dreams of General Jerusalem* concerns a team of European planners assembled by an international foundation to develop a thirty-year plan for the "metropolitan" area of a poor African country. A political assassination leads to the withdrawal of foundation support just as implementation is, albeit haltingly, underway. As the planners depart the country, the protagonist of the novel, George Eaton, comments:

> They had come without a text, a body of knowledge, but with a method. They left with the material for a text, if they ever chose to write one, and a store of experience, but the method all in doubt. Like so many before them, they had tested their system against Africa and discovered how limited was the context in which its meaning held. Africa had enlarged them, but they also felt diminished, knowing how little of what they had learned here would be valued in the jobs they would have to find. They did not want to stay, now. They were glad to be going home, because it was home, but they wanted to come back.

In this way, Eaton reflects not only on the clash between European and African cultures, but also on the conflicts engendered when a modernist planning project meets a nonmodernist reality.

Marris's theme echos the argument presented in John Friedmann's 1989 article "The Dialectic of Reason." In that article, Friedmann contends that an Enlightenment style of central planning, subsumed under the rubric of modernization, spread easily through Europe and the United States but has been vigorously resisted in developing countries, particularly in South America by a popular movement that he labels the "barrio economy." He claims that the "... attempt to *totalize the idea of modernity* ... is chiefly responsible for bringing the mod-

Abstract

Planning is currently suspended between a modernist sensibility whose validity is problematic and a postmodern reality posing serious challenges to planning's underlying assumptions. The result is an undesirable practical and intellectual ambivalence. The writings of Peter Marris and John Friedmann, Daniel Burnham and Frederic C. Howe, Clifford Geertz and James Clifford are used to elaborate and illustrate this argument and to forge links between planning and critical social theory.

Robert A. Beauregard is a Professor in the Graduate School of Public and International Affairs, University of Pittsburgh, and a member of Planners Network.

ernization project to a virtual halt in the third world and for its continuing and fundamental challenges in the west" and then concludes that the "Enlightenment project is on the verge of faltering" (Friedmann 1989, 218-219). The struggle is among an ostensibly transhistorical and transcultural reason carried by capitalism, a liberal democracy ultimately inhospitable to divergent cultural traditions, and a localized society negotiating its identity and survival within a hostile, indigenous as well as inimical "imported" environment.

Marris's fiction and Friedmann's critical empiricism reflect in quite different ways the clash between cultures in the southern hemisphere and the intrusion of European modernization (and capitalism) on African and South American sensibilities. For Friedmann, modernism's presence engenders political resistance. The process is not as much dialectical as it is oppositional. Either modernization will overcome or transform the barrio economy, or, the barrio economy will maintain its integrity. Marris, to the contrary, respects and represents the position ". . . that the very process of development, even as it transforms a wasteland into a thriving physical and social space, recreates the wasteland inside the developer himself" (Berman 1988, 68). For example, after George Eaton and his planners withdrew, Eaton established a doomed marriage with the wife of the assassinated politician. Eventually he attempted to cleanse himself of the tragedy of development, and the tragedy of his personal life, by co-authoring with his ex-wife a book that celebrated her former husband and his former friend.

The issue that concerns me is the challenge posed to the dominant culture of modernism in the West by alternative and oppositional cultures, of which the most frequently discussed is now postmodernism.

The challenge is complex and hardly clear; both modernism and postmodernism are conceptually and historically elusive. On the one hand, the political economy of modernity with its Fordist methods of mass production and consumption, reliance on manufacturing, welfare state policies, and economic growth is being superseded by a postmodernity characterized by post–Fordist methods of flexible accumulation and highly segmented consumption styles, shifts to financial services, conservative state policies, and increasing socioeconomic inequalities (Albertsen 1988; Harvey 1989; Soja 1989). In turn, the transformation includes a corresponding restructuring of space as modern cities and regions become postmodern ones (Cooke 1988; Zukin 1988). The industrial waterfronts of the former have been converted into places of conspicuous consumption for the middle class, areas of extreme wealth and poverty have become functionally integrated, and global cities now cast their influence over an international rather than subnational landscape.

On the other hand, the challenge is also to prevailing intellectual currents and cultural forms (Harvey 1989; Jameson 1984; Lyotard 1988). Postmodernism abandons

the critical distance of modernism, substituting an ironic commentary. Totalizing discourses, or master narratives, are criticized for their authoritarianism and failure to recognize the multiplicity of voices and communities that comprise society. Notions of progress and enlightenment are rejected, as is a commitment to the performativity of knowledge.

Much of the postmodern challenge makes the modernist planning project ambiguous (Beauregard 1989). That project endeavors to bring reason and, less so, democracy to bear on capitalist urbanization, guide state policy with technical rationality rather than political considerations, produce a coordinated and functional urban form through a unitary plan encapsulating collective goals, and use economic prosperity to create a middle class society.

Peter Marris makes this ambiguity clear through his positioning of the modernist development planners and their project within a narrative framework littered with postmodern sensibilities. First, Marris uses the notion of a text (not that of a plan) to characterize the commodity that planners produce. The text, though, is not simply a printed work (i.e., a document), but a body of knowledge. Marris also implies that a text is that which is written. He thus approaches but stops short of the text as an indeterminant, open, symbolic "methodological field" that is experienced in the act of production, a production that has no end, a production that even extends to its consumption, its reading (Barthes 1977). Note how this differs from a plan that is first written and then implemented, and a commodity that is produced, distributed, and consumed in sequential fashion.

In turn, Marris affects subtle changes in how we view planners and the act of planning itself. Rather than technical analysts whose plans emerge scientifically, he implies that planners are authors who create texts through imaginative acts. The planners imagine the Africans as incipient Europeans, the African city as stuck in an early stage of modernization, and the development plan as an eminently rational and thereby compelling document.

Marris also has George Eaton reflect upon the erosion of arrogance as the planners' totalizing discourse — their all-encompassing, internally coherent and unassailable method — is undermined by an alternative culture resistant to incorporation into the rigid plot of the planners' text. On the literal level of the story, the theme is certainly the clash between cultures that have emerged out of quite distinct social histories and been defined in nationalistic and racial terms. On another level, that of the text which "carries" the story, Marris is exploring a perspective quite foreign to planning, one in which multiple discourses exist simultaneously, and in interaction and without reconciliation, to produce action and inaction, even though certain discourses become dominant. "Progress," in the Enlightenment sense and from the planners' perspective, seems impossible, yet desirable, while from the viewpoint of the African citizenry it seems oppressive.

Finally, Marris opts to present his understanding of planners by way of a literary device that allows the emotional and subjective side of planners to be revealed. The planners' psychological make-up takes center stage: the conflict between a commitment to planning and an alienation from African reality which is the "object" subjected to their "process," the ambivalence that pervades their feelings for the country, and the unresolved emotional attachments that characterize their departure.

Marris conveys through a novel, rather than through academic research, a complex sense of what planners do and the multiple interpretations that surround their work. The perspective is profoundly postmodern. A leading postmodernist, Jean Francois Lyotard (1988, 19), argues that "[n]arration is the quintessential form of customary knowledge. . . ." It is the tradition ". . . through which the community's relationship to itself and its environment is played out" (p. 21). Or, consider briefly the argument of the Marxist cultural theorist Fredric Jameson: the world comes to us only through narration — it's all storytelling (Dowling 1984, 95). Modernist planners, then, can hardly enter communities and think about planning them democratically with analytical and causal frameworks that are incommensurate with and incomprehensible to those whose lives take on meaning in multivalent, multivocal, and intentional narratives.

Peter Marris has grasped this dilemma. *The Dreams of General Jerusalem* functions as the postmodern destination for a career that started as a modernist endeavor; early on, Peter Marris was one of those development planners. Later, however, his academic writings — specifically two wonderful books: *Loss and Change* (1974) and *Meaning and Action* (1987) — explore the meanings (rather than causes) and personal (rather than structural and objective) consequences of planning.

In *Loss and Change*, Marris develops the notion of a universal conservative impulse to explain not only resistances to disruptions ranging from slum clearance in Lagos to entrepreneurial innovations in Kenya, but the equally necessary sense of loss that follows such changes and our subsequent need to reconfigure our future in terms of such loss. The human consequences of planning take center stage. Almost a decade later, since *Meaning and Action* was originally published under another title in 1982, he explores the struggle to make sense of and give meaning to our existence and proposed changes to it is central to making social action not only relevant but also acceptable and ultimately successful. Again, the analysis is grounded in cases: community action in Coventry and planning in London's docklands. Stories are told, but their plots, unlike in the novel, are revealed as cause-and-effect structures. The quest is to resolve arguments in terms of action.

The fictional form of the novel allows Marris to explore the emotional and communicative in an intentional and multivocal format. Moreover, it enables him to leave ambiguities in place, thereby accepting the reality that planners too often deny. The various books thus represent a personal journey and reflect the transitions occurring in the larger realm of intellectual discourse. Marris, as postmoderns would applaud, travels to (and through) narrative and storytelling from origins in modernist planning, empirical research, and scientific analysis.

Consider Daniel Burnham, the famous Chicago architect, who wrote in 1909, "Make no little plans, they have no magic to stir men's [sic] blood and probably themselves will not be realized. Make big plans. . . ." *That* is a modernist statement. Its intent is action, and its subtext is a wide-ranging subjugation of society to the functional and aesthetic inclinations of a singular perspective. The statement verges on a totalizing discourse rooted in a belief that social progress emerges through a combination of a unique vision, central control, and scientific knowledge. In effect, Burnham presents the Enlightenment belief in man's ability to control nature, and does so with what postmodernists now call the master narrative.

Of course, Burnham was not alone in defining the modernist planning project in these terms. Just four years later, Frederic C. Howe published an essay titled "The Remaking of the American City" (Howe 1913). In his introduction to a review of city planning activities in cities throughout the world, Howe states very boldly his understanding of city planning: "In a big way, city planning is the first conscious recognition of the unity of society" (p. 186). (Karl Marx, among others, would certainly have disputed such a claim.) He goes on: [It] ". . . involves a new vision of the city: . . . new terms, a wider outlook, and the coordination of urban life in all of its relationships." Moreover, it means ". . . a city built by experts . . ." (p. 187).

One reads in Howe's article, then, the roots of the modernist planning project that Peter Marris fictionalized many years later: a totalizing and singular vision, the quest for an all-encompassing endeavor, and a pronounced elitism.

At the same time, however, and in what seems to be a contradiction, Howe maintains that "[M]odern city planning is a democratic movement. . . ." This perplexes. If the city is to be built by experts and their vision reigns, how is it that city building is democratic in the popular meaning of that term? Is not Howe's modernist version of reason, reason as embodied (only?) in planners, at odds with the sharing of information and decisionmaking that democracy requires?

City planning is democratic, Howe argues, because "[c]ity planning protects the rights of property, but restrains its license." More specifically, planning:

> . . . enlarges the power of the State to include the things men [sic] own as well as the men themselves, and widens the idea of sovereignty

so as to protect the community from him who abuses the rights of property, as it now protects the community from him who abuses his personal freedom (Howe 1913, 187).

By establishing restraints that legitimize the existence of private property and by vesting those restraints in planners as state actors, Howe articulates the role of planning in a capitalist democracy. Planners assume the existence of a consensual (or homogenizing) society whose interests ("public" interests) are waiting to be revealed, and a state whose neutrality is unquestioned. Moreover, both Howe and Burnham fail to appreciate how their plans are made possible and derive meaning from the capitalist society of which they are a part. A modernist choice is made; Howe opts for reason over democracy or, more accurately, reason as democracy.

Let us return to Daniel Burnham. If Burnham were reincarnated as a contemporary planning theorist, suspended between modernity and postmodernity, as I believe to be the case for planning, what would he now advise us? Most likely, he would suggest that we "Write no master narratives." His advice would be to avoid *making* plans. Rather, we should become authors of texts, authorities still, but less responsible for how our readers might respond, even relying on those readers to interpret what we mean and to determine for themselves whether or not to act, hardly the stance of a master planner.

The texts of the postmodernist planner, in fact, should be consciously fragmented and contingent, nonlinear, without aspiration to comprehensiveness, singularity, or even compelling authority. This clearly contrasts with the master plan of modernist planning; *it* is meant to be cohesive and visionary. Postmodern texts are to be written and interpreted and thus rewritten, master plans are to be made and followed.

These illustrations, then, reveal my project. At its most general, it is to strengthen the tenuous intellectual ties between planning thought and critical social theory. While planning theorists often draw upon a variety of academic disciplines for ideas, their forays are biased: economics and public administration but not anthropology and history, the social sciences but not cultural studies and literary theory.

Additionally, and in general, planning theorists are not public intellectuals (Jacoby 1987). Their work is written for and read by other planning theorists. Even planning practitioners avoid academic planning theory. To this extent, planning thought stands outside the intellectual currents that articulate the major themes of a period. Charles Mulford Robinson, at the turn of the century, was writing about city planning in national magazines such as *The Atlantic Monthly* and *The World's Work* as well as in professional journals such as *Architectural Record* and *Charities and the Commons*. Catherine Bauer published her ideas during the 1920s and 1930s in pop-

ular periodicals like *The American Scholar* and in *Architectural Forum*. Where are their contemporary counterparts? Few contributions can be made if planners isolate themselves from public debate. Though exceptions exist, a planning theorist is, more likely than not, to be a disciplinary and intellectual recluse.

More specifically, my objective is to set planning within the current spirited debate concerning postmodernity. The argument, as mentioned earlier, is that planning theory and practice are suspended between modernity and postmodernity, and that resolving this ambivalence is essential to making planning effective.

By "suspension" I do not mean interrupted or postponed, for that would imply an erroneous teleological view of planning history. Rather, I have in mind the image of the modernist planning project suspended not in time but in space — "hung up" as it were, in both a practical and psychological sense, between the understandings and methods of modernity and the challenges of postmodernity. (For a good illustration see Crow 1989.)

Notedly, postmodernism, as Jean-Francois Lyotard (1988, 79) has commented, is not "modernism at its end but in the nascent state, and this state is constant." In effect, I understand postmodernity to be either an oppositional or alternative movement — a verdict eludes — that sets forth arguments critical of the modernist project. As oppositional, postmodernism would attempt to displace modernism, destroying its roots in order to effectuate a paradigm shift. As alternative, it would challenge modernism but not displace it, possibly over the long term being absorbed into or ultimately transforming modernism (Williams 1980, 40).

Regardless, and to say this differently, the basic understandings, or worldview, of the modernist planning project no longer (if ever) wholly apply. Their utilization, depicted so vividly in Marris's novel, results in partial successes and embarrassing failures. The issue, moreover, extends along both dimensions of the challenge: first, modernist planners have lost touch with the prevailing political-economic forces that are restructuring cities and regions in a global context, and, second, have failed to keep pace with concomitant intellectual currents and cultural forms.

Let me illustrate with one example among many that could be selected. While my example begins in epistemology, it ends in the social role and political position that planners hold in contemporary society. (For a more extended discussion see Beauregard 1989.)

Take the very important link between knowledge and action that is so essential to planning as a social activity. The modernist planning project is basically built on Enlightenment assumptions concerning our ability to know and then to change the world, and, the centrality of reason and its derivative, science, to our ability to act effectively. Knowledge is important to us because it has performative characteristics; it is valued for its pragmatic consequences of prediction and control. With greater and more refined knowledge comes further enlightenment and progress, the Weberian rationalization of society. The scientific project thus dispels ignorance, while knowledge-directed action improves (or, reforms) social conditions. This, I would imagine, is all-too-familiar to you. Try, however, to imagine planning without such beliefs, without such basic tenets of the modernist project.

Postmodern critiques of this modernist perspective point out that knowledge is inherently unstable, that we only know the world through our arguments about it, and, therefore, that knowledge is not necessarily a reliable guide to effective action. Planners cannot be rational in a functional, that is modernist, sense.

Increased understanding can only reveal differences, not set direction. To this extent, what is important to a postmodernist is not causality — cause and effect relations — but meaning. Like the anthropologist Clifford Geertz, the postmodernist is concerned with symbolic representations of action and behavior. The task is to uncover the "historically transmitted pattern of meanings . . . [by] . . . which men [sic] communicate, perpetuate, and develop their knowledge about and attitudes toward life" (Geertz 1973, 5). The observer (or author) ". . . describes reality as a drama in which the focus is on symbolic exchanges, and not social consequences" (Walters 1980, 553). Knowledge of what an action means for someone, however, is not very useful in identifying the incentives that will cause that person to act in ways that achieve planning goals and the reasons that will justify those actions.

The postmodernist, in fact, rejects the plans themselves: those master narratives, those interpretations of reality that claim comprehensive understandings and exclusive insights into proper values and behavior. Master narratives violate the complexity and contingency of social reality, and impose exclusionary perspectives on individuals who are culturally diverse. Politically, totalizing discourses are oppressive; intellectually, they are maintained only through faith or power. As the historian James Clifford (1988, 15) has commented: "There is no master narrative that can reconcile the tragic and the comic plots of global cultural history." For postmodernists, then, there are only multiple narratives, a multiplicity of language games that are locally determined, none of which can be reconciled across speakers and all of which must be allowed their existence.

Clifford for one, however, goes on to point out that one can reject single master narratives and still respect the existence of pervasive global processes that set limits on local action. Still, the challenge to acknowledge "the authenticity of other voices" (Harvey 1989, 117) delegitimizes the type of authority that Frederick C. Howe wanted to adopt for planners; no single voice of reason can exist against, or in service of, a multivocal democracy.

The postmodern perspective in its various guises thus undermines the intellectual base of the modernist planning project. The modernist planning project is thereby suspended between a modernism whose validity is decaying and reconfiguring, and, a postmodernism whose arguments are convincing yet discomforting. As planning theorists we have failed to formulate a response and failed to work with practitioners to move the planning project from its ambivalent position.

In effect, we have opted to behave like the planners in Peter Marris's novel. As our failures multiply, we migrate to other locales: hoping that our method, despite its checkered history, will find a friendly reception; hoping to develop new plans that will not, when implementation stalls, simply become documents; hoping, eventually, to be accepted.

Nevertheless, this is only one response. We are not condemned to toil with a flawed modernist project, nor are we compelled to abandon it for a postmodernism that casts planners as authors of texts, eschews authoritative positions in public debates, succumbs to global forces, and, in a false respect for differences, remains politically silent in the face of objective conditions of inequality, oppression, ignorance, and greed.

Action can be unequivocal, knowledge can be helpful, and people can struggle successfully to improve their lives. As planners, we do have something to contribute. Our understandings and actions, however, must respect democratic practices that articulate the diversity of people's experiences and be communicated clearly and honestly (Forester 1989). Moreover, we must recognize that as George Eaton grappled with his love for a country and a woman, he did so, as a famous modernist once wrote, within historical conditions not of his own choosing.

Author's Note: *John Forester, Helen Liggett, Peter Marris and Daphne Spain read an earlier draft of this paper and provided critical comments in a modernist mode. That draft was presented on October 5, 1989 at the annual meeting of the Association of Collegiate Schools of Planning in Portland, Oregon.*   □

■ **References**

Albertsen, N. 1988. Postmodernism, post–Fordism, and critical social theory. *Society and Space* 6(3):339-365.

Barthes, R. 1977. From work to text. *Image, Music, Text*. New York: Hill and Wang.

Beauregard, R. A. 1989. Between modernity and postmodernity: The ambiguous position of U.S. planning. *Society and Space* 7(4):381-395.

Berman, M. 1988. *All That Is Solid Melts Into Air*. New York: Penguin Books.

Clifford, J. 1988. Introduction: The Pure Products Go Crazy. *The Predicament of Culture*. Cambridge: Harvard University Press.

Cooke, P. 1988. Modernity, postmodernity and the city. *Theory, Culture and Society*. 5(3):475-492.

Crow, D. 1989. LeCorbusier's postmodern plan. *Theory, Culture and Society*. 6(2):241-261.

Dowling, W. C. 1984. *Jameson, Althusser, Marx: An Introduction to "The Political Unconscious."* Ithaca, N.Y.: Cornell University Press.

Forester, J. 1989. *Planning in the Face of Power.* Berkeley: University of California Press.

Friedmann, J. 1989. The dialectic of reason. *International Journal of Urban and Regional Research.* 13(2):217-236.

Geertz, C. 1973. *The Interpretation of Cultures.* New York: Basic Books.

Harvey, D. 1989. *The Condition of Postmodernity.* Oxford: Basil Blackwell.

Howe, F. C. 1913. The remaking of the American city. *Harper's Monthly Magazine.* 127(758):186-196.

Jacoby, R. 1987. *The Last Intellectuals.* New York: The Noonday Press.

Jameson, F. 1984. Postmodernism, or the cultural logic of late capitalism. *New Left Review.* 146:53-92.

Lyotard, J. F. 1988. *The Postmodern Condition.* Minneapolis: University of Minnesota Press.

Marris, P. 1974. *Loss and Change.* New York: Pantheon.

———. 1987. *Meaning and Action.* London: Routledge & Kegan Paul.

———. 1988. *The Dreams of General Jerusalem.* London: Bloomsbury Publishing.

Soja, E. W. 1989. *Postmodern Geographies.* London: Verso.

Walters, R. G. 1980. Signs of the times: Clifford Geertz and historians. *Social Research.* 47(3):537-556.

Williams, R. 1980. Base and superstructure in Marxist cultural theory. *Problems in Materialism and Culture.* London: Verso.

Zukin, S. 1988. The postmodern debate over urban form. *Theory, Culture and Society.* 5(3):431-446.

[9]

NEW DIRECTIONS
IN PLANNING THEORY

SUSAN S. FAINSTEIN
Rutgers University

The author examines three approaches to planning theory: the communicative model, the new urbanism, and the just city. The first type emphasizes the planner's role in mediating among "stakeholders," the second paints a physical picture of a desirable planned city, and the third presents a model of spatial relations based on equity. Differences among the types reflect an enduring tension between a focus on the planning process and an emphasis on desirable outcomes. The author defends the continued use of the just-city model and a modified form of the political economy mode of analysis that underlies it.

The past decade has witnessed a reinvigoration of theoretical discussion within the discipline of planning. Inspired by postmodernist cultural critique and by the move among philosophers away from logical positivism toward a substantive concern with ethics and public policy, planning theorists have reframed their debates over methods and programs to encompass issues of discourse and inclusiveness. In the 1970s and 1980s, proponents of positivist scientific analysis battled advocates of materialist political economy. Although the divide between positivists and their opponents persists, other issues have come to define the leading edge of planning theory. Contemporary disagreements concern the usefulness of Habermasian communicative rationality, the effect of physical design on social outcomes (an old debate resurfaced), and the potential for stretching a postmarxist political economy approach to encompass a more complex view of social structure and social benefits than was envisioned by materialist analysis. Although discussions of

AUTHOR'S NOTE: *I thank Frank Fischer for helping me clarify the ideas presented in this article, even though he is not in full agreement with them, and Norman Fainstein, David Gladstone, Robert Beauregard, and Judith Innes for their comments on earlier drafts.*

452   URBAN AFFAIRS REVIEW / March 2000

communicative theory and political economy have transpired within academic journals and books,[1] the body of planning thought concerned with
physical design has grabbed public notice and received considerable attention within popular media.[2] Building on widespread dissatisfaction with the
anonymity and sprawl of contemporary urban growth, the "new urbanism"
espouses an outcome-based view of planning based on a vision of a compact,
heterogeneous city.

In this article, I discuss and critique contemporary planning theory in
terms of its usefulness in addressing what I believe to be its defining question:
What is the possibility of consciously achieving widespread improvement in
the quality of human life within the context of a global capitalist political
economy? I examine the three approaches referred to earlier under the rubrics
of (1) the communicative model, (2) the new urbanism, and (3) the just city. In
my conclusion, I defend the continued use of the just-city model and a modified form of the political economy mode of analysis that underlies it.

The first type, sometimes called the collaborative model, emphasizes the
planner's role in mediating among "stakeholders" within the planning situation; the second, frequently labeled neotraditionalism, paints a physical picture of a desirable city to be obtained through planning; and the third, which
derives from the political economy tradition, although also outcome oriented, is more abstract than the new urbanism, presenting a model of spatial
relations based on equity. This typology of planning theories is not exhaustive—there remain defenders of the traditionally dominant paradigm of the
rational model, as well as incrementalists who base their prescriptions on
neoclassical economics, and Corbusian modernists, who still promote for-
malist physical solutions to urban decay. Nor are the types wholly mutually
exclusive—each contains some elements of the others, and some theorists
cannot be fit easily into one of the types. Nevertheless, each type can claim
highly committed proponents, and each points to a distinctive path for both
planning thought and planning practice.

Differences among the types reflect the enduring tension within planning
thought between a focus on the planning process and an emphasis on desirable outcomes. In the recent past, neither tendency has fully dominated
because theoretical orientations toward process and outcome have respectively affected different aspects of practice. Thus the concept of the rational
model represented an approach based wholly on process, with little regard
either to political conflict or to the specific character of the terrain on which it
was working. As Beauregard (1987, 367) put it, "In its fullest development,
the Rational Model had neither subject nor object. It ignored the nature of the
agents who carried out planning and was indifferent to the object of their
efforts [i.e., the built environment]." This model has provided the metatheory

for planning activity in the decades since the 1960s, incorporating the faith in scientific method that swept through the social sciences during the cold war period. Within planning practice, it has primarily been used for forecasting impacts and for program evaluation. At the same time, however, as the rational model held sway among theorists, planning practitioners engaged in the development of zoning and environmental regulations, upholding an atheoretical, physical outcome–oriented vision of what Jacobs (1961, 22-25) sarcastically termed the "radiant garden city."[3] Outcome-oriented physical planning has left its mark on metropolitan areas in the form of urban renewal, low-density development, and spatial and functional segregation.

Although the rational model and the physical master plan were the dominant, late twentieth-century modes of planning practice throughout the world, they did not escape a powerful critique. Their opponents, who decried the distributional consequences of these approaches, generally adopted a political economic analysis. From this standpoint, critics persistently inquired into who benefited from planning efforts and associated themselves with social movements seeking to block displacement of low-income urban inhabitants, build affordable housing, halt the movement of capital out of distressed cities, and ameliorate racial, ethnic, and gender disadvantage.

The recent theoretical moves involved in the typology sketched earlier represent a reaction both to previously dominant modes of thought and also to events "on the ground." Thus the communicative model responds to the imposition of top-down planning by experts deploying an Enlightenment discourse that posits a unitary public interest to be achieved through application of the rational model, the new urbanism is a backlash to market-driven development that destroys the spatial basis for community, and the just-city formulation reacts to the social and spatial inequality engendered by capitalism. In common with earlier critics of the rational model (see Fainstein and Fainstein 1979), theorists within all three schools doubt the applicability of the scientific method to urban questions; none of the three approaches relies on scientific justification as the rationale for its vision. Whatever their differences, they are all three postpositivist.

THE COMMUNICATIVE MODEL

The communicative model draws on two philosophical approaches— American pragmatism as developed in the thought of John Dewey and Richard Rorty and the theory of communicative rationality as worked out by Jürgen Habermas.[4] The two strands differ somewhat in their methodologies. Neopragmatism tends toward empiricism, with its exemplars searching for

454   URBAN AFFAIRS REVIEW / March 2000

instances of best practices within planning from which generalizations can be drawn. Thus

> The big question for the pragmatic analysts is how practitioners construct the free spaces in which democratic planning can be institutionalized. The idea . . . is to uncover examples of planning that are both competent and democratic, and then to explore who the practitioners were who did it, what actions they took to make it happen, and what sorts of institutional conditions helped or hindered their efforts. (Hoch 1996, 42)

Communicative rationality starts instead with an abstract proposition. According to Healey (1996, 239),

> A communicative conception of rationality . . . replaces[s] that of the self-conscious autonomous subject using principles of logic and scientifically formulated empirical knowledge to guide actions. This new conception of reasoning is arrived at by an intersubjective effort at mutual understanding. This refocuses the practices of planning to enable purposes to be communicatively discovered.

Pragmatism and communicative rationality emerge from different philosophical traditions. Whereas Dewey's work comes out of British philosophical realism and empiricism, Habermas's original approach traces back to Hegelian idealism and marxist critical analysis and then later to Wittgenstein's scrutiny of language. Pragmatism and communicative rationality, however, converge when used to provide a guide for action to planners. This guide is the antithesis of Daniel Burnham's admonition to "make no small plans," an ambition that was once seen to embody the noblest aims of planning. Within communicative theory, the planner's primary function is to listen to people's stories and assist in forging a consensus among differing viewpoints. Rather than providing technocratic leadership, the planner is an experiential learner, at most providing information to participants but primarily being sensitive to points of convergence. Leadership consists not in bringing stakeholders around to a particular planning content but in getting people to agree and in ensuring that whatever the position of participants within the social-economic hierarchy, no group's interest will dominate.

Judith Innes (1998, 52) commented that "what planners do most of the time is talk and interact" and that "this 'talk' is a form of practical, communicative action." Innes (1995, 183) contended that the communicative model, which establishes the planner as negotiator and intermediary among stakeholders, has become so widely accepted as to form "planning theory's emerging paradigm."[5] Healey (1997, 29) summarized this theoretical turn as comprising the following emphases:

(1) all forms of knowledge are socially constructed; (2) knowledge and reasoning may take many different forms, including storytelling and subjective statements; (3) individuals develop their views through social interaction; (4) people have diverse interests and expectations and these are social and symbolic as well as material; (5) public policy needs to draw upon and make widely available a broad range of knowledge and reasoning drawn from different sources.

THEORETICAL AND PRACTICAL DEFICIENCIES

In its effort to save planning from elitist tendencies, communicative planning theory runs into difficulties. The communicative model should not be faulted for its ideals of openness and diversity. Rather, its vulnerability lies in a tendency to substitute moral exhortation for analysis. Although their roots, via Habermas, are in critical theory, once the communicative theorists move away from critique and present a manual for action, their thought loses its edge. Habermas posited the ideal speech situation as a criterion by which to register the distortion inherent in most interactions. As such, it supplies a vehicle for demystification. But when instead ideal speech becomes the objective of planning, the argument takes a moralistic tone, and its proponents seem to forget the economic and social forces that produce endemic social conflict and domination by the powerful. There is the assumption that if only people were reasonable, deep structural conflict would melt away. Although unquestionably many disagreements can be ameliorated through negotiation—the attainment of exactions or planning gain[6] from developers by community groups offers an example—persistent issues of displacement as a consequence of modernization and siting of unwanted facilities proximate to weak constituencies are less susceptible to resolution. Even when relatively powerless groups may prevail in individual instances—usually as a result of threat, not simply acknowledgment of their viewpoint within a planning negotiation—they still suffer from systemic bias and typically end up with meager, often symbolic benefits.[7]

The communicative theorists make the role of the planner the central element of discussion. Both the context in which planners work and the outcome of planning fade from view.[8] Unlike the rational modelers, the communicative theorists have found a subject, but like them, they lack an object. Whereas in legal theory the object of analysis is the relationship between the legal system and society and in medical theory the concern is with the human body, in communicative planning theory the spotlight is on the planner. Instead of asking what is to be done about cities and regions, communicative planners typically ask what planners should be doing, and the answer is that they should be good (i.e., tell the truth, not be pushy about their own judgments). Like the technocrats whom they criticize, they appear to believe that planners have a special claim on disinterested morality:

> Planners must routinely argue, practically and politically, about desirable and possible futures. . . . They may be sincere but mistrusted, rigorous but unappreciated, reassuring yet resented. Where they intend to help, planners may instead create dependency; and where they intend to express good faith, they may raise expectations unrealistically, with disastrous consequences.
>
> But these problems are hardly inevitable. When planners recognize the practical and communicative nature of their actions, they can devise strategies to avoid these problems and to improve their practice as well. (Forester 1989, 138-39)

The present trend among communicative planning theorists is to avoid broad examinations of the relationship between planning, politics, and urban development.[9] Much recent work in planning theory has been devoted to examining the meanings of planners' conversations with developers and city officials, deconstructing planning documents, and listening to planners' stories:

> The challenge we face, as planners and policy analysts more broadly, is . . . to listen carefully to practice stories [i.e., stories of planning in practice] and to understand who is attempting what, why, and how, in what situation, and what really matters in all that. That challenge is not just about words but about our cares and constraints, our real opportunities and our actions, our own practice, what we really can, and should, do now. (Forester 1993, 202)

Katha Pollitt (1999, 35), bemoaning a tendency toward solipsism among feminist writers, commented that

> "The personal is political" did not mean that personal testimony, impressions and feelings are all you need to make a political argument. The important texts of feminism have, in fact, been rather un-self-revealing. Simone de Beauvoir spent more than 700 pages in "The Second Sex" analyzing women's position in society through every conceivable lens: anthropological, economic, historical, literary, psychoanalytic, biological, philosophical, legal—except that of her own life.[10]

Similarly, the concern of communicative planning theory, itself influenced by feminism, has become subjective interpretation rather than the identification of causes, constraints, and substantive outcomes (see Campbell and Fainstein 1996). In fact, the search for explanation either gets lost in the thicket of hermeneutics or dismissed as totalizing (Milroy 1991; Beauregard 1991). The assumption is that explanation is necessarily reductionist. Yet even if we accept the premise that the purpose of planning theory is simply to tell planners what they ought to be doing, such knowledge depends on an accurate appraisal of the situation in which planners find themselves. Explanatory theory allows the observer to identify the general characteristics of a situation, and these characteristics cannot be inferred simply through the examination of discourse (Yiftachel forthcoming). This is not to deny the usefulness of experiential learning or of case analysis in contributing to understanding. But it does mean transcending individual experience, placing cases in a broad context, making comparisons, and not limiting analysis to exegesis.

In addition to questions of method, communicative theory runs into the fundamental issues of pluralist theory. Communicative theorists avoid dealing with the classic topic of what to do when open processes produce unjust results.[11] They also do not consider the possibility that paternalism and bureaucratic modes of decision making may produce desirable outcomes. Various studies of the European welfare states and of the New Deal in the United States have concluded that the principal measures for ensuring health and security were generated by state officials with little reference to interested publics (see Flora and Heidenheimer 1981; Mencher 1967; Skocpol 1985). Even though these measures would not have been approved without supportive constituencies and the threat of oppositional social movements, the actual formulation of policy (i.e., the planning of it) was highly insulated from stakeholder input.

Healey (1997) used the term *collaborative planning* to describe the process by which participants arrive at an agreement on action that expresses their mutual interests. She argued against a structuralist or political economy approach by contending that people do not have fixed interests. In other words, a particular structural position (e.g., capitalist) does not automatically produce a particular policy position (e.g., deregulation).[12] Discussion can lead capitalists to understand how they could benefit financially from environmental regulation when they might reflexively have opposed any attempt to restrict their freedom to pollute. And indeed, the vulgar marxist view that interests can be immediately inferred from relations to the means of production is indefensible. The marked differences between the attitudes of American and European business executives toward the interventionist state, whereby Europeans are much more accepting of state leadership, indicates the extent to which interpretations of interest by groups in similar structural positions can vary. Nevertheless, the different perceptions of interest held by those in different structural positions are not resolved simply through the exchange of ideas. If European and American business leaders have different perceptions of interest, ideas alone are not the cause. Rather, they exist in different historical contexts and different fields of power. Major changes in

458   URBAN AFFAIRS REVIEW / March 2000

perceptions of interest require restructuration as a consequence of crisis or of a social movement, not simply verbal assent (Lukacs 1971).

Even if perceptions of interest are biased or misdirected by distorted speech and even if structures are socially constructed, changing speech alone does not transform structures. An intervening stage of mobilization is required. Ideas can give rise to social movements that in turn change consciousness, ultimately resulting in the adoption of new public policy, but this is more than a matter of negotiation and consensus building among stakeholders.[13] In the instances of both environmentalism and neoliberalism, discontent among influential fractions of the population became a social force when mobilized by a set of ideas that seemed to define a reason for feelings of dissatisfaction. The aroused consciousness that puts ideas into practice involves leadership and the mobilization of power, not simply people reasoning together. Moreover, transformative social movements, whether conservative like neoliberalism or progressive like environmentalism, themselves contain distortions. Marx and Engels (1947), in their critique of the Hegelians, asserted that the world was changed through struggle, not the force of ideas. They did not mean, as they are often misinterpreted, that economic structures automatically determine outcomes and that human agency is helpless to affect them. But they did mean that words will not prevail if unsupported by a social force carrying with it a threat of disruption. To put this another way, the power of words depends on the power of the speakers. To quote Bent Flyvbjerg (1998, 234), "When we understand power we see that we cannot rely solely on democracy based on rationality to solve our problems."

The theoretical lacunae of communicative theory reveal themselves in practice. Scrutiny of efforts to base planning on dialogue reveals serious problems of implementation and the continued dominance of the already powerful. Perhaps the most interesting contemporary example of a conscious effort toward meaningful, inclusive, consensual planning has been in South Africa. There the transitional situation, after the elimination of apartheid and before the establishment of new local governments, presented a unique opportunity for developing policies outside normally constraining structures. Preexisting policies and institutions did not require typical deference, and huge policy areas were open to new determinations. Yet, as described by Mary Tomlinson (1998, 144–45),

> The loudly acclaimed "consensus" [on housing policy] supposedly hammered out by the stakeholders in the National Housing Forum which should have been achieved by hard bargaining among the parties was, in fact, the result of fudging vital differences between them. Faced with a conflict of vision between those who favoured a market-oriented strategy led by the private sector, and

those who preferred a more "people-centred" approach in which "communities" would be the central players—or at least retain a veto—the forum parties opted for both, despite their incompatibility. Thus all parties wanted immediate and visible delivery—but some also wanted "empowerment." So both were included, despite the fact that they would prove to be contradictory in practice.

By the second year of implementation of the housing subsidy scheme the consensus hammered out at the National Housing Forum had not, as its architects hoped, succeeded in binding all key housing interests to the policy: some key political actors had not been party to its formulation—and therefore did not feel bound by it—while crucial private interests proved ready to abandon it if it conflicted with their interests, or if it did not seem to produce the rate of delivery that had hoped to achieve.

A study of the implementation of the economic development plan for South Africa's Western Cape, which was also devised in a policy forum, comes to a strikingly similar conclusion:

> Amongst the public of Cape Town, the plan [produced by the Western Cape Economic Development Forum] is probably better known than any before it: it is frequently referred to, usually in a positive light. It remains, however, a paper plan and an abstract vision. On the ground large-scale private investors have continued to follow their own locational logic, and low-income housing has continued to spread in low-density fashion on the city edge, where cheaper land is available. Certain of the well located parcels of land earmarked by the plan for low-income housing were allocated to Olympic sports facilities or other upmarket developments, others still stand empty. (Watson 1998, 347)

Innes (1996) used the example of the New Jersey State Plan to demonstrate the efficacy of the communicative model. Here stakeholders from throughout the state participated in a series of meetings that produced a document targeting some areas for growth or redevelopment and others for conservation. Implementation depended on "cross acceptance," whereby localities, rather than being forced to conform to the statewide plan, would agree to conduct their planning in accordance with it in return for certain benefits.

Yet the same issues that cropped up in South Africa affected the implementation of the New Jersey State Plan. To start with, to win approval of the various participants in the planning process, the plan contained only weak requirements for the construction of affordable housing, suburban integration, and compact development, even though lack of housing for low-income residents, suburban exclusion of the poor and minorities, and lack of open space were identified as the principal problems that planning was supposed to overcome. Then, despite the moderate nature of the plan and the cross-acceptance process, its implementation has been half-hearted at best and

460   URBAN AFFAIRS REVIEW / March 2000

often strongly resisted by local planning boards. The principal result of consensual planning in New Jersey has been the continuance of a system whereby the market allocates land uses.[14]

These examples point to one problem of communicative planning in practice—the gap between rhetoric and action. The problem is perhaps most severe in the United States, where historic antagonism to a powerful administrative state has always limited the possibility of implementing any plan, regardless of how formulated (see Foglesong 1986). In Europe, where power is more centralized, corporatist bargaining has been institutionalized, and locally based interest groups are less able to block state action and the devolution of planning power to stakeholders; hence their assent to a plan is more likely to produce tangible results. Even there, however, agreement by participants to a document does not necessarily mean that anything will happen.

A second practical problem of communicative planning is the lengthy time required for such participatory processes, leading to burnout among citizen participants and disillusion as nothing ever seems to get accomplished. Cynical South Africans referred to the various policy forums as "talking shops." A third issue arises from the difficulties involved in framing alternatives when planners desist from agenda setting. Thus, for example, in Minneapolis, Minnesota, the city established a neighborhood planning process whereby residents formulated five-year plans for their neighborhoods and were allocated fairly substantial sums of money to spend. Planners assigned to facilitate the process were committed to a nondirective role and therefore only proposed actions when asked. The result was that some neighborhoods reached creative solutions, especially when participants were middle-class professionals, but others floundered in attempting to rank priorities and to come up with specific projects, sometimes taking as many as three years to determine a vague and hard-to-implement plan (Fainstein and Hirst 1996).

Finally, there is a potential conflict between the aims of communicative planning and the outcomes of participatory planning processes if planning is conducted within narrow spatial boundaries. The familiar specter of NIMBYism (not in my backyard) raises its head whenever participation is restricted to a socially homogeneous area.[15] Communicative theorists are committed to equity and diversity, but there is little likelihood that such will be the outcome of stakeholder participation within relatively small municipalities. Organizing planning across a metropolitan area to encompass diversity of class, race, and ethnicity requires extending the process through multiple political jurisdictions to escape the homogeneity imposed by spatial segregation. The obstacles to involving citizens in metropolitan-wide planning, however, are enormous, and doing so means sacrificing the local familiarity that is the rationale for participatory neighborhood planning.

The failures of planning during the heyday of massive urban renewal programs substantiate many of the objections to top-down, expert-driven planning and make desirable the communicative turn in planning. Nevertheless, the cruelties of massive clearance programs were not simply the result of deference to expertise. In the United States, business and political interests, not experts, constituted the power base on which the urban renewal endeavor was mounted, and the experts directing the programs were almost all physical determinists drawn from the design and engineering professions rather than planners and housing analysts (Gans 1968, chap. 18). The federal government terminated the program precisely when reforms, instigated by mobilized community groups and in reaction to urban civil disorder, had made it more sensitive to affected communities and less profitable for developers; this turn of events illustrates how problematic any policy is that circumvents power relations. Moreover, the present generation of planners is more likely to be responsive to the needs of neighborhood residents and ordinary citizens.[16] To the extent that they are not, the difficulty can only be partially remedied by open processes. City building for the benefit of nonelite groups requires empowering those who are excluded not just from discussions but from structural positions that allow them genuine influence. Ability to participate is one resource in the struggle for power, but it must be bolstered by other resources, including money, access to expertise, effective organization, and media coverage. Communicative theorists probably would not deny the importance of these resources, but neither do their analyses dwell on them. This omission constitutes the fundamental weakness of the theory.

THE NEW URBANISM

New urbanism refers to a design-oriented approach to planned urban development. Developed primarily by architects and journalists, it is perhaps more ideology than theory, and its message is carried not just by academics but by planning practitioners and a popular movement.[17] New urbanists have received considerable attention in the United States and, to a lesser extent, in Great Britain.[18] Their orientation resembles that of the early planning theorists—Ebenezer Howard, Frederic Law Olmsted, Patrick Geddes—in their aim of using spatial relations to create a close-knit social community that allows diverse elements to interact. The new urbanists call for an urban design that includes a variety of building types, mixed uses, intermingling of housing for different income groups, and a strong privileging of the "public realm." The basic unit of planning is the neighborhood, which is limited in physical size, has a well-defined edge, and has a focused center:

462   URBAN AFFAIRS REVIEW / March 2000

"The daily needs of life are accessible within the five minute-walk" (Kunstler 1996, 117).

The new urbanism stresses the substance of plans rather than the method of achieving them. In practice, it has stimulated the creation of a number of new towns and neighborhoods, of which Seaside, in Florida, is the best known.[19] Fundamental to its development has been a critique of American suburbia:

> In the postwar era, suburbia became the lifestyle of choice for most Americans.
>
> While this new way of living had many advantages, it also fragmented our society—separating us from friends and relatives and breaking down the bonds of community that had served our nation so well in earlier times. . . .
>
> The costs of suburban sprawl are all around us—they're visible in the creeping deterioration of once proud neighborhoods, the increasing alienation of large segments of society, a constantly rising crime rate and widespread environmental degradation. (Katz 1994, ix)

In this analysis, suburbia is responsible for far more than traffic congestion on the freeway and aesthetically unappealing strip-mall development. It is also the producer of crime and anomie.[20]

In its easy elision of physical form with social conditions, the new urbanism displays little theoretical rigor. Unlike other trends in planning, however, it is noteworthy for the popular response it has achieved. Although its appeal results partly from widespread dissatisfaction with suburban development and nostalgia for traditional forms, it also stems from the strong advocacy of its supporters, who have joined together in the Congress for the New Urbanism (CNU). The new urbanists do not fear playing the role disdained by the communicative theorists—that of persuasive salespersons for a particular point of view and deployers of strategies aimed at co-opting people. Thus Andres Duany unabashedly declared,

> Now, although it's important to be flexible, open to new ideas, it's also important, when you confront the world, to maintain principles that are inviolate—one thing you can learn from LeCorbusier is that to influence and persuade, you must be polemical. You can't convince people by equivocating, by saying "Well, on the one hand this, on the other that." You'll bore them, and they'll chew you up. As a polemicist, you have to clarify matters. . . . And you have to attack. Whenever I'm invited to speak to the Urban Land Institute [an organization of property developers], I try to destabilize them with my certainty that they are wrong. ("Urban or Suburban?" 1997, 48)

Duany did make a gesture toward participatory planning in his endorsement of citizen involvement in the *charette*, the lengthy design workshop that furnished the details of his developments. But one suspects that the purpose is as much co-optive as informative. When asked whether his use of neotraditional architectural styles was "like your use of language, a way of concealing what you're doing," he replied, "Yes, exactly." He commented that architects who insist on using a style without mass appeal, by which he meant high modernism, are "separating themselves from where the power really is, which is the ability of architecture to transform society, to be of genuine social benefit" ("Urban or Suburban?" 1997, 60).

Thus Duany and his confederates in the CNU did not fear distorted speech, nor did they shrink from using democratic procedures in responding to the public's stylistic preferences as a screen to achieve their desired sociospatial arrangements.

CRITIQUE

The new urbanism is vulnerable to the accusation that its proponents oversell their product, promoting an unrealistic environmental determinism that has threaded its way throughout the history of physical planning. Harvey (1997, 1) praised certain aspects of the new urbanism — its emphasis on public space, its consideration of the relationship between work and living, and its stance toward environmental quality. Nevertheless, his endorsement was mixed:

> But my real worry is that the movement repeats at a fundamental level the same fallacy of the architectural and planning styles it criticizes. Put simply, does it not perpetuate the idea that the shaping of spatial order is or can be the foundation for a new moral and aesthetic order? . . . The movement does not recognize that the fundamental difficulty with modernism was its persistent habit of privileging spatial forms over social processes. (Harvey 1997, 2)

As a consequence of its spatial determinism, the new urbanism runs into certain dangers. One frequently made criticism is that it merely calls for a different form of suburbia rather than overcoming metropolitan social segregation. Duany responded to this accusation by arguing that because most Americans are going to live in suburbs, planners need to build better suburbs. Moreover, he contended that it is not his philosophy but, rather, political opposition and obsolete zoning ordinances that prevent him from working in inner cities ("Urban or Suburban?" 1997). And indeed, the effort to overcome the environmentally destructive, wasteful form of American suburban development constitutes the most important contribution of the new urbanism to the commonweal.

464   URBAN AFFAIRS REVIEW / March 2000

The movement is less convincing in its approach to social injustice. Harvey (1997) feared that the new urbanism can commit the same errors as modernism—of assuming that changing people's physical environment will somehow take care of the social inequalities that warped their lives. To be sure, with its emphasis on community, it is unlikely to commit the principal sin of modernist redevelopment programs—destroying communities to put people in the orderly environments that were thought to enhance living conditions. The real problem replicates the one that defeated Ebenezer Howard's radical principles in the construction of garden cities. To achieve investor backing for his schemes, Howard was forced to trade away his aims of a socialist commonwealth and a city that accommodated all levels of society (Fishman 1977). The new urbanists must also rely on private developers to build and finance their visions; consequently, they are producing only slightly less exclusive suburbs than the ones they dislike. Although their creations will contain greater physical diversity than their predecessors, their social composition will not differ markedly.

Harvey (1997) also worried that the new urbanist emphasis on community disregards "the darker side" of communitarianism. He claimed that "'community' has ever been one of the key sites of social control and surveillance bordering on overt social repression. . . . As a consequence, community has often been a barrier to rather than facilitator of progressive social change" (p. 3). He was apprehensive that the enforced conformity of community blocks the creativity arising from diversity and conflict. He thus raised issues that have been major points of debate in discussions of institutionalized community participation among supporters of redistributive measures (see Fainstein 1990): Advocates argue that community power raises the self-esteem of members, whereas opponents fear that it produces parochialism and failure to recognize broader class interests (Katznelson 1981; Piven 1970).

Two problems come to the fore here. The classic and more important dilemma results from the two-edged quality of community, which in providing emotional sustenance to its members, necessarily excludes others. A second problem arises within theories of planning and urban design that urge the creation of exciting locales: Is planned diversity an oxymoron? Although Jacobs's (1961) critique of modernist planning undergirds much of the new urbanism, she would probably repudiate its effort to prescribe what in her view must be spontaneous. And truly, if one visits the world's planned new towns and downtown redevelopment projects, even those built with commitments to diversity and community, one is struck by their physical and social homogeneity:

> Sadly, the cornerstones of Jacobsian urbanism—picturesque ethnic shops piled high with imported goods, mustachioed hot-dog vendors in front of improvised streetcorner fountains, urban life considered as one enormous national-day festival—are cruelly mimicked in every Rouse market [i.e., festival marketplace developed by the Rouse Corporation] and historic district on the [American] continent. Contemporary developers have found it eminently easy to furnish such obvious symbols of urbanism, while at the same time eliminating the racial, ethnic, and class diversity that interested Jacobs in the first place. (Boddy 1992, 126n)

At the same time, relying on the market for an alternative to planning will not overcome the problem of homogeneity. The failure of the market to provide diversity in most places means that if planners do not attempt to foster it, the outcome will be increasingly segregated neighborhoods and municipalities. Nevertheless, the new urbanism, with its focus on physical form, will not do the job either:

> The reification of physical models is used by the architects of New Urbanism as a strategy to create local community, by reproducing a physical environment that fosters greater casual social contact within the neighborhood. However, these architects fail to sufficiently consider segregation within the greater urban area according to class, race and ethnicity, and may, in fact, help perpetuate it. (Lehrer and Milgrom 1996, 15)

Only a publicly funded effort to combine social groups through mixing differently priced housing with substantial subsidies for the low-income component can produce such a result. The new urbanists seek to create housing integration but, in their reliance on private developers, are unable to do so on a sufficient scale or across a broad enough range of housing prices to have a significant effect. However, a serious effort to attract public subsidy for the low-income component of their communities would involve the new urbanists in a political battle for which their architectural training and aesthetic orientation offer few resources. The appeal of Victorian gingerbread and Cape Cod shingle would not override the fear of racial and social integration.

For planning theory, the most interesting aspect of the new urbanism is that its assurance of a better quality of life has inspired a social movement. Its utopianism contrasts with communicative planning, which offers only a better process. Thus there is a model of planning practice that is based not on the picture of the sensitive planner who listens and engages in ideal speech but on the messianic promise of the advocate who believes in a cause and eschews neutrality. As in all such cases, the benefits are exaggerated. But there is an attraction to the doctrine, both because of its hopefulness and because the

466   URBAN AFFAIRS REVIEW / March 2000

places it seeks to create do appeal to anyone tired of suburban monotony and bland modernism.

THE JUST CITY

In *Socialism: Utopian and Scientific*, Engels ([1892] 1935, 54) presented the Marxian critique of utopianism:

> The final causes of all social changes and political revolutions are to be sought, not in men's brains, not in man's better insight into eternal truth and justice, but in changes in the modes of production and exchange.

For Marx and Engels, social transformation could occur only when the times were ripe, when circumstances enabled the forces for social amelioration to attain their objectives. In their view, utopian thinkers, such as Robert Owen and Charles Fourier, could not succeed because they developed a social ideal that did not coincide with a material reality still dominated by capitalist interests. Only smashing the structure of class domination could create the conditions for achieving a just society. Attainment of this goal, however, would not result from a passive acquiescence to historical forces. Engels laid out a role for intellectual understanding in bringing about a desirable transformation, as well as a picture of the future that only avoided the label of utopianism through an assertion of historic inevitability—the claim that once the working class seized power, it inevitably would create a just society:

> Once we understand [social forces] . . . when once we grasp their action, their direction, their effects, it depends only upon ourselves to subject them more and more to our own will, and by means of them to reach our own ends. . . . But when once their nature is understood, they can, in the hands of the producers working together, be transformed from master demons into willing servants. . . . With this recognition at last of the real nature of the productive forces of today, the social anarchy of production gives place to a social regulation of production upon a definite plan, according to the needs of the community and of each individual. (Engels [1892] 1935, 68-69)

At the millennium's end, one can hardly be sanguine that the hegemony of any social grouping will produce outcomes that will fulfill "the needs of the community and of each individual." By considering such an outcome as an inevitable consequence of proletarian revolution, Marx and Engels could simultaneously dismiss a nonconflictual path to socialism as unrealizable and present their teleological vision of revolutionary socialism as both realistic and desirable. If one does not accept their theory of historical development, however, one must either face the problem of formulating goals and identifying agents or capitulate to whatever structure of social domination exists. In this situation, a rigorous belief that people are helpless before forces such as globalization, sectarianism, and the repressive apparatus of the state produces either stasis or, at best, simply resistance.[21]

This crisis of action has led to the revival of utopian thought among some thinkers on the Left. Harvey (forthcoming), for example, has broken with the marxian critique of utopian idealism despite his continued adherence to other aspects of marxian analysis.[22] In his introduction to *Justice, Nature, and the Geography of Difference* (1996), he recounted his experience of attending an academic conference in an Atlanta hotel that was also hosting a convention of fundamentalist Christians. He was impressed by the much greater appeal of the Christians as compared to the academics, their greater joyfulness. Thus his new interest in utopias arises partly out of a recognition that creating a force for change requires selling a concept—as Duany so forthrightly pointed out—making people think that they want what you are offering.[23] Depicting a picture of a just city puts the planning theorist in the role of advocate—not necessarily the advocate for a particular group, as in Davidoff's concept of advocacy planning—but as the advocate of a program.

Just-city theorists fall into two categories: radical democrats and political economists. The former differ from communicative planning theorists in that they have a more radical concept of participation that goes beyond the involvement of stakeholders to governance by civil society, and they accept a conflictual view of society.[24] They believe that progressive social change results only from the exercise of power by those who previously had been excluded from power. Participation is the vehicle through which that power asserts itself. The political economy group, upon whom I shall focus in this section and among whom I include myself, takes an explicitly normative position concerning the distribution of social benefits. It goes beyond neomarxism, however, in analyzing distributive outcomes as they affect non-class-based groupings and refusing to collapse noneconomic forms of domination into class categories. Until recently, the political economy tradition involved a critique of urban and regional phenomena based on values that were rarely made explicit (Fainstein 1997; Sayer and Storper 1997). Although clearly the principal value underlying such analyses was equity, the discussion usually proceeded by identifying unfairness without positing what was fair. There has been, however, an effort of late, paralleling and drawing on work in philosophy (e.g., Nussbaum and Sen 1993; Young 1990), which has broken with positivism and with postmodernist relativism. The purpose of this project has been to specify the nature of a good city (Harvey 1992, 1996; Merrifield and Swyngedouw 1997; Beauregard forthcoming).

468   URBAN AFFAIRS REVIEW / March 2000

The audience for this endeavor has remained vaguely defined. By inference, however, one can deduce that the principal target group is the leadership of urban social movements. Because political economic analysis mostly condemns policy makers for being the captive of business interests, it is addressed primarily to insurgent groups, to officials in progressive cities (Clavel 1986), and to "guerrillas in the bureaucracy" (Needleman and Needleman 1974). Whereas the communicative planning theorists primarily speak to planners employed by government, calling on them to mediate among diverse interests, just-city theorists do not assume the neutrality or benevolence of government (Marcuse 1986). For them, the purpose of their vision is to mobilize a public rather than to prescribe a methodology to those in office.

A theory of the just city values participation in decision making by relatively powerless groups and equity of outcomes (see Sandercock 1998). The key questions asked of any policy by political economists have been, Who dominates? and Who benefits? The "who" has typically been defined by economic interest, but economic reductionism is not necessary to this mode of analysis; evaluation of outcomes can also be conducted with regard to groups defined by gender, race, and sexual orientation. Nor does the emphasis on material equality need to boil down to an expectation that redistribution should proceed to a point at which there is no reward to achievement.

The characteristic weakness of socialist analysis has been its dismissal of economic growth as simply capital accumulation that benefits only capitalists. Socialist doctrine fails to mobilize a following if it only ensures greater equality without also offering improved circumstances for most people. The market model and neoliberalism have proved popular because they promise increases in affluence for all even if within the context of growing inequality. Neomarxian analysis has shown that unregulated growth despoils the environment, primarily helps the upper echelons of the population, and even produces increased absolute deprivation at the bottom. Its attacks on the entrepreneurial state and its collaboration with private capital have delineated a collusion in which the interests of the majority have frequently been ignored (Squires 1989). Nevertheless, this critique did not point to a way in which the majority of the population can realize economic gains relative to their own previous position and, as a consequence, has lost popular support in the developed countries.

A persuasive vision of the just city needs to incorporate an entrepreneurial state that not only provides welfare but also generates increased wealth; moreover, it needs to project a future embodying a middle-class society rather than only empowering the poor and disfranchised. Whereas Marx dismissed the *lumpenproletariat* with contempt and placed his hopes with the working class, contemporary political economists tend to see society as consisting of the poor and the wealthy, ignoring the interests and desires of the vast middle mass and the aspirations for upward mobility of the working class. Yet, if substantive democracy is a constitutive element of a vision of social justice, then an antimajoritarian concept of society will not do. Recent work on industrial districts, social markets, local economic development, and national growth rates has pointed in a direction more sympathetic to middle-class aspirations (Storper 1997; Sayer and Walker 1991; Fainstein and Markusen 1993; Bluestone and Harrison 1997). Still, a great deal more attention needs to be paid to identifying a formula for growth with equity (Sanyal 1998).[25] And such an approach has to take into account the perseverance of a capitalist world economy and the evident success, at least for the moment, of a liberalized U.S. economy.

Participation in public decision making is part of the ideal of the just city, both because it is a worthy goal in itself and because benevolent authoritarianism is unlikely. At the same time, democracy presents a set of thorny problems that have never been theoretically resolved and can only be addressed within specific situations.[26] The almost exclusive preoccupation with participation that has come to characterize much of leftist thought since the demise of socialism in the Soviet bloc evades the problems that have vexed democratic theory throughout its history. Democratic pluralism, with its emphasis on group process and compromise, offers little likelihood of escape from dominance by those groups with greatest access to organizational and financial resources. Democratic rule can deprive minorities of their livelihood, freedom, or self-expression. Classic democratic theory deals with this problem through imbuing minorities with rights that cannot be transgressed by majorities. But what of the minority that seeks to exercise its rights to seize power and take away the rights of others in the name of religious authority or racial superiority? Democratic principles can easily accommodate ineffective or harmless minorities; they founder when confronted with right-wing militias, religious dogmatists, and racial purists. Thus the appropriate criterion for evaluating a group's claims should not be procedural rules alone; evaluation must comprise an analysis of whether realization of the group's goals is possible and, if so, whether such realization leaves intact the principle of social justice. Democracy is desirable, but not always.

Within a formulation of the just city, democracy is not simply a procedural norm but rather has a substantive content (see Pitkin 1967). Given the existing system of social domination, it cannot be assumed that participation by stakeholders would be transformative in a way that would improve most people's situation. Consequently, deliberations within civil society are not ipso facto morally superior to decisions taken by the state. Rather, "it is the

470   URBAN AFFAIRS REVIEW / March 2000

double-edged nature of the state, its ability to effect both regressive or progressive social change, that must be stressed" (Yiftachel 1998, 400).

The state can do both good and bad, and likewise, so can the citizenry. As Abu-Lughod (1998, 232) put it,

> When one considers the wide range of associational groups within civil society that seek empowerment . . . some of them are downright evil, while others seem very admirable. Furthermore, some forms of associational organization seem to be effective in achieving their goals whereas others, equally participatory, fail.

Storper (1998, 240) picked up on her theme:

> Abu-Lughod goes right to the heart of the matter in suggesting that the form of civil society—e.g. decentralized, embracing a diversity of voices—does not have a straightforward relation to the content of those voices. In this she mirrors an old debate in political philosophy, especially modern democratic political philosophy, between democracy as a set of procedures and democracy as content or substance.

Applying the just-city perspective, one must judge results, and furthermore, one must not forget that the results attainable through public policy are seriously constrained by the economy. Thus, even when the principal concern is not economic outcomes but ending discrimination or improving the quality of the environment, economic interests limit possible courses of action. To go back to the example of the New Jersey State Plan mentioned earlier, its primary purpose was environmental protection, not social integration or redistribution of land and property. Nevertheless, its content was affected by the state's dependence on private investors for new development and its implementation restricted by fears of landowners that their property values would be adversely affected by growth regulation. Thus economic interests impinge on planning even when the economy is not its foremost object.

As stated in the introduction to this article, the principal question of planning theory is the analysis of the possibility for attaining a better quality of human life within the context of a global capitalist political economy.[27] One way to approach this question is to frame a model of the good city and then to inquire how it is achievable. The model can be an abstract utopia—the cohesive city of the new urbanists' dreams—or be derived from the identification of places that seem to provide an exceptionally good quality of life (thus conforming to Hoch's 1996 description of pragmatic inquiry described earlier).

In a recent paper, I (Fainstein 1999) identified Amsterdam as comprising such an exemplar. Although not the embodiment of utopia, it contains many of the elements of the just city. If one considers the two other types of planning theory discussed here—communicative planning and the new urbanism—Amsterdam also conforms in many respects to their models. There is a highly consensual mode of decision making, with elaborate consultation of social groups and heavy reliance on third-sector organizations for implementation of policy. In conformity with the vision of the new urbanism, spatial forms are physically diverse, development is at very high density, and population is mixed by class and, to a lesser extent, ethnically. These achievements are within the context of a relatively equitable distribution of income, a very extensive welfare state, corporatist bargaining over the contours of the economy at the national level, and public ownership of urban land. All this came partly out of a tradition of planning and compromise but also out of militant struggle—by workers' parties for much of the century and by squatters and street demonstrators more recently.

Amsterdam is, of course, a wealthy Western city, and the theories discussed here derive primarily from a Western discourse rooted in the Enlightenment. Nevertheless, they are applicable to the developing world, where the goal of growth with equity has been a long-standing one. Despite the contention of various Asian dictators that the concepts of democracy and rights constitute Western values, the very active global human rights movement and the rapid spread of democratic ideas throughout much of the non-Western world indicate widespread acceptance of these values. Heller's analysis of the Indian state of Kerala supports this argument:

> Kerala is a striking example of equitable development: Successive governments in this southwestern state of 29 million inhabitants have successfully pursued social and redistributive strategies of development that has few, if any, parallels in the nonsocialist developing world. . . . The vigor and dynamism of civil society is matched only by the size and activism of the state. (Heller 1996, 1055)

In examining Amsterdam and Kerala, one can see that democratic procedure was crucial to their development but also that it was insufficient. Required also was a structural situation of relative material equality as both precondition and outcome of development and a culture of tolerance and commitment to equity. Put another way, both Amsterdam and Kerala operated within a mode of regulation that permitted private capital accumulation and a market economy while maintaining a large nonmarket sector. Citizens of Amsterdam and Kerala thus possess a set of social rights, not just political rights (see Marshall 1965).

472   URBAN AFFAIRS REVIEW / March 2000

RESURRECTING OPTIMISM

The three types of planning theory described in this article all embrace a
social reformist outlook. They represent a move from the purely critical perspective that characterized much theory in the 1970s and 1980s to one that
once again offers a promise of a better life. Whereas reaction to technocracy
and positivism shaped planning theory of that period, more recent planning
thought has responded to the challenge of postmodernism. It has therefore
needed to assert the possibility of a guiding ethic in the face of the postmodernist attack on foundationalism:

> The disrupting, enabling meaning of the postmodern is derived from the cri-
> tique of universalism and the placing of difference and heterogeneity in the
> foreground, but such an opening remains consistently incomplete for some dif-
> ferences we may want to struggle against when they encapsulate inequality,
> and the heterogeneous, plural or local do not of themselves carry any necessar-
> ily empowering or emancipatory meaning. Clearly, the locally or regionally
> particular can be as violently oppressive as the centrally or globally universal.
> (Slater 1997, 57)

Communicative planning theory has evaded the issue of universalism by developing a general procedural ethic without substantive content. The new urbanists claim that their design prescriptions incorporate diversity and provide
people what they really want rather than what archaic zoning laws and greedy
developers impose on them. Thus, even though they have been criticized for
imposing a particular formula on others, they defend themselves by arguing
that their conception incorporates difference. Just-city theorists work from
"the basic premise . . . that any distributional conception of social justice will
inevitably be linked to the broader way of life in which people engage"
(Smith 1997, 21). The argument is that although there may be no universal
standards of good and bad, there are criteria for judging better and worse
(Smith 1997; see also Fainstein 1997).

The progressives of the previous period spent much of their energy condemning traditional planning for authoritarianism, sexism, the stifling of
diversity, and class bias. More recent theorizing has advanced from mere critique to focusing instead on offering a more appealing prospect of the future.
For communicative planning, this means practices that allow people to shape
the places in which they live; for new urbanists, it involves an urban form that
stimulates neighborliness, community involvement, subjective feelings of
integration with one's environment, and aesthetic satisfaction. For just-city
theorists, it concerns the development of an urban vision that also involves

material well-being but that relies on a more pluralistic, cooperative, and decentralized form of welfare provision than the state-centered model of the bureaucratic welfare state.

At the millennium's end, then, planning theorists have returned to many of the past century's preoccupations. Like their nineteenth-century predecessors, they are seeking to interpose the planning process between urban development and the market to produce a more democratic and just society. The communicative theorists have reasserted the moral preoccupations that underlay nineteenth-century radicalism, the new urbanists have promoted a return to concern with physical form, and just-city theorists have resurrected the spirit of utopia that inspired Ebenezer Howard and his fellow radicals. Although strategic and substantive issues separate the three schools of thought described here, they share an optimism that had been largely lacking in previous decades. Sustaining this optimism depends on translating it into practice.

NOTES

1. See especially various issues of the journal *Planning Theory* and Lauria (1997).

2. An op-ed piece in the *New York Times* noted, "When [the chairman of the Metropolitan Atlanta Chamber of Commerce] . . . talks wistfully about the need to re-create the European town square in urban America, he is expressing sentiments that have spread through his entire business community with remarkable speed and intensity" (Ehrenhalt 1999).

3. By this she meant both the suburban legacy of Ebenezer Howard's garden city movement and the urban reconstruction schemes of LeCorbusier and the international movement.

4. The principal theorists who have developed communicative theory in planning are Judith Innes, John Forester, Jean Hillier, Patsy Healey, Charles Hoch, and Seymour Mandelbaum. See especially Mandelbaum, Mazza, and Burchell (1996) for an extensive collection of essays developing this theme. For critiques of communicative planning theory, see Flyvbjerg (1998), Yiftachel (forthcoming), Lauria and Whelan (1995), and Tewdwr-Jones (1998).

5. See Muller (1998) for a critique of the applicability of Kuhn's concept of the paradigm to planning theory.

6. The terms *exactions* (in the United States) and *planning gain* (in the United Kingdom) refer to the granting of benefits—for example, contributions to a housing fund, building of a public facility, and so on—by developers in return for the right to develop.

7. Stone (1989) chronicled the minor victories and overall defeat of the African-American population of Atlanta within a series of planning decisions dominated by a business-oriented regime. Despite a black mayor and a significant black leadership cadre, "the [governing] coalition is centered around a combination of explicit and tacit deals. Reciprocity is thus the hallmark of Atlanta's regime, and reciprocity hinges on what one actor can do for another. Instead of promoting redistribution toward equality, such a system perpetuates inequality" (p. 241).

8. Healey (1997) is bothered by this aspect of the theory and seeks to overcome it. Her work is distinguished by greater attention to the object of planning than is the case for most of her

colleagues in the communicative rationality group. Likewise, she is much less sanguine that good will triumph as a consequence of open discussion.

9. The first analytic case studies of planning were authored by political scientists (e.g., Altshuler 1965; Meyerson and Banfield 1955; Stone 1976) and did not contain this intense focus on the role of the planner.

10. It should be noted that much of Simone de Beauvoir's body of work did devote itself to an examination of her life; these writings, however, do not have the same theoretical importance or general applicability as *The Second Sex*. At the same time, they show the apparent contradictions between her general arguments and her life as lived, thereby raising important theoretical issues.

11. Healey (1997) again is an exception.

12. Lindblom (1990) took a similar position, arguing that interests are made, not discovered. He therefore preferred the term *volition* to interest.

13. The concept of stakeholder seems to imply that individuals and groups do have differing objective interests in a particular issue, even though the content of that interest is not fixed.

14. These conclusions are based on my own field observations.

15. American suburbs enjoy considerable autonomy and elicit substantial citizen participation in their planning processes. The outcome tends to be exclusionary zoning.

16. In a thesis examining four cases of military base conversion to peacetime uses, Hill (1998) found, contrary to her expectations, that in the most successful case, Boston's Charlestown Navy Yard, citizen participation did not play a significant role, but politicians and planners with a commitment to neighborhood development and environmental protection produced a desirable outcome.

17. Influential proponents of this body of thought include Peter Calthorpe, James Howard Kuntsler, Anton Nelessen, and especially Andres Duany and Elizabeth Plater-Zyberg.

18. Within the United Kingdom, Charles, the Prince of Wales, has been associated with the neotraditional movement and has sponsored development in accordance with principles of the new urbanism. In Britain and other parts of Europe, however, many of the tenets of the new urbanism have always formed the basis of planning regulation and thus do not represent as much of a reorientation as in the United States.

19. Katz's (1994) *The New Urbanism* contains pictures and plans of a number of these endeavors within the United States.

20. See Hamilton (1999) and Frantz and Collins (1999); these *New York Times* articles, published after the Littleton, Colorado, school massacre, traced problems of teenage alienation to suburban design and credited new urbanist forms with the potential to overcome them.

21. The reduction of oppositional action to simply resistance seems to be at the core of Foucault's philosophy. See Dreyfus and Rabinow (1983, 207).

22. Friedmann (forthcoming) has also recently written a paper exploring this theme, as have I (Fainstein 1999).

23. According to Kumar (1991, 31), "In the abstract schemes of conventional social and political theory, we are told that the good society will follow from the application of the relevant general principles; in utopia we are shown the good society in operation, supposedly as a result of certain general principles of social organization."

24. John Friedmann and Frank Fischer fit into this category. See Friedmann (forthcoming) and Fischer (forthcoming).

25. Healey (1998) emphasized the importance of institutional forms that will support economic development and tried to show how this can occur within the framework of collaborative planning. Her formulation is more applicable to those countries that already engage in corporatist decision making under the auspices of a social democratic state than it does to the United States.

26. See Day (1997) for the particular difficulties the concept presents to planners.

27. I do not deal here with the obviously fundamental issue of how one measures the quality of life, but see Nussbaum and Sen (1993) for a set of seminal essays on this subject.

REFERENCES

Abu-Lughod, J. 1998. Civil/uncivil society: Confusing form with content. In *Cities for citizens*, edited by M. Douglass and J. Friedmann, 227-38. London: Wiley.

Altshuler, A. A. 1965. *The city planning process*. Ithaca, NY: Cornell Univ. Press.

Beauregard, R. A. 1987. The object of planning. *Urban Geography* 8 (4): 367-73.

———. 1991. Without a net: Modernist planning and the postmodern abyss. *Journal of Planning Education and Research* 10 (3): 189-94.

———. Forthcoming. Resisting communicative planning: An institutional perspective. *Planning Theory*.

Bluestone, B., and B. Harrison. 1997. Why we can grow faster. *The American Prospect* 34:63-70.

Boddy, T. 1992. Underground and overhead: Building the analogous city. In *Variations on a theme park*, edited by M. Sorkin, 123-53. New York: Hill and Wang.

Campbell, S., and S. S. Fainstein, eds. 1996. A discussion on gender. *Readings in planning theory*, 441-74. Oxford, UK: Blackwell.

Clavel, P. 1986. *The progressive city*. New Brunswick, NJ: Rutgers Univ. Press.

Day, D. 1997. Citizen participation in the planning process: An essentially contested concept? *Journal of Planning Literature* 11 (3): 421-34.

Dreyfus, H. L., and P. Rabinow. 1983. *Michel Foucault: Beyond structuralism and hermeneutics*. 2nd ed. Chicago: Univ. of Chicago Press.

Ehrenhalt, A. 1999. New recruits in the war on sprawl. *New York Times*, 13 April.

Engels, F. [1892] 1935. *Socialism: Utopian and scientific*. New York: International Publishers.

Fainstein, S. S. 1990. The rationale for neighborhood policy. In *Neighborhood policy and programs*, edited by N. Carmon, 223-37. London: Macmillan.

———. 1997. Justice, politics and the creation of urban space. In *The urbanization of injustice*, edited by A. Merrifield and E. Swyngedouw, 18-44. New York: New York Univ. Press.

———. 1999. Can we make the cities we want? In *The urban moment*, edited by R. A. Beauregard and S. Body-Gendrot, 249-72. Thousand Oaks, CA: Sage.

Fainstein, S. S., and N. Fainstein. 1979. New debates in urban planning: The impact of marxist theory within the United States. *International Journal of Urban and Regional Research* 3:381-403.

Fainstein, S. S., and C. Hirst. 1996. Neighborhood organizations and community power: The Minneapolis experience. In *Revitalizing urban neighborhoods*, edited by D. Keating, N. Krumholz, and P. Star, 96-111. Lawrence: University Press of Kansas.

Fainstein, S. S., and A. R. Markusen. 1993. Urban policy: Bridging the social and economic development gap. *Univ. of North Carolina Law Review* 71:1463-86.

Fischer, F. Forthcoming. *Citizens, experts and the environment: The politics of local knowledge*. Durham, NC: Duke Univ. Press.

Fishman, R. 1977. *Urban utopias in the twentieth century*. New York: Basic Books.

Flora, P., and A. J. Heidenheimer, eds. 1981. *The development of welfare states in Europe and America*. New Brunswick, NJ: Transaction Books.

Flyvbjerg, B. 1998. *Rationality and power*. Chicago: Univ. of Chicago Press.

476   URBAN AFFAIRS REVIEW / March 2000

Foglesong, R. 1986. *Planning the capitalist city.* Princeton, NJ: Princeton Univ. Press.

Forester, J. 1989. *Planning in the face of power.* Berkeley: Univ. of California Press.

———. 1993. Learning from practice stories: The priority of practical judgment. In *The argumentative turn in policy analysis and planning,* edited by F. Fischer and J. Forester, 186-209. Durham, NC: Duke Univ. Press.

Frantz, D., and C. Collins. 1999. Breaking the isolation barrier. *New York Times,* 6 May, F4.

Friedmann, J. Forthcoming. The good city: In defense of utopian thinking. *International Journal of Urban and Regional Research.*

Gans, H. 1968. *People and plans.* New York: Basic Books.

Hamilton, W. L. 1999. How suburban design is failing teenagers. *New York Times,* 6 May, F1, F4.

Harvey, D. 1992. Social justice, postmodernism and the city. *International Journal of Urban and Regional Research* 16:588-601.

———. 1996. *Justice, nature, and the geography of difference.* Oxford, UK: Blackwell.

———. 1997. The new urbanism and the communitarian trap. *Harvard Design Magazine,* Winter/ Spring [Online]. Available: www.gsd.harvard.edu/hdm/harvey.htm.

———. Forthcoming. The spaces of utopia. In *Between law and justice,* edited by L. Bower, D. Goldberg, and M. Musheno. Minneapolis: Univ. of Minnesota Press.

Healey, P. 1996. Planning through debate: The communicative turn in planning theory. In *Readings in planning theory,* edited by S. Campbell and S. S. Fainstein, 234-57. Oxford, UK: Blackwell.

———. 1997. *Collaborative planning.* Hampshire, UK: Macmillan.

———. 1998. Building institutional capacity through collaborative approaches to urban planning. *Environment and Planning A* 30:1531-46.

Heller. 1996. Social capital as product of class mobilization and state intervention: Industrial workers in Kerala, India. *World Development* 24 (6): 1055-71.

Hill, C. 1998. Re-use of former military bases: An evaluation of converted naval bases. Ph.D. diss., Rutgers University, New Brunswick, NJ.

Hoch, C. 1996. A pragmatic inquiry about planning and power. In *Explorations in planning theory,* edited by S. J. Mandelbaum, L. Mazza, and R. W. Burchell, 30-44. New Brunswick, NJ: Center for Urban Policy Research, Rutgers University.

Innes, J. 1995. Planning theory's emerging paradigm: Communicative action and interactive practice. *Journal of Planning Education and Research* 14 (3): 183-89.

———. 1996. Group processes and the social construction of growth management: Florida, Vermont, and New Jersey. In *Explorations in planning theory,* edited by S. J. Mandelbaum, L. Mazza, and R. W. Burchell, 164-87. New Brunswick, NJ: Center for Urban Policy Research, Rutgers University.

———. 1998. Information in communicative planning. *Journal of the American Planning Association,* Winter, 52-63.

Jacobs, J. 1961. *The death and life of great American cities.* New York: Vintage.

Katz, P., ed. 1994. *The new urbanism: Toward an architecture of community.* New York: McGraw-Hill.

Katznelson, I. 1981. *City trenches.* New York: Pantheon.

Kumar, K. 1991. *Utopianism.* Minneapolis: Univ. of Minnesota Press.

Kunstler, J. H. 1996. *Home from nowhere.* New York: Simon & Schuster.

Lauria, M., ed. 1997. *Reconstructing urban regime theory.* Thousand Oaks, CA: Sage.

Lauria, M., and R. Whelan. 1995. Planning theory and political economy: The need for reintegration. *Planning Theory* 14:8-33.

Lehrer, U. A., and R. Milgrom. 1996. New (sub)urbanism: Countersprawl or repackaging the product. *Capitalism, Nature, Socialism* 7 (2): 1-16.

Lindblom, C. 1990. *Inquiry and change*. New Haven, CT: Yale Univ. Press.

Lukacs, G. 1971. *History and class consciousness*. Cambridge: MIT Press.

Marcuse, P. 1986. The myth of the benevolent state. In *Critical perspectives on housing*, edited by R. C. Bratt, C. Hartman, and A. Meyerson, 248-58. Philadelphia: Temple Univ. Press.

Marshall, T. H. 1965. *Class, citizenship, and social development*. Garden City, NY: Doubleday Anchor.

Marx, K., and F. Engels. [1846] 1947. *The German ideology*. Reprint. New York: International Publishers.

Mencher, S. 1967. *Poor law to poverty program*. Pittsburgh: Univ. of Pittsburgh Press.

Merrifield, A., and E. Swyngedouw, eds. 1997. *The urbanization of injustice*. New York: New York Univ. Press.

Meyerson, M., and E. C. Banfield. 1955. *Politics, planning and the public interest*. Glencoe, IL: Free Press.

Milroy, B. M. 1991. Into postmodern weightlessness. *Journal of Planning Education and Research* 10 (3): 181-88.

Muller, J. 1998. Paradigms and planning practice: Conceptual and contextual considerations. *International Planning Studies* 3 (3): 287-302.

Needleman, M. L., and C. E. Needleman. 1974. *Guerrillas in the bureaucracy*. New York: John Wiley.

Nussbaum, M. C., and A. Sen, eds. 1993. *The quality of life*. Oxford, UK: Oxford Univ. Press.

Pitkin, H. F. 1967. *The concept of representation*. Berkeley: Univ. of California Press.

Piven, F. F. 1970. Whom does the advocate planner serve? *Social Policy*, May/June, 32-37.

Pollitt, K. 1999. The solipsisters. *New York Times Book Review*, 18 April, 35.

Sandercock, L. 1998. *Toward cosmopolis: Planning for multicultural cities*. New York: John Wiley.

Sanyal, B. 1998. The myth of development from below. Paper presented at the annual meeting of the Association of Collegiate Schools of Planning, Pasadena, CA, November.

Sayer, A., and M. Storper. 1997. Ethics unbound: For a normative turn in social theory. *Environment and Planning D: Society and Space* 15 (1): 1-18.

Sayer, A., and R. Walker. 1991. *The new social economy*. Oxford, UK: Blackwell.

Skocpol, T. 1985. Bringing the state back in. In *Bringing the state back in*, edited by P. B. Evans, D. Rueschemeyer, and T. Skocpol, 3-43. Cambridge, UK: Cambridge Univ. Press.

Slater, D. 1997. Spatialities of power and postmodern ethics: Rethinking geopolitical encounters. *Environment and Planning D: Society and Space* 15:55-72.

Smith, D. M. 1997. Back to the good life: Towards an enlarged conception of social justice. *Environment and Planning D: Society and Space* 15:19-35.

Squires, G. D. 1989. *Unequal partnerships*. New Brunswick, NJ: Rutgers Univ. Press.

Stone, C. N. 1976. *Economic growth and neighborhood discontent*. Chapel Hill: Univ. of North Carolina Press.

————. 1989. *Regime politics*. Lawrence: University Press of Kansas.

Storper, M. 1997. *The regional world: Territorial development in a global economy*. New York: Guilford.

————. 1998. Civil society: Three ways into a problem. In *Cities for citizens*, edited by M. Douglass and J. Friedmann, 239-46. London: John Wiley.

Tewdwr-Jones, M. 1998. Deconstructing communicative rationality: A critique of Habermasian collaborative planning. *Environment and Planning A* 30:1975-89.

478   URBAN AFFAIRS REVIEW / March 2000

Tomlinson, M. R. 1998. South Africa's new housing policy: An assessment of the first two years, 1994-96. *International Journal of Urban and Regional Research* 22 (1): 137-46.

Urban or suburban? 1997. A discussion held at the Graduate School of Design in July 1996, with invited commentary. *Harvard Design Magazine*, Winter/Spring, 47-61.

Watson, V. 1998. Planning under political transition: Lessons from Cape Town's Metropolitan Planning Forum. *International Planning Studies* 3 (3): 335-50.

Yiftachel, O. 1998. Planning and social control: Exploring the dark side. *Journal of Planning Literature* 12 (4): 395-406.

———. Forthcoming. Rationality and theoretical power: Notes on Flyvbjerg's *Rationality and Power. Planning Theory.*

Young, I. M. 1990. *Justice and the politics of difference.* Princeton, NJ: Princeton Univ. Press.

Susan Fainstein is a professor of urban planning and policy development at Rutgers University. She is the author of a number of books and articles concerning urban revitalization, including The City Builders *(Blackwell, 1994), and is coeditor of* The Tourist City *(Yale University Press, 1999) with Dennis Judd and* Readings in Planning Theory *(Blackwell, 1996) with Scott Campbell.*

Part II
Inspirational Precursors

Introduction to Part II

... a city is more than a place in space, it is a drama in time. (Geddes, 1905, p. 107)

In Part II we present major contributions to the 'planning project' from the first part of the twentieth century. Authors such as Patrick Geddes and Ebenezer Howard belonged to a generation of international writers, thinkers and philanthropists who were critical of the social consequences of the Industrial Revolution. This was a period of, in Geddes' words, 'a new stirring of action, a new arousal of thought ... fraught with new policies and ambitions' (1968 [1915], p. 2) a period of vigorous hope for a future in which societies and cities could be reorganized to make them 'better' against a backdrop of urban slums, poverty, ill-health, exploitation of labour and the upheaval of the First World War. From the 1880s in Europe and the United States, several commissions, surveys and inquiries, together with various forms of philanthropic and faith-based social endeavour, had investigated and attempted to bring morality and improved living conditions to residents of inner cities. Many initiatives were founded by women, including Jane Addams in Chicago ('the face of compassion and do-goodism' according to Peter Hall (1988, p. 41)), although their contributions were not always appreciated.

The selected essays cover ideas about planning cities and regions, and about how to understand urban evolution, debates about planning society, and accounts of a highly influential integrated regional development programme. We have chosen essays that illustrate a genealogy of the main streams of thought, whilst recognizing that these 'civic dreams' (Geddes, 1968, p. 8) are but a few of the multiplicity of stories that could be represented. The development of the project of planning societies and cities in the late nineteenth century and the first half of the twentieth century was predominantly undertaken by male middle-class intellectuals and activists. As Leonie Sandercock (1995, 1996, 1998) has pointed out, the exclusion of women from anthologies of planning theory is certainly not because women were not interested in the built and social environments, but because they did not generally have any opportunities or connections to get their voices heard in the development of public policy and the 'expert' professions. We, too, are guilty of omitting women from our selection of material by 'inspirational precursors', simply due to restrictions on space and our consideration of what has been most influential in the field of planning theory. A rich vein of ideas about urban conditions and futures was contributed by women such as Jane Addams (2002 [1902], 1972 [1909], 1990 [1910]); Catherine Bauer (1934), Angela Burdett-Coutts (see E. Healey, 1978), Margaret Feilman (see Melotte, 1997), Octavia Hill (1877, 1899) and Mary Simkhovitch (1938), as is documented by Dolores Hayden (1981) and Daphne Spain (2001). African-American scholars, such as W.E.B. DuBois (1898, 1961), also made important contributions but were largely neglected in the documentation of mainstream planning history. So, although ours is, therefore, not a truly encompassing 'heroic narrative', but one which is necessarily fraught with tragic exclusions, we hope that people will take up our reference suggestions to follow the lines of thought for themselves.

Several of the essays in Part II demonstrate how the ideas and models with which we are familiar in spatial planning practice were often grounded in contexts and philosophies very different from those in which they have been used. The socialist anarchism of Ebenezer Howard, Patrick Geddes and Lewis Mumford, for example, has been significantly diluted and misapplied in its trajectory across time and space.

We offer more than just a chronology, aiming instead to illustrate how theories have evolved in relation to the practice challenges which the authors perceived. We are especially interested in the ways in which responses to such challenges, as demonstrated in the essays, led to shifts in thinking about the planning project. Whilst most of our authors were addressing issues of urbanization and industrialization at the beginning of the twentieth century or just after the Second World War, their understandings and recommendations for practice were quite different.

As mentioned above, it is possible to trace direct links between Ebenezer Howard, Patrick Geddes and Lewis Mumford. Geddes was probably the pivotal figure in this triumvirate. Influenced by the Russian, Piotr Kropotkin, the French geographer, Elisée Reclus, and familiar with the work of physicist Albert Einstein and mathematician Henri Poincaré, who were both looking at questions of relations and relativity, Geddes devised a vitalist form of socialist anarchism as a means of understanding and countering the appalling slum conditions he witnessed in Edinburgh and London in particular. He was the first to use the term 'conurbation' in 1915 in his appreciation of the city and region as an integrated whole.

The material we have chosen to include (as Chapter 11) comes not from Geddes' best-known work, *Cities in Evolution* (1968 [1915]), which is readily available, but from Part II of a paper which he read in 1905 to the Sociological Society in London, chaired by the social reformer Charles Booth, which included a response from Ebenezer Howard (Geddes, 1905; Howard, 1905) This paper outlines Geddes' conceptualization of civics – a methodological approach to social survey. Highly antipathetic to ideas of geographical determinism, which were popular throughout Europe at the time, Geddes viewed what he called 'civics' as a 'thinking-machine' for expressing 'the method of thought' of citizens (1968 [1915], p. 67). Geddes' idea of civics as social survey was to prepare for planning as social service, a diagnosis that would lead to a foreseeing of the future and a consequent treatment of ills to bring improvements in quality of life. Recognizing what we would now term complexities and relationalities between urban elements of place, work and folk, Geddes stressed the notion of the city as an organic entity with subjective life evolving from within towards 'creative synergies' of the biological, spatial, social and spiritual. The city 'proper' would be in continuous evolution through informed citizenship producing 'better human environments and better human beings' (Huxley, 2006, pp. 782–83).

Ebenezer Howard's response to what he described as Geddes' 'luminous and picturesque paper', was to welcome ideas that fitted so closely with his own. Howard's was a social, as well as a spatial, vision of reform. His aim was that 'cities would embody the values of a more just and equitable social order, and that they would set in train a process of social reform that would ultimately be a means of superseding the class conflicts of capitalism' (Pinder, 2005, p. 40). Howard argued in *To-Morrow: A Peaceful Path to Real Reform* (1898), for instance, that land should be owned by the whole community, with rents flowing back into communities to pay for public services, although by 1899, the date of the essay reproduced here as Chapter 10, his garden-city diagram had lost the call to 'Go Up and Possess the Land' (Pinder, 2005).

Howard's was not a form of state socialism but rather a 'cooperation' of decentralized and locally managed associations. Unfortunately, in the 1902 second edition of the book, the title had changed to *Garden Cities of To-Morrow* and the telling Social City diagram had been removed. As Peter Hall (1988, p. 88) has commented, the new version diverts people away from the truly radical nature of the message and demotes Howard from 'social visionary to physical planner'. The suite of regionally interrelated towns that Howard envisaged became middle-class suburbia.

Both Geddes and Howard were aware of the disadvantaged status of woman as 'utilitarian housewife' (Geddes, 1968 [1915], p. 8) in late nineteenth-century cities, which wasted women's abilities and energies. Both were interested in Howard's ideas for cooperative communal housekeeping arrangements which promised 'a juster and happier social order' for women who would then be free to play a 'far larger part' in society (Howard 1912 cited in Pinder, 2005, p. 276 n. 51).

Lewis Mumford shared Geddes' and Howard's ideas of the need for holistic, evolutionary analysis of the city in the region. Mumford (1917) espoused the notion of garden cities within a regional plan – a concept which became a firm foundation of the initial programme of the new Regional Planning Association of America in 1923 (Hall, 1988, p. 148). He believed in harnessing the great technological advances of the early twentieth century to 'a fuller quality of life' (1925, p. 151) through planned garden cities which would represent 'all that is good in our modern mechanical developments, but also all that was left out in this one-sided existence' (ibid., p. 152).

However, Mumford's idealism was dashed over the subsequent decades. By the time he wrote *The City in History* in 1961, his senses had been overwhelmed not only by the Second World War and the subsequent Cold War, but also by living in a world of apparently limitless increases in energy and productivity overshadowed by the threat of nuclear war and a car-driven formless 'urbanoid' sprawl of bitumen and rows of concrete box-type houses, all of which he regarded as the irrational misuse of science (Mumford, 1961). Mumford considered unrestricted urban expansion of conurbations into megalopolis as working against the possibility of social efficiency and human satisfaction. He saw bureaucracy as a 'miscarriage of effort' which meant well, but generally ended up as a diminution of purpose.

Mumford's vision, like that of Geddes and Howard, was of networks of small-scale associational civic institutions administering 'a different form of urban growth', responsive to human contact and based on the theory of the British New Towns. He, like Jane Jacobs writing some two years later (1963), wanted spatial planning to emphasize an organic relationship between people and space where people walked rather than drove: he wanted to 'restore human legs as a means of travel' and to 'forget the damned motor car and build the cities for lovers and friends' (Mumford, n.d.).

The Tennessee Valley Authority (TVA) was, in many ways, a development of Geddes' and Howard's city and regional ideas. Set in a context of Franklin D. Roosevelt's New Deal for America (1933 onwards), the TVA formed part of Roosevelt's ideas for a mass return to the land of people and industry. The TVA was a government-led 'experiment, an adventure' (Selznick, Chapter 13, this volume, p. 269) in both democratic planning and planning as a regional conception, based around a river basin as its integral unit. This represented a new, broader vision of agency, spatial scale and function. The TVA broke new ground by moving away from purely physical aspects of planning to 'assum[ing] responsibility' for the social consequences of specific activities. The administration saw a need for a strong sense of social responsibility, manifested through 'adjusting immediate urgencies to long-term social policy' – an approach largely absent today in many countries, where populist politics appear to be more the norm. However, Hall (1988, pp. 161–64) describes how the TVA's long-term vision did not exactly work out. Community development, health and education received only a minute amount of the promised funding and the 'new town' of Norris never really became more than a 'rural village'. As Hall comments, 'America – even New Deal America – was not politically ready for that vision' (1988, p. 164).

One of the key messages in Selznick's 1949 study of the TVA (the introduction to which is included here as Chapter 13) is that 'the instruments of planning are vitally relevant to the nature of the democratic process' (p. 267), an ideological framing completely at odds with that of Friedrich von Hayek for whom the very ideas of spatial planning and the 'common good' appear to be anathema. Written towards the end of the Second World War, Hayek's *Road to Serfdom* (1944) is dominated by a hatred of things German and Marxist and a search for 'freedom' and 'liberty'. In such a vein, planning becomes something pursued by 'single-minded idealists', which would 'make the very men who were most anxious to plan society the most dangerous if they were allowed to do so' (Hayek, 1944, p. 40). Hayek's enormously influential legacy, of neo-liberalist individualism and economic competition, manifest in monetarist economics and the privatization of much of the welfare state (in the UK, Australia and New Zealand at least) and once-nationalized industrial and commercial sectors, offers an ironic twist to the question of which might be a more 'dangerous' regime (see Chapter 14).

Karl Mannheim (Chapter 15), also writing during the Second World War, was more attuned to the idea of large-scale planned operations than was Hayek. He saw a need for 'planned freedom' and social control – 'the rational mastery of the irrational' – rather than Hayek's unplanned market 'freedom' or, indeed, Ebenezer Howard's cooperative 'freedom'. Mannheim's planned society would be scientifically based, working efficiently for 'the good of the whole' – a utilitarian concept in which some 'levels of society' would inevitably be more free than others.

All the authors represented in Part II were concerned with 'progress' – a substitution of some form of 'order' for perceived urban 'dis-order'. Even though the socialist anarchists seek to understand 'the method of thought' of citizens and the TVA seeks to be more democratic, they both express mainly physical and technical 'solutions' to their concerns, especially after the 1902 edition of Howard's *To-Morrow*. Spatial planning is regarded as an instrument for guiding or controlling society. Planners are seen as experts who can determine 'the public good' of hygiene, health, freedom and so on. There is little, if any, awareness of space as a dynamic, relational actor, despite Geddes' connections with European ideas, which seriously questioned Euclidean notions of space and time.

Furthermore all the authors argue for some form of what the French social thinker Michel Foucault would later regard as the regulation of bodies in space (see Volume 3). While Hayek argued for market-led regulation (see Chapter 14), the other authors recognized a need for 'common arrangements for life and health and efficiency' (Geddes, 1915, p. 26), whether this be regional, conurbation-wide, across networks of cities or in small-scale associations.

Geddes (Chapter 11) and Howard (Chapter 10) argue for the benefits of lower-density development, incorporating more access to the countryside and greater garden space, affording more sunlight and, by implication, less disease – Howard's 'healthy balance'. Mumford's 'balance', however, was for medium densities and less urban sprawl (see Chapter 12). However, whatever the 'balance', spatial planning would require Geddes' synoptic vision: seeing the city in its regional setting as an organic whole through direct observation and survey, and through bringing together experts and practitioners from disciplines including not only architecture and urban design, but also public health, civil engineering, sociology, geography, history and economics.

Broad vision would be required across a region, a city-region or even a city (Mumford's 'multi-centred container') as organic, differentiated entities. For the TVA, such a vision should be democratic and socially responsible. Policies should be integrative and also flexible in order to cope with changing circumstances. Practitioners would need not to be averse to risk and experimentation.

The indirect influence of all the authors continues to the present in the planning field. Whether in a strong belief in the ability of neoliberal markets found across much of the global North, the 'organic unity' of New Urbanism (Grant, 2006), or in interdisciplinary, integrative approaches to spatial planning, their often unrecognized legacies live on. The greatest casualty, it would appear, has been the Geddes–Howard–Mumford lineage of socialist anarchism, whose radical qualities of associational self-management, cooperative mutuality and decentralization have either been lost under the strong ties of state control or recently significantly resignified and realigned by right-wing, or centre-right, regimes in many parts of the world.

JEAN HILLIER AND PATSY HEALEY

References

Addams, J. (1972 [1909]), *The Spirit of Youth and the City*, Urbana, IL: University of Illinois Press.

Addams, J. (1990 [1910]), *Twenty Years at Hull-House*, Urbana, IL: University of Illinois Press.

Addams, J. (2002 [1902]), *Democracy and Social Ethics*, Urbana, IL: University of Illinois Press.

Bauer, C. (1934), *Modern Housing*, Boston, MA: Houghton Mifflin.

Dubois, W.E.B. (1898), *The Philadelphia Negro*, Philadelphia, PA: Lippincott.

Dubois, W.E.B. (1961), *The Black Frame*, 3 vols, New York: Mainstream.

Geddes P. (1905), 'Civics: As Applied Sociology', *Sociological Papers*, **1**, pp. 1–38.

Geddes, P. (1968 [1915]), *Cities in Evolution*, London: Ernest Benn.

Grant, J. (2006), *Planning the Good Community: New Urbanism in Theory and Practice*, London: Routledge.

Hall, P. (1988), *Cities of Tomorrow: An Intellectual History of Urban Planning and Design in the Twentieth Century*, Oxford: Blackwell.

Hayden, D. (1981), *The Grand Domestic Revolution: A History of Feminist Designs for American Homes, Neighbourhoods and Cities*, Cambridge MA: MIT Press.

Hayek, F. von (1944), *The Road to Serfdom*, London: Routledge and Kegan Paul.

Healey, E. (1978), *Lady Unknown: The Life of Angela Burdett-Coutts*, London: Sidgwick and Jackson.

Hill, O. (1877), *Our Common Land and Other Short Essays*, London: Macmillan and Co.

Hill, O. (1899), *Management of Homes for the London Poor*, London: Charity Organisation Society.

Hillier, J. and Healey, P. (2008), *Political Economy, Diversity and Pragmatism: Critical Essays in Planning Theory, Volume 2*, Aldershot: Ashgate.

Howard, E. (1898), *To-Morrow: A Peaceful Path to Real Reform*, London: Swan Sonnenschein.

Howard, E. (1905), 'Discussion: Response to Professor Geddes' Paper "Civics: As Applied Sociology"', *Sociological Papers*, **1**, pp. 119–22.

Howard, E. (1912), 'A New Outlet for Women's Energy', Howard Papers d/EHo F/10/5, cited in Pinder (2005).

Howard, E. (n.d.), 'Co-operative Housekeeping and the New Finance', Howard Papers d/EHo F/10/5, cited in Pinder (2005).

Huxley, M. (2006), 'Spatial Rationalities: Order, Environment, Evolution and Government', *Social and Cultural Geography*, **7**(5), pp. 771–87.

Jacobs, J. (1963), 'The Kind of Problem a City is', in J. Jacobs, *The Death and Life of Great American Cities*, New York: Vintage, pp. 428–48. Also published as Chapter 6 in Hillier and Healey (2008).

Melotte, B. (1997), 'Landscape, Neighbourhood and Accessibility: The Contributions of Margaret Feilman to Planning and Development in Western Australia', *Planning History*, **19**(2–3), pp. 32–41.

Mumford, L. (1917), 'Garden Civilizations in Preparing for a New Epoch', unpublished, cited in Hall (1988, p. 148).

Mumford, L. (1925), 'Regions – To Live In', *Survey*, **54**, pp. 151–52.

Mumford, L. (1961), *The City in History*, Harmondsworth: Pelican.

Mumford, L. (1982), *Sketches from Life: The Autobiography of Lewis Mumford: The Early Years*, New York: Dial Press.

Mumford, L. (n.d.), 'In his Own Words', website at: http://www.faculty.rsu.edu/~felwell/Theorists/Mumford/Words.htm. Accessed 20 November 2006.

Pinder, D. (2005), *Visions of the City*, Edinburgh: Edinburgh University Press.

Sandercock, L. (1995), 'Introduction', *Planning Theory*, **13**, pp. 10–33.

Sandercock, L. (1996), *Making the Invisible Visible: Insurgent Planning Histories*, Berkeley: University of California Press.

Sandercock, L. (1998), *Towards Cosmopolis*, New York: Wiley.

Selznick, P. (1949), *TVA and the Grass Roots*, Berkeley: University of California Press.

Simkhovitch, M. (1938), *Neighbourhood*, New York: W.W. Norton & Co.

Spain, D. (2001), *How Women Saved the City*, Minneapolis, MN: University of Minnesota Press.

[10]

The Town-Country Magnet

Ebenezer Howard

'I will not cease from mental strife,
  Nor shall my sword sleep in my hand,
Till we have built Jerusalem
  In England's green and pleasant land.'
                                              —BLAKE.

'Thorough sanitary and remedial action in the houses that we have;
and then the building of more, strongly, beautifully, and in groups of
limited extent, kept in proportion to their streams and walled round,
so that there may be no festering and wretched suburb anywhere, but
clean and busy street within and the open country without, with a
belt of beautiful garden and orchard round the walls, so that from
any part of the city perfectly fresh air and grass and sight of far
horizon might be reachable in a few minutes' walk. This the final
aim.'—JOHN RUSKIN, *Sesame and Lilies.*

The reader is asked to imagine an estate embracing an area
of 6,000 acres, which is at present purely agricultural, and
has been obtained by purchase in the open market at a cost of
£40[1] an acre, or £240,000. The purchase money is supposed to
have been raised on mortgage debentures, bearing interest at an
average rate not exceeding £4 per cent.[2] The estate is legally
vested in the names of four gentlemen of responsible position
and of undoubted probity and honour, who hold it in trust,
first, as a security for the debenture-holders, and, secondly, in

---

[1] This was the average price paid for agricultural land in 1898 : and,
though this estimate may prove far more than sufficient, it is hardly
likely to be much exceeded.

[2] The financial arrangements described in this book are likely to be
departed from in form, but not in essential principle. And until a
definite scheme has been agreed upon, I think it better to repeat them
precisely as they appeared in *To-morrow,* the original title of this
book—the book which led to the formation of the Garden City
Association. (Footnote to 1902 edition. *Ed.*)

THE TOWN-COUNTRY MAGNET

trust for the people of Garden City, the Town-country magnet, which it is intended to build thereon. One essential feature of the plan is that all ground rents, which are to be based upon the annual value of the land, shall be paid to the trustees, who, after providing for interest and sinking fund, will hand the balance to the Central Council of the new municipality,[1] to be employed by such Council in the creation and maintenance of all necessary public works—roads, schools, parks, etc.

The objects of this land purchase may be stated in various ways, but it is sufficient here to say that some of the chief objects are these: To find for our industrial population work at wages of *higher purchasing power*, and to secure healthier surroundings and more regular employment. To enterprising manufacturers, co-operative societies, architects, engineers, builders, and mechanicians of all kinds, as well as to many engaged in various professions, it is intended to offer a means of securing new and better employment for their capital and talents, while to the agriculturists at present on the estate as well as to those who may migrate thither, it is designed to open a new market for their produce close to their doors. Its object is, in short, to raise the standard of health and comfort of all true workers of whatever grade—the means by which these objects are to be achieved being a healthy, natural, and economic combination of town and country life, and this on land owned by the municipality.

Garden City, which is to be built near the centre of the 6,000 acres, covers an area of 1,000 acres, or a sixth part of the 6,000 acres, and might be of circular form, 1,240 yards (or nearly three-quarters of a mile) from centre to circumference. (Diagram 2 is a ground plan of the whole municipal area, showing the town in the centre; and Diagram 3, which represents one section or ward of the town, will be useful in following the description of the town itself—*a description which is, however, merely suggestive, and will probably be much departed from.*)

Six magnificent boulevards—each 120 feet wide—traverse the city from centre to circumference, dividing it into six equal parts or wards. In the centre is a circular space containing about

---

[1] This word, 'municipality', is not used in a technical sense.

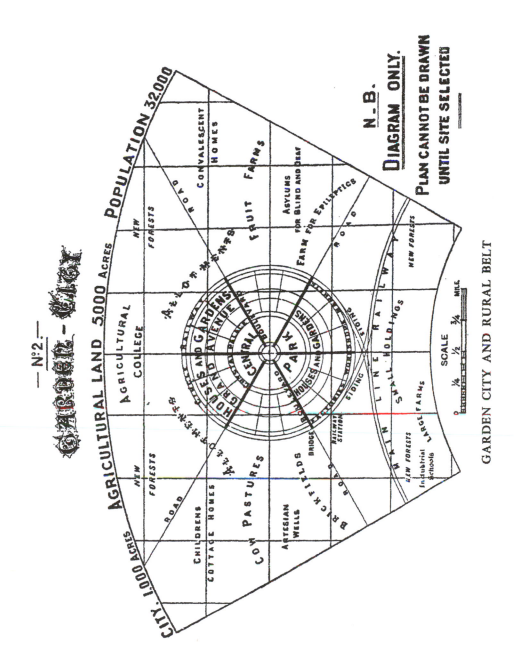

THE TOWN-COUNTRY MAGNET

five and a half acres, laid out as a beautiful and well-watered garden; and, surrounding this garden, each standing in its own ample grounds, are the larger public buildings—town hall,

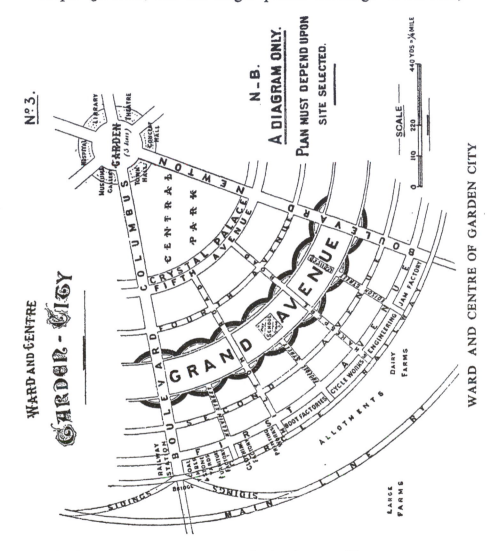

principal concert and lecture hall, theatre, library, museum, picture-gallery, and hospital.

The rest of the large space encircled by the 'Crystal Palace' is a public park, containing 145 acres, which includes ample recreation grounds within very easy access of all the people.

THE TOWN-COUNTRY MAGNET

Running all round the Central Park (except where it is intersected by the boulevards) is a wide glass arcade called the 'Crystal Palace', opening on to the park. This building is in wet weather one of the favourite resorts of the people, whilst the knowledge that its bright shelter is ever close at hand tempts people into Central Park, even in the most doubtful of weathers. Here manufactured goods are exposed for sale, and here most of that class of shopping which requires the joy of deliberation and selection is done. The space enclosed by the Crystal Palace is, however, a good deal larger than is required for these purposes, and a considerable part of it is used as a Winter Garden —the whole forming a permanent exhibition of a most attractive character, whilst its circular form brings it near to every dweller in the town—the furthest removed inhabitant being within 600 yards.

Passing out of the Crystal Palace on our way to the outer ring of the town, we cross Fifth Avenue—lined, as are all the roads of the town, with trees—fronting which, and looking on to the Crystal Palace, we find a ring of very excellently built houses, each standing in its own ample grounds; and, as we continue our walk, we observe that the houses are for the most part built either in concentric rings, facing the various avenues (as the circular roads are termed), or fronting the boulevards and roads which all converge to the centre of the town. Asking the friend who accompanies us on our journey what the population of this little city may be, we are told about 30,000 in the city itself, and about 2,000 in the agricultural estate, and that there are in the town 5,500 building lots of an *average* size of 20 feet x 130 feet —the minimum space allotted for the purpose being 20 x 100. Noticing the very varied architecture and design which the houses and groups of houses display—some having common gardens and co-operative kitchens—we learn that general observance of street line or harmonious departure from it are the chief points as to house building, over which the municipal authorities exercise control, for, though proper sanitary arrangements are strictly enforced, the fullest measure of individual taste and preference is encouraged.

Walking still toward the outskirts of the town, we come upon 'Grand Avenue'. This avenue is fully entitled to the name it

54

THE TOWN-COUNTRY MAGNET

bears, for it is 420 feet wide,[1] and, forming a belt of green upwards of three miles long, divides that part of the town which
lies outside Central Park into two belts. It really constitutes an
additional park of 115 acres—a park which is within 240 yards
of the furthest removed inhabitant. In this splendid avenue six
sites, each of four acres, are occupied by public schools and
their surrounding playgrounds and gardens, while other sites
are reserved for churches, of such denominations as the religious
beliefs of the people may determine, to be erected and maintained out of the funds of the worshippers and their friends. We
observe that the houses fronting on Grand Avenue have departed (at least in one of the wards—that of which Diagram 3
is a representation)—from the general plan of concentric rings,
and, in order to ensure a longer line of frontage on Grand
Avenue, are arranged in crescents—thus also to the eye yet further enlarging the already splendid width of Grand Avenue.

On the outer ring of the town are factories, warehouses,
dairies, markets, coal yards, timber yards, etc., all fronting on
the circle railway, which encompasses the whole town, and
which has sidings connecting it with a main line of railway which
passes through the estate. This arrangement enables goods to
be loaded direct into trucks from the warehouses and work-
shops, and so sent by railway to distant markets, or to be taken
direct from the trucks into the warehouses or factories ; thus not
only effecting a very great saving in regard to packing and
cartage, and reducing to a minimum loss from breakage, but
also, by reducing the traffic on the roads of the town, lessening
to a very marked extent the cost of their maintenance. The
smoke fiend is kept well within bounds in Garden City; for all
machinery is driven by electric energy, with the result that the
cost of electricity for lighting and other purposes is greatly
reduced.

The refuse of the town is utilized on the agricultural portions
of the estate, which are held by various individuals in large
farms, small holdings, allotments, cow pastures, etc.; the
natural competition of these various methods of agriculture,
tested by the willingness of occupiers to offer the highest rent

---

[1] Portland Place, London, is only 100 feet wide.

THE TOWN-COUNTRY MAGNET

to the municipality, tending to bring about the best system of husbandry, or, what is more probable, the best *systems* adapted for various purposes. Thus it is easily conceivable that it may prove advantageous to grow wheat in very large fields, involving united action under a capitalist farmer, or by a body of co-operators; while the cultivation of vegetables, fruits, and flowers, which requires closer and more personal care, and more of the artistic and inventive faculty, may possibly be best dealt with by individuals, or by small groups of individuals having a common belief in the efficacy and value of certain dressings, methods of culture, or artificial and natural surroundings.

This plan, or, if the reader be pleased to so term it, this absence of plan, avoids the dangers of stagnation or dead level, and, though encouraging individual initiative, permits of the fullest co-operation, while the increased rents which follow from this form of competition are common or municipal property, and by far the larger part of them are expended in permanent improvements.

While the town proper, with its population engaged in various trades, callings, and professions, and with a store or depot in each ward, offers the most natural market to the people engaged on the agricultural estate, inasmuch as to the extent to which the townspeople demand their produce they escape altogether any railway rates and charges; yet the farmers and others are not by any means limited to the town as their only market, but have the fullest right to dispose of their produce to whomsoever they please. Here, as in every feature of the experiment, it will be seen that it is not the area of rights which is contracted, but the area of choice which is enlarged.

This principle of freedom holds good with regard to manufacturers and others who have established themselves in the town. These manage their affairs in their own way, subject, of course, to the general law of the land, and subject to the provision of sufficient space for workmen and reasonable sanitary conditions. Even in regard to such matters as water, lighting, and telephonic communication—which a municipality, if efficient and honest, is certainly the best and most natural body to supply—no rigid or absolute monopoly is sought; and if any private corporation or any body of individuals proved itself

56

THE TOWN-COUNTRY MAGNET

capable of supplying on more advantageous terms, either the whole town or a section of it, with these or any commodities the supply of which was taken up by the corporation, this would be allowed. No really sound system of *action* is in more need of artificial support than is any sound system of *thought*. The area of municipal and corporate action is probably destined to become greatly enlarged; but, if it is to be so, it will be because the people possess faith in such action, and that faith can be best shown by a wide extension of the area of freedom.

Dotted about the estate are seen various charitable and philanthropic institutions. These are not under the control of the municipality, but are supported and managed by various public-spirited people who have been invited by the municipality to establish these institutions in an open healthy district, and on land let to them at a pepper-corn rent, it occurring to the authorities that they can the better afford to be thus generous, as the spending power of these institutions greatly benefits the whole community. Besides, as those persons who migrate to the town are among its most energetic and resourceful members, it is but just and right that their more helpless brethren should be able to enjoy the benefits of an experiment which is designed for humanity at large.

Note: The following quotation appeared at the head of this chapter in the edition of 1898. *Ed.*

'No scene is continuously and untiringly loved, but one rich by joyful human labour; smooth in field; fair in garden; full in orchard; trim, sweet and frequent in homestead; ringing with voices of vivid existence. No air is sweet that is silent; it is only sweet when full of low currents of under sound—triplets of birds, and murmur and chirp of insects, and deep-toned words of men, and wayward trebles of childhood. As the art of life is learned, it will be found at last that all lovely things are also necessary;—the wild flower by the wayside, as well as the tended corn; and the wild birds and creatures of the forest, as well as the tended cattle; because man doth not live by bread only, but also by the desert manna; by every wondrous word and unknowable work of God.'—JOHN RUSKIN, *Unto This Last* (1862).

57

[11]

CIVICS: AS CONCRETE AND APPLIED SOCIOLOGY, PART II.

By Professor GEDDES.

Read before the Sociological Society at a Meeting in the School of Economics and Political Science (University of London), Clare Market, W.C., on Monday, January 23rd, 1905, the Rt. Hon. CHARLES BOOTH, F.R.S., in the Chair.

A.—INTRODUCTION: THE NEED OF CIVIC SURVEYS.

To the previous discussion of this subject* the first portion of this present title, " Civics as Concrete Sociology," would have been more suitable than the second, (that of "Civics as Applied Sociology ") actually used. For its aim was essentially to plead for the concrete survey and study of cities, their observation and interpretation on lines essentially similar to those of the natural sciences. Since Comte's demonstration of the necessity of the preliminary sciences to social studies, and Spencer's development of this, still more since the evolution theory has become generally recognised, no one disputes the applicability of biology to

---

* "Sociological Papers," Vol. I., pp. 103–118.

sociology.   Many are, indeed, vigorously applying the conceptions of life in evolution, in geographical distribution and
environment, in health and disease, to the interpretations of the
problems of the times; while with the contemporary rise of
eugenics to the first plane of interest, both social and scientific,
these lines of thought, bio-social and bio-geographic, must
needs be increasingly utilised and developed.

But Comte and Spencer, with most other biologically-
minded sociologists have been more at home among biological
generalisations and theories than among the facts they arise
from, and hence it is ever needful to maintain and extend a
first-hand contact with these.   I seek, therefore, to press home
the idea that just as the biologist must earn his generalisations
through direct and first-hand acquaintance with nature, so
now must the sociologist work for his generalisations through
a period of kindred observation and analysis, both geographic
and historical; his " general laws " thus appearing anew as the
abstract of regional facts, after due comparison of these
as between region and region.

May not much of the comparative sterility of post-Comtean (or at
any rate post-Spencerian) sociology, which is so commonly reproached to us,
and to which the difficult formation and slow growth of sociological
societies and schools is largely due, be thus explained?   Is it not the case
that many able and persuasive writers, not only knowing the results, but
logically using the generalisations of Comte or Spencer, as of old of Smith
or now-a-days of List in the economic field, are yet comparatively sterile of
fresh contributions to thought, and still more to action?   In fact, must we
not apply to much of the literature of recent sociology, just as to traditional
economics, the criticism of Comte's well-known law of three states, and
inquire if such writers, while apparently upon the plane of generalised
science, are not really in large measure at least arrested upon Comte's
" metaphysical stage," Mill's " abstractional " one?

Conversely, the revival of sociological interest in this country at
present is obviously very largely derived from fresh and freshening work like
that of Mr Francis Galton and of the Right Hon. Charles Booth especially.
For here in Mr. Galton's biometrics and eugenics is a return to nature, a
keen scrutiny of human beings, which is really an orderly fruition of that
of the same author's " Art of Travel."   Similarly, Mr. Booth's " Survey of
London " is as truly a return to nature as was Darwin's Voyage, or his yet
more far-reaching studies in his garden and farmyard at home.

AS CONCRETE AND APPLIED SOCIOLOGY 59

Is it not the main support of the subtle theorisings and far-stretched polemic of Prof. Weismann that he can plague his adversaries with the small but literal and concrete mice and hydroids and water fleas with which his theories began? And is it not for a certain lack of such concrete matter of observation that the vast systematisations of M. de Greef, or M. de Roberty, or the original and ingenious readings of Prof. Simon Patten leave us too often unconvinced, even if not sometimes without sufficiently definite understanding of their meaning? The simplest of naturalists must feel that Comte or Spencer, despite the frequently able use of the generalisations of biology, themselves somewhat lacked this first-hand observation of the city and community around them, and suffered thereby; this part of their work obviously not being on a level with the historic interpretations of the one or the psychological productivity of the other. And if, without war-like intent, I may yet strike a conspicuous shield or two within these friendly lists, is it not this one element of concrete observation and illustration which is sometimes lacking to give its full effect to the encyclopædic learn-ing and the sympathetic insight of one of our recent papers, to the historic and poetic interpretations of another, or to the masterly logic of a third?

Before the polemics of our educationists, the voluminous argument-ation and casuistic subtlety of our professors of economics and ethics, yet more before the profound speculations of our epistemologists, the mere naturalist observer can but feel abashed like the truant before his school-masters; yet he is also not without a certain deep inward conviction, born of experience, that his outdoor world is yet more real, more vast, and more instructive than is theirs. And this impression becomes strengthened, nay verified and established, when he sees that the initiative thinkers from whom these claim to descend, have had in each and every case no merely academic record, but also a first-hand experience, an impulse and message from life and nature. Hence the contributions of Locke, of Comenius, and of Rousseau. Hence the Physiocrats found economics in peasant life; and thus too Adam Smith renewed their science, with due academic logic, doubtless, but from his experience of Glasgow and Kirkcaldy manufactures and trade. Even the idealist Berkeley owed much of his theory to his iridescent tar-water; while surely the greater ethicists are those who have not only been dialecticians, but moral forces in the world of men.

In such ways, then, I would justify the thesis that civics is no abstract study, but fundamentally a matter of concrete and descriptive sociology—perhaps the greatest field of this. Next, that such orderly study is in line with the preliminary sciences, and with the general doctrine of evolution from simple to complex; and finally with the general inquiry into the influence of geographical conditions on social development.

In short, the student of civics must be first of all an observer of cities; and, if so, of their origins and developments, from the small and simple beginnings of which the tiniest hamlet is but an arrested germ. The productive sociologist should thus be of all investigators a wandering student *par excellence;* in the first place, as far as possible, a literal tourist and traveller—and this although, like the homely Gilbert White or the world - voyaging Darwin, he may do his best work around his own home.

B.—INITIAL METHODS OF CONCRETE SURVEY.

Hence our civic studies began (vol. 1, p. 105) with the survey of a valley region inhabited by its characteristic types— hunter and shepherd, peasant and fisher—each on his own level, each evolving or degenerating within his own region. Hence the concrete picture of such a typical valley section with its types of occupation cannot be brought too clearly before our minds.*

What now of the causes of progress or decay? Are not these first of all the qualities and defects inherent in that particular social formation?—though we must also consider how these different types act and react, how they combine with, transform, subjugate, ruin or replace each other in region after region. We thus re-interpret the vicissitudes of history in more general terms, those of the differentiation, progress or degeneracy of each occupational and social type, and the ascending and descending oscillations of these types. In short, these occupational struggles underlie and largely interpret even that conflict of races, upon which Mr. Stuart-Glennie and other sociologists have so ably insisted. The fundamental importance of these initial factors of region and occupation to all studies of races and types, of communities and institu- tions, of customs and laws, indeed of language and literature, of religion and art, even of ideals and individualities, must be my excuse if I seem to insist, in season and out of season, upon

---

* Fig. I.

AS CONCRETE AND APPLIED SOCIOLOGY   61

the services of Le Play as one of the main founders of sociology ; and this not only *(a)* on account of his monographic surveys of modern industrial life — those " Monographies Sociales " from which our current economic studies of the condition of the worker, of the family budget, etc., descend—but *(b)* yet more on account of his vital reconstruction of anthropology, (albeit still far from adequately realised by most anthropologists) through his renewed insistence upon the elemental rustic origins of industry, family types, and social organisation alike, from these simplest reactions of man in his struggle for existence in varied and varying environment.

It does not suffice to recognise, with many economists, hunting, pastoral and agricultural formations, as states *preliminary* to our present industrial and commercial, imperial, and financial order of civilisation. This view, still too commonly surviving, is rather of hindrance than help ; what we need is to see our existing civilisation as the complex struggle and resultant of all these types and their developments to-day. So far, therefore, from leaving, as at present, these simple occupational types to the anthropologist, or at best giving him some scant hospitality within our city museum, we are learning to see how it is at one time the eager miner, or the conservative shepherd, or at another the adventurous fisher or hunter who comes concretely upon the first plane of national, imperial or international politics, and who awakens new strife among these. We not only begin to see, but the soldier frankly tells us, how the current sports of youth, and the unprecedented militarism of the past century, are alike profoundly connected with the hunting world. Hence the hope of peace lies not only, as most at present think, in the civilised and civilising development of international law, or of culture intercourse, excellent though these are, but also in a fuller and completer return to nature than has been this recent and persistent obsession of our governing classes with the hunter world almost alone ; in short, in adding the gentler, yet wider, experiences of the naturalist, the sterner experiences of other occupations also. Nor does such elementary recognition of these main social formations content us ; their local differentiations must be noted and compared—a comprehensive regional survey, therefore, which does justice to each local variety of these great types ; speaking henceforth of no mere abstract " hunter," but of the specific hunting types of each climate, and distinguishing these as clearly as do our own milder sportsmen of deer-forest and the turnip field from themselves and from each other. After such needed surveys in detail, we may, indeed must, compare and generalise them.

Similarly for the pasture, the forest. Every tourist in this country is struck by the contrast of Swiss towns and cities with our own, and notes too that on the Swiss pasture he finds a horde of cattle, while in Scotland or Yorkshire he left a flock of sheep. And not only the tourist, but the historian or the economist too often fail to see how Galashiels or Bradford are developments of the wool hamlet, now familiar to many in R. L. Stevenson's native Swanston. Again, not only Swiss wealth, but Swiss character and institutions, go back essentially to the high pasture and the well-filled byre. That this rich Swiss cow-pasture rests on limestone, and the poor Scottish sheep-grazing upon comparatively unmouldering and impermeable gneiss, is no mere matter of geologist's detail; it affords in each case the literal and concrete foundation-stone of the subsequent evolution of each region and population, and this not only in material and economic development, but even in higher and subtler outcomes, æsthetic, intellectual and moral.* It is for such reasons that one must labour and re-labour this geographic and determinist aspect of sociology, and this for no merely scientific reason, but also for practical ones. Nowhere perhaps have more good and generous souls considered how to better the condition of their people than in Swiss, or Irish, or Scottish valleys; yet it is one main reason of the continual failure of all such movements, and of such minds in the wider world as well, that they do not first acquaint themselves with the realities of nature and labour sufficiently to appreciate that the fundamental—I do not say the supreme—question is : what can be got out of limestone, and what can be got out of gneiss? Hence the rare educative value of such a concrete sociological diagram and model as was the Swiss Village at the Paris Exposition of 1900, for here geographic and economic knowledge and insight were expressed with artistic skill and sympathy as perhaps never before. Only as similar object-lessons are worked out for other countries, can we adequately learn, much less popularly teach, how from nature comes "rustics," and from this comes civics. But civics and rustics make up the field of politics; they are the concrete of which politics becomes the abstract—commonly the too remotely abstract.

For final illustration, let us descend to the sea-level. There again, taking the fisher, each regional type must be traced in his contribution to his town. Take for instance the salmon fisher of Norway, the whaler of Dundee, the herring-fisher of Yarmouth, the cod-fisher of Newfoundland, the coral fisher of the Ægean; each is a definite varietal type, one developing or at least tending to develop characteristic normal family relations, and corresponding social outcomes in institutions; in which again the appropriate qualities and defects must be expressed, even as is the quality and twist of the hemp in the strength of the cable, or as is the chemistry and the microscopic structure of the alloy in the efficiency of the great gun.

---

* For a fuller justification of this thesis as regards Switzerland, see the writer's "International Exhibitions," in *International Monthly*, October, 1900.

AS CONCRETE AND APPLIED SOCIOLOGY   63

Our neighbouring learned societies and museums, geographical, geological and the rest, are thus avowedly and consciously so many winter shelters in which respective groups of regional surveyors tell their tales and compare their observations, in which they meet to compare their generalisations from their own observations made in the field with those made by others. So it must increasingly be for this youngest of societies. We may, we should, know best our Thames valley, our London basin, our London survey ; but the progress of our science implies as increasingly varied and thorough an inquiry into rustic and civic regions and occupations and resultants throughout the whole world present and past, as does the corresponding world survey with our geologic neighbours.

I plead then for a sociological survey, rustic and civic, region by region, and insist in the first place upon the same itinerant field methods of notebook and camera, even for museum collections and the rest, as those of the natural sciences. The dreary manuals which have too long discredited those sciences in our schools, are now giving place to a new and fascinating literature of first-hand nature study. Similarly, those too abstract manuals of civics which are at present employed in schools * must be replaced by concrete and regional ones, their abstract counsels of political or personal perfection thus also giving place to a corresponding regional idealism which may then be supplemented from other regions as far as needs demand and circumstances allow.

C.—GEOGRAPHICAL DETERMINISM AND ITS DIFFICULTIES.

To interpret then our tangle of ideas, both of the city and its citizens, let us now bring more fully to our transverse valley sections, and to each occupation separately, the geographical view - point which we have found of service to elucidate the development of towns and cities upon its longi-

---

* For a fuller review of these, compare the writer's " City Development," in *Contemporary Review*, October, 1904.

tudinal slope. But this is neither more nor less than the method of Montesquieu, whose classic " Esprit des Lois " anticipates and initiates so much of that of later writers— Ritter, Buckle, Taine, or Le Play. Once more then let their common, or rather their resultant, doctrine be stated in terms expressing the latest of these more fully than the first. Given the region, its character determines the nature of the fundamental occupation, and this in turn essentially determines the type of family. The nature and method of the occupation must normally determine the mode of its organisation, *e.g.*, the rise and character of a specialised directive class, and the nature of these occupational chiefs as contrasted with the people and with each other. Similarly, the types of family tend to develop their appropriate types of institutions, *e.g.*, for justice, guidance, and of course notably in response to social environment as regards defence or attack.

Thus at this point in fact we seem to be pressing upon the student of sociology the essential argument of geographical and evolutionary determinism, in fact inviting him to adopt a view, indeed to commit himself to a method, which may be not only foreign to his habits, but repugnant to his whole view of life and history. And if able advocacy of this determinist view of society for at least the past five generations has not carried general conviction, why raise so controversial a suggestion, in the guise too of a method professing to harmonise all comers? Yet this is advisedly done ; and as no one will deny some civic importance to geographical factors, let patience be granted to examine this aspect of the city's map and shield, and to get from it what it can teach, under the present assurance to the philosophic and idealist critic that his view of other factors, higher and deeper, as supreme in human life, and therefore in city making, will not be forgotten, nor excluded from consideration when we come to them. All that is really insisted upon here is that if anything of naturalistic method of evolutionary conception is to be permitted at all, we must obviously proceed from this simple towards the more complex, and so begin with it here and now.

It is the appropriate slope or steppe, the needful rainfall, that conditions the growth of grass, this which conditions the presence of herds or flocks, and these again which determine the very existence of shepherds. These granted then, not only do the pastoral arts and crafts arise, but the patriarchal type and family develop, and this not only with their hospitality and other virtues, with their nomadic tendencies, at any rate, their unfixed land-tenure, very different from the peasant's, but their slow and skilful diplomacy (till the pasture is bared or grown again, as the negotiator's interests incline). The patriarch in his venerable age, the caravaneer in his nomadic and exploring youth, his disciplined maturity, thus naturally develop as different types of chief and leader; and it is therefore not until this stage, when all is ready for the entry of Abraham or Job, of Mohammed the camel-driver, or Paul the tent-maker, that any real controversy can arise between the determinist and his opponent, between the democratic and the great-man theories of history, towards which these respectively incline.* And at that stage, may not the controversy stimulate a fruitful analysis? After all, what is the claim of free-will but to select among the factors afforded by a given set of circumstances? And the utmost stretch of determinism to which geography and civics may lead us obviously cannot prove the negative of this. But whether the psychologic origins of new ideals be internal to the mind of genius, or imparted by some external source, is a matter obviously beyond the scope of either the geographer or the historian of civics to settle. Enough surely for both controversialists if we use such a means of tabulating facts as to beg the question for neither view; and still better if we can present the case of each without injustice to either, nay, to each with its clearness increased by the sharp edge of contrast. If the geographical determinist thesis on one hand, and its ethical and psychological antithesis on the other, can thus clearly be defined and balanced, their working equilibrium is at hand, even should their complete synthesis remain beyond us.

D.—NEED OF ABSTRACT METHOD FOR NOTATION AND FOR INTERPRETATION.

Not only such general geographical studies, but such social interpretations as those above indicated have long been in progress : witness the labours of whole schools of historians and critics, among whom Montesquieu and his immediate following, or in more recent times Buckle and Taine, are but the most prominent; witness the works of geographers like Humboldt, Ritter, Reclus, or of developmental technologists like Boucher de Perthes and regional economists like Le Play. The main lines of a concrete and evolutionary sociology (or at

---

* A fuller study, upon this method, of the essential origins of pastoral evolution, and of its characteristic modern developments, will be found in the writer's " Flower of the Grass," in *The Evergreen*, Edinburgh and Westminster, 1896. See also " La Science Sociale," *passim*, especially in its earlier vols. or its number for Jan. 1905.

least *sociography*) have thus been laid down for us; but the task now before us, in our time, in such a society as this—and indeed in such a paper as the present one—is that of extracting from all this general teaching its essential scientific method, one everywhere latent and implicit, but nowhere fully explicit, or at least adequately systematised.

It is in fact only as we can agree upon some definite and orderly method of description that our existing literature of social surveys can be adequately compared or new ones co-operatively undertaken. Hence the importance of discussions of scientific method such as those which have so largely occupied our first volume. Yet, I submit, here lies the means of escaping from these too abstract (and consequently too static) presentments of the general methodology of social science into which sociologists are constantly falling; and to which must be largely ascribed the prevalent distaste for sociology so general in this would-be practical-minded community in which we find ourselves, as indeed also the comparative unattractiveness of our studies to the body of specialist scientific workers, not even excepting those within what we consider sociological fields.

The history of each science, be it mathematics or astronomy, botany, zoology or geology, shows us that it is not enough to have the intelligent observer, or even the interpretative thinker with his personally expressed doctrine. This must be clearly crystallised into a definite statement, method, proposition, "law" or theory, stated in colourless impersonal form before it is capable of acceptance and incorporation into the general body of science. But while astronomer and geologist and naturalist can and do describe both the observational results and their general conceptions in literary form, requiring from the ordinary reader but the patience to master a few unfamiliar terms and ideas, they also carry on their work by help of definite and orderly technical methods, descriptive and comparative, analytic and synthetic. These, as far as possible, have to be crystallised beyond their mere verbal statement into formulæ, into tabular and graphic presentments, and thus not only acquire greater clearness of statement, but become more and more active agencies of inquiry—in fact, become literal *thinking-machines*. But while the mathematician has his notations and his calculus, the geographer and geologist their maps, reliefs and sections, the naturalist his orderly classificatory methods, it has been the misfortune and delay of political economy, and no small cause of that "notorious discord and sterility" with which Comte reproached it, that

AS CONCRETE AND APPLIED SOCIOLOGY   67

its cultivators have so commonly sought to dispense with the employment of any definite scientific notations; while even its avowed statisticians, in this country especially, have long resisted the consistent use of graphic methods.

I submit, therefore, for discussion, as even more urgent and pressing than that of the general and abstract methodology of the social sciences, the problem of elaborating a concrete descriptive method readily applicable to the study and comparison of human societies, to cities therefore especially. To do justice to this subject, not only the descriptive labours of anthropologists, but much of the literature of sociology would have to be gone through from the "Tableau Economique" of the Physiocratic School to the "Sociological Tables" of Mr. Spencer, and still more fruitfully to more recent writers. Among these, besides here recognising specially the work of Mr. Booth and its stimulus to younger investigators, I would acknowledge the helpful and suggestive impulse from the group of social geographers which has arisen from the initiative of Le Play,* and whose classification, especially in its later forms,† cannot but be of interest and value to everyone whose thought on social questions is not afloat upon the ocean of the abstract without chart or bearings.

Yet with all respect to each and all these classifications and methods, indeed with cordially acknowledged personal obligation and indebtedness to them from first to last, no one of these seems fully satisfactory for the present purpose; and it is therefore needful to go into the matter afresh for ourselves, though utilising these as fully as we can.

E.—THE CITY-COMPLEX AND ITS USUAL ANALYSIS.

In the everyday world, in the city as we find it, what is the working classification of ideas, the method of thought of its citizens? That the citizens no more think of themselves as using any particular sociological method than did M. Jourdain of talking prose does not really matter, save that it makes our observation, both of them and it, easier and more trustworthy.

They are speaking and thinking for the most part of

---

* La Nomenclature Sociale (Extrait de La Revue, "La Science Sociale," Dec. 1886) Paris, Firmin-Didot, 1887.

† Demoulins, La Science Sociale d'apres F. Le Play, 1882-1905 ; Classification Sociale, "La Science Sociale," Jan. 1905.

68   CIVICS:

People and of Affairs; much less of places. In the category of
People, we observe that individuals, self and others, and this
in interest, perhaps even more than in interests, commonly take
precedence of groups. Institutions and Government are, however, of general interest, the state being much more prominent
than is the church; the press, for many, acting as the modern
substitute for the latter. In the world of Affairs, commerce
takes precedence of industry, while sport runs hard upon
both. War, largely viewed by its distant spectators as the
most vivid form of sport, also bulks largely. Peace is not
viewed as a positive ideal, but essentially as a passive state,
at best, of non-war, more generally of latent war. Central
among places are the bank, the market (in its financial forms
before its material ones). Second to these stand the mines;
then the factories, etc.; and around these the fixed or floating
fortresses of defence. Of homes, that of the individual alone
is seriously considered, at most those of his friends, his " set,"
his peers, but too rarely even of the street, much less the
neighbourhood, at least for their own sake, as distinguished
from their reaction upon individual and family status or
comfort.

This set of views is obviously not easy of precise analysis
or exact classification. In broad outline, however, a summary
may be made, and even tabulated as follows :—

THE EVERYDAY TOWN AND ITS ACTIVITIES.

PEOPLE	AFFAIRS	PLACES
(a) INDIVIDUALS (Self and others).	(a) COMMERCE INDUSTRY, etc. SPORT.	(a) MARKET, BANK, etc. FACTORY, MINE, etc.
(b) GOVERNMENT(S) Temporal and Spiritual (State and Church).	(b) WAR and Peace (Latent War).	(b) FORT, FIELD, etc.

Next note how from the everyday world of action,
there arises a corresponding thought-world also. This has,

AS CONCRETE AND APPLIED SOCIOLOGY 69

of course, no less numerous and varied elements, with its resultantly complex local colour; but a selection will suffice, of which the headings may be printed below those of the preceding scheme, to denote how to the objective elements there are subjective elements corresponding—literal reflections upon the pools of memory—the slowly flowing stream of tradition. Thus the extended diagram, its objective elements expressed in yet more general terms, may now be read anew (noting that mirror images are duly reversed).

	PEOPLE	AFFAIRS	PLACES
"TOWN"	(a) INDIVIDUALS	(a) OCCUPATIONS	(a) WORK-PLACES
	(b) INSTITUTIONS	(b) WAR	(b) WAR-PLACES
"SCHOOLS"	(b) HISTORY ("Constitutional")	(b) STATISTICS and HISTORY ("Military")	(b) GEOGRAPHY
	(a) BIOGRAPHY	(a) ECONOMICS	(a) TOPOGRAPHY

Here then we have that general relation of the town life and its "schools," alike of thought and of education, which must now be more fully investigated.

Such diagrammatic presentments, while of course primarily for the purpose of clear expression and comparison, are also frequently suggestive —by "inspection," as geometers say—of relations not previously noticed. In both ways, we may see more clearly how prevalent ideas and doctrines have arisen as "reflections upon" the life of action, and even account for their qualities and their defects—their partial truth or their corresponding inadequacy, according to our own appreciative or depreciative standpoint. Thus as regards "People," in the first column we see expressed briefly how to (a) the individual life, with the corresponding vivid interest in biography, corresponds the "great man theory" of history. Conversely with (b) alone is associated the insistance upon institutional developments as the main factor. Passing to the middle column, that of "Affairs," we may note in connection with (b) say the rise of statistics in association with the needs of war, a point connected with its too empiric character; or note again, a too common converse weakness of economic theory, its inadequate induc-

tive verification.   Or finally, in the column of " Place," the long weakness
of geography as an educational subject, yet its periodic renewal upon the
field of war, is indicated.   We might in fact continue such a comparison of
the existing world of action and of ideas, into all the schools, those of thought
and practice, no less than those of formal instruction ; and thus we should
more and more clearly unravel how their complexity and entanglement, their
frequent oppositions and contradictions are related to the various and
warring elements of the manifold "Town" life from which they derive and
survive.   Such a fuller discussion, however, would too long delay the immediate problem—that of understanding " Town " and its " School " in their
origins and simplest relations.

F.—PROPOSED METHODICAL ANALYSIS.
(1) THE TOWN.

More fully to understand this two-fold development of
Town and School, we have first of all apparently to run counter
to the preceding popular view, which is here, as in so many
cases, the precise opposite of that reached from the side of
science.   This, as we have already so fully insisted, must set
out with geography, thus literally *replacing* People and Affairs
in our scheme above.

Starting then once more with the simple biological
formula :

ENVIRONMENT - - - - CONDITIONS - - - - ORGANISM

this has but to be applied and defined by the social
geographer to become

REGION - - - - OCCUPATION - - - - FAMILY-type and
                                        Developments

which summarises precisely that doctrine of Montesquieu and
his successors already insisted on.   Again, in but slight variation from Le Play's simplest phrasing (*"Lieu, travail, famille "*)
we have

PLACE - - - - - WORK - - - - - FOLK

It is from this simple and initial social formula that we have
now to work our way to a fuller understanding of Town and
School.

AS CONCRETE AND APPLIED SOCIOLOGY　　　71

Immediately, therefore, this must be traced upward towards its complexities. For Place, it is plain, is no mere topographic site. Work, conditioned as it primarily is by natural advantages, is thus really first of all *place-work*. Arises the field or garden, the port, the mine, the workshop, in fact the *work-place*, as we may simply generalise it; while, further, beside this arise the dwellings, the *folk-place*.

Nor are these by any means all the elements we are accustomed to lump together into Town. As we thus cannot avoid entering into the manifold complexities of town-life throughout the world and history, we must carry along with us the means of unravelling these; hence the value of this simple but precise nomenclature and its regular schematic use. Thus, while here keeping to simple words in everyday use, we may employ and combine them to analyse out our Town into its elements and their inter-relations with all due exactitude, instead of either leaving our common terms undefined, or arbitrarily defining them anew, as economists have alternately done—too literally losing or shirking essentials of Work in the above formula, and with these missing essentials of Folk and Place also.

Tabular and schematic presentments, however, such as those to which we are proceeding, are apt to be less simple and satisfactory to reader than to writer; and this even when in oral exposition the very same diagram has been not only welcomed as clear, but seen and felt to be convincing. The reason of this difficulty is that with the spoken exposition the audience sees the diagram grow upon the blackboard; whereas to produce anything of the same effect upon the page, it must be printed at several successive stages of development. Thus our initial formula,

PLACE - - - - - WORK - - - - - FOLK

readily develops into

		FOLK
PLACE-WORK	**WORK**	FOLK-WORK
(Natural advantages)		(Occupation)
PLACE		

This again naturally develops into a regular table, of which the filling up of some of the squares has been already suggested above, and that of the remaining ones will be intelligible on inspection :—

PLACE FOLK ("Natives")	WORK-FOLK ("Producers")	FOLK
PLACE-WORK	WORK	FOLK-WORK
PLACE	WORK-PLACE	FOLK-PLACE

So complex is the idea of even the simplest Town—even in such a rustic germ as the "farm-town" of modern Scottish parlance, the *ton* of place-names without number.

The varying development of the Folk into social classes or castes might next be traced, and the influence and inter-action of all the various factors of Place, Work, and Family tabulated. Suffice it here, however, for the present to note that such differentiation does take place, without entering into the classification and comparison of the protean types of patrician and plebeian throughout geography and history.

G.—ANALYSIS CONTINUED.—(2) THE SCHOOL.

Once and again we have noted how from the everyday life of action—the Town proper of our terminology—there arises the corresponding subjective world—the *Schools* of thought, which may express itself sooner or later in schools of education. The types of people, their kinds and styles of work, their whole environment, all become represented in the mind of the community, and these react upon the individuals, their activities, their place itself. Thus (the more plainly the more the community is a simple and an isolated one, but in appreciable measure everywhere and continually) there have obviously arisen local turns of thought and modes of speech, ranging from shades of accent and idiom to distinctive dialect or language. Similarly, there is a characteristic variety of occupational activity, a style of workmanship, a way of doing business. There are distinctive

AS CONCRETE AND APPLIED SOCIOLOGY   73

manners and customs—there is, in short, a certain recognisable likeness, it may be an indefinably subtle or an unmistakably broad and general one, which may be traced in faces and costumes, in tongue and literature, in courtesy and in conflict, in business and in policy, in street and in house, from hovel to palace, from prison to cathedral. Thus it is that every folk comes to have its own ways, and every town its own school.

While the complex social medium has thus been acquiring its characteristic form and composition, a younger generation has been arising. In all ways and senses, Heredity is commonly more marked than variation—especially when, as in most places at most times, such great racial, occupational, environmental transformations occur as those of modern cities. In other words, the young folk present not only an individual continuity with their organic predecessors which is heredity proper, but with their social predecessors also. The elements of organic continuity, which we usually think of first of all as organic, though of course psychic also, are conveniently distinguished as the *inheritance*—a term in fact which the biologist seeks to deprive of its common economic and social senses altogether, leaving for these the term *heritage*, material or immaterial alike. This necessary distinction between the inheritance, bodily and mental, and the heritage, economic and social, obviously next requires further elaboration, and with this further precision of language also. For the present, let us leave the term heritage to the economist for the material wealth with which he is primarily concerned, and employ the term *tradition* for these immaterial and distinctively social elements we are here specially considering. This in fact is no new proposal, but really little more than an acceptance of ordinary usage. Broadly speaking, tradition is in the life of the community what memory is for its individual units. The younger generation, then, not only inherits an organic and a psychic diathesis; not only has transmitted to it the accumulations, instruments and land of its predecessors, but grows up in their tradition also. The importance of imitation in this process, a matter of common experience, has been given the fullest sociological prominence, by M. Tarde especially.*
Thanks to these and other convergent lines of thought, we no longer consent to look at the acquirement of the social tradition as a matter requiring to be imposed upon reluctant youth almost entirely from without, and are learning anew as of old, with the simplest and the most developed peoples, the barbarians and the Greeks, to recognise and respect, and, if it may be, to nourish the process of self-instruction, viewed as normal accompaniment of each developing being throughout the phases of its

---

* Tarde, "L'Imitation Sociale," and other works.

organic life, the stages of its social life. Upon the many intermediate
degrees of advance and decline, however, between these two extremes of
civilisation, specific institutions for the instruction of youth arise, each in
some way an artificial substitute, or at least a would-be accelerant, for
the apprenticeship of imitation in the school of experience and the community's tradition, which we term a school in the restricted and pedagogic
sense. This whole discussion, however, has been in order to explain and
to justify the present use of the term "School" in that wide sense in
which the historian of art or thought—the sociologist, in fact—has ever
used the term, while yet covering the specialised pedagogic schools of all
kinds also.

Once more, then, and in the fullest sense, every folk has its own
tradition, every town its school.

We need not here discriminate these unique and characteristic elements to which the art-historians—say of Venice and
of Florence, of Barbizon or Glasgow—specially attend, from
those most widely distributed ones, in which the traditions
and schools of all towns within the same civilisation broadly
agree. Indeed, even the most widely distributed of these—say
from Roman law to modern antiseptic surgery—arose as local
schools before they became general ones.

Similarly for the general social tradition. The fundamental occupations and their division of labour, their differentiation in detail and their various interactions up to our
own day, at first separately considered, are now seen to be
closely correlated with the status of woman; while all these
factors determine not only the mode of union of the parents,
but their relation to the children, the constitution of the
family, with which the mode of transmission of property is
again thoroughly interwoven.

H.—TOWN AND SCHOOL COMPARED.

We may now summarise and tabulate our comparison
of Town and School,* and on the schema (p. 75) it will be seen

---

* For the sake of brevity, an entire chapter has been omitted, discussing the manifold
origins of distinct governing classes, whether arising from the Folk, or superimposed upon them
from without, in short, of that contrast of what we may broadly call patricians and plebeians,
which so constantly appears through history, and in the present also. These modes of origin are

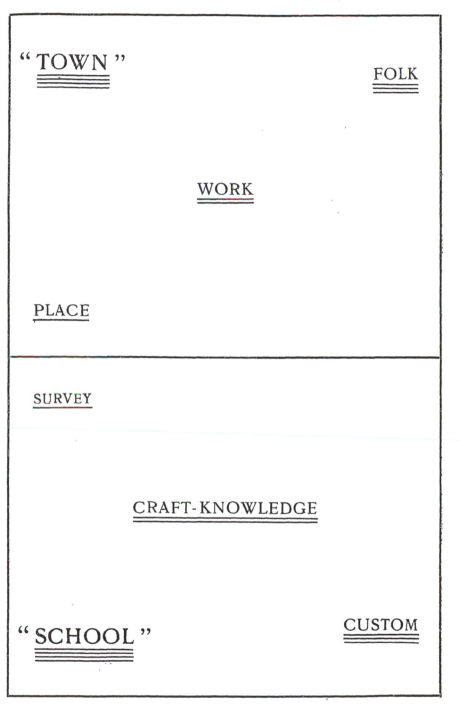

"**TOWN**"   FOLK

WORK

PLACE

SURVEY

CRAFT-KNOWLEDGE

"**SCHOOL**"   CUSTOM

that each element of the second is printed in the position of a mirror-reflection of the first. This gives but the merest outline, which is ready, however, to be applied in various ways and filled up accordingly. A step towards this is made in the next and fuller version of the scheme (p. 77). It will be noted in this that the lower portion of the diagram, that of School, is more fully filled up than is the upper. This is partly for clearness, but partly also to suggest that main elements in the origins of natural sciences and geography, of economics and . social science, are not always so clearly realised as they might be. The preceding diagram, elaborating that of Place, Work, Folk (p. 75), however, at once suggests these. Other features of the scheme will appear on inspection; and the reader will find it of interest and suggestiveness to prepare a blank schedule and fill it up for himself.

These two forms of the same diagram, the simple and the more developed, thus suggest comparison with the scheme previously outlined, that of People, Affairs, Places (p. 68), and is now more easily reconciled with this; the greater prominence popularly given to People and Affairs being expressed upon the present geographic and evolutionary scheme by the ascending position and more emphatic printing (or by viewing the diagram as a transparency from the opposite side of the leaf).

In the column of People, the deepening of custom into morals is indicated. Emphasis is also placed upon the development of law in connection with the rise of governing classes, and its tendency to dominate the standards previously taken as morals—in fact, that tendency of moral law to become static law, a process of which history is full.

In the present as in the past, we may also note upon the scheme the different lines of Place, Work and Folk on which respectively develop the natural sciences, the applied or

---

all in association respectively with Place, Work, and Family, or some of the various interactions of these. Origin and situation, migration, individual or general, with its conflict of races, may .be indicated among the first group of factors; technical efficiency and its organising power among the second; individual qualities and family stocks among the third, as also military and administrative aptitude, and the institutional privileges which so readily arise from them. Nor need we here discuss the rise of institutions, so fully dealt with by sociological writers. Enough for the present then, if institutions and social classes be taken as we find them.

AS CONCRETE AND APPLIED SOCIOLOGY 77

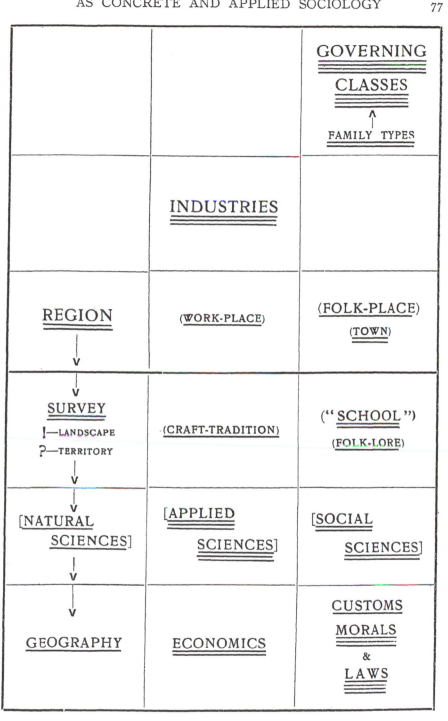

		GOVERNING CLASSES ^ FAMILY TYPES
	INDUSTRIES	
REGION v	(WORK-PLACE)	(FOLK-PLACE) (TOWN)
v SURVEY |—LANDSCAPE ?—TERRITORY v	(CRAFT-TRADITION)	("SCHOOL") (FOLK-LORE)
v [NATURAL SCIENCES] v	[APPLIED SCIENCES]	[SOCIAL SCIENCES]
v GEOGRAPHY	ECONOMICS	CUSTOMS MORALS & LAWS

technical sciences, and finally the social sciences, and the generalising of these respectively.

Thus, as we see the popular survey of regions, geography in its literal and initial sense, deepening into the various analyses of this and that aspect or element of the environment which we call the natural sciences—but which we might with advantage also recognise as what they really are, each a *geolysis*—so these sciences or geolyses, again, are tending to reunite into a higher geography considered as an account of the evolution of the cosmos.

Again, in the column of School, corresponding to Work, we have the evolution of craft knowledge into the applied sciences, an historic process which specialist men of science and their public are alike apt to overlook, but which is none the less vitally important. For we cannot really understand, say Pasteur, save primarily as a thinking peasant; or Lister and his antiseptic surgery better than as the shepherd, with his tar-box by his side; or Kelvin or any other electrician, as the thinking smith, and so on. The old story of geometry, as "*ars metrike*," and of its origin from land-surveying, for which the Egyptian hieroglyph is said to be that of "rope stretching," in fact, applies far more fully than most realise, and the history of every science, of course already thus partially written, will bear a far fuller application of this principle. In short, the self-taught man, who is ever the most fertile discoverer, is made in the true and fundamental school—that of experience.

The need of abbreviating the recapitulation of this, however, sooner or later develops the school in the pedagogic sense, and its many achievements, its many failures in accomplishing this, might here be more fully analysed.

Still more evident is this process in the column of Folk. From the mother's knee and the dame's school of the smallest folk-place, the townlet or hamlet, *ton* or home, up to the royal and priestly school of the law of ancient capitals, or from the "humanities" of a mediæval university to the "Ecole de Droit" of a modern metropolis, the series of essential evolutionary stages may be set down. Or in our everyday present,

AS CONCRETE AND APPLIED SOCIOLOGY 79

the rise of schools of all kinds, primary, secondary, higher, up to the current movement towards university colleges, and from these to civic and regional universities, might again be traced. The municipalisation of education is thus in fact expressed, and so on.

Leaving the schools in the main to speak for themselves of their advancing and incipient uses, a word may be said upon the present lines.

As a first and obvious application of this mode of geographic study of cities appears the criticism, and, when possible, the amendment of the city's plan; the monotonous rectangularity of the American city, and the petty irregularity more common in our own, being alike uneconomic and inartistic because ungeographic, irrational because irregional. With the improvement of communications, the physicist's point of view thus introduced—that of the economy of the energies of the community—is only beginning; the economy of fuel, the limitation of smoke and fogs being symptoms of this and pointing to a more economic organisation of industrial activities generally. But this next carries with it the improved efficiency of the producers themselves, with whom, however, the standpoint changes from the mere economisation of physical energies to the higher economy of organic evolution. The convention of traditional economics, that the productive capacity of the actual labourer is the sole concern of his science, thus gives place to what is at once the original conception of economics and the evolutionist one, viz., that the success of industry is ultimately measured neither by its return in wealth of the capitalist nor in money wages of the labourer, nor even by both put together, but in the results of industry upon the concrete environment, the family budget, the home, and the corresponding state of development of the family—its deterioration or progress. The organisation of industrial groups or of representative institutions found conducive to the well-being and progress of these prime civic units, the families, may now be traced into its highest outcome in city government. The method of analysis and graphic statement thus outlined may be shown to be even capable of useful application towards the statement of the best arguments of both progressive and moderate parties in city politics.

Passing from Politics to Culture, the needs of this also become clearer; each community developing a similar general series of culture institutions, from the simplest presentation of its geography, landscape and architecture, to the complex development of industrial, technical and scientific instruction; and for provision also for the institutions of custom and ethic in school, law, and church. Just as place, occupation, and family are intimately connected in the practical world, so their respective culture institutions must more and more be viewed as a whole. Civic improvers will find their ideals more realisable as they recognise the complex unity of the city as a social development of which all the departments of action and thought are in organic relation, be it of health or disease. The view of theoretic civics as concrete sociology, and of practical civics as applied sociology may be more simply expressed as the co-adjustment of social survey and social. service, now becoming recognised as rational, indeed in many cities being begun.

I.—DEVELOPMENT OF SCHOOL, AND ITS REACTION UPON TOWN.

The reactions of the School upon the Town are observed in practice to be of very different values;—how are these differences to be explained?

From the very first the school is essentially one of memory, the impress of the town-life, even at its best and highest individual quality and impressiveness, as in the work of a great master, the observation and memory of which may long give his stamp to the work of his followers. The fading of this into dulness, yet the fixing of it as a convention, is familiar to all in arts and crafts, but is no less real in the general lapse of appreciation of environment. Most serious of all is the fixation of habit and custom, so that at length "custom lies upon us with a weight heavy as death, and deep

AS CONCRETE AND APPLIED SOCIOLOGY 81

almost as life." This continual fixation of fashionable standards as moral ones is thus a prime explanation of each reformer's difficulty in making his moral standard the fashionable one, and also, when his doctrine has succeeded, of the loss of life and mummification of form which it so speedily undergoes.

Of conventional "education," considered as the memorisation of past records, however authoritative and classic, the decay is thus intelligible and plain, and the repetition of criticisms already adequately made need not therefore detain us here.

For this process is there no remedy? Science here offers herself— with senses open to observe, and intellect awake to interpret. Starting with Place, she explores and surveys it; from descriptive travel books at very various levels of accuracy, she works on to atlas and gazetteer, and beyond these to world-globe and "Geographie Universelle." With her charts and descriptions we are now more ready for a journey; with her maps and plans we may know our own place as never before; nay, rectify it, making the rough places plain and the crooked straight; even restoration may come within our powers.

Similarly as regards Work. Though mere empiric craft-mastery dies with the individual, and fails with his successors, may we not perpetuate the best of this? A museum of art treasures, a collection of the choicest examples of all times and lands, will surely raise us from our low level of mechanical toil; nay, with these carefully observed, copied, memorised, and duly examined upon, we shall be able to imitate them, to reproduce their excellencies, even to adapt them to our everyday work. To the art museum we have thus but to add a "School of Design," to have an output of more and less skilled copyists. The smooth and polished successes of this new dual institution, responding as they do to the mechanical elements of modern work and of the mechanical worker-mind, admitting also of ready multiplications as patterns, ensure the wide extension of the prevalent style of imitating past styles, designing patchwork of these; and even admit of its scientific reduction to a definite series of grades, which imitative youth may easily pass onwards from the age of rudest innocence to that of art-knowledge and certificated art-mastery. Our School of Design thus becomes a School of Art, at length a College, dominating the instruction of the nation, to the satisfaction not only of its promoters, but of the general public and their representatives, so that annual votes justly increase. Lurking discontent may now and then express itself, but is for practical purposes negligible.

The example of art accumulation and art instruction is thus natur-ally followed in other respects. For the commercial information of the public, varied representative exhibitions—primarily, therefore, international ones—naturally suggest themselves ; while so soon as expansion of imperial and colonial interests comes upon the first plane, a corresponding permanent Exhibition is naturally instituted. But when thus advancing commercial instruction, we must also recognise the claims of industry in all its crafts and guilds, and in fact the technical instruction of the community gener-ally. Hence the past, present, and promised rise of technical institutes upon increasing scales of completeness.

In the rise of such a truly encyclopædic system of schools, the university cannot permanently be forgotten. Since from the outset we have recognised the prime elements of the school in observation and memory, the testing of these by examinations—written, oral, and practical—however improvable in detail, must be fairly recognised, and the examining body or university has therefore to be adopted as the normal crown of our comprehensive educational system. Teaching, however, is found to be increasingly necessary, especially to examination ; and for this the main field left open is in our last column, that of People. Their lore of the past, whether of sacred or classical learning, their history, literature, and criticism, are already actively promoted, or at any rate adequately endowed at older seats of learning ; while the materials, resources, con-ditions and atmosphere are here of other kinds. Hence the accessibility of the new University of London to the study of sociology, as yet alone among its peers.

Hence, beside the great London, maritime, commercial and indus-trial, residential and governmental, there has been growing up, tardily indeed, as compared with smaller cities, yet now all the more massively and completely, a correspondingly comprehensive system of schools ; so that the historic development of South Kensington within the last half century, from International Exhibitions of Work, Natural History Museums of Place onwards to its present and its contemplated magnitude, affords a striking exemplification of the present view and its classification, which is all the more satisfactory since this development has been a gradual accretion.

Enough then has been said to show that the rise of schools, their qualities and their defects, are all capable of treatment upon the present lines ; but if so, may we not go farther, and ask by what means does thought and life cope with their defects, especially that fixation of memory, even at its best, that evil side of examination and the like, which we often call Chinese in the bad sense, but which we see arises so naturally everywhere ?

J.—FROM "SCHOOL" TO "CLOISTER."

The preceding view is, as yet, too purely determinist. The due place of ideals, individual and corporate, in their reaction upon the function and the structure of the city, and even upon its material environment, has next to be recognised. For where the town merely makes and fixes its industry and makes its corresponding schools, where its habits and customs become its laws, even its morality, the community, as we have just seen, sinks into routine, and therefore decay. To prevent this a twofold process of thought is ever necessary, critical and constructive. What are these? On the one hand, a continual and critical selection among the ideas derived from experience, and the formulation of these as Ideals; and further, the organisation of these into a larger and larger whole of thought; in fact, a Synthesis of a new kind. This critical spirit it is which produced the prophets of Israel, the questioning of Socrates, and so on, to the journalistic and other criticism of life to-day. The corresponding constructive endeavour is now no mere School of traditional learning or of useful information. It is one of science in a new and reorganised sense; one of philosophy also, one of ideals above all.

As from the Schools of the Law, as over against these, arise the prophets, so from the technical and applied sciences, the descriptive natural sciences, should arise the scientific thinkers, reinterpreting each his field of knowledge and giving us the pure sciences—pure geometry henceforth contrasted with mere land surveying, morphology with mere anatomy, and so on; while instead of the mere concrete encyclopædia from Pliny or Gesner to Diderot or Chambers, vast subjective reorganisations of knowledge, philosophic systems, now appear. Similarly, the mere observations of the senses and their records in memory become transformed into the images of the poet, the imagery too of the artist, for art proper is only thus born. That mere imitation of nature, which so commonly in the graphic arts (though happily but rarely in music) has been mistaken for art, thus modestly returns to its proper place—that of the iconography of descriptive science.

Thus from the Schools of all kinds of knowledge, past and present, we pass into the no less varied Cloisters of contemplation, meditation, imagination. With the historian we might explore the Cloisters of the past, built at one time from the current ideals of the Good, at another of the True, at another of the Beautiful; indeed, in widely varying measures and proportions, from all of these. How far each of these now expresses the present, how far it may yet serve the future, is obviously a question of questions, yet for that very reason one exceeding our present limits. Enough if in city life the historic place of what is here generalised under this antique name of Cloister be here recognised; and in some measure the actual need, the potential place be recognised also. Here is the need and use, beyond the fundamental claims of the material life of the Town, and the everyday sanity of the Schools, with all their observations and information, their commonsense and experience, their customs and conventions, even their morals and their law, for a deeper ethical insight than any rule or precedent can afford, for a fuller and freer intellectual outlook than that which has been derived from any technical experience or empiric skill, for an imagery which is no mere review of the phantasmagoria of the senses. In our age of the multiplication and expansion of towns, of their enrichment and their impoverishment, of the multiplication and enrichment of schools also, it is well for the sociologist to read from history, as he then may more fully see also around him that it is ever some fresh combination of these threefold products of the Cloister— ideal, theory, and imagery—emotional, intellectual, sensuous —which transforms the thought-world of its time.

The philosopher of old in his academic grove, his porch, the mediæval monk within his studious cloister's pale, are thus more akin ·to the modern scientific thinker than he commonly realises—perhaps because he is still, for the most part, of the solitary individualism of the hermit of the Thebaid, of Diogenes in his tub. Assuredly, they are less removed in essential psychology than their derived fraternities, their respective novices and scholars, have often thought. It is thus no mere play of language which hands on from the one to the other the "travail de Bénédictin;" though even here the phrase is inadequate, savouring too much of the school, into which each cloister of every sort declines sooner or later, unless even worse befall.

The decay of the cloister, though thus on the one hand into and with the school, may also take place within itself, since imagination and ideal may be evil, and theory false. That examples of all these decays abound in the history of religion, of philosophy, of art also, is a commonplace needing no illustration. Nor should the modern investigator think his science or himself immune to the same or kindred germs in turn.

K.—THE CITY PROPER.

Now, "at long last," we are ready to enter the city proper. This is not merely the Town of place and work and folk, even were this at their economic best. It is not enough to add the School, even at its completest; nor the cloister, though with this a yet greater step towards the city proper is made. For though this is not itself the City, its ideals of human relations, its theory of the universe and man, its artistic expression and portrayal of all these, ever sooner or later react upon the general view and conduct of life. Hence the Academe of Plato and the Lyceum of Aristotle, the mediæval cloister and the modern Research Institute, have been so fertile, so creative in their influence upon the city's life, from which they seemed to be retired. Hence it is ever some new combination of the threefold product of the cloister—ideal, idea, and image—which transforms the world, which opens each new epoch. Each new revelation and vision, each system of thought, each new outburst of poetry and song, has moved the men of its age by no mere mechanical pressure of economic need or external force, by no mere scholastic instruction, but in a far subtler way, and into new and unexpected groupings, as the sand upon Chladon's vibrating plate leaps into a new figure with each thrill of the violinist's bow.

Instead of simply developing our morals from custom, and therefore codifying them into law as in the school, they are now boldly criticised, as in part if not in whole, hindrances to a better state of things. As this becomes more and more clearly formulated as an ideal, its ethic transcendence of convention and law not only becomes clear, but the desire for its realisation becomes expressed. This may be with all degrees of clearness of reason and vividness of imagery, yet may remain long or altogether in the plane of literature, as has Plato's Republic or More's Utopia—standard and characteristic types of the cloister library as we may call it, one of inestimable value to the world in the past, and perhaps in our time needed as much as ever to help us to see somewhat beyond the output of the busy presses of town and school. Yet our ideal, our "Civitas Dei," "Civitas Solis," need not remain unrealised: it may be not only seriously planned towards realisation, as was Platonopolis of old, but bravely founded, as has been done in cases without number, from the ancient world to modern communities, by no means wholly unsuccessful. Though in our great industrial towns, our long settled regions, such new departures seem less easy, the principle remains valid—that it is in our ideal of polity and citizenship, and in our power of realising this, that the city proper has its conception and its birth. Again, instead of simply deriving our thought from experience, we now project our clarified thought into action and into education; so that from cloister of philosophy, and from its long novitiate of silence, there grows up the brotherhood of culture, the culture-city itself. Similarly in art, we no longer imitate nature, nor copy traditional designs. Art proper appears, shaping bronze and marble into images of the gods, and on a burnt and ruined hill-fort renewing the Parthenon. In general terms, instead of simply adjusting, as in the school, our mental picture to the outward facts, we reverse the process; and with a new art conception, be it good or bad, we transform the outward world, like wax under the seal. Thus from the

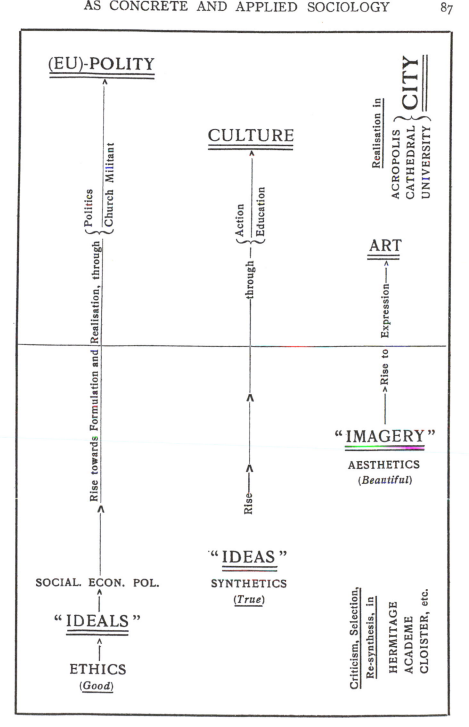

cloister and chapel of the musician, the studio-cell of the artist, the scriptorium of the poet, comes forth the architect, remodelling the city around his supreme material expression and home of its moral and material reorganisation, its renewed temporal and spiritual powers. Of this, the city proper, the Acropolis of Athens, the Temple of Jerusalem, the Capitol and Forum of Rome are classic and central examples, and in the mediæval city, pre-eminently the cathedral; though beside this we must not forget the town house and its belfry, the guild houses, the colleges, the great place, the fountains, the city cross, and if last, still best if good at all, the streets and courts and homes. Returning once more to the history of educational development, we have here a means of unravelling the apparently perplexing history of universities. For the university past or present has but its foundations in the school, with its local and its general tradition, whatever may be the accordance of these with well-ascertained fact, its true novitiate can only be afforded in the cloister of reflection and research, of interpretation and synthesis; while for its full development it needs the perpetual renewal of that generous social life—that inspiring intercourse "of picked adolescents and picked senescents"—which has marked the vital periods of every university worthy of the name.

In summary then, to the town has been added the school, with its advantages, its increasingly obvious limitations also, which it is for the cloister to remedy—even the advantages of the barrack finding a main element of its claim in this no less than in its professed training as regards citizenship. But here also it is for few to remain; albeit free for each to return at will. Ideals, to survive, must surely live, that is, be realised; hence for full life one needs "to meditate with the free solitary; yet to live secular, and serve mankind."

L.—THE CITY COMPLETED: TOWN, SCHOOL, CLOISTER, AND CITY PROPER.

In course of this fourfold analysis, it is plain that we have reached the very converse—or at all events the comple-

CITY	ART	IMAGERY	CLOISTER
CULTURE		IDEAS	
POLITY		SOC. ECON. IDEALS ETHICS	
FOLK		MORALS LAW	
WORK		KNOWLEDGE	
TOWN	PLACE	SURVEY	SCHOOL

ment—of that geographical determinism with which we started, and that we have returned to a view corresponding to the popular one (of " People, Affairs, Places," p. 69), which we then set aside for the reasons given. The "great man theory" of history, at best less crudely stated, thus reappears ; in short, to the initial thesis we have now the distinct antithesis. It is time, therefore, to bring these together towards the needed synthesis. Hence to the page (p. 77) on which was summarised the determinist view of Town and School, we now require the complemental statement upon page (p. 87) of Cloister and City proper. Nor must we be content, with too many controversialists hitherto, to keep in view only one at a time ; but by folding back the pages of print between these two half-schemes, as the book lies open, to take in both together.

We may thus finally compress the essentials of this whole paper into a simple formula—

TOWN			CITY
	FOLK	POLITY	
WORK			CULTURE
PLACE			ART
LORE			IMAGERY
LEAR		IDEA	
	LOVE	DEAL	
SCHOOL			CLOISTER

or most briefly—

TOWN	CITY
SCHOOL	CLOISTER

—noting in every case the opposite direction of the arrows. The application of this formula to different types of town, such as those already indicated in the former instalment of this paper (Vol. I., p. 107) or in the present one, will not be found to present any insuperable difficulty. It must, however, be kept clearly in view that the city of each day and generation subsides or decays more or less completely into the mere town anew, as the cloister into the schools. The towns and cities of the world are thus classifiable in terms of their past development and present condition.

SUMMARY.

Condensing now this lengthy, yet compressed and abbreviated series of analyses into a single page of summary, we may briefly define the main aspects and departments of civics from the present point of view. First then, comes the study of civics as fundamentally (and ever anew) an orderly development—at once geographic, economic, and anthropologic in its nature—a survey of place, work, and folk ; and these not merely or mainly as broken up into the fine dust of censuses and statistics, nor even of the three too separate sciences above named, but as a living unity, the human hive, the Town.

Corresponding to this objective and organic life we reorganise its fundamental subjective life. This is fundamentally, and ever partially, the record and reflex of the life of the hive, the Town ; of all its general and particular environment and function, its family type and development ; and, however overlaid by imported culture or by decayed ideals, it is fundamentally expressed in local knowledge, in craft tradition, in kinship and its associated kindness, in habits and customs, and their developments up to morals and law. Simple terms corresponding to place, work, and folk, are hard to find ; say, however, till better be suggested, that in close relation to the maternal arms in which general social thought and its utmost pedagogic developments alike begin, it is place-lore, work-lear, and folk-love, which are the essentials of every

92   CIVICS:

School.[*]   That existing educational machineries may not adequately recognise these is not of course the question here.

These three terms, lore, lear, and love are thus well related to their respectively deepening levels of sense, intelligence and feeling; and their respective relation is thus more plain to the imagery, the theory, and the idealism above defined as the essentials of the Cloister. The psychology of the processes of poetic, philosophic and spiritual awakening and renewal is in these days being approached anew, both from the individual and social side, but cannot here be entered upon.

Finally and supremely arises the City proper—its individuality dependent upon the measure and form in which ideals are expressed and harmonised in social life and polity, ideas synthetised in culture, and beauty carried outwards from the study or chamber of the recluse into the world of art.

PRACTICAL CONCLUSION.

The investigation of the City thus tends towards the practice of citizenship. Thus social survey prepares for social service, as diagnosis towards treatment and hygiene; and these react fruitfully upon our knowledge and understanding anew. Beyond social observations, and the needed observatories for making them more adequately, we need social activities and the laboratories for preparing them, or at least the leavens of them; or, again, in happier phrase, at once simple and more synthetic, we need some shelter † into which to gather the best

---

[*] The use of *lore* as primarily empirical, and derived from the senses, is traditional; it is well therefore to restrict it to this, and to revive the old word *lear*, still understood in Scotland in these precise senses—intellectual, rational, yet traditional, occupational also.

† Without forgetting the many institutions and workers in almost all departments of the field of civics, the rise of definite surveys and of scientific groupings like this Society, without ignoring also the many admirable workers and institutions of social endeavour, and their progressive integration into Social Unions, Institutes of Service, and the like, I may be permitted to press for the need of uniting both types, the scientific and the practical, into a single one—a civic museum and active centre in one. Of this type, my own Outlook Tower at Edinburgh is, so far as I am aware, the earliest beginning; and, despite its rudimentary condition, may thus serve to suggest a type of institution which will be found of service alike to the sociologist and the citizen.

seed of past flowerings and in which to raise and tend the seedlings of coming summers. We need definitely to acquire such a centre of survey and service in each and every city—in a word, a Civicentre for sociologist and citizen.

M.—THE HISTORIC CITY-COMPLEX.

The criticism may have already arisen in the reader's mind that the "Town" and "School" of our analysis are by no means so simple as we have assumed them. Our surveys of antique towns ever disclose the material survivals, at least the vestiges, of the cloister or the acropolis of the past, of its cathedral or its forum. The processes of our industries, in what is now their daily artisan routine, include, repeat, condense what were yesterday or longer ago living inventions, each instinct with Promethean fire. The hackneyed ornament of our homes was once glowing with beauty, radiant or dark with symbolism. So it is for our everyday customs and institutions, and so for living languages; our own, perhaps, most of all. These, of course, are facts made familiar by investigators of all orders, from the scholar and antiquary of old, the historian and philologist of yesterday, to the geographer or the sociologist of our own time : witness Mr. Spencer's masterly treatment of their main results. How, then, shall we correlate this process of all things growing old with the analysis of cities above attempted? In other words, how shall we interpret the course of their historic evolution, their renewed growth and decay, progress and degeneracy, their present condition, crowded with residues of the past, with those potentialities which our outline discloses? This is the more necessary since this fourfold analysis applies in principle to all human groupings, from the simplest village to the Eternal City. To this, indeed, we have in principle already traced it, onwards from our primitive valley-section with its humble hamlets, its fundamental occupations.

Returning then to our main diagram, with its four-fold analysis of the City, so soon as we have completed this, and carried its progress up to the level of city life proper, we must next turn over the leaf and begin a new page, with place and work and folk once more. This simplest of acts expresses with graphic significance the very process of history; for in closing our diagram page its " Cloister " has been folded down on the "School," our cathedral and forum, our " City " proper, upon the " Town." Thus it is that the ideals and the achievements of one day and generation and city are ever melting away, and passing out of sight of the next; so that to the joy or sorrow of the successors the new page seems well nigh bare, though ever there comes faintly through some image or at least blurred suggestion of the fading past. Hence each page of history is a palimpsest. Hence our modern town, even when yesterday but prairie, was no mere vacant site, but was at once enriched and encumbered by the surviving traditions of the past; so that even its new buildings are for the most part but vacant shells of past art, of which now only the student cares to trace the objective annals, much less penetrate to the inner history. So for the decayed Renaissance learning of our schools, for the most part so literally dead since the "Grammarian's Funeral"; and so, too, for the unthinking routines, the dead customs and conventions, and largely too the laws and rituals of our urban lives. Hence, then, it is that for the arrest and the decay of cities we have no need to go for our examples to the ancient East. These processes, like those of individual senility and death, are going on everywhere day by day.

Upon the new page, then, it is but a complexer " Town " and "School" anew : we have no continuing City. This too commonly has existed at its best but for the rare generation which created it, or little longer; though its historic glories, like those of sunset and of after-glow, may long shed radiance and glamour upon its town, and linger in the world's memory long after not only these have faded, but their very folk have vanished, their walls fallen, nay their very site been buried or forgotten. Upon all these degrees of dying, all these faint and fading steps between immortality and oblivion, we may arrange what we call our historic cities. Obviously in the deeper and more living sense the city exists only in actualising itself; and thus to us it is that the ideal city lies ever in the future. Yet it is the very essence of this whole argument that an ideal city is latent in every town. Where shall we in these days find our cloistered retreats to think out such ideals as may be applicable in our time and circumstances: the needed kinetic ethics, the needed synthetic philosophy and science, the needed vision and imagery and expression of them all?

N.—THE EVILS OF THE CITY.

DISEASE, DEFECT, VICE AND CRIME.

I have spoken little of town evils, and much of town ideals, primarily for the reason that even to recognise, much less treat, the abnormal, we must know something of the normal course of evolution. Hence, the old and useful phrase by which physiology used to be known, that of " the institutes of medicine." Sociology has thus to become " the institutes of citizenship."

Often though philanthropists forget this, diagnosis should precede treatment. The evils of the city, by the very nature of our hypothesis, demand special survey, and this no less thoroughly than do the normal place and work and industry. It is only our most permanent intellectual impulse, that of seeking for unity, which excuses the cheap unitary explanations so often current; as, for instance, that social evils are mainly to be explained by intemperance, as for one school of reformers; by poverty or luxury, for a second and third; by Tammany or other form of party government, by socialism or by individualism for yet others; that they are due to dissent or to church, to ignorance or to the spread of science, and so on almost indefinitely—doubtless not without elements of truth in each!

Yet let me offer as yet another explanation of civic evils, this more general one—distinguished from the preceding by including them all and more—that not only is our "Town" in itself imperfect, but the other three elements we have been

characterising as school, cloister and city, are yet more imperfect, since disordered, decayed, or undeveloped anew. It is
because of each and all of these imperfect realisations of our
civic life, that the evils of life sink down, or flame out, into
these complex eruptions of social evils with which our human
aggregations are as yet cursed.

Hence, to those who are struggling with disease and
pain, with ignorance and defect, with vice, and with crime,
but for the most part too separately, it is time to say that all
these four evils are capable of being viewed together, and
largely even treated together. They are not unrelated, but
correspond each as the negative to that fourfold presentment
of ideals we have hitherto been raising. To this ideal unity
of healthy town, with its practical and scientific schools of
all kinds, with its meditative cloister of ethical and social
idealism, of unified science and philosophy, of imagination and
drama, all culminating in the polity, culture, and art which
make a city proper, we have here the corresponding defects
in detail.

The evils of existing city life are thus largely re-
interpreted; and if so more efficiently combated; since the
poverty, squalor and ugliness of our cities, their disease and
their intemperance, their ignorance, dulness and mental defect,
their vice and crime are thus capable not only of separate
treatment but of an increasingly unified civic hygiene, and
this in the widest sense, material and moral, economic and
idealist, utilitarian and artistic. Even the most earnest and
capable workers towards civic betterment in these many fields
may gain at once in hope and in efficiency as they see their
special interests and tasks converging into the conception of
the city as an organic unity, and this not fixed and settled,
nor even in process of progress or degeneration from causes
beyond our ken, but as an orderly development which we may
aid towards higher perfection, geographic and cultural alike.

Our modern town is thus in a very real sense, one not
hopeless, but as hopeful as may be, a veritable purgatory; that
is a struggle of lower and higher idealisms, amid the respective
expressions and outcomes of these. Indeed, in our own present

cities, as they have come to be, is not each of us ever finding his own Inferno, or it may be his Paradise? Does he not see the dark fate of some, the striving and rising hope of others, the redemption also?

The supreme poetic utterance of the mediæval world is thus in great measure, as each thoughtful reader sees, an expression of impassioned citizenship, and this at one of the golden moments of the long history of city life. This expression—this exiled citizen's autobiographic thought-stream— is resumed at every level, from youthful home and local colour, from boyish love and hopes, from active citizenship and party struggle, to the transfiguration of all these. Hence these mystic visions, and these world ambitions, temporal and spiritual; hence this rise from cloistered faith and philosophy into many-sided culture; hence the transformation of all these, through intensest symbol-visions into enduring song.

Am I thus suggesting the *Divina Comedia* as a guide-book to cities? Without doubt, though not necessarily for beginners. Yet who can see Florence without this, though we may pack below it Baedeker and Murray? Or who, that can really read, can open a volume of Mr. Booth's severely statistical Survey of London, with all its studious reserve, its scientific repression, without seeing between its lines the Dantean circles; happy if he can sometimes read them upward as well as down?

O.—A CIVIC SYMBOL AND ITS MEANING.

But such books of the city, whether of the new and observant type, from Baedeker to Booth, or of the old and interpretative Dantean one, are too vast and varied to keep open before us. Even the preceding open page of diagram is complex enough with its two-fold, indeed four-fold city; and we are called back to our daily work in the first of these divisions, that of the everyday town. Since its subjective aspects of school and cloister may fade from memory, its higher aspect also, that of city proper, how can we retain this four-fold analysis, and how test if it be true? Take then one final illustration; this time no mere logical skeleton, however simple or graphic, but an image more easily retained, because a concrete and artistic one, and moreover in terms of that form of life-labour and thought-notation—that of current coin— which, in our day especially, dominates this vastest of cities; and hence inherits for the region of its home and centre— "the Bank," which has so thoroughly taken precedence of the town-house and cathedral, of the fortress and palace—the honoured name of "City." The coinages of each time and place combine concrete and social use with statements of historic facts; and they add to both of these a wealth of emblematic suggestions: but that is to say, they express not only their town, and something of its *school*, but much of its thought also, its *cloister* in my present terminology.

So before me lies an old "bawbee" of my own home city. On one side stands the hammerman at his anvil, below him the motto of his guild, *"Non marte sed arte."* Here then the industrial "Town" and its "School" express themselves plainly enough, and precisely as they have been above defined. But on the other side spreads the imperial double eagle; since Perth *(Bertha aurea)* had been the northmost of all Rome's provincial capitals, her re-named ".Victoria" accordingly, as the mediæval herald must proudly have remembered, so strengthened his associations with the Holy Roman Empire with something of that vague and shadowy historic dignity which the Scot was wont to value so much, and vaunt so high. On the ·eagle's breast is a shield, tressured like the royal standard, since Perth was the national capital until the "King's Tragedy" of 1457; but instead of the ruddy lion the shield bears the lamb with the banner of St. John, the city's saint. This side, too, has its motto, and one befitting an old capital of King and Commons, both in continual strife with the feudal nobles, *"Pro Rege, Lege, et Grege."* Here then, plain upon this apparent arbitrarily devised trifle, this petty provincial money-token, this poor bawbee, that is, this coin not only of the very humblest order, but proverbially sordid at that, we find clearly set down, long generations ago, the whole

AS CONCRETE AND APPLIED SOCIOLOGY   99

four-fold analysis and synthesis of civic life we have been above labouring for. For what makes the industrial Town, what can better keep it than strenuous industry at its anvil ? How better express its craft school, its local style and skill, its reaction too upon the town's life in peace and war, than by this Hal o' the Wynd by his forge ? Nay, what better symbol than this hammer, this primitive tool and ever typical one, of the peaceful education of experience, from Prometheus to Kelvin, of the warlike, from Thor to modern cannon-forge ? Turning now from Town and School to Cloister, to the life of secluded peace and meditation—from which, however, the practical issues of life are ever renewed—what plainer symbol, yet what more historic or more mystic one can we ask than this of the lamb with the banner ? While of the contrasted yet complemental civic life of fullest, broadest action, what expression like the Roman eagle—the very eyes of keenness, and the spreading wings of power ?

So rarely perfect then is this civic symbol, that I must not omit to mention that it has only come to my notice since the body of this paper, with its four-fold analysis of cities as above outlined, was essentially finished. Since it thus has not in any particular suggested the treatment of cities here advocated, it is the more interesting and encouraging as a confirmation of it. It is also to my mind plain that in this, as in many other of our apparent "advances in science," and doubtless those in social studies particularly, we are but learning to think things anew, long after our forefathers have lived them, even expressed them—and these in their ways no less clear and popular than can ever be ours. That we may also again live them is once more curiously expressed by the same symbol ; for its re-appearance is due to its having been appropriately revived, in a fitting art form, that of the commemorative and prize medal of the local arts and crafts exhibition, held in the new Public Library, under civic auspices. Little scrutiny of this last sentence will be needed to see the four-fold completeness of the civic event which it describes.

For just as we have seen on the old coin the hammer-

CIVICS :

man and his motto answer to the town and school; so now on its reissue do the renascent local arts and crafts, with their commemoration in this library. And as the greater motto, that of widest policy, corresponds to the cloister of reflection and resolve, so we note that this new impulse to civic betterment is associated with the new library—no mere school-house of memory, but also the open cloister of our day. Finally, note that this impulse is no longer merely one of æsthetic purpose, of "art for art's sake," nor its execution that of a cultured minority merely ; it announces a re-union of this culture and art with the civic polity. What fitter occasion, then, for the striking of a medal, than this renewal of civic life, with municipal organisation and polity, art and culture, renascent in unison. That such events are nowadays far from exceptional is so true that we are in danger of losing sight of their significance. Yet it is amid such city developments that the future Pericles must arise.

We thus see that our analysis is no mere structural one, made post-mortem from civic history ; but that it applies to the modern functioning of everyday life in an everyday city, so soon as this becomes touched anew towards cultural issues. Furthermore, it is thus plain that civic life not only has long ago anticipated and embodied our theories of it, but once more outruns them, expressing them far better than in words—in life and practice. In this way the reader who may most resent these unfamiliar methods of exposition, alternately by abstract diagram or concrete illustration—which may seem to him too remote from ordinary life and experience, perhaps too trivial—may now test the present theory of the city, or amend it, by means of the ample illustrations of the processes and results of social life which are provided by his daily newspaper, and these on well-nigh all its fields and levels.

Note finally that it is the eagle and lamb of temporal and spiritual idealism that form the "head" of this coin, the craftsman and anvil but the modest "tail." The application is obvious.

Thus even numismatics revives from amid the fossil

sciences. For from this to our own common coinage, or notably to that of France, America, Switzerland, etc., the transition is easy, and still better to that of the noblest civic past, both classic and mediæval. Without pursuing this further here, my present point is gained, if we see, even in the everyday local details of work and people, the enduring stamp, the inextinguishable promise, of the flowering of our everyday industries and schools into worthier ideals than they at present express, and of the fruition of these in turn upon nobler heights of life and practice. It expresses the essential truth of the popular view of the city; that in terms of the formula—People . . . . . Affairs . . . . . Places—above referred to (page 69). It also explains the persistent vitality of this view, despite its frequent crudity, and lack of order in detail, in face of the more scientific treatment here at first employed, that in the elementary geographic order—Place . . . . Work . . . . People. For though this objective order be fundamental, it is the complementary subjective evolution which throughout history has ever become supreme; so that our scheme must combine the outward geographic presentment with the inward psychological one. This may be graphically expressed by changing the order of presentment from that used hitherto :—

Town	City		City	Town
School	Cloister	to	Cloister	School

P.—FORECAST OF CITY DEVELOPMENT. SPECIAL AND GENERAL.

The dual and four-fold development of the city, as above sketched, is by no means far advanced in most of our present towns or cities, which have obviously but scanty expression of the ideas shadowed forth for the modern equivalents of cloister and cathedral, of academe and acropolis. But this is to say that such towns, however large, populous, and rich according to conventional economic standards, are to that extent small and poor, indeed too often little better than cities by courtesy. Yet their further development, upon this

four-fold view of civic evolution, though in principle the same
for each and all, has always been, and let us hope may always
be, in large measure an individual (because regional) one. For
if each human individuality be unique, how much more must
that of every city?

In one concrete case, that of Dunfermline, I have already
submitted definite suggestions towards the realisation of the
civic Utopia, and even architectural designs towards its execution,* so that these may at any rate suffice to show how local
study and adaptive design are needed for each individual city,
indeed for every point of it. It is thus, and thus only, that we
can hope to have a city development truly evolutionary, that is,
one utilising the local features, advantages, and possibilities
of place, occupation, and people. Of course, it is needful to
supplement these by the example of other cities; but it is no
less needful to avoid weighting down the local life with replicas
of institutions, however excellent elsewhere, if really irregional
here. With the re-awakening of regional life in our various
centres, and of some comprehension of its conditions among
our rulers, they will cease to establish, say, a school of mines
in Piccadilly, or again one of engineering and the like in
South Kensington. The magistrates of Edinburgh have long
abandoned their old attempt to plant mulberries and naturalise
silk culture upon their wind-swept Calton Hill; albeit this
was a comparatively rational endeavour, since a population of
Huguenot refugee silk-weavers had actually come upon their
hands.

Similarly, it is plain that we must develop Oxford as
Oxford, Edinburgh as Edinburgh, and so on with all other
cities, great or small—York or Winchester, Westminster or
London. And so with Chelsea or Hampstead, with Woolwich
or Battersea. Has not the last of these grown from a mere
outlying vestry, like so many others, into a centre of genuine
vitality and interior progress, indeed of ever-widening interest
and example; and all this in half a generation, apparently
through the sagacious leadership—say, rather the devoted, the

---

* Cf. the writer's "City Development," Edinburgh and Westminster, 1904.

AS CONCRETE AND APPLIED SOCIOLOGY   103

impassioned citizenship—of a single man ? And does not his popular park at times come near giving us a vital indication of the needed modern analogue of cathedral and forum ? Civic development is thus no mere external matter, either of " Hauss-mannising " its streets, or of machine-educating its people ; the true progress of the city and its citizenship must alike grow and flower from within, albeit alive and open to every truly fertilising impulse from without.

Yet since national interests, international industry, commerce, science, and therefore progress are nowadays and increasingly so largely one, may we not in conclusion foresee something at least of the great lines of development which are common to cities, and generalise these as we are accustomed to do in history ? Witness the Classical, Mediæval, and Renaissance types to which historic cities preponderatingly belong, and within which we group their varied individualities, as after all of comparative detail.

Here then it is time to recall the presentment of ancient, recent and contemporary evolution already outlined in the part of this paper previously read (Vol. I, p. 109), dealing with the historic survey of cities. We have now to face the question, then postponed, indeed left in interrogation-marks—that of seeking not indeed sharply to define the future order of things, yet in some measure to discern such elements of progress as may be already incipient in the existing order, if not yet largely manifest there. Such elements may be reasonably expected to grow in the near future, perhaps increasingly, and whatever be their rate of growth are surely worthy of our attention.

Contemporary science, with its retrospective inquiries into origins in the past, its everyday observation of the present, is apt practically to overlook that the highest criterion and achievement of science is not to decipher the past, nor record the present, not even to interpret both. It is to foresee : only thus can it subserve action, of which the present task ever lies towards the future, since it is for this that we have to provide. Why then should not Comte's famous aphorism—" *Voir pour prévoir, prévoir pour pourvoir,*" become applicable in our civic studies no less than in the general social and political fields to which he applied it? In navigation or engineering, in agriculture or hygiene, prevision and provision alike are ever increasing; yet these are no mere combinations of the preliminary sciences and the fundamental occupations, but obviously contain very large social elements.

It is proverbially safe to prophesy when one knows; and it is but this safe prediction which we make every day of child or bud, where we can hardly fail to see the growing man, the coming flower. Yet do not most people practically forget that even now, in mid-winter, next summer's leaves are already waiting, nay, that they were conceived nine months ago? That they thus grow in small, commonly unnoticed beginnings, and lie in bud for a period twice as long as the summer of their adult and manifest life, is yet a fact, and one to which the social analogies are many and worth considering.

While recognising, then, the immense importance of the historic elements of our heritage, renaissance and mediæval, classic and earlier; recognising also the predominance of contemporary forces and ideas, industrial and liberal, imperial and bureaucratic, financial and journalistic, can we not seek also, hidden under all these leaves, for those of the still-but-developing bud, which next season must be so much more important than they are to-day? It is a commonplace, yet mainly of educational meetings, to note that the next generation is now at school; but how seldom do we recognise its pioneers, albeit already among our own contemporaries? At any rate we may see here and there that their leaven is already at work.

In this respect, cities greatly differ—one is far more initiative than another. In the previous paper (vol. 1, p. 109), we saw how individuals, edifices, institutions, might represent all past phases; these, therefore, often predominate in different cities sufficiently to give its essential stamp. Why then should we not make a further survey and seek to see something of the cities of the future; though we may have to look for these in quarters where at first sight there may seem as yet scanty promise of flower?

To recall an instance employed above, probably every member of this Society is old enough to remember incredulous questionings of whether any good thing could come out of Battersea. Again, how few, even in America, much less than in Europe, a few years ago, foresaw the rapid growth of those culture-elements in St. Louis, of which the recent World-Exposition will not have been the only outcome?

Only a few years earlier, it was Chicago which, for New England no less than for the Old World, seemed but the byword of a hopelessly materialised community. So Birmingham or Glasgow has won its present high position among cities in comparatively recent times ; so it may now be the turn of older cities, once far more eminent, like Newcastle or Dundee, to overtake and in turn, perhaps, outstrip them. But all this is still too general and needs further definition : let us attempt this, therefore, somewhat more fully, in the concrete case of Glasgow.

Q.—GLASGOW AS TYPICAL OF CIVIC TRANSITION— FROM "PALEOTECHNIC" TO "NEOTECHNIC."

My own appreciation of the significance of Glasgow was first really awakened over twenty years ago by William Morris, who in his vivid way pointed out to me how, despite the traditional culture - superiority of Edinburgh, Glasgow was not only the Scottish capital, but, in his view, in real progressiveness the leading and initiative city of the whole United Kingdom. And this for him was not merely or mainly in its municipal enterprise, then merely in its infancy —although he expressed this development in the phrase "In London, people talked socialism without living it ; but in Glasgow, they were socialists without knowing it !" Despite all the ugliness which had so repelled Ruskin, the squalor which moved Matthew Arnold to the fiercest scorn in all his writings, Morris's appreciation arose from his craftsman's knowledge and respect for supreme craftsmanship. The great ships building upon the Clyde were for him "the greatest achievement of

humanity since the days of the cathedral-builders," nay, for
him actually surpassing these, since calling forth an even more
complex combination and "co-operation of all the material
arts and sciences" into a mighty and organic whole; and
correspondingly of all their respective workers also, this being
for him of the very essence of his social ideal.

For these reasons he insisted, to my then surprise, that
the social reorganisation he then so ardently hoped for "was
coming faster upon the Clyde than upon the Thames": he
explained as for him the one main reason for his then dis-
couragement as to the progress of London that there East and
West, North and South, are not only too remote each from the
other, but in their occupations all much too specialised—there
to finance, there to manufactures, or here to leisure, and so on;
while on the Clyde industrial organisation and social progress
could not but develop together, through the very nature of the
essential and working unity of the ship.

Since Morris's day, a local art movement, of which he
knew little, has risen to eminence, a foreign critic would say
to pre-eminence, in this country at least. Since Ruskin's
savage response to a Glasgow invitation to lecture—"first
burn your city, and cleanse your river,"—a new generation of
architects and hygienists have not a little transformed the one,
and vigorous measures have been taken towards the purifica-
tion of the other. That the city and university pre-eminently
associated with the invention of the steam-engine, and consequently with the advent of the industrial revolution throughout the world, should, a century later, have produced a scarcely
less pre-eminent leader of applied science towards the command of electricity is thus no isolated coincidence. And as
political economy, which is ever the theory corresponding to
our phase of industrial practice, had there some of its foremost
pioneers, and later its classical exponent, Adam Smith himself,
so once more there are signs at least of a corresponding wave
of theoretic progress.

Students of primitive civilisation and industry have
now long familiarised us with their reinterpretation of what
was long known as the stone age, into two very distinct

periods, the earlier characterised by few and rough implements, roughly used by a rude people; the second by more varied tools, of better shape, and finer edge, often of exquisite material and polish.   We know that these were wielded more skilfully, by a people of higher type, better bred and better nourished ; and that these, albeit of less hunting and militant life, but of pacific agricultural skill, prevailed in every way in the struggle for existence ; thanks thus not only to more advanced arts, but probably above all to the higher status of woman.   This distinction of Paleolithic and Neolithic ages and men, has long passed into the terminology of sociological science, and even into current speech : is it too much then, similarly, to focus the largely analogous progress which is so observable in what we have been wont to generalise too crudely as the modern Industrial Age ?   All are agreed that the discoveries and inventions of this extraordinary period of history constitute an epoch of material advance only paralleled, if at all, in magnitude and significance by those of prehistory with its shadowy Promethean figures.   Our own advance from a lower industrial civilisation towards a higher thus no less demands definite characterisation, and this may be broadly expressed as from an earlier or *Paleotechnic* phase, towards a later or more advanced *Neotechnic* one.   If definition be needed, this may be broadly given as from a comparatively crude and wasteful technic age, characterised by coal, steam, and cheap machine products, and a corresponding *quantitative* ideal of " progress of wealth and population "—towards a finer civilisation, characterised by the wider command, yet greater economy of natural energies, by the predominance of electricity, and by the increasing victory of an ideal of *qualitative* progress, expressed in terms of skill and art, of hygiene and of education, of social polity, etc.

This Neotechnic phase, though itself as yet far from completely replacing the paleotechnic order which is still quantitatively predominant in most of our cities, begins itself to show signs of a higher stage of progress, as in the co-ordination of the many industries required for the building of a ship, or in the yet more recent developments which begin to renew for us the conception of the worthy construction of a city.   As the former period may be characterised by the predominance of the relatively unskilled workman and of the skilled, so this next incipient age by the development of the chief workman proper, the literal *architectos* or architect ; and by his companion the rustic improver, gardener and forester, farmer, irrigator, and their correspondingly evolving types of civil engineer.

To this phase then the term *Geotechnic* may fairly be applied. Into its corresponding theoretic and ideal developments we need not here enter, beyond noting that these are similarly of synthetic character ; on the concrete side the sciences unifying as geography, and on their more abstract side as the classification and philosophy of the sciences,—while both abstract and concrete movements of thought are becoming more and more thoroughly evolutionary in character.

But evolutionary theories, especially as they rise towards comprehensiveness, cannot permanently content themselves with origins, or with classifications merely, nor with concentrating on nature rather than on man. Nature furnishes after all but the stage for evolution in its highest terms ; of this man himself is the hero ; so that thus our Geotechnic phase, Synthetic age (call it what we will) in its turn gives birth to a further advance—that concerned with human evolution, above all, subordinating all things to him ; whereas in all these preceding industrial phases, even if decreasingly, " things are in the saddle and ride mankind." This age, now definitely evolutionist in policy, as the geotechnic was in theory and in environment we may term the *Eugenic*. For its theory, still less advanced, the term *Eupsychic* may complete our proposed nomenclature.

Thus then our conception of the opening future may be increasingly defined, since all these apparently predicted phases are already incipient among us, and are thus really matters of observed fact, of social embryology let us say ; in short, of city development.

In summary, then, the diagram of the former instalment of this paper (vol. 1, p. 109)

ANCIENT			RECENT			CONTEMPORARY			INCIPIENT
Primitive	Matri- archal	Patri- archal	Greek and Roman	Mediæval	Renaissance	Revolution	Empire	Finance	? ? ?

AS CONCRETE AND APPLIED SOCIOLOGY 109

has thus its interrogations filled up. Omitting the left-hand half, that generalised as Ancient and Recent in the above diagram, so as to give more space to the Contemporary and Incipient phases, these now stand as follows :—

CONTEMPORARY			INCIPIENT		
Revolution	Empire	Finance	Neotechnic	Geotechnic	Eugenic

To elaborate this farther would, of course, exceed my present limits ; but I may be permitted to say that long use of this schematic outline, especially of course in more developed forms, has satisfied me of its usefulness alike in the study of current events and in the practical work of education and city betterment. I venture then to recommend it to others as worth trial.

R.—A PRACTICAL PROPOSAL—A CIVIC EXHIBITION.

How shall we more fully correlate our theoretic civics, *i.e.*, our observations of cities interpreted as above, with our moral ideas and our practical policy—*i.e.*, our Applied Civics. Our ideals have to be selected, our ideas defined, our plans matured ; and the whole of these applied ; that is realised, in polity, in culture, and in art. But if this be indeed the due correlation of civic survey and civic service, how may we now best promote the diffusion and the advancement of both ? At this stage therefore, I venture to submit to the Society a practical proposal for its consideration and discussion ; and if approved, I would fain hope for its recommendation to towns and cities, to organisations and to the public likely to be interested.

Here then is my proposal. Is not the time ripe for bringing together the movements of Civics and Eugenics, now here and indeed everywhere plainly nascent, and of setting these before the public of this country in some such large and concrete ways, as indeed, in the latter subject at least, have been so strongly desiderated by Mr. Galton ? As regards Civics, such have been afforded to America during the summer of 1904 by the Municipal Section of the St. Louis Exhibition ; in

Dresden also, at the recent Towns Exhibition ; and by kindred Exhibitions and Congresses in Paris and elsewhere.

All these have taken form since the Paris Exposition of 1900, with its important section of social economy and its many relevant special congresses. Among these may be specially mentioned here as of popular interest, and civic stimulus, the *Congrès de L'Art Public* ; the more since this also held an important Exhibition, to which many Continental cities sent instructive exhibits.

Other exhibitions might be mentioned ; so that the fact appears that in well-nigh every important and progressive country, save our own, the great questions of civics have already been fully opened, and vividly brought before their public, by these great contemporary museums with their associated congresses.

With our present Chairman, the Rt. Hon. Charles Booth, with Canon Barnett, Mr. Horsfall, and so many other eminent civic workers among us ; with our committee and its most organising of secretaries, might not a real impulse be given in this way by this Society towards civic education and action?

Let me furthermore recall the two facts ; first, that in every important exhibition which has been held in this country or abroad, no exhibits have been more instructive and more popular than have been (1) the picturesque reconstructions of ancient cities, and the presentment of their city life, and (2) the corresponding surveys of the present conditions of town life, and of the resources and means of bettering them.

Even as a show then, I venture to submit that such a " Towneries " might readily be arranged to excel in interest, and surpass in usefulness, the excellent " Fisheries," " Healtheries," and other successful exhibitions in the record and recent memory of London. The advantages of such an exhibition are indeed too numerous for even an outline here ; but they may be easily thought out more and more fully. Indeed, I purposely abstain for the present from more concrete suggestion ; for the discussion of its elements, methods, plans, and scale will be found to raise the whole range of civic questions, and to set these in freshening lights.

AS CONCRETE AND APPLIED SOCIOLOGY   III

At this time of social transition, when we all more or less feel the melting away of old divisions and parties, of old barriers of sects and schools, and the emergence of new possibilities, the continual appearance of new groupings of thought and action, such a Civic Exhibition would surely be specially valuable. In the interest, then, of the incipient renascence of civic progress, I plead for a Civic Exhibition.*

Of such an exhibition, the very catalogue would be in principle that *Encyclopædia Civica*, into which, in the previous instalment of this paper (vol. 1, p. 118) I have sought to group the literature of civics. We should thus pass before us, in artistic expression, and therefore in universal appeal, the historic drama of the great civic past, the mingled present, the phantasmagoria and the tragi-comedy of both of these. We should then know more of the ideals potential for the future, and, it may be, help onward some of the Eutopias which are already struggling towards birth.

---

* Since the preceding paper was read, it is encouraging to note the practical beginnings of a movement towards a civic exhibition, appropriately arising, like so many other valuable contributions to civic betterment, from Toynbee Hall. The Cottages Exhibition initiated by Mr. St. Loe Strachey at Garden City, and of course also that admirable scheme itself, must also be mentioned as important forces in the directions of progress and propaganda advocated above.

[12]

The Myth of Megalopolis

Lewis Mumford

1: ACCRETIONS OF POWER

The increase in the area of arable land, the improvement of agriculture, the spread of population, and the multiplication of cities have gone hand in hand throughout history: never more so than during the last century. Many countries are now entering an era when the urban population will not merely be greater than the rural population, but when the actual area occupied or pre-empted by urban growth will rival that devoted to cultivation. One of the signs of this change has been the increase in the number, area, and population of great cities. Megalopolis is fast becoming a universal form, and the dominant economy is a metropolitan economy, in which no effective enterprise is possible without a close tie to the big city.

Does this represent a final stage in urban development? Those who believe that there are no alternatives to the present proliferation of metropolitan tissue perhaps overlook too easily the historic outcome of such a concentration of urban power: they forget that this has repeatedly marked the last stage in the classic cycle of civilization, before its complete disruption and downfall. There is surely no evidence of stability in a civilization that has, within forty years, undergone two world wars and prematurely terminated the lives of some sixty million people, on the lowest careful estimate: a civilization that has resurrected the most barbarous forms of compulsion, torture, and wholesale extermination, and that now threatens, in future struggles to 'extend communism' or 'preserve freedom,' to annihilate the population of entire continents and perhaps make the whole planet permanently uninhabitable. This metropolitan civilization contains within itself the explosive forces that will wipe out all traces of its existence; and to make plans for the future without taking account of this fact is to betray one of the typical symptoms of that divorce from reality which has characterized the current exploitation of the scientific agents of mass extermination and mass destruction.

Before we can assess the more vital resources at the disposal of mankind, which may at last save it from its irrational misuse of science and technological invention, we must look more closely into the forces that have produced this metropolitan economy, and have battened on its proudly disastrous success. Perhaps a consciousness of the historic evolution of cities will provide an insight, hitherto lacking, that will enable new measures of control to be introduced into their otherwise automatic, because unconscious, processes. Even many present factors that now seem blind and spontaneous may prove, in fact, to be conscious and calculated efforts to stimulate growth that should be curbed, or to concentrate functions and powers that should be diffused.

Possibly one of the reasons for the oft-repeated urban cycle of growth, expansion, and disintegration, as I suggested earlier, lies in the very nature of civilization itself. We have seen that in many instances the city tends to encase the organic, many-sided life of the community in petrified and overspecialized forms that achieve continuity at the expense of adaptation and further growth. The very structure of the city itself, with the stone container dominating the magnet, may in the past have been in no small degree responsible for this resistance. In the end it has made physical disintegration—through war, fire, or economic corrosion and blight—the only way of opening the city up to the fresh demands of life.

If this is true, the prime need of the city today is for an intensification of collective self-knowledge, a deeper insight into the processes of history, as a first step toward discipline and control: such a knowledge as is achieved by a neurotic patient in facing a long-buried infantile trauma that has stood in the way of his normal growth and integration.

Cities like Rome, which historically came to the full end of their cycle before resuming growth again at a lower stage, afford an abundance of data for studying the rise and fall of Megalopolis. But unfortunately that data is too scattered and much of it is too illegible to provide a full insight into the facts. Though in our time Warsaw, Berlin, Tokyo, and many other cities were close to physical extinction, enough of the living tissue of the culture was preserved elsewhere to make possible their swift reconstruction, with many minor improvements, if with no decisive functional alteration. The persistence of these overgrown containers would indicate that they are concrete manifestations of the dominant forces in our present civilization; and the fact that the same signs of overgrowth and overconcentration exist in 'communist' Soviet Russia as in 'capitalist' United States shows that these forces are universal ones, operating almost without respect to the prevailing ideologies or ideal goals.

While one must recognize such facts, it would be premature to believe that these processes are final and irreversible: we have already surveyed a vast amount of data that demonstrates that, even in cultures far less committed to quantitative growth than our own, there comes a point when the tumorous organ will destroy the organism at whose expense it has reached such swollen dimensions. Meanwhile normal birth, growth, and renewal may elsewhere shift the balance.

Sociologists and economists who base their projects for future economic and urban expansion on the basis of the forces now at work, projecting only such changes as may result from speeding up such forces, tend to arrive at a universal megalopolis, mechanized, standardized, effectively dehumanized, as the final goal of urban evolution. Whether they extrapolate 1960 or anticipate 2060 their goal is actually '1984.' Under the guise of objective statistical description, these social scientists are in fact leaving out of their analysis the observable data of biology, anthropology or history that would destroy their premises or rectify their conclusions. While rejecting the scholastic doctrine of final causes, these observers have turned Megalopolis itself into a virtual final cause.

Much of the thought about the prospective development of cities today has been based upon the currently fashionable ideological assumptions about the nature and destiny of man. Beneath its superficial regard for life and health lies a deep contempt for organic processes that involve maintaining the complex partnership of all organic forms, in an environment favorable to life in all its manifestations. Instead of regarding man's relation to air, water, soil, and all his organic partners as the oldest and most fundamental of all his relations—not to be constricted or effaced, but rather to be deepened and extended in both thought and act—the popular technology of our time devotes itself to contriving means to displace autonomous organic forms with ingenious mechanical (controllable! profitable!) substitutes.

Instead of bringing life into the city, so that its poorest inhabitant will have not merely sun and air but some chance to touch and feel and cultivate the earth, these naïve apostles of progress had rather bring sterility to the countryside and ultimately death to the city. Their 'city of the future' is one levelled down to the lowest possibility of active, autonomous, fully sentient life: just so much life as will conform to the requirements of the machine. As we shall see, this would only carry the present forces at work in Megalopolis to their ultimate goal—total human annihilation. Such prophecies tend to be self-fulfilling. The more widely they are believed the better they work. But by the same token the more swiftly they work, the sooner they may come to a dire climax.

Today the end of our whole megalopolitan civilization is all-too-visibly in sight. Even a misinterpreted group of spots on a radar screen might trigger off a nuclear war that would blast our entire urban civilization out of existence and leave nothing behind to start over with—nothing but death by starvation, pandemic disease, or inexorable cancer from strontium 90 for the thrice-miserable refugees who might survive. To build any hopes for the future on such a structure could occur only to the highly trained but humanly under-dimensioned 'experts' who have contrived it. Even if this fate does not overtake us, many other forms of death, equally sinister, if more insidious and slow, are already at work.

But the cyclic process we are in the midst of is not necessarily a fixed and fatal one. On this fact all wise plans must be based. Our modern world culture, with its ever deepening historic sources and its ever widening contacts, is far richer in still unused potentialities, just because it is world-wide, than any other previous civilization.

Our problem in every department is to slow down or bring to a halt the forces that now threaten us: to break into the cycle of expansion and disintegration by establishing new premises, closer to the demands of life, which will enable us to change our direction and in many areas, to make a fresh start. The very existence of the New Towns of England and Sweden, though they have not yet altered the dominant metropolitan pattern, still bears witness to the possibility of a different mode of urban growth. That small sign may be the harbinger of a larger transformation.

In the present chapter, I purpose to look more closely at some of the formidable negative aspects of metropolitan civilization. This will serve as a prelude to a fresh analysis of the role of the city as magnet, container, and transformer, in modern culture.

2: "THE SLAVERY OF LARGE NUMBERS"

The basis for metropolitan agglomeration lay in the tremendous increase of population that took place during the nineteenth century: this probably surpassed, relatively as well as absolutely, that in neolithic times which made possible the original conquests of urbanism. The peoples of European stock multiplied from about two hundred million during the Napoleonic Wars to about six hundred million at the outbreak of the First World War. This stock, which accounted for only about one-sixth of the population of the earth in Malthus' day, rose to about a third of it in a little over a century, though meanwhile some of the other peoples who came under their influence, like the population of the Netherlands East Indies, likewise reproduced and survived as never before.

In 1800 not a city in the Western World had even a million people: London, the biggest, had only 959,310, while Paris had little more than half a million, far less than Amsterdam today. By 1850, London had over two million and Paris over a million inhabitants; and though other cities increased rapidly, too, they were still without serious rivals. But by 1900 eleven metropolises with more than a million inhabitants had come into existence, including Berlin, Chicago, New York, Philadelphia, Moscow, St. Petersburg, Vienna, Tokyo, and Calcutta.

Thirty years later, as the result of a feverish concentration of capital and financial direction, along with the profitable mechanical means for urban congestion and extension, there were twenty-seven cities with more than a million inhabitants, headed by New York and grading down to Birmingham, England, including metropolises on every continent, even Australia. By the middle of the twentieth century there were a host of new metropolitan areas, with bulging and sprawling suburban rings that brought many more within the general metropolitan picture.

The rise of cities with a population of over a hundred thousand was equally marked; and these smaller cities, too, had their suburban rings: even in such areas as North Carolina, where there was an almost providential opportunity to create a regional balance, in separated constellations of cities, no one of which might be more than 100,000 in number, these separate entities tended to coalesce into an undifferentiated, formless urban mass, or "conurbation." By 1930 nearly half of the population of the United States lived within a radius of twenty to fifty miles of cities with over a hundred thousand population; while by 1950 they were to be found in 168 urban areas with 50,000 or more people: in all 83,929,863. Similar tendencies prevailed everywhere: by 1950 13.1 per cent of the world population lived in cities of 100,000 or over, as against 1.7 in 1800.

This alteration in numbers, scale, and area under urbanization, resulted in qualitative changes in all these centers and in addition, extended the sphere of urban influence, bringing the goods, the habits, and the ideological values of the city to hitherto almost self-contained villages, still pursuing a round of life basically similar in content to that of the neolithic culture. Even the chief tools of primitive life in the jungle, the ax and the machete of the South American Indians, were no longer produced close at hand, but in Newark or Sheffield. These changes likewise affected the natural range of sizes in cities: for this apparently varies in numbers and distribution roughly with the size of the biggest city in the series. Above all, this building and multiplication of cities altered the whole balance between the urban and the agricultural population. Cities had once been islands dotting a wide agricultural sea. But now, in the more populated parts of the earth, the productive agricultural areas tended to be isolated green islands, slowly disappearing under a sea of asphalt, concrete, brick, and stone, either entirely covering up the the soil, or reducing its value for any purpose other than more paving, piping, and building.

To give an account of all the factors that brought about this change, would be to paint a much fuller picture of the development of our mechanical civilization during the last three centuries than I have attempted here: let my account in 'Technics and Civilization' supplement the previous chapters in this book. But in brief one may say that by a process of substitution and forced growth, mechanical processes had supplanted organic processes, in one department after another; and that the total result was to displace living forms and to encourage only those human needs and desires that could be profitably attached to the productive mechanism, whether for profit and power, as in early risk capitalism, for security and luxury, as under welfare capitalism, or for security and power together as under the monopolistic state capitalism of the so-called communist countries.

In any event the final result was much the same. Along with this change went a shift to more distant sources of supply, and from the producing towns to the financial centers, where the market was manipulated and the profits spent. 'Free competition' which was the slogan that broke the old feudal and municipal monopolies gave way to large-scale efforts to achieve monopoly or quasi-monopoly, now called 'oligopoly,' so that a minority of organizations could control the market and fix prices almost as successfully as if they were in fact one unit. The great metropolis was both an agent of this process and a symbol of its overwhelming success.

This general movement brought the various sectors of modern society within the same large urban container; and so it broke down in no little degree the separation between the various ruling groups and classes. Land, industry, finance, the armed forces, and officialdom formed a coalition in the leading Western countries, to effect the maximum amount of pecuniary exploitation and the maximum exercise of effective political control. Governmental agents of power began to direct 'national interests' toward the service of the industrialist and the financier, for, as Cecil Rhodes observed, "Expansion is everything."

Thus the specific forces naturally promoting the expansion of the metropolis were augmented by a general push in the same direction. The industrialist, abandoning his creed of laissez-faire and free enterprise, came to rely upon his imperialist allies to protect industry against the instabilities of the market: hence every form of 'protection,' from tariffs and subsidies to armies and navies that opened up closed markets or collected debts.

If the original form of the city was effected through the union of paleolithic and neolithic economies, that of the ultimate metropolis would seem the result of two forces that detached themselves in institutional forms very swiftly after the seventeenth century: a productive economy (industrial) utilizing energies on a scale never before available, and a consumption economy (commercial) heretofore confined to the court and the aristocracy, quickly multiplying the comforts and luxuries available to the few and gradually widening the entire circle of consumers.

Both economies became hyper-active under the pressure of continued invention: power, speed, quantity, and novelty became ends in themselves, and no effective attempt was made to control power and quantity with respect to other human needs than expanding production and consumption. Thus the great metropolises brought into one vast complex the industrial town, the commercial town, and the royal and aristocratic town, each stimulating and extending its influence over the other.

The standards of the factory and the market quickly spread to every other institution in the metropolis. To have the biggest museum, the biggest university, the biggest hospital, the biggest department store, the biggest bank, the biggest financial corporation was to fulfill the ultimate urban requirement: and to produce the maximum number of inventions, the maximum number of scientific papers, the maximum number of books became as much a mark of metropolitan success as the maximum number of tons of pig-iron in Pittsburgh or Essen. In short, every successful institution of the metropolis repeats in its own organization the aimless giantism of the whole. In reacting against the ancient conditions of dearth and scarcity, the metropolitan economy thus went to the other extreme and concentrated on quantity, without paying attention to the necessity for regulating the tempo, distributing quantity, or assimilating novelty. The organic, the qualitative, the autonomous were reduced to a secondary position, if not obliterated in every department.

Both the citadel and the wall had long been obsolescent in the great capitals; but at the very moment they disappeared, a network of organizational controls centering in the dominating capital city, ramifying by instant communication everywhere, came into existence and performed the same functions more effectively. Just to the extent that the new powers were shadowy, impossible to pin down or come to grips with, etherialized, they were all the more effective. One might breach a city wall or kill a king: but how could one assault an international cartel? Only when one national capital came into conflict with another capital did it become apparent that all the archaic and disruptive forces in the old citadels were still active—and indeed had become grossly magnified and increasingly irrational.

The growth and multiplication of great metropolises were both the proofs of this general tendency toward monopolistic concentration and the means by which it was effected. Even in the most self-complacent provincial town, the pattern of institutional life became increasingly that of the metropolis: the shibboleths of power politics, the orgiastic surges of nationalism, the general acceptance of both the commercial and the cultural trade-marks of the metropolis, to the shame-faced exclusion of local products, became well-nigh universal by the beginning of the twentieth century.

To the great consternation of Herbert Spencer and his followers, who innocently believed that industrialism made for peace, it became plain by the end of the nineteenth century that just the opposite had happened: it had widened the magnitude and destructive efficiency of war, by giving it the benefits of mass production and mechanization. Once more the soldier appeared in the center of the city and with him, the colors of life, ebbing from the insensate milieu of the industrial town, flowed back into the metropolis, in the gay uniforms of the Guards and the Cuirassiers. No part of life could escape this general regimentation. Under the peaceful surface and orderly routine of the metropolis, all the dimensions of violence had suddenly enlarged. As these forces developed, the metropolis became more and more a device for increasing the varieties of violent experience, and every citizen became a connoisseur in the arts of death.

This negative picture of metropolitan organization does not, let me emphasize, tell the whole story. One must judge what has happened during the past century, and what threatens us so banefully now, not only by the actual transformations that have taken place, but by many brave potentialities that may, in the long run, offset them and lift the whole level of life to a higher plane. Some of these potentialities have indeed, alas! already been wiped out. Thus the preservation and transmission of primitive cultures, for the contributions that they might have made in overcoming the sterilities now so painfully evident in our own, was not attempted till irreparable damage was done. So, too, many humane procedures and discoveries in medicine and education that have been perverted by metropolitan civilization, still await their full service in a culture directed to more human ends. But if the history of the nineteenth-century city is, as Lavedan has well said, the history of an illness, that of the twentieth-century city might be called the story of a strange kind of medical care and treatment which sought to allay the symptoms, while sedulously maintaining all the agonizing conditions that caused the disease—and actually produced side reactions that were as bad as the disease.

With a few outstanding exceptions, like Patrick Geddes, Peter Kropotkin, Ebenezer Howard, and Max Weber, one still looks in vain for fullness of understanding of the normal processes that the city furthers. Though there have been a multitude of studies of urban disorder and decay, the few that attempt to deal with urban health and to establish better norms for growth and development are still, for the most part, innocently utopian in their unqualified belief in the dubious imperatives of an expanding economy; likewise in their conceiving as all-important and all-sufficient the role science and technics would play in the city's future development.

Yes: the present metropolis, even in its most confused and corrupted form, reveals certain fresh achievements in diffusing human culture that hardly existed in earlier times, when all the higher forms were a monopoly of citadel and temple. The historic metropolitan core still has a function to perform, once its members understand that neither its original monopoly, nor its present disintegration can be indefinitely maintained. The great problem of today, if one may borrow a cliché from physics, is to transmute physical mass into psychic energy. We must invent new agencies for turning automatic congestion into purposeful mobilization: for etherializing the container, for repolarizing the magnet and widening the field. These possibilities will perhaps become more tangible, if we examine the miscarriages of effort that have taken place.

3 : THE TENTACULAR BUREAUCRACY

The hypnotic attraction of the big city derives from its original position as an instrument of the national state, and a symbol of its sovereign power: one of the earliest of all urban functions. Except for Washington and Canberra, the cities that first set the pattern for inordinate and unrestricted growth were the national or imperial capitals: through their grandeur and wealth they drew both population and trade away from the smaller centers whose traditional ways of life were forced to yield to the immense prestige of king and court.

But political and military power must be sustained by economic organization. The means of continued urban agglomeration were the world-wide lanes of commerce that were opened from the sixteenth century on, tapping the hinterland by means of canals and rivers, then in the nineteenth century by continental railroad systems, and finally, in the middle of the twentieth century, by airlines whose very speed on non-stop flights caused smaller urban aggregations to be by-passed, and favored further concentration at a few terminals.

These varied means brought an endless flow of distant foods and raw materials into the metropolis, along with workers and intellectuals, traders and travellers, drawn from remote areas. "All roads lead to Rome," and railroads promoting regional diffusion were abandoned, or allowed to become obsolete and pushed into bankruptcy, in order to favor main-line travel and terminal congestion. Even the later motor expressways, potentially admirable agents of diffusion, have been planned, or rather adroitly misplanned, for this purpose.

The political condition that hastened the pace of this concentration and established it in sub-centers as well, was the increasing importance of the process of administration itself in every type of enterprise: industry, business, philanthropy, education. In its later phases, the growth of the big city is a by-product of the growth and widening influence of the bureaucracy, which pushed into every sphere the controls and regimentations we examined first in the baroque city.

Once the means of instantaneous communication were available, there was a fresh incentive to concentrate the organs of administration: production could now be directed, the shipment of goods routed, orders given and cancelled, sales made, credits extended and drafts cleared, at a single spot. Remote control, first embodied in the separation of staff and line in the army, spread to business operations. With the manufacture of the typewriter in the eighteen-seventies, and the coincident spread of high-speed stenography, more and more business could be conducted profitably on paper. Mechanical means of communication: mechanical means of making and manifolding the permanent record: mechanical systems of audit and control—all these devices aided the rise of a vast commercial bureaucracy, capable of selling in ever-remoter territories by establishing the fashionable patterns of the metropolis as identical with civilization itself, or with anything that could be called 'real life.'

The word bureaucracy had indeed become a discouraging by-word for tortuous inefficiency by the middle of the nineteenth century. Dickens needed no special powers of invention to create Sir Tite Barnacle and the Circumlocution Office. Everyone experienced, throughout the financial and the political world, the difficulty of getting things done by direct action. The simplest civil act required legal sanctions, documents, verifications. From the searching of a deed up to the establishment of civil rights in marriage, no one could move without the aid and slow consent of special functionaries. Lawyers who knew the prescribed forms and technicalities formed a large part of the growing professional population: their services were needed in the observance, and even more in the tactful breach, of the law.

In all this development the political bureaucracy served as a special target for chronic disparagement: it was supposed to have a monopoly of roundabout methods and a finicking, time-wasting attention to form. But the business man's self-righteous indignation about the monstrous growth of political bureaucracy was extremely humorless. Such an attitude overlooked the fact that the greatest development of bureaucracy during the last century took place within the realm of business itself: this put to shame the punier additions to the governmental bureaucracy. Plainly no great corporate enterprise with a worldwide network of agents, correspondents, market outlets, factories, and investors could exist without relying upon the services of an army of patient, clerkly routineers in the metropolis: stenographers, filing clerks, and book-keepers, office managers, sales managers, advertising directors, accountants, and their varied assistants, right up to the fifth vice-president whose name or O.K. sets the final seal of responsibility upon an action.

The housing of this bureaucracy in office buildings and tenements and residential suburbs constituted one of the major tasks of metropolitan expansion. Their transportation to and from work, within a limited time-span, raised one of the difficult technical problems that confronted the city planner and the engineer. And not merely did the bureaucracy itself require office space and domestic space: the by-products of its routine demanded an increasing share of the new quarters: files, vaults, places for live storage and dead storage, parade grounds and cemeteries of documents, where the records of business were alphabetically arrayed, with an eye to the possibility of future exploitation, future reference, future lawsuits, future contracts.

This age found its form, as early as the eighteen-eighties in America, in a new type of office building: symbolically a sort of vertical human filing case, with uniform windows, a uniform façade, uniform accommodations, rising floor by floor in competition for light and air and above all financial prestige with other skyscrapers. The abstractions of high finance produced their exact material embodiment in these buildings, and the tendency to multiply bureaucratic services and extend the far-reaching system of controls has not, even now, reached a terminus; for as members increase and transactions become more complicated, mechanical bureaucratic processes must replace direct human contact and personal intercourse. While in England and Wales, for example, between 1931 and 1951 total employment grew by eight per cent, office employment grew by sixty-three per cent; and in London the number of persons employed in offices is twice the national average.

With this development, a new trinity dominated the metropolitan scene: finance, insurance, advertising. By means of these agents, the metropolis extended its rule over subordinate regions, both within its own political territory and in outlying domains: directly or indirectly, they expedited the flow of tribute back into the big centers. Economic enterprise, political power, social authority, once divided over the length and breadth of the land, now concentrated in the new Romes. To obtain money, one must go to the metropolis: to exercise influence, one must achieve a prominent financial position in the metropolis. Here and there, a lone wolf, like the senior Henry Ford, would temporarily remain outside the system, or, like Walter Rathenau, would try to control it for higher human ends. But such isolation, such control, would be largely an illusion. Mark how Ford himself, who once manufactured a car adapted to popular needs and rural life, finally succumbed to the lure of metropolitan style.

Monopolistic organization: credit finance: pecuniary prestige—these are the three sides of the metropolitan pyramid. (Each has its equivalent in the planned, state-managed economies of 'communist' countries.) Whatever goes on in the big city ultimately traces back to one or another of these elements. The metropolis is the natural reservoir of capital under this economic phase; for its banks, its brokerage offices, its stock exchanges, serve as a collecting point for the savings of the surrounding country, and in the case of world capitals, for the surplus capital of foreign investors. Investors and manufacturers both gravitate to the metropolis. The more constant the need for credit capital, the more important for the borrower to be close to the big banks that can advance it.

The concentration of financial power in national or semi-national banks, like the august Bank of England, and in the hands of politically irresponsible private bankers, like the Houses of Rothschild and Morgan, was a characteristic early feature of this regime: but in turn even greater banking networks of national scope arose; so that sooner or later a large part of the population, as investors, depositors, borrowers, speculators, were drawn into the metropolitan scheme. As Balzac saw clearly at the very beginning of this concentration, the banker was supreme. Directly or indirectly the banker manipulated the puppets that appeared on the political stage: he contributed to the funds of the political parties and his sanction was as necessary to the success of a political policy or an industrial enterprise as his veto was fatal.

Now, mortgages on metropolitan real estate, whose values are 'secured' by the continued prosperity and growth of the metropolis, became a mainstay of savings banks and insurance companies. In order to protect their investments, these institutions must combat any attempt to lessen congestion; for this would also deflate the values that are based on congestion. Note how the program for slum replacement and suburban re-settlement mapped out by the Roosevelt administration after 1933 was undermined by the fact that the administration created at the same time another agency whose main purpose was to keep intact the existing structure of mortgages and interest rates. This policy made it impossible to scale down the burden of inflated urban land values and fixed urban debt to the general level of prices. Note, further, how the generous provisions for writing off part of high slum land values, in the interest of urban renewal, by the Federal government has resulted, not in lower densities and better housing for the poor people thus displaced, but often in even higher densi-

THE TENTACULAR BUREAUCRACY 537

ties and larger profits through housing upper-income groups. (Characteristically, not the slum dwellers but the speculative financiers and builders have been the main beneficiaries.)

Though based on dynamic expansion, the whole system becomes cumulatively rigid and less capable of meeting new situations: it can neither maneuver nor retreat. Not the least rigid part of it, indeed, is the compulsion to carry through the processes of expansion. In the medieval order, the fatalities and insecurities of life were offset by the organization of guilds and friendly societies. In the metropolitan regime, these services are mainly performed by special financial corporations: insurance companies. Fire, flood, sickness, disability, accident, and death are all covered by one or another form of insurance. In the calculations made to ascertain the rates of insurance the first advances in statistical sociology took place; and in intensive work toward health maintenance and disease prevention, great organizations like the Metropolitan Life Insurance Company have demonstrated the cash value of improvement in these departments by education and medical aid.

Unfortunately, within the current metropolitan scheme, insurance is an attempt to achieve security by piling together at one point the maximum number of risks. In the short run the insurance company may be solvent: in the long run it becomes itself one of the elements contributing to the bankruptcy of the regime as a whole. As long as the productive mechanism is in working order, the flow of goods and services is continuous. But a drought, a dust-storm, an earthquake, a glut of commodities, to say nothing of a war, will shake the fabric; and the assertion of these implacable metropolitan claims then stands in the way of rational political adjustment. If this held before the invention of nuclear weapons, what shall we say of this form of security now? If the system had in fact a rational basis, all the surplus funds of insurance organizations would be addressed to the one risk that now makes all other risks microscopic: insurance for world peace, a prudent proposal that the philosopher, Josiah Royce, broached long ago.

To complete the process of metropolitan monopoly, its one-sided control must be pushed even further: by buying up and assembling local enterprises, forming chains of hotels or department stores that may be placed under centralized control and milked for monopoly profits. To seal this control one further step is necessary: the effective monopoly of advertising, news, publicity, periodical literature, and above all, of the new channels of mass communication, radio and television. These various departments have diverse points of origin and represent various initial interests; but historically they have been loosely tied together since the beginning and within the metropolitan framework they finally coalesce.

All these media work to a common end: to give the stamp of authenticity and value to the style of life that emanates from the metropolis. They establish the national brand: they control the national market: they make every departure from the metropolitan pattern seem deplorably provincial, uncouth, and what is even more heinous, out-of-date. The final goal of this process would be a unified, homogeneous, completely standardized population, cut to the metropolitan pattern and conditioned to consume only those goods that are offered by the controllers and the conditioners, in the interests of a continuously expanding economy. In countries like the United States where this development has been swiftest, that goal is already clearly in sight. Need one wonder that in this country, during the past decade, something like twice the sum was spent per family on advertising as was spent on primary and secondary public education? Control without kingship: conformity without choice: power without the intervention of personality.

Where the organs of finance and publicity are concentrated, the possessing classes, no matter where they originate, are likewise brought together; for the ritual of their life, as lived in public for the benefit of the illustrated newspapers and the television programs, is an essential part of the pecuniary lure. Montesquieu, observing this regime at an early stage, described the social consequences with his usual insight and precision. "Luxury," he noted, "is also in proportion to the populousness of towns, and especially of the capital; so that it is in proportion to the riches of the states, to the inequality of private fortunes, and to the number of people settled in particular places." The concentration of the rich is a typical metropolitan phenomenon. The princely ritual of conspicuous expenditure, no longer confined to the royal court, gives rise to the special luxury industries of the metropolis: dress, food, adornment, cosmetics. Because of the universal nature of metropolitan standards, the exotic fashions of the rich are presently copied and reproduced on a mass scale for the benefit of the entire populace: that indeed is a necessary pillar of an expanding economy.

Though greed, avarice, and pride are the main motivators of the metropolitan regime, in the second and third generations of money-making philanthropy itself becomes an auxiliary business of high repute. In countries where the supertax on income is high, charitable and educational foundations serve the new art of giving away money and yet retaining a firm control over its disposition, so as to protect the system that makes it possible. Just as a few hundred great corporations control about half the industrial capital in the United States, so do a relatively small group from the financial and managerial classes control the organs of culture. When new lines of activity are to be promoted in the arts and sciences, it is to the swollen purses of the metropolis that the promoters direct themselves: there, more often than not, the new foundation settles.

THE TENTACULAR BUREAUCRACY   539

Thus a multitude of associations and organizations of national and international scope naturally have their headquarters in New York, London, or Paris. Here patrons and clients come together: here competitive patronage increases the opportunity for special interests to find support. Since a disproportionate share of power and influence and wealth has been drained away from the hinterland, it is necessary for the provincial who would recapture any of these things to leave his home and fight for a place in the metropolis.

Still a third condition abets the insensate agglomeration of population. Victor Branford suggested that the growth of imperial bureaucracies, coming as a result of political centralization in war, was one of the agents that either transformed the industrial town or caused it to yield in power and influence to the metropolis. War is the forcing house of political bureaucracy. During the nineteenth century, as population heaped further into a few great centers, they were forced to rely more fully on distant sources of supply: to widen the basis of supplies and to protect the 'life-line' that connects the source with the voracious mouth of the metropolis, became the functions of the army and navy.

In so far as the metropolis, by fair means or foul, is able to control distant sources of food and raw materials, the growth of the capital can proceed indefinitely. Even in a country like the United States, the outlying rural areas were for long treated as colonial possessions, and deprived by metropolitan bankers of the capital necessary to build their own steel works, even' to further local consumption. It needed the Second World War to force the establishment of steel mills on the Pacific Coast.

Do not suppose that these efforts to promote agglomeration and congestion are wholly spontaneous. On the contrary, strenuous efforts were made—and continue to be made—to ensure it. Railroad systems were deliberately designed to compel passengers and goods to pass through the metropolis before going elsewhere. Each great metropolis still sits like a spider in the midst of a transportation web, though the railroads themselves have been sacrificed to the motor car and the jet plane. In the United States, in addition, as Warren Thompson long ago pointed out, the railroad rate structure is not based on the actual cost of service; the charges are arbitrarily equalized in such a fashion as to give a subsidy to the big cities at the expense of rival towns that are perhaps nearer the shipping point, even though the cost of handling freight in big cities has always, by reason of their very congestion, been disproportionately high— and is now almost prohibitive.

The public subsidy of air transportation works to the same end: that of achieving the maximum amount of congestion and nullifying the very improvements that the technological advances themselves have, potentially, brought about. Thus many of the boasted advantages of the metropolis, with its command of every resource of technology, turn out to be illusory: like Alice's Red Queen, by great exertion and utmost speed the metropolis barely manages to remain in the same position: in fact many of its services, for the last half century, have gone backward. Technological adroitness is no cure for political incompetence and social uninventiveness.

4: THE REMOVAL OF LIMITS

Let us now view the situation of the metropolis in more general terms: what some have called the urban explosion is in fact a symptom of a more general state—the removal of quantitative limits. This marks the change from an organic system to a mechanical system, from purposeful growth to purposeless expansion.

Until the nineteenth century the limitations of both local and regional transportation placed a natural restriction upon the growth of cities. Even the biggest centers, Rome, Babylon, Alexandria, Antioch, were forced to respect that limit. But by the middle of the nineteenth century the tendency toward metropolitan monopoly was supplemented with a new factor brought in by the effective utilization of coal and iron and the extension of the railroad: in terms of purely physical requirements the area of settlement coincided with the coal beds, the ore beds, the railroad network. Patrick Geddes, early in the present century, pointed out the significance of the new population maps, which graphically disclosed a general thickening and spreading of the urban mass: he showed that entire provinces and counties were becoming urbanized, and he proposed to differentiate such diffused formations by a name that would distinguish them from the historic city: the 'conurbation.'

Meanwhile the original forces that created the conurbation were supplemented by the electric power grid, the electric railway, and still later by the motor car and the motor road: so that a movement that was at first confined largely to the area accessible to the railroad now is taking place everywhere. Whereas the first extension of the factory system produced a multitude of new cities and greatly augmented the population of existing centers, the present diffusion of the area of settlement has largely halted this growth and has enormously increased the production of relatively undifferentiated urban tissue, without any relation either to an internally coherent nucleus or an external boundary of any sort.

The result threatens to be a universal conurbation. Those who ignored Geddes's original definition half a century ago have recently re-discovered

the phenomenon itself, and treated it as if it were an entirely new development. Some have even misapplied to the conurbation the inappropriate
term Megalopolis, though it represents, in fact, the precise opposite of
the tendency that brought the original city of this name into existence. The
overgrown historic city was still, residually, an entity: the conurbation is
a nonentity, and becomes more patently so as it spreads.

What this removal of limits means can perhaps best be grasped by
referring to the extension of historic centers. When Rome was surrounded
by the Aurelian Wall in A.D. 274, it covered a little more than five square
miles. The present area of London is 130 times as great as this; while
it is roughly 650 times as big as the area of medieval London, which was
677 acres. The conurbation of New York is even more widespread: it
covers something like 2,514 square miles. If no human purposes supervene
to halt the blotting out of the countryside and to establish limits for the
growth and colonization of cities, the whole coastal strip from Maine to
Florida might coalesce into an almost undifferentiated conurbation. But
to call this mass a 'regional city' or to hold that it represents the new
scale of settlement to which modern man must adapt his institutions and
his personal needs is to mask the realities of the human situation and
allow seemingly automatic forces to become a substitute for human
purposes.

These vast urban masses are comparable to a routed and disorganized
army, which has lost its leaders, scattered its battalions and companies,
torn off its insignia, and is fleeing in every direction. "Sauve qui peut."
The first step toward handling this situation, besides establishment of an
over-all command, is to re-group in units that can be effectively handled.
Until we understand the function of the smaller units and can bring them
under discipline we cannot command and deploy the army as a whole
over a larger area. The scale of distances has changed, and the 'regional
city' is a potential reality, indeed a vital necessity. But the condition for
success in these endeavors lies in our abilities to recognize and to impose
organic limitations. This means the replacement of the machine-oriented
metropolitan economy by one directed toward the goods and goals of life.

Though the removal of limits is one of the chief feats of the metropolitan
economy, this does not imply any abdication of power on the part of the
chiefs in charge: for there is one countervailing condition to this removal,
and that is the processing of all operations through the metropolis and
its increasingly complicated mechanisms. The metropolis is in fact a processing center, in which a vast variety of goods, material and spiritual, is
mechanically sorted and reduced to a limited number of standardized
articles, uniformly packaged, and distributed through controlled channels
to their destination, bearing the approved metropolitan label.

'Processing' has now become the chief form of metropolitan control;

and the need for its constant application has brought into existence a whole range of inventions, mechanical and electronic, from cash registers to electronic computers, which handle every operation from book-keeping to university examinations. Interests and aptitudes that do not lend themselves to processing are automatically rejected. So complicated, so elaborate, so costly are the processing mechanisms that they cannot be employed except on a mass scale: hence they eliminate all activities of a fitful, inconsecutive, or humanly subtle nature—just as 'yes' or 'no' answers eliminate those more delicate and accurate discriminations that often lie at one point or another in between the spuriously 'correct' answer. That which is local, small, personal, autonomous, must be suppressed. Increasingly, he who controls the processing mechanism controls the lives and destinies of those who must consume its products, and who on metropolitan terms cannot seek any others. For processing and packaging do not end on the production line: they finally make over the human personality.

In short the monopoly of power and knowledge that was first established in the citadel has come back, in a highly magnified form, in the final stages of metropolitan culture. In the end every aspect of life must be brought under control: controlled weather, controlled movement, controlled association, controlled production, controlled prices, controlled fantasy, controlled ideas. But the only purpose of control, apart from the profit, power, and prestige of the controllers, is to accelerate the process of mechanical control itself.

The priests of this regime are easy to identify: the whole system, in its final stages, rests on the proliferation of secret, and thus controllable, knowledge; and the very division of labor that makes specialized scientific research possible also restricts the number of people capable of putting the fragments together. But where are the new gods? The nuclear reactor is the seat of their power: radio transmission and rocket flight their angelic means of communication and transportation: but beyond these minor agents of divinity the Control Room itself, with its Cybernetic Deity, giving His lightning-like decisions and His infallible answers: omniscience and omnipotence, triumphantly mated by science. Faced with this electronic monopoly of man's highest powers, the human can come back only at the most primitive level. Sigmund Freud detected the beginnings of creative art in the infant's pride over his bowel movements. We can now detect its ultimate manifestation in paintings and sculpture whose contents betray a similar pride and a similar degree of autonomy—and a similar product.

One of the ancient prerogatives of the gods was to create man out of their flesh, like Atum, or in their own image, like Yahweh. When the accredited scientific priesthood go a little farther with their present activities, the new life-size homunculus will be processed, too: one can already see anticipatory models in our art galleries. He will look remarkably like a man accoutered in a 'space-suit': outwardly a huge scaly insect. But the face inside will be incapable of expression, as incapable as that of a corpse. And who will know the difference?

5: SPRAWLING GIANTISM

Circle over London, Buenos Aires, Chicago, Sydney, in an airplane or view the cities schematically by means of an urban map and block plan. What is the shape of the city and how does it define itself? The original container has completely disappeared: the sharp division between city and country no longer exists. As the eye stretches toward the hazy periphery one can pick out no definite shapes except those formed by nature: one beholds rather a continuous shapeless mass, here bulging or ridged with buildings, there broken by a patch of green or an unwinding ribbon of concrete. The shapelessness of the whole is reflected in the individual part, and the nearer the center, the less as a rule can the smaller parts be distinguished.

Failing to divide its social chromosomes and split up into new cells, each bearing some portion of the original inheritance, the city continues to grow inorganically, indeed cancerously, by a continuous breaking down of old tissues, and an overgrowth of formless new tissue. Here the city has absorbed villages and little towns, reducing them to place names, like Manhattanville and Harlem in New York; there it has, more happily, left the organs of local government and the vestiges of an independent life, even assisted their revival, as in Chelsea and Kensington in London; but it has nevertheless enveloped those urban areas in its physical organization and built up the open land that once served to ensure their identity and integrity. Sometimes the expanding street system forms an orderly pattern, sometimes it produces only a crazy network that does not even serve traffic: but the difference between one type of order and another is merely a difference in the degree of sprawl, confusion, de-building.

As one moves away from the center, the urban growth becomes ever more aimless and discontinuous, more diffuse and unfocussed, except where some surviving town has left the original imprint of a more orderly life. Old neighborhoods and precincts, the social cells of the city, still maintaining some measure of the village pattern, become vestigial. No human eye can take in this metropolitan mass at a glance. No single gathering place except the totality of its streets can hold all its citizens. No human mind can comprehend more than a fragment of the complex and minutely specialized activities of its citizens. The loss of form, the loss of autonomy, the constant frustration and harassment of daily activities, to say nothing of gigantic breakdowns and stoppages—all these become normal attributes of the metropolitan regime. There is a special name for power when it is concentrated on such a scale: it is called impotence.

The giantism of the metropolis is not the result of technological progress alone. Contrary to popular belief, the growth of great cities preceded the decisive technical advances of the last two centuries. But the metropolitan phase became universal only when the technical means of congestion had become adequate—and their use profitable to those who manufactured or employed them. The modern metropolis is, rather, an outstanding example of a peculiar cultural lag within the realm of technics itself: namely, the continuation by highly advanced technical means of the obsolete forms and ends of a socially retarded civilization. The machines and utilities that would lend themselves to decentralization in a life-centered order, here become either a means to increase congestion or afford some slight temporary palliation—at a price.

The form of the metropolis, then, is its formlessness, even as its aim is its own aimless expansion. Those who work within the ideological limits of this regime have only a quantitative conception of improvement: they seek to make its buildings higher, its streets broader, its parking lots more ample: they would multiply bridges, highways, tunnels, making it ever easier to get in and out of the city, but constricting the amount of space available within the city for any other purpose than transportation itself. Frank Lloyd Wright's project for a skyscraper a mile high was the ultimate reduction to absurdity of this whole theory of city development. The ultimate form of such a city would be an acre of building to a square mile of expressways and parking lots. In many areas this is rapidly approaching fulfillment.

When both the evil and the remedy are indistinguishable, one may be sure that a deep-seated process is at work. An expanding economy, dedicated to profit, not to the satisfaction of life-needs, necessarily creates a new image of the city, that of a perpetual and ever-widening maw, consuming the output of expanding industrial and agricultural production, in response to the pressures of continued indoctrination and advertising. Two centuries ago the need for such an economy was indisputable, and in many poverty-stricken countries that need still remains, to lift the population above the margin of starvation and helpless depression. But in the countries of the West, particularly in the United States, the problem of scarcity has been solved, apart from distribution and relation to organic needs, only to create a new set of problems just as embarrassing: those of surfeit and satiety. Today, accordingly, expansion has become an end in itself: to make it possible the rulers of this society resort to every possible device of pyramid-building.

For unfortunately, once an economy is geared to expansion, the means rapidly turn into an end, and "the going becomes the goal." Even more unfortunately, the industries that are favored by such expansion must, to maintain their output, be devoted to goods that are readily consumable, either by their nature, or because they are so shoddily fabricated that they must soon be replaced. By fashion and built-in obsolescence the economies of machine production, instead of producing leisure and durable wealth, are duly cancelled out by mandatory consumption on an ever larger scale.

By the same token, the city itself becomes consumable, indeed expendable: the container must change as rapidly as its contents. This latter imperative undermines a main function of the city as an agent of human continuity. The living memory of the city, which once bound together generations and centuries, disappears: its inhabitants live in a self-annihilating moment-to-moment continuum. The poorest Stone Age savage never lived in such a destitute and demoralized community.

Now organic processes are purposeful, goal-seeking, self-limiting: indeed all organisms have built-in controls that serve to co-ordinate action and limit growth. The expanding economy, like the technological system on which it is so largely based, has no such limitations: its stabilization takes the form of multiplying the number of consumers and intensifying their wants. But to ensure continued productivity, it limits these wants to those that can be supplied at a profit by the machine. Thus this economy produces motor cars and refrigerators galore; but has no motive to supply durable works of art, handsome gardens, or untrammelled, nonconsuming leisure. Our economic establishment is better equipped to destroy the product outright than to give it away or to limit the output at source.

The image of modern industrialism that Charlie Chaplin carried over from the past into 'Modern Times' is just the opposite of megalopolitan reality. He pictured the worker as an old-fashioned drudge, chained to the machine, mechanically fed while he continued to operate it. That image belongs to Coketown. The new worker, in the metropolis, has been progressively released from the productive process: the grinding, impoverished toil that made the nineteenth-century factory so hideous has been lifted by social services and security, by mechanical aids and by complete automation. Work is no longer so brutal in the light industries: but automation has made it even more boring. The energy and application that once went into the productive process must now be addressed to consumption.

By a thousand cunning attachments and controls, visible and subliminal, the workers in an expanding economy are tied to a consumption mechanism: they are assured of a livelihood provided they devour without undue selectivity all that is offered by the machine—and demand nothing that is not produced by the machine. The whole organization of the metropolitan community is designed to kill spontaneity and self-direction. You stop on the red light and go on the green. You see what you are supposed to see, think what you are supposed to think: your personal contributions, like your income and security taxes, are deductible at source. To choose, to select, to discriminate, to exercise prudence or continence or forethought, to carry self-control to the point of abstinence, to have standards other than those of the market, and to set limits other than those of immediate consumption—these are impious heresies that would challenge the whole megalopolitan myth and deflate its economy. In such a 'free' society Henry Thoreau must rank as a greater public enemy than Karl Marx.

The metropolis, in its final stage of development, becomes a collective contrivance for making this irrational system work, and for giving those who are in reality its victims the illusion of power, wealth, and felicity, of standing at the very pinnacle of human achievement. But in actual fact their lives are constantly in peril, their wealth is tasteless and ephemeral, their leisure is sensationally monotonous, and their pathetic felicity is tainted by constant, well-justified anticipations of violence and sudden death. Increasingly they find themselves "strangers and afraid," in a world they never made: a world ever less responsive to direct human command, ever more empty of human meaning.

[13]

TVA AND DEMOCRATIC PLANNING

Philip Selznick

In this country we are very vain of our political institutions, which are singular in this, that they sprung, within the memory of living men, from the character and condition of the people, which they still express with sufficient fidelity...

EMERSON

WHATEVER the ultimate outcome, it is evident that modern society has already moved rather far into the age of control. It is an age marked by widening efforts to master a refractory industrial system. That a technique for control will emerge, that there is and will be planning, is hardly in question. What is more doubtful is the character and direction of the new instruments of intervention and constraint. For these have been born of social crisis, set out piecemeal as circumstances have demanded; they have not come to us as part of a broad and conscious vision. As a consequence, the foundations of a clear-cut choice between totalitarian and democratic planning have not been adequately laid; nor has the distinction been altogether clear between planning directed toward some acceptable version of the common good and planning for the effective maintenance of existing and emerging centers of privilege and power.

Democracy has to do with means, with instruments, with tools which define the relation between authority and the individual. In our time, new and inescapable tasks demand a choice among available means within the framework of increased governmental control. It is therefore especially important to examine those organizations which are proposed as contributions to the technique of democratic planning. An example of such a proposed contribution is the Tennessee Valley Authority.

On June 25, 1942, *The Times* (London) published a brief review of TVA under the heading "The Technique of Democratic Planning." *The Times* correspondent reported that he was impressed by the physical accomplishments of dam and power plant construction, but what interested him most was "the technique which the TVA had adopted with the deliberate aim of reconciling over-all planning with the values of democracy." Here *The Times* reflected what many feel to be the enduring significance of this much discussed government agency. The theme of democracy in government administration was also prominent in a widely distributed book, *TVA: Democracy on the March*, written by David E. Lilienthal, and in numerous speeches and pamphlets emanating from the Authority. In addition, much of the comment friendly to the agency has stressed its contribution to a new synthesis, one which would unite positive government—the welfare or service state—with a rigorous adherence to the principles of democracy.

What is this organization which is thought to embody an ideal so eagerly sought? What is the nature of this democratic technique? What are its implications and consequences? What will a close and critical study of the organization in action tell us about these problems? These questions have yet to be satisfactorily answered. To seek a partial answer, a study was undertaken, during 1942–1943, with attention focused primarily upon the Authority's "democratic" or "grass roots" method. This inquiry was based upon the assumption that no prior personal commitment to the TVA as a political symbol ought to interfere with a realistic examination. It was an inquiry which did not hesitate to seek out informal and unofficial sources of information. And it began with certain ideas about the nature of the administrative process which seem helpful in uncovering the underlying forces shaping leadership and policy.

The Tennessee Valley Authority was created by Congress in May, 1933, as a response to a long period of pressure for the disposition of government-owned properties at Muscle Shoals, Alabama. During the First World War, two nitrate plants and what was later known as Wilson Dam were constructed, at a cost of over $100,000,000. For the next fifteen years, final decision as to the future of these installations hung fire. The focal points of contention related to the production and distribution of fertilizer and electric power, and to the principle of government versus private ownership. Two presidential commissions and protracted congressional inquiries recorded the long debate. At last, with the advent of the Roosevelt administration in 1933, the government assumed responsibility for a general resolution of the major issues.

The TVA Act as finally approved was a major victory for those who favored the principle of government operation. The Muscle Shoals investment was to remain in public ownership, and this initial project was to be provided with new goals and to be vastly extended. A great public power project was envisioned, mobilizing the "by-product" of dams built for the purpose of flood control and navigation improvement on the Tennessee River and its tributaries. Control and operation of the nitrate properties, to be used for fertilizer production, was also authorized, although this aspect was subordinated in importance to electricity. These major powers—authority to construct dams, deepen the river

Selznick: TVA and the Grass Roots 5

channel, produce and distribute electricity and fertilizer—were delegated by Congress to a corporation administered by a three-man board of directors.

If this had been all, the project would still have represented an important extension of government activity and responsibility. But what began as, and what was generally understood to be, primarily the solution of a problem of fertilizer and power emerged as an institution of far broader meaning. A new regional concept—the river basin as an integral unit—was given effect, so that a government agency was created which had a special responsibility neither national nor state-wide in scope. This offered a new dimension for the consideration of the role of government in the evolving federal system. At the same time, the very form of the agency established under the Act was a new departure. There was created a relatively autonomous public corporation free in important aspects from the normal financial and administrative controls exercised over federal organs. Further, and in one sense most important, a broad vision of regional resource development—in a word, planning— informed the conception, if not the actual powers, of the new organization.

The Message of the President requesting the TVA legislation did much to outline that perception : "It is clear," wrote Mr. Roosevelt, "that the Muscle Shoals development is but a small part of the potential public usefulness of the entire Tennessee River. Such use, if envisioned in its entirety, transcends mere power development : it enters the wide fields of flood control, soil erosion, afforestation, elimination from agricultural use of marginal lands, and distribution and diversification of industry. In short, this power development of war days leads logically to national planning for a complete river watershed involving many States and the future lives and welfare of millions. It touches and gives life to all forms of human concerns." To carry out this conception, the President recommended "legislation to create a Tennessee Valley Authority—a corporation clothed with the power of government but possessed of the flexibility and initiative of private enterprise. It should be charged with the broadest duty of planning for the proper use, conservation, and development of the natural resources of the Tennessee River drainage basin and its adjoining territory for the general social and economic welfare of the Nation."

This special regional focus and broad scope of the project have given it a character which reflects one of the major motifs of our time : the need for some sort of integral planning, especially in key problem areas.

It is that character which has been caught up as a model for similar projects in other areas. For the uniqueness of TVA is not that it is a government-owned power business or conservation agency, but that it was given some responsibility for the unified development of the resources of a region.

Yet it must be said that although the agency and its program have symbolized concentrated effort and planning, in fact the TVA has had little direct authority to engage in large-scale regional planning. The powers delegated to it were for the most part specific in nature, related to the primary problems of flood control, navigation, fertilizer, and power. In addition, authority to conduct studies and demonstrations of a limited nature, but directed toward general welfare objectives, was delegated to the President and by him to the Authority. This became the basis for some general surveys and demonstration work in forestry, local industrial development, community planning, and for work with coöperatives.

More important, however, is that the Act permitted such discretion in the execution of the primary purposes as would invite those in charge to recognize the social consequences of specific activities—such as the effect upon farm populations and urban communities of the creation of large reservoirs—and to assume responsibility for them. This assumption of responsibility invests the administration with an important planning function, though it is indirect and remains modifiable as circumstances may demand. In addition, there remained administrative freedom to devise methods of dealing with local people and institutions which would reflect the democratic process at work. Perhaps of equal importance is that the idea of planning associated with TVA accords this agency a central status in the consideration of the problems and the future of the Tennessee Valley region.

In the light of this weak delegation of broad planning powers, and the tendency of Congress to restrict developmental functions, it is probable that the significance of TVA in relation to democratic planning comes primarily from the infusion of specific tasks with a sense of social responsibility. In the purchase of lands, in the distribution of fertilizer and power, in personnel policy—in those functions which are a necessary part of the execution of its major and clearly delegated responsibilities—the TVA has normally taken account of the people of the area, with a view to adjusting immediate urgencies to long-term social policy. This, of course, is not the same as devising and executing a frontal plan for the reconstruction of the economy or institutions of an area. And yet, whichever view is emphasized—whether one conceives of TVA's limited regional planning as a portent of fuller ventures along that line, or whether one thinks of planning as simply an adjunct of specific responsibilities—we have something to learn from a study of the organization itself and of the methods developed in the execution of its tasks.

"Organization" and "method" are key words. Wherever we turn in considering the implications of a program for democracy these terms are inevitably involved. No democratic program can be unconcerned about the objectives of a course of action, especially as they affect popular welfare. But the crucial question for democracy is not what to strive for, but by what means to strive. And the question of means is one of what to do now and what to do next—and these are basic questions in politics.

If the problem of means is vital, it is also the most readily forgotten. "Results," "achievement," and "success" are heady words. They induce submission and consent, thus summoning rewards for diligence and labor—and they also enfeeble the intellect. For the results which most readily capture the imagination are external, colorful, concrete. They are the stated goals of action. Their achievement lends reality, wholesomeness, and stature to the enterprise as a whole.

But methods are more elusive. They have a corollary and incidental status. A viable enterprise is sustained in the public eye by its goals, not its methods. Means are variable and expedient. Their history is forgotten or excused. Here again the concrete and colorful win easiest attention. Where incorrect methods leave a visible residue—a rubbled city or wasted countryside,—then methods may gain notice. But those means which have long-run implications for cultural values, such as democracy, are readily and extensively ignored.

When we speak of methods, we speak in the same breath of instruments. Policies, decisions as to "how to proceed," require execution. Execution in turn implies a technology. We are familiar with the kind of technology which includes machines and tools of all sorts, handled and manipulated in more or less obvious ways. We are even reasonably familiar with the technology of economic and military organization, geared to the achievement of technical objectives, qualified and informed by the criteria of efficiency. But when we move into that area of technology which is related to the creation, defense, or reintegration of values, such as democracy, we find ourselves less assured. Yet the significance of this noneconomic technology, under the conditions of mass society and cultural disintegration, is of primary importance for whatever we may wish to do about that vague but demanding reality which we call our "way of life." Propaganda agencies, mass parties, unions, educational systems, churches, and governmental structures have a common aspect in that, more or less directly, they work upon and seriously affect the evolving values, the spirit, of contemporary society. Furthermore, there is a growing tendency for this effect to be conscious, to become an ordered technology available to those who have a stake in changing sentiment or social policy.

One of the pervasive obstacles to the understanding and even the inspection of this technology is ideology or official doctrine. By the very nature of their function, all those forces which are concerned about the evolution of value-impregnated methods, or public opinion itself, have a formal program, a set of ideas for public consumption. These ideas provide a view of the stated goals of the various organizations—political or industrial democracy, or decentralization, or the like—as well as of the methods which are deemed crucial for the achievement of these goals. It is naturally considered desirable for the attention of observers to be directed toward these avowed ideas, so that they may receive a view of the enterprise consistent with the conception of its leadership. All this in the often sincere conviction that precisely this view is in accord with the realities of the situation and best conveys the meaning and significance of the project under inspection.

However much we may be impressed by what a group says about its methods or its work, there is adequate justification for uneasiness and doubt. This doubt has its source in our general understanding of the persistent tendency for words to outrun deeds, for official statement and doctrine to raise a halo over the events and activities themselves. That this is a natural disposition among responsible men is well understood, and a gap of some sort between the idea and the act is normally expected. But what is less well understood, or at least less generally applied to objects of public esteem, is the tendency for ideas to reflect something more than enthusiasm or more or less pardonable pride. The functions of a doctrine may be more subtle and more significant, related to the urgent needs of leadership and to the security of the organization itself. Such functions, when relevant, cast a deeper shadow and indicate the need for more searching questions. In Part I of this study, we have critically analyzed TVA's official doctrine in relation to democratic planning—the policy of grass-roots administration as a contribution to democracy. The analysis points to underlying issues and problems not directly evident when we speak of the normal and anticipated gap between avowed statement and actual practice.

Though official statements and theories are important, an undue concentration upon what men say diverts attention from what they do. This is especially true with respect to the methods utilized in the execution of a program, for these are particularly difficult to view realistically. It is often sufficiently troublesome to attain a clear picture of the formal, stated methods in use, without pressing inquiry as to the less obvious but vital informal behavior of key participants. Yet it is precisely into the realm of actual behavior and its significance for evolving structures and values that we must move if this kind of inquiry is to realize its possibilities.

The instruments of planning are vitally relevant to the nature of the democratic process. The TVA is many things, but most significant for our purposes is its status as a social instrument. It is this role as instrument with which this study is directly concerned. Or, to emphasize another word, it is TVA as an organization to which our attention is directed. Thus it is not dams or reservoirs or power houses or fertilizer as such, but the nature of the Authority as an ordered group of working individuals, as a living institution, which is under scrutiny.

In searching out organizational behavior and problems as keys to understanding the implications of TVA for democratic planning, we are entering a field of inquiry which probes at the heart of the democratic dilemma. If democracy as a method of social action has any single problem, it is that of enforcing the responsibility of leadership or bureaucracy. A faith in majorities does not eliminate the necessity for governance by individuals and small groups. Wherever there is organization, whether formally democratic or not, there is a split between the leader and the led, between the agent and the initiator. The phenomenon of abdication to bureaucratic directorates in corporations, in trade unions, in parties, and in coöperatives is so widespread that it indicates a fundamental weakness of democracy. For this trend has the consequence of thrusting issues theoretically decided by a polity into the field of bureaucratic decision.

The term "bureaucracy" has an invidious connotation, signifying arbitrary power, impersonality, red tape. But if we recognize that all administrative officials are bureaucrats, the bishop no less than the tax collector, then we may be able to understand the general nature of the problem, separating it from the personal qualities or motives of the individuals involved. Officials, like other individuals, must take heed of the conditions of their existence. Those conditions are, for officials, organizational: in attempting to exercise some control over their own work and future they are offered the opportunity of manipulating personnel, funds, and symbols. Among the many varied consequences of this manipulation, the phenomena of inefficiency and arbitrariness are ultimately among the least significant. The difference between officials and ordinary members of an organized group is that the former have a special access to and power over the machinery of the organization; while those outside the bureaucratic ranks lack that access and power.

If we are to comprehend these bureaucratic machines, which must play an indispensable role in any planning venture, it is essential to think of an organization as a dynamic conditioning field which effectively shapes the behavior of those who are attempting to remain at the helm. We can best understand the behavior of officials when we are able to trace that behavior to the needs and structure of the organization as a living social institution.

The important point about organizations is that, though they are tools, each nevertheless has a life of its own. Though formally subordinated to some outside authority, they universally resist complete control. The use of organizational instrumentalities is always to some degree precarious, for it is virtually impossible to enforce automatic response to the desires or commands of those who must employ them. This general recalcitrance is recognized by all who participate in the organizational process. It is this recalcitrance, with its corollary instability, which is in large measure responsible for the enormous amount of continuous attention which organizational machinery requires. There are good reasons, readily grasped, for this phenomenon.

The internal life of any organization tends to become, but never achieves, a closed system. There are certain needs generated by organization itself which command the attention and energies of leading participants. The moment an organization is begun, problems arise from the need for some continuity of policy and leadership, for a homogeneous outlook, for the achievement of continuous consent and participation on the part of the ranks. These and other needs create an intricate system of relationships and activities, formal and informal, which have primarily an internal relevance. Thus leadership is necessarily turned in upon itself. But at the same time, no organization subsists in a vacuum. Large or small, it must pay some heed to the consequences of its own activities (and even existence) for other groups and forces in the community. These forces will insist upon an accounting, and may in self-defense demand a share in the determination of policy. Because of this outside pressure, from many varied sources, the attention of any bureaucracy must be turned outward, in defending the organization against possible encroachment or attack.

These general considerations, which have been stated here in a summary way, should lead to a more discerning study of any administrative agency. They direct us (1) to seek the underlying implications of the official doctrine of the agency, if it has one; (2) to avoid restriction to the formal structure of the organization, as that may be outlined in statutes, administrative directives, and organization charts; and (3) to observe the interaction of the agency with other institutions in its area of operation. Throughout, a search for the internally relevant in organizational behavior, especially that which is related to self-defensive needs, is a primary tool of such analysis.[1]

It will probably bear emphasis that the significance of TVA for democratic planning lies not so much in its program, or in its accomplishments, as in its methods and in its nature as an organization. Even though its planning powers are limited, the TVA does represent an experiment, an adventure in executing broad social responsibilities for the development of a unified area. Furthermore, its type of organization is proffered as a model for governmental planning in other areas. This point has been clearly recognized within TVA itself:

Few of the activities of TVA are unique as public responsibilities. The Government of the United States has been constructing waterways and building works for flood control for more than a century. State and Federal agencies have engaged in technical research, and surveys of mineral and forestry resources have been carried on with public funds for many years. The TVA is not the first instance in which the Federal Government has sold electric power. Aid to and stimulation of business opportunities in industrial development, employment, farming, and other fields has become a familiar role of Government, State and National.

---

[1] It appears that this institutional approach (not, of course, original with the author) to the study of administrative organization may be the avenue to an enlargement of the horizon of inquiry in this field. In a sense, this approach and this study are a response to such criticism as that voiced by Donald Morrison in his review of the series, *Case Reports in Public Administration:* "To put the matter succinctly, the subject-matter of public administration has been defined so as to leave a no-man's land of significant problems, flanked on one side by the students of administration and on the other by political theorists. The problems thus isolated have their origin in the fact that in its fundamental aspect administration is governance. . . . One such problem, perhaps the most urgent, is to develop and strengthen ways of insuring that government by the bureaucracy does not destroy the democratic pattern of our society. Unless it is assumed that such insurance lies in the perfection of organizational structure and techniques of fiscal and personnel management, the present series of case studies does not deal with this matter. Many persons believe that the TVA experiment is suggestive of ways of democratizing bureaucratic government. Ten TVA studies are published in *Case Reports*, but none deals with the integration of the TVA program into the social and economic life of the area" (*Public Administration Review*, V, 1 [Winter, 1945], 85).

12   *University of California Publications in Culture and Society*

It is in the integration and the correlation on a regional basis of these various activities under a single, unified management that the Tennessee Valley Authority represents a pioneer undertaking of government. For the first time a President and Congress created an agency which was directed to view the problems of a region as a whole.[2]

If the power granted to the Authority was not sufficient fully to execute that broad responsibility, still the vision has remained. It is the conception of an administrative instrument created to fulfill necessary planning functions within the framework of democratic values.

If TVA as instrument is the focus of attention, and if we are prepared to think of the Authority as a living social organization, we may expect that in one way or another the Authority will have been caught up in and shaped by its institutional environment. This expectation becomes especially relevant as we note (1) the TVA's official avowal of a special democratic relation to certain local institutions "close to the people," a doctrine which will be discussed in detail below; and (2) that TVA did not arise out of the expressed desires of the local area, and consequently was faced with a special problem of adjustment. Each of these points lends weight to the anticipation that in the Authority's relation to its own grass roots we may find significant material of general interest to those who wish to learn the lessons of the TVA experience.

Given such an anticipation, the problem for this inquiry became one of finding a significant vantage point from which to examine this grass-roots relationship. The question thus posed required some sort of theory, a set of ideas which could point a way to the most vital aspects of the situation. The theory which seemed to make sense in the light of a general understanding of the materials was so formulated as to bring together in a single over-all analysis (1) the avowed contribution of TVA to democratic planning, through a grass-roots method of executing its responsibilities; (2) the self-defensive behavior of the organization as it faced the need to adjust itself to the institutions of its area of operation; (3) the consequences for policy and action which must follow upon any attempt to adjust an organization to local centers of interest and power. Put in a few words, this involved the hypothesis that the Authority's grass-roots policy as doctrine and as action must be understood as related to the need of the organization to come to terms with certain local and national interests; and that in actual practice this procedure resulted in commitments which had restrictive consequences for the policy and behavior of the Authority itself.

[2] "The Widening of Economic Opportunity through TVA," pamphlet adapted from an address by David E. Lilienthal, Director, TVA, at Columbia University, New York, N.Y., January, 1940 (Washington: Government Printing Office, 1940), p. 15.

In order to handle this problem most effectively, it has been found necessary to introduce a concept which, while not new, is somewhat unfamiliar. This is the idea of *coöptation*[3]—often the realistic core of avowedly democratic procedures. To risk a definition: *coöptation is the process of absorbing new elements into the leadership or policy-determining structure of an organization as a means of averting threats to its stability or existence.* With the help of this concept, we are enabled more closely and more rigorously to specify the relation between TVA and some important local institutions and thus uncover an important aspect of the real meaning and significance of the Authority's grass-roots policy. At the same time, it is clear that the idea of coöptation plunges us into the field of bureaucratic behavior as that is related to such democratic ideals as "local participation."

Coöptation tells us something about the process by which an institutional environment impinges itself upon an organization and effects changes in its leadership, structure, or policy. Coöptation may be formal or informal, depending upon the specific problem to be solved.

Formal coöptation.—When there is a need for the organization to publicly absorb new elements, we shall speak of formal coöptation. This involves the establishment of openly avowed and formally ordered relationships. Appointments to official posts are made, contracts are signed, new organizations are established—all signifying participation in the process of decision and administration. There are two general conditions which lead an organization to resort to formal coöptation, though they are closely related:

1. When the legitimacy of the authority of a governing group or agency is called into question. Every group or organization which attempts to exercise control must also attempt to win the consent of the governed. Coercion may be utilized at strategic points, but it is not effective as an enduring instrument. One means of winning consent is to coöpt into the leadership or organization elements which in some way reflect the sentiment or possess the confidence of the relevant public or mass and which will lend respectability or legitimacy to the organs of control and thus reëstablish the stability of formal authority. This device is widely used, and in many different contexts. It is met in colonial countries, where the organs of alien control reaffirm their legitimacy by coöpting native leaders into the colonial administration. We find it in

---

[3] With some modifications, the following statement of the concept of coöptation is a repetition of that presented in the author's "Foundations of the Theory of Organization," *American Sociological Review,* XIII, 1 (February, 1948), pp. 33–35. For further discussion of coöptation see below, pp. 259–261.

the phenomenon of "crisis-patriotism" wherein normally disfranchised groups are temporarily given representation in the councils of government in order to win their solidarity in a time of national stress. Coöptation has been considered by the United States Army in its study of proposals to give enlisted personnel representation in the courts-martial machinery—a clearly adaptive response to stresses made explicit during World War II. The "unity" parties of totalitarian states are another form of coöptation; company unions or some employee representation plans in industry are still another. In each of these examples, the response of formal authority (private or public, in a large organization or a small one) is an attempt to correct a state of imbalance by formal measures. It will be noted, moreover, that what is shared is the responsibility for power rather than power itself.

2. When the need to invite participation is essentially administrative, that is, when the requirements of ordering the activities of a large organization or state make it advisable to establish the forms of self-government. The problem here is not one of decentralizing decision but rather of establishing orderly and reliable mechanisms for reaching a client public or citizenry. This is the "constructive" function of trade unions in great industries where the unions become effective instruments for the elimination of absenteeism or the attainment of other efficiency objectives. This is the function of self-government committees in housing projects or concentration camps, as they become reliable channels for the transmission of managerial directives. Usually, such devices also function to share responsibility and thus to bolster the legitimacy of established authority. Thus any given act of formal coöptation will tend to fulfill both the political function of defending legitimacy and the administrative function of establishing reliable channels for communication and direction.

In general, the use of formal coöptation by a leadership does not envision the transfer of actual power. The forms of participation are emphasized but action is channeled so as to fulfill the administrative functions while preserving the locus of significant decision in the hands of the initiating group. The concept of formal coöptation will be utilized primarily in the analysis of TVA's relation to the voluntary associations established to gain local participation in the administration of the Authority's programs.

Informal coöptation.—Coöptation may be, however, a response to the pressure of specific centers of power within the community. This is not primarily a matter of the sense of legitimacy or of a general and diffuse lack of confidence. Legitimacy and confidence may be well established with relation to the general public, yet organized forces which are able to threaten the formal authority may effectively shape its structure and policy. The organization faced with its institutional environment, or the leadership faced with its ranks, must take into account these outside elements. They may be brought into the leadership or policy-determining structure, may be given a place as a recognition of and concession to the resources they can independently command. The representation of interests through administrative constituencies is a typical example of this process. Or, within an organization, individuals upon whom the group is dependent for funds or other resources may insist upon and receive a share in the determination of policy. This type of coöptation is typically expressed in informal terms, for the problem is not one of responding to a state of imbalance with respect to the "people as a whole" but rather one of meeting the pressure of specific individuals or interest groups which are in a position to enforce demands. The latter are interested in the substance of power and not necessarily in its forms. Moreover, an open acknowledgment of capitulation to specific interests may itself undermine the sense of legitimacy of the formal authority within the community. Consequently, there is a positive pressure to refrain from explicit recognition of the relationship established. This concept will be utilized in analyzing the underlying meaning of certain formal methods of coöperation initated in line with the TVA's grass-roots policy.

Coöptation reflects a state of tension between formal authority and social power. This authority is always embodied in a particular structure and leadership, but social power itself has to do with subjective and objective factors which control the loyalties and potential manipulability of the community. Where the formal authority or leadership reflects real social power, its stability is assured. On the other hand, when it becomes divorced from the sources of social power its continued existence is threatened. This threat may arise from the sheer alienation of sentiment or because other leaderships control the sources of social power. Where a leadership has been accustomed to the assumption that its constituents respond to it as individuals, there may be a rude awakening when organization of those constituents creates nucleuses of strength which are able to effectively demand a sharing of power.

The significance of coöptation for organizational analysis is not simply that there is a change in or a broadening of leadership, and that this is an adaptive response, but also *that this change is consequential for the character and role of the organization or governing body.* Coöptation results in some constriction of the field of choice available to the organization or leadership in question. The character of the coöpted elements will necessarily shape the modes of action available to the group which has won adaptation at the price of commitment to outside elements. In other words, if it is true that the TVA has, whether as a defensive or as an idealistic measure, absorbed local elements into its policy-determining structure, we should expect to find that this process has had an effect upon the evolving character of the Authority itself. From the viewpoint of the initiators of the project, and of its public supporters, the force and direction of this effect may be completely unanticipated.

The important consideration is that the TVA's choice of methods could not be expected to be free of the normal dilemmas of action. If the sentiment of the people (or its organized expression) is conservative, democratic forms may require a blunting of social purpose. A perception of the details of this tendency is all important for the attempt to bind together planning and democracy. Planning is always positive—for the fulfillment of some program,—but democracy may negate its execution. This dilemma requires an understanding of the possible unanticipated consequences which may ensue when positive social policy is coupled with a commitment to democratic procedure. The description and analysis which follows, in tracing the consequences of TVA's grass-roots policy for the role and character of the organization, may cast some light upon that problem.[4]

---

[4] The notion of "unanticipated consequence" referred to in this section is central to this study. See below, pp. 253–259, for a theoretical statement of the problem.

[14]

PLANNING AND DEMOCRACY

F.A. Hayek

> The statesman who should attempt to direct private people in what manner they ought to employ their capitals, would not only load himself with a most unnecessary attention, but assume an authority which could safely be trusted to no council and senate whatever, and which would nowhere be so dangerous as in the hands of a man who had folly and presumption enough to fancy himself fit to exercise it.
>
> *Adam Smith.*

THE common features of all collectivist systems may be described, in a phrase ever dear to socialists of all schools, as the deliberate organisation of the labours of society for a definite social goal. That our present society lacks such "conscious" direction towards a single aim, that its activities are guided by the whims and fancies of irresponsible individuals, has always been one of the main complaints of its socialist critics.

In many ways this puts the basic issue very clearly. And it directs us at once to the point where the conflict arises between individual freedom and collectivism. The various kinds of collectivism, communism, fascism, etc., differ between themselves in the nature of the goal towards which they want to direct the efforts of society. But they all differ from liberalism and individualism in wanting to organise the whole of society and all its resources for this unitary end, and in refusing to recognise autonomous spheres in which the ends of the individuals are supreme. In short, they are totalitarian in the true sense of this new word which we have adopted to describe the unexpected but nevertheless inseparable manifestations of what in theory we call collectivism.

The "social goal", or "common purpose", for which society is to be organised, is usually vaguely described as the "common good", or the "general welfare", or the "general interest". It does not need much reflection to see that these terms have no sufficiently definite meaning to determine a particular course of action. The welfare and the happiness of millions cannot be measured on a single scale of less and more. The welfare of a people, like the happiness of a man, depends on a great many things that can be provided in an infinite variety of combinations. It cannot be adequately expressed as a single end, but only as a hierarchy of ends, a comprehensive scale of values in which every need of every person is given its place. To direct all our activities according to a single plan presupposes that

PLANNING AND DEMOCRACY   43

every one of our needs is given its rank in an order of values
which must be complete enough to make it possible to decide
between all the different courses between which the planner has
to choose.   It presupposes, in short, the existence of a complete
ethical code in which all the different human values are allotted
their due place.

The conception of a complete ethical code is unfamiliar and
it requires some effort of imagination to see what it involves.
We are not in the habit of thinking of moral codes as more or
less complete.   The fact that we are constantly choosing between
different values without a social code prescribing how we ought
to choose, does not surprise us, and does not suggest to us that
our moral code is incomplete.   In our society there is neither
occasion nor reason why people should develop common views
about what should be done in such situations.   But where all the
means to be used are the property of society, and are to be used
in the name of society according to a unitary plan, a " social " view
about what ought to be done must guide all decisions.   In such
a world we should soon find that our moral code is full of gaps.

We are not concerned here with the question whether it would
be desirable to have such a complete ethical code.   It may
merely be pointed out that up to the present the growth of
civilisation has been accompanied by a steady diminution of the
sphere in which individual actions are bound by fixed rules.
The rules of which our common moral code consists have progressively become fewer and more general in character.   From
the primitive man who was bound by an elaborate ritual in
almost every one of his daily activities, who was limited by innumerable taboos, and who could scarcely conceive of doing things
in a way different from his fellows, morals have more and more
tended to become merely limits circumscribing the sphere within
which the individual could behave as he liked.   The adoption
of a common ethical code comprehensive enough to determine
a unitary economic plan would mean a complete reversal of this
tendency.

The essential point for us is that no such complete ethical
code exists.   The attempt to direct all economic activity according to a single plan would raise innumerable questions to which
the answer could be provided only by a moral rule, but to which
existing morals have no answer and where there exists no agreed
view on what ought to be done.   People will have either no
definite views or conflicting views on such questions, because
in the free society in which we have lived there has been no
occasion to think about them and still less to form common
opinions about them.

*   *   *   *   *

44   THE ROAD TO SERFDOM

Not only do we not possess such an all-inclusive scale of values : it would be impossible for any mind to comprehend the infinite variety of different needs of different people which compete for the available resources and to attach a definite weight to each. For our problem it is of minor importance whether the ends for which any person cares comprehend only his own individual needs, or whether they include the needs of his closer or even those of his more distant fellows—that is, whether he is egoistic or altruistic in the ordinary senses of these words. The point which is so important is the basic fact that it is impossible for any man to survey more than a limited field, to be aware of the urgency of more than a limited number of needs. Whether his interests centre round his own physical needs, or whether he takes a warm interest in the welfare of every human being he knows, the ends about which he can be concerned will always be only an infinitesimal fraction of the needs of all men.

This is the fundamental fact on which the whole philosophy of individualism is based. It does not assume, as is often asserted, that man is egoistic or selfish, or ought to be. It merely starts from the indisputable fact that the limits of our powers of imagination make it impossible to include in our scale of values more than a sector of the needs of the whole society, and that, since, strictly speaking, scales of value can exist only in individual minds, nothing but partial scales of values exist, scales which are inevitably different and often inconsistent with each other. From this the individualist concludes that the individuals should be allowed, within defined limits, to follow their own values and preferences rather than somebody else's, that within these spheres the individual's system of ends should be supreme and not subject to any dictation by others. It is this recognition of the individual as the ultimate judge of his ends, the belief that as far as possible his own views ought to govern his actions, that forms the essence of the individualist position.

This view does not, of course, exclude the recognition of social ends, or rather of a coincidence of individual ends which makes it advisable for men to combine for their pursuit. But it limits such common action to the instances where individual views coincide ; what are called " social ends " are for it merely identical ends of many individuals—or ends to the achievement of which individuals are willing to contribute in return for the assistance they receive in the satisfaction of their own desires. Common action is thus limited to the fields where people agree on common ends. Very frequently these common ends will not be ultimate ends to the individuals, but means which different persons can use for different purposes. In fact, people are most

PLANNING AND DEMOCRACY 45

likely to agree on common action where the common end is not an ultimate end to them, but a means capable of serving a great variety of purposes.

When individuals combine in a joint effort to realise ends they have in common, the organisations, like the state, that they form for this purpose, are given their own system of ends and their own means. But any organisation thus formed remains one " person " among others, in the case of the state much more powerful than any of the others, it is true, yet still with its separate and limited sphere in which alone its ends are supreme. The limits of this sphere are determined by the extent to which the individuals agree on particular ends ; and the probability that they will agree on a particular course of action necessarily decreases as the scope of such action extends. There are certain functions of the state on the exercise of which there will be practical unanimity among its citizens ; there will be others on which there will be agreement of a substantial majority ; and so on, till we come to fields where, although each individual might wish the state to act in some way, there will be almost as many views about what the government should do as there are different people.

We can rely on voluntary agreement to guide the action of the state only so long as it is confined to spheres where agreement exists. But not only when the state undertakes direct control in fields where there is no such agreement is it bound to suppress individual freedom. We can unfortunately not indefinitely extend the sphere of common action and still leave the individual free in his own sphere. Once the communal sector, in which the state controls all the means, exceeds a certain proportion of the whole, the effects of its actions dominate the whole system. Although the state controls directly the use of only a large part of the available resources, the effects of its decisions on the remaining part of the economic system become so great that indirectly it controls almost everything. Where, as was, for example, true in Germany as early as 1928, the central and local authorities directly control the use of more than half the national income (according to an official German estimate then, 53 per cent.) they control indirectly almost the whole economic life of the nation. There is, then, scarcely an individual end which is not dependent for its achievement on the action of the state, and the " social scale of values " which guides the state's action must embrace practically all individual ends.

* * * * *

It is not difficult to see what must be the consequences when democracy embarks upon a course of planning which in its execution requires more agreement than in fact exists. The

THE ROAD TO SERFDOM

people may have agreed on adopting a system of directed economy because they have been convinced that it will produce great prosperity. In the discussions leading to the decision, the goal of planning will have been described by some such term as " common welfare " which only conceals the absence of real agreement on the ends of planning. Agreement will in fact exist only on the mechanism to be used. But it is a mechanism which can be used only for a common end ; and the question of the precise goal towards which all activity is to be directed will arise as soon as the executive power has to translate the demand for a single plan into a particular plan. Then it will appear that the agreement on the desirability of planning is not supported by agreement on the ends the plan is to serve. The effect of the people agreeing that there must be central planning, without agreeing on the ends, will be rather as if a group of people were to commit themselves to take a journey together without agreeing where they want to go : with the result that they may all have to make a journey which most of them do not want at all. That planning creates a situation in which it is necessary for us to agree on a much larger number of topics than we have been used to, and that in a planned system we cannot confine collective action to the tasks on which we can agree, but are forced to produce agreement on everything in order that any action can be taken at all, is one of the features which contribute more than most to determining the character of a planned system.

It may have been the unanimously expressed will of the people that parliament should prepare a comprehensive economic plan, yet neither the people nor its representatives need therefore be able to agree on any particular plan. The inability of demo-cratic assemblies to carry out what seems to be a clear mandate of the people will inevitably cause dissatisfaction with democratic institutions. Parliaments come to be regarded as ineffective " talking shops ", unable or incompetent to carry out the tasks for which they have been chosen. The conviction grows that if efficient planning is to be done, the direction must be " taken out of politics " and placed in the hands of experts, permanent officials or independent autonomous bodies.

The difficulty is well known to socialists. It will soon be half a century since the Webbs began to complain of " the increased incapacity of the House of Commons to cope with its work ".[1] More recently, Professor Laski has elaborated the argument :

> It is common ground that the present parliamentary machine is quite unsuited to pass rapidly a great body of complicated legislation.

---

[1] S. and B. Webb, *Industrial Democracy*, 1897, p. 800, footnote.

The National Government, indeed, has in substance admitted this by implementing its economy and tariff measures not by detailed debate in the House of Commons but by a wholesale system of delegated legislation. A Labour Government would, I presume, build upon the amplitude of this precedent. It would confine the House of Commons to the two functions it can properly perform : the ventilation of grievances and the discussion of general principles of its measures. Its Bills would take the form of general formulæ conferring wide powers on the appropriate government departments ; and those powers would be exercised by Order in Council which could, if desired, be attacked in the House by means of a vote of no confidence. The necessity and value of delegated legislation has recently been strongly reaffirmed by the Donoughmore Committee ; and its extension is inevitable if the process of socialisation is not to be wrecked by the normal methods of obstruction which existing parliamentary procedure sanctions.

And to make it quite clear that a socialist government must not allow itself to be too much fettered by democratic procedure, Professor Laski at the end of the same article raised the question " whether in a period of transition to Socialism, a Labour Government can risk the overthrow of its measures as a result of the next general election "—and left it significantly unanswered.[1]

* * * * *

It is important clearly to see the causes of this admitted ineffectiveness of parliaments when it comes to a detailed administration of the economic affairs of a nation. The fault is neither with the individual representatives nor with parliamentary institutions as such, but with the contradictions inherent in the task with which they are charged. They are not asked to act where they can agree, but to produce agreement on everything—the whole direction of the resources of the nation. For such a task the system of majority decision is, however, not suited. Majorities will be found where it is a choice between limited alternatives ; but it is a superstition to believe that there must be a majority view on everything. There is no reason why there should be

[1] H. J. Laski, " Labour and the Constitution ", *The New Statesman and Nation*, No. 81 (New Series), Sept. 10th, 1932, p. 277. In a book (*Democracy in Crisis*, 1933, particularly p. 87) in which Professor Laski later elaborated these ideas, his determination that parliamentary democracy must not be allowed to form an obstacle to the realisation of socialism is even more plainly expressed : not only would a socialist government " take vast powers and legislate under them by ordinance and decree " and " suspend the classic formulæ of normal opposition ", but the " continuance of parliamentary government would depend on its [i.e. the Labour Government's] possession of guarantees from the Conservative Party that its work of transformation would not be disrupted by repeal in the event of its defeat at the polls " !
As Professor Laski invokes the authority of the Donoughmore Committee it may be worth recalling that Professor Laski was a member of that committee and presumably one of the authors of its report.

a majority in favour of any one of the different possible courses of positive action if their number is legion. Every member of the legislative assembly might prefer some particular plan for the direction of economic activity to no plan, yet no one plan may appear preferable to a majority to no plan at all.

Nor can a coherent plan be achieved by breaking it up into parts and voting on particular issues. A democratic assembly voting and amending a comprehensive economic plan clause by clause, as it deliberates on an ordinary bill, makes nonsense. An economic plan, to deserve the name, must have a unitary conception. Even if parliament could, proceeding step by step, agree on some scheme, it would certainly in the end satisfy nobody. A complex whole where all the parts must be most carefully adjusted to each other, cannot be achieved through a compromise between conflicting views. To draw up an economic plan in this fashion is even less possible than, for example, successfully to plan a military campaign by democratic procedure. As in strategy it would become inevitable to delegate the task to the experts.

Yet the difference is that, while the general who is put in charge of a campaign is given a single end to which, for the duration of the campaign, all the means under his control have to be exclusively devoted, there can be no such single goal given to the economic planner, and no similar limitation of the means imposed upon him. The general has not got to balance different independent aims against each other ; there is for him only one supreme goal. But the ends of an economic plan, or of any part of it, cannot be defined apart from the particular plan. It is the essence of the economic problem that the making of an economic plan involves the choice between conflicting or competing ends—different needs of different people. But which ends do so conflict, which will have to be sacrificed if we want to achieve certain others, in short, which are the alternatives between which we must choose, can only be known to those who know all the facts ; and only they, the experts, are in a position to decide which of the different ends are to be given preference. It is inevitable that they should impose their scale of preferences on the community for which they plan.

This is not always clearly recognised and delegation is usually justified by the technical character of the task. But this does not mean that only the technical detail is delegated, or even that the inability of parliaments to understand the technical detail is the root of the difficulty.[1] Alterations in the structure

---

[1] It is instructive in this connection briefly to refer to the Government document in which in recent years these problems have been discussed. As long as thirteen years ago, that is before this country finally abandoned economic liberalism, the process of delegating legislative powers had already been carried

of civil law are no less technical and no more difficult to appreciate in all their implications ; yet nobody has yet seriously suggested that legislation there should be delegated to a body of experts. The fact is that in these fields legislation does not go beyond general rules on which true majority agreement can be achieved, while in the direction of economic activity the interests to be reconciled are so divergent that no true agreement is likely to be reached in a democratic assembly.

It should be recognised, however, that it is not the delegation of law-making power as such, which is so objectionable. To oppose delegation as such is to oppose a symptom instead of the cause and, as it may be a necessary result of other causes, to weaken the case. So long as the power that is delegated is merely the power to make general rules, there may be very good reasons why such rules should be laid down by local rather than by the central authority. The objectionable feature is that delegation is so often resorted to because the matter in hand cannot be regulated by general rules but only by the exercise of discretion in the decision of particular cases. In these instances delegation means that some authority is given power to make with the force of law what to all intents and purposes are arbitrary decisions (usually described as " judging the case on its merits ").

The delegation of particular technical tasks to separate bodies, while a regular feature, is yet only the first step in the process whereby a democracy which embarks on planning progressively relinquishes its powers. The expedient of delegation cannot really remove the causes which make all the advocates of comprehensive planning so impatient with the impotence of democracy. The delegation of particular powers to separate agencies creates

to a point where it was felt necessary to appoint a committee to investigate " what safeguards are desirable or necessary to secure the sovereignty of Law ". In its report the " Donoughmore Committee " (*Report of the* [Lord Chancellor's] *Committee on Ministers' Powers*, Cmd. 4060, 1932) showed that even at that date Parliament had resorted " to the practice of wholesale and indiscriminate delegation " but regarded this (it was before we had really glanced into the totalitarian abyss !) as an inevitably and relatively innocuous development. And it is probably true that delegation as such need not be a danger to freedom. The interesting point is why delegation had become necessary on such a scale. First place among the causes enumerated in the report is given to the fact that " Parliament nowadays passes so many laws every year " and that " much of the detail is so technical as to be unsuitable for Parliamentary discussion ". But if this were all there would be no reason why the detail should not be worked out *before* rather than after Parliament passes a law. What is probably in many cases a much more important reason why, " if Parliament were not willing to delegate law-making power, Parliament would be unable to pass the kind and quantity of legislation which public opinion requires " is innocently revealed in the little sentence that " many of the laws affect people's lives so closely that elasticity is essential " ! What does this mean if not conferment of arbitrary power, power limited by no fixed principles and which in the opinion of Parliament cannot be limited by definite and unambiguous rules ?

a new obstacle to the achievement of a single co-ordinated plan. Even if, by this expedient, a democracy should succeed in planning every sector of economic activity, it would still have to face the problem of integrating these separate plans into a unitary whole. Many separate plans do not make a planned whole—in fact, as the planners ought to be the first to admit—they may be worse than no plan. But the democratic legislature will long hesitate to relinquish the decisions on really vital issues, and so long as it does so it makes it impossible for anyone else to provide the comprehensive plan. Yet agreement that planning is necessary, together with the inability of democratic assemblies to produce a plan, will evoke stronger and stronger demands that the government or some single individual should be given powers to act on their own responsibility. The belief is becoming more and more widespread that, if things are to get done, the responsible authorities must be freed from the fetters of democratic procedure.

The cry for an economic dictator is a characteristic stage in the movement towards planning, not unfamiliar in this country. It is now several years since one of the most acute of foreign students of England, the late Elie Halévy, suggested that "if you take a composite photograph of Lord Eustace Percy, Sir Oswald Mosley, and Sir Stafford Cripps, I think you would find this common feature—you would find them all agreeing to say : ' We are living in economic chaos and we cannot get out of it except under some kind of dictatorial leadership '."[1] The number of influential public men whose inclusion would not materially alter the features of the " composite photograph " has since grown considerably.

In Germany, even before Hitler came into power, the movement had already progressed much further. It is important to remember that for some time before 1933 Germany had reached a stage in which it had, in effect, had to be governed dictatorially. Nobody could then doubt that for the time being democracy had broken down, and that sincere democrats like Brüning were no more able to govern democratically than Schleicher or von Papen. Hitler did not have to destroy democracy ; he merely took advantage of the decay of democracy and at the critical moment obtained the support of many to whom, though they detested Hitler, he yet seemed the only man strong enough to get things done.

*   *   *   *   *

The argument by which the planners usually try to reconcile us with this development is that so long as democracy retains

[1] " Socialism and the Problems of Democratic Parliamentarism ", *International Affairs*, vol. XIII, p. 501.

PLANNING AND DEMOCRACY 51

ultimate control, the essentials of democracy are not affected. Thus Karl Mannheim writes :

> The only [*sic*] way in which a planned society differs from that of the nineteenth century is that more and more spheres of social life, and ultimately each and all of them, are subjected to state control. But if a few controls can be held in check by parliamentary sovereignty, so can many. . . . in a democratic state sovereignty can be boundlessly strengthened by plenary powers without renouncing democratic control.[1]

This belief overlooks a vital distinction. Parliament can, of course, control the execution of tasks where it can give definite directions, where it has first agreed on the aim and merely delegates the working out of the detail. The situation is entirely different when the reason for the delegation is that there is no real agreement on the ends, when the body charged with the planning has to choose between ends of whose conflict parliament is not even aware, and when the most that can be done is to present to it a plan which has to be accepted or rejected as a whole. There may and probably will be criticism ; but as no majority can agree on an alternative plan, and the parts objected to can almost always be represented as essential parts of the whole, it will remain quite ineffective. Parliamentary discussion may be retained as a useful safety-valve, and even more as a convenient medium through which the official answers to complaints are disseminated. It may even prevent some flagrant abuses and successfully insist on particular shortcomings being remedied. But it cannot direct. It will at best be reduced to choosing the persons who are to have practically absolute power. The whole system will tend towards that plebiscitarian dictatorship in which the head of the government is from time to time confirmed in his position by popular vote, but where he has all the powers at his command to make certain that the vote will go in the direction he desires.

It is the price of democracy that the possibilities of conscious control are restricted to the fields where true agreement exists, and that in some fields things must be left to chance. But in a society which for its functioning depends on central planning, this control cannot be made dependent on a majority being able to agree ; it will often be necessary that the will of a small minority be imposed upon the people, because this minority will be the largest group able to agree among themselves on the question at issue. Democratic government has worked successfully where, and so long as, the functions of government were, by a widely accepted creed, restricted to fields where agreement among a

---

[1] K. Mannheim, *Man and Society in an Age of Reconstruction*, 1940, p. 340.

majority could be achieved by free discussion ; and it is the great merit of the liberal creed that it reduced the range of subjects on which agreement was necessary to one on which it was likely to exist in a society of free men. It is now often said that democracy will not tolerate " capitalism ". If " capitalism " means here a competitive system based on free disposal over private property, it is far more important to realise that only within this system is democracy possible. When it becomes dominated by a collectivist creed, democracy will inevitably destroy itself.

* * * * *

We have no intention, however, of making a fetish of democracy. It may well be true that our generation talks and thinks too much of democracy and too little of the values which it serves. It cannot be said of democracy, as Lord Acton truly said of liberty, that it " is not a means to a higher political end. It is itself the highest political end. It is not for the sake of a good public administration that it is required, but for the security in the pursuit of the highest objects of civil society, and of private life." Democracy is essentially a means, a utilitarian device for safeguarding internal peace and individual freedom. As such it is by no means infallible or certain. Nor must we forget that there has often been much more cultural and spiritual freedom under an autocratic rule than under some democracies—and it is at least conceivable that under the government of a very homogeneous and doctrinaire majority democratic government might be as oppressive as the worst dictatorship. Our point, however, is not that dictatorship must inevitably extirpate freedom, but rather that planning leads to dictatorship because dictatorship is the most effective instrument of coercion and the enforcement of ideals, and as such essential if central planning on a large scale is to be possible. The clash between planning and democracy arises simply from the fact that the latter is an obstacle to the suppression of freedom which the direction of economic activity requires. But in so far as democracy ceases to be a guarantee of individual freedom, it may well persist in some form under a totalitarian regime. A true " dictatorship of the proletariat ", even if democratic in form, if it undertook centrally to direct the economic system, would probably destroy personal freedom as completely as any autocracy has ever done.

The fashionable concentration on democracy as the main value threatened is not without danger. It is largely responsible for the misleading and unfounded belief that so long as the ultimate source of power is the will of the majority, the power cannot be arbitrary. The false assurance which many people

PLANNING AND DEMOCRACY   53

derive from this belief is an important cause of the general
unawareness of the dangers which we face. There is no justification for the belief that so long as power is conferred by democratic procedure, it cannot be arbitrary ; the contrast suggested
by this statement is altogether false : it is not the source but the
limitation of power which prevents it from being arbitrary.
Democratic control *may* prevent power from becoming arbitrary,
but it does not do so by its mere existence. If democracy resolves
on a task which necessarily involves the use of power which
cannot be guided by fixed rules, it must become arbitrary power.

[15]

THE CONCEPT OF SOCIAL CONTROL

Planning as the Rational Mastery of the Irrational

Karl Mannheim

Society is almost ready to pass into a new stage. Unless we realize this, we shall lose the boundless opportunities which a co-ordination of social techniques would put into our hands.

Planned freedom can only be achieved by a deliberate and skilful handling of these techniques, so that every kind of

[1] I have dealt with the opportunities which planned society could offer for the growth of personality in three public lectures " Planned Society and the Problem of Human Personality " given at the London School of Economics. These lectures are as yet unpublished.

influence which can be brought to bear on human beings must be theoretically understood.   The planning authority should be able to decide on empirical grounds what sort of influence to use in a given situation, basing its judgments on the scientific study of society, coupled if possible with sociological experiments.   Such a tendency is already apparent in certain fields. For example, to-day we are developing a new kind of scientific study, e.g. the sociology of taxation,[1] in order to discover which methods work best in different countries. In the same way it is to be hoped that we shall be able to decide by experience what tactics to adopt in other spheres of society in view of the customs prevailing at the time. For just as different citizens in different countries feel differently about moral obligations when it comes to paying taxes, so there are different habits of thought, beaten tracks in the psychology of nations, which lead them to do some things in obedience to military orders, others in a spirit of free co-operation.

   Social science in pondering the right techniques will obviously have to work with varying conceptions of efficiency. Apart from the purely technical conception which could be defined as " achieving the maximum effect by the minimum of effort ", other more human considerations must be taken into account. A drastic form of taxation may be efficient for the moment from the purely technical point of view because it extorts the largest sum in the shortest possible time, but psychologically and in the long run it may be inefficient, because it may shake the confidence of the tax-payer on which every future collection of taxes depends. Thus every economic, administrative, and educational code must be ready to consider not only the short-lived technical efficiency but the deeper psychological effects. A society in which profit is not the only criterion of economic production will prefer to work by methods which, though less effective from the point of view of output, give the workers more psychological satisfaction.   Has not even our own brand of capitalist society, although it is prepared to fight for purely economic ends, been forced to cut down its profits

---

[1] On the Sociology of taxation, cf. Sultan, H., *Die Staatseinnahmen,* Versuch einer soziologischen Finanztheorie als Teil einer Theorie der politischen Ökonomie. Tübingen, 1932 ; and Mann, F. K., *Finanzsoziologie,* Kölner Vierteljahreshefte für Soziologie, vol. 12, No. 1, 1933.

THE CONCEPT OF SOCIAL CONTROL 267

in favour of the social services ? A planned society would be still more likely to invent new forms of calculation owing to its greater interest in the good of the whole. The changed conception of efficiency which we have just discussed would not confine itself to the economic sphere. The psychological, social, and technical means applied should be judged by their effect on character and individuality as well as by their purely technical efficiency. Why should not a planned society which could deal not only with economy proper, but with human economy as well, make allowance for this point of view ? We can go even further. A finer mastery of the social keyboard, a more accurate knowledge of social technique, does not necessarily result in excessive interference. I believe that the wisdom of the planner would very often lead to a deliberate refusal to interfere in many fields. I can perhaps explain what I have in mind by giving an example on a smaller scale. An experimental boarding school for instance which aimed at planning the whole scope of its activities, might proceed to think out its syllabus and time-table in detail, but at the same time would see that recreation hours should be provided in which the children were invariably left to themselves without advice or interference so that they could develop their own initiative. Arrangements could at the same time be made for the boys to go off for a tramp on their own, or find themselves work in which their individual initiative would have free play. This is by no means contrary to the principle that educational influences should be carefully controlled. Even in our present society sheltered zones and open battlefields exist side by side. In a planned society they will still be there, but they will be brought into harmony by a deeper understanding of the contribution they make, both to the formation of character and to the efficiency of society.

This rational mastery of the irrational which does not rob it of its peculiar charm, this deliberate recognition of irrationality is only possible when there is a thorough grasp not only of the standardized techniques involved, but also of the spontaneous forms which develop in life when it is left to itself. The keyboard and the polyphonic harmony of musical instruments of which we spoke were no chance metaphors. The analogy is justified in so far that only the man who has fully mastered musical technique can really express the irrationality of musical experience. In the same way a truly planned society does not suppress the genuine dynamics of life or intellectualize them, but tries through a skilful handling of situations to make a fuller use of organic forces than was possible at a stage of more-primitive, inflexible control.

Even the greatest expert in social technique does not imagine that he himself creates the elementary psychological and social processes. The greater his knowledge, the more clearly will he see that a genuine improvement in social technique means an ever fuller use, an ever increasing mastery of the original material. Real skill will not make us inhuman, but human in a deeper sense. Only those who feel that the present state of society is " natural " because they were born into it will oppose true planning, thereby completely overlooking the fact that this alleged naturalness is the chance product of spasmodic interference with the course of social events and the development of the individual—an interference which usually does more harm than good because it is not consciously applied. The clumsiness of our society in which different man-made institutions frequently clash and different moral codes continuously lead to conflicts, is reflected in the rising tide of neurosis in the individual and in disastrous panics and crises in international relations.

If society can be controlled, we must ask ourselves how we can improve our technique of intervention in human affairs, and where this intervention ought to begin. The problem of this " where ", the right point of attack, brings us to the conception of social control.[1] The societies of the past made use of this control in many forms, and we are

[1] C. F. Ross, E. A., *Social Control : A Survey of the Foundations of Order* (New York, 1901), a book which has the merit of having directed attention very early to that problem. But I think in that early stage it was not yet possible to see its ultimate implications, which only become visible as soon as one discusses them in the context of social techniques and planning. Cf. also Cooley, Ch. H., *Social Organization*, New York, 1909, and his *Social Process*, New York, 1918 ; MacIver, R. M., *Society, a Textbook of Sociology*, esp. Book II, part ii, New York, 1937 ; Case, C. M., " Some Sociological Aspects of Coercion," *Publications of the Amer. Sociological Society*, 1922, vol. 117, pp. 75–88 ; Lumley, F. E., *Means of Social Control*, New York, 1925 ; Bernard, L. L., *The Transition as an Objective Standard of Social Control Thesis*, Chicago, 1911 ; " Social Control," *Publications of the American Sociol. Society*, vol. 12, Chicago, 1918 ; Smith, W. R., " School Discipline as Training for the Larger Social Control," *Publ. of the Amer. Sociol Soc.*, vol. 17, 1923 ; Mead, G. H., " The Genesis of the Self and Social Control," *Intern. Journ. of Ethics*, vol. 35, 1924–5. Cf. also I, 1 in the Bibliography.

THE CONCEPT OF SOCIAL CONTROL   269

justified in speaking of the " key positions of social control " in the sense that there have always been foci from which the most important influences emanated.   A new approach to history will be achieved when we are able to translate the main structural changes in terms of a displacement of the former systems of control.   Looking at society as a whole, the replacement of individual controls is never due solely to immediate causes but is a function of changes in the whole configuration.

The question emerges whether in the past the controls grew up side by side haphazard, or whether even then they were unconsciously co-ordinated, and whether in the future such a co-ordination could be deliberately encouraged.   The key to an understanding of shifting social controls lies partly in the changing nature of social techniques and partly in the transformation of human beings themselves.

In a society where the technique of social control is still in its infancy the influence comes from near at hand, from the father, the neighbour, the chieftain.   Standards of behaviour must be inculcated and everybody must conform to them if the society is to work.   This kind of primitive group with its narrow range of social influence will tend to impose too many taboos and will anxiously insist on what Durkheim calls a " mechanical solidarity ".

But in a society in which a more detailed division of labour occurs human conduct can be influenced by subtler and less obvious means.   As Durkheim points out, division of labour creates functions which are complementary to each other, so that everyone is much more dependent on his neighbours than in a society where no such division exists and each as it were produces for himself.   Owing to the division of labour and the consequent dependence of the individual on society, new kinds of pressure come into being which continue to take effect when there is no one to give orders.   Certain situations constantly recur and exert a pressure from which there is little chance of escape.   This " pressure of circumstances " admittedly allows the individual to make his own adjustment, but the number of possible adjustments is limited.   Even if society is not in a position to deal with these situations, they can nevertheless be foreseen and are easily recognizable in the most important spheres of life.   This similarity appears in its most striking form

when we study the biographies of men who belong to the
same period and class : they are usually confronted with the
same type of situation even when they believe their circumstances are unique. It is clear that the social control which
consists in confronting certain social classes with certain
definite situations is radically different from that of primitive
society where the individual is directly affected.   Only
when the social structure has reached a fairly complex
stage of development can the social controls become flexible
enough to provoke a number of possible reactions to typical
conditions instead of laying down hard and fast rules of
behaviour. The types of social control which work through
situations or through force of circumstances are only to be
found at a certain level of society, and their significance
increases as its complexity grows.   In the same way the
vital question whether social control is exercised by a central
group of leaders or is democratically diffused throughout
society depends for its answer both on the social order and
on the social techniques.

In this connection it again becomes clear that discussion
of the problem of social control is hopelessly abstract
when it is not related to the workings of society as a whole
but is artificially divided into water-tight compartments
such as economics, political science, administration, and
education. As long as we specialize only in one of these fields
its nature is hidden from us.   We do not realize that all
these seemingly separate sciences are in fact interrelated,
that they refer to social techniques whose ultimate aim
is to secure the functioning of the social order by bringing
an appropriate influence to bear on the behaviour and attitudes of men.

Once this unity of purpose is recognized the political and
social character of all human institutions becomes clear.
They are not as they seem at first sight designed simply to
achieve a limited object, they are permanent elements in the
political organization of society and have grown up side by
side. Economics in their broader aspect are not merely
a device for regulating production and consumption, they are
also an efficient means of regulating human behaviour as well,
and in some spheres of action they help to adjust it to the
general trend of affairs.   Administration is not merely a
form of social organization created for the purpose of carrying

THE CONCEPT OF SOCIAL CONTROL   271

out certain decisions ; it is becoming more and more obvious to-day that administration is turning into an instrument of political interference and that the methods used in executing the prescribed regulations can serve as an indirect means of altering the balance of power in a society. The dogmatic distinction between making the law (legislation) and expounding it (jurisdiction) does not seem to be as clear cut as it used to be, and we see ever more plainly that in the process of jurisdiction the judges are creating the law. Sociologists do not regard education solely as a means of realizing abstract ideals of culture, such as humanism or technical specialization, but as part of the process of influencing men and women. Education can only be understood when we know for what society and for what social position the pupils are being educated.[1]

If, instead of studying every branch of activity separately, we consider all social activities as a whole we shall be able to classify them as social techniques, whose sole *raison d'être* is to influence human behaviour as society thinks fit.[2] This leads us on to the working hypothesis that the quantum of mental energy needed to produce the habits and outlook of a society remains constant and that only the concrete forms of expression change. In this sense we can speak of a transmutation (metamorphosis) of this energy.

Let us now proceed to examine this transformation of mental energy in greater detail and give an example to show how the same activity (manual labour) was enforced in different ways in two successive phases of history. It is well

---

[1] K. Mannheim, "Mass Education and Group Analysis," op. cit. ; and cf. in the Bibliography III 3*a*, III 4, and III 7*a*.

[2] We will only indicate here what we have explained in another place— why it should be in the liberal age that a tendency arose to divorce the spheres from one another. The habit of thinking in terms of pure economics, the unquestioning distinction between legislature, executive, and judiciary, the autonomy of education, mark only a certain stage in the evolution of society, in which, for structural reasons, co-ordination takes place through checks and balances. But even in this sense the different spheres of action were not so simple and unpolitical as they appeared to be in an abstract analysis. The regulation of property for instance was always political, for it was not only a means of guaranteeing a certain standard of living but regulated human activities in different spheres. Even when there was no authority which consciously set the different parts of the social mechanism in motion, they constantly influenced each other and tended towards equilibrium. This equilibrium was not totalitarian, however, in the sense that it was planned beforehand on theoretical principles to function as a single machine.

known that in Roman society, especially on the great estates (*latifundia*), the work was done by slaves and the principal incentive was the whip. Towards the end of Roman rule, at the beginning of the Middle Ages, this system of slave economy was transformed into serfdom, and now instead of brute force a combination of methods was used to arouse the will to work. First the slaves, once condemned to celibacy, were allowed to marry, so that instead of living in barracks they could have a home and family. This was a more or less deliberate attempt to mobilize the instinct of self-preservation in the economic interests of their masters by strengthening it through family ties. Then this motive was reinforced from another side and a strip of land was given them with a share in the harvest, so that they would take an interest in the output. And finally they were bound to the soil by law, and thus the ambition which society itself had aroused was checked by social regulation, for they had no hope of moving to the best manors in the country. These restrictions on their freedom of movement were further reinforced by the lack of communications.

The transformation of slaves into serfs is an example of the different incentives employed in these two solutions to the labour problem. Instead of the primitive method of brute force applied in slavery, in serfdom there is a combination of stimuli. Blood ties, an emotional attachment to the land, the legal inability to leave it and a vested interest in its produce, all combined to create a skilfully balanced system for arousing the necessary will to work. The particular course which human initiative takes, the changing forms of incentives, are once more functions of the changing social techniques and can only be completely understood with reference to the whole social order. People turned in our example to the more complicated system, not merely because it gave the serf a keener interest in his work but because imperialistic wars, which were a kind of slave-hunting, ceased and with them the source of slave labour.[1]

In this example the transmutation of social energy (metamorphosis) is obvious when we notice how certain systems

---

[1] Cf. Max Weber, " Die sozialen Gründe des Unterganges der antiken Kultur," in his *Gesammelte Aufsätze zur Sozial- und Wirtschaftsgeschichte*, Tübingen, 1924.

THE CONCEPT OF SOCIAL CONTROL   273

used different methods of pressure and stimulation in order to achieve the same result. In spite of its relevance in this particular case the principle of the transmutation of social energy is only a metaphor ; it would be a mistake to carry it too far.[1] It would also be foolish to attempt to measure the quantum of energy[2] ; we might be led into theoretical trifling. For the vital element in the physical principle of the conservation of energy is that quanta of energy can be measured as they actually occur in various forms. Here the analogy of the conservation of energy only serves to emphasize two important facts : First, there is only one single principle underlying all social techniques, that of influencing human behaviour, causing people to act in a desired way. Secondly, the same behaviour (manual labour, in the case we have just analysed) can be obtained sometimes by a single act of direct compulsion, sometimes by a combination of social controls, expanding throughout the whole social texture.

---

[1] C. J. Friedrich, *Constitutional Government and Politics*, New York, London, 1937, pp. 12 ff., speaks of interpreting human action by the power principle, but forgets to emphasize that the idea of the conservation of energy is only adequate if it can be measured. Moreover, he ignores the primary assumption of the unity of social techniques, which in spite of their external differences have in our opinion a single task to fulfil—the influencing of human behaviour. Only if one makes this the basis of one's study is it possible to speak of the transmutation of energy. Otherwise it is impossible to interpret the changing expression of the same tendency as variations of that tendency. Certainly Friedrich has taken an important step in this direction in so far as he regards not merely the compulsory activities but also the spontaneous ones as an expression of this energy. Indeed, obtaining obedience to a distasteful order is a method of influencing behaviour just as much as creating agreement or a spontaneous desire to do one's duty. It is just in this ability to create agreement where authoritarian methods only obtain obedience, that the greater efficiency of democratic methods lies.

[2] In order to measure the mental energy expended in the above mentioned two methods of making people work, the results obtained by slave labour would have to be compared with the energy consumed by the overseers, and then with the results produced by the serfs, in order to contrast the energy expended by the overseers with the energy needed to keep the whole system going. It is clear that these quanta are not measurable, so, as we explained in the text, it is not the equality of the energy expended on which we lay such stress but on the question by what means (pride in one's work, enterprise) and through what combinations of social techniques, identical functions are created in different societies.

As to the psychological effects of spontaneous and authoritarian methods, cf. the following recent contributions : Lewin, K., and Lippitt, R., "An Experimental Approach to the Study of Autocracy and Democracy : A Preliminary Note," *Sociometry* I, Nos. 3–4, 1934. Lewin, K., and White, R. K., "Patterns of Aggressive Behaviour in Experimentally Created Social Climates," *Journal of Soc. Psychol.*, May, 1939.

Part III
Planning as Rational
Scientific Management

Introduction to Part III

Planning and science propel this process of man becoming master over his world and himself along a path towards future human growth. (Faludi, 1973, p. 35)

The set of ideas presented in Part III centre on the conception of planning as a process of societal management. Making a selection from what was a dominating perspective in the planning field in the 1950s and 1960s inevitably means that we have had to omit many significant contributions. Here we present essays which provide clear outlines of positions and developments, many of which have often been referred to in later debate.

These ideas developed in the United States in the mid-twentieth century (see the main Introduction to this volume) and were advocated as a way of realizing, in public policy, the Western 'Enlightenment' project (Friedmann, 1987) and, in particular, the American national 'dream' of a democratic society following an ongoing upward trajectory of material and moral progress (Menand, 2002). The challenge, as understood by proponents of the conception of planning as a process of rational scientific management in the public realm, was to develop an appropriate approach to societal development for a democratic society, guided by 'intelligence' that was informed by scientific methods of inquiry and conducted in open and transparent ways. Proponents argued that policy options and decisions about the guidance of development trajectories could be evaluated in terms of the relation between ends and means and the assessment of potential consequences. These ideas were developed in part to correct what proponents saw as an overemphasis on the substance of policy in planning programmes emerging in the United States in the 1950s (Davidoff and Reiner, Chapter 16, this volume), and in part as a challenge to the practices of political manipulation evident in many US urban governance situations (Meyerson and Banfield, 1955).

As illustrated in Part III of Volume 2 (Hillier and Healey, 2008a), the initial conception of planning as a process of societal management owed much to early twentieth-century pragmatist philosophy. By the 1950s in the United States it had become grounded in a belief in shared social goals, encapsulated in Daniel Bell's (1962) claim that the era of ideological debate was over. But the pragmatic influence was sidelined as ideas about the democratic potential of scientific inquiry were turned into the techniques of 'scientific management' (Churchman, [1968]1979), and the consensus assumptions were undermined by the social critiques of the systemic injustices in US society, which unfolded in the 1960s.

Many advocates of the idea of planning as 'scientific' societal management recognized that they presented a 'heroic' or 'Promethean' endeavour (Faludi, 1973; Etzioni, 1967). The ideas were deliberately normative, intended to develop and transform governance towards more democratic and more effective societal guidance. Proponents hoped to inspire better governance practices (Dyckman, 1961), just as the ideas discussed in Part II were intended to inspire new ways of thinking about society and cities. Yet this transformative agenda was strongly influenced by parallel developments in economics and management science, which drew the technical operationalization of the conception of rational procedures towards a strong emphasis on efficiency and effectiveness, rather than on democracy as a social and moral project (Dyckman, Chapter 21). This influence also encouraged proponents to treat the world of government agencies and public policy-making as if it consisted of agencies that acted like individuals, with interests and preferences already pre-given. The challenge then was to find a procedure for making 'democratic' choices between different preferences in terms of their impacts on different interests.

Even in the 1950s, this led to a debate between those aiming to achieve transformation by 'big leaps', encapsulated in societal or urban transformation strategies, and those who advocated the established economic methods of comparing strategies at the margins, focusing on incremental change rather than on major transformations. This 'incrementalist' alternative to the comprehensive, rational, social choice process was progressively developed by Charles Lindblom into a strategy of 'partisan mutual adjustment' as an alternative 'intelligence of democracy' (Lindblom, Chapter 17 and 1965). Amitai Etzioni sought to reconcile the rationalist and incrementalist approaches in his metaphor of mixed-scanning (Etzioni, 1967). He suggested that what governments needed was a capacity for large-scale decisions in some situations and for incremental decisions in the routine flow of policy-making activity. Both approaches assumed that social choices – choices made by public agencies on behalf of citizens – should be conducted through careful argument that was in turn informed by scientific inquiry.

Planners and development economists carrying the banner of 'rational' ideas of policy-making entered two practice arenas which opened up in the 1950s – national economic development in the so-called 'developing' world and urban development in US cities. As the approach evolved, it spun out into a policy development technology which influenced the world of international aid agencies and public administration in many 'developed' countries (Friedmann and Weaver, 1979; Hillier and Healey, 2008a, Part I). In Europe, its principles underlay the reforms to urban and regional planning legislation in several countries in the 1960s and 1970s, and traces of it can be found in the reformulation of public administration in the 1990s, known as the 'new public management', with its vocabulary of impact analysis, indicators, targets and monitoring (Ferlie *at al.*, 1996).[1] But as the technology and practice of 'rational' policy-making procedures developed, the original transformative aims were slowly eroded, just as the American dream of progressive democracy itself faltered.

The critical notion underlying the rational approach is that public policy decisions about development futures should be made in 'rational' ways. Planning, according to Davidoff and Reiner (Chapter 16), is a 'set of procedures' for making social choices in rational ways (p. 307). By 'rational' in this context, proponents meant not just that they involve processes of reasoned argument, but that such argument proceeds through systematic, deductive logic. Starting from goals to be achieved, impediments to goal-achievement are analysed using 'scientific' methods. From this analysis a range of policy options can be identified. These are then evaluated by criteria derived from the value premises embodied in the goals. Such a linear and logical form of argumentation gives transparency to decision-makers and those who judge them, and, in theory, provides a countervailing force to political manipulation. Planning

---

[1]   NPM principles aim to shift attention from the design of policy processes to the setting of criteria through which to assess outputs and outcomes, but its link to neoclassical assumptions about individual behaviour and to a positivist conception of knowledge and scientific inquiry remains strong.

thus offers a kind of superior rationality, buttressing public policy decisions with technical information. When focused on societal development or urban development, it enables a more holistic, comprehensive and long-term perspective to develop (Dyckman, 1961). Its objective, often rather vaguely expressed, was the progressive development of individual potential in democratic societies. Faludi (1973) attempted to specify this goal more precisely in his conception of 'human growth'.

Advocates of this rational approach understood well the potential for conflict over values in a democratic society and the complexity of social choices focused on development futures. But they believed that a joint effort by politicians and experts could arrive at well-grounded choices. Politicians were allotted their role as elected representatives in the making of judgements between values. Expert planners, using scientific methods of inquiry, provided a structured basis for making such choices (Davidoff and Reiner, Chapter 16). This relationship thus contrasted with that advocated in continental European public administration, where politicians made laws that were then 'administered' by officials who converted the laws into bureaucratic rules. This also, in theory, imbued public decision-making with a form of transparency, but assumed that future demands, needs and contextual conditions could be fixed in advance and fitted into a regulatory development plan. This did not allow for unforeseen evolutions. Expert planners following the rational procedure were expected to conduct analyses which looked into the emerging future in more informed and innovative ways, so that politicians could be encouraged to make more flexible policies rather than follow fixed rules. Goals and objectives – that is, expressions of values – rather than administrative rules were to become guiding principles of development policy.

'Scientific method' was central to this notion of 'rational' decision-making. This concept had both a broad and a narrow meaning. In its broad meaning, it referred to an attitude and practice of continuous critical inquiry, informed by empirical investigation and probing argumentation. This echoed the conception of scientific method advocated by pragmatist John Dewey ((1910), and see Hillier and Healey, 2008a, Part III). In its narrower meaning, the method proposed was that of 'logical positivism', which centred on the formulation and testing of hypotheses in relation to empirical evidence through which principles and laws of social processes could be developed (Davidoff and Reiner, Chapter 16). This in turn led to the anticipation that such laws and principles could be used to construct models of social 'systems'. The relations of these systems, some advocates believed, could be expressed in the language of mathematics, enabling the testing of policy options experimentally in a model which mirrored the 'real' world.[2]

This conception of the 'science' needed for rational social choice of development trajectories unleashed a stream of work among planners and others, who sought to construct holistic and dynamic models of urban systems in order to assist, in particular, in major transport and land development decisions. In this way, the actions of individuals and individual agencies, such as firms, were set in the context of some kind of systemic relation that connected parts to wholes. These ideas drew on conceptions from the natural science of 'ecosystems' and the military science of self-steering missiles. They were then developed, in particular, in the fields of operations research and management science, migrating from there into the planning

---

[2] Advocates of urban systems modelling held great hopes of stochastic, probabilistic mathematics as a way to build complex, multivariate open systems models: see Chadwick (1971).

field. Some proponents of a 'systems' perspective were well aware of the limits of building determinist, predictive models of phenomena as complex as urban systems, notably C.W. Churchman (1971, [1968]1979), but others, such as Jay Forrester (1969), promoted the model-building enterprise vigorously. As developed in the work of British contributors, McLoughlin (1969) and Chadwick (1971) in Manchester University, urban systems were understood as being hierarchically ordered, with parts linking into a system, which was in turn a part of a larger order. A system was not to be understood as a machine that works, but as a system that evolves (McLoughlin, 1969). The dynamics of such systems involved ongoing interaction with a wider environment, generating a continual need to re-establish a moving equilibrium in order to keep the system 'on course'. This course was the upward development trajectory, 'human growth', achieved by continuous learning and growth in 'intelligence' accumulated by the processes of dynamic interaction with the system environment. The model-building efforts of the 1960s were sharply criticized in the 1970s.[3] However, some proponents of a less determinist understanding of system dynamics provided the inspiration for later work on modelling complex systems, which were infused by developments in complexity science (see Hillier and Healey, 2008b, Part III).[4]

Somewhat paradoxically, these self-regulating, learning systems needed 'steering'. McLoughlin (1969) equated steering mechanisms not just with government action, but also with the role of a British local government planning department. Such an agency, he imagined, provided the 'cybernetic control system' that prevented urban and regional systems swinging out of balance. Such control systems held the system on course like, in McLoughlin's famous analogy, a 'helmsman steering a ship' (1969, p. 86). The 'plan' – McLoughlin had in mind a typical urban development plan of the period – served as a critical ordering device, a basis of argumentation and a guidance manual for these cybernetically steering planners. Through such systematic ordering, the messy complexity of evolving urban dynamics was to be steered back into 'equilibrium'.

Those advocating this conception of the planning task raised issues that have continued to reverberate in the planning field. But they quickly attracted criticism, too. For many, the problem was one which afflicts all advocates of a different way of doing things. The 'heroic ideal' seemed a long way from the 'practical realities' of government and public policy practice, as revealed in case studies of societal economic development and of urban planning and urban renewal strategies (Meyerson and Banfield, 1955; Wildavsky, Chapter 3). Well-established governance practices were not just going to fade away in the face of the better knowledge and logic of rational scientific management. Instead, the encounter between different modes of politics and governance was a terrain of struggle, where the culture of administrative bureaucracy and patronage battled with the new ideas, which in turn were challenged by those who doubted that the separation between experts as guardians of 'science' and politicians as guardians of 'values' could be sustained and who felt that, in a democratic society, more space should be given to citizens' involvement in policy-making.[5]

---

[3]   See Lee (1973); also Rittel and Webber (Chapter 4) and Wildavsky (Chapter 3).

[4]   Work inspired by the 'Manchester School' of systems thinking continued throughout the rest of the century, led in particular by Michael Batty, as editor of *Environment and Planning B: Planning and Design*.

[5]   This critique was reinforced by the developing philosophical critique of the claims of 'logical positivism' as a scientific method.

Paul Davidoff, who had originally argued for the analytical separation of fact and value (see Davidoff and Reiner, Chapter 16), changed his mind a few years later. Instead, he turned to the significance of lively and informed debate among citizens in a democratic society. If facts and values are really intertwined, then, in a society with a plurality of social groups, there are likely to be a plurality of different ways of framing what facts to consider, as well as a multiplicity of conclusions about policy options and their impacts. This led Davidoff (Chapter 20) to argue that all kinds of groups should be encouraged to prepare urban development plans and that democratic argument should then proceed on the relative merits of different plans. Planners, rather than giving expert advice to representative government as the apex of democratic decision-making, should instead work in advocate mode as consultants to different groups. This led many planners into advocacy and community development work on behalf of disadvantaged communities (Goodman, 1972).

Other critics followed Davidoff's conclusion that there was no value-neutral ground in the processes of scientific inquiry and system-building on which an expert planner could stand. Faludi argued that, by dedicating planning effort to the project of 'human growth', planning as rational scientific management should not, in any case, be value-neutral. But others noted that, throughout the process of apparent logical deduction from goals to analyses, the formation and evaluation of means and the structuring of choices for politicians, all kinds of assumptions and logical leaps had to be made by the 'experts'. How these were made depended significantly on conceptions and values locked into the particular epistemologies used to describe systems and analyse relations. As Dyckman (Chapter 21) argued, these were dominated by the discipline of economics, especially by mid-twentieth-century welfare economics. Dyckman thought that this seriously neglected understanding of the impact of policies on particular social groups, some of whom were systematically disadvantaged in American society. Like Davidoff, Dyckman was thinking in particular not just of working-class groups and poorer immigrants, but also of those disadvantaged by the deeply embedded racial injustices of American society. In the 1960s, as the civil rights movement gathered pace, these criticisms seemed increasingly salient. Dyckman argued that the remedy in the United States was a restatement of American societal goals. In contrast, Arnstein advocated radical grassroots mobilization. In her famous metaphor of a ladder of citizen participation opportunities (see Chapter 22), she advises protest groups to resist attempts at consultation, which merely give an aura of participative legitimacy to public policies, and instead to take control of agenda-setting through political mobilization.[6]

The existence of systematic injustice supported criticism of the notion of a 'pluralistic' democratic, yet capitalist, society. In the US democratic ideal, a plurality of different social groups coexisted within a cohesive belief in the values of the possibility of material progress for all in a democratic context. But systematic disadvantage undermined this ideal. In Europe, in the late 1960s, systematic inequalities were identified with the workings of the capitalist system itself. A vigorous revival of Marxist political economy identified a range of structural injustices locked into the institutional arrangements of Western societies in order to enable capitalist exploitation of workers' labour (see Hillier and Healey, 2008a, Part I). Although Marx's historical materialism was informed by a similar faith in the potential of scientific

---

[6]   Such mobilization was, in any case, happening in the urban social movements of the 1970s: see Fainstein and Hirst (1995) and Mayer (2000).

inquiry to uncover laws of social development, the Marxist notion of development trajectories as evolving through struggles between classes was very different to the 'American Dream' conceptions of progress that shaped the notion of planning as rational scientific management. The urban political economists criticized the rational model as idealized, abstracted not only from the particular contingencies of context and content, but also from the general processes of struggle over control of the means of production, consumption and exchange (Thomas, 1982; Scott and Roweis, 1977). Yet, as Taylor (1984) observed, this critique was itself typically conducted in the language of abstract ideological struggle.

Turning away from this terrain, other policy analysts and planners began to look elsewhere for inspiration, and in particular to how policy work was actually done. Inspired by Wildavsky's work in the early 1970s (Pressman and Wildavsky, 1973), researchers began to explore policy 'implementation' processes and the social worlds of actors in governance situations. Barrett and Fudge (Chapter 23) argued that it is not enough to make a policy; it has to be made to happen. This meant looking at the micro-dynamics of how people acted in institutional settings to see how links between policy-making, resource allocation and regulatory practices were actually made. Barrett and Fudge concluded that the relation between policy and action was not linear, but interactive. Through such micro-political interactions, social orders are negotiated and institutional cultures created. This opened the way for more attention to sociological and institutionalist perspectives on governance processes in the planning field. By the 1980s the planning project had become much less 'heroic'. Operations researchers Friend and Hickling (Chapter 24), still developing a form of planning as rational scientific management, present it as a craft which helps to develop capacities to think and act creatively when faced with uncertainties and complexities. The practice arena that informs Friend's and Hickling's ideas centres on the work of stakeholder partnerships, a much less ambitious activity than comprehensive urban planning or societal development.

Reading the essays in Part III, and in particular those of the advocates of planning as a set of procedures for rational scientific management, gives a feeling of the intellectual vigour and hope for the future, which their authors felt in the mid-twentieth century. The crude portrayals of these ideas by later critics often miss the points they made, and also misinterpret their project. Advocates of planning as rational scientific management struggled over the nature of reason and the complex relations between ends and means, facts and values. They debated the relation of individuals and social orders. They were aware that any planning endeavour had to address the complexity of societal development processes, whether of nations or cities. And they wondered about how societies and governance processes changed. Perhaps their most important legacy for the twenty-first century is the message that the way in which governance is carried out matters, that the what, why and how of policy-making are interrelated and that *how* policies are made should be as much a subject for normative proposals as *what* policies are made.

PATSY HEALEY AND JEAN HILLIER

References

Bagnasco, A. and Le Galés, P. (eds) (2000), *Cities in Contemporary Europe*, Cambridge: Cambridge University Press.

Barrett, S. and Fudge, C. (1981), *Policy and Action*, London: Methuen.

Bell, D. (1962), *The End of Ideology: On the Exhaustion of Political Ideas in the Fifties*, New York: Free Press.

Chadwick, G. (1971), *A Systems View of Planning*, Oxford: Pergamon Press.

Churchman, C.W. ([1968]1979), *The Systems Approach* (2nd edn), New York: Dell Publishing.

Churchman, C.W. (1971), *Design of Inquiring Systems: Basic Concepts of Systems and Organization*, New York: Basic Books.

Dewey, J. (1910/1997), *How we Think*, New York: Dover Publications.

Dyckman, J.W. (1961), 'Planning and Decision Theory', *Journal of the American Institute of Planners*, XXVII, pp. 335–45.

Etzioni, A. (1967), 'Mixed-Scanning: A "Third" Approach to Decision-making', *Public Administration Review*, **27**, pp. 5, 385–92.

Fainstein, S. and Hirst, C. (1995), 'Urban Social Movements', in D. Judge *et al.* (eds), *Theories of Urban Politics*, London: Sage.

Faludi, A. (1973), *A Reader Planning Theory*, Oxford: Pergamon Press.

Ferlie, E., Ashburner, L., Fitzgerald, L. and Pettigrew, A. (1996), *The New Public Management in Action*, Oxford: Oxford University Press.

Forrester, J. (1969), *Urban Dynamics*, Cambridge, MA: MIT Press.

Friedmann, J. (1987), *Planning in the Public Domain*, Princeton, NJ: Princeton University Press.

Friedmann, J. and Weaver, C. (1979), *Territory and Function*, London: Edward Arnold.

Friend, J. and Hickling, A. (1987), *Planning under Pressure: The Strategic Choice Approach*, Oxford: Pergamon Press.

Goodman, R. (1972), *After the Planners*, Harmondsworth: Penguin.

Hillier, J. and Healey, P. (2008a), *Political Economy, Diversity and Pragmatism: Critical Essays in Planning Theory, Volume 2*, Aldershot: Ashgate.

Hillier, J. and Healey, P. (2008b), *Contemporary Movements in Planning Theory: Critical Essays in Planning Theory, Volume 3*, Aldershot: Ashgate.

Lee, D.B. (1973), 'Requiem for Large-Scale Models', *Journal of the American Institute of Planners*, **39**, pp. 163–78.

Lindblom, C.E (1965), *The Intelligence of Democracy*, New York: Free Press.

McLoughlin, J.B. (1969), *Urban and Regional Planning: A Systems Approach*, London: Faber and Faber.

Mayer, M. (2000), 'Social Movements in European Cities: Transitions from the 1970s to the 1990s', in A. Bagnasco and P. Le Galés (eds), pp. 131–52.

Menand, L. (2002), *The Metaphysical Club*, London: Flamingo, Harper Collins.

Meyerson, M. and Banfield, E. (1955), *Politics, Planning and the Public Interest*, New York: Free Press.

Pressman, J.L. and Wildavsky, A.B. (1973), *Implementation: How Great Expectations in Washington are Dashed in Oakland*, Berkeley: University of California Press.

Scott, A.J. and Roweis, S.T. (1977), 'Urban Planning in Theory and Practice: A Reappraisal', *Environment and Planning A*, **9**, pp. 1097–119. Also published as Chapter 1 in Hillier and Healey (2008a).

Taylor, N. (1984), 'A Critique of Materialist Critiques of Procedural Planning Theory', *Environment and Planning B: Planning and Design*, **11**, pp. 103–26.

Thomas, M. (1982), 'The Procedural Planning Theory of A. Faludi', in C. Paris (ed.), *Critical Readings in Planning Theory*, Oxford: Pergamon Press, pp. 13–26.

[16]

A Choice Theory of Planning*

Paul Davidoff and Thomas A. Reiner

PLANNING is a set of procedures. The theory we present rests on this belief. We will analyze the implications of this assertion and then identify the steps comprising these procedures. Further, we will show the bearing of these steps on behavior in fields where planning, as we define it, is practiced. What we have to say applies equally well to such diverse endeavors as urban land use planning, national economic planning, business planning, and others, for the same steps are followed no matter what the substantive or geographic focus.[1]

Planning Defined

We define planning as a process for determining appropriate future action through a sequence of choices. We use *determining* in two senses: *finding out* and *assuring*. Since appropriate implies a criterion for making judgments concerning preferred states, it follows that planning incorporates a notion of goals. *Action* embodies specifics, and so we face the question of relating general ends and particular means. We further note from the definition that *action* is the eventual outcome of planning efforts, and, thus, a theory of planning must be directed to problems of effectuation.

The choices which constitute the planning process are made at three levels: first, the selection of ends and criteria; second, the identification of a set of alternatives consistent with these general prescriptives, and the selection of a desired alternative; and, third, guidance of action toward

* Reprinted by permission of the *Journal of the American Institute of Planners*, Vol. 28, May 1962.

[1] However, the substantive is important and gives a particular instance of planning its special character. We leave a discussion of this point to another time, and focus in this paper on the ground common to all types of planning.

12   *A Reader in Planning Theory*

determined ends. Each of these choices requires the exercise of judgment; judgment permeates planning.[2] We will show the need for and some means of rendering judgments explicitly and with reason.[3]

Having introduced the definitional base, we now turn to three sets of propositions that are prerequisites for our planning theory. The first set refers to the subject-matter of planning and the environment in which it takes place, and is offered as postulates depicting the world-as-it-is. The second set of propositions describes the purposes for which planning is employed. We infer the purposes of planning, as defined above, from the uses to which it is put in dealing with the conditions set forth in the first set of propositions. The third set identifies elements which in their inter-relation compose the planning act and distinguish it from other forms of behavior. This set is derived from consideration of planning's purposes and the environmental postulates.

The Environment Surrounding Planning

The following set of postulates, describing aspects of the world-as-it-is, rests in part on axioms that have been found helpful in economic theory. The remaining postulates in this set also are statements on which there is general agreement.

1. Individuals have preferences and behave in accordance with them.[4] Actors are to some extent able to order their preferences. Different objects of preference, for any actor, may substitute for or complement each other.[5] Preferences express comparisons between wants: these wants have several features. An actor never experiences complete satisfaction of all his wants. Further, man finds that enjoyment brought on by addition to those goods and services already held pales with possession of increasing amounts.

---

[2] The judgment basis of decision-making in general is analyzed by Churchman [7]. Numbers in brackets refer to the Bibliography at the end of this article.

[3] We are concerned with the problem, so trenchantly posed by Haar [13], that a major task confronting the planner is to see that he acts in a nonarbitrary manner, administratively as well as conceptually. We develop in these pages a theory of non-arbitrary planning.

[4] Preferences are not absolute, yet they can be measured with tools of probability analysis.

[5] An individual's consumption of fuel would rise with purchase of a car: gas and autos are complementary goods. Use of public transit facilities will decline with the acquisition of a car: these are substitutable entities.

This is the familiar notion of diminishing marginal utility. To say that man is able to order his preferences among all alternatives is an exaggeration. For example, "poverty of desires" may limit his preference field. This problem becomes even more acute where alternative future goal situations are to be compared.

2. Actors vary in their preferences. The fact that men do not appraise things similarly complicates the allocation problem in society. It does so in two ways: the aggregation of individual preferences is sometimes a highly complex matter.[6] Second, there is considerable dispute whether there is any group interest or common welfare other than the sum of individual preferences.[7] It is often possible, however, to group the individuals with similar preference patterns. Such, for example, is the practice of economic determinists as well as of social analysts accustomed to draw conclusions from observation of manifest behavior.

3. Goods are produced and services, including labor, are performed subject to the constraint that diminishing returns set in at a given level. Beyond a certain point, "another buck just doesn't give as big a bang as it used to". This idea corresponds, on the supply side, to the notion on the demand side of diminishing marginal utility from goods and services.

4. Resources are scarce and consequently output is limited. Factors which go into the production of goods and services are, at any one point in time, limited in supply. This is the essence of the problem of priorities; we cannot achieve all things that need doing, or are desirable, at any one time.

5. The entity for which planning is undertaken—be it a production unit or a metropolitan area—will typically consist of interrelated parts generally in flux. Any action has consequences that add additional reverberations to such a system. To describe this condition we use terms such as "network effect", "organic structure", or "the need for coordination".

6. Man operates with imperfect knowledge. He also is often illogical (by formal canons), as where his preferences are not transitive,[8] or where

---

[6] This is the aggregation paradox analyzed by Arrow [2]. See also Baumol [5], ch. 13.

[7] Meyerson and Banfield [20], pp. 322–9, present the contending viewpoints.

[8] The transitivity assumption appears in various deductive systems. A transitive preference scheme will posit that where an individual prefers X to Y, and Y to Z, he also prefers X to Z.

14   *A Reader in Planning Theory*

his several values, at least at the levels at which he perceives them, are in conflict with each other. Thus, his abilities to calculate and control are ever limited. Severe, too, is conflict between demands for immediate action and for non-arbitrary decision. Kaplan [16] has well illustrated this predicament. "We are playing a game in a taxi with the meter running; even though we may possess a theory of the game, the cost of computing the optimal strategy may be too great." Man will doubtlessly continue to operate somewhere in the realm of bounded rationality, rather than reach perfect rationality.[9]

Planning's Purposes

Given these postulates, which describe the environment in which planning takes place, we move on to discuss why the planning act is undertaken. Ultimate purposes cannot be appraised from within a system: there is need to rely on outside criteria to evaluate such ends. We shall limit our discussion to presentation of objectives implicit in planning endeavors.

We refer to ultimate objectives of planning (external purposes), not to substantive matters (internal purposes) such as urban renewal, harmonious land use relations, or most profitable output. What reasons might institutions have for calling on planners to help them achieve their specific objectives?

Planning has been employed for a number of reasons, any one of which can serve independently or in combination with others as the objective of planning. Critics of the direction, efficacy, and value of contemporary planning should recognize the possibility of such a variety of perspectives; they might then see that the means in question are appraised differently for different purposes.

Three classes of objectives seem to exist. The first is efficiency and rational action; the second is market aid or replacement; and the third may be labeled change or widening choice.

1. *Efficiency and rational action.* In a world of scarcity there is a need to conserve resources and also to allocate them in an efficient manner. Planning is seen as a means of reducing waste or producing the greatest return

---

[9] For example, Schoeffler's [24] is a model of full rationality: Simon's [26] model postulates "satisficing," a more limited concept of rationality.

from employment of resources, although the line between these is not always clear. The distinction may rest on the amount of control that is exercised.[10] Definitions of waste or of optimum allocation hinge on assessment of wants. As we postulated above, different clients have different patterns of preference. Therefore the efficient utilization of resources would be that which satisfied the particular preferences of individual actors—as such preferences are determined and aggregated in a manner accepted in a given society. Efficiency thus is measured in terms of the purpose it serves.

Rationality is sometimes conceived as (a) referring to increasing the reasonableness of decisions, and sometimes as (b) involving full knowledge of the system in question. In the former sense (a) the task of planning may be to provide information to decision-makers, and, in certain cases, to the clients and the public at large about what presently exists and what may be expected in the future under alternative conditions. With this information the actors can better satisfy their own wants. The latter concept of rationality (b) is far more demanding of planning, for it requires identification of the best of all alternatives evaluated with reference to all ends at stake. The alternative thus selected as optimal implies, and is implied by, an efficient course of action.

2. *Market aid or replacement.* Planning would be of little, if any, use for an environment where an open, fully competitive market (either political or economic) operated perfectly. Such a market would imply that both buyers and sellers knew fully the relative worth over time of the items and services they sought and possessed, bought and sold, and of all the alternatives they had. Such a market would also require free entry and each participant's having, as it were, a single vote, with no party exercising monopolistic control over any segment of the market. Although such a market system does not exist, it remains a goal for some purpose: particularly as a model for optimum allocation of sets of goods and services in

---

[10] Waste itself involves notions of efficiency or optimum output per input. Efficiency, waste, and optimizing are interrelated; fruitful discussion of their relation depends on the particular model or ideal employed. Thus these terms take on one meaning in a competitive market model and quite another in a model which has, underlying, an objective that investments not be retired until their physical usefulness has been exhausted.

response to preferences of participants. Planning may be desired precisely in order to bring the society a few steps closer to such a goal. On the other hand, certain critics deny the possibility of a working competitive market. Their objective is to replace an imperfectly operating market system with some other scheme for distribution of scarce resources in response to claims upon them. Seen from this perspective, planning is to serve a new and controlling system of pricing and distribution.

Either of these objectives seizes on planning as a vehicle which collects, analyzes, and publicizes information (such as forecasts and assessment of third-party costs and benefits) required to make reasoned decisions. Those who favor the use of planning to make the market operate effectively do not see planning as a direct agent of change, but rather as providing the factual basis that will permit various value alternatives to be confronted and tested. Those who seek a market substitute view the planning act as more directly responsible for change. In this view planning becomes a "directive" method that will in itself yield rational order; the planner's task is enlarged to include examining value alternatives and, in some instances, suggesting particular courses of action.

3. *Change or widening of choice.* Given scarcities, social and individual choices must be made about the manner in which resources are to be allocated: how, when, to whom, to what purpose, and in what combination. The pure democratic ethic posits that no one has the wisdom or ability to make decisions for the society or for another individual; choice-making is left to the individual or to a majority of the individual voters.

In today's world, the inadequacy of this position is self-evident. Individuals increasingly delegate decision-making powers to legislative bodies; legislatures delegate to administrative and executive hands. This is specifically clear in the public realm; analogous conditions prevail in industry and in other institutions. Delegation often decreases individual opportunity to choose, but this decrease has limits; the decision-maker can both question and inform the individual client about the issues at hand. The planning process can be specifically employed to widen and to publicize the range of choice of future conditions or goals, as well as of means. This function may be extended to include opening opportunities where choice can be exercised. Lack of techniques and of willingness often holds back urban planners in this realm.

Widening of choice may overlap objectives of rational action. Those choices between alternatives that are central to the rational decision-making model clearly cannot be made in the absence of knowledge about such alternatives. The chooser must be informed of the range of choices and of the implications of each of the choices open. This suggests that the planner ought to render explicit the implications of proposals.

Planning can serve as a vehicle for the portrayal of utopian solutions. As distinct from plans expressing incremental improvements or even large-scale modifications along familiar lines, utopian plans show courses of action or end states involving fundamental change in values or environmental reconstruction. The utopian plan may open choice in several ways. It may give meaning to an old value by placing it in an unfamiliar setting. It may spell out the implications of total commitment to one or more values. It may shake belief in the *status quo* and suggest possibility of change and the directions this may take.[11]

A belief in the possibility of effective planning rests on the assumption that man controls his destiny: either by affecting the rate and direction of ongoing change or by initiating such motion. Planning is often relied on to achieve such control. Many of the reform features of city planning can be traced to a conviction that it is possible to improve man's conditions or to arrest decline.

Planning Characteristics

We next consider those elements which, in their interrelations, characterize the planning act. Though we wish to use these elements to distinguish planning from other forms of behavior, we recognize the considerable overlap between such fields as operations research, decision-making, or problem-solving, and planning.

We suggest the following as necessary components of the planning act.

1. *The achievement of ends.* Our definition of planning incorporates a concept of a purposive process keyed to preferred, ordered ends. Such ends may be directions or rates of change, as well as terminal states. Means

---

[11] On the relations between utopias and urban planning, see: Dahl and Lindblom [9], pp. 86–88; Meyerson [19]; Reiner [22]; and Riesman [23].

are not proposed for their own sake, but as instruments to accomplish these. The ends are not given, irrevocable, but are subject to analysis.

2. *Exercise of choice.* Planning is behavior which sees—at many levels—values formulated, means established, and alternatives selected. Our definition of planning stresses exercise of choice as its characteristic intellectual act.

3. *Orientation to the future.* Time is a valued and depletable resource consumed in effecting any end. Planning, an end-directed process, is therefore future oriented. Each of the ultimate objectives of planning implies a need in the present for information about the future. Estimates of future states are also important for what they imply for present behavior; thus, points are identified where control is required if ends are to be achieved. Moreover, planning involves assigning costs to deferred goal satisfaction and to losses arising from postponed actions. The task of calculating interest rates thus implicitly incorporates planning.

4. *Action.* Planning is employed to bring about results. It is a step in an ends-means chain leading to that which is desired.

5. *Comprehensiveness.* Planning serves to relate the components of a system. In order to allow decision-makers to choose rationally among alternative programs, the planner must detail fully the ramifications of proposals. In a world of imperfect knowledge this requirement must be balanced with that of action.

The Planning Process

As he faces these realities and concerns, and as he strives to identify appropriate courses of action, the planner engages in choice at three fundamental levels. These jointly constitute the process of planning. They are: *value formulation, means identification,* and *effectuation.* They are the necessary and sufficient steps constituting planning. We believe each represents an analytically useful category, for associated with each step are distinct methods of operation and problems of theory.

VALUE FORMULATION

Fact and Value

Our analysis of the value-formulation process and of the planner's responsibilities in dealing with values has as its basis the philosophical distinction between fact and value.

A fact is a descriptive statement involving definitions and postulates, and a relationship. It is an assertion of the truth of the relationship. "X is Y" is one characteristic form of a factual statement.

Values may be expressed as moral statements, or as statements of preference, of criteria, or of ends—more particularly goals. For our purposes, each of these can be related to, or transformed into, any of the others. Moral statements take the form of "X ought to Y", or, in terms more familiar to urban planners, "metropolitan areas ought to be surrounded by greenbelts". Statements of preference take the form "X is preferred to Y", or, "I would rather live in a single-family detached house than in a multifamily dwelling". Statements of ends or goals take the form "X is the end state sought", or, "Our goal in housing is the re-creation of New York as the first major city of the world without a slum". Criteria statements take the form, "when confronted with a choice between X and Y, apply rule M", or "when choosing between possible urban renewal sites, select the one with the highest reuse potential".

We further maintain that a given nondefinitional assertion would belong either to the category of facts or that of values and that any discourse could be divided in this manner. There are, on the one hand, uses, tests, and criticisms singularly appropriate to values and, on the other, those singularly appropriate to facts.[12]

Yet fact and value are closely related. The separation of fact and value in itself requires certain assumptions and possibly violation of the dictates of reason.[13] Let us consider some of the ways in which fact and value may be related.

1. Factual statements and their analysis invariably reflect the values of

---

[12] The position presented thus far rests on logical positivism, see: Ayer [3] and Carnap [6].

[13] In the last analysis, judgment, choice, and values enter into any verification. On this point, see Churchman [7], chaps. 4–6.

their makers; if only in the importance attached to them or the sequence in which they are studied.[14]

2. Our personal experiences show that our values are colored by our understanding of facts.[15]

3. We can make factual assertions about values: for example, their distribution in a given group. Conversely, one can make value assertions about facts, as does the city planner who desires to counter the fact of public apathy about a public program.

Verification of facts and verification of values, nevertheless, involve different techniques. The definition of a fact requires the possibility of disproving the assertion. Further, the true measures of facts lie on a probabilistic continuum; we cannot be absolutely certain of any assertion. Disconfirming and verifying value statements are highly complex issues that are by no means resolved. How then can the imperative of a value statement be tested? Disagreement on a value position cannot be resolved by recourse to facts.[16] We can speak of verification of values only in terms of their consistency with values of a higher level. Eventually, however, there must be reference to ultimate values which are essentially assumed and asserted as postulates.

The many goals within a system of values can be viewed in terms of their interrelations, although we can at times conveniently focus on individual goals. Considering an individual goal as a part, rather than as the entirety, of a system of ends has important analytic consequences. One goal may appear as superior to an alternative goal when both are measured against a higher value; however, the alternative may appear as a better means of satisfying a system-wide set of ends. This suggests that goals can be compared in terms of both their intrinsic and their instrumental worth. Values exist in a hierarchy. The hierarchical relation of values provides a means for whatever testing of values is possible. A value may be tested, that is, understood and its reasonableness assessed, by specifying values of a lower level it subsumes and by comparing it with other lower-level values as a means to achieve values of a higher level. We emphasize that a given value may be viewed both as a means and an end.

---

[14] See, for example, Merton [18] and Myrdal [21].

[15] Stevenson [29] gives one formulation of this problem.

[16] This position has been developed by a large number of contemporary philosophers: in particular we find support in Churchman [7].

The planner, as an agent of his clients, has the task of assisting them in understanding the range of the possible in the future and of revealing open choices. He does this in two ways—one involving facts and the other, values. The planner deals with facts to predict the nature of the future. Such predictions take account of a variety of different factors in the environment as well as likely effects of alternative controls. Such predictions permit comparison with conditions that are desired. Knowledge of gaps between desired and predicted conditions may suggest the nature of further controls needed.

The planner deals with values to discover which future conditions are presently desired and which may be desired by future clients. The environment desired for the future is, *in the first instance*, purely a matter of values. There is nothing in the factual side of the planner's work which, *in the first instance*, can reveal to him the desired nature of the future. But once a particular set of values concerning the future is posited, knowledge of facts is needed to determine the relative weight of a particular value. For example, value X might be preferred in the first instance, but subsequent knowledge of the costs of achieving X might lead to heightened consideration of another value. We agree with Kaplan [16] who has written of the importance of "confronting values with facts" in order to make "valuation realistic".

Constraints should be imposed only after choices are expressed. All too often planners first predict the nature of the future, then help set in motion programs that fulfill this prophecy, and thus limit men's aspirations. Planners should not let such predictions about the future limit the range of choice, for controls can alter the future and can make predicted outcomes improbable. However, evidence revealed through prediction can suggest undesirable aspects of a given course of control. Thus, prediction and control are complementary.

We would prefer to see planning operate under the assumption that all things are possible, given the willingness to meet their costs. Only when the client of the planner reveals that the costs are excessive should the future condition be excluded from consideration. If this procedure is followed, the planner's client remains in control.

Responsibility

Although we propose that the planner become vitally involved with values, we must make clear our belief that the planner should act with a keen sense of responsibility. He cannot, as an agent of his clients, impose his own ideas of what is right or wrong. We do not wish to see the planner's influence on decisions limited, but we would argue strongly that the planner's role in dealing with values must be constrained so that he acts as a responsible agent.

If an ultimate objective of planning is to widen choice, and the opportunity to choose, then the planner has the obligation not to limit choice arbitrarily. If an ultimate objective of planning is efficiency, then the planner cannot afford prematurely to dismiss any set of means. An examination of current goal-setting practice would show that planners as a rule fail to reject explicitly alternatives not included within their final plans. Thus, a proposed master plan contains a list of goals, but not a list of rejected goals. Further, such plans seldom indicate why the accepted goals were selected. If the planner is to be permitted to reject alternatives it must be because he has some knowledge or skill that provides a rational basis for such acts of rejection. This basis can be provided only by the values of the clients. Our contention rests on the thesis that goals are value statements, that value statements are not objectively verifiable, and, therefore, that the planner, by himself, cannot reasonably accept or reject goals for the public. This is crucial: we maintain that neither the planner's technical competence nor his wisdom entitles him to ascribe or dictate values to his immediate or ultimate clients. This view is in keeping with the democratic prescriptive that public decision-making and action should reflect the will of the client; a concept which rejects the notion that planners or other technicians are endowed with the ability to divine either the client's will or a public will.[17]

Clients

It is not for the planner to make the final decision transforming values into policy commitments. His role is to identify distribution of values

---

[17] Another reason for interest in clients' values is that their assessment permits prediction of aggregate private decisions and behavior, and thus leads to more effective planning.

among people, and how values are weighed against each other. To do this, the planner must determine relevant client groups. We can speak of two general classes: the immediate client, or the planner's employer; and the ultimate clients, those affected by the proposals.

The values sought are the clients; we reject the notion that individuals express the values of an institution, or what has been called the organismic view of the public interest. Values are personal; institutions do not hold values and purported expressions of institutional will cannot be proved or disproved. An institution does not have a will separate from that of its members; otherwise, man is the ward of that which he can master and control. Institutions exist to serve man. It is important to state our position explicitly (although ours is not an uncommon one) because of its meaning for the planning process we describe. It implies that the planner should not search for the "interest" of the entity for which he works, be it Philadelphia, General Motors, or the United States.

The planner therefore must take a preliminary step: the identification of his clients. Often, terms of employment prescribe the reference group for the planner's activity. But in public planning, with intervening administrative and legislative levels, to identify clients is a difficult task, and one that is often sidestepped.[18] The failure properly to identify relevant clients lies at the bottom of many of the current difficulties of the urban renewal program.[19]

In some situations the planner's perspective is limited to the values given by his immediate client, for his employer may exclude the planner from what might be deemed a political area. When the planner is permitted (or, as is frequently the case, asked and urged) to study the larger client group, serious problems confront him. What type of information should be elicited from the clients? Should the planner study the values of a random sample of the population, or should he classify the relevant population and then sample the different groups, or should he otherwise assign values to these aggregations? If he has chosen the second course, the planner will be required to establish explicit criteria for the definition of groups.

---

[18] Likewise, is management or the stockholder the immediate client in a corporate planning situation? See *Dodge* vs. *Ford Motor Co.*, 204 Mich. 459, 170 N.W. 688. See also, operation research literature, viz. Churchman, Ackoff, and Arnoff [8], chap. 1.

[19] As documented by Gans [12] and Seeley [25].

One such criterion should be to aggregate individuals expected to have similar cost-benefit expectations.

Clients might thus be grouped according to income, race, age, occupational characteristics, location, or by roles in various institutions. Any one individual might fall in several or all such categories. Just as we deny an institutional will, neither shall we find a group interest. That which expresses the values of a majority of a group need neither represent that class's permanent view nor the views of each member.

Analysis of Values

Let us now identify what information about the values of clients should be sought and analyzed. Values are not self-evident, simple entities, but, though complex, neither do they defy analysis. The planner should consider values from two perspectives: first, as the clients' internal states of valuation: second, externally, as the entities which are valued. It is easy to slip into a position where internal and external values are not distinguished, where the preference structure of an individual is not separated analytically from the commodities, services, or conditions which are the objects of his preference. We may find that for some purposes value analysis should concentrate on the internal states, such as those previously discussed, while, for other purposes, study can more fruitfully focus on the external. As one proceeds from more general to more specific values, the external elements seem more evident, dominant, and measurable.

To lend substance to our discussion of internal states, let us focus on values such as health, wealth, and power,[20] which might be considered values at a middle range of generality. These values should be considered in the following ways.

1. For a given value: how widely is it held? What is its spread and distribution in the institution and amongst client groups?

2. What is the intensity of the value? Techniques of measurement are not sharply developed here. The only meaningful intensity scale may be

---

[20] We sidestep the question of the selection of these values; they are taken from Lasswell and Kaplan [17] who offered these as part of a plausible value system.

one measuring overt behavior, for example, migration. It may also be desirable to distinguish between those values held in private and those shared as when attitudes are publicly voiced or voted. The planner might be particularly concerned with identifying conditions under which privately held values become public. This is related to whether a value is strongly held by an individual, or whether he is amenable to changing it.

3. Does the individual believe he can or cannot influence the achievement or a goal?

What are the characteristics of the external value entities? The stock of such things as wealth or health that an individual possesses at any one time, in combination with his internal values, provides a significant basis for planning analysis. An individual's well-being is measured by:

(a) his absolute stock of valued entities;

(b) divergence of his stock from his own goals (his aspirations); and

(c) divergence of the stock of valued entities from a level set by others (this is the familiar notion of standards).

The difference noted in (b) and (c) need not be equal.[21] For purposes of analysis, information on both gaps is desirable. A criterion for planning action would give a directive to narrow either the subjective gap, the objective gap, or some combination.

Valued entities can be measured in several ways. First, regarding the amount held or desired: is possession a 'yes-no' phenomenon, does it exist in discrete lumps, or is it measured along a continuum?[22] Second, how easily is the valued item transferred from person to person?[23] Third, along the continuum which measures the individual or social origin of a value: is the valued entity internalized, or is it other-directed?[24] Fourth,

---

[21] For example, the political theorist asks: Can freedom be measured objectively, or is it purely a subjective state? Or, in the urban planner's world: How is adequacy of municipal services to be measured?

[22] Survival might be in the first category, days at work without interruptions due to illness in the second, and degree of health in the third.

[23] Wealth has low transfer costs, whereas health or rectitude have high costs of transfer.

[24] Thus, affection may be totally other-directed, whereas, depending on market conditions and assumptions, wealth is only partly so. Health is largely internalized, although not exclusively so: subjective well-being reflects knowledge of others' states, and identification of well-being hinges partly on publicly held criteria.

measurement of valued objects also must embody recognition that some are not subject to restrictions of finiteness.[25]

Planning analysis of an entire value system would lead to portrayal of value hierarchies. It is by study of such structures and by defining the levels therein that it is possible to identify, reduce, or even eliminate the inconsistencies in pursuit of a system of goals. With knowledge of the hierarchy, the planner can better pinpoint specific means.

Ideally, for purposes of planning analysis, value hierarchies should be formulated to provide criteria for specific action or inaction in all cases. We recognize that this sets a highly demanding requirement, for it must account for discord and inconsistencies within and among people. Yet, there are at least three processes the planner may employ to resolve value conflict and efficiently attain plural goals. First, assigning exchange prices to several goals permits their joint pursuit. Second, posing alternatives, analyzing ramifications, and disseminating information contribute to effective bargaining between proponents of contending values. Third, rendering value meanings explicit provides common grounds for appraisal.

Though the planner tries to formulate unitary hierarchies, these may not be attainable, and, in any case, are not desirable in their monolithically consistent form. For there is virtue in highlighting conflict of values and goals: a richer, if only temporary, synthesis grows out of advocacy.

Evaluation of Values

Although a value statement cannot be verified by empirical data, it can be referred to other value statements in the hierarchical structure. Furthermore, implications of values can be detailed to permit greater understanding of their meanings. The process of rendering a value explicit also reveals the way in which the value may be transformed into a goal statement. Let us illustrate the different ways of treating a value by reference

---

[25] Wealth would be quite finite, given a particular technological and capital context, a pricing system, and a fixed time period. Health may be finite, but only within some of its definitions. It is harder to assign such ceilings to affection (if, however, this were to be measured in sociometric terms, there is a ceiling, a very high one, on interaction possibilities). Justice or skill would seem to defy notions of a maximum, although it may be possible to set a minimum. Finiteness is related to depletability. Thus, commodities constituting wealth are generally consumed in use, while skills grow with exercise.

to a currently popular aim: "It is desirable to maintain the level of investment in, and the output from, centrally located business districts." The transformation of this statement into a planning goal is: "The preservation of the C.B.D." For purposes of analysis, we might begin by defining the key terms in either the moral statement or the goal statement. For example, what is meant by the term "preserve"?[26] Next we would seek the reasons underlying the goal. We could ask what benefits and costs would arise under each alternative. Or, we might observe that the value was related to others.[27] In sum, the process of explaining the possible reasons underlying a value and the possible effects of its pursuit would permit more intelligent choices between such a value and other similarly treated values.

The final product of the value formulation stage of planning should be alternative sets of objectively measurable goals and criteria. Objective measures are prescribed first because they limit the possibility of abuse through arbitrary decision. Second, if an objective of planning action is to achieve ends, then the ends selected must be achievable. Some ends may be unattainable because of their generality, vagueness, or ambiguity. We do not assert that such ends do not have importance in value formulation, but an objectively measurable end must be deduced from them if a specific direction is to be given to planning means. Criteria are employed for choosing the best means to achieve stated ends. Only where criteria are stated in objective form can alternative means be reliably compared, with assurance that the means selected are directed toward the same goals.

We have suggested that value formulation yields alternative sets of goals. This requirement is supported by the following reasoning. We plan in a world of limited knowledge, a world in which facts are probabilistic and values debatable. Under such circumstances "correct" decisions do not

---

[26] In speaking of preserving a C.B.D., is the implication that the C.B.D.'s activity should be maintained at its current level, or at its current level relative to a certain region as a whole? Or, does "preserve" mean that the older business district should be maintained as a central focus for particular functions: trade, exchange, recreation, etc.?

[27] Preservation of the C.B.D. may be sought in order to enlarge the assessment base so as to permit reduction of taxes. Or, it may be sought out of the belief that scale factors operate which require a central complex as a necessary condition for provision of desired facilities. Both these hypotheses are subject to evaluation and the validity of the initial goal (preserve the C.B.D.) may thus be tested.

exist. The merit of a decision can only be appraised by values held individually or in a collectivity, but such values, as we have pointed out, are
not verifiable. In such a situation, the goal for decision-making should be
increasing the degree of assurance (of decision-makers and clients) that
the choice made was at least as reasonable or more reasonable than any
other alternative. This goal is best attained by bringing to bear on every
decision the greatest amount of relevant information concerning the
ramifications of all alternatives.

In general, if the planner is not to make final decisions (and even where
he is delegated the power to make such decisions), alternative possibilities
should be explicitly scrutinized. We object strenuously to the current
practice in urban planning of excluding all but the selected alternatives
from consideration.[28] Even if the planner prefers a single alternative, a
preference we believe he should assert as strongly as desired and permitted,
he has the obligation to detail objectively and explicitly the meaning and
implication of each alternative. We recognize that the planner must exercise judgment as to which alternatives should be considered as possibilities.
But this can be done discreetly through explication of the criteria he
employs.

Time Perspective of Plans

We have espoused widening clients' choices. The planner, to do so,
must offer value alternatives not currently given great weight in society.
The planner should be called upon to present tentative objectives—
new, radical, or even absurd alternatives. This involves creative and
utopian thought and design. The planner can engage in such thought; possibilities for significant societal change are great (although the immediate
willingness may be lacking). Significant planned change generally takes
a long time. For this reason, a long-range plan should embody consideration
of alternatives which set forth values of a higher level and include some
which are distinctly different from those currently approved.

A short-term plan on the other hand will suffer from constraints of time
and from necessity for action. This being true, it should focus on purposes

---

[28] Attempts to display alternatives prove worthless where there is a failure to
compare the relative costs and benefits of the posed alternatives.

which are fairly certain to receive political approval. The short-range plan must include consideration of values which have been approved and given expression in past programs, for in part it is a plan showing an efficient way of moving into the immediate future. The preparation of the short-term plan thus calls for identification and analysis of currently pursued goals (as they may be found, for example, in explicit or implicit form in budgets and other public documents). Goals in opposition to the accepted ones, when held by those with significant power, must also be given attention.

A middle-range plan (perhaps for a five-year period) provides an opportunity to mesh the extreme points of view regarding societal change which are expressed in the other two plans. Estimates of future conditions can be made with greater assurance than in the long-range plan. There is more accurate knowledge of what may occur under different controlled situations. Alternatives posed in such a five-year plan should be those carrying some commitment to implementation, as opposed to mere intention (such as might set the criterion for inclusion in the long-range plan).

For each of the three plans, a number of methods are available to the planner seeking to identify possible values and value groupings. These methods include: market analyses, public opinion polls, anthropological surveys, public hearings, interviews with informed leaders, press-content analyses, and studies of current and past laws, of administrative behavior, and of budgets. Singly, and more so in combination, these are superior to reliance on planners' intuition or guesswork.

In each plan, the importance of placing value formulation first cannot be overstated, though there is great reluctance in urban planning to start with a search for ends. Even where goal selection is placed first, there is a tendency to underplay this and to return to familiar territory—"survey and analysis."[29] We do not understand the logic that supports ventures in research before the objectives of the research have been defined.[30] Such emphasis on research is premised on an ill-founded belief that knowledge of facts will give rise to appropriate goals or value judgments. Facts by

[29] There is one legitimate and necessary exception: survey and analysis of client values. Study of their shape, incidence, and intensity makes a valid starting point for planning studies.

[30] A practical reason to delay research studies is to avoid unnecessary or unproductive studies. Planning agencies, as is painfully known, are the repositories of many unutilized surveys.

themselves will not suggest what would be good or what should be preferred. To illustrate this point, a factual survey of housing conditions in a given area would not give rise to a value judgment or a goal in the absence of an attitude about the way people ought to live in residential structures.

Values are inescapable elements of any rational decision-making process or of any exercise of choice. Since choice permeates the whole planning sequence, a clear notion of ends pursued lies at the heart of the planner's task, and the definition of these ends thus must be given primacy in the planning process.

MEANS IDENTIFICATION

In the next stage of the planning process, ends are converted into means. The crucial question is: how to proceed, by nonarbitrary steps, from a general objective to a specific program? We stress that the hierarchy of means be deduced logically from ends.

The process of means identification commences once an attempt is made to identify an instrument to a stated end. It terminates when all the alternative means have been appraised in terms of their costs and benefits (as calculated by criteria referring to all relevant goals) and, in certain cases, where the power is delegated, a particular implementing means is chosen to be the desired alternative to achieve the stated purpose. The identification of a best alternative implies a need for operational criteria for such choices.[31]

The most general end and the most specific means represent extreme points along a continuum. The task of deducing from a value the tools for its implementation is not a one-step operation. A particular program may serve either as a means or as an end, depending on its relation to other values, programs, or tasks, and depending on the perspectives of the relevant individuals.

Methods for the identification of means conveniently fall into two

---

[31] We distinguish decision-making from planning: the former is usually restricted to choices among given alternatives, whereas we see the latter as a process incorporating the formulation of ends, as well as ways of identifying and expanding the universe of alternatives. On decision-making literature see the recent article by Dyckman [11].

categories. The first is the identification of a universe of alternate means consistent with the value. The alternatives identified would be those which were conditions sufficient for achievement of the goal. This is the deductive element of the model, a task which may take the form of identifying all the feasible alternatives, or a finite number, or possibly only one for comparison with existing conditions. The choice depends on the planner's skills, technical as well as creative. At this point, we are not familiar with any rigorous techniques, either in the natural or the social sciences or in philosophy, which would enable us to identify the full set of possible alternatives to the achievement of an end.[32]

Certain steps might be taken to reduce the number of alternatives to be considered, such as the aggregation, into a few representative alternatives, of all the alternatives constituting a continuum or series of continua. Where alternatives refer to policies in a short-range perspective, a useful approach is review and evaluation of the set of programs currently in use, at several levels of operation and in various combinations.

The second task in means identification is the weighing of alternatives identified in the first step. Two types of weights are involved. One refers to the degree to which a given means satisfies the end sought. The other is a probability score: an estimate of the likelihood that the end will be associated with the means employed. At this point, the planner must pay close heed to the subtleties and complexities of causal, producer-product, and correlation relationships.[33] Using criteria developed in the value formulation stage, such weights are attached to each alternative. One alternative may then be identified as superior to others: that is, optimal by preestablished criteria. However, this last step should be taken only if an explicit delegation of power has been made. In all cases there is a clear

---

[32] The one exception might be some classes of programming: given a set of restrictive constraints, all feasible solutions are implicitly identified. However, two types of problems arise with programming. Programming is not operational or even relevant to many aspects of planning. More important, the approach requires that explicit constraints be set: there often is loss in precisely that flexibility needed for meaningful expansion of the set of alternatives. For a review of programming literature, see Stevens [28]. An excellent recent introduction to this topic will be found in Baumol [5], chap. 5.

[33] For definition and discussion of these terms, see, for example, Ackoff [1], pp. 65–68.

32   *A Reader in Planning Theory*

responsibility to reveal to the decision-maker the grounds for selecting the particular alternative.

Legal procedures adopted in our society reject the thesis that ends justify any means; furthermore, means vary in their effects on different client groups. Hence, the process of means identification is politically charged and must be resolved without arbitrariness. The technician has an important role to play in assessing the impact of alternative means. However, the tasks of adopting criteria for evaluation (during the value-formulation stage) and determining finally the appropriate alternatives are not his, unless these functions have been expressly delegated.

The technician should make explicit to the clients all the information he can muster as to hypothetical consequences resulting from adoption of each of the means considered. Two classes of verifiable, nonarbitrary planning techniques are relevant in this regard. These may be labeled "optimizing" studies, and "comparative impact" analyses. The former would select the best solution out of all possible courses of action, given a criterion of "best" and given explicit constraints. The optimizing study itself would identify all alternatives; these do not have to be determined beforehand. Linear programming is such a technique.

Comparative impact analyses have a more modest aim: weighing already identified alternatives subject to some criteria. The simplest form is comparison between the effects of a single improvement, as against maintenance of the *status quo*. An input-output study is an example, provided a rule is added which allows assessment of the merits of the consequent states. Other examples are comparative cost and cost-benefit studies.

At the moment, our means-identification skills are limited. Nevertheless, we can state standards for such endeavors, whether conducted in contemporary handicraft manner or using more sophisticated techniques which may develop.

1. We seek to identify a set of means so related to the given purpose as to include the one that is "best". Thus, the set of alternatives identified by a means-identification effort must not omit one (identified by some other method than that used) clearly superior to the one selected.

2. The alternatives identified must possess certain features of measurability. There must be "success indicators", which, at a later stage, make it possible to assess the effectiveness of means programs.

3. Means identification should be consistent. That is, alternatives

selected as optimal in the pursuit of a goal should be consistent with the alternatives employed in pursuit of another goal, or least inconsistent with achievement of other goals.

4. Finally, we seek to develop mean-identification methods that are manageable, ones that do not burden us with irrelevant and excessive alternatives. Analysis must be possible, and also productive to actors constrained by time.

EFFECTUATION

In effectuation, the third step in the planning process, the planner guides previously selected means toward attainment of goals adopted in the first stage. Effectuation is concerned with administration of programs and with control; it has been discussed at great length, and from various points of view, in administration theory. We limit our discussion to those aspects of effectuation so essential or peculiar to the planning process that a theory of planning requires their consideration.

There is some question whether concern with effectuation belongs in a theory of planning for it can be held that planning ceases with identification of means and is not concerned with their application. This position implies a cleavage separating policy and administration. Such separation assumes that, once commitments are secured to accomplish intended objectives, policy making terminates and administrators carry out the programs. Contemporary administrative thought has strongly undercut this distinction between policy and administration[34] by showing, for example, how administration of a program can lead to unwanted results. Thus, we pose for the planner the role of an overseer, one who aids policy makers by observing the direction programs are given and by suggesting means for redirecting these toward their intended goals. If circumstances are unusual and significant, unanticipated consequences are likely to occur, the planner will suggest immediate reconsideration of goals or means. There are several reasons why the undesired and unanticipated may arise:

1. Administrators consciously or unconsciously redirect programs. This is not surprising where, typically, several bureaucratic levels are involved in implementing an objective. Each of these levels may involve a separate

---

[34] For a review of this issue, see Simon [27].

set of actors with unique interpretations of facts, ends, and personal responsibilities.

2. Programmatic means are general and in their application to specific areas or individuals may cause injustice. A whole program may be jeopardized where such injustice is sufficiently grave.[35] Variance procedures, for example, represent explicit recognition of the need to apply equity in certain specific circumstances, yet variables may cumulatively thwart program ends.

3. Not every consequence can be predicted. If (previously) unanticipated events do arise (or are later predicted) they may have significant impact. In some cases the impact will lead to pressures sufficient to alter goals or to introduce new controls.

In serving as an overseer of programs the planner's role is analogous to a feedback control mechanism. The ultimate recipient of information is the policy maker, but in some circumstances the planner may be delegated the task of redirecting a program's administration so that it stays on course. Another significant aspect of the planner's feedback role is the storing of information regarding client reaction to programs and to total or partial achievement of various goals. In this fashion the planner performs a value formulation task, understanding contemporary reaction to the world as it is. This coincidence of value formulation and effectuation stages suggest the ongoing nature of the planning process.

Aspects of effectuation actually commence with agreement on goals and criteria in the value formulation stage: in urban planning, for example, with publication of the first part of a master plan. The function we see for the master plan is to set forth basic accepted policies, the goals and criteria of the government. The master plan need not contain details of programs derived during the means-identification stage. But it must include the criteria necessary to control exercise of administrative discretion.

We conceive of the master plan as an amendable document, one that reflects the political consensus at a given moment as to desired change over the short-, middle-, and long-range periods. The master plan serves as an instrument for evaluating and overseeing the use of controls and functions as a yardstick against which progress toward goals can be

---

[35] The relocation problems arising from urban renewal programs are examples in point.

measured. Ideally, all the controls employed to effectuate a plan could be deduced from the criteria set forth in the master plan, but specific control need not be part of the master plan. The task and methods of deducing controls from the master plan belong to the means-identification stage. Languages such as "in accordance with a comprehensive plan" would mean "deducible from" such a plan.

We have reserved our consideration of controls until this discussion of effectuation because of their importance for action. However, values as to the nature of controls and the criteria to guide their use are formulated in the earlier stages of the planning process. There are many forms of control from which to choose: those that are directed (such as ones relying on immediate impact on identified clients) as well as those that are automatic (as those that depend on the operation of a free market). Both directed and automatic controls may be imposed by strict regulations or by more subtle means, such as influence or prediction posed to fulfill itself. In our society the Constitution and the positive and common laws embody values governing use of controls. Controls may be exercised from many points within a system.[36]

The planner should establish for his clients' consideration alternative criteria in reference to controls. One set of criteria might deal with the location and character of controls and of the planning function. Such a set would resolve for a particular institution the question of whether controls and planning functions should be centralized or decentralized.[37] Still another set of criteria might deal with relations between controller and controlled. Thus, for example, where individual freedom was highly valued the criterion might be: the control employed should be one which achieves the desired end with the least restriction of the prevailing rights of individuals. Other criteria in this set might answer such questions as:

1. What consideration, if any, should be given to those proximately affected by a control? Should there be compensation?

2. Should the accepted limits of control be a function of the purposes it seeks to achieve? Under which circumstances do ends justify means?

3. What rights will be afforded individuals to question or contest

---

[36] For a thorough study of types, costs, benefits, and other aspects of controls, see Dahl and Lindblom [9].

[37] This question has been debated by a number of urban planners: Bassett [4], Walker [31], Howard [15], Tugwell and Banfield [30], and also Dunham [10].

particular controls? For example, what should be the content and requirements of a public hearing, or under what circumstances could the consti-
tutionality of legislation or legality of administrative discretion be
challenged?

The planner, however, does not have total authority and is himself
subject to many constraints. Within any institution, forces, some rational,
some irrational, are at work affecting decisions; only some of these are
subject to the controls developed by the planner. Planning calculations
are set against those arising out of market processes and are either
challenged or relied upon by power groups with their own interests.
Furthermore, a given planning agency often coexists with others responsible
for parts or the whole planning process. Thus, a city planning department
may work in co-operation (or conflict) with planning divisions of other
departments. In a pluralistic society this is inevitable and acts to limit the
planner's activities. But, again, it also can contribute to that higher synthesis we saw arising from conflict of ideas and values.

CONCLUSIONS

The theory presented in this paper has numerous implications both for
the education of planners and for the role planners play in public affairs,
industry, welfare organizations, and other areas. It is our conviction that
contemporary urban planning education has been excessively directed to
substantive areas and has failed to focus on any unique skills or responsibilities of the planner. Such planning education has emphasized understanding of subject-matter: cities, regions, facilities, housing, land use,
zoning, transportation, and others. In fact, the student has had thrust
upon him a growing list of courses and is perennially in danger of becoming a Jack-of-all-trades (almost all, but never enough), and a master of
none. In a few years on the job he sinks into an uninspired and intellectually blunted administrator-generalist or public relations semiexpert.
Planning education, until now, has paid little or no attention to methods
for determining ends and relating ends to means. And although some tools
of effectuation are studied, their relation to a planning process is largely
neglected. The very obvious shortcomings of current master plans reflect
both the bias and the inadequacy of their formulators' training.

The back issues of this and other planning journals are replete with self-conscious consideration of the urban planner's role as a professional. Planners frequently assert their status of a profession and so implicitly claim a distinct body of knowledge and procedures. Is this claim premature ?

It has been our intent to set forth a theory of planning complete in the sense that it defines the field, its purpose, its methods, and the constraints imposed on it by its surrounding environment. Though we do not contend that planning is a task which any one individual can perform in its entirety, we do believe that a curriculum can be developed to prepare each planner to engage in the process and analyses described. There would have to be much reliance on skills and accumulated knowledge in related social sciences, law, ethics, statistics, and applied mathematics. We also believe there is possibility for fruitful exploitation of the common ground between planning and such new fields as operations research and decision theory. However, it should be noted that operations researchers, in their quest for optimal processes, have shown relatively little interest in formulating goal alternatives, and that decision-making theory has largely focused on ways to make the best choice from among given alternatives in response to set criteria. The task we have outlined for planning clearly transcends these in scope.

Attempts are currently under way in a number of universities to teach aspects of planning theory. However, no school has, as yet, focused on planning methods. Our conclusions suggest that, at least for the present, departments of planning should be separated from departments of subject-matter, for example, urbanism, regionalism, welfare programs, industry. Planners should be trained to apply their methods to a variety of subject areas, though any given institution may have to limit its scope to one or a few such areas. We do not mean to suggest, though, that a planner's education should ignore study in subject areas. Rather, we urge that such areas become the testing ground for the application of planning.

Our colleague Britton Harris recently wrote in these pages [14] that "at least for the moment there can be no theory of city planning which is wholly divorced from a theory of cities, and hence no wholly general theory of planning as such". We have taken up his call for reaction to this thesis, and hope that the discussion will continue. We have arrived at a different conclusion. In the long run, we would assert that procedures and substance cannot be treated separately. For the present, the need is great for widespread attention to planning method.

38   *A Reader in Planning Theory*

BIBLIOGRAPHY

1. ACKOFF, RUSSELL L. *The Design of Social Research*, University of Chicago Press, Chicago, 1953.
2. ARROW, KENNETH J. "A difficulty in the concept of social welfare", *Journal of Political Economy*, Vol. LVIII, No. 4 (August 1950), pp. 328–46.
3. AYER, ALFRED J., *Language, Truth and Logic*, Dover Publications, Inc., New York, 2nd ed., 1946.
4. BASSETT, EDWARD M., *The Master Plan*, The Russell Sage Foundation, New York, 1938.
5. BAUMOL, WILLIAM J., *Economic Theory and Operations Analysis*, Prentice-Hall, Inc., Englewood Cliffs, N.J., 1961.
6. CARNAP, RUDOLF, "Logical positivism", in MORTON WHITE (ed.), *The Age of Analysis: 20th Century Philosophers*, Mentor Books, New York, 1955, pp. 203–25.
7. CHURCHMAN, C. WEST, *Prediction and Optimal Decision*, Prentice-Hall, Inc., Englewood Cliffs, N.J., 1961.
8. CHURCHMAN, C. WEST, RUSSELL L. ACKOFF and E. LEONARD ARNOFF, *Introduction to Operations Research*, New York, John Wiley & Sons, Inc., 1957.
9. DAHL, ROBERT A. and CHARLES E. LINDBLOM, *Politics, Economics, and Welfare*, Harper & Brothers, New York, 1953.
10. DUNHAM, ALLISON. "City planning: an analysis of the content of the master plan", *The Journal of Law & Economics*, Vol. I (October 1958), pp. 170–86.
11. DYCKMAN, JOHN W., "Planning and decision theory", *Journal of the American Institute of Planners*, Vol. XXVII, No. 4 (November 1961), pp. 335–45.
12. GANS, HERBERT, "The human implications of current redevelopment and relocation planning", *Journal of the American Institute of Planners*, Vol. XXV, No. 1 (February 1959), pp. 15–25.
13. HAAR, CHARLES M., "The Master Plan: an inquiry in dialogue form", *Journal of the American Institute of Planners*, Vol. XXV, No. 3 (August 1959), pp. 133–42.
14. HARRIS, BRITTON, "Plan or projection", *Journal of the American Institute of Planners*, Vol. XXVI, No. 4 (November 1960), pp. 265–72.
15. HOWARD, JOHN T., "In defense of planning commissions", *Journal of the American Institute of Planners*, Vol. XVII, No. 2 (Spring 1951), pp. 89–94.
16. KAPLAN, ABRAHAM, "On the strategy of social planning", "a report submitted to the Social Planning Group of the Planning Board of Puerto Rico, September 10, 1958", mimeographed.
17. LASSWELL, HAROLD D. and ABRAHAM KAPLAN, *Power and Society*, Yale University Press, New Haven, 1950.
18. MERTON, ROBERT K., "The role of applied social science in the formation of policy", *Philosophy of Science*, Vol. XVI, No. 3 (July 1949), pp. 161–81.
19. MEYERSON, MARTIN, "Utopian tradition and the planning of cities," *Dædalus*, Vol. XC, No. 1 (Winter 1961), pp. 180–93.
20. MEYERSON, MARTIN and EDWARD C. BANFIELD, *Politics, Planning and the Public Interest*, The Free Press, Glencoe, Ill., 1955.
21. MYRDAL, GUNNAR, *Value in Social Theory*, Harper & Brothers, New York, 1958.
22. REINER, THOMAS A., *The Place of the Ideal Community in Urban Planning*, University of Pennsylvania Press, Philadelphia, 1962 (in press).

23. RIESMAN, DAVID, "Some observations on community plans and utopia", *The Yale Law Journal*, Vol. LVII (December 1947), pp. 173–200; reprinted in *Individualism Reconsidered*, The Free Press, Glencoe, Ill., 1954.

24. SCHOEFFLER, SIDNEY, "Toward a general definition of rational action", *Kyklos*, Vol. VII, No. 3 (1954), pp. 245–73; reprinted in *The Failure of Economics*, Harvard University Press, Cambridge, Massachusetts, 1955: Appendix A.

25. SEELEY, JOHN R., "The slum: Its nature, use and users", *Journal of the American Institute of Planners*, Vol. XXV, No. 1 (February 1959), pp. 7–14.

26. SIMON, HERBERT A., "A behavioral model of rational choice", *Quarterly Journal of Economics*, Vol. LXIX, No. 1 (February 1955), pp. 99–118; reprinted in *Models of Man*, John Wiley & Sons, Inc., New York, 1957; ch. 14.

27. SIMON, HERBERT A., *Administrative Behavior*, Macmillan, New York, rev. ed., 1956.

28. STEVENS, BENJAMIN H., "A review of the literature on linear methods and models for spatial analysis", *Journal of the American Institute of Planners*, Vol. XXVI, No. 3 (August 1960), pp. 253–9.

29. STEVENSON, CHARLES L., *Ethics and Language*, Yale University Press, New Haven, 1953.

30. TUGWELL, REXFORD G. and EDWARD C. BANFIELD, Book Review of Walker's "The planning function in urban government", *Journal of the American Institute of Planners*, Vol. XVII, No. 1 (Winter 1951), pp. 46–49.

31. WALKER, ROBERT A., *The Planning Function in Urban Government*, 2nd ed., University of Chicago Press, Chicago, 1950.

[17]

The Science of "Muddling Through"*

Charles E. Lindblom

SUPPOSE an administrator is given responsibility for formulating policy with respect to inflation. He might start by trying to list all related values in order of importance, e.g. full employment, reasonable business profit, protection of small savings, prevention of a stock market crash. Then all possible policy outcomes could be rated as more or less efficient in attaining a maximum of these values. This would of course require a prodigious inquiry into values held by members of society and an equally prodigious set of calculations on how much of each value is equal to how much of each other value. He could then proceed to outline all possible policy alternatives. In a third step, he would undertake systematic comparison of his multitude of alternatives to determine which attains the greatest amount of values.

In comparing policies, he would take advantage of any theory available that generalized about classes of policies. In considering inflation, for example, he would compare all policies in the light of the theory of prices. Since no alternatives are beyond his investigation, he would consider strict central control and the abolition of all prices and markets on the one hand and elimination of all public controls with reliance completely on the free market on the other, both in the light of whatever theoretical generalizations he could find on such hypothetical economies.

Finally, he would try to make the choice that would in fact maximize his values.

An alternative line of attack would be to set as his principal objective,

* Reprinted by permission of the *Public Administration Review*, Spring 1959

either explicitly or without conscious thought, the relatively simple goal of keeping prices level. This objective might be compromised or complicated by only a few other goals, such as full employment. He would in fact disregard most other social values as beyond his present interest, and he would for the moment not even attempt to rank the few values that he regarded as immediately relevant. Were he pressed, he would quickly admit that he was ignoring many related values and many possible important consequences of his policies.

As a second step, he would outline those relatively few policy alternatives that occurred to him. He would then compare them. In comparing his limited number of alternatives, most of them familiar from past controversies, he would not ordinarily find a body of theory precise enough to carry him through a comparison of their respective consequences. Instead he would rely heavily on the record of past experience with small policy steps to predict the consequences of similar steps extended into the future.

Moreover, he would find that the policy alternatives combined objectives or values in different ways. For example, one policy might offer price-level stability at the cost of some risk of unemployment; another might offer less price stability but also less risk of unemployment. Hence, the next step in his approach—the final selection—would combine into one the choice among values and the choice among instruments for reaching values. It would not, as in the first method of policy-making, approximate a more mechanical process of choosing the means that best satisfied goals that were previously clarified and ranked. Because practitioners of the second approach expect to achieve their goals only partially, they would expect to repeat endlessly the sequence just described, as conditions and aspirations changed and as accuracy of prediction improved.

BY ROOT OR BY BRANCH

For complex problems, the first of these two approaches is of course impossible. Although such an approach can be described, it cannot be practiced except for relatively simple problems and even then only in a somewhat modified form. It assumes intellectual capacities and sources of information that men simply do not possess, and it is even more absurd as an approach to policy when the time and money that can be allocated to a policy problem is limited, as is always the case. Of particular importance to public administrators is the fact that public agencies are in effect usually instructed not to practice the first method. That is to say, their prescribed functions and constraints—the politically or legally possible—restrict their attention to relatively few values and relatively few alternative policies among the countless alternatives that might be imagined. It is the second method that is practiced.

Curiously, however, the literatures of decision-making, policy formulation, planning, and public administration formalize the first approach rather than the second, leaving public administrators who handle complex decisions in the position of practicing what few preach. For emphasis I run some risk of overstatement. True enough, the literature is well aware of limits on man's capacities and of the inevitability that policies will be approached in some such style as the second. But attempts to formalize rational policy formulation—to lay out explicitly the necessary steps in the process—usually describe the first approach and not the second.[1]

The common tendency to describe policy formulation even for complex problems as though it followed the first approach has been strengthened by the attention given to, and successes enjoyed by, operations research, statistical decision theory, and systems analysis. The hallmarks of these procedures, typical of the first approach, are clarity of objective, explicitness of evaluation, a high degree of comprehensiveness of overview, and, wherever possible, quantification of values for mathematical analysis. But these advanced procedures remain largely the appropriate techniques of relatively small-scale problem-solving where the total number of variables to be considered is small and value problems restricted. Charles Hitch, head of the Economics Division of RAND Corporation, one of the leading centers for application of these techniques, has written:

> I would make the empirical generalization from my experience at RAND and elsewhere that operations research is the art of sub-optimizing, i.e. of solving some lower-level problems, and that difficulties increase and our special competence diminishes by an order of magnitude with every level of decision making we attempt to ascend. The sort of simple explicit model which operations researchers are so proficient in using can certainly reflect most of the significant factors influencing traffic control on the George Washington

---

[1] James G. March and Herbert A. Simon similarly characterize the literature. They also take some important steps, as have Simon's recent articles, to describe a less heroic model of policy-making. See *Organizations*, John Wiley & Sons, 1958, p. 137.

Bridge, but the proportion of the relevant reality which we can represent by any such model or models in studying, say, a major foreign-policy decision, appears to be almost trivial.[2]

Accordingly, I propose in this paper to clarify and formalize the second method, much neglected in the literature. This might be described as the method of *successive limited comparisons*. I will contrast it with the first approach, which might be called the rational-comprehensive method.[3] More impressionistically and briefly—and therefore generally used in this article—they could be characterized as the branch method and root method, the former continually building out from the current situation, step-by-step and by small degrees; the latter starting from fundamentals anew each time, building on the past only as experience is embodied in a theory, and always prepared to start completely from the ground up.

Let us put the characteristics of the two methods side by side in simplest terms.

Rational-Comprehensive (Root)	Successive Limited Comparisons (Branch)
1a. Clarification of values or objectives distinct from and usually prerequisite to empirical analysis of alternative policies.	1b. Selection of value goals and empirical analysis of the needed action are not distinct from one another but are closely intertwined.
2a. Policy-formulation is therefore approached through means-end analysis: first the ends are isolated, then the means to achieve them are sought.	2b. Since means and ends are not distinct, means-end analysis is often inappropriate or limited.

---

[2] "Operations research and national planning—a dissent", *Operations Research*, Vol. 5, p. 718 (October 1957). Hitch's dissent is from particular points made in the article to which his paper is a reply; his claim that operations research is for low-level problems is widely accepted.

For examples, of the kind of problems to which operations research is applied, see C. W. Churchman, R. L. Ackoff and E. L. Arnoff, *Introduction to Operations Research*, John Wiley & Sons, 1957; and J. F. McCloskey and J. M. Coppinger (eds.), *Operations Research for Management*, Vol. II, The Johns Hopkins Press, 1956.

[3] I am assuming that administrators often make policy and advise in the making of policy and am treating decision-making and policy-making as synonymous for purposes of this paper.

3a. The test of a "good" policy is.that it can be shown to be the most appropriate means to desired ends.

3b. The test of a "good" policy is typically that various analysts find themselves directly agreeing on a policy (without their agreeing that it is the most appropriate means to an agreed objective).

4a. Analysis is comprehensive; every important relevant factor is taken into account.

4b. Analysis is drastically limited:
   (i) Important possible outcomes are neglected.
   (ii) Important alternative potential policies are neglected.
   (iii) Important affected values are neglected.

5a. Theory is often heavily relied upon.

5b. A succession of comparisons greatly reduces or eliminates reliance on theory

Assuming that the root method is familiar and understandable, we proceed directly to clarification of its alternative by contrast. In explaining the second, we shall be describing how most administrators do in fact approach complex questions, for the root method, the "best" way as a blueprint or model, is in fact not workable for complex policy questions, and administrators are forced to use the method of successive limited comparisons.

INTERTWINING EVALUATION AND EMPIRICAL ANALYSIS (1b)

The quickest way to understand how values are handled in the method of successive limited comparisons is to see how the root method often breaks down in *its* handling of values or objectives. The idea that values should be clarified, and in advance of the examination of alternative policies, is appealing. But what happens when we attempt it for complex social problems? The first difficulty is that on many critical values or objectives, citizens disagree, congressmen disagree, and public administrators disagree. Even where a fairly specific objective is prescribed for the administrator, there remains considerable room for disagreement on sub-objectives. Consider, for example, the conflict with respect to locating public housing, described in Meyerson and Banfield's study of the Chicago

Housing Authority[4]—disagreement which occurred despite the clear
objective of providing a certain number of public housing units in the
city. Similarly conflicting are objectives in highway location, traffic control,
minimum wage administration, development of tourist facilities in national
parks, or insect control.

Administrators cannot escape these conflicts by ascertaining the
majority's preference, for preferences have not been registered on most
issues; indeed, there often *are* no preferences in the absence of public
discussion sufficient to bring an issue to the attention of the electorate.
Furthermore, there is a question of whether intensity of feeling should be
considered as well as the number of persons preferring each alternative.
By the impossibility of doing otherwise, administrators often are reduced
to deciding policy without clarifying objectives first.

Even when an administrator resolves to follow his own values as a
criterion for decisions, he often will not know how to rank them when they
conflict with one another, as they usually do. Suppose, for example, that
an administrator must relocate tenants living in tenements scheduled for
destruction. One objective is to empty the buildings fairly promptly,
another is to find suitable accommodation for persons displaced, another
is to avoid friction with residents in other areas in which a large influx
would be unwelcome, another is to deal with all concerned through persuasion if possible, and so on.

How does one state even to himself the relative importance of these
partially conflicting values? A simple ranking of them is not enough; one
needs ideally to know how much of one value is worth sacrificing for some
of another value. The answer is that typically the administrator chooses—
and must choose—directly among policies in which these values are combined in different ways. He cannot first clarify his values and then choose
among policies.

A more subtle third point underlies both the first two. Social objectives
do not always have the same relative values. One objective may be highly
prized in one circumstance, another in another circumstance. If, for
example, an administrator values highly both the dispatch with which his
agency can carry through its projects *and* good public relations, it matters
little which of the two possibly conflicting values he favors in some abstract

---

[4] Martin Meyerson and Edward C. Banfield, *Politics, Planning and the Public
Interest*, The Free Press, 1955.

or general sense. Policy questions arise in forms which put to administrators such a question as: Given the degree to which we are or are not already achieving the values of dispatch and the values of good public relations, is it worth sacrificing a little speed for a happier clientele, or is it better to risk offending the clientele so that we can get on with our work? The answer to such a question varies with circumstances.

The value problem is, as the example shows, always a problem of adjustments at a margin. But there is no practicable way to state marginal objectives or values except in terms of particular policies. That one value is preferred to another in one decision situation does not mean that it will be preferred in another decision situation in which it can be had only at great sacrifice of another value. Attempts to rank or order values in general and abstract terms so that they do not shift from decision to decision end up by ignoring the relevant marginal preferences. The significance of this third point thus goes very far. Even if all administrators had at hand an agreed set of values, objectives, and constraints, and an agreed ranking of these values, objectives, and constraints, their marginal values in actual choice situations would be impossible to formulate.

Unable consequently to formulate the relevant values first and then choose among policies to achieve them, administrators must choose directly among alternative policies that offer different marginal combinations of values. Somewhat paradoxically, the only practicable way to disclose one's relevant marginal values even to oneself is to describe the policy one chooses to achieve them. Except roughly and vaguely, I know of no way to describe—or even to understand—what my relative evaluations are for, say, freedom and security, speed and accuracy in governmental decisions, or low taxes and better schools than to describe my preferences among specific policy choices that might be made between the alternatives in each of the pairs.

In summary, two aspects of the process by which values are actually handled can be distinguished. The first is clear: evaluation and empirical analysis are intertwined; that is, one chooses among values and among policies at one and the same time. Put a little more elaborately, one simultaneously chooses a policy to attain certain objectives and chooses the objectives themselves. The second aspect is related but distinct: the administrator focuses his attention on marginal or incremental values. Whether he is aware of it or not, he does not find general formulations of objectives very helpful and in fact makes specific marginal or incremental comparisons. Two policies, X and Y, confront him. Both promise the same degree of attainment of objectives *a*, *b*, *c*, *d*, and *e*. But X promises him somewhat more of *f* than does Y, while Y promises him somewhat more of *g* than does X. In choosing between them, he is in fact offered the alternative of a marginal or incremental amount of *f* at the expense of a marginal or incremental amount of *g*. The only values that are relevant to his choice are these increments by which the two policies differ; and, when he finally chooses between the two marginal values, he does so by making a choice between policies.[5]

As to whether the attempt to clarify objectives in advance of policy selection is more or less rational than the close intertwining of marginal evaluation and empirical analysis, the principal difference established is that for complex problems the first is impossible and irrelevant, and the second is both possible and relevant. The second is possible because the administrator need not try to analyze any values except the values by which alternative policies differ and need not be concerned with them except as they differ marginally. His need for information on values or objectives is drastically reduced as compared with the root method; and his capacity for grasping, comprehending, and relating values to one another is not strained beyond the breaking point.

RELATIONS BETWEEN MEANS AND ENDS (2b)

Decision-making is ordinarily formalized as a means–ends relationship: means are conceived to be evaluated and chosen in the light of ends finally selected independently of and prior to the choice of means. This is the means–ends relationship of the root method. But it follows from all that has just been said that such a means–ends relationship is possible only to the extent that values are agreed upon, are reconcilable, and are stable at the margin. Typically, therefore, such a means–ends relationship is absent from the branch method, where means and ends are simultaneously chosen.

Yet any departure from the means–ends relationship of the root method

---

[5] The line of argument is, of course, an extension of the theory of market choice, especially the theory of consumer choice, to public policy choices.

will strike some readers as inconceivable. For it will appear to them that only in such a relationship is it possible to determine whether one policy choice is better or worse than another. How can an administrator know whether he has made a wise or foolish decision if he is without prior values or objectives by which to judge his decisions? The answer to this question calls up the third distinctive difference between root and branch methods: how to decide the best policy.

THE TEST OF "GOOD" POLICY (3b)

In the root method, a decision is "correct", "good", or "rational" if it can be shown to attain some specified objective, where the objective can be specified without simply describing the decision itself. Where objectives are defined only through the marginal or incremental approach to values described above, it is still sometimes possible to test whether a policy does in fact attain the desired objectives; but a precise statement of the objectives takes the form of a description of the policy chosen or some alternative to it. To show that a policy is mistaken one cannot offer an abstract argument that important objectives are not achieved; one must instead argue that another policy is more to be preferred.

So far, the departure from customary ways of looking at problem-solving is not troublesome, for many administrators, will be quick to agree that the most effective discussion of the correctness of policy does take the form of comparison with other policies that might have been chosen. But what of the situation in which administrators cannot agree on values or objectives, either abstractly or in marginal terms? What then is the test of "good" policy? For the root method, there is no test. Agreement on objectives failing, there is no standard of "correctness". For the method of successive limited comparisons, the test is agreement on policy itself, which remains possible even when agreement on values is not.

It has been suggested that continuing agreement in Congress on the desirability of extending old-age insurance stems from liberal desires to strengthen the welfare programs of the federal government and from conservative desires to reduce union demands for private pension plans. If so, this is an excellent demonstration of the ease with which individuals of different ideologies often can agree on concrete policy. Labor mediators report a similar phenomenon: the contestants cannot agree on criteria for settling their disputes but can agree on specific proposals. Similarly, when one administrator's objective turns out to be another's means, they often can agree on policy.

Agreement on policy thus becomes the only practicable test of the policy's correctness. And for one administrator to seek to win the other over to agreement on ends as well would accomplish nothing and create quite unnecessary controversy.

If agreement directly on policy as a test for "best" policy seems a poor substitute for testing the policy against its objectives, it ought to be remembered that objectives themselves have no ultimate validity other than they are agreed upon. Hence agreement is the test of "best" policy in both methods. But where the root method requires agreement on what elements in the decision constitute objectives and on which of these objectives should be sought, the branch method falls back on agreement wherever it can be found.

In an important sense, therefore, it is not irrational for an administrator to defend a policy as good without being able to specify what it is good for.

NON-COMPREHENSIVE ANALYSIS (4b)

Ideally, rational-comprehensive analysis leaves out nothing important. But it is impossible to take everything important into consideration unless "important" is so narrowly defined that analysis is in fact quite limited. Limits on human intellectual capacities and on available information set definite limits to man's capacity to be comprehensive. In actual fact, therefore, no one can practice the rational-comprehensive method for really complex problems, and every administrator faced with a sufficiently complex problem must find ways drastically to simplify.

An administrator assisting in the formulation of agricultural economic policy cannot in the first place be competent on all possible policies. He cannot even comprehend one policy entirely. In planning a soil bank program, he cannot successfully anticipate the impact of higher or lower farm income on, say, urbanization—the possible consequent loosening of family ties, possible consequent eventual need for revisions in social security and further implications for tax problems arising out of new federal responsibilities for social security and municipal responsibilities for urban services. Nor, to follow another line of repercussions, can he work through the soil bank program's effects on prices for agricultural products in foreign markets and consequent implications for foreign markets and consequent implications for foreign relations, including those arising out of economic rivalry between the United States and the U.S.S.R.

In the method of successive limited comparisons, simplification is systematically achieved in two principal ways. First, it is achieved through limitation of policy comparisons to those policies that differ in relatively small degree from policies presently in effect. Such a limitation immediately reduces the number of alternatives to be investigated and also drastically simplifies the character of the investigation of each. For it is not necessary to undertake fundamental inquiry into an alternative and its consequences; it is necessary only to study those respects in which the proposed alternative and its consequences differ from the status quo. The empirical comparison of marginal differences among alternative policies that differ only marginally is, of course, a counterpart to the incremental or marginal comparison of values discussed above.[6]

Relevance as Well as Realism

It is a matter of common observation that in Western democracies public administrators and policy analysts in general do largely limit their analyses to incremental or marginal differences in policies that are chosen to differ only incrementally. They do not do so, however, solely because they desperately need some way to simplify their problems; they also do so in order to be relevant. Democracies change their policies almost entirely through incremental adjustments. Policy does not move in leaps and bounds.

The incremental character of political change in the United States has often been remarked. The two major political parties agree on fundamentals; they offer alternative policies to the voters only on relatively small points of difference. Both parties favor full employment, but they define it somewhat differently; both favor the development of water-power resources, but in slightly different ways; and both favor unemployment

---

[6] A more precise definition of incremental policies and a discussion of whether a change that appears "small" to one observer might be seen differently by another is to be found in my "Policy Analysis", *American Economic Review*, Vol. 48, p. 298 (June 1958).

compensation, but not the same level of benefits. Similarly, shifts of policy within a party take place largely through a series of relatively small changes, as can be seen in their only gradual acceptance of the idea of governmental responsibility for support of the unemployed, a change in party positions beginning in the early thirties and culminating in a sense in the Employment Act of 1946.

Party behavior is in turn rooted in public attitudes, and political theorists cannot conceive of democracy's surviving in the United States in the absence of fundamental agreement on potentially disruptive issues, with consequent limitation of policy debates to relatively small differences in policy.

Since the policies ignored by the administrator are politically impossible and so irrelevant, the simplification of analysis achieved by concentrating on policies that differ only incrementally is not a capricious kind of simplification. In addition, it can be argued that, given the limits on knowledge within which policy-makers are confined, simplifying by limiting the focus to small variations from present policy makes the most of available knowledge. Because policies being considered are like present and past policies, the administrator can obtain information and claim some insight. Non-incremental policy proposals are therefore typically not only politically irrelevant but also unpredictable in their consequences.

The second method of simplification of analysis is the practice of ignoring important possible consequences of possible policies, as well as the values attached to the neglected consequences. If this appears to disclose a shocking shortcoming of successive limited comparisons, it can be replied that, even if the exclusions are random, policies may nevertheless be more intelligently formulated than through futile attempts to achieve a comprehensiveness beyond human capacity. Actually, however, the exclusions, seeming arbitrary or random from one point of view, need be neither.

Achieving a Degree of Comprehensiveness

Suppose that each value neglected by one policy-making agency were a major concern of at least one other agency. In that case, a helpful division of labor would be achieved, and no agency need find its task beyond its capacities. The shortcomings of such a system would be that one agency might destroy a value either before another agency could be activated to safeguard it or in spite of another agency's efforts. But the possibility that important values may be lost is present in any form of organization, even where agencies attempt to comprehend in planning more than is humanly possible.

The virtue of such a hypothetical division of labor is that every important interest or value has its watchdog. And these watchdogs can protect the interests in their jurisdiction in two quite different ways: first, by redressing damages done by other agencies; and second, by anticipating and heading off injury before it occurs.

In a society like that of the United States in which individuals are free to combine to pursue almost any possible common interest they might have and in which government agencies are sensitive to the pressures of these groups, the system described is approximated. Almost every interest has its watchdog. Without claiming that every interest has a sufficiently powerful watchdog, it can be argued that our system often can assure a more comprehensive regard for the values of the whole society than any attempt at intellectual comprehensiveness.

In the United States, for example, no part of government attempts a comprehensive overview of policy on income distribution. A policy nevertheless evolves, and one responding to a wide variety of interests. A process of mutual adjustment among farm groups, labor unions, municipalities and school boards, tax authorities, and government agencies with responsibilities in the fields of housing, health, highways, national parks, fire, and police accomplishes a distribution of income in which particular income problems neglected at one point in the decision processes become central at another point.

Mutual adjustment is more pervasive than the explicit forms it takes in negotiation between groups; it persists through the mutual impacts of groups upon each other even where they are not in communication. For all the imperfections and latent dangers in this ubiquitous process of mutual adjustment, it will often accomplish an adaptation of policies to a wider range of interests than could be done by one group centrally.

Note, too, how the incremental pattern of policy-making fits with the multiple pressure pattern. For when decisions are only incremental—closely related to known policies, it is easier for one group to anticipate the kind of moves another might make and easier too for it to make correction for injury already accomplished.[7]

Even partisanship and narrowness, to use pejorative terms, will sometimes be assets to rational decision-making, for they can doubly insure that what one agency neglects, another will not; they specialize personnel to distinct points of view. The claim is valid that effective rational coordination of the federal administration, if possible to achieve at all, would require an agreed set of values[8]—if "rational" is defined as the practice of the root method of decision-making. But a high degree of administrative coordination occurs as each agency adjusts its policies to the concerns of the other agencies in the process of fragmented decision-making I have just described.

For all the apparent shortcomings of the incremental approach to policy alternatives with its arbitrary exclusion coupled with fragmentation, when compared to the root method, the branch method often looks far superior. In the root method, the inevitable exclusion of factors is accidental, unsystematic, and not defensible by an argument so far developed, while in the branch method the exclusions are deliberate, systematic and defensible. Ideally, of course, the root method does not exclude; in practice it must.

Nor does the branch method necessarily neglect long-run considerations and objectives. It is clear that important values must be omitted in considering policy, and sometimes the only way long-run objectives can be given adequate attention is through the neglect of short-run considerations. But the values omitted can be either long-run or short-run.

SUCCESSION OF COMPARISONS (5b)

The final distinctive element in the branch method is that the comparisons, together with the policy choice, proceed in a chronological series. Policy is not made once and for all; it is made and re-made endlessly. Policy-making is a process of successive approximation to some desired

---

[7] The link between the practice of the method of successive limited comparisons and mutual adjustment of interests in a highly fragmented decision-making process adds a new facet to pluralist theories of government and administration.

[8] Herbert Simon, Donald W. Smithburg, and Victor A. Thompson, *Public Administration*, Alfred A. Knopf, 1950, p. 434.

objectives in which what is desired itself continues to change under reconsideration.

Making policy is at best a very rough process. Neither social scientists, nor politicians, nor public administrators yet know enough about the social world to avoid repeated error in predicting the consequences of policy moves. A wise policy-maker consequently expects that his policies will achieve only part of what he hopes and at the same time will produce unanticipated consequences he would have preferred to avoid. If he proceeds through a *succession* of incremental changes, he avoids serious lasting mistakes in several ways.

In the first place, past sequences of policy steps have given him knowledge about the probable consequences of further similar steps. Second, he need not attempt big jumps toward his goals that would require predictions beyond his or anyone else's knowledge, because he never expects his policy to be a final resolution of a problem. His decision is only one step, one that if successful can quickly be followed by another. Third, he is in effect able to test his previous predictions as he moves on to each further step. Lastly, he often can remedy a past error fairly quickly—more quickly than if policy proceeded through more distinct steps widely spaced in time.

Compare this comparative analysis of incremental changes with the aspiration to employ theory in the root method. Man cannot think without classifying, without subsuming one experience under a more general category of experiences. The attempt to push categorization as far as possible and to find general propositions which can be applied to specific situations is what I refer to with the word "theory". Where root analysis often leans heavily on theory in this sense, the branch method does not.

The assumption of root analysts is that theory is the most systematic and economical way to bring relevant knowledge to bear on a specific problem. Granting the assumption, an unhappy fact is that we do not have adequate theory to apply to problems in any policy area, although theory is more adequate in some areas—monetary policy, for example—than in others. Comparative analysis, as in the branch method, is sometimes a systematic alternative to theory.

Suppose an administrator must choose among a small group of policies that differ only incrementally from each other and from present policy. He might aspire to "understand" each of the alternatives—for example, to know all the consequences of each aspect of each policy. If so, he would indeed require theory. In fact, however, he would usually decide, that *for policy-making purposes*, he need know, as explained above, only the consequences of each of those aspects of the policies in which they differed from one another. For this much more modest aspiration, he requires no theory (although it might be helpful, if available), for he can proceed to isolate probable differences by examining the differences in consequences associated with past differences in policies, a feasible program because he can take his observations from a long sequence of incremental changes.

For example, without a more comprehensive social theory about juvenile delinquency than scholars have yet produced, one cannot possibly understand the ways in which a variety of public policies—say on education, housing, recreation, employment, race relations, and policing—might encourage or discourage delinquency. And one needs such an understanding if he undertakes the comprehensive overview of the problem prescribed in the models of the root method. If, however, one merely wants to mobilize knowledge sufficient to assist in a choice among a small group of similar policies—alternative policies on juvenile court procedures, for example—he can do so by comparative analysis of the results of similar past policy moves.

THEORISTS AND PRACTITIONERS

This difference explains—in some cases at least—why the administrator often feels that the outside expert or academic problem-solver is sometimes not helpful and why they in turn often urge more theory on him. And it explains why an administrator often feels more confident when "flying by the seat of his pants" than when following the advice of theorists. Theorists often ask the administrator to go the long way round to the solution of his problems, in effect ask him to follow the best canons of the scientific method, when the administrator knows that the best available theory will work less well than more modest incremental comparisons. Theorists do not realize that the administrator is often in fact practicing a systematic method. It would be foolish to push this explanation too far, for sometimes practical decision-makers are pursuing neither a theoretical approach nor successive comparisons, nor any other systematic method.

It may be worth emphasizing that theory is sometimes of extremely limited helpfulness in policy-making for at least two rather different reasons. It is greedy for facts; it can be constructed only through a great collection of observations. And it is typically insufficiently precise for application to a policy process that moves through small changes. In contrast, the comparative method both economizes on the need for facts and directs the analyst's attention to just those facts that are relevant to the fine choices faced by the decision-maker.

With respect to precision of theory, economic theory serves as an example. It predicts that an economy without money or prices would in certain specified ways misallocate resources, but this finding pertains to an alternative far removed from the kind of policies on which administrators need help. On the other hand, it is not precise enough to predict the consequences of policies restricting business mergers, and this is the kind of issue on which the administrators need help. Only in relatively restricted areas does economic theory achieve sufficient precision to go far in resolving policy questions; its helpfulness in policy-making is always so limited that it requires supplementation through comparative analysis.

SUCCESSIVE COMPARISON AS A SYSTEM

Successive limited comparisons is, then, indeed a method or system; it is not a failure of method for which administrators ought to apologize. None the less, its imperfections, which have not been explored in this paper, are many. For example, the method is without a built-in safeguard for all relevant values, and it also may lead the decision-maker to overlook excellent policies for no other reason than that they are not suggested by the chain of successive policy steps leading up to the present. Hence, it ought to be said that under this method, as well as under some of the most sophisticated variants of the root method—operations research, for example—policies will continue to be as foolish as they are wise.

Why then bother to describe the method in all the above detail? Because it is in fact a common method of policy formulation, and is, for complex problems, the principal reliance of administrators as well as of other policy analysts.[9] And because it will be superior to any other decision-making

[9] Elsewhere I have explored this same method of policy formulation as practiced by academic analysts of policy ("Policy analysis", *American Economic Review*, Vol. 48, p. 298 [June, 1958]). Although it has been here presented as a method for public administrators, it is no less necessary to analysts more removed from

method available for complex problems in many circumstances, certainly superior to a futile attempt at superhuman comprehensiveness. The reaction of the public administrator to the exposition of method doubtless will be less a discovery of a new method than a better acquaintance with an old. But by becoming more conscious of their practice of this method, administrators might practice it with more skill and know when to extend or constrict its use. (That they sometimes practice it effectively and sometimes not may explain the extremes of opinion on "muddling through", which is both praised as a highly sophisticated form of problem-solving and denounced as no method at all. For I suspect that in so far as there is a system in what is known as "muddling through", this method is it.)

One of the noteworthy incidental consequences of clarification of the method is the light it throws on the suspicion an administrator sometimes entertains that a consultant or adviser is not speaking relevantly and responsibly when in fact by all ordinary objective evidence he is. The trouble lies in the fact that most of us approach policy problems within a framework given by our view of a chain of successive policy choices made up to the present. One's thinking about appropriate policies with respect, say, to urban traffic control is greatly influenced by one's knowledge of the incremental steps taken up to the present. An administrator enjoys an intimate knowledge of his past sequences that "outsiders" do not share, and his thinking and that of the "outsider" will consequently be different in ways that may puzzle both. Both may appear to be talking intelligently, yet each may find the other unsatisfactory. The relevance of the policy chain of succession is even more clear when an American tries to discuss, say, antitrust policy with a Swiss, for the chains of policy in the two countries are strikingly different and the two individuals consequently have organized their knowledge in quite different ways.

---

immediate policy questions, despite their tendencies to describe their own analytical efforts as though they were the rational-comprehensive method with an especially heavy use of theory. Similarly, this same method is inevitably resorted to in personal problem-solving, where means and ends are sometimes impossible to separate, where aspirations or objectives undergo constant development, and where drastic simplification of the complexity of the real world is urgent if problems are to be solved in the time that can be given to them. To an economist accustomed to dealing with the marginal or incremental concept in market processes, the central idea in the method is that both evaluation and empirical analysis are incremental. Accordingly I have referred to the method elsewhere as "the incremental method".

If this phenomenon is a barrier to communication, an understanding of it promises an enrichment of intellectual interaction in policy formulation. Once the source of difference is understood, it will sometimes be stimulating for an administrator to seek out a policy analyst whose recent experience is with a policy chain different from his own.

This raises again a question only briefly discussed above on the merits of like-mindedness among government administrators. While much of organization theory argues the virtues of common values and agreed organizational objectives, for complex problems in which the root method is inapplicable, agencies will want among their own personnel two types of diversification: administrators whose thinking is organized by reference to policy chains other than those familiar to most members of the organization and, even more commonly, administrators whose professional or personal values or interests create diversity of view (perhaps coming from different specialties, social classes, geographical areas) so that, even within a single agency, decision-making can be fragmented and parts of the agency can serve as watchdogs for other parts.

[18]

The Guidance and Control of Change: Physical Planning as the Control of Complex Systems

J. Brian McLoughlin

The following chapters of the book deal with planning techniques: the planning process in outline, the identification of goals and objectives, information for planning, projection, simulation and modelling, the design of plans, their evaluation and implementation.

Systems in general
This present chapter lays the foundation with an introduction to notions fundamental to this book—*the environment as a system and its control by the application of cybernetic principles.*

In general usage a system is understood as a 'complex whole', a 'set of connected things or parts', an 'organised body of material of immaterial things' and as a 'group of objects related or interacting so as to form a unity'.* In recent years bodies of thinking have grown up known as *General Systems Theory* (von Bertalanffy, 1951) which deal with the notion of systems in general just as *Operations Research* (Churchman, Ackoff and Arnoff, 1957) applies systems thinking via *systems analysis* to real-life situations, whilst *Cybernetics* (Wiener, 1948; Ashby, 1956) is the study of the control of complex systems, both living and inanimate.

In Chapter 1 of this book we saw the relationships of man (and other creatures) with the environment could be identified in system terms—as an ecological or *eco-system* in fact. Stafford Beer

* Oxford English Dictionary.

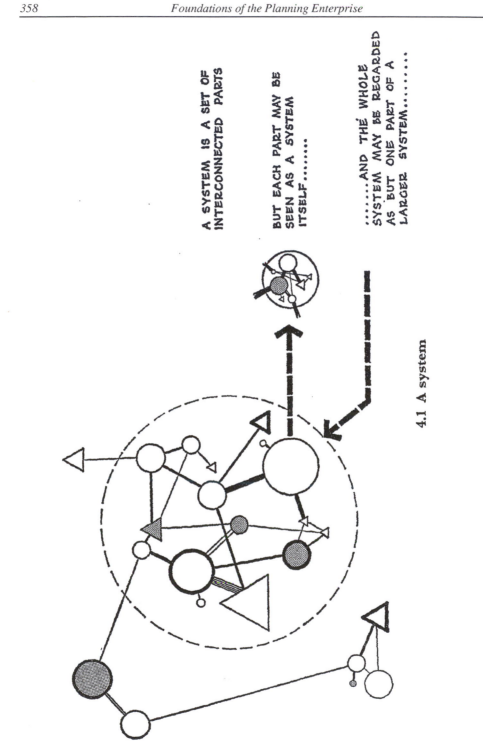

A SYSTEM IS A SET OF
INTERCONNECTED PARTS

BUT EACH PART MAY BE
SEEN AS A SYSTEM
ITSELF........

.......AND THE WHOLE
SYSTEM MAY BE REGARDED
AS BUT ONE PART OF A
LARGER SYSTEM........

4.1 A system

The Guidance and Control of Change

(1959, Chapter II) reminds us 'that the definition of any particular system is arbitrary . . . the universe seems to be made up of sets of systems, each contained within one somewhat bigger, like a set of hollow building blocks [Figure 4.1]. Just as it is always possible to expand the system to a scope of wider perspective, it is also possible to cut down the system to a smaller version . . . the point to seize on here is that if we wish to consider the interactions affecting one simple entity, then we shall have to define that entity as part of a system. The system we choose to define is a system because it contains interrelated parts, and is in some sense a complete whole in itself. But the entity we are considering will certainly be part of a number of such systems, each of which is a sub-system of a series of larger systems. So the problem of stating the system we wish to study is by no means easy'.

The human environment as a system
We can now attempt to define the system with which we will deal in the remainder of the book. This we must do by identifying the parts or components on the one hand and the connections or interactions on the other. The parts of our system are persistent *human activities* and especially those that tend to occur and recur at specific locations or within particular zones or areas (Chapin, 1965, pp. 90–5). Within the vast range of human activity there is a continuous gradation between those activities that are very strongly 'place-related' and those which are totally random with respect to place. For example, family life, the nurture and care of children, the welcoming of friends, these are strongly place-related; by contrast a hobby such as taking photographs, where the whole environment may be grist to the mill, is of itself very weakly related to place. Although there is gradation between extremes, considerable shifts occur. Webber (1963, 1964) has given us a full and provocative account of the way some human activities are becoming more and others less place-related. Whilst the components of our system, being an *eco-* system are those activities which are more recurrent and more strongly related to place, we must bear in mind the fluid nature of the distinction.

The connections between these parts are *human communications* and once again, our concern is mainly with those that

77

The Guidance and Control of Change

are recurrent and spatially clustered (in 'channels'—see below) (Meier, 1962). The communications enable the various activities to interact, to link up and cross-connect so that necessary patterns of human behaviour can occur. These communications take many forms. Radio communication is a good example of interaction which is wholly unrelated to place whilst railway transport is obviously at the opposite extreme. Communication involves many types of interaction: the transmission of material goods, of persons, of messages and of impressions received by the sense-organs of sight, sound and smell. It is useful to distinguish *transport* as a sub-system of communications concerned with material interaction (goods and persons). Just as activities may be more or less place-related, so with communications. We are familiar with messages sent by letter, (material and so involving place-related transport) being substituted by telephone messages. Television enables the sense impressions of sights and sounds at a football game to be received almost anywhere on earth, (though it cannot convey the smell of grease paint from a theatrical performance). Once again our main concern is to see the system's connections in those communications which are more recurrent and strongly patterned spatially.

So, the first step in defining the system with which we deal is to recognise *activities* linked by *communications*. We can imagine this graphically—in the words of Beer (1959): 'We will now represent the "bits and pieces" which make up this by a series of dots of paper. The connectiveness of the system can now be introduced into this picture by drawing lines between the dots; some dots may well be connected to all other dots, but in some cases a dot may be connected to only one of its fellows. In this way, we come to look upon a system as a kind of network'.

Proceeding further; our system takes physical form. The activities occur within adapted *spaces*. These include buildings, arenas, parks, seashores, lakes, quarries, forests and airfields. The adjective 'adapted' does not necessarily imply physical construction or development; fields used by a motor-cycle club for 'scrambling' meets, seashores and sand-dunes by holiday-makers, a natural lake by sailing enthusiasts, and a mountain by hill-walkers are all examples. It is their conscious and regular

The Guidance and Control of Change

use rather than building and engineering work which earns them the title 'adapted spaces' (Lynch, 1960).

Similar remarks apply to the physical forms for communications—the *channels*. These too may be deliberately constructed as are roads, footpaths, railways, canals, pipelines, cables and ski-lifts; or they may be borrowed from nature as are rivers, air corridors, ridges and valleys.

Systems and Structure

The parts of our system are activities linked by communications, and many of these use the physical forms of adapted spaces and channels. But we must not think that there is a fixed, unchanging correspondence between these two aspects of the system (Buchanan, 1966, Chapter 3 and Supplementary Volume 2). Very many activities take place within adapted spaces which were originally intended for some quite different purpose and channels become used for new forms of communication (Cowan, 1966). The whole history of towns and the countryside is witness to this: churches become warehouses then bingo-halls; houses become shops, then offices; royal parks may become partly used for underground car parking. Equally, many different activities may use the same space or channel—a phenomenon sometimes called 'multiple use'. A lake is used for water supply, fisheries and water sport; roads are used not only for transport but also for parking, retailing and public assembly.

We must not be disheartened by these conceptual problems. The key point to remember is that a system is *not* the real world, but a way of looking at it. Definitions of systems therefore depend in part on the purposes and objectives for which they are to be used. The reader who is not accustomed to thinking in system terms should have patience; increasing familiarity will almost certainly bring great clarification. We believe that for planners, one of the main difficulties arises from an undue emphasis to date on the physical side, on spaces and channels. We would advise a corrective emphasis which whilst remaining fully aware of the great importance of the material equipment, lays stress on the *human activities and communications* which are the key to understanding and control of the system. In addition to giving understanding, the systems view helps in practical situations and many of the problems of defining

79

The Guidance and Control of Change

our system, its components and its linkages will in large measure be resolved when discussing planning techniques in the chapters which follow.

We can further describe our system components and connections by *type or mode*. For example, activities include domestic, productive, recreational and educational types. If we adopt a finer 'grain' of typology we might wish to distinguish such activities as stock-holding for distribution, soft fruit-growing, youth clubs and carburettor manufacturing. Connections can be described by either the content or the medium or both. For example we might identify material goods movements, person movements and message flows; among modes there are road vehicle transport, radio signals, pipeline flows, telephone messages and visual sense-impressions transmitted from the objects to the human eye. Finer grain reveals private-car passenger movements for recreational purposes, pipeline-flows of natural gas, police VHF radio transmissions and so on.

By way of illustration here, we can quantify both the components and connections of our system in varying ways. Activities have measures of *stock*, e.g. amounts of population, employment, fixed capital, standing timber, floor space, and of *density*, e.g. persons per acre, workers per acre, sales per square foot.

Communications are measured by *flow*, e.g. vehicles, messages, kilovolts, trains, passengers, and by *flow density* or *interactance*, e.g. passenger-car-units (p.c.u.) per hour, million gallons per day (m.g.d.).

Refinement of the systems view of settlements

The Detroit and Chicago transportation studies about fifteen years ago interpreted the city as this kind of system, a view which was confirmed by Mitchell and Rapkin (1954). In the view of those men and their colleagues the city was a system whose component parts were small zones of land uses or activity, and whose connections were all forms of communication and especially road traffic. A series of transportation plans was then based on this view since, it was argued, if a future land use pattern could be defined, then the resultant traffic pattern could be derived and a suitable transport system designed to fit it.

In the late fifties and early sixties fundamental objections

The Guidance and Control of Change

were raised to this view (Wingo and Perloff, 1961). In essence, they amounted to this: because land uses and traffic flows are interdependent, each affecting the other, we cannot push forward land use in one giant stride of, say, twenty years and derive a traffic flow pattern or vice versa; for the simple reason that traffic flows alter in response to changing land use patterns while at the same time (though at different rates of response), land uses tend to relocate themselves in relation to the movement opportunities that are available; the city evolves through time in ways which depend upon the sequences in which changes in land use and movement facilities are introduced (Beesley and Kain, 1964).

Within a decade, then, we moved from a view of the city as a machine-like system—a system that *works*—to a view of the city as a system that evolves. To analyse the city as a complex system that evolves has profound consequences for many aspects of planning thought and practice.

When we seek to control any dynamic system we must try to foresee how that system might evolve—how it would develop if left severely alone, and also what the outcomes of many different kinds of stimuli and intervention might be. Anyone who seeks to control anything must ask the question, 'what would happen if . . .?' Effective control must be based on understanding and is often gained through learning by experiment.

But it is not always possible to experiment with the actual situation—sometimes it is too dangerous, sometimes too costly, sometimes too slow. In such cases we have to simulate the situation as best we can and carry out our experiments and learn to know the system's responses by way of analogues or models of real the thing (Harris, 1965). Examples are numerous: wind-tunnels and model planes in aero-engineering, the water-tank models in hydraulic engineering and naval architecture, experiments (which many people deplore) in which living creatures are used as 'models' in order to discover more about possible human responses. If the model is a good one (and often time alone will tell) it will reproduce the behaviour of the real thing with sufficient accuracy to answer questions of the 'what will happen if . . .?' kind.

Of course it has long been possible for planners to foresee

The Guidance and Control of Change

aspects of the future of the city—we can project population, employment and spending power, we can forecast complex travel patterns and shopping centre sales. Many professions and skills have contributed greatly to our ability to make such forecasts.

But until recently it has not been possible to foresee the city as a whole, its future shape, the disposition of its activities and linkages, and its resulting character in the round. Thus, we have been lacking in our ability to answer the 'what would happen if . . .?' questions in the most important way—with a synoptic view of the future. We should like to know the city-wide effects of certain policies or trends—of green belts, green wedges and conservation areas, of different programmes and patterns of road construction and parking policy, of expansion of entrenchment of central area shopping and employment, of different timings of similar proposals.

We want to experiment within the whole range of the possible in order to discover what is most desirable. Of course to some extent we have always tried to do this sort of thinking. We have considered alternative policies, and different likely responses, we have approached the private sector's industrial, commercial and residential developers to find out their aims and to test their response to various public policy alternatives. The trouble is that when we try to take into account the inter-relations of more than about a dozen or so of these issues, their scores of immediate side effects, their hundreds of indirect effects all merging and overlapping with different time-lags, we find the human brain cannot cope without assistance. We cannot model the city in our heads—its complexity overwhelms us.

We know that the city is comprised of a myriad relationships, but if we have the vision to identify and describe these in the right way they can be expressed in mathematical terms. The way changes occur through time can be built into the equations, and the computer, handling the instructions provided, can in a matter of minutes enable us to observe decades of growth in a large city. In effect, changes in the location of many kinds of activity in the city, the flows along roads and railway lines, the accompanying shifts in land values, clearance and renewal operations, the growth, change and shifting of manufacturing and commercial enterprises, the evolving life of the city in out-

The Guidance and Control of Change

line is mirrored in the model or 'family' of models. We can study the results for any point in time–asking 'how will things be in 1985 on this basis?'–or we can see a whole trajectory of the city's evolution like a series of frames in a cine-reel of the future. The extent to which we have a correct and appropriate method of forecasting the city's future depends on how clearly we have been able to describe the system we are simulating in the models. Simulation exercises have the very salutory effect of forcing us to find out how the real world actually works. Projection and simulation are discussed in Chapter 8.

The system view of plans

So, if we see the city as a dynamic system that evolves in response to many influences, it follows that plans for it must be cast in similar form; as Mitchell (1961) says, they

'will be plans for the nature, rate, quantity and quality of urban change–for a process of development. They will be expressed in dynamic rather than in static terms. They will start with present conditions and point the direction of change'.

Following experiments about the stages through which it could pass plans will essentially show the steps through which the city ought to pass–they will be the charts of a course to be steered. We will thus focus our attention on the well-being of the city at all times and not simply at some distant future date.

The basic form of plans should be statements which describe how the city should evolve in a series of equal steps–of say, five years at a time. These statements would be a series of diagrams, statistics and written matter, which would set out for each five-yearly interval the intended disposition of the principal activities–agricultural, industrial, commercial, residential, recreational–together with the intended communication and transport networks. The land uses and the flows on the networks would be described in quantitative and qualitative terms. There would be enough information about such matters as the distribution of population, car ownership, spending power, industrial and shopping floor-space, car parks and traffic volumes to make clear the intentions and expectations of the plan. Also the information should be in such a form as to be

83

The Guidance and Control of Change

directly usable in implementation and control (a very important point which will be developed in some detail later). The figures would be expressed as probabilities over a range—narrower in the near future where we can be more certain, widening out as the 'horizon year' is approached to broader ranges in acceptance of the fact that forecasting of human behaviour is a hazardous job.

Of course, all this refers to the basic plan documents only—they would be supplemented by a host of more detailed studies of land development, redevelopments, road construction, school-building and housing programmes. In some areas dereliction and restoration, in others holiday development and tourism would be the subjects of special studies. They would in part derive from and in turn help to refine and correct the broad and general view put forward here; such detailed studies would have already helped in the construction of models to simulate the growth of the study area as a whole. The mapped or diagrammatic part of the plan should also resemble a cinefilm of the future—each frame showing a picture of the city as it should be at some future date, the whole reel showing a process of change which we want the city to undergo. Using the same metaphor, the statistical and verbal parts of the plan are the sound track giving a full commentary on the city's planned course; Buchanan (1966, foldout sheets 7–13) has provided a splendid example.

Such plans are the necessary description of the course or trajectory we wish a dynamic system to follow. They bring together land use and communications at all times; they show where the city should go and how it can get there. Methods of formulating plans and the details of their form and content are dealt with in Chapter 9, whilst Chapter 10 discusses problems and methods of choosing between a number of alternative possible plans—that is with plan *evaluation*.

Implementation, guidance and control

The implementation of such a plan falls within the general province of control—control as understood in systems engineering and in the biological sciences; not in the narrow and restrictive sense of the use of the veto but in the fullest sense which includes 'positive' stimulus and intervention. Control has been defined as

The Guidance and Control of Change

'that ... which provides direction in conformance to the plan, or in other words, the maintenance of variations from system objectives within allowable limits' (Johnson, Kast and Rosenzweig, 1963).

This is a general definition and can be applied to any control situation whether biological, economic, industrial or political and whether the system is simple and determinate or probabilistic and highly complex (Rose, 1967). We shall see how it can be applied to urban and regional systems. To implement a plan of the kind described here requires that the city shall follow 'within allowable limits' the course which the plan has charted in all important aspects. Such control processes are very familiar. They occur in such simple devices as thermostats where the heat source is controlled by deviations from the prescribed temperature; in more complex industrial processes and in highly complex man/machine systems such as driving a car.

The general principle involved here is called 'error-controlled regulation' (Ashby, 1956, Chapter 12); the system is actuated by a control device which is supplied with information about its *actual state* compared with the *intended state* (Figure 4.2). There are four common features of all control:

1. The system to be controlled.
2. The intended state or states of the system.
3. A device for measuring the actual state of the system and thus its deviation from the intended state.
4. A means of supplying correcting influences to keep the system within the limits set.

In our own situation, the city of course is the system we wish to control, the desired states are expressed in the plan, we measure the actual state at any time by all forms of survey and can thus compare the actual conditions with those intended by the plan. So far, so good, but what about the correcting influences to keep the system on course? By the nature of the city, it is influenced by the addition, removal or alteration of component parts or connections—that is, land uses and communications. It follows then, that the evolution of the city can be influenced by regulating the flow of additions, removals and alterations to land uses and communications (McLoughlin, 1965). This can be done in two ways: first by directly carrying out changes and here we think of the very wide range of public

85

The Guidance and Control of Change

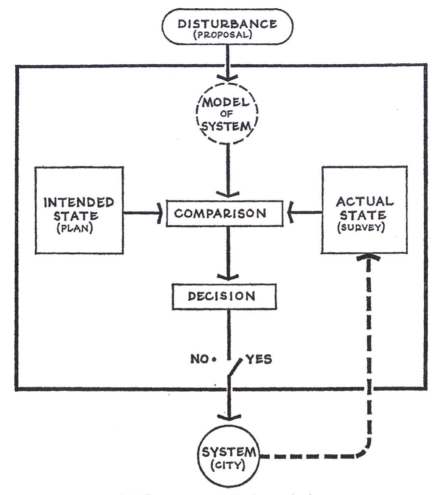

4.2 Error-controlled regulation

influence over hospitals, schools, housing, utilities, roads, bus services, railways, car parking, airports and so on; and second, indirectly, by regulating the flow of changes proposed by others through all the processes of development control–the power to say 'yes' or 'no' to a very wide range of private (and certain public) proposals (Llewelyn-Davies, 1967).

We can picture the planner now as a helmsman steering the city. His attention focuses on the plan–the charted course–the future states through which the city should pass–and on the

The Guidance and Control of Change

survey observations which indicate its actual state. In order to steer, he has two main controls—one is his influence over public investment, development and policy, and the other can be visualised as a switch marked 'on/off' of 'yes/no' by which he releases or blocks private proposals for change (Figure 4.2).

One problem remains: how does the planner know at any point whether he should say 'yes' or 'no', or what his response should be to public proposals? The car driver must see the road ahead—he has learned by experience what sorts of response to expect from steering, throttle, brakes and gears. As the PAG report said,

> 'the planning authorities must consider whether the develop-
> ment proposed would advance or hinder (or have no effect
> on) the policies and objectives set out in the plan' (Planning
> Advisory Group, 1965 p. 46).

Now such questions can be answered partly by experience as in driving a car, but to control more complex systems like the city we once again need help of analogues or models. Just as these devices helped us to experiment in the drawing up of the plan, they will help in its implementation; in control and implementation we are asking, 'what would happen if we approve, or refuse this application? Will the city continue on course or not?' We must have the means to foresee the possible effects because by the time they occur, the system may have gone outside the limits set in the plan and corrective action may then be too late (Figure 4.3). We can refer such questions to our models which can simulate the responses in the city over a period of time. Single large proposals for change or the aggregate of a number of smaller proposals can be treated in this way.

These models augment or amplify the planner's experience. They can also be an early-warning device, indicating needs for corrective action that may lie ahead and enabling the planner to experiment with different forms of public intervention or policies which would keep the system in control or put it back on course again. First, because time is simulated in the model we can see the different effects of short, medium and long-term actions. As Mitchell (1961, p. 171) has put it,

> 'this continuous planning process of the future will incor-
> porate a feedback of information on community change and
> on the results of planned and programmed action. In this

87

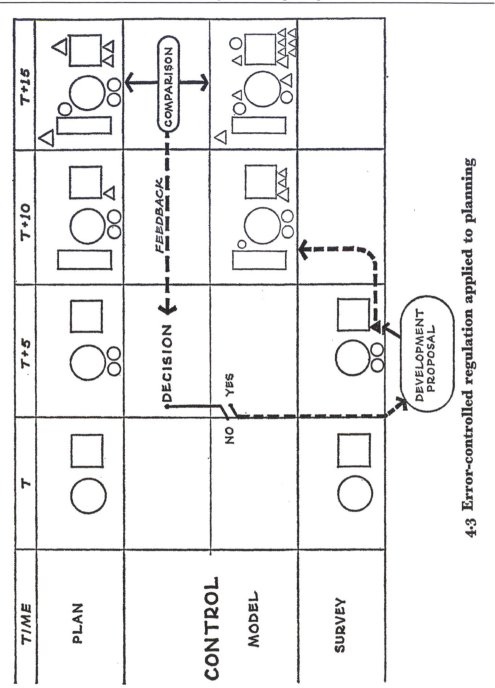

4·3 Error-controlled regulation applied to planning

The Guidance and Control of Change

way, as progress is measured, the planning process can adjust to guide development, much as the course of a missile is guided by a feedback of information on its deviation from a projected course.'

He goes on to say that,

'the planning process thus becomes time-oriented in three ways:

(a) it is continuous, without termination in a "final plan";

(b) it seeks to affect and make use of change, rather than to picture a static, future condition; and

(c) it is expressed partly in long-range and short-range programmes of action to be taken and of capital and other resources to be utilised.'

Finally, serious deviations and the discovery that major interventions are necessary might well suggest a review of the plan because its aims and assumptions may be due for overhaul. This could result in the charting of a modified course to be followed; and so the endless cycle is closed. The detailed treatment of these issues—implementation, control and review—is to be found in Chapter 11. Control depends on the handling of appropriate *information* about the system's intended and actual states, and in the form of models of its possible behaviour. The kinds of information needed in planning are the subject of Chapter 7.

The promise of cybernetics

But let us return to the view of our system as a whole, with its property of 'connectiveness', to use Beer's word. In Chapter 1 we showed that our system was ecological in nature. By any standards it is extremely complex. Beer (1959, p. 10) shows that a system of n components can take up $2^{n(n-1)}$ *states* if we define a state to be the pattern produced when each of the connections is either 'on' or 'off' (a gross simplification). Thus a system of seven parts could have 2^{42} states!

It is no good our being either impressed or frightened by this realisation; in any case, we know already that human relations with the environment are complex. But it must surely make us realise the nature of the planner's position. The largely intuitive and informal methods with which we have grown up cannot in honesty survive the admission of the complexity of the task.

The Guidance and Control of Change

But is it not hopeless? Should we not simply admit defeat and throw up our hands at the futility of it all? We think not, and for a number of reasons. Until very recently science has attempted to deal with complex systems in ways which were almost doomed to failure from the start. Situations in which complexity and randomness were inherent (e.g. that of most living organisms) have been studied by varying one factor at a time. Unfortunately for scientists (and they knew it) *many* factors of the system under study were varying at once in mutual interactions. In recent years the new science of cybernetics has grown up defined by one of its founders, Norbert Wiener (1948), as 'the science of control and communication, in the animal and the machine'. Cybernetics, rather than shrinking from complex systems has made the study of complexity and control its own field. Astonishing progress is being made. Cybernetic techniques have enabled us to postulate the structure of control mechanisms in living tissues (e.g. the connections between the retina and the optic nerve) which have later been confirmed by improved microscopic examination. Lord Snow, recently addressing the Historical Association, expressed his view that we are now living through the latest of three spurts of progress. The first was the agro-urban revolution which resulted in the first literate cities supported by advanced agriculture about 10,000 years ago. The second was the dramatic increase in available energy in the eighteenth and nineteenth centuries which enabled us to transform the earth with machinery and create undreamed-of material wealth. Now, says Snow, we are experiencing the 'Cybernetic Revolution' in which we are beginning to understand complexity and its control for human purposes. He believes that this will be by far the most significant change of all. Dr. Ashby (1956, pp. 5–6) tells us that 'cybernetics offers the hope of providing effective methods for the study, and control, of systems that are intrinsically extremely complex. It will do this by first marking out what is achievable (for probably many investigations of the past attempted the impossible), and then providing generalised strategies, of demonstrable value, that can be used uniformly in a variety of special cases. In this way it offers the hope of providing the essential methods by which to attack the ills–psychological, social, economic–which at present are defeating us by their intrinsic complexity.'

The Guidance and Control of Change

In medicine and in management, in astronautics and in biology, cybernetics is showing its astonishing and growing powers. It is able to do this because its field is the study of complex and probabilistic systems and their control. We have tried to show in this and the preceeding chapter how the study of human location behaviour, originating as a facet of work in many other fields, has recently been regarded as a study of a system in its own right. This has happened because of closer links between theoreticians with a systems approach and practical projects in which personnel, with or without a systems view, found it an increasingly useful and powerful aid to understanding action. The latest insights (which we would stress are completely untried in practice) concern the evolutionary character of the system which is the planner's concern and the potential offered for its control by the methods of cybernetics.

These are difficult notions. Many attitudes of a lifetime may have to be modified, even rejected, if the systems view is adopted. We put this framework forward then simply because it is our belief that it solves far more problems than it creates and is at the same time an elegant and beautiful means to understanding the man-environment relationship, and a potentially powerful means for its control and guidance.

We would urge the reader not only to study the works we have listed but also to relate these notions to the world around, to his own daily experience. Only by making this attempt to relate these insights to the 'real world' will the fullest benefits be gained. From here on, this book is concerned with planning techniques. Many of these are well-tried and familiar, others are new, even experimental; we shall always make the distinction clear. We hope that many of the points discussed in this section will be better understood in retrospect when the following chapters have been read.

References

ASHBY, W. ROSS (1956) *An introduction to cybernetics* London

BEER, STAFFORD (1959) *Cybernetics and Management* London

BEESLEY, M.E. AND J.F. KAIN (1965) Forecasting car ownership and use. *Urban studies, 2*, 163–185

VON BERTALANFFY, LUDWIG (1951) An outline of general system theory *British Journal of the Philosophy of Science*, I, 134–65

BUCHANAN, COLIN in association with ECONOMIC CONSULTANTS LTD. (1966) *South Hampshire Study: A report on the feasibility of major urban growth.* 3 vols. London

CHAPLIN, F. STUART (jr.) and HENRY C. HIGHTOWER (1965) Household activity patterns and land use *Journal of the American Institute of Planners, 31*, 222–31

CHURCHMAN, C.W., R.L. ACKOFF, and E.L. ARNOFF (1957) *Introduction to operations research* New York

COWEN, PETER (1966) Institutions, activities and accommodation in the city *Journal of the Town Planning Institute, 52*, 140–1

HARRIS, BRITTON (ed.) (1965) Urban development models: new tools for planning. Complete issue of the *Journal of the American Institute of Planners, 31*, No. 2

JOHNSON, R.A., F.E. KAST and J.E. ROSENZWEIG (1963) *The theory and management of systems* New York

LLEWELYN-DAVIES, RICHARD (1967) Research for planning *Journal of the Town Planning Institute, 53*, 221–25

LYNCH, KEVIN (1960) *The image of the city* Cambridge, Mass.

McLOUGHLIN, J. BRIAN (1965) Notes on the nature of physical change *Journal of the Town Planning Institute, 51*, 397–400

MEIER, RICHARD L. (1962) *A communications theory of urban growth* Cambridge, Mass.

MITCHELL, ROBERT B. and CHESTER RAPKIN (1954) *Urban traffic: a function of land use.* New York

MITCHELL, ROBERT B. (1961) The new frontier in metropolitan planning *Journal of the American Institute of Planners, 27*, 169–75

PLANNING ADVISORY GROUP (1965) *The future of development plans* London

ROSE, JOHN (1967) *Automation: its anatomy and physiology* Edinburgh

WEBBER, MELVIN M. (1963a) Order in diversity: community without propinquity *Cities and Space, the future use of urban land*, pp. 23–54 Baltimore, Md.

WEBBER, MELVIN M. (1963b) Comprehensive planning and social responsibility *Journal of the American Institute of Planners, 29*, 232–41

WEBBER, MELVIN M. (ed.) (1964) *Explorations into urban structure* Philadelphia

WIENER, NORBERT (1948) *Cybernetics* New York

WINGO, LOWDON AND HARVEY S. PERLOFF (1961) The Washington transportation plan: technics or politis? *Papers and proceedings of the Regional Science Association, 7*

91a

[19]

The Rationale of Planning Theory

Andreas Faludi

IN THIS chapter, I shall try to specify the rationale of planning theory as that of planning promoting *human growth* by the use of rational procedures of thought and action. This requires prior discussion of the concept of human growth itself, and the reasons for putting it forward as a worthwhile ideal. We shall examine human growth both as a *product*, and as a *process*. But not even as a product may we see human growth as co-terminous with numerical growth and an increase in economic wealth. It stands rather for a continuing enrichment of human life, and the widening of the range of goals which human beings are capable of pursuing.

Planning promotes human growth as a product in two ways. Firstly, it identifies the best way of attaining ends. Secondly, it contributes to learning, and hence to future growth. Lastly, as regards human growth as a process, planning may be identified as a vehicle for controlling and accelerating that process. In all this, I perceive planning as analogous to that other activity which has resulted in unparalleled human growth: science. Planning and science can be seen as twin sisters born from the same desire of man to free himself from the strictures of ignorance and fear. Planning and science propel this process of man becoming master over his world and himself along a path towards further human growth. Planning theory improves upon the process by providing guidelines for meta-planning.

PLANNING AS RATIONAL ACTION

Planning has always meant taking intelligent, rational action. However, what constitutes intelligent action is the subject of much argument. Often, people identify it with responding to problems in specific and, to their proponents, obvious ways. Thus, it might be argued that: the environment ought to be protected; scarce resources should be preserved; help should be

36   *Planning Theory*

given to underprivileged groups; public transport ought to be given priority over private transport; certain patterns of urban growth should underlie the future development of a region. What I wish to argue is that, in presenting proposals such as these, the proponents of substantive policies imply that they have gone through a rational thought process. The planning literature calls this the *rational planning process* of going through generation of alternatives, evaluation, and choice based on that evaluation.[1]

Proponents of policies invoke this rational planning process because presenting an argument means to reconstruct and communicate a conclusion in such a way that somebody else is led to draw the same inferences. Rationality in this context is ". . . a shorthand way of pointing out . . . the . . . standards which I and others appeal to when we try, individually or collectively, to give our 'reasons' in a clear and demonstrable form" (Gould, 1971). To achieve this we present our proposals as superior to the alternatives. An environmentalist may therefore support a demand for controls on industrial effluents discharged into rivers by painting a picture of their state if such measures are not taken; the advocate of better welfare benefits may describe the consequences of not giving these benefits. More sophisticated advocates consider many alternatives. But they still claim that their proposals are demonstrably superior to other conceivable courses of action, "demonstrably" referring to a, if only crude, process of rational thought which they claim to have followed.

Of course, very often proposals do not originate from a truly rational thought process at all, and the arguments advanced are as has been described above: reconstructions for the purpose of communicating ideas in a way which will gain their acceptance. The moving force behind a proposal may be different from what is said explicitly. For instance, it may be a feeling of threat against which a proposal appears to provide a remedy.[2] In other cases, there may be hidden motives behind the painting of bleak pictures which the advocate of a certain policy may not even be aware of. Some such motive is occasionally imputed to the environmental lobby, namely that by decrying the effects of economic growth, they

---

[1] For an early statement of what rational planning involves, see the "Note on conceptual scheme" in Meyerson and Banfield (1955). See also Banfield (1959).

[2] In the case of the neighbourhood community idea, it has been argued by Dennis (1958) and Glass (1959) that to break urban settlements up into small neighbourhoods seemed to alleviate fears of an uprising of the urban proletariat.

implicitly wish to preserve their own privileged positions. In other cases, it may simply be that the members of a skilled group wish to underline the importance of the means which they have to offer, means which promise solutions to allegedly serious problems. This is common amongst professionals, and the case has been argued extensively in relation to town planners and their "physical determinism" (Broady, 1968).

Uncovering and analysing motives as they underlie practical proposals is very interesting. The sociology of knowledge provides concepts for doing so which say, basically, that men think the way they do because of their relative positions in society. In the field of planning, this line has been taken recently by a number of writers (Dennis, 1970; Davies, 1972). Young planners are prone to reduce their findings to the formula of planning being "middle class". This verdict combines with slightly romantic notions concerning "the people", thus strangely implying that somehow or other the middle class are not people.

Undoubtedly, such an ideological critique of planning proposals enriches intellectual discussion. But ideological critique has relatively little to contribute to the essential rôle of planning as making decisions. A decision-taker presented with a multitude of arguments made by the advocates of particular courses of action is faced with the problem of judging which course of action to accept as worth implementing. He must resolve, if only tentatively, to accept some reasons put before him as valid grounds for adopting one line in preference to others. For him, the information provided by ideological criticisms is a useful signpost to what may underlie a proposal, but it must not paralyse him lest he should become defunct as a decision-taker. He is more likely, therefore, to evaluate the arguments as they are manifestly made (meaning in their reconstructed form), judging premises for their acceptability and conclusions for whether proper inferences have been drawn. Furthermore, the decision-taker will combine these premises of individual courses of action into more holistic conceptions, balancing demands on the use of scarce resources against each other and thus coming to conclusions which may be judged intelligent in terms of his total situation. In short, he will combine particular demands and proposals into one overall rational choice.

The form which I have suggested advocates of particular courses of action would use in presenting their argument, and the procedure used by an intelligent decision-taker in determining the practical desirability of

38   *Planning Theory*

any one of a number of proposals is thus the same, namely that of the rational planning process. Since, in making the intelligence of a course of action plausible one always has to take recourse to this standard, the definition of an intelligent proposal as one that can be reconstructed as having resulted from a rational planning process is primary to any other one. This argument has particular relevance to public decision-making where choices, and the reasons leading up to them, must be communicated to allow for public discussion and democratic control.

Planning may therefore be defined as deciding on a course of action by satisfying oneself that it is possible to present one's choice in a form which could have resulted from a rational planning process, even if this has not actually been the case. Much as in science, where the form of presenting findings does not necessarily correspond to the process of their discovery (Medawar, 1967), the effort of presenting a course of action in this way has the advantage of facilitating criticism and of establishing an unambiguous basis for agreement or conflict.[3]

This notion of planning is identical to what, in different contexts, has been termed *systems analysis* and *operational research*. Thus, Quade (1968) defines systems analysis as

> ...a systematic approach to helping a decision-maker choose a course of action by investigating his full problem, searching out objectives and alternatives, and comparing them in the light of their consequences, using an appropriate framework—in so far as is possible analytic—to bring expert judgement and intuition to bear on the problem.

Similarly, Beer (1966) describes operational research as follows:

> Operational research is the attack of modern science on complex problems arising in the direction and management of large systems of men, machines, materials and money in industry, business, government and defence. Its distinctive approach is to develop a scientific model of the system, incorporating measures of factors such as chance and risk, with which to predict and compare the outcome of alternative decisions, strategies and controls. The purpose is to help management determine the policy and actions scientifically.

[3]It is rare for practising planners to forego the appeal which advocating particular solutions has with the public and to emphasize the central obligation of the planner to the process by which decisions are made. Amos (1971) is surely an exception when he says that rather than to pronounce official views on "residential density, public participation, land ownership, or any other topic ..." the Royal Town Planning Institute "could seek to ensure that the processes of critical analysis are as exhaustive and unbiased as possible".

During the sixties, therefore, what could be observed was a confluence between systems analysis, operational research and planning (Robinson, 1972). For instance, in Britain a distinct school of thought emerged which took a "systems view" of planning (McLoughlin, 1969; Chadwick, 1971) thereby drawing on the literature in these related fields. This was challenged recently for its attempt to arrogate to planning an area that had hitherto been considered a prerogative of the polity: the formulation of goals against which to evaluate alternatives (Dimitriou, 1972). With this goes a deep distrust of the very attempt to take rational, "scientific", approaches, so that Kahn (1969) even talks of a "political science challenge" to planning. Certainly, formulations like Friedmann's (1969) describing planning as the application of "scientific-technical intelligence" to the solution of practical problems are therefore liable to be criticized, much as my, basically identical, view of planning as a rational form of decision-making outlined above. However, it will become obvious throughout this book that I see politics and rational planning as complementary, and not as conflicting: as with "scientific method", by facilitating criticism, the requirements of presenting decisions as following from certain presuppositions improves the quality of debates and ultimately also that of the choices made in planning matters.[4]

HUMAN GROWTH

Having shown that planning means to present choices as if one had made them going through a rational planning process, we now turn to the central question of this chapter: why should one plan? The answer is that the aim of planning is human growth. At the same time, this is also the rationale of planning theory, that is the point of view taken in building a conceptual framework for planning thought.

In this section I shall describe what I mean by human growth (leaving aside for the moment the establishment of the link between rational planning and human growth). In giving reasons for seeing it as an ideal worth pursuing I shall draw on a number of authors, most of whom have been influenced by cybernetics. Since this discipline promises to offer explanations of processes of growth, this influence is not surprising. Indeed, the

---

[4]Dyckman (1961) draws the analogy between planning and science, extending it even to their morality.

40   *Planning Theory*

very existence of models of growth which, as their proponents claim, fit
the growth even of social systems is itself a supportive argument for
accepting human growth as an ideal.

Defining Human Growth

Human growth is not a simple concept. It has two aspects: growth as a
product, and as the *process* leading to the same product. Of these, one may
feel inclined to emphasize one or the other. But the continuing process of
growth utilizes the products of previous growth. Also, the aim of a growth
process may sometimes not be that of obtaining material products, but the
ability to achieve still further growth. For instance, Diesing (1962) describes growth as an "... increase of integrative power, or mastery, or
creativeness, as well as increased complexity of the problems and materials
to be mastered". Deutsch (1966) also links his concept of growth to learning
capacity. Growth for him refers to: the application of learning capacity to
increase a system's openness; the increase of a system's ability to make
effective responses to the environment; the increase in the range and
diversity of goals which we are capable of following.

The last point is particularly relevant in our present climate of *pluralism*.
Opponents of rational planning will probably find my concept of planning
as leading to human growth questionable because of its connotation of
"mankind", of "the social system", or some other reified collective entity,
growing without adequate attention being paid to the individual or to sub-
groups in society. But my concept of growth, like that of Deutsch, means
the fulfilment of an increasingly diverse range of goals.[5] Similarly,
Etzioni's normative model, *The Active Society* (1968), includes the notion of
widening the area of choice, and in particular of increasing the range of
goals pursued. The active society is hence *responsive*, aiming at "... the

---

[5]Deutsch spells this out in the last chapter of his book discussing the "politics
of growth". There he says that growth not only refers to the system growing,
but also to the growth of sub-groups. Thus, the "dimensions of growth" include
growth in sheer man-power; economic growth; growth in operational resources
("uncommitted resources" which are essential for growth); growth in self-determination; growth in the ability to change patterns of communication and organization; *and* the growth of goal-seeking ability, including the facility of selecting
new goals.

uninhibited, authentic, educated expression of an unbounded member-ship".

It is therefore plain that, as a product, growth cannot solely be measured in numerical terms such as population increase, GNP, and standard of living indices. It also refers to increase in the variety of goals attained, as well as to capacity for future goal attainment. Therefore the recent arguments concerning the *Limits to Growth* (Meadows *et al.*, 1972), directed as they are against continuing expansion, do not apply to the concept of growth which is advanced here. If one were to conclude that such limits threatened the future of mankind, then it would be possible within the concept of growth proposed to justify limiting numerical growth in the name of future goal-seeking ability. Likewise, it seems plausible that, since this would enable more people to attain their ends, one could argue for a more equal distribution of economic assets within the same concept, even if this was to the detriment of overall growth.

The production of material goods apart, growth as a *process* refers mainly to learning and creativity, defined as the gaining of insights into the existing order of things, and the transformation of that order into a new one (Diesing, 1962). It is that process by which man creates himself which brings us to reasons for putting forward human growth as the rationale of planning theory.

Reasons for Regarding Human Growth as an Ideal

The reasons for my regarding human growth as the end of planning, and thus as a suitable rationale of planning theory, are: my view of man as guiding his own development; the interpretation which human growth gives to past developments; the availability of models of growth.

Views of man. Such views of man and of the development of mankind have been advocated in the past. But the bane of concepts like growth, and of similar ones like progress, has been their lack of empirical relevance. Without this, whether growth takes place or not remains very much a question of faith. With the availability of models of growth, this has changed. Hence, an exciting range of books like Deutsch's *The Nerves of Government* (1966), Buckley's *Sociology and Modern Systems Theory* (1967), and Etzioni's *The Active Society* (1968) has appeared which try to synthesize cybernetic thinking with social and political theory. These

42   *Planning Theory*

authors present growth as an empirically verifiable concept, and the conditions of growth as open to analysis and manipulation. Therefore, the argument will be that the very availability of models of growth, though in itself not an adequate reason for viewing it as an ideal worth pursuing, makes growth as a concept more meaningful than it has been up until now.

Human growth is inextricably linked with the notion of man perpetually shaping this world, including the guidance of his own development. I personally find this view an appealing one because it seems to me that to guide one's own development consciously is a value in itself and justification for regarding human growth as a worthwhile ideal. I shall therefore demonstrate the link which I think exists between human growth and self-guidance. However, both aspects of this Promethean view of man presuppose something else: consciousness, or the awareness of knowledge (Etzioni, 1968). Being aware of knowledge, including the process by which it is created, and by which it results in action, adds an entirely new dimension to human growth: "When reason becomes self-conscious it changes into something it never was before. It becomes capable of studying its own working . . . and of improving this working by changing the structure" (Diesing, 1962).

Broadly speaking, the argument concerning human growth and self-guidance as based in consciousness which these authors advance is this: many of the existing barriers to further human growth (for instance in the sense of a more equitable distribution of resources) must be sought in our ways of doing things. If these could be changed, human growth could continue. Such change often involves changing habits and even whole world outlooks. Therefore, to remove some of the barriers to human growth means to change ourselves. But only by being aware of our own habits, our ways of looking at this world, including how they affect our actions, may we deliberately guide our own development towards the removal of barriers to human growth. Such self-awareness one calls one's consciousness. Since research designs have been based on it, consciousness is a respectable concept even in experimental psychology (Young, 1971). This book assumes that processes analogous to individual consciousness exist in society. They result in societal self-awareness which, much as individual consciousness, can be inferred from observations.

The three authors quoted have a common emphasis on consciousness. Deutsch (1966) discusses it as a kind of feedback. Feedback, in turn, is the central notion of cybernetics, that is the science of communication and control. In feedback, ". . . some of the out-put energy of an apparatus or machine is returned as in-put . . .". This input then controls the future output of the machine or process so that, in cybernetics ". . . we now have an array of self-controlling machines that react to their environment, as well as to the result of their own behavior; that store, process and apply information; and that have, in some cases, a limited capacity to learn".

Because human beings possess consciousness, their capacity to learn is infinitely greater than that of even the most sophisticated machine. But this consciousness need not be regarded as something completely beyond our understanding. Deutsch presents consciousness as the *highest level of feedback* and hence as a process of information resulting in action. He thereby links consciousness to other types of (lower-order) information processes. There is the simplest one (the thermostat is often quoted as an example) whereby a variable (such as temperature) is kept constant. There is the second type whereby the "behaving object" (be it a more complex mechanism or a living being) finds that it cannot achieve its ends and therefore adapts them. This is called goal-changing feedback or learning. There is, finally, the third type of feedback which Deutsch emphasizes as central to the social and political processes which he is interested in, that is the scanning of internal data, or consciousness. Consciousness is important to Deutsch because it relates to self-determination:

> A society or community that is to steer itself must continue to receive a full flow of three kinds of information: first information about the world outside; second, information from the past, with a wide range of recall and re-combination; and third, information about itself and its own parts . . ..

The test of functioning on all these levels would be the capacity to learn, that is to produce internal rearrangements so as to bring about changes in the system's behaviour. This is linked to Deutsch's concept of growth as presented earlier, and he refers to a "theory of growth" going with his "theory of self-determination".

Similarly with Buckley (1967) who builds on Deutsch, and who first of all emphasizes the importance of the social over the physical environment:

> As we progress from lower to higher biological adaptive systems we note, as a general rule, the gradually increasing role of other biological units . . as part of the significant environment. The variety and the constraints represented

44   *Planning Theory*

by the behavior of these units must be mapped, as well as that of the physical environment. With the transition from the higher primate social organization to the full-blown human, symbolically mediated, socio-cultural system, the mapping of the subtle behaviors, gestures and intentions of the individuals making up the effective social organization becomes increasingly central, and eventually overshadows the mapping of the physical environment.

But to operate in a social environment not only requires developing images of the behaviour of others, it also depends on the development of an awareness of which images one projects oneself. Such a reflective quality leads to self-awareness. It enables actors ". . . to map, store, and selectively or normatively act towards not only the external variety and constraints of the social and physical environment but also to their internal states". This again means that an actor possessing consciousness is able to change himself in a deliberate manner, thereby to improve his chances of attaining his ends, and hence to grow.

Finally, in his book on *The Active Society*, Etzioni (1968) also links the concept of self-guidance with those of consciousness and growth. Firstly, he describes his active society clearly as one which is growing: "The study of the active society is the study of a society realizing *its* values and an exploration of the barriers which deter society from realizing these values and investigating ways to accelerate their fulfilment." Many of these barriers to continuing growth in society lie in society itself. For realizing his values, and thereby guiding his future development, man must therefore turn his attention to society:

> Man is *not* unless he is social; what he is depends on his social being, and what he makes of his social being is irrevocably bound to what he makes of himself. He has the ability to master his internal being, *and the main way to self-mastery leads to his joining with others like himself in social acts.*

Etzioni's book thus has as its sub-title "A theory of societal and political processes". These processes are subject to social laws, laws which penetrate the individual's mind by way of socialization. But social laws, as opposed to the laws of the natural sciences, may be *changed* collectively. Society is "malleable"; as Diesing (1962) says, it is the prime object of the creative exercise of reason.

Societal malleability implies a danger. Change may result in more freedom for members of society but may also transform it so that man's domination over man is increased. The active society is one which has opted for the first alternative, drawing on its consciousness, the commitment of its members, and on power that "allows resetting of the social code". However, the resetting of the social code in an active society means that it exercises collective self-guidance in the pursuit of its own growth. Hence, the active society is one that is master of itself.

Like these authors I am proposing to regard human growth as an ideal in the sense of man firstly transforming his physical environment and utilizing its resources; and secondly shaping human institutions, thus including the social environment into the orbit of his control. Because growth in the latter sense also means self-guidance, this concept incorporates a view of man as gaining mastery over himself by power of his faculty of reason.

Growth as an evolutionary principle. Growth, in the sense of an increase in the variety of goals which living organisms can achieve, is a principle underlying the process of evolution. Human growth provides an interpretation to the historical development of mankind, explaining secular trends such as technological and economic progress, the expansion of the human habitat, institutional differentiation, urbanization and scientific progress, as forming part of an overall process. Combining the evolution of life with that of mankind, it is even possible to interpret the progression of life-forms from the most primitive organisms to the most complex socio-cultural systems as one overall process of growth. Buckley (1967) argues this way, unifying the evolution of life and of mankind by identifying in them a common thread of continuing growth in terms of an increase in learning capacity. Equating this with intelligence, one is reminded of Diesing's interpretation of what growth and historical development may mean: "If history does move toward a goal, that goal can only be intelligence . . . because intelligence (which makes all other values achievable— AF) is the only unconditional value" (Diesing, 1962).

Learning, Buckley says, is achieved by natural selection in the case of biological adaptive systems; by behavioural change in the case of animals; and by people or social organizations anticipating future possibilities and exercising conscious choice. In this ascending scale, complexity increases along three dimensions: the time-span for the results of learning to take effect becomes shorter; the fidelity of the information becomes greater;

46   *Planning Theory*

the methods of storage are refined until, eventually, what one finds are the "entirely extrasomatic socio-cultural depositories" of libraries and data banks.

So one could construct indices of growth which relate to the capacity of exercising control over the environment, and ultimately also to that of exercising self-guidance. Growth thus becomes a measurable concept: we can apply it to interpret past developments. For instance, Buckley's dimensions of growth may be related to indicators like the reduction of the time taken for information retrieval and the greater precision of data. These signal growth because they increase learning capacity. Their development can be measured over time, giving a clear idea of the historical process of growth.

Intuitively, one might expect that such observations would confirm the view of life progressing, and of man developing from lower to higher cultural forms. Thus, the existence of measurable concepts of growth could amplify the many philosophical views of history as embodying the principle of human growth (and, incidentally, of developing towards democracy as a form of political organization enabling still further growth, such as Buckley suggests). Therefore, empirically relevant concepts make growth as a principle underlying evolution, and human growth as the end towards which history has striven, intellectually more palatable than they have been thus far. This brings me to the third, supportive, reason for regarding human growth as the rationale of planning theory.

Models of growth. Models of growth belong to the family of cybernetic models. Cybernetic models are capable of explaining goal-seeking behaviour. Hitherto, the explanation of such behaviour has caused problems, especially as regards social organizations. In the past, one has sought to explain such behaviour by reference to the goals pursued. However, this means invoking the end of a process or activity to explain its existence, which is methodologically unsound. Cybernetic models turn this explanation on its head by inferring *the existence of ends from manifest behaviour* such as feedback processes. The end of such a process is simply that condition under which the mechanism or being stops receiving feedback because it is on course (Deutsch, 1966). Even where this is never actually the case, this state may be deduced from the pattern of information flows.

One may not only discern lower-order feedback processes and their effects (as with a domestic thermostat), but also higher-order ones, like Deutsch's learning. This is because learning means changing the end of action. But with ends being related to patterns of information flows, changing them must involve changes to the channels forming these patterns. To invoke a simple example, when a learner driver develops the habit of glancing at the rear mirror, we take this as evidence for his having adopted the end of avoiding danger from the rear as one worth entertaining simultaneously with others. In its own way, even this small example of learning contributes to growth of the chances of survival, and one may therefore say that one has observed a process of growth.

Similarly with consciousness which one can observe much as one observes learning simply by looking at patterns of information flows. For instance, when a management consultant is called in to assist a firm in making its own "corporate appraisal" (Hussey, 1971), and when this appraisal results in changes to the procedures by which decisions are made, one can observe a highest-order feedback, or consciousness, in action leading to further growth.

Models of growth do not only provide leads in observing growth, they also indicate concrete steps to be taken for the promotion of growth. Buckley (1967) provides one such model. He distinguishes between two processes building on two different types of feedback: morphostasis and morphogenesis. Morphostasis is the process whereby a system preserves its given form. The type of feedback associated with this is called *negative* feedback whereby information concerning the system going "off course" results in counter-action. As against this, morphogenesis refers to those processes which tend to elaborate a system, that is which lead to growth. It relies on *positive* feedback whereby information concerning the system going "off course" results in more action of the same type, thus amplifying the original movement. An example which Buckley quotes and which is a familiar one to urban planners is that of urbanization: the more land-use activities are concentrated in one locality, the greater its attraction as a location of further activities.

The problem of guiding growth is then that of identifying the deviation-amplifying mechanisms which propel it along. This is what Maruyama (1970) describes as the "second cybernetics" of growth. In identifying concrete steps to be taken in the pursuit of further growth one can draw

48   *Planning Theory*

on this second cybernetics. One does not depend on those "Inexorable Laws of Historical Destiny" which Popper (1961) claims are often inherent to the idea of planning.[6]

THE CHOICE TO BE MADE

Having outlined my reasons for seeing human growth as an ideal worth pursuing let me add that I do not claim that one *has* to pursue it. In addition to having reasons what is needed is the optimism required to face up to the perpetual challenge which human growth poses: the challenge to pursue growth relentlessly, and to fight the obstacles of growth, wherever they may be; the challenge to abandon or check certain types of growth where they develop pathological aspects, however dear they may be to one's heart; the challenge of facing up to the anxieties involved in making decisions in the pursuit of growth; the challenge of sharing responsibility for mankind's future. It also requires having faith in man's ability, and in particular in his faculty of reason.

Therefore, as Etzioni (1968) says, there is this very real choice to be made between accepting a challenge and letting mankind drift into the future. New powers are becoming available for self-destruction, and subtle and persuasive means of opinion moulding may further extend the control of man over man. This arises out of fear, of man's unwillingness to face up to the challenges of growth, of his efforts to close himself to the possibilities lying ahead of him. Grauhan and Strudelt (1971) elaborate on this choice drawing on most of the authors quoted above. They consider the question of whether a purely procedural definition of rationality is adequate or not, and come down very strongly on the side of a substantive definition: the goals of rational choice must themselves be rational. These must contribute to "self-enhancement" (in my terms: to growth), that is: "... the principle of on-going enrichment of the life of the individual in society and of on-going reduction of its destructive elements". But

---

[6]For instance, it is perfectly conceivable to accept the emerging concern for the human environment, and the ensuing elaboration of institutions and procedures to protect it (including their self-justification, and their struggle for a clientele) as yet another incidence of the widening of the range of goals that we are capable of pursuing, without in any way having to accept the doomsday philosophy that often seems to accompany it.

whether the individual, or society, opt for self-enhancement as a goal is, in principle, an open question:

> The fact that an individual can deliberately commit suicide shows that the more conscious he is about his own choices, the more clearly he has to choose existence first in order to choose any other goal. It is not by chance that even the proponents of a procedural concept of rationality give as the only material standard of appraisal, the survival quality (Grauhan and Strudelt, 1971).

If we apply this to society, there are, as with individuals, pathological aspects of societal choices made in furtherance of self-enhancement. This, for instance, is the case when élites attain high levels of self-enhancement at the expense of others. Also Grauhan and Strudelt give the concept of self-enhancement a further, historical dimension. They recognize it as a dynamic concept to be measured in terms of "the potentialities realizable at any given time in history".

This turns the choice for or against self-enhancement, for human growth or, in the last consequence, death, into the perpetual challenge which I have earlier described. It is a challenge which is exacerbated by the un-certainty which characterizes any choice, uncertainty that concerns, amongst others, the possibility of choices having counterproductive implica-tions. Even given the best of intentions, choices may lead to unintended consequences, and to the closure of future opportunities. Therefore, choices carry elements of risk. This, incidently, is an important reason why choices must ultimately be made in a political arena (Grauhan, 1973). But to shy away from choices means to shy away from that responsibility which a secular view of man squarely places upon him: the responsibility for his own fate.

THE RATIONAL PLANNING PROCESS AND HUMAN GROWTH

Having argued for human growth as an ideal, I must now link it with planning. More precisely, I shall demonstrate that (distinguishing be-tween human growth as a *product* and as a *process*) rational planning results in growth as a product, and that the rational planning process may itself be viewed as a vehicle for the very process of growth.

As regards growth as a product, one may take both a narrow and a wide view. The narrow view is that the goals in the planning process represent

50   *Planning Theory*

an operational definition of what human growth means in concrete situations. As argued earlier, there is no better way for any decision-taker to satisfy himself that he will attain his ends then to present his choices as if he had arrived at them by a rational planning process. As Davidoff and Reiner (1963) put it: ". . . intuition or experiences unsupported by reason are weak reeds on which to rest".

So, the rational planning process leads to growth in this narrow sense. But we must not be satisfied with this narrow view of human growth. Goals may very well change, even whilst the planner is engaged busily in identifying the means for their attainment, and many plans become irrelevant long before they are implemented. Nevertheless, even planning efforts that lead to no action may still result in human growth. This is because the rational planning process forces one to make assumptions explicit about oneself, one's environment, and how one relates to it, and it to oneself. In doing so, these thoughts become cast into the mould of an ordered argument thereby improving awareness of the structure of what, in Chapter 5, I shall term the action space, and the way its structure relates to preferences held. Ultimately, because in planning one must reflect on one's goals, it also increases awareness of oneself.

Awareness thus results from deliberations made during the process. It is improved as a result of feedback concerning the effects of actions on the environment. Overall, the result of engaging in rational planning is therefore learning, including self-learning, and hence an increase in the capacity to attain *future* growth.[7]

Lastly, the rational planning process is itself part of the *process* of growth, in line with that concept as outlined above. Following Diesing (1962), this process has been described as one of order being changed creatively into new order. However, this is precisely what the rational planning

---

[7]For instance, urban planners have learnt from the unintended consequences of urban renewal that a city does not only consist of houses, but that the people inhabiting them, together with these houses in their relative locations, constitute a "system". Similarly, as a result of deliberations following the publication of the Greater London Council's plan for a "motorway box" in and around London, planners, politicians and sections of the public have learnt that the problem of urban transport is inextricably linked with that of the distribution of life-chances amongst the inhabitants of a city. In both cases, the outcome is an enlarged concept of the end of planning but also of the nature of society, thus preparing the ground for action being taken with a view to further growth.

process does: it identifies a (future) order, together with the steps which must be taken to bring it about, based on knowledge concerning the present order of things. This order is constantly modified by newly received information.

In all this I see the rational planning process as analogous to another learning vehicle: *scientific method* meaning a set of procedural requirements which propositions must meet in order to pass as scientifically valid (Ackoff, 1962; Olsen, 1968). By imposing stringent requirements, scientific method forces the scientist to be explicit, to submit all his considerations to public scrutiny, thereby facilitating their testing. In doing so, science contributes to the solution of particular problems; it results in a general growth of knowledge; and, from a different standpoint, scientific pursuit may itself be regarded as another form which the process of growth takes.

HUMAN GROWTH AND META-PLANNING

There is a final gloss which one can put on this as it concerns planning theory. Since planning, like learning, is an information process, it is observable and, within limits, capable of manipulation and thus itself potentially the *object of planning*. Indeed, the basic idea underlying this book is that of providing a planning theory to guide this, what has been called meta-planning.

In one form or another, the authors quoted above have come to the conclusion that ways of going about decision-making may be improved on the basis of insights gained from consciousness. For instance, Diesing (1962) claims that, out of the five types of rationality which he identifies, *political* rationality concerned with "decision structures" (like planning agencies), is the most important:

> Negatively, a rational decision structure removes internal obstacles to decision, such as conflict, rigidity, and disproportionate influence. Positively, a decision structure so organizes a person's or group's perceptive, creative and communicative faculties as to enable him to reach effective decisions.

Deutsch (1966) and Buckley (1967) even provide models of "self-guiding systems" which incorporate highest-order feedback loops or consciousness. These models have their normative aspects. By identifying what a self-guiding system would be, they give a direction to the consciousness of any decision-maker. Finally, Etzioni (1968) links the same concern

52   *Planning Theory*

for increasing self-awareness of decision-makers with his belief in the potential of the social sciences for providing a firm basis for such awareness:

> As an intellectual process overlaying normative commitments, as a critical evaluator of existing social combinations, as an explorer of alternative combinations and their transformation, the social sciences are able to clarify basic commitments and to make them more realistic and, thus, more sustained.

The views of these authors converge with the concept of planning theory advanced. This convergence we may characterize as follows: the ultimate objective of planning theory is meta-planning. This must be based on the consciousness of planning agencies, that is on their awareness of their structure and procedures and their effects on planning, thereby taking cognizance of social-science findings. Meta-planning may thus be described as the most direct pursuit of human growth. Only where growth is based on consciousness is it truly deliberate. Therefore, the Promethean view of man as guiding his own growth may be interpreted as meaning man planning his own planning, thus underlining the importance of planning theory.

REFERENCES

ACKOFF, R. *et al.* (1962) *Scientific Method: Optimizing Applied Research Decisions*, John Wiley, New York.

AMOS, F. J. C. (1971) Presidential Address, *Journal of the Royal Town Planning Institute*, Vol. 57, pp. 397–9.

*BANFIELD, E. C. (1959) Ends and means in planning, *International Social Science Journal*, Vol. 11, pp. 361–8.

BEER, S. (1966) *Decision and Control*, John Wiley, New York.

BROADY, M. (1968) *Planning for People*, The Bedford Square Press, London.

BUCKLEY, W. (1967) *Sociology and Modern Systems Theory*, Englewood Cliffs, New Jersey.

CHADWICK, G. (1971) *A Systems View of Planning*, Pergamon, Oxford.

DAVIDOFF, P. and REINER, T. A. (1963) A reply to Dakin, *Journal of the American Institute of Planners*, Vol. 29, pp. 27–8.

DAVIES, J. G. (1972) *The Evangelist Bureaucrat: A Study of a Planning Exercise in Newcastle upon Tyne*, Tavistock Publications, London.

DENNIS, N. (1958) The popularity of the neighbourhood community idea, *Sociological Review*, Vol. 6, pp. 191–206.

DENNIS, N. (1970) *People and Planning*, Faber & Faber, London.

DEUTSCH, K. W. (1966) *The Nerves of Government—Models of Political Communication and Control*, 2nd ed. Macmillan, New York–London.

DIESING, P. (1962) *Reason in Society*, University of Illinois Press, Urbana.

DIMITRIOU, B. (1972) The interpretation of politics and planning, *The Systems View of Planning* (DIMITRIOU, B. *et al.*), Oxford Working Papers in Planning Education and Research, No. 9. Department of Town Planning, Oxford Polytechnic, Oxford.

*DYCKMAN, J. W. (1961) What makes planners plan? *Journal of the American Institute of Planners*, Vol. 27, pp. 164–7.

ETZIONI, A. (1968) *The Active Society*, Collier-Macmillan, London.

FRIEDMANN, J. (1969) Notes on societal action, *Journal of the American Institute of Planners*, Vol. 35, pp. 311–18.

*GLASS, R. (1959) The evaluation of planning: some sociological considerations, *International Social Science Journal*, Vol. 11, pp. 393–409.

GOULD, S. J. (1971) *The Rational Society* (August Comte Memorial Lecture) The Athlone Press, London.

*GRAUHAN, R. R. (1973) Notes on the structure of planning administration, *A Reader in Planning Theory* (edited by FALUDI, A.), Pergamon, Oxford.

GRAUHAN, R. R. and STRUDELT, W. (1971) Political rationality reconsidered, *Policy Sciences*, Vol. 2, pp. 249–70.

HUSSEY, D. E. (1971) *Introducing Corporate Planning*, Pergamon, Oxford.

KAHN, J. (1969) *Studies in Social Policy and Planning*, Russell Sage Foundation, New York.

KAPLAN, A. (1964) *The Conduct of Inquiry: Methodology for Behavioral Science*, Chandler, Scranton, Penn.

MARUYAMA, M. (1970) Cybernetics, *Planning Programming Budgeting* (edited by LYDEN, F. J. and MILLER, E. G.), 3rd ed. Markham Publishing Company, Chicago.

McLOUGHLIN, J. B. (1969) *Urban and Regional Planning—A Systems Approach*, Faber & Faber, London.

MEADOWS, D. H. *et al.* (1972) *Limits to Growth*, Earth Island, London.

MEDAWAR, P. B. (1967) Scientific method, *The Listener*, Vol. 78, pp. 453–6.

MEYERSON, M. and BANFIELD, E. C. (1955) *Politics, Planning and the Public Interest*, Free Press, Glencoe.

OLSEN, M. E. (1968) *The Process of Social Organization*, Holt, Rinehart & Winston, London.

POPPER, K. (1961) *The Poverty of Historicism*, Routledge & Kegan Paul, London.

QUADE, E. S. (1968) Introduction, *Systems Analysis and Policy Planning* (edited by QUADE, E. S. and BOUCHER, W. I.), Elsevier, New York.

ROBINSON, I. M. (1972) Introduction, *Decision-making in Urban Planning* (edited by ROBINSON, I. M.), Sage Publications, Beverly-Hills-London.

YOUNG, J. Z. (1971) *An Introduction to the Study of Man*, Clarendon Press, Oxford.

*Included in FALUDI, A. (1973) *A Reader in Planning Theory*, Pergamon, Oxford.

ADVOCACY
AND PLURALISM
IN PLANNING

Paul Davidoff

City planning is a means for determining policy. Appropriate policy in a democracy is determined through political debate. The right course of action is always a matter of choice, never of fact. Planners should engage in the political process as advocates of the interests of government and other groups. Intelligent choice about public policy would be aided if different political, social, and economic interests produced city plans. Plural plans rather than a single agency plan should be presented to the public. Politicizing the planning process requires that the planning function be located in either or both the executive and legislative branches and the scope of planning be broadened to include all areas of interest to the public.

The present can become an epoch in which the dreams of the past for an enlightened and just democracy are turned into a reality. The massing of voices protesting racial discrimination have roused this nation to the need to rectify racial and other social injustices. The adoption by Congress of a host of welfare measures and the Supreme Court's specification of the meaning of equal protection by law both reveal the response to protest and open the way for the vast changes still required.

The just demand for political and social equality on the part of the Negro and the impoverished requires the public to establish the bases for a society affording equal opportunity to all citizens. The compelling need for intelligent planning, for specification of new social goals and the means for achieving them, is manifest. The society of the future will be an urban one, and city planners will help to give it shape and content.

The prospect for future planning is that of a practice which openly invites political and social values to be examined and debated. Acceptance of this position means rejection of prescriptions for planning which would have the planner act solely as a technician. It has been argued that technical studies to enlarge the information available to decision makers must take precedence over statements of goals and ideals:

> We have suggested that, at least in part, the city planner is better advised to start from research into the functional aspects of cities than from his own estimation of the values which he is attempting to maximize. This suggestion springs from a conviction that at this juncture the implications of many planning decisions are poorly understood, and that no certain means are at hand by which values can be measured, ranked, and translated into the design of a metropolitan system.[1]

While acknowledging the need for humility and openness in the adoption of social goals, this statement amounts to an attempt to eliminate, or sharply reduce, the unique contribution planning can make: understanding the functional aspects of the city and recommending appropriate future action to improve the urban condition.

Paul Davidoff is Professor of City Planning at Hunter College of the City University of New York City, where he is developing a graduate program in city planning to begin in 1966. He is also a member of the faculty of City Planning at the University of Pennsylvania. He holds a law degree and a master's degree in planning from the University of Pennsylvania.

Another argument that attempts to reduce the importance of attitudes and values in planning and other policy sciences is that the major public questions are themselves matters of choice between technical methods of solution. Dahl and Lindblom put forth this position at the beginning of their important textbook, *Politics, Economics, and Welfare:*[2]

> In economic organization and reform, the "great issues" are no longer the great issues, if they ever were. It has become increasingly difficult for thoughtful men to find meaningful alternatives posed in the traditional choices between socialism and capitalism, planning and the free market, regulation and laissez faire, for they find their actual choices neither so simple nor so grand. Not so simple, because economic organization poses knotty problems that can only be solved by painstaking attention to technical details—how else, for example, can inflation be controlled? Nor so grand, because, at least in the Western world, most people neither can nor wish to experiment with the whole pattern of socio-economic organization to attain goals more easily won. If for example, taxation will serve the purpose, why "abolish the wages system" to ameliorate income inequality?

These words were written in the early 1950's and express the spirit of that decade more than that of the 1960's. They suggest that the major battles have been fought. But the "great issues" in economic organization, those revolving around the central issue of the nature of distributive justice, have yet to be settled. The world is still in turmoil over the way in which the resources of nations are to be distributed. The justice of the present social allocation of wealth, knowledge, skill, and other social goods is clearly in debate. Solutions to questions about the share of wealth and other social commodities that should go to different classes cannot be technically derived; they must arise from social attitudes.

Appropriate planning action cannot be prescribed from a position of value neutrality, for prescriptions are based on desired objectives. One conclusion drawn from this assertion is that "values are inescapable elements of any rational decision-making process"[3] and that values held by the planner should be made clear. The implications of that conclusion for planning have been described elsewhere and will not be considered in this article.[4] Here I will say that the planner should do more than explicate the values underlying his prescriptions for courses of action; he should affirm them; he should be an advocate for what he deems proper.

Determinations of what serves the public interest, in a society containing many diverse interest groups, are almost always of a highly contentious nature. In performing its role of prescribing courses of action leading to future desired states, the planning profession must engage itself thoroughly and openly in the contention surrounding political determination. Moreover, planners should be able to engage in the political process as advocates of the interests both of government and of such other groups, organizations, or individuals who are concerned with proposing policies for the future development of the community.

The recommendation that city planners represent and plead the plans of many interest groups is founded upon the need to establish an effective urban democracy, one in which citizens may be able to play an active role in the process of deciding public policy. Appropriate policy in a democracy is determined through a process of political debate. The right course of action is always a matter of choice, never of fact. In a bureaucratic age great care must be taken that choices remain in the area of public view and participation.

Urban politics, in an era of increasing government activity in planning and welfare, must balance the demands for ever-increasing central bureaucratic control against the demands for increased concern for the unique requirements of local, specialized interests. The welfare of all and the welfare of minorities are both deserving of support; planning must be so structured and so practiced as to account for this unavoidable bifurcation of the public interest.

The idealized political process in a democracy serves the search for truth in much the same manner as due process in law. Fair notice and hearings, production of supporting evidence, cross examination, reasoned decision are all means employed to arrive at relative truth: a just decision. Due process and two- (or more) party political contention both rely heavily upon strong advocacy by a professional. The advocate represents an individual, group, or organization. He affirms their position in language understandable to his client and to the decision makers he seeks to convince.

If the planning process is to encourage democratic urban government then it must operate so as to include rather than exclude citizens from participating in the process. "Inclusion" means not only permitting the citizen to be heard. It also means that he be able to become well informed about the underlying reasons for planning proposals, and be able to respond to them in the technical language of professional planners.

A practice that has discouraged full participation by citizens in plan making in the past has been based on what might be called the *"unitary plan."* This is the idea that only one agency in a community should prepare a comprehensive plan; that agency is the city planning commission or department. Why is it that no other organization within a community prepares a plan? Why is only one agency concerned with establishing both general and specific goals for community development, and with proposing the strategies and costs required to effect the goals? Why are there not plural plans?

If the social, economic, and political ramifications of a plan are politically contentious, then why is it that those in opposition to the agency plan do not prepare one of their own? It is interesting to observe that "rational" theories of planning have called for consideration of alternative courses of action by planning agencies. As a matter of rationality it has been argued that all of the alternative choices open as means to the ends sought be examined.[5] But those, including myself, who have recommended agency consideration of alternatives have placed upon the agency planner the burden of inventing "a few representative alternatives."[6] The agency planner has been given the duty of constructing a model of the political spectrum, and charged with sorting out what he conceives to be worthy alternatives. This duty has placed too great a burden on the agency planner, and has failed to provide for the formulation of alternatives by the interest groups who will eventually be affected by the completed plans.

Whereas in a large part of our national and local political practice contention is viewed as healthy, in city planning where a large proportion of the professionals are public employees, contentious criticism has not always been viewed as legitimate. Further, where only government prepares plans, and no minority plans are developed, pressure is often applied to bring all professionals to work for the ends espoused by a public agency. For example, last year a Federal official complained to a meeting of planning professors that the academic planners were not giving enough support to Federal programs. He assumed that every planner should be on the side of the Federal renewal program. Of course government administrators will seek to gain the support of professionals outside of government, but such support should not be expected as a matter of loyalty. In a democratic system opposition to a public agency should be just as normal and appropriate as support. The agency, despite the fact that it is concerned with planning, may be serving undesired ends.

In presenting a plea for plural planning I do not mean to minimize the importance of the obligation of the public planning agency. It must decide upon appropriate future courses of action for the community. But being isolated as the only plan maker in the community, public agencies as well as the public itself may have suffered from incomplete and shallow analysis of potential directions. Lively political dispute aided by plural plans could do much to improve the level of rationality in the process of preparing the public plan.

The advocacy of alternative plans by interest groups outside of government would stimulate city planning in a number of ways. First, it would serve as a means of better informing the public of the alternative choices open, *alternatives strongly supported by their proponents.* In current practice those few agencies which have portrayed alternatives have not been equally enthusiastic about each.[7] A standard reaction to rationalists' prescription for consideration of alternative courses of action has been "it can't be done; how can you expect planners to present alternatives which they don't approve?" The appropriate answer to that question has been that planners like lawyers may have a professional obligation to defend positions they oppose. However, in a system of plural planning, the public agency would be relieved of at least some of the burden of presenting alternatives. In plural planning the alternatives would be presented by interest groups differing with the public agency's plan. Such alternatives would represent the deep-seated convictions of their proponents and not just the mental exercises of rational planners seeking to portray the range of choice.

A second way in which advocacy and plural planning would improve planning practice would be in forcing the public agency to compete with other planning groups to win political support. In the absence of opposition or alternative plans presented by interest groups the public agencies have had little incentive to improve the quality of their work or the rate of production of plans. The political consumer has been offered a yes—no ballot in regard to the comprehensive plan; either the public agency's plan was to be adopted or no plan would be adopted.

A third improvement in planning practice which might follow from plural planning would be to force those who have been critical of "establishment" plans to produce superior plans, rather than only to carry out the very essential obligation of criticizing plans deemed improper.

The Planner as Advocate

Where plural planning is practiced, advocacy becomes the means of professional support for competing claims about how the community should develop. Pluralism in support of political contention describes the process; advocacy describes the role performed by the professional in the process. Where unitary planning prevails, advocacy is not of paramount importance, for there is little or no competition for the plan prepared by the public agency. The concept of advocacy as taken from legal practice implies the opposition of at least two contending viewpoints in an adversary proceeding.

The legal advocate must plead for his own and his client's sense of legal propriety or justice. The planner as advocate would plead for his own and his client's view of the good society. The advocate planner would be more than a provider of information, an analyst of current trends, a simulator of future conditions, and a detailer of means. In addition to carrying out these necessary parts of planning, he would be a *proponent* of specific substantive solutions.

The advocate planner would be responsible to his client and would seek to express his client's views. This does not mean that the planner could not seek to persuade his client. In some situations persuasion might not be necessary, for the planner would have sought out an employer with whom he shared common views about desired social conditions and the means toward them. In fact one of the benefits of advocate planning is the possibility it creates for a planner to find employment with agencies holding values close to his own. Today the agency planner may be dismayed by the positions affirmed by his agency, but there may be no alternative employer.

The advocate planner would be above all a planner. He would be responsible to his client for preparing plans and for all of the other elements comprising the planning process. Whether working for the public agency or for some private organization, the planner would have to prepare plans that take account of the arguments made in other plans. Thus the advocate's plan might have some of the characteristics of a legal brief. It would be a document presenting the facts and reasons for supporting one set of proposals, and facts and reasons

indicating the inferiority of counter-proposals. The adversary nature of plural planning might, then, have the beneficial effect of upsetting the tradition of writing plan proposals in terminology which makes them appear self-evident.

A troublesome issue in contemporary planning is that of finding techniques for evaluating alternative plans. Technical devices such as cost-benefit analysis by themselves are of little assistance without the use of means for appraising the values underlying plans. Advocate planning, by making more apparent the values underlying plans, and by making definitions of social costs and benefits more explicit, should greatly assist the process of plan evaluation. Further, it would become clear (as it is not at present) that there are no neutral grounds for evaluating a plan; there are as many evaluative systems as there are value systems.

The adversary nature of plural planning might also have a good effect on the uses of information and research in planning. One of the tasks of the advocate planner in discussing the plans prepared in opposition to his would be to point out the nature of the bias underlying information presented in other plans. In this way, as critic of opposition plans, he would be performing a task similar to the legal technique of cross-examination. While painful to the planner whose bias is exposed (and no planner can be entirely free of bias) the net effect of confrontation between advocates of alternative plans would be more careful and precise research.

Not all the work of an advocate planner would be of an adversary nature. Much of it would be educational. The advocate would have the job of informing other groups, including public agencies, of the conditions, problems, and outlook of the group he represented. Another major educational job would be that of informing his clients of their rights under planning and renewal laws, about the general operations of city government, and of particular programs likely to affect them.

The advocate planner would devote much attention to assisting the client organization to clarify its ideas and to give expression to them. In order to make his client more powerful politically the advocate might also become engaged in expanding the size and scope of his client organization. But the advocate's most important function would be to carry out the planning process for the organization and to argue persuasively in favor of its planning proposals.

Advocacy in planning has already begun to emerge as planning and renewal affect the lives of more and more people. The critics of urban renewal [8] have forced response from the renewal agencies, and the ongoing debate [9] has stimulated needed self-evaluation by public agencies. Much work along the lines of advocate planning has already taken place, but little of it by professional planners. More often the work has been conducted by trained community organizers or by student groups. In at least one instance, however, a planner's professional aid led to the development of an alternative renewal approach, one which will result in the dislocation of far fewer families than originally contemplated.[10]

Pluralism and advocacy are means for stimulating consideration of future conditions by all groups in society. But there is one social group which at present is particularly in need of the assistance of planners. This group includes organizations representing low-income families. At a time when concern for the condition of the poor finds institutionalization in community action programs, it would be appropriate for planners concerned with such groups to find means to plan with them. The plans prepared for these groups would seek to combat poverty and would propose programs affording new and better opportunities to the members of the organization and to families similarly situated.[11]

The difficulty in providing adequate planning assistance to organizations representing low-income families may in part be overcome by funds allocated to local anti-poverty councils. But these councils are not the only representatives of the poor; other organizations exist and seek help. How can this type of assistance be financed? This question will be examined below, when attention is turned to the means for institutionalizing plural planning.

The Structure of Planning

PLANNING BY SPECIAL INTEREST GROUPS

The local planning process typically includes one or more "citizens" organizations concerned with the nature of planning in the community. The Workable Program requirement for "citizen participation"[12] has enforced this tradition and brought it to most large communities. The difficulty with current citizen participation programs is that citizens are more often *reacting* to agency programs than *proposing* their concepts of appropriate goals and future action.

The fact that citizens' organizations have not played a positive role in formulating plans is to some extent a result of both the enlarged role in society played by government bureaucracies and the historic weakness of municipal party politics. There is something very shameful to our society in the necessity to have organized "citizen participation." Such participation should be the norm in an enlightened democracy. The formalization of citizen participation as a required practice in localities is similar in many respects to totalitarian shows of loyalty to the state by citizen parades.

Will a private group interested in preparing a recommendation for community development be required to carry out its own survey and analysis of the community? The answer would depend upon the quality of the work prepared by the public agency, work which should be public information. In some instances the public agency may not have surveyed or analyzed aspects the private group thinks important; or the public agency's work may reveal strong biases unacceptable to the private group. In any event, the production of a useful plan proposal will require much information concerning the present and predicted conditions in the community. There will be some costs associated with gathering that information, even if it is taken from the public agency. The major cost involved in the preparation of a plan by a private agency would probably be the employment of one or more professional planners.

What organizations might be expected to engage in the plural planning process? The first type that comes to mind are the political parties; but this is clearly an aspirational thought. There is very little evidence that local political organizations have the interest, ability, or concern to establish well developed programs for their communities. Not all the fault, though, should be placed upon the professional politicians, for the registered members of political parties have not demanded very much, if anything, from them as agents.

Despite the unreality of the wish, the desirability for active participation in the process of planning by the political parties is strong. In an ideal situation local parties would establish political platforms which would contain master plans for community growth and both the majority and minority parties in the legislative branch of government would use such plans as one basis for appraising individual legislative proposals. Further, the local administration would use its planning agency to carry out the plans it proposed to the electorate. This dream will not turn to reality for a long time. In the interim other interest groups must be sought to fill the gap caused by the present inability of political organizations.

The second set of organizations which might be interested in preparing plans for community development are those that represent special interest groups having established views in regard to proper public policy. Such organizations as chambers of commerce, real estate boards, labor organizations, pro- and anti-civil rights groups, and anti-poverty councils come to mind. Groups of this nature have often played parts in the development of community plans, but only in a very few instances have they proposed their own plans.

It must be recognized that there is strong reason operating against commitment to a plan by these organizations. In fact it is the same reason that in part limits the interests of politicians and which limits the potential for planning in our society. The expressed commitment to a particular plan may make it difficult for groups to find means for accommodating their various interests. In other terms, it may be simpler for professionals, politicians, or lobbyists to make deals if they have not laid their cards on the table.

There is a third set of organizations that might be looked to as proponents of plans and to whom the foregoing comments might not apply. These are the ad hoc protest associations which may form in opposition to some proposed policy. An example of such a group is a neighborhood association formed to combat a renewal plan, a zoning change, or the proposed location of a public facility. Such organizations may seek to develop alternative plans, plans which would, if effected, better serve their interests.

From the point of view of effective and rational planning it might be desirable to commence plural planning at the level of city-wide organizations, but a more realistic view is that it will start at the neighborhood level. Certain advantages of this outcome should be noted. Mention was made earlier of tension in government between centralizing and decentralizing forces. The contention aroused by conflict between the central planning agency and the neighborhood organization may indeed be healthy, leading to clearer definition of welfare policies and their relation to the rights of individuals or minority groups.

Who will pay for plural planning? Some organizations have the resources to sponsor the development of a plan. Many groups lack the means. The plight of the relatively indigent association seeking to propose a plan might be analogous to that of the indigent client in search of legal aid. If the idea of plural planning makes sense, then support may be found from foundations or from government. In the beginning it is more likely that some foundation might be willing to experiment with plural planning as a means of making city planning more effective and more democratic. Or the Federal Government might see plural planning, if carried out by local anti-poverty councils, as a strong means of generating local interest in community affairs.

Federal sponsorship of plural planning might be seen as a more effective tool for stimulating involvement of the citizen in the future of his community than are the present types of citizen participation programs. Federal support could only be expected if plural planning were seen, not as a means of combating renewal plans, but as an incentive to local renewal agencies to prepare better plans.

THE PUBLIC PLANNING AGENCY

A major drawback to effective democratic planning practice is the continuation of that non-responsible vestigial institution, the planning commission. If it is agreed that the establishment of both general policies and implementation policies are questions affecting the public interest and that public interest questions should be decided in accord with established democratic practices for decision making, then it is indeed difficult to find convincing reasons for continuing to permit independent commissions to make planning decisions. At an earlier stage in planning the strong arguments of John T. Howard[1x] and others in support of commissions may have been persuasive. But it is now more than a decade since Howard made his defense against Robert Walker's position favoring planning as a staff function under the mayor. With the increasing effect planning decisions have upon the lives of citizens the Walker proposal assumes great urgency.[14]

Aside from important questions regarding the propriety of independent agencies which are far removed from public control determining public policy, the failure to place planning decision choices in the hands of elected officials has weakened the ability of professional planners to have their proposals effected. Separating planning from local politics has made it difficult for independent commissions to garner influential political support. The commissions are not responsible directly to the electorate and in turn the electorate is, at best, often indifferent to the planning commission.

During the last decade in many cities power to alter community development has slipped out of the hands of city planning commissions, assuming they ever held it, and has been transferred to development coordinators. This has weakened the professional planner. Perhaps planners unknowingly contributed to this by their refusal to take concerted action in opposition to the perpetuation of commissions.

Planning commissions are products of the conservative reform movement of the early part of this century. The movement was essentially anti-populist and pro-aristocracy. Politics was viewed as dirty business. The commissions are

relics of a not-too-distant past when it was believed that if men of good will discussed a problem thoroughly, certainly the right solution would be forthcoming. We know today, and perhaps it was always known, that there are no right solutions. Proper policy is that which the decision-making unit declares to be proper.

Planning commissions are responsible to no constituency. The members of the commissions, except for their chairman, are seldom known to the public. In general the individual members fail to expose their personal views about policy and prefer to immerse them in group decision. If the members wrote concurring and dissenting opinions, then at least the commissions might stimulate thought about planning issues. It is difficult to comprehend why this aristocratic and undemocratic form of decision making should be continued. The public planning function should be carried out in the executive or legislative office and perhaps in both. There has been some question about which of these branches of government would provide the best home, but there is much reason to believe that both branches would be made more cognizant of planning issues if they were each informed by their own planning staffs. To carry this division further, it would probably be advisable to establish minority and majority planning staffs in the legislative branch.

At the root of my last suggestion is the belief that there is or should be a Republican and Democratic way of viewing city development; that there should be conservative and liberal plans, plans to support the private market and plans to support greater government control. There are many possible roads for a community to travel and many plans should show them. Explication is required of many alternative futures presented by those sympathetic to the construction of each such future. As indicated earlier, such alternatives are not presented to the public now. Those few reports which do include alternative futures do not speak in terms of interest to the average citizen. They are filled with professional jargon and present sham alternatives. These plans have expressed technical land use alternatives rather than social, economic, or political value alternatives. Both the traditional unitary plans and the new ones that present technical alternatives have limited the public's exposure to the future states that might be achieved. Instead of arousing healthy political contention as diverse comprehensive plans might, these plans have deflated interest.

The independent planning commission and unitary plan practice certainly should not co-exist. Separately they dull the possibility for enlightened political debate; in combination they have made it yet more difficult. But when still another hoary concept of city planning is added to them, such debate becomes practically impossible. This third of a trinity of worn-out notions is that city planning should focus only upon the physical aspects of city development.

An Inclusive Definition of The Scope of Planning
The view that equates physical planning with city planning is myopic. It may have had some historic justification, but it is clearly out of place at a time when it is necessary to integrate knowledge and techniques in order to wrestle effectively with the myriad of problems afflict-

ing urban populations.

The city planning profession's historic concern with the physical environment has warped its ability to see physical structures and land as servants to those who use them.[15] Physical relations and conditions have no meaning or quality apart from the way they serve their users. But this is forgotten every time a physical condition is described as good or bad without relation to a specified group of users. High density, low density, green belts, mixed uses, cluster developments, centralized or decentralized business centers are per se neither good nor bad. They describe physical relations or conditions, but take on value only when seen in terms of their social, economic, psychological, physiological, or aesthetic effects upon different users.

The profession's experience with renewal over the past decade has shown the high costs of exclusive concern with physical conditions. It has been found that the allocation of funds for removal of physical blight may not necessarily improve the over-all physical condition of a community and may engender such harsh social repercussions as to severely damage both social and economic institutions. Another example of the deficiencies of the physical bias is the assumption of city planners that they could deal with the capital budget as if the physical attributes of a facility could be understood apart from the philosophy and practice of the service conducted within the physical structure. This assumption is open to question. The size, shape, and location of a facility greatly interact with the purpose of the activity the facility houses. Clear examples of this can be seen in public education and in the provision of low cost housing. The racial and other socio-economic consequences of "physical decisions" such as location of schools and housing projects have been immense, but city planners, while acknowledging the existence of such consequences, have not sought or trained themselves to understand socio-economic problems, their causes or solutions.

The city planning profession's limited scope has tended to bias strongly many of its recommendations toward perpetuation of existing social and economic practices. Here I am not opposing the outcomes, but the way in which they are developed. Relative ignorance of social and economic methods of analysis have caused planners to propose solutions in the absence of sufficient knowledge of the costs and benefits of proposals upon different sections of the population.

Large expenditures have been made on planning studies of regional transportation needs, for example, but these studies have been conducted in a manner suggesting that different social and economic classes of the population did not have different needs and different abilities to meet them. In the field of housing, to take another example, planners have been hesitant to question the consequences of locating public housing in slum areas. In the field of industrial development, planners have seldom examined the types of jobs the community needed; it has been assumed that one job was about as useful as another. But this may not be the case where a significant sector of the population finds it difficult to get employment.

"Who gets what, when, where, why, and how" are the basic political questions which need to be raised about every allocation of public resources. The questions cannot be answered adequately if land use criteria are the sole or major standards for judgment.

The need to see an element of city development, land use, in broad perspective applies equally well to every other element, such as health, welfare, and recreation. The governing of a city requires an adequate plan for its future. Such a plan loses guiding force and rational basis to the degree that it deals with less than the whole that is of concern to the public.

The implications of the foregoing comments for the practice of city planning are these. First, state planning enabling legislation should be amended to permit planning departments to study and to prepare plans related to any area of public concern. Second, planning education must be redirected so as to provide channels of specialization in different parts of public planning and a core focussed upon the planning process. Third, the professional planning association should enlarge its scope so as to not exclude city planners not specializing in physical planning.

A year ago at the AIP convention it was suggested that the AIP Constitution be amended to permit city planning to enlarge its scope to all matters of public concern.[16] Members of the Institute in agreement with this proposal should seek to develop support for it at both the chapter and national level. The Constitution at present states that the Institute's "particular sphere of activity shall be the planning of the unified development of urban communities and their environs and of states, regions and the nation as *expressed through determination of the comprehensive arrangement of land and land occupancy and regulation thereof.*" [17]

It is time that the AIP delete the words in my italics from its Constitution. The planner limited to such concerns is not a city planner, he is a land planner or a physical planner. A city is its people, their practices, and their political, social, cultural and economic institutions as well as other things. The city planner must comprehend and deal with all these factors.

The new city planner will be concerned with physical planning, economic planning, and social planning. The scope of his work will be no wider than that presently demanded of a mayor or a city councilman. Thus, we cannot argue against an enlarged planning function on grounds that it is too large to handle. The mayor needs assistance; in particular he needs the assistance of a planner, one trained to examine needs and aspirations in terms of both short and long term perspectives. In observing the early stages of development of Community Action Programs, it is apparent that our cities are in desperate need of the type of assistance trained planners could offer. Our cities require for their social and economic programs the type of long range thought and information that have been brought forward in the realm of physical planning. Potential resources must be examined and priorities set.

What I have just proposed does not imply the termination of physical planning, but it does mean that physical planning be seen as part of city planning. Uninhibited by limitations on his work, the city planner will be able to add his expertise to the task of coordinating the operating and capital budgets and to the job of relating effects of each city program upon the others and upon the social, political, and economic resources of the community.

An expanded scope reaching all matters of public concern will make planning not only a more effective administrative tool of local government but it will also bring planning practice closer to the issues of real concern to the citizens. A system of plural city planning probably has a much greater chance for operational success where the focus is on live social and economic questions instead of rather esoteric issues relating to physical norms.

The Education of Planners

Widening the scope of planning to include all areas of concern to government would suggest that city planners must possess a broader knowledge of the structure and forces affecting urban development. In general this would be true. But at present many city planners are specialists in only one or more of the functions of city government. Broadening the scope of planning would require some additional planners who specialize in one or more of the services entailed by the new focus.

A prime purpose of city planning is the coordination of many separate functions. This coordination calls for men holding general knowledge of the many elements comprising the urban community. Educating a man for performing the coordinative role is a difficult job, one not well satisfied by the present tradition of two years of graduate study. Training of urban planners with the skills called for in this article may require both longer graduate study and development of a liberal arts undergraduate program affording an opportunity for holistic understanding of both urban conditions and techniques for analyzing and solving urban problems.

The practice of plural planning requires educating planners who would be able to engage as professional advocates in the contentious work of forming social policy. The person able to do this would be one deeply committed to both the process of planning and to particular substantive ideas. Recognizing that ideological commitments will separate planners, there is tremendous need to train professionals who are competent to express their social objectives.

The great advances in analytic skills, demonstrated in the recent May issue of this *Journal* dedicated to techniques of simulating urban growth processes, portend a time when planners and the public will be better able to predict the consequences of proposed courses of action. But these advances will be of little social advantage if the proposals themselves do not have substance. The contemporary thoughts of planners about the nature of man in society are often mundane, unexciting or gimmicky. When asked to point out to students the planners who have a developed sense of history and philosophy concerning man's situation in the urban world one is hard put to come up with a name. Sometimes Goodman or Mumford might be mentioned. But planners seldom go deeper than acknowledging the goodness of green space and the soundness of proximity of linked activities. We cope with the problems of the alienated man with a recommendation for reducing the time of the journey to work.

Conclusion

The urban community is a system comprised of interrelated elements, but little is known about how the elements do, will, or should interrelate. The type of knowledge required by the new comprehensive city planner demands that the planning profession be comprised of

groups of men well versed in contemporary philosophy social work, law, the social sciences, and civic design Not every planner must be knowledgable in all these areas, but each planner must have a deep understanding of one or more of these areas and he must be able to give persuasive expression to his understanding.

As a profession charged with making urban life more beautiful, exciting, and creative, and more just, we have had little to say. Our task is to train a future generation of planners to go well beyond us in its ability to prescribe the future urban life.

NOTES

1 Britton Harris, "Plan or Projection," *Journal of the American Institute of Planners*, XXVI (November 1960) 265-272.

2 Robert Dahl and Charles Lindblom, *Politics, Economics, and Welfare* (New York: Harper and Brothers, 1953) p. 3.

3 Paul Davidoff and Thomas Reiner, "A Choice Theory of Planning," *Journal of the American Institute of Planners*, XXVIII (May 1962) 103-115.

4 *Ibid.*

5 See, for example, Martin Meyerson and Edward Banfield *Politics, Planning and the Public Interest* (Glencoe: The Free Press 1955) p. 314 ff. The authors state "By a *rational* decision, we mean one made in the following manner: 1. the decision-maker considers all of the alternatives (courses of action) open to him; . . . 2. he identifies and evaluates all of the consequences which would follow from the adoption of each alternative; . . . 3. he selects that alternative the probable consequences of which would be preferable in terms of his most valued ends."

6 Davidoff and Reiner, *Op. cit.*

7 National Capital Planning Commission, *The Nation's Capital a Policies Plan for the Year 2000* (Washington, D.C.: The Commission, 1961).

8 The most important critical studies are: Jane Jacobs, *The Life and Death of Great American Cities* (New York: Random House 1961); Martin Anderson, *The Federal Bulldozer* (Cambridge: M.I.T Press, 1964); Herbert J. Gans, "The Human Implications of Current Redevelopment and Relocation Planning," *Journal of the American Institute of Planners*, XXV (February 1959) 15–26.

9 A recent example of heated debate appears in the following set of articles: Herbert J. Gans, "The Failure of Urban Renewal," *Commentary* 39 (April 1965) p. 29; George Raymond "Controversy," *Commentary* 40 (July 1965) p. 72; and Herbert J. Gans, "Controversy," *Commentary* 40 (July 1965) p. 77.

10 Walter Thabit, *An Alternate Plan for Cooper Square*, (New York: Walter Thabit, July 1961).

11 The first conscious effort to employ the advocacy method was carried out by a graduate student of city planning as an independent research project. The author acted as both a participant and an observer of a local housing organization. See Linda Davidoff, "The Bluffs: Advocate Planning," *Comment*, Dept. of City Planning. University of Pennsylvania, (Spring 1965) p. 59.

12 See Section 101(c) of the United States Housing Act of 1949, as amended.

13 John T. Howard, "In Defense of Planning Commissions," *Journal of the American Institute of Planners*, XVII (Spring 1951).

14 Robert Walker, *The Planning Function in Urban Government*; Second Edition (Chicago: University of Chicago Press, 1950). Walker drew the following conclusions from his examination of planning and planning commissions. "Another conclusion to be drawn from the existing composition of city planning boards is that they are not representative of the population as a whole." p. 153. "In summary the writer is of the opinion that the claim that planning commissions are more objective than elected officials must be rejected." p. 155. "From his observations the writer feels justified in saying that very seldom does a majority of any commission have any well-rounded understanding of the purposes and ramifications of planning." p. 157. "In summary, then, it was found that the average commission member does not comprehend planning nor is he particularly interested even in the range of customary physical planning." p. 158. "Looking at the planning commission at the present time, however, one is forced to conclude that, despite some examples of successful operations, the unpaid board is not proving satisfactory as a planning agency," p. 165. ". . . (it) is believed that the most fruitful line of development for the future would be replacement of these commissions by a department or bureau attached to the office of mayor or city manager. This department might be headed by a board or by a single director, but

the members or the director would in any case hold office at the pleasure of the executive on the same basis as other department heads." p. 177.

15 An excellent and complete study of the bias resulting from reliance upon physical or land use criteria appears in David Farbman, *A Description, Analysis and Critique of the Master Plan*, an unpublished mimeographed study prepared for the Univ. of Pennsylvania's Institute for Urban Studies, 1959-1960. After studying more than 100 master plans Farbman wrote:

"As a result of the predominantly physical orientation of the planning profession many planners have fallen victims to a malaise which I suggest calling the "Physical Bias." This bias is not the physical orientation of the planner itself but is the result of it. . . . "The physical bias is an attitude on the part of the planner which leads him to conceive of the principles and techniques of *his profession* as the key factors in determining the particular recommendations to be embodied in his plans. . . .

"The physically biased planner plans on the assumption (conviction) that the physical problems of a city can be solved within the framework of physical desiderata; in other words, that physical problems can be adequately stated, solved and remedied according to physical criteria and expertise. The physical bias produces both an inability and an unwillingness on the part of the planner to 'get behind' the physical recommendations of the plan, to isolate, ex-

amine or discuss more basic criteria. . . ."

". . . There is room, then, in plan thinking, for physical principles, i.e., theories of structural inter-relationships of the physical city; but this is only a part of the story, for the structural impacts of the plan are only a part of the total impact. This total impact must be conceived as a web of physical, economic and social causes and effects." pp. 22–26.

16 Paul Davidoff, "The Role of the City Planner in Social Planning," *Proceedings of the 1964 Annual Conference*, American Institute of Planners (Washington, D.C.: The Institute, 1964) 125–131.

17 Constitution of AIP, Article II "Purposes," in *AIP Handbook & Roster—1965*, p. 8.

Author's Note:
The author wishes to thank Melvin H. Webber for his insightful criticism and Linda Davidoff for her many helpful suggestions and for her analysis of advocate planning. Special acknowledgment is made of the penetrating and brilliant social insights offered by the eminent legal scholar and practitioner, Michael Brodie, of the Philadelphia Bar.

[21]

SOCIAL PLANNING, SOCIAL PLANNERS, AND PLANNED SOCIETIES

John W. Dyckman

The name "social planning" has been bestowed on the remedial patch-up of unplanned social consequences of public and private programs, to the neglect of other aspects of social planning. An analysis of social planning must distinguish societal planning, programming for selected social goals, and the deliberate introduction of social values into economic or political processes. The relation of the planner to his client spotlights the conflict between social goals and program requirements, and leads to various formulations of social planning. These versions cannot avoid the choice of social ideology, which guides social plans and relates them to societal plans.

Social planning is a belated and tentative response of American planners to functional lag. Physical planning, particularly of cities, has been accepted as a legitimate activity at the governmental level for more than half a century. Economic planning, though partial and inconstant, has been an established part of the governmental scene since the 1930's. Social planning, on the other hand, has been openly recognized only more recently, and then it has proceeded under a cover of confusion which has prevented public debate on its scope and its intentions.

For the most part, social planning in the USA is defensive, and arises from the crises which are spun off as by-products of action programs of government. Public intervention in urban development and renewal, for example, has cast up problems of relocation which are so intertwined in the fabric of social life of the affected communities that "social" planners are called upon for relief.

At the same time, the residual issues of the affluent society are so clearly social issues that earlier concerns of physical and economic planning have in some cases given way to priorities for direct planning of social outcomes. The Poverty Program, for example, recognizes that the problem of poverty is not merely a problem of economics, but is also a problem of the culture of poverty which can be addressed only by direct social action. Juvenile delinquency, mental health, and a range of other social ills are, in the view of the behavioral scientists who examine them, more than economic problems. Indeed, there are many who argue that a planned economy cannot eliminate these problems. The presence of social pathology alongside planning then becomes an argument against an excessively "materialistic" view of society. Paradoxically, opponents of the excessive economic determinism often attributed to Marxism are cast in the role of advocates of increasing planning in the social sphere.

Other types of social planning have been made necessary by rejection of the "planned society" of socialist economists. The whole complex of welfare services which have grown up in the United States were traditionally, and still remain, devices to compensate for the wastage and breakage in a competitive, individual-serving, industrial society. They have existed to cushion the blow of this competitive struggle for those so disadvantaged as to be unable to compete effectively. The traditional social services, both privately and publicly provided, are ad hoc solutions for specific problems. They have not, until recently, drawn upon a common context or comprehensive planning outlook.

The notion of coordinated social services, of planned cooperation between agencies, is relatively recent in the field of social welfare and social work. But even where such coordinating councils exist in cities or metropolitan areas, their planning is roughly advisory (except for determinations which enter into the division of the Community Chest) and lacks measures of progress which would

John Dyckman is professor of City and Regional Planning, and Chairman of the Center for Planning and Development Research at the University of California at Berkeley. He is interested in ideas of planning, and in their social manifestations.

guide the allocative decisions. Even more important, the social goals which planning would presumably help to advance are vague and are often stated so as to obscure rather than to adjudicate differences between the goals of the independent agencies.

As a result, there is a great deal of remedial social action, and some social planning in the United States, but this goes on in the absence of even a schematic societal plan which will guide the individual plans of the operating agencies. Societal planning in the United States is principally hortatory, as in the National Goals Reports issued during the Eisenhower Administration.

Some of the most thoughtful work on the meaning of social planning in the American context was instituted several years ago under the direction of Everett Reimer for the Puerto Rican Planning Board. Reimer, assisted by Janet Reiner, commissioned thoughtful papers by Herbert Gans, Abraham Kaplan, and other consultants, and produced many useful internal memoranda. In one of these papers Gans clearly distinguished "societal planning" from "social programs." The former is much more difficult to treat, since it entails some specification of the goals of the society, while the latter are farther along in the "means" end of the means–ends continuum. Gans developed a paradigm for locating programs and actions in this framework which is an excellent statement for orientation to the problem of social planning in the context of the remedial actions of social agencies traditional in the United States.[1]

Let us extend this line of reasoning, and take *social planning* to mean the effort to plan for the fate of a whole society. This view emphasizes the interdependence of activities and the shared consequences of program actions. It recognizes that there may be unplanned consequences of planned actions, and that these may deserve attention equal to that given the programs themselves. Much of the concern with social planning among city planners in the United States stems from the unplanned social dislocations and stresses that follow upon public programs such as redevelopment. In a comparable vein, the interest in social planning in developing economies arises from similar stresses that follow upon planned economic development. Indeed, the former draws heavily on the literature developed in the latter, and both have made liberal use of studies developed in crisis situations such as bombings, floods, and deportations. The problems of disrupted working class urban neighborhoods described by Gans and others are in one perspective a pale copy of the disruptions and strains on social goals of political realization, social justice, and cultural self-expression which have accompanied pursuit of the goal of economic development in preindustrial societies.

When societal goals are advanced by unilateral programs of service agencies, unexpected or perverse results may emerge. Thus the goals of economic justice may dictate an emphasis on low-cost meritorious consumer goods such as housing, and the goals of social justice may indicate that the housing should be placed in neighborhoods as favored as those claimed by higher income groups, but the actual programs for achieving these goals may make for outcomes that disturb the harmonious relations between groups, aggravate class tension, and encourage some forms of antisocial actions. Programs of economic development have almost inevitably favored certain classes whose cooperation was vital to the program, to the relative disadvantage of others. More specifically, these programs have been concerned with incentives necessary to realization of the goals, such as high rewards to entrepreneurs, which may have been paid for by relatively disadvantaged groups. One can proliferate examples of this kind, both in economic development and in urban renewal. These examples dramatize the need for a true social planning framework in which to evaluate the social consequences of individual programs.

To clarify these relations, we might distinguish three operational meanings of *social planning*, and three levels of action.

      1. At the societal planning level, social planning means the selection of the social goals of the nation or state, and the setting of targets for their achievement. It requires a ranking of these goals, and assessment of the cost (in terms of other objectives) of achieving them, and judgments of the feasibility of such programs.

2. Social planning, in a closely related meaning, involves the application of social values and action criteria to the assessment of programs undertaken in the pursuit of economic or political goals. Thus, it can mean the testing of the consequences—in terms of intergroup or interpersonal relations—of everything from broad economic development programs to specific redevelopment projects.

3. Social planning can mean specifically "social" programming arising from the broad social goals of the community. The traditional welfare activities of public and private agencies have been the principal focus of such planning in the United States. The coordination of programming for and by the multitude of caretaker agencies that have grown up in our free enterprise economy is a popular task for this type of social planning.

Much of the discussion of social planning, and the identification of activities under this label, belongs in the third category. It is my contention that this category has developed in a variety of directions without an adequately specified set of objectives at the first and second levels. This view is independent of considerations of the planned society, though subsequent discussion will make clear that the latter are not irrelevant to it.

Social planning has long been treacherous ground for the city planner because of the ever present danger that the expert determination of need might degenerate into the imposition of class or professional prejudices upon a resistant clientele. Social planning, in the sense of determination of the social needs of a community or a group within the community is torn between the desire to require certain levels of consumption of merit goods on the one hand, and the recognition of the legitimacy of individual choice on the other. Many social planners assert that their interest is in the maximization of opportunity, or freedom of choice. But as a practical matter, no society has found a feasible way of maximizing choice for all groups or individuals at all times. For the exercise of one man's choice is a limitation on the freedom of choice of another.

It is not surprising that social planning has often turned away from goals, in the direction of means. For one thing, it is firmly in the tradition of modern clinical psychology, and the positivism of sociology, to accept individually determined ends as legitimate, and to emphasize means of realizing these ends. But it is a matter of some subtlety, worthy to challenge the professional social actionist, or clinical caretaker, to emphasize the manipulation of behavior, rather than the alteration of goals of behavior. Let us consider some of the problems encountered in these tasks.

FINDING APPROPRIATE REMEDIES: DIAGNOSIS OF THE CLIENT

Remedial social planning is necessary in our society because the major forces shaping our lives are unplanned. Social planning has come to the fore because we have been unable to predict, control, or shape the repercussions of technological change or of our planned programs. Because we do not plan our technology, but allow it to follow opportunistic lines, we do not control the repercussions of its development. These repercussions cast up many of the persistent social problems of our times, such as the sharp segregation of the poor, the aged, and the minorities in the cities; the left-behind regions of economic depression; the unemployable cadres of displaced workers; and the great gaps in educational attainment. In many respects, the advanced technological societies need therapeutic social planning as badly as the countries experiencing the stresses of early technological change. For example, urban renewal, which was embraced avidly by liberals and city planners in 1949 at passage of the Housing Act, has proven a specific source of embarrassment and friction to liberal politicians for fifteen years. It is the realization of this fact that has created the call for a Domestic Peace Corps in the United States.

These problems have traditionally been easier to identify in the newly developing economies. One might swiftly recognize the particular problems raised for Puerto Rican planning by a host of world and hemispheric developments: the emergence of a new stage in world industrialization; the extension of the urban life style and the obliteration of differences between city and country in the most industrially developed nations; the sharpening of differences between the "educated" and "uneducated"; the development of new technological advances in transportation and communication. Until a Michael Harrington, or some other prophet, calls attention to the lags in our perception, we are likely to miss the similar phenomena which take place in societies starting from a more favored base. It is the merit of urban renewal that it called attention to problems of the city, to implications of public intervention in the city, and to undeveloped perspectives in city planning.

Further, the issue of relocation in urban redevelopment emphasizes the interdependence of the social fabric of communities. It has underlined the reality that one cannot intervene in any important portion of this web without disrupting the structure and entangling himself in the consequences.

But the urban renewal issue is complicated by the complexity of modern government and its ingrown bureaucracy in response to technological pressures operating through the inexorable drive of organizational efficiency. In the course of this transformation of government, many of the more purely "social" concerns, which were adequately handled in the days when political community and social community were identical, have disappeared in the larger governmental apparatus. As a result, the need for social planning is one symptomatic side effect of the organizational conquest of government. This bureaucratization is present at all levels—the distance between the local communities and city government is evident at a public hearing in a major city on the subject of a freeway location or a redevelopment proposal—though it is most intense at the federal level, where the bureaucracies are relatively rationalized and professionalized. Because we have not been conscious of the organizational and technological revolutions in our modern life, we approach the discovery of disparities between local community feeling and bureaucratic objectives with indignation. Truly effective social planning, even in a limited therapeutic sense, would need to deal more self-consciously with the relation between local social objectives and larger organizational requirements.

It is largely this sense of bureaucratic distance, which exists between city planners and citizens, almost equally with practitioners of welfare services and their clients, that has led to the social planning emphasis on *client analysis*. Presumably, by detailed sociological analysis of the client population, akin to the market analysis conducted by firms seeking outlets for their products, social planning can be equipped to overcome this bureaucratic disability. Client analysis has drawn upon, and has developed, substantial insights into the aspirations and motives of the target populations. Presumably, client analysis will also help uncover and recognize the interest of groups who are disenfranchised of power, and whose real aspirations would rarely be reflected in public programs. This more dynamic, or even revolutionary, aspect of client analysis has been widely stressed by social planners operating in minority group areas. It may be likened to a caretaker variant of the civil rights position that the society must do some things to help disadvantaged groups which have not yet been discovered by the disadvantaged groups themselves. In the advertising analogy, client analysis thus leads to taste-making, as well as taste-serving.

In this latter formulation, the client analysis position strikes a responsive note in the ideology of city planners, who have commonly felt that the citizens of the megapolitan world must be saved from themselves. In the social planning context, the inarticulate disadvantaged are saved from a temporary ignorance of their own best interests in order that they can more effectively express those interests over time.

The client analysis position, however, has one great advantage over that of traditional city planning. It explicitly identifies these interests, and neither subsumes them in vague categories of public interest, nor freely ascribes the prejudices of the bureaucracy to the long run best interest of the poor. Client analysis, moreover, begins from the presupposition that many of the bureaucratic standards will be ill-suited to serve the real client population. Nevertheless, one cannot escape the reality that social planning with client analysis merely substitutes market research for the operations of the market. That is, client analysis notwithstanding, social planning is the antithesis of laissez-faire.

Social planning, in fact, cannot escape the ire of the conservatives by adopting some of the instruments of the market. Indeed, the violence of objections to the rent supplements included in last year's Housing Bill is evidence that indirectness and subtlety in social programs, which place a greater premium on planning than on direct action, may be more deeply resented by opponents of the programs' purposes. One is reminded that the late Senator Bricker belaboured his compatriot Senator from Ohio, Robert Taft, for introducing the "Trojan Horse" of private redevelopment into the publicly subsidized 1949 Housing Act. There is no particular ground for believing that social planning and market mechanisms make public spending any more palatable to enemies of the programs. The very informational requirements of social planning may make the priests of that planning more suspect of hoarding secrets.

CARETAKERS AND LONG-RUN CLIENT INTERESTS   Most social planners have at least a modified "caretaker" orientation. In his statement on "Meeting Human Needs" in *Goals for Americans,* the report of the President's Commission in 1960, James P. Dixon, Jr. wrote, "[society] can develop ways by which people can meet their own needs more readily and fruitfully, and it can develop ways by which society as a whole can meet needs that would otherwise be unmet. There are individuals who will not meet their own needs, and others who cannot." [2] The caretaker responsibility presumably extends to those who will not as well as those who cannot. Few societies take a wholly permissive view towards freedom of choice. In addition to the collective goods which we make available for the use of all citizens, from national defense to national parks, there are public programs encouraging the consumption of certain goods and services, and discouraging others. Economists recognize that societies encourage the consumption of the "merit" goods and discourage the consumption of demerit goods. Thus we exempt certain foods from sales taxes and place punitive taxes on alcohol, tobacco, and other products, and severely restrict the use of narcotics.

Americans have been understandably wary of social planning, since these responsibilities place the planners in the role of caretakers of "safety," "health," and "morals." The technological competence of highly organized government is today so great that there is widespread suspicion and apprehension about government power. We are afraid of the information handling capabilities which modern technology has placed at the disposal of government, for the "disutopians" have warned us of the threat to liberty which may lurk in such power. We all tend to be slightly apprehensive about the governmental capacity for storing information about the individual and recalling it by means of his social security number, zip code, or other identification. These fears may be legitimate even when it is recognized that the information technology is itself morally indifferent, and can be used with equal effect for widely approved and undesirable social purposes. The issue of what is "desirable" is an openly divisive one. Humanists have never been reluctant to prescribe remedies for fellow humans, but a central problem of democratic planning, as Davidoff and Reiner have emphasized, is that of preserving an adequate area of individual choice in the face of expert judgments of the "good." [3]

This issue is a persistent stumbling block in all social planning programs aimed at overcoming some of the undesirable consequences of our great technical efficiency. The Poverty Program is split, from the very start, on disagreement over the meaning of poverty. The traditional libertarian nineteenth century economists argue that the problem of poverty is one of inadequate income, and the provision of that income will eliminate the poverty. Some of the contemporary liberals argue the contrary, maintaining that there is a culture of poverty independent of income which cannot be redressed by simple money payments. The choice of a measurement of poverty engages this issue. A "market basket" approach as contrasted with an income level approach commits one to a definition of poverty in terms of merit goods, and required consumption, rather than income payment. In short, it takes some of the choice away from the poor, and refers the determination to an objective standard.

In social planning, the caretaker issue directly confronts choice. The case of

70

planning for mental health, for example, is fraught with instances of value conflict. Even at the margin, where relatively clear-cut issues of community interest can be adduced, there are few clear-cut policy directions. Take the control of dischargees from mental hygiene programs. It serves the cause of effective treatment to continue the contact with the patient over a period of time. To maintain this contact normally requires a legal hold on the patient. But it is a matter of great administrative delicacy to decide when the imposition of that hold, usually by court order, is genuinely "protective," and when it is a violation of the patient's civil liberties.

In such cases, the welfare economics rule, crudely paraphrased, would be to restrain the patient only when the marginal social benefit from the continuing contact exceeds the marginal social cost of diminishing individual liberty. In practice, the probability of relapse once removed from contact is the decisive "factual" input. When the social cost of relapse, weighted by the probability of relapse once the patient is removed from contact, exceeds the social cost of deprivation of liberty multiplied by the probability of such deprivation in enforced contact, the restraint is justified. Clearly, administrators may be divided on their relative valuation of the social damage of the behavior of the mentally ill and of freedom to come and go at will. But it is sometimes overlooked that the social sciences, on which such calculus is dependent for its "factual" inputs, are often equally at variance over the behavioral probabilities. As Hans Morgenthau once observed, social sciences are not only uncertain about the nature of causes, given effects, but are also uncertain about the evaluation of the effects, given the causes.

The problem of choice is therefore shifted uncomfortably to the social planner. He finds that he must have a theory of long-run client interests. If he is to engage in this perilous activity, he cannot afford the luxury of positivist detachment. He will not be handed a ready-made packet of goals in the form of a set of well-ordered preference functions, and the task of discerning "latent" goals will take great patience and much free interpretation. The enterprise of social planning has always been facilitated by strong ideology. At the least, it requires determined leadership.

SOCIAL PLANNING AND
SOCIAL LEADERSHIP

If the democratic ideals of decentralized decision and individual choice are to be pursued concurrently with the officially defined community goals of health and welfare, including increased consumption of meritorious goods and services, extraordinary efforts must be made to bulwark the choosing processes of the disadvantaged with vast amounts of technical information, political leverage, and economic means. In particular, it may be necessary for the poor and disadvantaged to have their own planners. This realization is quickly forced upon those who hold uncompromisingly democratic goals, and who become engaged in the action processes. For example, Paul Davidoff has on various occasions urged that planners take up the role of advocates for the disadvantaged.[4]

The problem is closely analogous to that of foreign aid. In making grants or loans to undeveloped nations, the donors are always faced with the difficult task of insuring efficient use of the funds, without imposing imperialistic controls. The difficulties in such action may account for the predilection in Soviet aid programs for concrete development projects, rather than outright grants. If the projects chosen are popular, some of this difficulty can be avoided. Presumably, if federal programs followed indigenous market choice rather than bureaucratic determination of merit, they would provide freedom schools, key club memberships, and cut-rate Cadillacs rather than public housing, Job Corps camps, and school lunches. It would then be up to local planners, working in the community as advocates, to both extend the impact of the actual choices of the community, and to reshape the choice, by dramatizing the relations between means and ends.

Taken seriously programs like the rent subsidy provisions of the present Housing Act, which are aimed at encouraging the consumption of merit goods, entail a basic reeducation of consumers. Indeed, real incomes measured by consumer satisfaction, may not go up in the short run under such programs even if the objective level of consumption is raised. (In the case of relocation of slum dwellers in housing estates in England, Ireland, and elsewhere, there is even some evidence that the objective level of living has at times declined slightly with the increased consumption of a particular merit good, housing.)

The closer one gets to the community level, and the closer to the client, the more acute are these problems of individual liberty and choice. [The main problem of social planning at the national level is to establish social goals which are attainable, or at least approachable, which can be given some hierarchical ordering, and which can be programmed.] National planners should use program guides, standards, and other bureaucratic controls sparingly, lest they make demands on localities which are unreasonable in this sense.

At the local level, where these goals are to be implemented, the democratic ideal would hold out the opportunity for citizens to participate in defining the operational form of their goals. In practice, however, there is a tendency toward organizational efficiency which requires each local agency action to be measured against the operating rules of output which are established by the national bureaucracies. While planning as an activity is independent of the issue of centralization, the same organizational forces that make for planning push for the efficiencies realizable by central control. What is more, the planners are often impatient with the delays, losses, and frictional costs imposed by decentralized administration. The conduct of the Antipoverty Program is an example of such costs, and the uneasiness which these arouse in the planners.

SOCIAL PLANNING AND ADMINISTRATIVE EFFICIENCY	The Great Society is determined to be The Efficient Society, not content to provide butter with its guns, but bent on having the most Bang for the Buck and the smoothest spreading, high-score product in Dairyland.

The success of economic thinking in the Defense Department's planning and the great growth of efficiency analysis techniques supported by government contract effort have encouraged governmental planners to apply performance tests to social welfare programs as well as to military procurement. The city planning profession, which has long vacillated between social utopianism and managerial efficiency aims, now must increasingly accommodate to the imposition of the latter by the administering federal bureaucracies. Local social planning has barely begun to digest the implications of this trend.

The drive for evaluation of the effectiveness of social service programs is eminently reasonable. In the absence of well articulated national social goals, individual program progress is difficult to measure; in a society only recently concerned with defining more subtle measures of social progress than income and employment some confusion of direction is to be expected. The presence of established bureaucracies poised to soak up the new program funds does not reassure the operations analyst. After all, what percentage of applicants to the U.S. Employment Service are placed in jobs by that service? What percentage of referrals to Mental Health clinics are successfully treated? Existing welfare agencies tend to be audited in terms of operations performed, not results achieved. Senator Ribicoff's recent observation that federal agencies may lack the competence to administer the new social programs enacted by Congress is only half the picture; Congress has failed to give clearly the direction of results expected from these programs. Administrative audits may be premature until these purposes are clarified. There is even a danger that too-hasty efficiency measures will impede the development of these goals, for the latter must be defined by the interactions between the clients and the supply agencies.

Since a prime goal of administration is efficiency, and since individuals may be legitimately indifferent to the efficiency of the system or organization, individual behavior is a friction to be overcome in administration. Resistance to the imposition of preference rankings from above is a fundamental democratic tenet, but it is almost inevitably in conflict with programs planned by experts, whether social planners or physical planners. Efficiency-minded physical planners become impatient at the economic and engineering inefficiencies produced by obdurate human behavior, and the social planners, since the origins of the settlement house movement, have marvelled at the capacities of the poor for resisting "self-betterment." Robert Moses, one of the more impatient of planners, recently gave vent to this common annoyance, commenting on an engineering feasibility report for a proposed Long Island Sound crossing which he favors. Since the feasibility depends, to some extent, on the ability of the planners to persuade people to use the crossing at times other than summer months and week-ends, Mr. Moses complained that "the usual short season, dependent on the opening and closing of schools, and occasional mid-summer peak loads due to silly, gregarious travel hours, are the despair and curse of those who operate our seashore." The stickiness of this behavior puzzled Mr. Moses, for he continued, "as to hourly schedules, why should motorized lemmings instinctively crawl in huge armies to cast themselves into the sea just at high noon, instead of staggering their arrivals? Why can't they listen to radio and other mechanical instruction? Why must a driver behave like an ant, and if he must, why isn't he an obedient ant?" [5]

The administrative, or management, sciences differ in their approach to planning, depending on the scope and degree of control exercised by the management. More centralized management leans to a "hard" style, with decentralized or democratic management styles featuring a "soft" approach. The mnemonic public administration acronym POSDOORB (plan, organize, staff, direct, coordinate, report, budget) is appropriate to the hard style, while its counterpart DECOCOMO (decide, communicate, coordinate, motivate) is more representative of the soft. The soft style in administrative planning does not ask why man is not an obedient ant, it assumes that strict obedience is not feasible, and that manipulation of the actor's motives will be necessary to achieve the desired performance. But both POSDOORB and DECOCOMO are "top-down" procedures, as the words "direct" and "decide" reveal. The ends, in either case, are given.

The Community Action Committees set up by the Office of Economic Opportunity in its "Poverty Program" wish to have a hand in setting these ends. They wish to exploit the "maximum feasible participation" phrase in the enabling legislation to take a major part in the direction of the program. The Bureau of the Budget, guardian of administrative efficiency and witting or unwitting ally of the established big-city political machinery, has moved to curb the power of the clients in policy-making. Administrative efficiency and mass democracy have often been in conflict; Veblen's Engineers could not leave the conduct of the economy to so anarchic a mechanism as the Price System. Elites and the electorate are constantly in tension, both about the proper ends of the society and the appropriate forms of participation in decision-making.

SOCIAL PLANNING AND
RADICAL REFORM

Proponents of social planning in the United States are impeded from developing a coherent plan of action by the ideological strictures of the society in which they operate. Our pragmatic, conservative, democratic ideology holds that *one*, the structure of power cannot be changed from below, and *two*, behavior and taste cannot be changed from above. Under the first, not only are revolutionary *means* excluded, but radical ends are ruled out as well. By the canons of presupposition *two*, democracies must resist the imposition of preferences upon the weak by the strong. Despite welfare economists' demonstration that aggregation of individual values into a community value function is greatly facilitated by acceptance of the preference of authority as the preference of the group (the dictatorship case) this convenience is denied social planners.

Given these limitations, social planning is split, with its left wing rejecting presupposition *one* and accepting *two;* an administrative right accepting *one* but altering *two;* and a political right accepting both *one* and *two* and insisting on confining operations within the alternatives of the status quo. Only the last mentioned has no crisis of legitimation. Radical social planners bent on changing the distribution of power and available actions to maximize individual choice and administrative social planners accepting the power distribution and attempting to secure behavior of the wards to conform to the tastes of their guardians are both pushing for social change. The left wishes substantial redistribution so that its clients will be allowed to transform themselves (along lines of their choosing) while the administrative right wants the clients to transform themselves so that the whole game will work more smoothly, even if the chief beneficiaries of

73

smoother functioning prove to be the more powerful. Examples of these ideal types are not hard to find in city planning.

The task of the radical social planners is difficult. Society is less tolerant of those who would tamper with the goals than of those who would alter the means, and its organized apparatus is especially uneasy at efforts to incorporate machinery for regularly changing the goals, through radical indulgence of free choice, even when the rhetoric of the social planners uses venerated slogans. The experience of Mobilization For Youth in New York is evidence that revolutionary programs guided by social planners are not likely to be treated by the custodians of civil order with the degree of indulgence sometimes accorded illegal sit-ins. Mobilization For Youth, moreover, was challenging the local governmental administration more directly than it was threatening some vague "power structure." This was true even when it supported tenant movements, for the slum landlords "power" is vested in their relations with local political figures rather than in connections with financial and economic powers.

In comments at the workshop on "Centrally Planned Change" two years ago, John R. Seeley expressed the fear that the federal involvement in traditional local social planning would create a more formidable bureaucratic administrative barrier to the "grass roots" choice school of social planning. Observing that "a number of the executive departments of the federal government have moved into a species of planning and plan-forcing on a scale so massive as to constitute almost a new force in American life, and, incidentally, to render peripheral and probably powerless the previous incumbents of "the social planning activity," he went on to cite Karl Mannheim as labelling "correctly the major danger on which would turn the fate of planning as between the dictatorial and democratic varieties. The former fate would be sealed if planning fell into the hands of the bureaucracies." [6] But the dilemma for social planning leadership is clearly not "bureaucracy or grass roots," but "what bureaucracy?" In a society in which the "establishment" has vast bureaucratic, rationalizing, technically competent apparatus at its disposal, can a more tolerant, permissive, choice-maximizing movement succeed in redistributing power? And if the radical social planners are allowed to keep presupposition *two* on condition that they give up their opposition to *one*, that is, that they retain democratic choice at the price of foregoing revolutionary redistribution, will they not become the leaders of the lost, the counselors of despair?

This tension in the leadership condition of the radical social planners in the American ghetto slums has been bared by the anarchic outbreaks of Harlem last summer and Los Angeles this year. The democratic social planner resists being made a recruitment officer for the Establishment. He wants the client to be taken on his own terms, to be taken seriously as an arbiter of his own values. He may even attempt to protect indigenous forms and life styles when they are illegal. But he has no revolutionary role or power. In a direct confrontation of authority and the frustrated aspirations of his clients, he has no function, for he cannot relinquish or curb his doctrine of self-determination—that would mean rejection of position *two*—and he cannot speedup the transfer of power.

SOCIAL PLANNING, SOCIAL SCIENCE, AND SOCIETAL GOALS

At best, our contemporary social planning can achieve some coordination of welfare agency efforts, some limited participation by community groups in welfare planning, and a readiness to be measured against such goals as the discerning savants of our society can muster. Positive social science, which is steadfastly descriptive, and determined to be value-free, can play an important diagnostic role, but without the informing graces of ideology it is remarkably mute on prescription. Social scientists tell us of the plight of the bottom fifth of our society, of the obstacles to social mobility, of the frustrating flight of meaningful work, of intergenerational transmission of dependency, and even of the private grasp of public decision, but they leave program to the reformers and ideologues. Ideologically sustained societal planning, as the socialist experiments show, virtually dispenses with social science.[7]

The ideological socialists are steadfast in their commitment to equity principles, though in practice efficiency considerations of economic development may be allowed to supersede these as "temporary" expedients. The utilitarian postulates of the economic-efficiency administrative analysts are regarded by social critics as convenient oversimplifications. As a nation we have slipped into a program of broad social reform which involves the organization of our economy, of the space organization of our cities, and even of interpersonal relations, without benefit of societal planning. At the same time our social scientists have compiled some of the best social statistics in the world, and have supported these with unexcelled social analysis and a great deal of partial social theory. At the local community level we are on the verge of comprehensive social accounts.[8]

We are now in an increasingly good position to measure the impact of public programs on their various clients, to establish the benefits and costs of programs, and to measure, in limited terms, the efficiency of public actions, thanks to a host of social studies, social measurements, and social accounts. Our social intelligence system is potentially powerful. Some, like Seeley, fear that this power will be manipulated by the planner-bureaucrats. Others feel, somewhat wryly, that the bureaucrats will keep this knowledge from being mobilized for social action. The "broad citizen involvement and participation" sought in community social planning is frustrated by the lack of basic social democracy. Without this involvement, the political legitimacy of social planning is open to challenge, for we have no consensus on a national social program to guide the community effort.

In any event, the social democracy which is a precondition to collective social planning in a political democracy depends on social gains which will be engineered, for the most part, from Washington, The achievement of economic democracy, the securing of equality in civil rights, the abolition of gross regional differences in education, and other major social gains will be forged by federal power, or not at all. But the societal plan which will set the targets against which all the ad hoc programs will be measured does not exist.

If such national social planning were to be instituted in the USA, substantial reorganization and improvement of our social data might be required. It is obvious, for example, that the relation of economic planning to social planning requires a national manpower policy, and that the latter, in turn, requires a national manpower budget with great regional and local detail. The material for such a budget is abundantly available, but the policy—which would require the setting of targets on full employment, local and regional labor force mobility, and similar matters—is not available to organize the data.

Social science can inform policy directly, as well as contribute to social accounting. The findings of social scientists have influenced the highest councils in the land, as the wholesale citation of Myrdal's *American Dilemma* by the Supreme Court in its civil rights decisions showed, and the revival of brain-trusting style in the executive branch is now graced by richer social science material than was available to the New Deal. At times it seems we have fallen back on "objective" social science findings because our political ideology offers so few positive guides to social reconstruction. Thus a program which might be openly embraced in other countries out of commitment to an ideology might be introduced in the USA under the seemingly nonarbitrary cloak of social "science." There is a danger in this process, for it could lead to the tyrannical "scientism" predicted by intellectual opponents of planning.

More likely, however, it would lead to much ad hoc social planning. For the social scientists cannot supplant the goal-making role of ideology, or relieve the political decision makers of their responsibility for setting the public preference scale and the targets to be embodied in a societal plan. The protection of the citizen against administrative abuses, the biases of planners, the condescension of caretakers, and all arbitrariness in social planning depends upon the open articulation of coherent national social goals, and the public acceptance of social planning targets. The Poverty Program, Appalachia Bill, aid to education, and other "Great Society" Acts need a national social accounting against which to be measured. Even more, they need a national social plan which articulates policy, and target dates, for achieving minimum levels of income and consumption, direction and amount of redistribution of population, reduction of intergenerational dependency, equalization of education, and a host of other social goals.

NOTES

Author's Note: Parts of this article are based on "Memorandum on Social Issues in Planning in Puerto Rico," which I prepared while on a consulting team under the leadership of Professor Robert B. Mitchell in San Juan in July of 1963.

[1] Herbert Gans, "Memorandum," an unpublished paper of the Puerto Rican Planning Board.

[2] James P. Dixon, Jr., "Meeting Human Needs," *Goals for Americans,* The Report of the President's Commission on National Goals (Prentice-Hall, 1960), p. 249.

[3] P. Davidoff and T. Reiner, "A Choice Theory of Planning," *Journal of the American Institute of Planners,* XXVIII (May, 1962), 103–115.

[4] Good statements of the Davidoff position may be found in: Paul Davidoff, "The Role of the City Planner in Social Planning," *Proceedings of the American Institute of Planners, 1964 Annual Conference,* pp. 125–131, and, "Advocacy and Pluralism in Planning," *Journal of the American Institute of Planners,* XXX (November, 1964), 331–338.

[5] Remarks by Robert Moses on the proposed Long Island Sound Crossing, Triborough Bridge Authority, 1965.

[6] John R. Seeley, "Central Planning: Prologue to a Critique," *Centrally Planned Change: Prospects and Concepts,* ed. Robert Morris (New York: National Association of Social Workers, 1964), p. 58.

[7] A well-documented case for this conclusion appears in a yet-unpublished paper on Soviet Social Science prepared by Peter R. Senn for the Annual Meeting of the American Association for the Advancement of Science at Berkeley, December, 1965.

[8] See Harvey Perloff, "New Directions in Social Planning," *Journal of the American Institute of Planners* XXXI (November, 1965), 297–303.

[22]

A LADDER OF CITIZEN PARTICIPATION

Sherry R. Arnstein

The heated controversy over "citizen participation," "citizen control," and "maximum feasible involvement of the poor," has been waged largely in terms of exacerbated rhetoric and misleading euphemisms. To encourage a more enlightened dialogue, a typology of citizen participation is offered using examples from three federal social programs: urban renewal, anti-poverty, and Model Cities. The typology, which is designed to be provocative, is arranged in a ladder pattern with each rung corresponding to the extent of citizens' power in determining the plan and/or program.

The idea of citizen participation is a little like eating spinach: no one is against it in principle because it is good for you. Participation of the governed in their government is, in theory, the cornerstone of democracy—a revered idea that is vigorously applauded by virtually everyone. The applause is reduced to polite handclaps, however, when this principle is advocated by the have-not blacks, Mexican-Americans, Puerto Ricans, Indians, Eskimos, and whites. And when the have-nots define participation as redistribution of power, the American consensus on the fundamental principle explodes into many shades of outright racial, ethnic, ideological, and political opposition.

There have been many recent speeches, articles, and books [1] which explore in detail *who* are the have-nots of our time. There has been much recent documentation of *why* the have-nots have become so offended and embittered by their powerlessness to deal with the profound inequities and injustices pervading their daily lives. But there has been very little analysis of the content of the current controversial slogan: "citizen participation" or "maximum feasible participation." In short: *What* is citizen participation and what is its relationship to the social imperatives of our time?

Citizen Participation is Citizen Power

Because the question has been a bone of political contention, most of the answers have been purposely buried in innocuous euphemisms like "self-help" or "citizen involvement." Still others have been embellished with misleading rhetoric like "absolute control" which is something no one—including the President of the

Sherry R. Arnstein is Director of Community Development Studies for The Commons, a non-profit research institute in Washington, D.C. and Chicago. She is a former Chief Advisor on Citizen Participation in HUD's Model Cities Administration and has served as Staff Consultant to the President's Committee on Juvenile Delinquency, Special Assistant to the Assistant Secretary of HEW, and Washington Editor of *Current Magazine.*

United States—has or can have. Between understated euphemisms and exacerbated rhetoric, even scholars have found it difficult to follow the controversy. To the headline reading public, it is simply bewildering.

My answer to the critical *what* question is simply that citizen participation is a categorical term for citizen power. It is the redistribution of power that enables the have-not citizens, presently excluded from the political and economic processes, to be deliberately included in the future. It is the strategy by which the have-nots join in determining how information is shared, goals and policies are set, tax resources are allocated, programs are operated, and benefits like contracts and patronage are parceled out. In short, it is the means by which they can induce significant social reform which enables them to share in the benefits of the affluent society.

EMPTY RITUAL VERSUS BENEFIT

There is a critical difference between going through the empty ritual of participation and having the real power needed to affect the outcome of the process. This difference is brilliantly capsulized in a poster painted last spring by the French students to explain the student-worker rebellion.[2] (See Figure 1.) The poster highlights the fundamental point that participation without redistribution of power is an empty and frustrating process for the powerless. It allows the power-holders to claim that all sides were considered, but makes it possible for only some of those sides to benefit. It maintains the status quo. Essentially, it is what has

FIGURE 1   *French Student Poster. In English, I participate; you participate; he participates; we participate; you participate . . . **They profit.***

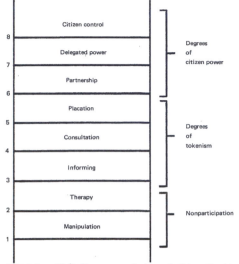

FIGURE 2   *Eight Rungs on a Ladder of Citizen Partici-*
               pation

been happening in most of the 1,000 Community Action Programs, and what promises to be repeated in the vast majority of the 150 Model Cities programs.

Types of Participation and "NonParticipation"
A typology of eight *levels* of participation may help in analysis of this confused issue. For illustrative purposes the eight types are arranged in a ladder pattern with each rung corresponding to the extent of citizens' power in determining the end product.[3] (See Figure 2.)

The bottom rungs of the ladder are (1) *Manipulation* and (2) *Therapy*. These two rungs describe levels of "non-participation" that have been contrived by some to substitute for genuine participation. Their real objective is not to enable people to participate in planning or conducting programs, but to enable powerholders to "educate" or "cure" the participants. Rungs 3 and 4 progress to levels of "tokenism" that allow the have-nots to hear and to have a voice: (3) *Informing* and (4) *Consultation*. When they are proffered by powerholders as the total extent of participation, citizens may indeed hear and be heard. But under these conditions they lack the power to insure that their views will be *heeded* by the powerful. When participation is restricted to these levels, there is no followthrough, no "muscle," hence no assurance of changing the status quo. Rung (5) *Placation,* is simply a higher level tokenism because the groundrules allow have-nots to advise, but retain for the powerholders the continued right to decide.

Further up the ladder are levels of citizen power with increasing degrees of decision-making clout. Citizens

can enter into a (6) *Partnership* that enables them to negotiate and engage in trade-offs with traditional powerholders. At the topmost rungs, (7) *Delegated Power* and (8) *Citizen Control,* have-not citizens obtain the majority of decision-making seats, or full managerial power.

Obviously, the eight-rung ladder is a simplification, but it helps to illustrate the point that so many have missed—that there are significant gradations of citizen participation. Knowing these gradations makes it possible to cut through the hyperbole to understand the increasingly strident demands for participation from the have-nots as well as the gamut of confusing responses from the powerholders.

Though the typology uses examples from federal programs such as urban renewal, anti-poverty, and Model Cities; it could just as easily be illustrated in the church, currently facing demands for power from priests and laymen who seek to change its mission; colleges and universities which in some cases have become literal battlegrounds over the issue of student power; or public schools, city halls, and police departments (or big business which is likely to be next on the expanding list of targets). The underlying issues are essentially the same —"nobodies" in several arenas are trying to become "somebodies" with enough power to make the target institutions responsive to their views, aspirations, and needs.

LIMITATIONS OF THE TYPOLOGY
The ladder juxtaposes powerless citizens with the powerful in order to highlight the fundamental divisions between them. In actuality, neither the have-nots nor the powerholders are homogeneous blocs. Each group encompasses a host of divergent points of view, significant cleavages, competing vested interests, and splintered subgroups. The justification for using such simplistic abstractions is that in most cases the have-nots really do perceive the powerful as a monolithic "system," and powerholders actually do view the have-nots as a sea of "those people," with little comprehension of the class and caste differences among them.

It should be noted that the typology does not include an analysis of the most significant roadblocks to achieving genuine levels of participation. These roadblocks lie on both sides of the simplistic fence. On the powerholders' side, they include racism, paternalism, and resistance to power redistribution. On the have-nots' side, they include inadequacies of the poor community's political socioeconomic infrastructure and knowledge-base, plus difficulties of organizing a representative and accountable citizens' group in the face of futility, alienation, and distrust.

Another caution about the eight separate rungs on the ladder: In the real world of people and programs, there might be 150 rungs with less sharp and "pure" distinctions among them. Furthermore, some of the characteristics used to illustrate each of the eight types might be applicable to other rungs. For example, employment of the have-nots in a program or on a planning staff could occur at any of the eight rungs and could represent either a legitimate or illegitimate characteristic of citizen participation. Depending on their motives, powerholders can hire poor people to coopt them, to placate them, or to utilize the have-nots' special skills and insights.[4] Some mayors, in private, actually boast of their strategy in hiring militant black leaders to muzzle them while destroying their credibility in the black community.

Characteristics and Illustrations

It is in this context of power and powerlessness that the characteristics of the eight rungs are illustrated by examples from current federal social programs.

1. MANIPULATION

In the name of citizen participation, people are placed on rubberstamp advisory committees or advisory boards for the express purpose of "educating" them or engineering their support. Instead of genuine citizen participation, the bottom rung of the ladder signifies the distortion of participation into a public relations vehicle by powerholders.

This illusory form of "participation" initially came into vogue with urban renewal when the socially elite were invited by city housing officials to serve on Citizen Advisory Committees (CACs). Another target of manipulation were the CAC subcommittees on minority groups, which in theory were to protect the rights of Negroes in the renewal program. In practice, these subcommittees, like their parent CACs, functioned mostly as letterheads, trotted forward at appropriate times to promote urban renewal plans (in recent years known as Negro removal plans).

At meetings of the Citizen *Advisory* Committees, it was the officials who educated, persuaded, and advised the citizens, not the reverse. Federal guidelines for the renewal programs legitimized the manipulative agenda by emphasizing the terms "information-gathering," "public relations," and "support" as the explicit functions of the committees.[5]

This style of nonparticipation has since been applied to other programs encompassing the poor. Examples of this are seen in Community Action Agencies (CAAs) which have created structures called "neighborhood councils" or "neighborhood advisory groups." These bodies frequently have no legitimate function or power.[6] The CAAs use them to "prove" that "grassroots people" are involved in the program. But the program may not have been discussed with "the people." Or it may have been described at a meeting in the most general terms; "We need your signatures on this proposal for a multiservice center which will house, under one roof, doctors from the health department, workers from the welfare department, and specialists from the employment service."

The signators are not informed that the $2 million-per-year center will only refer residents to the same old waiting lines at the same old agencies across town. No one is asked if such a referral center is really needed in his neighborhood. No one realizes that the contractor for the building is the mayor's brother-in-law, or that the new director of the center will be the same old community organization specialist from the urban renewal agency.

After signing their names, the proud grassrooters dutifully spread the word that they have "participated" in bringing a new and wonderful center to the neighborhood to provide people with drastically needed jobs and health and welfare services. Only after the ribbon-cutting ceremony do the members of the neighborhood council realize that they didn't ask the important questions, and that they had no technical advisors of their own to help them grasp the fine legal print. The new center, which is open 9 to 5 on weekdays only, actually adds to their problems. Now the old agencies across town won't talk with them unless they have a pink paper slip to prove that they have been referred by "their" shiny new neighborhood center.

Unfortunately, this chicanery is not a unique example. Instead it is almost typical of what has been perpetrated in the name of high-sounding rhetoric like "grassroots participation." This sham lies at the heart of the deep-seated exasperation and hostility of the have-nots toward the powerholders.

One hopeful note is that, having been so grossly affronted, some citizens have learned the Mickey Mouse game, and now they too know how to play. As a result of this knowledge, they are demanding genuine levels of participation to assure them that public programs are relevant to their needs and responsive to their priorities.

2. THERAPY

In some respects group therapy, masked as citizen participation, should be on the lowest rung of the ladder because it is both dishonest and arrogant. Its administrators—mental health experts from social workers to psychiatrists—assume that powerlessness is synonymous with mental illness. On this assumption, under a masquerade of involving citizens in planning, the experts subject the citizens to clinical group therapy. What makes this form of "participation" so invidious is that citizens are engaged in extensive activity, but the focus of it is on curing them of their "pathology" rather than changing the racism and victimization that create their "pathologies."

Consider an incident that occurred in Pennsylvania less than one year ago. When a father took his seriously ill baby to the emergency clinic of a local hospital, a young resident physician on duty instructed him to take the baby home and feed it sugar water. The baby died that afternoon of pneumonia and dehydration. The overwrought father complained to the board of the local

218

Community Action Agency. Instead of launching an investigation of the hospital to determine what changes would prevent similar deaths or other forms of malpractice, the board invited the father to attend the CAA's (therapy) child-care sessions for parents, and promised him that someone would "telephone the hospital director to see that it never happens again."

Less dramatic, but more common examples of therapy, masquerading as citizen participation, may be seen in public housing programs where tenant groups are used as vehicles for promoting control-your-child or cleanup campaigns. The tenants are brought together to help them "adjust their values and attitudes to those of the larger society." Under these groundrules, they are diverted from dealing with such important matters as: arbitrary evictions; segregation of the housing project; or why is there a three-month time lapse to get a broken window replaced in winter.

The complexity of the concept of mental illness in our time can be seen in the experiences of student/civil rights workers facing guns, whips, and other forms of terror in the South. They needed the help of socially attuned psychiatrists to deal with their fears and to avoid paranoia.[7]

3. INFORMING

Informing citizens of their rights, responsibilities, and options can be the most important first step toward legitimate citizen participation. However, too frequently the emphasis is placed on a one-way flow of information —from officials to citizens—with no channel provided for feedback and no power for negotiation. Under these conditions, particularly when information is provided at a late stage in planning, people have little opportunity to influence the program designed "for their benefit." The most frequent tools used for such one-way communication are the news media, pamphlets, posters, and responses to inquiries.

Meetings can also be turned into vehicles for one-way communication by the simple device of providing superficial information, discouraging questions, or giving irrelevant answers. At a recent Model Cities citizen planning meeting in Providence, Rhode Island, the topic was "tot-lots." A group of elected citizen representatives, almost all of whom were attending three to five meetings a week, devoted an hour to a discussion of the placement of six tot-lots. The neighborhood is half black, half white. Several of the black representatives noted that four tot-lots were proposed for the white district and only two for the black. The city official responded with a lengthy, highly technical explanation about costs per square foot and available property. It was clear that most of the residents did not understand his explanation. And it was clear to observers from the Office of Economic Opportunity that other options did exist which, considering available funds, would have brought about a more equitable distribution of facilities. Intimidated by futility, legalistic jargon, and prestige of

the official, the citizens accepted the "information" and endorsed the agency's proposal to place four lots in the white neighborhood.[8]

4. CONSULTATION

Inviting citizens' opinions, like informing them, can be a legitimate step toward their full participation. But if consulting them is not combined with other modes of participation, this rung of the ladder is still a sham since it offers no assurance that citizen concerns and ideas will be taken into account. The most frequent methods used for consulting people are attitude surveys, neighborhood meetings, and public hearings.

When powerholders restrict the input of citizens' ideas solely to this level, participation remains just a window-dressing ritual. People are primarily perceived as statistical abstractions, and participation is measured by how many come to meetings, take brochures home, or answer a questionnaire. What citizens achieve in all this activity is that they have "participated in participation." And what powerholders achieve is the evidence that they have gone through the required motions of involving "those people."

Attitude surveys have become a particular bone of contention in ghetto neighborhoods. Residents are increasingly unhappy about the number of times per week they are surveyed about their problems and hopes. As one woman put it: "Nothing ever happens with those damned questions, except the surveyer gets $3 an hour, and my washing doesn't get done that day." In some communities, residents are so annoyed that they are demanding a fee for research interviews.

Attitude surveys are not very valid indicators of community opinion when used without other input from citizens. Survey after survey (paid for out of antipoverty funds) has "documented" that poor housewives most want tot-lots in their neighborhood where young children can play safely. But most of the women answered these questionnaires without knowing what their options were. They assumed that if they asked for something small, they might just get something useful in the neighborhood. Had the mothers known that a free prepaid health insurance plan was a possible option, they might not have put tot-lots so high on their wish lists.

A classic misuse of the consultation rung occurred at a New Haven, Connecticut, community meeting held to consult citizens on a proposed Model Cities grant. James V. Cunningham, in an unpublished report to the Ford Foundation, described the crowd as large and "mostly hostile:"[9]

Members of The Hill Parents Association demanded to know why residents had not participated in drawing up the proposal. CAA director Spitz explained that it was merely a proposal for seeking Federal planning funds—that once funds were obtained, residents would be deeply involved in the planning. An outside observer who sat in the audience described the meeting this way:

"Spitz and Mel Adams ran the meeting on their own. No representatives of a Hill group moderated or even sat on the stage. Spitz told the 300 residents that this huge meeting was an example of 'participation in planning.' To prove this, since there was a lot of dissatisfaction in the audience, he called for a 'vote' on each component of the proposal. The vote took this form: 'Can I see the hands of all those in favor of a health clinic? All those opposed?' It was a little like asking who favors motherhood."

It was a combination of the deep suspicion aroused at this meeting and a long history of similar forms of "window-dressing participation" that led New Haven residents to demand control of the program.

By way of contrast, it is useful to look at Denver where technicians learned that even the best intentioned among them are often unfamiliar with, and even insensitive to, the problems and aspirations of the poor. The technical director of the Model Cities program has described the way professional planners assumed that the residents, victimized by high-priced local storekeepers, "badly needed consumer education." [10] The residents, on the other hand, pointed out that the local storekeepers performed a valuable function. Although they overcharged, they also gave credit, offered advice, and frequently were the only neighborhood place to cash welfare or salary checks. As a result of this consultation, technicians and residents agreed to substitute the creation of needed credit institutions in the neighborhood for a consumer education program.

5. PLACATION

It is at this level that citizens begin to have some degree of influence though tokenism is still apparent. An example of placation strategy is to place a few hand-picked "worthy" poor on boards of Community Action Agencies or on public bodies like the board of education, police commission, or housing authority. If they are not accountable to a constituency in the community and if the traditional power elite hold the majority of seats, the have-nots can be easily outvoted and outfoxed. Another example is the Model Cities advisory and planning committees. They allow citizens to advise or plan ad infinitum but retain for powerholders the right to judge the legitimacy or feasibility of the advice. The degree to which citizens are actually placated, of course, depends largely on two factors: the quality of technical assistance they have in articulating their priorities; and the extent to which the community has been organized to press for those priorities.

It is not surprising that the level of citizen participation in the vast majority of Model Cities programs is at the placation rung of the ladder or below. Policy-makers at the Department of Housing and Urban Development (HUD) were determined to return the genie of citizen power to the bottle from which it had escaped

(in a few cities) as a result of the provision stipulating "maximum feasible participation" in poverty programs. Therefore, HUD channeled its physical-social-economic rejuvenation approach for blighted neighborhoods through city hall. It drafted legislation requiring that all Model Cities' money flow to a local City Demonstration Agency (CDA) through the elected city council. As enacted by Congress, this gave local city councils final veto power over planning and programming and ruled out any direct funding relationship between community groups and HUD.

HUD required the CDAs to create coalition, policy-making boards that would include necessary local power-holders to create a comprehensive physical-social plan during the first year. The plan was to be carried out in a subsequent five-year action phase. HUD, unlike OEO, did not require that have-not citizens be included on the CDA decision-making boards. HUD's Performance Standards for Citizen Participation only demanded that "citizens have clear and direct access to the decision-making process."

Accordingly, the CDAs structured their policy-making boards to include some combination of elected officials; school representatives; housing, health, and welfare officials; employment and police department representatives; and various civic, labor, and business leaders. Some CDAs included citizens from the neighborhood. Many mayors correctly interpreted the HUD provision for "access to the decision-making process" as the escape hatch they sought to relegate citizens to the traditional advisory role.

Most CDAs created residents' advisory committees. An alarmingly significant number created citizens' policy boards and citizens' policy committees which are totally misnamed as they have either no policy-making function or only a very limited authority. Almost every CDA created about a dozen planning committees or task forces on functional lines: health, welfare, education, housing, and unemployment. In most cases, have-not citizens were invited to serve on these committees along with technicians from relevant public agencies. Some CDAs, on the other hand, structured planning committees of technicians and parallel committees of citizens.

In most Model Cities programs, endless time has been spent fashioning complicated board, committee, and task force structures for the planning year. But the rights and responsibilities of the various elements of those structures are not defined and are ambiguous. Such ambiguity is likely to cause considerable conflict at the end of the one-year planning process. For at this point, citizens may realize that they have once again extensively "participated" but have not profited beyond the extent the powerholders decide to placate them.

Results of a staff study (conducted in the summer of 1968 before the second round of seventy-five planning grants were awarded) were released in a December 1968 HUD bulletin.[11] Though this public document uses much more delicate and diplomatic language, it

220

attests to the already cited criticisms of non-policy-making policy boards and ambiguous complicated structures, in addition to the following findings:

1. Most CDAs did not negotiate citizen participation requirements with residents.

2. Citizens, drawing on past negative experiences with local powerholders, were extremely suspicious of this new panacea program. They were legitimately distrustful of city hall's motives.

3. Most CDAs were not working with citizens' groups that were genuinely representative of model neighborhoods and accountable to neighborhood constituencies. As in so many of the poverty programs, those who were involved were more representative of the upwardly mobile working-class. Thus their acquiescence to plans prepared by city agencies was not likely to reflect the views of the unemployed, the young, the more militant residents, and the hard-core poor.

4. Residents who were participating in as many as three to five meetings per week were unaware of their minimum rights, responsibilities, and the options available to them under the program. For example, they did not realize that they were not required to accept technical help from city technicians they distrusted.

5. Most of the technical assistance provided by CDAs and city agencies was of third-rate quality, paternalistic, and condescending. Agency technicians did not suggest innovative options. They reacted bureaucratically when the residents pressed for innovative approaches. The vested interests of the old-line city agencies were a major—albeit hidden—agenda.

6. Most CDAs were not engaged in planning that was comprehensive enough to expose and deal with the roots of urban decay. They engaged in "meetingitis" and were supporting strategies that resulted in "projectitis," the outcome of which was a "laundry list" of traditional programs to be conducted by traditional agencies in the traditional manner under which slums emerged in the first place.

7. Residents were not getting enough information from CDAs to enable them to review CDA developed plans or to initiate plans of their own as required by HUD. At best, they were getting superficial information. At worst, they were not even getting copies of official HUD materials.

8. Most residents were unaware of their rights to be reimbursed for expenses incurred because of participation—babysitting, transportation costs, and so on.

9. The training of residents, which would enable them to understand the labyrinth of the federal-state-city systems and networks of subsystems, was an item that most CDAs did not even consider.

These findings led to a new public interpretation of HUD's approach to citizen participation. Though the requirements for the seventy-five "second-round" Model City grantees were not changed, HUD's twenty-seven page technical bulletin on citizen participation repeatedly advocated that cities share power with residents.

It also urged CDAs to experiment with subcontracts under which the residents' groups could hire their own trusted technicians.

A more recent evaluation was circulated in February 1969 by OSTI, a private firm that entered into a contract with OEO to provide technical assistance and training to citizens involved in Model Cities programs in the northeast region of the country. OSTI's report to OEO corroborates the earlier study. In addition it states: [12]

> In practically no Model Cities structure does citizen participation mean truly shared decision-making, such that citizens might view themselves as "the partners in this program. . . ."
> In general, citizens are finding it impossible to have a significant impact on the comprehensive planning which is going on. In most cases the staff planners of the CDA and the planners of existing agencies are carrying out the actual planning with citizens having a peripheral role of watchdog and, ultimately, the "rubber stamp" of the plan generated. In cases where citizens have the direct responsibility for generating program plans, the time period allowed and the independent technical resources being made available to them are not adequate to allow them to do anything more than generate very traditional approaches to the problems they are attempting to solve.
> In general, little or no thought has been given to the means of insuring continued citizen participation during the stage of implementation. In most cases, traditional agencies are envisaged as the implementors of Model Cities programs and few mechanisms have been developed for encouraging organizational change or change in the method of program delivery within these agencies or for insuring that citizens will have some influence over these agencies as they implement Model Cities programs. . . .
> By and large, people are once again being planned *for*. In most situations the major planning decisions are being made by CDA staff and approved in a formalistic way by policy boards.

6. PARTNERSHIP

At this rung of the ladder, power is in fact redistributed through negotiation between citizens and powerholders. They agree to share planning and decision-making responsibilities through such structures as joint policy boards, planning committees and mechanisms for resolving impasses. After the groundrules have been established through some form of give-and-take, they are not subject to unilateral change.

Partnership can work most effectively when there is an organized power-base in the community to which the citizen leaders are accountable; when the citizens group has the financial resources to pay its leaders reasonable honoraria for their time-consuming efforts; and when the group has the resources to hire (and fire) its own technicians, lawyers, and community organizers. With these ingredients, citizens have some genuine bargaining influence over the outcome of the plan (as long as both parties find it useful to maintain the partnership). One community leader described it "like coming to city hall with hat on head instead of in hand."

In the Model Cities program only about fifteen of the so-called first generation of seventy-five cities have reached some significant degree of power-sharing with residents. In all but one of those cities, it was angry citizen demands, rather than city initiative, that led to the negotiated sharing of power.[18] The negotiations were triggered by citizens who had been enraged by previous forms of alleged participation. They were both angry and sophisticated enough to refuse to be "conned" again. They threatened to oppose the awarding of a planning grant to the city. They sent delegations to HUD in Washington. They used abrasive language. Negotiation took place under a cloud of suspicion and rancor.

In most cases where power has come to be shared it was *taken by the citizens,* not given by the city. There is nothing new about that process. Since those who have power normally want to hang onto it, historically it has had to be wrested by the powerless rather than proffered by the powerful.

Such a working partnership was negotiated by the residents in the Philadelphia model neighborhood. Like most applicants for a Model Cities grant, Philadelphia wrote its more than 400 page application and waved it at a hastily called meeting of community leaders. When those present were asked for an endorsement, they angrily protested the city's failure to consult them on preparation of the extensive application. A community spokesman threatened to mobilize a neighborhood protest *against* the application unless the city agreed to give the citizens a couple of weeks to review the application and recommend changes. The officials agreed.

At their next meeting, citizens handed the city officials a substitute citizen participation section that changed the groundrules from a weak citizens' advisory role to a strong shared power agreement. Philadelphia's application to HUD included the citizens' substitution word for word. (It also included a new citizen prepared introductory chapter that changed the city's description of the model neighborhood from a paternalistic description of problems to a realistic analysis of its strengths, weaknesses, and potentials.)

Consequently, the proposed policy-making committee of the Philadelphia CDA was revamped to give five out of eleven seats to the residents' organization, which is called the Area Wide Council (AWC). The AWC obtained a subcontract from the CDA for more than $20,000 per month, which it used to maintain the neighborhood organization, to pay citizen leaders $7 per meeting for their planning services, and to pay the salaries of a staff of community organizers, planners, and other technicians. AWC has the power to initiate plans of its own, to engage in joint planning with CDA committees, and to review plans initiated by city agen-cies. It has a veto power in that no plans may be submitted by the CDA to the city council until they have been reviewed, and any differences of opinion have been successfully negotiated with the AWC. Representatives of the AWC (which is a federation of neighborhood organizations grouped into sixteen neighborhood "hubs") may attend all meetings of CDA task forces, planning committees, or subcommittees.

Though the city council has final veto power over the plan (by federal law), the AWC believes it has a neighborhood constituency that is strong enough to negotiate any eleventh-hour objections the city council might raise when it considers such AWC proposed innovations as an AWC Land Bank, an AWC Economic Development Corporation, and an experimental income maintenance program for 900 poor families.

7. DELEGATED POWER

Negotiations between citizens and public officials can also result in citizens achieving dominant decision-making authority over a particular plan or program. Model City policy boards or CAA delegate agencies on which citizens have a clear majority of seats and genuine specified powers are typical examples. At this level, the ladder has been scaled to the point where citizens hold the significant cards to assure accountability of the program to them. To resolve differences, powerholders need to start the bargaining process rather than respond to pressure from the other end.

Such a dominant decision-making role has been attained by residents in a handful of Model Cities including Cambridge, Massachusetts; Dayton, and Columbus, Ohio; Minneapolis, Minnesota; St. Louis, Missouri; Hartford and New Haven, Connecticut; and Oakland, California.

In New Haven, residents of the Hill neighborhood have created a corporation that has been delegated the power to prepare the entire Model Cities plan. The city, which received a $117,000 planning grant from HUD, has subcontracted $110,000 of it to the neighborhood corporation to hire its own planning staff and consultants. The Hill Neighborhood Corporation has eleven representatives on the twenty-one-member CDA board which assures it a majority voice when its proposed plan is reviewed by the CDA.

Another model of delegated power is separate and parallel groups of citizens and powerholders, with provision for citizen veto if differences of opinion cannot be resolved through negotiation. This is a particularly interesting coexistence model for hostile citizen groups too embittered toward city hall—as a result of past "collaborative efforts"—to engage in joint planning.

Since all Model Cities programs require approval by the city council before HUD will fund them, city councils have final veto powers even when citizens have the majority of seats on the CDA Board. In Richmond, California, the city council agreed to a citizens' counter-

AIP JOURNAL JULY 1969

veto, but the details of that agreement are ambiguous and have not been tested.

Various delegated power arrangements are also emerging in the Community Action Program as a result of demands from the neighborhoods and OEO's most recent instruction guidelines which urged CAAs "to exceed (the) basic requirements" for resident participation.[14] In some cities, CAAs have issued subcontracts to resident dominated groups to plan and/or operate one or more decentralized neighborhood program components like a multipurpose service center or a Headstart program. These contracts usually include an agreed upon line-by-line budget and program specifications. They also usually include a specific statement of the significant powers that have been delegated, for example: policymaking; hiring and firing; issuing subcontracts for building, buying, or leasing. (Some of the subcontracts are so broad that they verge on models for citizen control.)

8. CITIZEN CONTROL

Demands for community controlled schools, black control, and neighborhood control are on the increase. Though no one in the nation has absolute control, it is very important that the rhetoric not be confused with intent. People are simply demanding that degree of power (or control) which guarantees that participants or residents can govern a program or an institution, be in full charge of policy and managerial aspects, and be able to negotiate the conditions under which "outsiders" may change them.

A neighborhood corporation with no intermediaries between it and the source of funds is the model most frequently advocated. A small number of such experimental corporations are already producing goods and/or social services. Several others are reportedly in the development stage, and new models for control will undoubtedly emerge as the have-nots continue to press for greater degrees of power over their lives.

Though the bitter struggle for community control of the Ocean Hill-Brownsville schools in New York City has aroused great fears in the headline reading public, less publicized experiments are demonstrating that the have-nots can indeed improve their lot by handling the entire job of planning, policy-making, and managing a program. Some are even demonstrating that they can do all this with just one arm because they are forced to use their other one to deal with a continuing barrage of local opposition triggered by the announcement that a federal grant has been given to a community group or an all black group.

Most of these experimental programs have been capitalized with research and demonstration funds from the Office of Economic Opportunity in cooperation with other federal agencies. Examples include:

1. A $1.8 million grant was awarded to the Hough Area Development Corporation in Cleveland to plan economic development programs in the ghetto and to develop a series of economic enterprises ranging from a novel combination shopping-center-public-housing project to a loan guarantee program for local building contractors. The membership and board of the nonprofit corporation is composed of leaders of major community organizations in the black neighborhood.

2. Approximately $1 million ($595,751 for the second year) was awarded to the Southwest Alabama Farmers Cooperative Association (SWAFCA) in Selma, Alabama, for a ten-county marketing cooperative for food and livestock. Despite local attempts to intimidate the coop (which included the use of force to stop trucks on the way to market), first year membership grew to 1,150 farmers who earned $52,000 on the sale of their new crops. The elected coop board is composed of two poor black farmers from each of the ten economically depressed counties.

3. Approximately $600,000 ($300,000 in a supplemental grant) was granted to the Albina Corporation and the Albina Investment Trust to create a black-operated, black-owned manufacturing concern using inexperienced management and unskilled minority group personnel from the Albina district. The profit-making wool and metal fabrication plant will be owned by its employees through a deferred compensation trust plan.

4. Approximately $800,000 ($400,000 for the second year) was awarded to the Harlem Commonwealth Council to demonstrate that a community-based development corporation can catalyze and implement an economic development program with broad community support and participation. After only eighteen months of program development and negotiation, the council will soon launch several large-scale ventures including operation of two supermarkets, an auto service and repair center (with built-in manpower training program), a finance company for families earning less than $4,000 per year, and a data processing company. The all black Harlem-based board is already managing a metal castings foundry.

Though several citizen groups (and their mayors) use the rhetoric of citizen control, no Model City can meet the criteria of citizen control since final approval power and accountability rest with the city council.

Daniel P. Moynihan argues that city councils are representative of the community, but Adam Walinsky illustrates the nonrepresentativeness of this kind of representation: [15]

> Who . . . exercises "control" through the representative process? In the Bedford-Stuyvesant ghetto of New York there are 450,000 people—as many as in the entire city of Cincinnati, more than in the entire state of Vermont. Yet the area has only one high school, and 80 per cent of its teen-agers are dropouts; the infant mortality rate is twice the national average; there are over 8000 buildings abandoned by everyone but the rats, yet the area received not one dollar of urban renewal funds

during the entire first 15 years of that program's operation; the unemployment rate is known only to God.

Clearly, Bedford-Stuyvesant has some special needs; yet it has always been lost in the midst of the city's eight million. In fact, it took a lawsuit to win for this vast area, in the year 1968, its first Congressman. In what sense can the representative system be said to have "spoken for" this community, during the long years of neglect and decay?

Walinsky's point on Bedford-Stuyvesant has general applicability to the ghettos from coast to coast. It is therefore likely that in those ghettos where residents have achieved a significant degree of power in the Model Cities planning process, the first-year action plans will call for the creation of some new community institutions entirely governed by residents with a specified sum of money contracted to them. If the groundrules for these programs are clear and if citizens understand that achieving a genuine place in the pluralistic scene subjects them to its legitimate forms of give-and-take, then these kinds of programs might begin to demonstrate how to counteract the various corrosive political and socioeconomic forces that plague the poor.

In cities likely to become predominantly black through population growth, it is unlikely that strident citizens' groups like AWC of Philadelphia will eventually demand legal power for neighborhood self-government. Their grand design is more likely to call for a black city hall, achieved by the elective process. In cities destined to remain predominantly white for the foreseeable future, it is quite likely that counterpart groups to AWC will press for separatist forms of neighborhood government that can create and control decentralized public services such as police protection, education systems, and health facilities. Much may depend on the willingness of city governments to entertain demands for resource allocation weighted in favor of the poor, reversing gross imbalances of the past.

Among the arguments against community control are: it supports separatism; it creates balkanization of public services; it is more costly and less efficient; it enables minority group "hustlers" to be just as opportunistic and disdainful of the have-nots as their white predecessors; it is incompatible with merit systems and professionalism; and ironically enough, it can turn out to be a new Mickey Mouse game for the have-nots by allowing them to gain control but not allowing them sufficient dollar resources to succeed.[16] These arguments are not to be taken lightly. But neither can we take lightly the arguments of embittered advocates of community control—that every other means of trying to end their victimization has failed!

NOTES

[1] The literature on poverty and discrimination and their effects on people is extensive. As an introduction, the following will be

224

helpful: B. H. Bagdikian, *In the Midst of Plenty: The Poor in America* (New York: Beacon, 1964); Paul Jacobs, "The Brutalizing of America," *Dissent*, XI (Autumn 1964), p. 423–8; Stokely Carmichael and Charles V. Hamilton, *Black Power: The Politics of Liberation in America* (New York: Random House, 1967); Eldridge Cleaver, *Soul on Ice* (New York: McGraw-Hill, 1968); L. J. Duhl, *The Urban Condition; People and Policy in the Metropolis* (New York: Basic Books, 1963); William H. Grier and P. M. Cobbs, *Black Rage* (New York: Basic Books, 1968); Michael Harrington, *The Other America: Poverty in the United States* (New York: Macmillan, 1962); Peter Marris and Martin Rein, *Dilemmas of Social Reform: Poverty and Community Action in the United States* (New York: Atherton Press, 1967); Mollie Orshansky, "Who's Who Among the Poor: A Demographic View of Poverty," *Social Security Bulletin*, XXVII (July 1965), 3–32; and Richard T. Titmuss, *Essays on the Welfare State* (New Haven: Yale University Press, 1968).

[2] The poster is one of about 350 produced in May or June 1968 at Atélier Populaire, a graphics center launched by students from the Sorbonne's École des Beaux Art and École des Arts Decoratifs.

[3] This typology is an outgrowth of a more crude typology I circulated in March 1967 in a HUD staff discussion paper titled "Rhetoric and Reality." The earlier typology consisted of eight levels that were less discrete types and did not necessarily suggest a chronological progression: Inform, Consult, Joint Planning, Negotiate, Decide, Delegate, Advocate Planning, and Neighborhood Control.

[4] For an article of some possible employment strategies, see, Edmund M. Burke, "Citizen Participation Strategies," *Journal of the American Institute of Planners*, XXXIV, No. 5 (September 1968), 290–1.

[5] U.S., Department of Housing and Urban Development, *Workable Program for Community Improvement, Answers on Citizen Participation*, Program Guide 7, February, 1966, pp. 1 and 6.

[6] David Austin, "Study of Resident Participants in Twenty Community Action Agencies," CAP Grant 9499.

[7] Robert Coles, "Social Struggle and Weariness," *Psychiatry*, XXVII (November 1964), 305–15. I am also indebted to Daniel M. Fox of Harvard University for some of his general insights into therapy being used as a diversion from genuine citizen participation.

[8] See, Gordon Fellman, "Neighborhood Protest of an Urban Highway," *Journal of the American Institute of Planners*, XXXV, No. 2 (March 1969), 118–22.

[9] James V. Cunningham, "Resident Participation, Unpublished Report prepared for the Ford Foundation, August 1967, p. 54.

[10] Interview with Maxine Kurtz, Technical Director, Denver CDA.

[11] U.S., Department of Housing and Urban Development, "Citizen Participation in Model Cities," *Technical Assistance Bulletin*, No. 3 (December 1968).

[12] Organization for Social and Technical Innovation, *Six-Month Progress Report to Office of Economic Opportunity, Region 1*, February 1, 1969, pp. 27, 28, and 35.

[13] In Cambridge, Massachusetts, city hall offered to share power with residents and anticipated the need for a period in which a representative citizens' group could be engaged, and the ambiguities of authority, structure, and process would be resolved. At the request of the mayor, HUD allowed the city to spend several months of Model Cities planning funds for community organization activities. During these months, staff from the city manager's office also helped the residents draft a city ordinance that created a CDA composed of sixteen elected residents and eight appointed public and private agency representatives. This resident-dominated body has the power to hire and fire CDA staff, approve all plans, review all model city budgets and contracts, set policy, and so forth. The ordinance, which was unanimously passed by the city council also includes a requirement that all Model City plans must be approved by a majority of residents in the neighborhood through a referendum. Final approval power rests with the city council by federal statute.

[14] U.S., Office of Economic Opportunity, *OEO Instruction, Participation of the Poor in the Planning, Conduct and Evaluation of Community Action Programs* (Washington, D.C.: December 1, 1968), pp. 1–2.

[15] Adam Walinsky, "Review of *Maximum Feasible Misunderstanding*" by Daniel P. Moynihan, New York Times *Book Review*, February 2, 1969.

[16] For thoughtful academic analyses of some of the potentials and pitfalls of emerging neighborhood control models, see, Alan Altshuler, "The Demand For Participation in Large American Cities," An Unpublished Paper prepared for the Urban Institute, December 1968; and Hans B. C. Spiegel and Stephen D. Mittenthal, "Neighborhood Power and Control, Implications for Urban Planning," A Report prepared for the Department of Housing and Urban Development, November 1968.

[23]

Examining the policy-action relationship

Susan Barrett and Colin Fudge

Public agencies often tend to be viewed as rule-bound and inflexible bureaucratic machines which grind on regardless of changing problems and circumstances, concerned more with their own procedures than with the public they are intended to serve. It is easy to find anecdotal horror stories: examples of 'buck-passing' between welfare agencies, exasperating delay in obtaining planning permission, or housing allocation rules applied to the level of absurdity. Public agencies cannot expect to be immune from public scrutiny and criticism, and failure or crisis is inevitably more newsworthy than adequacy, efficiency or success. However, it is not easy to find ways of measuring the relative incidence of 'failure' among the whole range of activities and services performed satisfactorily by public agencies. As far as the more routine services are concerned, these may only be noticed when something goes wrong – or they fail to be provided. At the same time, the image is perhaps symptomatic of a more fundamental anxiety about the effectiveness of public policy and government in general. Government, whether national, regional or local, appears to be adept at making statements of intention, but what happens on the ground often falls a long way short of the original aspirations. Government either seems unable to put its policy into effect as intended, or finds that its interventions and actions have unexpected or counter-productive outcomes which create new problems. Blame for the ineffectiveness of government intervention tends to be directed either at those responsible for policy-making, for constantly producing the 'wrong' policy, or at the implementing agencies for being, apparently, unable or unwilling to act.

At one level, concern about effectiveness centres around the question of the role and scope of government in an advanced industrial society. This includes differing ideological positions about the role of the state in society and debate focusing on the appropriate level of intervention assuming the continuation of a mixed economy. Even from the latter point of view, it has been argued that

Policy and Action

government is trying to influence and control more than it has the material or political resources to achieve, resulting in diminishing marginal returns and policy failure.[1] It has also been argued that uncertain or counter-productive policy outcomes can be attributed to increasing social and economic complexity and inter-relatedness of activities in society.[2] At a more prosaic level, lack of effectiveness is equated with incompetence and inefficiency. It is suggested that the bureaucratic structure and style of government agencies are intrinsically unsuited to many of the tasks such agencies attempt or are expected to perform.[3] Alternatively, it is argued, lack of competence, resulting in unresponsiveness or inappropriate responses, is due to an absence of appropriate skills and adequate management in the public sector,[4] or, at worst, the fact that public agencies provide a protected environment for the inept.

Two distinct themes run through debates about government effectiveness. On the one hand, concern centres on the appropriateness of public intervention and the relevance of public policy in relation to problems and issues, implying the need for a better understanding of the implications of public intervention and, thence, 'better' policy. On the other hand, criticism focuses on the *processes* of policy-making and administration, implying the need for increased policy-making skills and better management and co-ordination amongst public agencies.

This is our starting point. In this introductory review we begin by looking at the way in which practitioners and academics have responded to criticism and these expressions of concern and at how, through developments in the study of policy, policy-making processes and the management of public sector organizations and agencies,[5] attention has become focused on the 'problem' of implementation and the processes of putting policy into effect. We then go on to examine in more detail some recent approaches to the study of implementation with reference to selected literature, and to consider how well the conceptualization of implementation as 'putting policy into effect' seems to fit with what happens in practice. We argue that much of the existing literature tends to take a 'managerial' perspective; the problems of implementation are defined in terms of co-ordination, control or obtaining 'compliance' with policy. Such a policy-centred or 'top down' view of the process treats implementers as 'agents' for policy-makers and tends to play down issues such as power relations, conflicting interests and value systems between individuals and agencies responsible for making policy and those responsible for taking action. In the final sections of the chapter, we introduce two alternative ways of viewing the policy-action relationship: as a negotiating process and as a process of action and response. We suggest that, rather than treating implementation as the transmission of policy into a series of consequential actions, the policy-action relationship needs to be regarded as a process of interaction and negotiation, taking place over time, between those seeking to put policy into effect and those upon whom action depends.

4

Examining the policy-action relationship

This chapter is intended to form a background for the individual contributions which follow in Part Two. In the concluding chapter (Part Three), we attempt to draw out some of the themes and issues raised by the contributions and to suggest some avenues for further work.

Effectiveness, administrative efficiency and the development of policy studies

Those in government, whether elected representatives or employees, are only too aware of their public image and share at least some of the above concerns about the effectiveness of government. Over the last ten years or so, increasing attention has been paid within government agencies to improving and enhancing what might be termed the 'policy content' of government decision-making; to improving decision-making processes and the co-ordination of policy and to streamlining management structures, administrative operations and service delivery. For example, in the mid-1960s, the Planning Advisory Group's[6] review of the land use planning system resulted in the introduction, in the Town and Country Planning Act of 1968,[7] of the concept of a strategic plan that was a statement of reasoned policy, rather than a map of land use zones. Similar developments have occurred in the field of social services, transport, the health service and housing.[8] Policy 'capacity' has been increased by the employment of research staff in both central and local government, whose function is to review, evaluate and formulate alternative courses of action (whether in a service department or in special Research and Intelligence Units). Within central government, these developments are exemplified by the post-Fulton creation of departmental Policy Units, the establishment of the Central Policy Review Staff (CPRS) within the Cabinet Office, and the development of Programme Analysis Review (PAR) in the early 1970s.[9] At the same time there has been an increasing tendency for central government to require or ask for statements of policy and a reasoned justification of the public programmes carried out at local level, as a basis for resource allocation decisions – for example in Housing Strategies and Investment Programmes.[10]

The explicit linkage of policy objectives and resource allocation derives from the Planning Programming and Budgeting System (PPBS) concept developed in a number of American business schools and the Rand Corporation and used first in the public sector in the United States Defence Department in 1961.[11] PPBS was aimed at improving both the *rationality* of public decision-making and the *effectiveness* of action via the purposive direction of expenditure towards clear objectives and the monitoring of performance in relation to those objectives. These ideas, and the techniques imported with them, have had a strong influence on the whole approach to managing British central and local government activities, for example in the corporate philosophy which blossomed in the early 1970s,[12] and which was endorsed in the Bains report.[13]

5

Policy and Action

Corporate planning and management also attempted to improve awareness of the interconnectedness of public policy and the co-ordination of service delivery. Corporate plans – the comprehensive statement of an agency's policies and programmes – aimed not only to provide an explicit statement of policy against which performance could be measured and evaluated (and policy thereby improved), but also to avoid problems of contradictory policy being operated by different departments and to assist in the dovetailing of interdependent programmes.

Opinions vary about the effects and effectiveness of these developments.[14] There may be more rational processes, but it is argued that through the proliferation of planning activity more energy has been expended in producing plans and programmes and in reorganizing management structures than in actually getting things done or paying attention to fundamental questions of policy relevance.

So far we have focused on government's attempts to respond to criticisms of its effectiveness by placing more emphasis on policy development, on increasing the rationality of decision-making processes and on administrative efficiency. The same concerns have also been taken up in the academic arena and are reflected in the development of 'policy studies' as an academic and applied subject for study and research.[15] Perhaps three main dimensions of intellectual concern can be identified, although these overlap, are interconnected and are not necessarily as clearly distinguished as the categorization would make them appear:

1 *Policy analysis*, concerned with understanding and explaining the substance of policy content and policy decisions and the way in which policy decisions are made, and including the prescription of methodological frameworks and techniques for improving the substance and process of decision-making.

2 *Evaluative studies*, concerned with the understanding and assessment of policy outcomes and impacts as a basis for evaluating policy performance – its relevance and effectiveness. This area embraces the development of economic and social indicators, performance measures, evaluative techniques, for example, cost benefit analysis, and issues concerning the methodology of evaluative research and its application in political decision-making environments.

3 *Organizational studies*, concerned with understanding the operation of political and administrative organizations, the relationship between structures, functions and systems of management, the behaviour of individuals and groups within organizational frameworks, and inter-organizational relationships and behaviour. This area, too, includes the prescription of organizational and management structures and styles of administration aimed at improving performance.

6

Examining the policy-action relationship

Heclo has identified three sources of impetus for the study of policy: 'downwards from a comparative politics seeking to become more empirical, upwards from a decision making approach seeking to become more generalized, and across from either disciplines seeking to become more truthful to the complexity of events'.[16] Whilst economics and political science can be regarded as the key 'parent' disciplines of policy studies, more recent commentators point to the need for a synthesis of the various theoretical strands contributing to explanatory developments, involving the interaction of political, economic, environmental and organizational variables.[17] This kind of approach to the study of policy is associated with a shift in emphasis from comparative studies, which provide explanations of relationships at a high level of generality, to the use of detailed case studies of particular policies or events. Such studies examine in detail the origins and objectives of a particular 'piece of policy' and seek to explain how and why decisions came to be made, or events turned out the way they did.[18] Inevitably, by turning to the detail of events, such studies point to the need for theories that take account of individual and group behaviour within institutional settings. Similarly, they focus attention on administrative structures and the way in which individuals respond and behave in bureaucratic organizations, involving issues such as accountability, rewards and incentives, organizational and professional 'cultures' and limits of authority and control. They also raise questions about the environment in which policy is being made – the context of physical, economic, political and social circumstances – and the individuals, groups and interests upon which policy impinges.

In the field of applied policy analysis, analysts concerned to prescribe for the improvement of public policy-making still espouse concepts of rational choice as an ideal for professional policy-makers and administrators, perhaps, notably, in the case of Dror.[19] At the same time, various attempts (starting with Charles Lindblom's ideas on incrementalism)[20] have been made to relate the process of decision-making to its political and organizational context, and to take on board theories about political and organizational behaviour and response. Ideas about strategic choice and coping with complex interagency inter-dependence,[21] or Etzioni's 'mixed scanning' approach to decision-making,[22] can be regarded as attempts to find *practical methodologies* that utilize more behavioural explanations of the policy-making process.

Concern with complexity and the capability to respond have perhaps been the other main stimuli for development in the prescriptive field. Two main directions can be distinguished: a cybernetics approach, and a behavioural approach. The cybernetics approach applies systems theory to organizational and political systems, and also embraces theories of organizational behaviour. Its prescriptions seek to achieve efficient and effective responses by creating organizational and management structures and processes that are capable of dealing with the variety of demands placed upon them. On the one hand, the

7

Policy and Action

cybernetics approach has been taken up by political scientists interested in exploring models of political communication and control;[23] on the other hand, it is associated with developing the technological capacity to assimilate, process and communicate information through the use of real-time computer systems, for example, as advocated by Beer.[24] An alternative perspective is that taken by such people as Vickers or Schon[25] and, on a more prescriptive note, by Etzioni and Friedman.[26] They are really arguing that responsiveness is a matter of attitude – individual and organizational – and that new attitudes and patterns of behaviour are required to shake off conventional bureaucratic responses. Much of the prescriptive content is concerned with altering systems of rewards and incentives in order to effect changes of this kind.

A number of points seem to us to emerge from developments in the policy studies field which have particular relevance for our consideration of implementation and the policy-action relationship. First, the study of policy indicates the complexity of the policy process. Its elements might be described as:

1   an environmental system, from which demands and needs arise, and upon which policy seeks to have an effect
2   a political system in which policy decisions are made
3   an organizational system through which policy is mediated and executed

The problem is to understand and explain how these systems operate and interact – what influences what, when, and how. Since each system is dynamic, the nature of interaction will also vary over time.

Second, there is a distinction between explanation and prescription. It may be difficult to find robust explanations which hold in a wide variety of circumstances, but it is even more difficult to prescribe in a way which accommodates reality without merely mirroring its ineffectiveness.

Third, linked to this is the question of methodologies and perspectives. Allison summarizes the problem thus:

> Conceptual models not only fix the mesh of the nets through which the analyst drags the material in order to explain a particular action; they also direct him to cast his nets in select ponds, at certain depths, in order to catch the fish he is after.[27]

If what you see depends on where you are standing and which way you are looking, then a pluralist approach – both in the use of conceptual models or theories and in type of studies undertaken (comparative as well as in-depth case studies) – seems an essential prerequisite to understanding what is going on, especially if it is complicated.

Fourth, and of most significance to the study of implementation, until recently most policy analysts (whether operating in a descriptive or prescriptive mode) have tended to equate policy *decisions* with action.

8

Examining the policy-action relationship

Decisions are seen as the outputs of the policy process, the assumption being that once made they will be translated into action. Only lately (and largely through the influence of detailed case studies of the type cited earlier) have policy analysts started to focus on what practitioners are only too well aware of, and what Dunsire has termed the 'implementation gap'.[28] Policy does not implement itself, and attention is now being directed beyond policy *making* towards the processes by which policy is translated into action and the factors influencing those processes. This leads on to our last point.

A great deal of research and a huge literature exist on the analysis of organizations: understanding the way they operate, prescribing administrative structures, examining the behaviour of groups and individuals in an organizational setting. Dunsire has pointed out that some of this literature recognizes a distinct implementation process, and that many of the issues and ideas currently being seized upon as 'new' by policy analysts and practitioners have actually been around for a long time.[29] However, therein lies part of the problem. Much of the organizational literature treats the implementation of policy as a separate process more or less in a vacuum. Policy is made somewhere else and handed in, so to speak, to the administrative system which then executes it. The implementation process is seen as inextricably bound up with organizational structures and processes, that is, policy comes in at the top and is successively refined and translated into operating instructions as it moves down the hierarchy to the 'operatives' at the bottom. The desire to separate 'politics' and 'administration', whilst in many ways discredited at an intellectual level,[30] still forms part of the conventional wisdom among professionals and administrators in the public service. Similarly, the stages of implementation tend to be associated automatically with a hierarchical 'chain of command' and this association has no doubt had an influence on the way in which the process of policy implementation is perceived, by practitioners and researchers alike, and hence the tendency to take it for granted as an automatic follow-on from policy decisions. Whilst the literature has much to say about such matters as the way in which controls and incentives operate to ensure compliance or the operation of discretion, behavioural issues tend to be dealt with in terms of a single organization whose basic purpose is to administer policy or to carry out specific functions. Thus implementation is regarded as a matter of communication, channels of communication and control systems to ensure compliance.

Weberian ideas about hierarchical organization and management are so firmly embedded in the conventional wisdom of public organizations that it is difficult to stand back and examine critically some of the assumptions being made. Many of the attempts to improve the performance of public agencies follow the logic of organizational studies, assuming that if management structures and processes, channels of communication and clarity of communication are 'right', effective action will be assured.

9

Policy and Action

Implementation and action

So, how do we start to look at the problem? What is meant by 'implementation'? Pressman and Wildavsky, in their study of the attempts of the US Economic Development Agency to implement a job creation programme in Oakland, California, initially defined the process thus: 'Implementation may be viewed as a process of interaction between the setting of goals and actions geared to achieving them.'[31]

However, they qualified the definition in the following terms:

> Implementation does not refer to creating the initial conditions. Legislation has to be passed and funds committed before implementation takes place to secure the predicted outcome. . . . To emphasise the actual existence of initial conditions we must distinguish a program from a policy. . . . A program exists when the initial conditions – the 'if' stage of the policy hypothesis – have been met. The word program signifies the conversion of a hypothesis into *governmental* action. The initial premises of the hypothesis have been authorised. The degree to which the predicted consequences (the 'then' stage) take place we will call implementation.
> [emphasis added]

They go on to say:

> Programs make the theories operational by forging the first link in the causal chain connecting actions to objectives. Given X we act to obtain Y. *Implementation, then, is the ability to forge subsequent links in the causal chain so as to obtain the desired results.*[32]
> [emphasis added]

We have quoted their definition at some length because it embodies assumptions most commonly held about implementation.[33] First, they assume a series of logical steps – a progression from intention through decision to action – and clearly see implementation starting where policy stops. Second, they distinguish two steps in formulating intentions: policy-making – their 'initial conditions' – and the creation of programmes which form the 'inputs' to their implementation process.[34] We shall return to this point presently. Third, they see implementation as a process of putting policy (or in their case, programmes) into effect, mainly concerned with co-ordinating and managing the various elements required to achieve the desired ends.

Other definitions follow a similar logic. For example, Walter Williams says: 'The agency implementation process includes both *one-time* efforts to convert decisions into operational terms and continuance of efforts over time to raise the quality of the agency's staffs and organisational structure in the field.'[35] And later, in the context of implementation as a research question, he states: 'In its most general form, an inquiry about implementation capability . . .

10

Examining the policy-action relationship

seeks to determine whether an organisation can bring together men and material in a cohesive organisational unit and motivate them in such a way as to carry out the organisation's stated objectives.'[36] This is echoed by Van Meter and Van Horn in an article which reviews the field and attempts to provide a conceptual framework or model of the implementation process: 'policy implementation encompasses those actions by public and private individuals (or groups) that are directed at the achievement of objectives set forth in prior policy decisions.'[37]

One immediate issue is raised by comparing Pressman and Wildavsky's definition with the others. They take programmes – the means or proposed activities by which intentions are to be translated into action – rather than policy (in the sense of a statement of intentions or objectives) as inputs to the process. They state that implementation cannot start until policy has been made operational through the passing of legislation and the committing of resources to it, whereas the others refer more loosely to 'decisions' and 'objectives'. Pressman and Wildavsky thus explicitly exclude from the implementation process what they nevertheless refer to as 'governmental action' to convert policy intentions into programmes. Williams, on the other hand, explicitly includes 'efforts to convert decisions into operational terms' in the implementation process. This is not merely semantic juggling, but raises some fundamental questions about the definition of policy itself. What is being implemented and where does policy-making stop and implementation start?

What do we mean by policy? A political intention as expressed, say, in a political party manifesto? A formal decision expressed as legislation or a local council resolution? Operational policy expressed in government circulars, managerial statements or detailed administrative procedures providing 'rules' for the carrying out of specific tasks? Clearly, policy is all these things and where policy stops and implementation starts depends on where you are standing and which way you are looking. To some politicians, policy is synonymous with the party manifesto and everything that follows is implementation. For executive officers involved in local service delivery, administrative procedures may well appear to be policy in so far as they comprise the framework governing the scope for action. On this basis, implementation is the process of successive refinement and translation of policy into specific procedures and tasks directed at putting policy intentions into effect. In any study of implementation, it seems important to examine the various stages in this process, who is involved, in what roles and with what motives. It is particularly important to investigate what is happening to policy as it is successively refined and translated. How far do detailed frameworks for action – legislative, administrative, procedural – reflect or relate to original intentions; that is, what exactly *is* being implemented? If what is being implemented is different from the original policy intention, is this 'good', for example, demonstrating that policy was flexible enough to be tailored to the

11

Policy and Action

local circumstances, or 'bad' in that the original policy goals have been distorted in the process?

These questions are considered, directly or indirectly, in several of the contributions to this volume, notably in the chapters by Barrett (examining local authorities' implementation of the Community Land Act 1975), Fudge (focusing on local elected members' experience in implementing a political manifesto), and Bishop (looking at the process of briefing architects for school building programmes). Indeed, Hill returns to the theme of the policy-implementation distinction for a more general examination of the validity and implications of attempts to conceptualize implementation as a 'rational' process of putting policy into effect. Even where studies are undertaken to evaluate outcomes in relation to policy intentions, there is no guarantee that the results of such studies will be utilized by policy-makers. Smith, in his chapter, discusses how and why this situation arises.

Our discussion has so far centred on this definition of implementation: a policy-centred approach, by which policy is the starting point, the trigger for action, and implementation a logical step-by-step progression from policy intention to action. This approach might be defined as 'the policy-makers' perspective', since it represents what policy-makers are trying to do to put policy into effect. As noted earlier, this perspective tends to be associated with hierarchical concepts of organization; policy emanates from the 'top' (or centre) and is transmitted down the hierarchy (or to the periphery) and translated into more specific rules and procedures as it goes to guide or control action at the bottom (or on the ground). However, in our view this perspective is open to question. It assumes that policy comes from the top and is the starting point for implementation and action. This, we would argue, is not necessarily the case: policy may be a response to pressures and problems experienced on the ground. Equally, policy may be developed from specific innovations, that is, action precedes policy. Not all action relates to a specific or explicit policy.[38] The hierarchical view of implementation also implies that implementers are agents for policy-makers and are therefore in a *compliant* relationship to policy-makers. But in many instances – especially in the public policy field – those upon whom action depends are *not* in any hierarchical association with those making policy. By definition, public policy is often aimed at directing or intervening in the activities of private interests and agencies. Implementation agencies will thus, in many instances, be autonomous or semi-autonomous, with their own interests and priorities to pursue and their own policy-making role.

We would thus argue that it is essential to look at implementation not solely in terms of putting policy into effect, but also in terms of observing what actually happens or gets done and seeking to understand how and why. This kind of action perspective takes 'what is done' as central, focuses attention on the behaviour or actions of groups and individuals and the determinants of that

12

Examining the policy-action relationship

behaviour, and seeks to examine the degree to which action relates to policy, rather than assuming it to follow from policy. From this perspective, implementation (or action) may be regarded as a series of *responses*: to ideological commitment, to environmental pressures, or to pressures from other agencies (groups) seeking to influence or control action.

Distinguishing between a 'policy-centred' and an 'action-centred' approach to implementation also points to the importance of the interaction between those seeking to influence the actions of others and those upon whom influence is being brought to bear to act in a particular way, whether within or between organizations. This involves considering implementation in terms of *power relations* and different mechanisms for gaining or avoiding influence or control.

In the next section, we look in more detail at what is involved in 'putting policy into effect' before moving on to consider alternative ways of conceptualizing the implementation process.

Implementation as putting policy into effect

This is what policy-makers are concerned about; what they are trying to do. It is, therefore, not surprising that much of the implementation literature, particularly that using policy case studies, takes policy as its starting point and considers implementation in terms of the problems or factors that 'get in the way' of its execution.

So what is involved in putting policy into effect? Take, for example, building a house extension. The task will require money, materials, skills and time; it will also involve obtaining building regulations consent. In some circumstances it may involve obtaining planning permission or complying with public health regulations; it will certainly demand planning and management to make sure that the job is done effectively. Only the most intrepid DIY expert is likely to tackle such a job him or herself. Most people would hire a builder, in which case the task will involve communicating what is wanted to the builder, deciding how much discretion will be left to him or her in the execution and deciding whether and how to check or control performance.

Putting policy into effect is therefore basically dependent on:

1   knowing what you want to do
2   the availability of the required resources
3   the ability to marshal and control these resources to achieve the desired end
4   if others are to carry out the tasks, communicating what is wanted and controlling their performance

Just thinking for a moment about what can go wrong in the execution of this kind of job provides a useful starting point for the more general consideration

13

Policy and Action

of implementation issues. In the first place, the householder's aspirations may exceed the resources he has available to carry out the job. In public policy terms, it is certainly not unknown for central government to pass legislation (apparently) without considering the manpower implications for the local agencies which will be responsible for its implementation, or for inadequate financial resources to be allocated in relation to the original policy goals. For example, in her chapter, Barrett argues that one of the reasons for local authorities' lack of activity in buying and selling development land under the Community Land Act 1975 was the low level of financial resources devoted to the scheme by central government. Another example might be the low level of local authority activity in response to the part of the Control of Pollution Act 1974 which empowers them to obtain and make public information about emissions to the air from industrial processes. This was included in the Act in response to suggestions from a Royal Commission, an official committee and various pressure groups, yet it is costly for local authorities to implement and the government provided no new resources for this purpose.[39] Indeed, it is frequently argued (particularly in central-local government debates) that 'central' policy-makers show a certain duplicity in exhorting local agencies, or in passing legislation which requires local agencies to provide services which the 'centre' knows are unlikely to be afforded, at the same time as other policy is being promulgated to cut public expenditure or reduce manpower. Such an argument, of course, raises further questions about the nature and role of policy, and reinforces our argument that implementation cannot be treated as an administrative process in a vacuum. Indeed, the issue of policy intentions crops up in several of the contributions and we return to this theme in our concluding chapter.

Linked to the availability or provision of resources is the 'legitimation' or obtaining of clearance for action. Going back to the house extension, what if planning permission is refused? It is quite probable that the householder's original ideas do not comply with some public policy or regulation and he will have to negotiate a compromise and modify his original intentions. Alternatively, his neighbour may object to the proposed extension and put pressure on the householder to modify his plans. Government policy, too, is likely to come up against problems of obtaining a mandate, and the process of legitimizing action is also likely to involve compromise and modification of the original intentions, either as a condition for obtaining an electoral or parliamentary mandate, or as a result of pressure from powerful interests affected by the policy concerned. The chapter on the Community Land Scheme again provides a useful example. The policy was highly controversial, both ideologically and in terms of development industry interests potentially affected. The original intentions (as set out in the Land White Paper) were substantially modified during the drafting of legislation and the passage of the Bill through Parliament as a result of pressures stemming from these sources.

14

Examining the policy-action relationship

It is interesting in this context to recap on Pressman and Wildavsky's definitions, whereby they regard both the legitimation and provision of resources as 'starting conditions' *preceding* implementation proper. We would argue, certainly on the basis of the material in this volume, that what happens during these processes is fundamental in helping to explain subsequent actions and reactions, and should therefore be included in any study of 'implementation'. Montjoy and O'Toole go even further, to argue from an analysis of evidence of implementation problems in the US General Accounting Office's reports that: 'From one perspective it appears that the surest way to avoid intra-organisational implementation problems is to establish a specific mandate and provide sufficient resources.'[40] By 'mandate' they refer to the legitimizing and operationalizing of policy objectives.

Assuming that Pressman and Wildavsky's starting conditions are satisfied, the process is then a matter of assembling, co-ordinating and managing the resources necessary to implement the policy or purpose. To organize the building of the house extension, it will be necessary to assemble the appropriate skills for the job to be done, to co-ordinate them in the correct sequence and to programme the activities over time. If a small builder is being used, he will probably employ bricklayers, plasterers and decorators, but may need to subcontract specialist parts of the work, for example, joinery, plumbing or electrical installations. He has to sort out the best way in which to order the various tasks involved in the job, to co-ordinate manpower and materials and to programme the whole series of activities over time. He also has to instruct or brief all those involved. The example demonstrates that even a relatively straightforward job involves a considerable amount of planning and co-ordination where a variety of 'actors' or implementation agencies is involved. The situation would be even further complicated if the house owner in fact owned several properties, was attempting to improve them all at the same time, and was operating through a firm of managing agents. Obvious parallels can be drawn with public policy implementation: many of the problems of putting policy into effect stem from the multiplicity of agencies involved in implementation. Such problems have been well illustrated in Pressman and Wildavsky's study referred to earlier.

Pressman and Wildavsky argue that one of the key reasons for 'policy failure' is that policy-makers generally underestimate the complexity and difficulty of co-ordinating the tasks and agencies involved in implementing programmes. One reason may be the tendency to equate implementation with the execution of policy in a hierarchical organizational context – the 'top down' model already referred to. Both Hood[41] and Dunsire[42] have shown how difficult are the problems of organizational control, even within unitary hierarchical organizations. It therefore follows that these problems will be multiplied by inter-organizational complications.

Lack of co-ordination often tends to be equated with lack of, or inadequate,

15

Policy and Action

communication; the assumption being that if intentions are spelled out clearly, and the right organizational channels established for the transmission of policy to those responsible for its implementation, then the policy will be put into effect. It is certainly true that one of the most frequent complaints from those 'in the field' is that it is difficult to tell what a particular piece of policy really means. For example, development controllers in a local authority planning department may find it difficult to operate the planning policies set out in the development plan if these are presented as general intentions such as 'to safeguard local employment opportunities', rather than being spelled out in terms of how the development controllers are expected to act when faced with applications for development, for example: 'priority should be given to applications for extension or rebuilding of existing industrial concerns'. Some of the problems of interpreting policy at the 'street' level are discussed by Underwood in her chapter on development control.

However, pleas for better communication or 'briefing' often mask more fundamental issues, such as policy ambiguity; conflict of value systems between professions or agencies; ambiguity of roles and responsibilities between individuals or agencies; scope or limits of discretion. This is well illustrated in Bishop's chapter on the briefing of architects for educational building programmes in a sample of local authorities, and in Towell's account of attempts to implement improvements in the psychiatric services of a large mental hospital. Indeed, we shall presently be arguing that these more 'political' aspects of interpersonal and interagency relations are crucial in explaining policy outcomes or understanding the implementation process.

However, communication figures strongly as an implementation issue not only in terms of making it clear to implementers what they are supposed to do, but also because of the *view* of implementation as separate from policy-making, in which policy is made by the policy-makers and has to be transmitted to those responsible for carrying it out, who may be in a variety of different agencies. Hence the association of communication with co-ordination. Dunsire points to the importance of distinguishing a hierarchy of *tasks*, meaning the 'unbundling' of policy into the whole collection and sequence of tasks necessary for its execution (which he sees as a progression from the general to the specific), from a hierarchy of *authority*. He refers back to the ideas of March and Simon, who distinguished between hierarchies of command related to the central functions of an organization, and the co-ordination of activities to execute particular programmes.[43]

For example, going back to our house extension, the householder or builder who is subcontracting the various parts of the job sees each task as part of an interconnected programme. However, those to whom the tasks are being assigned will tend to see the tasks as separate jobs to be fitted in to their own programmes and priorities. The builder wants the electrical wiring to be fitted in after the basic structure is completed but before the plastering and joinery.

Examining the policy-action relationship

The electrical contractor, however, does not organize his business around the building of house extensions, but takes on a wide variety of electrical installation jobs. He will have his own 'rating' of different jobs, his own problems of managing skills and manpower to meet different requirements. He will thus assign an electrician to the house extension job according to where that job sits in his 'queue' of work and when the particular skills required become available. Successful co-ordination of the electrical work into the whole building will thus require not only communication, in the sense of transmitting to the electrician what is wanted and in the feedback of information about the electrician's workload and capability to take on the job, but also co-ordination and perhaps compromise to arrive at a mutually satisfactory programme. Pressman and Wildavsky place a great deal of emphasis on this idea of implementation as a complicated assembly job of tasks and agencies, which Dunsire refers to as:

> creating and establishing links between separate bodies – *making* a chain, not just using one; a chain which, in principle, might be made up of different sets of bodies for each implementation exercise, though the more often a chain is 'forged' the more easily it is 'forged' the next time, until it may be virtually permanent.[44]

From this view of the process, the main thrust of the argument is that things have to be *made* to happen. Implementation will not automatically follow from policy decisions but needs to be treated as a positive, purposive process in itself. The theme is echoed by Bardach; one of the main conclusions he draws from the study of a relatively successful programme of mental health reform in California is that substantial effort and continuity of effort is required to follow policy through from intention to action – to keep up the momentum and maintain the 'links in the chain'.[45] These aspects are highlighted, in particular, in two of our contributions: Davies' account of the development and implementation of employment policy in a local authority, and Fudge's account of local council members' involvement in the implementation of their party manifesto. Whilst written from very different perspectives, both these contributions focus on policy *innovation* and implementation at the local level and both point to the importance of actively seeking out or *creating* resources, maintaining or *re-creating* legitimacy and motivation during the implementation process, even where these factors were present when the policy was initiated.

So here we have a view of the implementation process as a sequence of events 'triggered off' by a policy decision, involving the translation of policy into operational tasks to be carried out by a variety of actors and agencies, and substantial co-ordinating activity to ensure that resources are available and that things happen as intended. This conceptualization strongly underlies some of the more recent literature which has shifted from the diagnosis of policy failure

17

Policy and Action

to attempts to identify ways in which failure can be prevented. For example, Williams exhorts policy-makers to pay more attention to 'implementation capacity' and sets out a checklist of questions:

(a) How well articulated is the policy to the implementers?
(b) How capable are the policy-makers of developing meaningful guidelines for and assistance to implementers?
(c) How capable are the implementers to develop and carry out new policy?
(d) How much ability/power do either have to change the other?[46]

Sabatier and Mazmanian take an even bolder line in an article entitled 'The conditions of effective implementation: a guide to accomplishing policy objectives'.[47] They identify five conditions which must be satisfied if implementation is to be effective:

1. The program is based on a sound theory relating changes in target group behaviour to the achievements of the desired end state (objectives).
2. The statute (or other basic policy decision) contains unambiguous policy directives and structures the implementation process so as to maximize the likelihood that target groups will perform as desired.
3. The leaders of the implementation agencies possess substantial managerial and political skill and are committed to statutory goals.
4. The program is actively supported by organized constituency groups and by a few key legislators (or the chief executive) throughout the implementation process, with the courts being neutral or supportive.
5. The relative priority of statutory objectives is not significantly undermined over time by the emergence of conflicting public policies or by change in relevant socio-economic conditions that undermine the statute's 'technical' theory or political support.[48]

This article demonstrates only too clearly the weakness of this 'recipe book' approach; the sort of 'conditions' for effective implementation prescribed are precisely those which empirical evidence suggests are not met in the real world. The authors' underlying argument is that problems can be avoided by anticipating complications and difficulties in advance. But this assumes that those responsible for administering policy are in a position of total and 'rational' control, that implementation takes place in a static environment and in a politics-free world.[49]

Looking, for example, at Sabatier and Mazmanian's list of conditions, expressions like 'desired end state', 'unambiguous policy directives', 'statutory objectives' rightly imply that if only policy goals are unambiguous then implementation will be easier. However, there are many good reasons for expecting ambiguity. Even when policy-makers are able to express their policy goals clearly, relating means to ends, they are likely to face a policy-making process in which compromise with other actors and their interests undermine

Examining the policy-action relationship

this clarity.. Many of the features which Sabatier and Mazmanian identify as essential for 'good' policies are precisely those which political processes are likely to undermine. Sabatier and Mazmanian themselves refer to many of the leading American implementation studies dealing with issues like air pollution control, job creation, urban renewal and education reform. These are all issues which were controversial from their initial introduction into the political agenda, and have remained so throughout their history. To suggest that there could have been better policies if attention had been paid to Sabatier and Mazmanian's prescription is to say that they should have been depoliticized. This is like the plaintive cry often heard in Britain that politics should be 'kept out' of education or planning or the health service. Little account appears to be taken of the political processes already referred to earlier by which policy is formulated and 'legitimized'. These processes do not stop when initial policy decisions are made, but continue to influence policy during implementation in terms of the behaviour of those implementing policy and those affected by policy. This is one of the main themes of Barrett's chapter on the implementation of the Community Land Scheme, and is also discussed in Boddy's account of the relations between central government and the Building Societies between 1974 and 1979.

In particular, the presumptions skate over the whole question of consensus, either in a party political or ideological sense, or in terms of organizational/ sectional interests affected by policy. Whilst Chase,[50] in a recent article, does recognize the difficulty of obtaining compliance where policy or a programme is to be implemented by agencies whose interests do not necessarily coincide with those of the policy-makers, solutions to this difficulty are seen in terms of:

* gaining credibility
* reference to higher authority
* financial incentives

He still tends to ignore the relationship between interests, politics and the balance of power between those making, implementing and affected by policy.

We have discussed at some length the concept of implementation as putting policy into effect, since it is the prevailing perspective from which implementation and its problems tend to be viewed – reflecting, perhaps, the origins of concern with 'policy failure'. Seeing implementation as a series of logical steps from intention to action also provides a useful heuristic device through which to identify issues and questions about 'what is going on'. We have thus attempted in this section both to outline the conventional wisdoms and to point to the strengths and weaknesses of this view of the process. Although we have been critical of the 'recipe book' approach presented in some of the recent literature, its analysis has helped us to sharpen our own focus and pinpoint more clearly alternative avenues of investigation. First, it has focused our attention on the need to examine more closely the whole question of

19

Policy and Action

consensus, control and compliance as essentially a *political*, rather than *managerial* issue. Second, it has led us to re-examine the conceptualization of the implementation process itself.

If we are faced with the phenomenon of agencies upon whom action depends, but which are ideologically hostile and/or not susceptible to direct control, then implementation must be considered in terms of the nature of inter- and intra-organizational power relations, the interests of implementing agencies and the people in them. At the same time, it is clear that the political processes shaping policy have an important bearing on what actually gets done, when and by whom, and we need to look more closely at what might be termed the 'politics of policy'. In the remaining two sections of this introductory chapter, we put forward some ideas about alternative ways of conceptualizing implementation

* as a negotiating process
* as action and response

and look briefly at the issues that come to the fore from these different points of view. In doing this, we are raising questions for readers to take forward to Part Two, rather than offering the kind of critical review undertaken so far, and we return to a more detailed discussion of the issues in our concluding chapter.

Implementation as a negotiating process

The preceding conceptualization suggests that control over policy execution or the ability to ensure compliance with policy objectives is a key factor determining implementation 'success' or 'failure'. We have already made reference to one or two examples of the substantial literature that exists on questions of administrative control and compliance within and between organizations. Some of the literature oriented towards public administration focuses specifically on issues such as the range of controls available to government and factors affecting their choice, the choice of appropriate agencies to execute policy, the limits of control and how to cope with discretion.[51] However, much of this material tends to treat problems of control or compliance as purely administrative and 'policy free'. Lack of compliance is seen as recalcitrance, a deliberate and 'natural' reaction to authority. It is assumed that those subject to an administrative system will tend to try to avoid interference with their freedom of action and will look for ways of outwitting the system.[52] It is assumed that control or compliance can only be achieved by producing the 'right' incentives, or through recourse to sanctions and enforcement mechanisms. On this basis, the 'limits' of control depend on the amount of power (resources, legitimacy, authority) to operate sanctions and incentives possessed by one agency *vis-à-vis* those it is seeking to control. Hence, many of the problems which arise in the implementation of public

Examining the policy-action relationship

policy arise because much public policy is dependent for its execution on a variety of actors and agencies which

> whether or not they all belong to a single organisation, exhibit a degree of independence, a relative 'autonomy' as among themselves: either because they are specialised, by skill and equipment or by jurisdiction, and so not substitutable for one another, or because they have their own 'legitimacy' or lines to the outside.[53]

But we would argue that compliance is not only a matter of control, and that compliance in this sense needs to be distinguished from the issue of *consensus* – the degree to which different actors and agencies share value systems and objectives and are thus more or less willing to support and execute particular policies and programmes. For example, going back to the house extension, getting the builder to comply with the specification for the extension may be a matter of incentives and sanctions; but gaining acceptance (or consensus) for the proposal or avoiding conflict and resistance from the next door neighbour is quite a different matter.

Both issues, however, involve notions of negotiation, bargaining and compromise. In order to gain acceptance for his proposal, the householder may have to negotiate and make compromises with his neighbour. Similarly, he may need to bargain with the builder over what will be done for how much. Without total control over resources, agencies and the whole implementation 'environment', those wanting to do something may be forced to compromise their original intentions in order to get any action at all.

If implementation is defined as 'putting policy into effect', that is, action in conformance with policy, then compromise will be seen as policy failure. But if implementation is regarded as 'getting something done', then *performance* rather than conformance is the central objective, and compromise a means of achieving performance albeit at the expense of some of the original intentions. Emphasis thus shifts to the *interaction* between policy-makers and implementers, with negotiation, bargaining and compromise forming central elements in a process that might be characterized as 'the art of the possible'.

What do we mean by negotiation? Who is bargaining with what, for what? Different commentators appear to use the terms in different ways. Pressman and Wildavsky see bargaining as a method of obtaining compliance in the sense of arriving at a shared purpose, that is, consensus:

> Since other actors cannot be coerced, their consent must be obtained. Bargaining must take place to reconcile the differences, with the result that the policy may be modified, even to the point of compromising its original purpose. Coordination in this sense is another word for consent.[54]

Dunsire similarly looks at bargaining as a means of resolving conflicts of objectives or surmounting opposition to a particular course of action. For him,

Policy and Action

bargaining is a process of negotiation where objectives are *traded*, taking place in the interests of reaching agreement when 'none wishes to sacrifice any objectives, yet all have interest in resolving the conflict in the group'.[55] He goes on to say: 'Continuing conflict is acknowledged but immediate problems are resolved without destroying the group.[56]

Thus, these writers see bargaining as a specific form of negotiation which takes place in a context of shared purpose or in recognition of the need to work together. Similar ideas about the exchange or trading of resources within a framework of interdependence underlie recent analyses of intergovernmental relations in Britain.[57] Government agencies are operating, by and large, within a formal or constitutional framework of interdependence which, at least, specifies the distribution and general scope of functions (*intra* and *ultra vires*). Whilst the 'balance of power' inevitably rests with central government (in terms of its constitutional right to establish, disband and determine the functions of other public agencies), it is argued that central government is, nevertheless, dependent on local government agencies of one kind or another to carry out its policy, both by virtue of the autonomy and discretion granted to such agencies by statute, and because of the political and informational resources 'possessed' by the periphery.

Yet Dunsire (referring once more to the ideas of March and Simon) also distinguishes negotiations involving the bargaining or trading of objectives from those aimed at *persuading* some of a group to relinquish voluntarily some or all of their objectives, and from a process of *recourse to power* in which:

> Resolution of an impasse is sought by enlarging the group, or (the same thing) taking the issue out of the small arena into a larger arena, each interest seeking alliances and combinations in the larger arena on the strength of whatever persuading or bargaining counters they hold, perhaps to do with quite other issues than the one in dispute.[58]

The distinctions made here between persuasion, bargaining and 'power games' aimed at increasing leverage (or ability to enforce compliance) are important ones to which we shall return presently. Nevertheless, it must be noted that Dunsire is explicitly writing about implementation within a bureaucratic context. He takes a 'top down' view of the process and sees implementation problems as essentially problems of policy control in a bureaucracy (indeed, this is the title and focus of his second volume). He discusses at length different systems of controls, sanctions and incentives which may be brought into play to achieve compliance with policy; whilst the resolution of conflict features as an aspect of this, it is treated rather as a side issue to the main concern with establishing an effective administrative system.

Bardach, in his book *The Implementation Game*, takes a more machiavellian view of the implementation process. He sees this as:

22

Examining the policy-action relationship

1) a process of assembling the elements required to produce a particular
programmatic outcome, and 2) the playing out of a number of loosely
interrelated games whereby these elements are withheld from or delivered to
the program assembly process on particular terms.[59]

In other words, whilst viewing implementation as an assembly job, he sees the
interaction between the parts as a struggle for influence going on between one
set of actors trying to put policy into effect by influencing and controlling the
actions of others, and another set of actors trying to avoid being influenced or
controlled, except in so far as it fits in with or furthers their own interests.
Bardach, too, regards 'control' as a central concept, but defines control as
being: 'exercised through bargaining, persuasion and maneuvering under
conditions of uncertainty. "Control", therefore, resolves into strategies and
tactics – hence the appropriateness of "games" as the characterisation of the
"control" aspects of the process.'[60] Basically, the games which he identifies
relate to the administrative processes and procedures usually employed to gain
compliance, or to promote activity among implementation agencies, and the
way in which both policy-makers and implementers attempt to 'play the
system' to their own advantage. The importance of this approach is that it sees
implementers not as passive *agents* on the receiving end of policy, but as
semi-autonomous groups actively pursuing their own goals and objectives (i.e.
engaging in self-interested behaviour) which may or may not be in accord with
those of the policy-makers.

Whilst talking about 'bargaining, persuasion and maneuvering' (similar to
Dunsire's categories discussed earlier), Bardach characterizes the interactions
between agencies as a struggle for control or self-determination. This differs
from the earlier conceptualizations where interactions are, by and large, seen
as means of resolving conflict. The distinction hinges around whether or not
consensus is regarded as important or necessary, which in turn depends on the
view taken of inter-agency relations. Both Dunsire and Pressman and
Wildavsky assume a degree of interdependence and recognition of the need to
work together between those negotiating or interacting. Bardach assumes that
the more powerful will act in a self-interested way; strategies and tactics are
aimed at preserving or enhancing autonomy and power, regardless of the
degree of organizational interdependence in a formal sense.

In practice, this apparent distinction between power play (zero sum games
in which goals have to be sacrificed by the less powerful) and bargaining (the
more gentlemanly exchange of resources or search for a mutually satisfactory
compromise) may not be so clear-cut. We have already referred to literature
concerned with the limits of control, even within highly 'rulebound' and
formally structured situations. Bardach himself illustrates the power games
played by actors in governmental settings *within* a formal framework of
interdependence and apparently 'shared purpose'. Perhaps less attention has

23

Policy and Action

been given to the converse situation, where the possession of power does not always appear to be the most relevant factor in setting the rules of the game, or a necessary 'bargaining counter' to achieve compliance with a specific policy. Agencies which are not apparently dependent on one another seem in certain circumstances to behave as if they were. Questions of this kind are raised in a number of contributions to this volume (notably in Stewart and Bramley's examination of the implementation of public expenditure cuts and in Boddy's chapter concerning the relations between government and the Building Societies).

This paradox has been central to much of the work carried out by Strauss and leads to his analysis of negotiations.[61] He suggests that 'social orders' – the framework of norms and rules within which groups and individuals operate (including organizational contexts) – are changing all the time, and argues that negotiation plays a big part in the process. From detailed studies of psychiatric institutions he concluded that, even in a highly institutional setting operated in accordance with formal rules and hierarchies, negotiations were constantly taking place (overtly and covertly) which basically set the pattern of *actual* organizational relationships. His later work has extended this thesis to inter-organizational and even international situations.

As well as arguing that social order is 'negotiated order', Strauss points to the importance of the context within which negotiations take place; the limits which different structural situations may place on the room for manoeuvre, and the influence of such factors as power, 'stakes' or interests and experience with the issues and with negotiations, in determining both the negotiation processes and their outcomes.

These aspects seem particularly relevant to the concept of implementation as a negotiating process. It may be useful to view what goes on between actors and agencies in the policy/action arena as bargaining *within* negotiated order. Specific issues may be haggled over, but within broader limits. The limits themselves will vary both in kind and over time, and are themselves subject to negotiation in relation to the wider social setting. For example, at one end of the spectrum limits may be provided by a formal constitutional/legal frame-work (as in central/local government relations). At the other, there may be no formal rules or sanctions, but limits of operation are set by accepted (or negotiated) 'norms' of behaviour.

A specific event or a specific policy may not 'fit' into the current negotiated order and require renegotiation. The question is how far the policy itself is 'renegotiated' – modified or compromised – to fit in with the existing order, or whether it is the order itself which is renegotiated in order to get policy implemented. We return in Part Three to a further discussion of Strauss's concepts and their application to the policy-action relationship.

Ideas about negotiation and bargaining between actors and agencies involved in the policy process lead to a redefinition of 'implementation'. Policy

Examining the policy-action relationship

cannot be regarded as a 'fix', but more as a series of intentions around which bargaining takes place and which may be modified as each set of actors attempts to negotiate to maximize its own interests and priorities. Interests and pressures may alter over time in relation to changing circumstances and in response to the way that continuing activities of the organizational environment impinge on the 'outside world'. Thus it becomes difficult to identify a distinct and sequential 'implementation process' which starts with the formulation of policy and ends with action. Rather, it is appropriate to consider implementation as a policy/action continuum in which an interactive and negotiative process is taking place over time, between those seeking to put policy into effect and those upon whom action depends. Diagrammatically, the process can be seen in Figure 1.

policy ⟶ reformulation

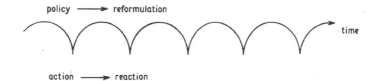

action ⟶ reaction

Figure 1   *The policy-action relationship*

This is more appropriate than a simple linear progression indicated by the 'conventional' formulation:

policy $\xrightarrow{\text{time}}$ action.

At any point in time it may not be clear whether policy is influencing action or whether action is influencing policy.

For us, the value of a 'negotiating' perspective for the study of implementation is that it suggests a new way to operate the policy/implementation dichotomy. If we take implementation to describe the day-by-day working of an agency (whether it involves relations between organizations or relations within organizations), then policy-making may be seen as attempts to structure this operation in a way which limits the discretionary freedom of other actors. As such, it may be seen either from a top-down or a bottom-up perspective. It is the former which is most frequently identified as policy-making: the setting of parameters (perhaps by means of the law) by actors at the 'top', who have the power to constrain those 'lower down'. But we may also identify the phenomenon the other way round, when lower level actors take decisions which effectively limit hierarchical influence, pre-empt top decision-making, or alter 'policies'.

This perspective also necessitates changing the way in which implementation 'success' or 'failure' is viewed: if policy is modified as a result of inter- or intra-agency negotiation, then how can 'conformance' or 'compliance' be

25

Policy and Action

judged? What may appear to be failure in the policy-makers' terms may be regarded as success by the implementing agencies in negotiating a policy which fitted their own definition of the problem or situation. This raises questions about the possibility of evaluating outcomes in any 'objective' sense. Who is undertaking such studies and for whom are they being undertaken? Again some of these points are developed by Smith in his chapter.

Implementation as action and response

We have identified a need to consider implementation as an *interactive* process whereby the response may itself influence and change policy in the course of implementation, particularly where co-operation or compliance can only be achieved by negotiation and bargaining. We would thus argue that under-standing the relationship between policy and action also requires an *action* perspective, which takes what is going on as central, seeks to understand how and why, and from that base explores the different kinds of frameworks within which action takes place.

To understand actions and responses we need to look at the groups of actors involved, the agencies within which they operate, and the factors which influence their behaviour. We need to consider actors and agencies, not just in single roles as the makers of policy for others to implement or the im-plementers of someone else's policy (which tends to be the case when taking a policy-centred perspective or implementation), but in a *combination* of roles, including a third, that of interested parties affected by the outcomes of policy made and implemented by themselves or others.

Thus the focus of attention shifts from policy to the organizations them-selves (or parts of organizations), to what is going on, who is doing it and why? Some activities will be dependent on policy innovation (either from within the organization or from outside), other activities will not. Day-to-day activities do not necessarily appear to relate to explicit or purposive policy and may appear to operate without control or the need to refer to a higher level of the organization. Agencies also respond to crises or to *ad hoc* issues and events without necessarily first formulating a 'policy'. Within what kind of frame-work do such activities take place?

We also need explanations for:

1   Why apparently similar agencies respond differently to the same policy.
2   Why some agencies innovate and others do not.
3   Why there is variation in priorities at the operational level for different issues.
4   Why some organizations succeed in inter-agency co-ordination and others do not.

26

Examining the policy-action relationship

To answer some of these questions, it is necessary to 'get inside' organizations or agencies and to look at the way in which goals and priorities are arrived at, the interests being promoted or protected by different groups and to try to build up a picture of the way in which practice or the particular way of doing things has evolved. In other words, we are saying that, since actors and agencies operate in a variety of roles, the factors which shape their *own* decisions and actions will also be important determinants of their response to the policy or actions of others.

Two themes seem particularly important to explore as a basis for understanding action and response:

1   the differential scope for autonomous action amongst agencies
2   the use made of it

Scope for action includes such factors as: the functions, responsibilities and statutory power conferred upon agencies from 'above'; political structure and accountability; environmental pressures and constraints – social, economic, physical and political; access to resources – constitutional, legal, hierarchical, financial, technological and information (in other words, bargaining power). Such factors provide the setting within which groups of actors are operating: the 'formal' limits of responsibility or control which one group may have *vis-à-vis* another; the structural relations and interdependency between agencies and machinery for communication; the contexts for negotiations. As such these factors are the focus of attention in most studies of organizational behaviour. However, much of the material tends to be holistic and 'policy free' in the sense of taking the organization as the unit of analysis.[62] As we have discussed earlier, policy and its implementation are likely to involve specific groups of actors and parts of organizations, the 'forging of links' and creation of instances within and between parts of organizations which are distinct from the 'chain of command' within an organization or the formal structural relations between organizations. The scope for action in any particular policy area may well depend on a variety of contexts devised from the different configuration and combination of 'limiting' factors affecting the different organizations or parts of organizations involved. Lewis and Flynn, in their study of the implementation of urban and regional planning policies,[63] pointed to the variety of modes of action adopted by central government for the implementation of different policies emanating from the same department. This analysis points to the need for more attention to be paid to the interaction between the subject matter of policy (and thus the specific groups and interests likely to be involved in or affected by it) and the organizational contexts in shaping the scope and limits for action.

However, the existence of opportunities for action does not necessarily mean that action will be taken, or determine the nature of action or response. We therefore also need to consider what factors may determine action or inaction

27

Policy and Action

in a given situation. Three aspects seem of particular relevance:

1   perceptions of the scope for action
2   perceptions of the need for action
3   motivation to act

Different values, attitudes and experiences combine to form the 'perceptions of the situation' held by different groups of actors which will shape their whole approach to defining problems and issues and to determining whether or not action is needed or cannot be avoided.[64] How far are attitudes and values shaped by political ideology, professional education or the organizational environment? Similarly, attitudes and values at both individual and agency level will affect the way in which different individuals or groups perceive and interpret their scope for autonomous action. For example, is the local authority lawyer's caution in interpreting a particular legal clause as an enabling framework due to his lawyer's training, his own reluctance to act in this particular instance because he doesn't agree with the proposal, or a reflection of the prevailing 'culture' in the authority as a whole which tends to wait and see what others do, rather than initiate or break any new ground? These considerations open up the whole field of theories and ideas about perception, motivation and the 'institutionalization' of ideologies.[65] They also lead back to political theories concerning the determinance of action and non-action.[66]

The way in which different 'actors' perceive and make sense of the world helps to explain organizational behaviour and response. Individuals and groups of actors, via the rules they establish (or absorb) for their own behaviour and the roles they occupy in organizations, not only influence the specific decisions of those organizations, but also 'embed' institutional structures with certain values and norms which will result in a distinctive organizational 'culture' and a tendency to promote certain interests rather than others. These phenomena are illustrated in Davies's description of the attempt to introduce and implement a workers' co-operative within a district authority, and are discussed further in Underwood's chapter on development control, Bishop's chapter on the briefing of architects for educational building and in the chapter by Towell on the implementation of improved services for the mentally ill.

Concluding note

In this chapter we have tried to do three things; to review some of the approaches to policy analysis and the study of implementation, with reference to existing literature; to suggest alternative views of the implementation process and the questions which such approaches bring to the fore; and to raise questions about how well the 'conventional wisdom' seems to fit with what goes on in reality. We have thus dealt in some detail with a 'rational model' of

28

Examining the policy-action relationship

the policy-action relationship – the steps involved in putting policy into effect – and have used this analysis as a basis for pointing up key issues of importance in understanding implementation processes

* multiplicity and complexity of linkages
* questions of control and coordination
* issues of conflict and consensus

From this we have suggested that the policy-action relationship needs to be considered in a political context and as an interactive and negotiative process taking place over time between those seeking to put policy into effect and those upon whom action depends. From this perspective, more emphasis is placed on issues of power and dependence, interests, motivations and behaviour, and we suggested the need to consider a third perspective, focusing on action itself, factors affecting individuals' and agencies' scope for action and the perception and use of that scope.

These different perspectives do not necessarily introduce entirely distinct issues; rather, they each place more or less emphasis on particular issues and thereby help to widen the avenues for exploration. We do not regard them as mutually exclusive conceptualizations, but rather as complementary approaches to understanding the policy-action relationship and, in the context of this book, as providing a 'backcloth' against which to look at the cases and themes discussed in the detailed contributions forming Part Two.

Perhaps one further point needs to be made before moving on to Part Two. Throughout our own discussions, whilst assembling the material for this chapter, we have found ourselves coming back again and again to the question of policy as the 'key' to the whole debate about implementation. Policy has been seen as the starting point for action, the focus of negotiations, or the expression of values, stances and practices which frame organizational activity. Most of the contributions in Part Two raise questions, albeit in a variety of ways, about the nature of policy – what it is, where it comes from, how it is used. We have, therefore, deliberately left discussion of this important theme to our concluding chapter.

Notes and references

1 For general arguments about 'government overload' see, for example, King 1975: 162–74; Rose 1978. See also Brittan 1975: 129–60.
2 See, for example, Forrester 1969; La Porte 1975.
3 See, for example, Crozier 1964; Perrow 1972; Litwak and Meyer 1974; Beer 1974.
4 These kinds of assumptions underlie many of the prescriptions and recommendations to be found in 'official' reviews and reports such as the Fulton Report on the Civil Service (HMG Cmnd 3638, 1968), the Redcliffe-Maude Report on the reorganization of local government in England (HMG Cmnd 4040, 1969) and the Bains Report on the management of reorganized local government (DoE 1972), and

Policy and Action

   in many of the management reviews undertaken by consultants for individual agencies, e.g. that carried out by McKinsey & Company Ltd for Sunderland as part of the Department of the Environment's three towns initiative in the early 1970s (DoE 1973).

5 The term agency implies a body or organization acting as an agent to carry out specific tasks on behalf of another body. However, throughout the book we shall be using the term in a looser sense as a shorthand for any body or organization or part thereof involved in the policy-making relationship.

6 Ministry of Housing and Local Government 1965.

7 Town and Country Planning Act 1968.

8 These systems were introduced in the following circulars: DHSS Circular 35/72, 1972; DoE Circular 104/73, 1973; DHSS Health Circular (76)30, 1976 (introducing the DHSS Manual entitled *The NHS Planning System* issued at the same time); DoE Circular 63/77, 1977.

9 For an account of these developments and their origins see Chapman 1975; McDonald and Fry 1980: 421–37. Programme Analysis Review (PAR) (along with the Public Expenditure Survey Committee) originated from the recommendations of the Plowden Committee on the Control of Public Expenditure (HMG Cmnd 1432, 1962). The introduction of PAR – a form of PPBS – into central government departments tended to reinforce the need for the kind of policy planning units recommended by the Fulton Report (HMG Cmnd 3638, 1968). These were intended to be concerned with long-term policy planning and their major objective was envisaged to be to provide a capacity for assessing the longer term implications of day-to-day policy decisions.

   The Central Policy Review Staff (CPRS) was established as part of the proposals set out in the 1970 White Paper (HMG Cmnd 4506, 1970).

10 The key HIPS circular was listed under (8) above. For an appraisal of the HIPS system, see Bramley, Leather and Murie 1980.

11 This 'orthodox' version of the antecedents and purpose of PPBS is challenged by Harvey Sapolsky. He argues that PPBS was the creation of the US Defense Department and that its real purpose was to provide a smokescreen around a new weapons development agency. Sapolsky 1972.

12 See, for example, Stewart 1970; Eddison 1973; Skitt 1975.

13 DoE 1972.

14 See, for example, Wildavsky 1979; Stewart 1969: 313–19; Armstrong 1969: 454–66; Cockburn 1977: 5–40.

15 Gordon, Lewis and Young 1977: 26–35.

16 Heclo 1972: 83–108.

17 For a comprehensive review of the field, see Jenkins 1978.

18 Notable examples of the case study approach are: Meyerson and Banfield 1955; Selznick 1966; Derthick 1972; Allison 1971; Crenson 1972; Pressman and Wildavsky 1973; Hood 1976; Hood 1968.

19 Dror 1968; Dror 1971.

20 Lindblom 1959; Lindblom 1965.

21 Friend and Jessop 1969; Friend, Power and Yewlett 1974.

22 Etzioni 1967: 385–92. See also Etzioni 1968.

23 See, for example, Deutsch 1966.

30

Examining the policy-action relationship

24 Beer 1971; Beer 1975.
25 Vickers 1965; Vickers 1970; Schon 1971.
26 Etzioni 1968; Friedman 1973.
27 Allison 1971: 4.
28 Dunsire 1978a: 18.
29 Dunsire 1978a: chapter 2.
30 Dunsire 1978a. For a discussion of this issue, see chapter 1.
31 Pressman and Wildavsky 1973: (Preface) xiv.
32 Pressman and Wildavsky 1973: xv.
33 However, it is important to point out that these definitions are only the starting point of Pressman and Wildavsky's study. They go on to say 'We oversimplify. Our working definition of implementation will do as a sketch of the earliest stages of the program, but the passage of time wreaks havoc with efforts to maintain tidy distinctions' (xv). 'The study of implementation requires understanding that apparently simple sequences of events depend on complex chains of reciprocal action' (xvii).
   Wildavsky has subsequently revised his conceptualization of the implementation process, in Majone and Wildavsky 1978.
34 The American literature uses the term 'program' to describe the means and proposed activities by which policy intentions are to be translated into action. Unless quoting directly from literature, we use the British spelling of the word in this context – programme.
35 Williams 1971: 131.
36 Williams 1971: 144.
37 Van Meter and Van Horn 1975: 445–88.
38 See, for example, Keeling 1972; Hill *et al.* 1979.
39 For discussion of the implementation of the Control of Pollution Act 1974, see Hill 1980; Levitt 1980.
40 Montjoy and O'Toole 1979: 465–76.
41 Hood 1976.
42 Dunsire 1978a.
43 Dunsire 1978a: 48. On this point, Dunsire refers specifically to p. 161 of March and Simon 1958 and their use of the ideas in Bakke 1950.
44 Dunsire 1978a: 85.
45 Bardach 1977.
46 Williams 1971: 147–8.
47 Sabatier and Mazmanian 1979: 481–3.
48 Sabatier and Mazmanian 1979: 484–5.
49 These points are developed further in Gunn 1978: 169–76.
50 Chase 1979: 385–435.
51 See, for example, Griffith 1966; Lewis and Flynn 1979: 123–44; Hood 1976; Hill 1972; Argyris 1960; Burns and Stalker 1961; Dunsire 1978b.
52 Hood 1976, especially chapter 5.
53 Dunsire 1978a: 85.
54 Pressman and Wildavsky 1973: 134.
55 Dunsire 1978b: 106.
56 Dunsire 1978b: 106.

Policy and Action

57 See, for example, Rhodes 1979 and Rhodes 1980: 289–322.
58 Dunsire 1978b: 107.
59 Bardach 1977: 57, 58.
60 Bardach 1977: 56.
61 Strauss 1978.
62 For a critique of this approach, which we return to in our concluding chapter, see Hjern and Porter 1980.
63 Lewis and Flynn 1979.
64 See, for example, Young 1979 and Young and Mills 1980.
65 See, for example, Berger and Luckman 1966.
66 See, for example, Bachrach and Baratz 1970.

Bibliography

Allison, G. T. (1971) *Essence of Decision,* Boston, Little, Brown.

Argyris, C. (1960) *Understanding Organisational Behaviour,* London, Tavistock.

Armstrong, R. H. (1969) 'The approach to PPBS in local government', *Local Government Finance,* August.

Bardach, E. (1977) *The Implementation Game: What Happens After A Bill Becomes A Law,* London, MIT Press.

Beer, S. (1971) *Decision and Control: The Meaning of Operational Research and* Management Cybernetics, New York, Wiley.

Beer, S. (1974) *Designing Freedom,* New York, Wiley.

Beer, S. (1975) *Platform for Change,* New York, Wiley.

Bramley, G., Leather, P. and Murie, A. (1980) *Housing Strategies and Investment Programmes,* SAUS Working Paper 7, Bristol, School for Advanced Urban Studies.

Brittan, S. (1975) 'The economic contradictions of democracy' , *British Journal of Political Science,* 5(2), April.

Burns, T. and Stalker, G. M. (1961) *The Management of Innovation,* London, Tavistock.

Chapman, R. (1975) 'The role of central or departmental policy and planning units: recent developments in Britain', *Public Administration* (Sydney), 34(2), June.

Chase, G. (1979) 'Implementing a human services program: how hard will it be?', *Public Policy,* 27(4), Fall.

Cockburn, C. (1977) *The Local State,* London, Pluto Press.

Crenson, M. (1972) *The Unpolitics of Air Pollution,* Baltimore, Johns Hopkins University Press.

Crozier, M. (1964) *The Bureaucratic Phenomenon,* London, Tavistock. Department of Health and Social Security (DHSS) (1972) Circular 35/72, *Local Authority Social Services: 10 Year Development Plans 1973-1983,* London, DHSS.

DHSS (June 1976) Health Circular (76)30, *Health Services Management, The NHS Planning System: Planning Activity in* 1976/77, London, DHSS.

Department of the Environment (DoE) (1972) *The New Local Authorities:* Management and Structure, London, HMSO.

DoE (1973) Circular 104/73, *Local Transport Grants,* London, HMSO. DoE (1977) Circular 63/77, *Housing Strategies and Investment Programmes:* Arrangements for 1978/79, London, HMSO.

Derthick, M. (1972) *New Towns In-Town,* Washington D.C., the Urban Institute.

Deutsch, K. W. (1966) *The Nerves of Government: Models of Political Communication and Control,* New York, Free Press.

Dror, Y. (1968) *Public Policy Making Re-examined,* Scranton, Penn., Chandler.

Dror, Y. (1971) *Design for Policy Sciences,* New York, Elsevier.

Dunsire, A. (1978a) *Implementation in a Bureaucracy: The Execution Process, I,* Oxford, Martin Robertson.

Dunsire, A. (1978b) *Control in a Bureaucracy: The Execution Process,* II, Oxford, Martin Robertson.

Eddison, T. (1973) *Local Government: Management and Corporate Planning,* London, Leonard Hill Books.

Etzioni, A. (1967) 'Mixed scanning: a "third" approach to decision making', Public Administration Review.

Etzioni, A. (1968) *The Active Society,* New York, Free Press.

Forrester, J. W. (1969) *Urban Dynamics,* Cambridge, MIT Press. Friedman, J. (1973) *Retracking America: A Theory of Transactive Planning,* New York, Anchor Books.

Friend, J. K. and Jessop, W. M. (1969) *Local Government and Strategic Choice,* London, Tavistock.

Friend, J., Power, J. M. and Yewlett, C. (1974) *Public Planning: The Intercorporate Dimension,* London, Tavistock.

Gordon, I., Lewis, J. and Young, K. (1977) 'Perspectives on policy analysis', *Public Administration Bulletin,* 25, December.

Griffiths, J. A. G. (1966) *Central Departments and Local Authorities,* London, Allen & Unwin.

Gunn, L. (1978) 'Why is implementation so difficult?' *Management Services in Government,* November.

Heclo, H. H. (1972) 'Review article: policy analysis', *British Journal of Political Science,* vol. 2.

H.M. Government (HMG) (1962) Cmnd 1432, *Control of Public Expenditure,* London, HMSO.

HMG (1968) Cmnd 3638, *The Civil Service,* vol. 1, Report of the Committee 1966-68, London, HMSO.

HMG (1969) Cmnd 4040, *Royal Commission on Local Government in England* 1966-69, London, HMSO.

HMG (1970) Cmnd 4506, *The Reorganisation of Central Government,* London, HMSO.

Hill, M. J. (1980a) 'The role of British local government in the control of air pollution – a growing gap between policy and implementation?', paper presented to the European Consortium for Political Research (ECPR) Workshop on Environment Politics and Policies, Florence.

Hill, M. J. *et al.* (1979) 'Implementation and the central-local relationship', Appendix II in *Central-Local Government Relationships,* A Panel Report to the Research Initiatives Board, Social Science Research Council.

Hood, C. C. (1968) *Public Policy Making Re-examined,* Scranton, Penn., Chandler.

Hood, C. C. (1976) *The Limits* of *'Administration,* London, John Wiley. Jenkins, W. I. (1978) *Policy Analysis: a political and organisational perspective,* London, Martin Robertson.

Keeling, D. (1972) *Management in Government,* London, Allen & Unwin.

King, A. (1975) 'Overload: problems of governing in the 1970s', *Political Studies,* 23.

La Porte, T. (1975) *Organised Social Complexity,* Princeton, NJ, Princeton University Press.

Levitt, R. (1980) Implementing Public Policy, London, Croom Helm.

Lewis, J. and Flynn, R. (1979) 'The implementation of urban and regional planning policies', *Policy and Politics,* 7(2), April.

32c   *Bibliograghy*

Lindblom, C. E. (1959) 'The science of muddling through', *Public Administration Review,* Spring.

Lindblom, C. E. (1965) *The Intelligence of Democracy;* New York, Free Press.

Litwak, E. and Meyer, H. J. (1974) *School, Family and Neighborhood: The Theory and Practice of School-Community Relations,* New York, Columbia University Press.

McDonald, J. and Fry, G. K. (1980) 'Policy planning units – ten years on', *Public Administration,* 58.

Majone, G. and Wildavsky, A. (1978) 'Implementation as evolution', in Freeman, H. E. (ed.) *Policy Studies Review Annual,* vol. 2, Beverly Hills, Sage Publications.

March, J. G. and Simon, H. A. (1958) *Organizations,* New York, Wiley.

Meyerson, M. and Banfield, E. C. (1955) *Politics, Planning and the Public,* New York, Free Press of Glencoe.

Montjoy, R. S. and O'Toole, L. J. (1979) 'Towards a theory of policy implementation: an organisational perspective', *Public Administration Review,* 39(5), September/October.

Perrow, C. (1972) *Complex Organisms: A Critical Essay,* Glenview, Illinois, Scott Foresman & Co.

Pressman, J. and Wildavsky, A. (1973) *Implementation,* Berkeley, University of California Press.

Rose, R. (1978) 'Ungovernability: is there fire behind the smoke?', *Studies in Public Policy,* no. 16, Strathclyde, Centre for the Study of Public Policy.

Sabatier, P. and Mazmanian, D. (1979) 'The conditions of effective implementation: a guide to accomplishing policy objectives, *Policy Analysis,* Fall.

Sapolsky, H. (1972) *The Polaris System Development,* Cambridge, Mass., Harvard University Press.

Schon, D. A. (1971) *Beyond the Stable State,* London, Temple Smith.

Selznick, P. (1966) IV *A and the Grass Roots,* New York, Harper & Row.

Skin, J. (ed.) (1975) *Practical Corporate Planning in Local Government,* London, Leonard Hill Books.

Stewart, J. D. (1969) 'Programme budgeting in British local government', *Local Government Finance,* August.

Stewart, J. D. (1970) *Management in Local Government,* London, Charles Knight.

Van Meter, D. and Van Horn, C. E. (1975) 'The policy implementation process, a conceptual framework', *Administration and Society,* 6(4), February.

Vickers, G. (1965) *The Art o/Judgement,* London, Methuen.

Vickers, G. (1970) *Value Systems and the Social Process,* Harmondsworth, Penguin.

Wildavsky, A. (1979) 'Rescuing policy analysis from PPBS', *Public Administration Review,* March/April.

Williams, W. (1971) *Social Policy Research and Analysis,* New York, Elsevier.

[24]

Foundations

John Friend and Allen Hickling

A Philosophy of Planning

There are many possible ways in which to approach the challenge of planning in an uncertain world.

The approach to be introduced in this chapter is one in which planning is viewed as a continuous process: a process of choosing strategically through time. This view of planning as a process of strategic choice is, however, not presented as a set of beliefs which the reader is expected to embrace uncritically at this stage. That would be too much to expect — especially of an introductory chapter, which is intended merely to open the door for the more specific concepts, methods and guidelines to be offered in those that follow. People involved in any kind of planning activity of course build up their own sets of beliefs about the practice of planning in the course of their working lives: beliefs which they will not wish to set aside lightly. Yet experience in applying the approach offered here has shown that its fundamentals can usually be accepted without much difficulty by those planners or managers whose working philosophy draws more on their own practice than on taught beliefs. This is because, in essence, the approach sets out to do no more than to articulate, as clearly as possible, the kinds of dilemma that experienced decision-makers repeatedly face in the course of their work, and the often intuitive judgements they make in choosing how to respond.

In practice, such judgements may sometimes be accompanied by a sense of discomfort or even guilt. For the decision-makers may feel they are departing from certain principles of rational behaviour which they have been taught to respect. Indeed, the view of planning as strategic choice is found to offer more of a challenge to such idealised principles of rationality than it does to the intuitive judgements and compromises that seem characteristic of planning practice. If this point can be accepted, the reader should be able to relax in following the ideas put forward in this chapter, and view them as offering perspectives that can help make sense of current practice — without necessarily demanding any revolutionary change in familiar ways of working.

2   Planning Under Pressure

The Craft of Choosing Strategically

It is important to emphasise that the view of strategic choice presented here is essentially about choosing in a strategic *way* rather than at a strategic *level*. For the idea of choosing at a strategic level implies a prior view of some *hierarchy* of levels of importance in decision-making; while the concept of strategic choice that will be developed here is more about the *connectedness* of one decision with another than about the level of importance to be attached to one decision relative to others.

It is not too surprising that these two senses of the word *strategic* have tended to fuse together in common usage. For it is often the more weighty and broader decisions which are most obviously seen to be linked to other decisions, if only because of the range of their implications and the long time horizons over which their effects are expected to be felt. This, in turn, can lead to a view that any process of strategic decision-making should aspire to be comprehensive in its vision and long-range in its time horizon, if it is to be worthy of its name.

But such a view of strategic choice can become a restrictive one in practice; for it is all too rarely that such idealistic aspirations can be achieved. The approach to strategic choice to be built up in this chapter is not only about making decisions at a supposedly strategic level. It goes beyond this in addressing the making of *any* decisions in the light of their links to other decisions, whether they be at a broader policy level or a more specific action level; whether they be more immediate or longer term in their time horizons; and no matter who may be responsible for them. This concept of strategic choice indicates no more than a readiness to look for patterns of connectedness between decisions in a manner that is selective and judgemental — it is *not* intended to convey the more idealistic notion that everything should be seen as inextricably connected to everything else.

So this view of planning as a process of strategic choice implies that planning can be seen as a much more *universal* activity than is sometimes recognised by those who see it as a specialist function associated with the preparation of particular sorts of plans. At the same time, it allows planning to be seen as a *craft*, full of subtlety and challenge; a craft through which people can develop their capacity to think and act creatively in coping with the complexities and uncertainties that beset them in practice.

Organisational Contexts of Strategic Choice

This relatively modest interpretation of the word *strategic* means that the view of planning as strategic choice is one that can be applied not only to decision-making in formal organisational settings, but to the choices and uncertainties which people face in their personal, family and community lives. For example, any of us might find ourselves involved in a process of strategic choice in addressing the problem of where and when to go on holiday next year, or how to sell an unwanted vehicle, or how to deal with a difficult request from a relative or friend. Of course, the craft of choosing strategically becomes more complicated where it involves elements of *collective* choice — of negotiation with others who view problems and possibilities in different ways. Indeed, most of the more demanding problems to which the strategic choice approach has been applied have involved challenges of collective decision-making, either in organisational or inter-organisational settings; and this can have the effect of blurring many of the familiar distinctions of task and discipline around which organisational structures are usually designed. For the skill of choosing strategically through time is one that can become just as essential to the manager or executive as to those in more formal planning roles. This point is illustrated schematically in Figure 1, through which is presented a view of planning under the practical pressures of organisational life. It is a view in which an organisation's arrangements for making plans, and those for making day-to-day decisions, tend to merge together into a less clearly bounded process through which progress is sustained. This is a process of choosing strategically in coping with difficult problems, amidst all the complex realities — or perceptions of reality — which contribute to organisational life.

The larger and more complex the organisation, the more it is to be expected that decision-making responsibilities will have become differentiated according to a multitude of operational, managerial or entrepreneurial roles. The more likely it is too that specialised plan-making functions will have been developed in an effort to maintain a co-ordinated, longer-term view isolated from everyday management pressures. However, no plan-making activity will remain valued within an organisation unless it can provide support for the more difficult and important of the decisions people face; and it is a common experience that carefully prepared plans can quickly lose their relevance under the pressures of day-to-day events. The combined pressures of urgency, competition for resources and turbulence in the world outside can soon lead to disenchantment and confusion in the arrangements for making plans; while the pressures of complexity, conflict and overload can lead to vacillation and inconsistency in the making of day-to-day decisions. To counter the resulting personal and organisational stresses, those responsible for organisational guidance sometimes look towards some overarching framework of *policies* or aims. But, in practice, such policy guidelines can often be difficult to agree — especially when working in inter-organisational settings — and their contributions towards sorting out the predicaments of day-to-day management can be disappointingly small.

The making of generalised policies is therefore given its place in Figure 1; but it is not given pride of place. Instead, the emphasis is on the more subtle

FIGURE 1

Planning Under Pressure: A View of the Realities

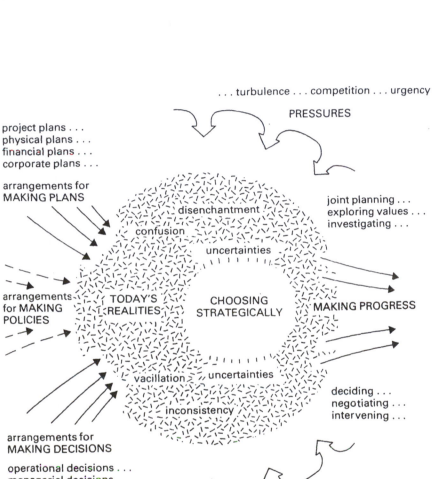

... turbulence ... competition ... urgency

PRESSURES

project plans ...
physical plans ...
financial plans ...
corporate plans ...

arrangements for
MAKING PLANS

disenchantment

confusion

uncertainties

joint planning ...
exploring values ...
investigating ...

arrangements
for MAKING
POLICIES

TODAY'S
REALITIES

CHOOSING
STRATEGICALLY

MAKING PROGRESS

vacillation   uncertainties

inconsistency

deciding ...
negotiating ...
intervening ...

arrangements for
MAKING DECISIONS

operational decisions ...
managerial decisions ...
resource decisions ...
entrepreneurial decisions ...

PRESSURES

... complexity ... conflict ... overload

FOUNDATIONS

process of making progress through time by choosing strategically; and on the creative management of multiple *uncertainties* as a crucial means towards this end. And progress through time can, itself, take many forms. Immediate progress can take the form of intervening, or negotiating with others, as well as taking decisions on matters where direct action is possible. Meanwhile, progress in building a base for later decisions can also take different forms — not only investigations but also clarification of values and cultivation of working relationships with other decision-makers.

So the term 'planning' will be used in this book to refer generally to this more loosely defined process of *choosing strategically*, in which the activities of making plans, decisions and policies can come together in quite subtle and dynamic ways. But with a wide variety of ways of making progress to be considered, the process can soon begin to appear as one not so much of planning but of scheming — to introduce a term which has a similar literal meaning but which carries very different undertones in its everyday usage. Whereas the notion of planning may invoke a sense of idealism and detachment, the notion of scheming tends to suggest working for sectional advantage in an often devious way. So there is a case to be made that people involved in planning must learn to become effective schemers; and furthermore that it is possible to exercise scheming skills in a responsible way. Those who are troubled about social responsibility in planning — and that includes both the authors of this book — may wonder whether there must always be a divide between responsible planners and irresponsible schemers — and if so, whether it must always be the latter who will win. As Chapter 10 will demonstrate, the concept of *responsible scheming* need not be considered a contradiction in terms. Indeed, it is towards the search for a theory and a practice of responsible scheming that the strategic choice view of planning can be said to be addressed.

It is, however, one thing for an individual to embrace a philosophy of planning as strategic choice; and quite another thing for a group of people working together to share such a philosophy as an unequivocal foundation for their work. Experience has shown that there are some settings where a sense of shared philosophy can indeed emerge — either where a set of close colleagues has learnt to work together as a coherent team, or where they discover that a common professional background allows them to proceed on shared assumptions as to how decisions should be made. Yet those whose work involves cutting across organisational boundaries must expect often to find themselves working alongside people with whom they do not share a philosophical base. So it is important to think of the philosophy presented in this chapter as a helpful frame of reference in making use of the more specific concepts and methods to be introduced in this book, rather than as a necessary foundation from which to build.

Indeed, it is a common enough experience, when working with strategic choice concepts, that people of quite diverse backgrounds can make solid

6   Planning Under Pressure

progress towards decisions based on shared understandings, with little or no explicit agreement at a more philosophical level. Often it is only through the experience of working together on specific and immediate problems that they find they are beginning to break through some of the philosophical barriers which may have inhibited collaboration in the past.

Dilemmas of Practice

The view of strategic choice presented in this book gained its original impetus from the experience of a particular research project, which offered unusually extensive opportunities to observe the kinds of organisational processes indicated in Figure 1.

The setting of this research was the municipal council of a major English city — Coventry — which, between 1963 and 1967, agreed to act as host to a wide-ranging project on the processes of policy-making and planning in local government, viewed as a microcosm of government as a whole. This seminal research was supported by a grant from the Nuffield Foundation, and has been more fully reported elsewhere (Friend and Jessop, 1969/77). Over the four-year period, the research team was able to follow a wide range of difficult issues including the review of the city's first development plan; the redesign of its urban road network; the reorganisation of its school system; the renewal of its housing stock; the finance of public transport; and the scheduling of capital works. The researchers were able to hold many discussions with the various politicians, administrators, planners and professional experts involved, and to observe the processes of collective decision-making in which they came together — not only in the departmental offices and the formal meetings of Council and its committees, but also in the smoke-filled rooms of the opposing political groups.

Through these experiences, some impressions of the persistent *dilemmas* of decision-making in such complex circumstances gradually came to the fore. Among the clearest impressions were:

— that people held different and continually shifting views about the **shape** of the issues they faced and, not least, about how closely or widely the boundaries of their concern should be drawn;
— that there were persistent pressures for them to arrive at commitments to action in an **incremental** or piecemeal way, however committed they might be in theory to the idea of taking a broader, more comprehensive view of the issues before them;
— that there was a continuing dilemma of balancing **urgency** against **uncertainty** in decision-making through time;
— and that there were persistent difficulties in distinguishing the **technical** from the **political** aspects of the decision process, even

though the entire organisational structure was built around the maintenance of distinctions of this kind.

These impressions of the practical difficulties of choosing strategically in organisations facing complex problems have been strengthened and extended by many other experiences since the conclusion of the Coventry project — not only in the world of local government but in other public sector organisations, in industry and commerce, in voluntary organisations, and in the increasingly wide range of problem situations where these different domains of decision-making tend to converge. On the strength of this broader experience, a view is presented in Figure 2 of five broad dimensions in which difficult choices of *balance* tend to arise in the management of a continuing process of strategic choice. There is a choice between:

- a more **focussed** and a more **synoptic** treatment of problem *scope*;
- a more **simplifying** and a more **elaborating** treatment of *complexity*;
- a more **reactive** and a more **interactive** treatment of *conflict*;
- a more **reducing** and a more **accommodating** treatment of *uncertainty*;
- and a more **exploratory** and a more **decisive** treatment of progress through time.

The practical task of choosing a position in each of these five dimensions is not one of making a firm and lasting commitment to one extreme or the other. It is more a task of maintaining an appropriate *balance* in continually shifting circumstances, shifting from time to time in one direction or another, according to the — often intuitive — judgements of those involved. In the chapters that follow, the picture presented in Figure 2 will be used as a point of reference in building more structured frameworks of ideas through which to expand further on the view of planning as a process of strategic choice. These frameworks will give deeper significance to the various contrasts which, at this stage, can only be indicated in outline terms.

In later chapters, fuller interpretations will be offered of other related aspects of the dilemmas of practice observed in Coventry and elsewhere, which are not brought out so clearly in the comparatively broad set of balances presented in Figure 2. In particular, later chapters will have more to say about the issues of urgency and incrementality, and about the relationship of the political arena to the technical domain. This is a dichotomy which, in Coventry City Council, could be seen as the fundamental organising principle on which the formal structures of accountability were designed; but it is a relationship with far wider implications for decision-making, even in contexts where such distinctions may become more blurred.

Judgements of Balance in Strategic Choice

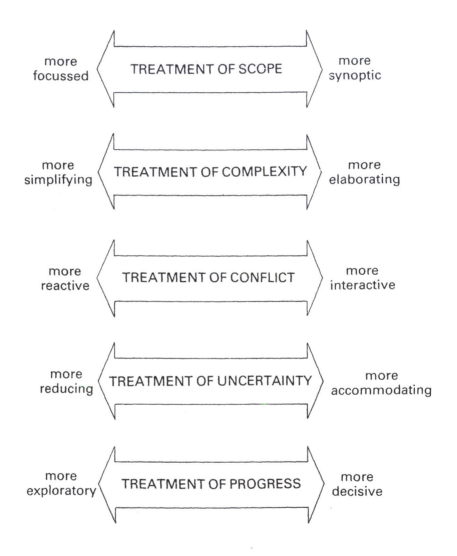

FOUNDATIONS

Responding to Difficulty in Making Decisions

The view of planning as a process of strategic choice is, above all, a dynamic one. However, in building up a view of the way this process works, it is useful to begin with a more static picture. This picture, which is quite simple yet also quite general in its application, has as its focus any situation in which one or more decision-makers are experiencing *difficulty* in choosing how they should act in response to some particular *decision problem* with which they are currently concerned. A snapshot view of such a decision situation is presented in Figure 3. The decision problem itself is depicted as a cloud, to indicate that its shape will often be in some degree obscure. However, what makes it problematic to the decision-makers is that they are experiencing some pressure to arrive at a decision, yet it is not clear to them what course of action they should choose.

Where a group of people find themselves collectively in such a situation, then it is often found that different members of the group will advocate different ways of responding; so some degree of conflict of opinion may emerge. Three types of response which are repeatedly offered in practice are indicated by the three different 'bubbles' shown emerging from the central cloud in Figure 3.

Very often, people will see the way out of their present difficulties in terms of explorations of a more or less technical nature. The suggestions offered typically include various forms of costing or forecasting exercises, surveys, technical analyses, research studies; or, in some circumstances, proposals for investment in more ambitious forms of mathematical or economic modelling. Whatever the form of investigation, however, the purpose is to reduce the difficulties of making decisions by investing in a process of *exploration* into particular aspects of the decision-makers' working environment about which it is felt that too little is currently known.

Other people, meanwhile, may see the way out of the difficulty in terms of other, less technical, kinds of exploration designed to establish more clearly what policy values should guide their choice of action. Typically, they may call for investment in activities designed to clarify goals, objectives, aims or policy guidelines, whether through formal or informal channels. In some situations, this may mean simply consulting decision-takers who bear more direct responsibility for organisational policy; in others it could mean deliberately seeking fuller involvement in the process by a range of affected interest groups or their representatives.

A third response is to seek the way out of the difficulty by moves to extend the current agenda of decision-making concern. People advocating this response will often argue that the decision problem currently in view is one that cannot realistically be addressed in isolation, because it is connected to one or more other decision problems which lie ahead. So the demand here is likely to be for some form of co-ordination, negotiation or

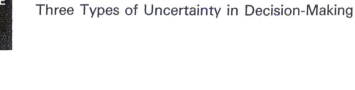
Three Types of Uncertainty in Decision-Making

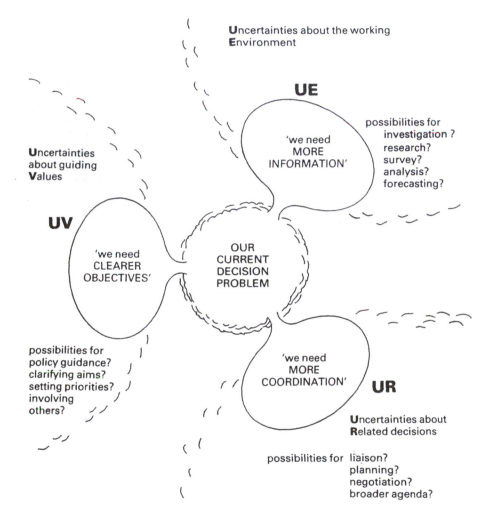

planning exercise that will allow the current decision problem to be explored alongside others within a broader, more synoptic problem focus.

Each of the three kinds of demand — most typically expressed as demands for *more information*, for *clearer objectives* and for *more co-ordination* — can be regarded as a different kind of attempt to manage the current state of **uncertainty** over what should be done about the current decision situation. Indeed, it is possible to go on to identify three general *categories* of uncertainty along the lines indicated below, which are distinguished by the different forms of response that can be made. These three types of uncertainty play an important part in the philosophy of planning as a process of strategic choice; they can be formally described as follows:

Uncertainties about the working Environment: **UE** for short
Uncertainties about guiding Values: **UV** for short
Uncertainties about Related decisions: **UR** for short

It is important to stress that the idea of uncertainty in strategic choice is normally viewed in *relative* rather than absolute terms. It is treated as an attribute of particular situations and people rather than something with an objective reality of its own. In practice it is often far from easy for people to agree which of the three kinds of uncertainty are most crucial in a particular decision situation; and, therefore, how much attention should be given to each possible form of response. For instance, members of a city planning team, considering whether to recommend approval of an application to build a new hotel, might see possibilities either for calling for deeper investigation of its traffic implications; or for seeking clearer guidance on the Council's policies in relation to this particular kind of development; or for initiating a wider review of tourism possibilities within the city as a whole. They might of course want to move in all three directions more or less at the same time; however, this is not always possible where there are pressures to make a speedy decision. Nor will it necessarily be desirable to invest resources in all possible ways of responding to uncertainty — especially if some of them are expected to be less effective than others, in terms of reducing the feelings of uncertainty among the decision-makers involved.

Managing Uncertainty : A Dynamic View

So, in practice, it may be far from easy to judge how uncertainty is to be *managed* at any moment, even in situations where the sources of that uncertainty have been clearly identified.

To consider further the possible ways of managing uncertainty through time, it becomes necessary to move to a more *dynamic* view. Such a view is presented in Figure 4 which builds on the 'snapshot' picture of Figure 3 by

FIGURE 4

Opportunities for Managing Uncertainty through Time

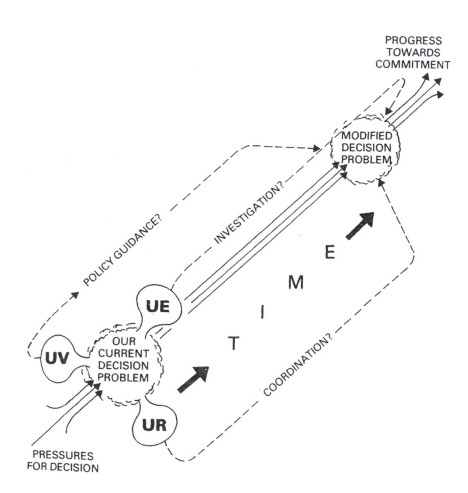

introducing the reality that any form of investigative, policy clarifying or co-ordinating initiative must take some time to carry through. Indeed, explorations in some of these directions may, in practice, take longer to carry out than others. However, the intended consequence of pursuing any chosen exploratory path is to make the decision situation less difficult to deal with once the outcome of the exploration is known — in other words, to lessen the feelings of uncertainty being experienced by the decision-makers, and thus to increase the level of *confidence* with which they can act. In practice, however, it will not often be realistic to expect that the feelings of uncertainty surrounding a difficult decision problem can be made to vanish altogether, however much effort may be invested in exploratory activities. In terms of the symbolism used here, the process can be pictured as one whereby the original cloud becomes smaller in its dimensions and, by implication, less obscure.

Sometimes, of course, feelings of uncertainty may be reduced through time without any conscious action on the part of the decision-makers. Expected events may or may not unfold; trends may become more apparent; the intentions of other parties may be revealed; policy positions may become more clear cut. In general, however, uncertainty can only be reduced at a cost — whether this be merely the cost of delay when there may be urgent issues to be settled, or whether it also includes more direct costs in terms of money, skills or other scarce resources.

So the management of uncertainty through time is rarely simple in the types of judgement it entails. It is the raising of these judgements to a more conscious level that is one of the most distinctive characteristics of the strategic choice approach.

Interconnected Agendas of Decision-Making

Of the three exploratory routes indicated in Figure 4, it is the co-ordinative (UR) route which is of most far-reaching significance in developing the idea of planning as strategic choice.

The demand to move in this direction arises when there is a sense that the present agenda of decision-making is too restricted — that the decision problem currently in view is significantly influenced by uncertainties to do with intended actions in other fields of choice. Such a concern for a wider view will also often lead to an extension in the time frame as well, because the pressures for decision may be less immediate in some of these related areas. The concern for co-ordination may also shift the process in the direction of some form of liaison or joint working with other sections or departments, and sometimes, also, with other decision-makers quite outside the organisational framework within which the current problem is being addressed.

Extending the Problem Focus

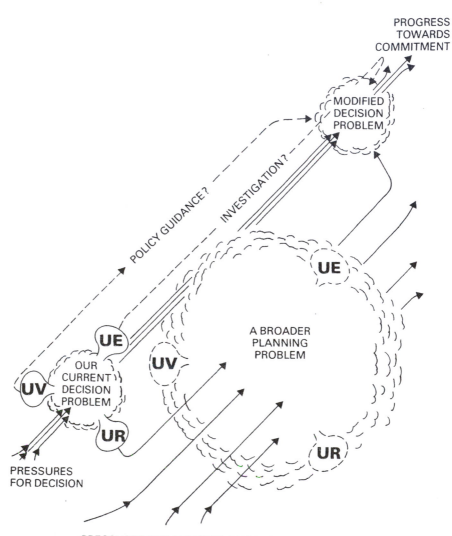

The concern for co-ordination in dealing with related fields of choice does not, however, inevitably mean transcending organisational boundaries in this way. At a more modest level, it may simply be a matter of the same decision-maker recognising that an issue to be dealt with today should be considered in relation to some other issue to be dealt with next week. In the case of the hotel development mentioned earlier, for instance, it could be that a proposal to develop an indoor leisure centre is known to be pending on a neighbouring site, suggesting that either proposal could affect the other.

In general, the pursuit of the co-ordinative (UR) route implies forging a relationship between one decision process or planning process and others, in the manner indicated in Figure 5. The dynamic view is here taken a step further than in Figure 4, by showing the fuller implications of a shift from a more limited to a broader decision focus. The investment in 'more co-ordination' can be seen as shifting the focus, temporarily at least, from the original decision problem to a broader and more complex problem within which it is contained.

Incremental Progress in Planning

One of the most important points about this shift to a broader problem focus is that it does not automatically mean that those involved should be aiming for early decision in respect of all the related choices now brought into view. It is perfectly possible that the shift to a broader focus will help to reduce uncertainty in the original decision problem and so enable firm commitment to be agreed, without leading to simultaneous commitments in any or all of the other related areas. Indeed, the issue of balance between exploratory and decisive progress has already been highlighted (Figure 2) as one of the main areas of judgement in strategic choice; and it is a balance of critical importance in managing uncertainty through time.

The broader the focus of the problem within the larger cloud in Figure 5, the more it is likely to be thought of not simply as a decision problem but as a *planning problem* because it contains elements of both immediate and longer-term decision. But the distinction is not so much an absolute one as one of degree. This point is made in Figure 5 by showing the three kinds of uncertainty surfacing again at the broader level of the more complex planning problem. Indeed, if uncertainties of type UR again appear important at this level, this may trigger off concerns to move to an even broader level of concern, and to begin to explore the shape of an even larger and more obscure cloud. But this process of continually enlarging the scope of the problem will always have its limits in practice; and, if useful pointers to action are to emerge, then the focus of concern must be kept within manageable bounds.

Two Contexts for Sequential Decision-Making

It is not hard to see how planning procedures conceived with ambitions towards comprehensiveness can develop their own internal momentum. Such tendencies can be found in corporate planning procedures for the guidance of large and diffuse commercial enterprises, and also in exercises in the production of land-use plans or economic planning frameworks, through which public agencies endeavour to set a context for the actions of other parties. The danger is always that such activities will become separated from other management processes and so cease to exercise any real influence on the more immediate decisions they were designed to inform. This risk of disengagement between arrangements for planning and for management has already been suggested in the keynote diagram (Figure 1); it is a risk that can be confronted directly from the perspective of planning as a process of strategic choice.

Human Settings for Decision-Making

The shift from a 'snapshot' view of decision-making (Figure 3) to a more dynamic, multi-level picture (Figures 4 and 5) implies that the imagery of the cloud should itself be conceived in more realistic, multi-dimensional terms. To extend the metaphor, clouds in reality are not flat: they have length, depth and breadth; their edges may be blurred; they progress across the sky, changing shape as time passes; they dissolve, they merge, they break up; and, in so doing, they assume new and often unpredictable forms.

With such a picture in mind, it is possible to look more closely at some different kinds of human context for decision, as a step towards a closer examination of the processes of thought and communication which go on 'within the cloud'. Figure 6 begins by looking at an organisational context of the most simple and restricted kind: an individual sits on a chair (symbolising a defined organisational role), with successive matters for decision arriving in an 'in' tray on a table (symbolising an agenda). The matters are dealt with in sequence, agreed rules are applied, and decisions are then transferred to the 'out' tray one at a time.

If the rules are unambiguous in their bearing on the issue currently being dealt with, then the cloud representing the thought process of the decision-maker is a small one, and quickly evaporates, to be replaced by the next. Indeed, the symbolism of the cloud can be replaced by the more mechanistic image of the black box — and the decision-maker at the table is at risk of being superseded by an electronic counterpart. Of course, the cloud may sometimes become larger, when a more complex case arrives. The decision-maker now experiences uncertainty and, as in the case of the public official dealing with the application to build a new hotel, this uncertainty may be in part due to awareness of links to other related cases — as symbolised perhaps by some matters marked for further attention in a 'pending' tray.

Figure 6 then demonstrates another context of sequential decision-making, by contrasting the situation of a single decision-maker sitting at his or her small table with that of a collective decision-making body — a committee or management board — grouped around a larger table. Such a group will often have a pre-circulated agenda, presenting an ordered list of issues to discuss and where possible resolve, corresponding to the 'in' tray of the single decision-maker. Among the occupants of the roles symbolised by the chairs around the larger table, there will usually be someone in a 'chairing' role, responsible for ensuring that the business is dealt with in an orderly and expeditious way. In place of the 'out' tray, there will usually be a running record of decisions kept by a committee secretary or clerk; while the occupants of at least some of the other chairs around the table will sometimes be recognised as having different representative or expert roles to play.

The decision-making process is now not purely one of cogitation within an individual's head; it embraces processes of communication, verbal and non-verbal, among the members of the group. For the observer of the process, the elongated cloud above the large table in Figure 6 takes on additional substance, in that it becomes possible to follow the dynamics of information sharing, negotiation and — if decisions are to be reached — compromise between conflicting views. For instance, if the issue of permission to build a new hotel has been brought up on the planning committee's agenda, there may be a variety of financial, aesthetic, engineering and commercial considerations to be exposed and shared. Further, there may be various conflicts of interest to be managed; for instance, there could be conflicts between the committee's responsibilities to the local community and the relationships of some members with the developer, who could perhaps be a well-known and influential local figure.

However, many decision processes in practice fail to conform to either of the tidy, sequential models. If the issues are complex and their boundaries unclear, then organisational responsibilities too are likely to be diffuse and probably confused. Communications may take place not just around tables but on the telephone, in corridors, in small back rooms. The inputs and outputs can no longer be seen as falling into any clear sequence, and the image of the single cloud may have to be replaced by one of several separate clouds which continually come together, drift apart, coalesce or disappear. For instance, the hotel developer, in making his or her own investment decisions, may have a series of meetings with planners and other public officials, as well as finance houses, landowners and other commercial interests. The developer as well as the committee members will have uncertainties to manage in some or all of the three categories of UE, UV and UR; and the extent to which the different planning processes can be linked may begin to raise a host of difficult administrative, political, ethical and legal issues.

Modes of Decision-Making

In developing further the view of planning as a process of strategic choice, it is helpful to see the process within any 'cloud' as continually shifting between different and complementary 'modes' of decision-making activity. In the simple situation of sequential decision-making, where the nature of the problem inputs and the expected decision outputs is well defined, this movement can be seen in terms of only two complementary modes: the one concerned with *designing* possible courses of action, and the other with *comparing* them in the light of some view of what their consequences might be. This relatively simple view is indicated in Figure 7.

The process may not in practice be strictly linear because a comparison of the consequences of any pair of alternatives — for instance a straight 'yes' or 'no' to the application to build a hotel — may reveal that either response could have undesirable consequences and so trigger off a search for some other compromise solution. So it becomes necessary to allow for the possibility of a feedback loop returning from the comparing to the designing mode. So, in Figure 7 the single 'cloud' is shown as tending to change shape into two smaller clouds — clouds which may still not be clearly separable in practice, insofar as the interplay between designing and comparing may become rapid and difficult to trace.

This picture has much in common with other, more orthodox models of decision-making processes, which tend to present stages or activities in logical sequence, having a beginning and an end, while allowing for elements of feedback or recycling in between. However, the more diffuse, continuous kind of process which is characteristic of the making of complex decisions in practice involves coping with multiple problem inputs and multiple decision outputs, with no clear sequential relationships between the two. To represent this kind of process, it is necessary to move to a rather more elaborate picture of the process within the cloud, introducing two additional modes as shown in Figure 8.

The two further modes of decision-making activity which make their appearance in Figure 8 are both of a more subtle and political kind. One of these is concerned with the *shaping* of problems; a mode within which judgements about the possible connections between one field of choice and another can have a crucial role to play. The other, referred to as the *choosing* mode, is concerned with the formation of proposed commitments to action progressively through time. Here it has to be kept in mind that the more complex the shape of the problem, the wider the choices that have to be faced. There will be choices, not only about what courses of action are preferred, but also about what degree of commitment is appropriate at this stage; which decisions should be deferred until later; and what explorations could be set in train in response to different types of uncertainty.

So, instead of two partially overlapping foci within the cloud, there now

A Process of Simple Choice

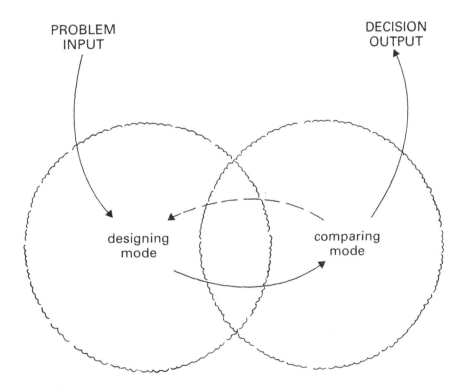

PROBLEM
INPUT

DECISION
OUTPUT

designing
mode

comparing
mode

appear four, with a variety of possible directions of movement between one mode and another. The most orthodox progression might appear to be from shaping problems, through designing possibilities, to comparing their consequences and then on to a final choosing of actions. However, such a progression is likely to be neither straightforward nor realistic, insofar as the process is to be seen as a continuous and incremental one, with no clear beginning and no single end. For the choice of actions to deal with some parts of the problem situation will leave other choices open for the future, creating opportunities for future reshaping of problems as unexpected events occur and new connections begin to appear.

Challenges to Management and Planning Norms

Already, the ideas presented here can be seen to pose some direct challenges to long-established management and planning norms: norms which have indeed been under sustained challenge from other sources, yet remain extremely persistent in the design of formal management and planning procedures — often for reasons of organisational stability and accountability which cannot be lightly criticised. Among the more deeply-established norms in any management system are those of *linearity, objectivity, certainty* and *comprehensiveness*. These can be summarised as follows:

> aim for **linearity** — "Tackle one thing at a time";
> aim for **objectivity** — "Avoid personal or sectional bias";
> aim for **certainty** — "Establish the full facts of the situation";
> aim for **comprehensiveness** — "Don't do things by halves".

Such norms may usually be adequate enough for the functionary sitting at a desk, working to highly constrained terms of reference. However, even here the system of rules can rarely be exhaustive in representing the situations that could arise; so feelings of uncertainty about how to act will sometimes surface and, with them, will arise difficulties in conforming to the norms of linearity and objectivity in their pristine forms. When a shift is made from decision-making to plan-making, the same four norms tend to show a remarkable persistence, even though the language may change. Yet the experience of working on difficult and complex planning problems is that the norms of linearity, objectivity, certainty and comprehensiveness keep on breaking down. So, in this book, they will be replaced by less simple prescriptions of the following form:

> don't aim for linearity — learn to work with **cyclicity**;
> don't aim for objectivity — learn to work with **subjectivity**;
> don't aim for certainty — learn to work with **uncertainty**;
> don't aim for comprehensiveness — learn to work with **selectivity**;

FIGURE 8

A Process of Strategic Choice

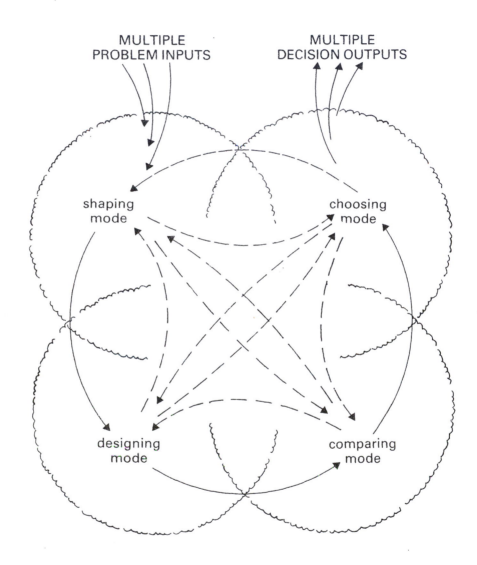

These alternative prescriptions may appear to be less straightforward to interpret in practice than the more familiar norms. But experience demonstrates that they offer a much more effective guide for people in attempting to choose strategically in practice. What is more, once they are stated and developed more fully, they can help people cope constructively with any sense of residual guilt they may feel in failing to apply simple management and planning norms when they encounter problems of a more complex kind.

Implications for a Technology of Strategic Choice

There are many forms of management and planning technique which have been devised to help people deal with difficult decision problems. Indeed, systematic methods of designing courses of actions, and comparing their likely consequences, have reached a considerable level of sophistication in some professional fields. For instance, systematic methods have been developed for assessing investment proposals in the light of predictions of not only their economic but also their social and environmental implications, while there are various computer-aided methods which can help generate a range of alternatives within some of the better understood fields of technological design. Meanwhile, mathematical programming techniques can allow analysts to conduct a systematic search for better solutions within a complex, multi-dimensional field, provided certain stringent assumptions about the structure of the problem can be met.

As yet, however, there has been much less investment in the development of techniques to support the two modes of decision-making which appear in the upper part of Figure 8 — even though these two modes take on special significance in confronting decision problems of a less clearly-structured kind, where it becomes necessary to cope with multiple inputs and outputs in a highly flexible, cyclic and, necessarily, subjective way.

Just as a distinction can be drawn between the two lower, more technical, modes in Figure 8 and the upper, more political modes, so another kind of distinction can be drawn between the two modes to the left of the diagram and the two modes to the right. Whereas the former two modes are primarily addressed towards the task of opening up the field of choice facing the decision-makers, the latter two modes can be seen as addressed towards the complementary task of narrowing that field down again in order to work towards agreement on action.

This distinction will be used as a basis for the organisation of the next two chapters. These will introduce and illustrate a series of basic concepts and techniques which have been developed, tested and modified progressively

A Structure for Subsequent Chapters

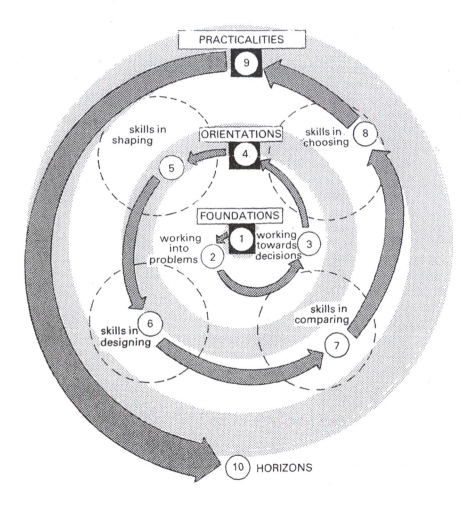

STRUCTURE

through repeated application to a range of applied planning problems. Together, these concepts and techniques can be seen as constituting an *appropriate technology* for strategic choice: appropriate in the sense that it is not intended as an advanced technology for use primarily by the expert. Rather the technology is designed to support the interactive work of groups of people who have different perspectives to contribute to a problem; who face quite daunting challenges in communicating with each other; yet who may appreciate the importance of working quickly and informally under the pressures of day-to-day events.

So, the concepts to be introduced in the next two chapters will only occasionally be worth applying with a high level of analytical sophistication by specialists in a back-room setting. Indeed, the more complex and unclear become the issues and their relationships, the more problematic become the more political modes of shaping problems and choosing actions, and the more vital it becomes that any technology of strategic choice be capable of use in a flexible and relatively non-technical way.

Implications for Chapter Structure

The emphasis in the chapters that follow will therefore be on quite simple and *transparent* concepts and techniques — most of them involving graphical forms of representation. These are intended to aid the processes of communication between people whose perspectives, attitudes and experiences may differ, as much as to help individuals in structuring their own personal thought processes. Working on these principles, Figure 9 presents a preview of the way in which the content of the nine chapters that follow will relate to the four modes of strategic choice which were distinguished in Figure 8. This picture can be used in conjunction with the Quick Access Guide at the beginning, by the reader who wishes to refer at any moment to the principles of structure on which this book has been designed.

Chapter 2, which is concerned with concepts and techniques for working into complex problems, will begin with the shaping mode, and will introduce some simple concepts which can help in structuring areas of choice and the interconnections between them. It will then move down to the designing mode, to introduce some further ideas to help in organising views about the options available and the patterns of compatibility or incompatibility between them. Chapter 3 is concerned with the complementary process of working towards decisions; it will begin with some concepts intended to help in comparing the foreseeable consequences of alternative courses of action, taking uncertainty explicitly into account. It then moves on to introduce further concepts addressed to the explicit

26   Planning Under Pressure

management of uncertainty and the choice of incremental actions through time, drawing on the UE/UV/UR framework which has already been introduced. Together, the two chapters provide a foundation for the discussion, in later chapters, of the many different ways in which the basic concepts and methods can be brought into play in practice.

References

FRIEND JK and JESSOP WN (1977) Local Government and Strategic Choice: An Operational Research Approach to the Processes of Public Planning (Second Edition). Oxford:Pergamon. [First Edition (1969) – London:Tavistock Publications]

[25]

Re-examining the International Diffusion of Planning

Stephen V. Ward

An intriguing footnote in the life of Ildefons Cerdà, author of the 1859 plan for Barcelona's *Eixample* (Extension), is that Georges-Eugène Haussmann, simultaneously engaged on the remodelling of Paris, is reported to have offered to buy Cerdà's plans and studies (Estapé, 1996, p. 55). Cerdà apparently refused, saying that he had drawn them up for Catalonia. If true, and the evidence rests on family recollection rather than a documentary source, this episode suggests that there was some degree of international linkage at a very early stage in the development of modern planning. In turn, Cerdà's refusal to sell may also partially explain why his remarkable innovatory work including, in 1867, the *Teoría General de la Urbanización* (General Theory of Urbanization), effectively the first modern theoretical work on urban planning, had a negligible international impact.

Within a few decades, however, there was abundant evidence that much more effective international flows of ideas and practices were becoming well established (Albers, 1997; Collins and Collins, 1965; Sutcliffe, 1981). Many cities, in Europe and beyond, sought to replicate the great new boulevards which Haussmann had driven through the old Paris at the behest of his Emperor. The emerging practices of *Stadterweiterungen* (town extension) in Germany, associated particularly with Reinhard Baumeister and Joseph Stübben, were also beginning to attract interest in Britain and the United States. So too was the notion of a more organic approach to town design, developed by Camillo Sitte and, to a lesser extent, Charles Buls from Austria and Belgium respectively. In England, Ebenezer Howard contributed a conceptually rich vision of the garden city in 1898, soon to be given a tangible form at Letchworth. Other seminal works followed in the new century, from Eugène Hénard and Tony Garnier in France, Charles Mulford Robinson and Daniel Burnham in the United States, Raymond Unwin in England, and Patrick Geddes in Scotland. Reflecting the nationalities of the authors of most of these works, four main innovatory planning traditions – Germany (*Städtebau*), Britain (town planning), France (*urbanisme*) and the United States (city planning) – were clearly apparent by 1914.

The key point, however, is that virtually all these works and the ideas they contained were also part of an emergent international discourse of planning. Written in German, French or English, many were translated within a few years of their publication into at least one other of the three languages. Some also appeared in other languages as well. The ideas they contained were interpreted, albeit selectively, into specific national contexts by a host of intermediaries throughout the world. Individual planners began to work in other countries, taking with them their own national planning conceptions and, in some cases, receiving others.

These early years set a pattern for the twentieth century. Despite the disruptive effects of major wars, internationalism has remained a powerful theme in urban planning. The dominant centres of innovation and patterns of emulation have not remained static, however. The balance of exchange between the main innovatory nations has shifted. Everywhere the influence of American ideas and practices has strengthened, paralleling the United States' rise to world dominance (Cody, 1998). The creation of the Soviet Union in 1917 unleashed a periodically innovative planning tradition, influential to some extent in Western Europe in the 1930s and 1940s and more directly so in Eastern Europe in the third quarter of the century.

Yet planning innovation has not been the exclusive prerogative of world powers. New innovators such as the Netherlands and Scandinavia emerged, to some extent replacing Germany as its influence waned in the Nazi years and their aftermath (e.g. Hall, 1991). Moreover, the decline of formal colonialism since 1945 has been paralleled by a weakening of the direct influence of British and French planning. A neo-colonialism built around foreign aid and international institutions such as the United Nations or the World Bank has, however, perpetuated a mainly (but not entirely) one way flow of planning ideas and practices from the developed to the developing world (e.g. Armstrong, 1987; Okpala, 1990; Sanyal, 1990). The European Union has also tried to play an important role in producing convergence in the planning repertoires of its member states (Williams, 1996).

INTERNATIONAL DIFFUSION AS A HISTORICAL THEME

Not surprisingly, the international character of the twentieth century planning movement has been a strong theme in historical writing. In particular, historians have been obliged to consider how and why planning ideas and practices came to spread between different countries. The best known works in English dealing with this theme are Anthony Sutcliffe's *Towards the Planned City* (1981) and Peter Hall's *Cities of Tomorrow* (1988, revised 1996). In fact, there is a significant volume of other work from many countries dealing to some extent with diffusion. The main concern has been to show how their principal subject, usually a particular city, country or group of countries, encountered key planning ideas or practices from elsewhere. This is apparent, for example, in Freestone (1989), Home (1997), King (1976, 1990), Smets (1977), Watanabe (1980, 1992), Wynn (1984), Yeoh (1996) and Yerolympos (1996).

Another approach to diffusion is that found in Buder (1991), Gold (1997) and Hardy (1991). These works have explored how the ideas and practices of particular planning traditions (namely the garden city and modern movements) have spread to different countries. In other cases the emphasis has been much more the exchange of planning ideas and practices, implying more complex diffusional flows between particular places. We can find this expressed in Albers (1997), Bosma and Hellinga (1997), Hall, P. (1996), Hall, T. (1997), Schubert (1997) and Sutcliffe (1981). It has also been the subject of a major international conference on planning history held in Tokyo in 1988 (TIPHC, 1988).

But, whatever the exact treatment of diffusion, we can identify three major concerns recurring throughout all these studies:

1. The mechanisms of diffusion. For example, key personalities, reformist or professional milieux, intergovernmental actions.

2. The extent to which ideas and practices are changed in their diffusion. How are they applied in specific national settings and why are differences apparent?

3. The fundamental causation of diffusion. For example, how much does it mirror the larger economic, political or cultural contexts of international relations? How far is the 'text' of planning's international diffusion more autonomous or reliant on chance actions?

No universal answers to these questions have emerged from historical studies and planning historians have adopted a variety of perspectives. We can illustrate this by reference to three planning historians whose work has been particularly influential. Thus Peter Hall's narrative, though acknowledging the role of structure and context, is largely one of great men with big ideas that spread because of the potency of message and the charisma and energy of those who carried it. By contrast, Anthony King's explanation rests much more on the global hegemony of Western imperialism, exporting its conception of planning in both the colonial and post-colonial eras. Between these two, Sutcliffe's account of the emergence of urban planning in the great powers of the late nineteenth century acknowledges both the larger impersonal forces and charismatic visionaries. Yet he stresses the critical intermediary role of the reformist and expert milieux, where imported ideas were distilled into locally relevant practices.

It will be immediately clear, however, that these different perspectives are not merely products of the interpretative stances of the historians concerned. They reflect real differences in the experiences of different countries. India's encounters with external planning models, the basis of King's work, were objectively different to those of Western Europe or the United States. In contrast to the pattern of promiscuous borrowing of external models that was typical amongst the latter group, planning in imperial India was externally imposed from one source. Significantly, when he deals with New Delhi, Nairobi or Lusaka, Hall readily acknowledges the central importance of this imperial domination. Here, at least, the ideas of the great men were triumphant because they were imposed by colonial power.

A wider review of writing about countries that were neither the major Western world powers nor their colonies increases this sense of real variety in experiences of diffusion. Thus the planning histories of southern European countries or the smaller countries of north western Europe, of Japan or the self-governing white Dominions of the British Empire typically show a high dependence on externally developed planning models. Yet such models were certainly not imposed in the classic imperial manner, without opportunity for indigenous political discretion. We can go further and note a growing awareness of the many subtleties of colonial planning, between imperial powers, between different parts of their Empires, and over time (e.g. Home, 1997; Wright, 1991). Also, it is clear that post-colonial experiences of planning imported as part of foreign aid, though replicating many features of the colonial era, have differed in some important respects.

These cases underline the general point that diffusion needs to be understood as highly variable, rather than as a single, uniform process. All the major dimensions of diffusion – the agencies and mechanisms by which it occurs, the extent to which ideas and practices are changed and, though it is more a matter of interpretation, its fundamental causation – have shown great diversity. Without denying that there will always be unique features in every episode of diffusion, it is possible (and indeed valuable) to generalize the different varieties.

A TYPOLOGY OF DIFFUSION

The remainder of the chapter elaborates on this general point, drawing widely on relevant historical writing to develop a typology for the diffusion of planning. It consists of a series of 'ideal types' of episodes of diffusion, highlighting salient features and giving some examples that reflect these features. Table 3.1 summarizes the different types. They fall into two distinct groups – 'borrowing' and 'imposition' – each having three types. This grouping thus marks a fundamental distinction between those episodes of diffusion where the 'importing' country has the greater role in shaping and controlling the diffusion process (borrowing) and those where the 'exporting' country is the main determining force (imposition).

As this rather implies, the essential basis of the typology is that of context,

44

Table 3.1 Typology of diffusion.

Type	Indigenous Role	External Role	Typical Mechanisms	Level of Diffusion	Key Actors	Potential for Distinctiveness	Characteristic Examples
Synthetic borrowing	Very high	Very low	Indigenous planning movements plus wide external contacts	Theory and practice	Indigenous	Very high	Major countries of of Western Europe & USA
Selective borrowing	High	Low	External contact with innovative planning traditions	Practice and some theory	Indigenous	High	Smaller countries of Western Europe
Undiluted borrowing	Medium	Medium	Indigenous deference to innovative external planning traditions	Practice with little or no theory	External with some indigenous	Fairly Low	Dominions of British Empire, Japan, & some European examples
Negotiated imposition	Low	High	Dependence on external planning tradition(s)	Practice	External with some indigenous	Low	Aid-dependent countries (e.g. Africa)
Contested imposition	Very low	Very high	High dependence on one external planning tradition	Practice	External	Low	'Enlightened' colonial planning
Authoritarian imposition	None	Total	Total dependence on one external planning tradition	Practice	External	None	Newly subjugated territories

specifically the power relationship between the countries originating and receiving planning models, is always of critical importance. By power relationship is meant simply the degree of domination, however expressed, of the one by the other. The individual types are, of course, rather generalized and certainly do not capture the subtléties of actual diffusion episodes. They merely represent the principal gradations of borrowing and imposition during the twentieth century. Thus the great Western powers, equivalents and rivals rather than deferential to each other, borrowed in creative rather than slavish fashion. Where the sense of deference was greater, then the borrowing became progressively less selective.

As deference graded into dependence, in colonial or post-colonial situations, then the power balance and the diffusional type shifted to imposition. Yet there are degrees of dependence and thus of imposition. In most cases receiving countries have been able to negotiate or contest the process of external imposition, thereby moderating its nature. However, in extreme cases, few in number in this century, dominance has been so complete as to eliminate any hint of indigenous modification. In all such situations the power balance, whether measured in governmental, economic or cultural terms, was very uneven as between the dominated colony and dominant imperial power. Among the rival great Western powers in the early twentieth century, however, the power relationship was more nearly equal.

DIFFUSION BY BORROWING

Synthetic Borrowing

Most familiar is the type of diffusion which has occurred between the main innovative planning traditions. As we have already noted of the early years, the patterns have typically been very open. Each of these innovatory countries drew on several external planning models, while the other innovators for their part borrowed back from them. To a greater extent than in other types of diffusion, the trade in ideas was closer to a state of balance. Before 1914, for example, Britain borrowed heavily from German town extension, zoning and organic approaches to urban design. In turn, the Germans (having already borrowed British public health innovations) looked admiringly on British housing design and, above all, the garden city. The United States, for its part, borrowed German zoning, the British garden city, and the French approach to grand urban design. It gave back to Europe the notion of the city-wide master plan and the grand approach to urban landscape design.

One of the key points about this form of diffusion is that the borrowed external models have typically been filtered through highly developed indigenous reformist movements and professional expertise. This filtering process has tended to deconstruct the models, breaking them down into component elements, and integrating them with planning ideas and practices that are already present. This deconstruction has occurred both consciously and unconsciously, through misunderstanding or partial understanding. In either case, though, the outcome has been that the diffused models were almost never transferred unaltered. Indigenous ideas and ideas already received from other sources were combined with newly-received models to create something distinctive and new. The overall effect was a process of synthetic innovation, with the further possibility that the resultant innovations might themselves be diffused elsewhere.

The history of the neighbourhood unit provides a classic example of how this process operated. The starting point was Britain, with Ebenezer Howard's indicative but barely elaborated concept of the 5000 population ward within his larger formulation of the garden city. It was, however, Clarence Perry in the United States who fashioned it into a workable physical model, sticking to Howard's 5000 population, in the 1920s. These ideas were further elaborated to reflect the growing importance of automobile traffic by Henry Wright and Clarence Stein. Their efforts culminated in the Radburn layout in the late 1920s.

Both ideas then spread back to Western Europe, where they were further overlain with new aspects and meanings. For the moment, Radburn principles were not applied, although there were signs of some German interest, especially in Hermann Jansen's road safety residential plans of the late 1920s (Hass-Klau, 1992). In Britain, however, planners were becoming more concerned with the neighbourhood as a device to promote social cohesion. Increasingly more ambitious objectives, involving a social class mix, were gradually added. Particularly influential was Barry Parker's plan for the Wythenshawe satellite town in Manchester, part of the garden city mainstream. Meanwhile in the Soviet Union there were some innovations that echoed Perry's ideas, though without apparent knowledge of Western developments (Tetlow, 1959). British modernists, in the shape of the MARS (Modern Architectural Research) group, began to experiment with Soviet-influenced neighbourhood ideas in the later 1930s (Gold, 1997). These two strands came together in the 1940s. Neighbourhoods, now with a notional population of up to 10,000, occupied a central place in Britain's wartime and early postwar plans, particularly in the first new towns.

American and British thinking had by then begun to influence planners in Sweden during the early 1940s. As a neutral country, Sweden suffered less wartime privation than other parts of Europe. This allowed it to assume an especially important role in the empirical elaboration of neighbourhood ideas in the immediate postwar years. Accordingly, Swedish experience became extremely important in the physical design of neighbourhoods. By 1947, variants of Radburn layouts were being planned, a few years before their first British use (Parsons, 1992). By 1950, Swedish experiences had also shown that 10,000 was far too low a population for an effective social unit in an affluent society (Sidenbladh, 1964).

Meanwhile, Dutch planners secretly replanning the devastated city of Rotterdam during the Nazi occupation had already come to similar conclusions but for quite different reasons (Lock, 1947). Aware to some extent of pre-war thinking on neighbourhood units but without knowledge of the important Anglo-American developments of the 1940s, the Rotterdam planners had already by 1945 proposed a socially mixed neighbourhood unit of 20,000. This reflected some very specific features of Dutch society, relating to the church's extensive role in social provision. Although planners from other countries, ever fascinated by Rotterdam's reconstruction, soon became aware of this variant of the neighbourhood, it did not seem as generalizable as the Swedish experience.

The most extraordinary aspect of the diffusion of the neighbourhood unit at this time involved its deployment in wartime Nazi Germany. Thus planners in Hamburg particularly made extensive use of a concept called the 'local group as neighbourhood cell' (Schubert, 1995). This reflected the idiosyncrasies of Nazi ideology, yet it also leaned on the Anglo-American concept of the neighbour-hood. In part, this connection reflected pre-war links. Yet there was also a keen awareness of wartime developments in London and other cities. Via neutral Stockholm, the German intelligence services had secured copies of Patrick Abercrombie's plans for London, making them available to Hamburg's chief planner. The similarities ensured that, stripped of their Nazi overtones, they could therefore be perpetuated into the postwar years.

After 1945 all versions of the idea became the subject of even more international cross-fertilization, with Radburn principles being widely adopted and adapted. However enough has been said to show how this synthetic process gave an innovative dimension to diffusion, in circumstances where planning models came into countries which already had highly developed planning traditions.

Selective Borrowing

Where innovatory synthesis of imported and existing ideas and practices has been lacking, diffusion has often taken the form of a rather simpler process of borrowing. A characteristic feature of this non-innovatory borrowing has been a relatively shallow engagement within the importing country with the theoretical and conceptual bases of the borrowed model. This has limited the possibilities of deconstructing the ideas and reassembling them, with other ideas, to make something different. Instead planners in the receiving country have tended, rather atheoretically, to emulate specific aspects of external planning practice in a simple and direct manner.

This is not to say, however, that the borrowing has necessarily been slavish or uncritical. There has often been some degree of selection. Parts of the borrowed model may be discarded if they seem less appropriate. The main point, though, is that the importing country has added nothing significant to what is imported. In turn this offers little that is sufficiently distinctive for other countries to borrow. Yet countries which habitually borrow selectively may sometimes play an important intermediary role, facilitating the movement of innovations between more distinctive (and possibly competitive) planning traditions.

In fact, this type of diffusion episode can be found throughout the century in many different countries. It is, perhaps, most characteristic of the development of planning in the smaller and less powerful Western and Central European countries. These countries would have enjoyed fairly good access to more than one of the major innovative planning traditions. Typically they would also have had reformist movements pressing for planning and substantial indigenous professional expertise. Together these were capable of exercising some discretion over what was borrowed from external planning models. Yet the critical mass needed to innovate in more thoroughgoing fashion was absent.

A good example is Belgium. This small country was not entirely devoid of genuine innovation of international significance. Yet its planning tradition depended heavily on external sources of theory and practice, mainly French, German and British (Smets, 1977). Thus Parisian Haussmannism was emulated in the later nineteenth century (Hall, 1997). The early twentieth century brought growing awareness of the British garden city tradition, implemented through a combination of French-style social housing organizations and the British co-partnership model. More generally, Belgium (along with Switzerland) apparently played significant parts in moving British and German urban reformist ideas into the Francophone world (Claude, 1989). Another case is Norway, where traditional dependence on Swedish design in the early twentieth century was leavened, though not supplanted, by other influences, especially from Britain, the United States, France and the Netherlands (Lorange and Myhre, 1991). Again, however, no significant innovations arose from these borrowings.

Yet it would be incorrect to imply that selective borrowing has occurred only in smaller countries. Although there has always been a strong tendency in the major innovative planning traditions to use imported models in a more adaptive fashion, episodes of selective borrowing can be found everywhere. A recent example would be the rapid adoption throughout the developed world of the American approach to waterfront redevelopment. Pioneered in cities such as Baltimore and Boston in the 1970s, the model had by the 1990s appeared throughout Europe and beyond, with varying (but often very close) correspondence to the originals (Breen and Rigby, 1996).

Overall, however, examples of this type do not negate the main point: if synthetic innovation has been the dominant means of receiving externally generated ideas and practices, the cumulative result will be a national planning tradition that soon becomes distinct. If selective borrowing has been usual, particularly from more than one source, then differences will certainly arise, but more slowly. The cumulative result will also appear as an altogether more derivative planning tradition.

Undiluted Borrowing

This derivative quality has been even more marked where external ideas and practices have been received without conscious selectivity – where the borrowing, in other words, is undiluted. In such cases, the tendency has been to receive not just individual ideas or innovations but substantial packages of planning practice. As this implies, such borrowing has been rather uncritical and frequently with only very limited awareness of the full range of alternative external planning models that are available. In turn, this reflects a rather underdeveloped indigenous planning movement and, quite often, a high reliance on foreign planners to supply leadership. There is a real difference here from previous types, where imported ideas and practices were filtered through indigenous planning movements (and in some cases, intermediate countries).

This diffusional type has been characteristic of countries which exhibit a more general deference to ideas arising in those countries from which they borrow. The relationship between the two parties is therefore markedly more uneven than in the previous two types. Yet we should not exaggerate the aspect of external dependence. This type should be still understood, very definitely, as *borrowing*, clearly implying that the power to make decisions remains in the importing country.

The clearest examples of undiluted borrowing have undoubtedly been the white settled Dominions of the British Empire, whose early encounters with twentieth century planning came largely through the prism of British experience (Ward, 1997). These were self governing by the time modern planning thought and practice developed. Yet they had relatively small populations, underdeveloped reform movements and limited professional resources. When combined with more general ethnic and cultural affinities, these factors created a strong initial dependence on planning models from the imperial homeland. At varying rates, this was then overlain with what, initially at least, was an almost equally uncritical admiration for ideas and practices from the United States.

Canada borrowed uncritically from British planning in the first two decades of the century, to the extent of adopting planning legislation and founding a British-style professional body for planning (Simpson, 1983). Then, in the 1920s, American influences, often copied in an equally direct way, became dominant, coinciding exactly with the American replacement of Britain as the main foreign investor in Canada (Ward, 1999). After 1945, there was a resurgence of British planning (though not economic) influences. Yet external ideas were by then being received in a more critical and selective fashion. Canadian awareness of other European planning traditions, particularly the French, also increased.

There were many similarities between Canada and Australia. In the latter, however, British connections were dominant for much longer (Freestone, 1989; 1997). In part, this reflected the persistence of Australia's economic and cultural ties with Britain. Nor was the American model as conveniently located as it was for Canadian planners, who often found it easier to consult American planners than fellow Canadians. Thus the Australian planning system developed very much in the British image, with extensive British professional leadership. Although there was early awareness of American planning models (most strongly apparent in the chosen plan for the new federal capital at Canberra), it was not until the 1960s that they even began to match the extent of British influence.

Yet we should not see undiluted borrowing as a manifestation only of late imperialism. It could also arise in quite different circumstances, sometimes even in countries with relatively advanced planning traditions. Thus the replanning of the historic French city of Reims, devastated in World War One, became an exercise in scientific American city planning. United States' wartime relief had brought a leading American planner, George B. Ford, on the scene who quickly assumed technical dominance in the reconstruction debate (Bédarida, 1990; Wright, 1991). Ironically, very similar circumstances at almost exactly the same time allowed the French *urbaniste*, Ernest Hébrard, to assume an even more dominant role in the replanning of Thessaloniki in Greece, following its destruction by fire in 1917 (Yerolympos, 1996). The resultant plan was a grand exercise in French urban design. Such uncritical absorption of external models was not usual in either country, however, especially France.

An example of a more habitual uncritical borrowing that did not depend on imperial ties or emergency situations, was early twentieth century Japan. Here Western, especially German, British and American, planning practices were borrowed and applied with a surprising lack of adaptation to Japanese conditions (Hein and Ishida, 1998; Watanabe, 1988, 1992). The context was the rapid modernization of Japan from the later nineteenth century, which encouraged a fairly systematic trawling of the advanced Western countries for progressive practices which could be adopted.

What was particularly striking, however, was the rather imperfect conceptual grasp of the models that were being received. Having only a weakly developed reformist movement and professional skills in planning, the possibilities of conscious selection or synthesis were quite limited. Initially, at least, Western planning was copied quite slavishly, the only adaptations arising unconsciously from misunderstanding. In some aspects, what was borrowed was an even purer version of Western ideas than was actually adopted in the West. The land readjustment proposals incorporated in the first Japanese planning legislation of 1919, for example, were a more radical version of the widely admired German *Lex Adickes* than the German parliament had been prepared to adopt (Ishida, 1988).

Over time Japanese planning began to assume a more distinctive character, not least because Japanese planners, unlike those in Australia, had always looked to the West as a whole. Even so, as late as the 1950s, Tokyo's planners were still directly mimicking a planning model drawn directly from another country

(TMG, 1994). This was the archetypal British metropolitan planning solution, with encircling green belt and planned decentralization. Ironically, the Tokyo plan was very similar to proposals for Sydney adopted a decade earlier and on the point of being substantially abandoned (Winston, 1957). The Japanese plan proved even more short-lived. In both cases the failures reveal the weakness of over reliance on imported models. They failed entirely to grasp political and growth realities that were quite different to those of British cities.

DIFFUSION BY IMPOSITION

The dangers of inappropriate transfers were (and are) much higher when the balance of power is such that the exporting country can exert more control than the importing country over the diffusion process. Thus, instead of authorities in the importing countries deciding themselves what they wish to borrow from foreign planning repertoires, relevant agencies in the exporting countries make the key decisions. This inherently limits the opportunities for local participation in the planning process within the countries receiving planning. Even more than in cases of undiluted borrowing, the importing countries will typically have very underdeveloped planning and reform movements. They will also be heavily, often almost totally, reliant on imported planning expertise. In most cases, of course, imposition is symptomatic of colonial or neo-colonial relationships. Beyond these underlying characteristics, there have been several distinct varieties of diffusion through imposition.

Negotiated Imposition

The post-colonial period for many former colonies in some cases encouraged greater scepticism about external planning ideas. The more affluent and determined former colonies were quickly able to cross that critical divide between imposition and borrowing. In Singapore, for example, the post-independence State constructed a distinctive form of planning that borrowed freely from Western planning practice (Perry, Kong and Yeoh, 1997). The original base was British, yet ideas and practices were seemingly drawn from a variety of sources. They were applied, however, with a relentless discipline rarely matched in the West, inspired by distinctively Asian social and political ideologies.

Yet Singapore was exceptional, not least because of an extraordinary material progress that no other recent ex-colonies have matched. Many other ex-colonies in Asia and, above all, in Africa experienced a mode of diffusion that can be called negotiated imposition. It was characterized by continued dependence on external technical expertise and, often more importantly, material aid. Nominally the independent governments actually took the decisions about the acceptance of external aid and assistance. Yet such was the extent of dependence that the process went beyond borrowing. If these countries wanted the aid, the technical assistance went along with it. The offer could scarcely be refused.

It was a diffusional relationship that perpetuated some aspects of colonialism. At the outset, at least, there were slightly more options. In cases where the transition to independence had been peaceful and without active resentment, planning and aid flowed smoothly from former colonial masters. Thus from the late 1940s many British and French consultants began to find work in former colonies in this way, funded substantially by their own governments or United Nations agencies (e.g. MLCERG, 1997). Independence could also mean seeking aid and expertise from sources other than (or at least, in addition to) former colonial masters. Indonesia, for example, turned sharply away from the Netherlands for fifteen years after independence (van der Heiden, 1988). While maintaining fairly strong connections with Britain, India began to develop other linkages (Evenson, 1989). Its great size and economic and strategic potential gave it a negotiating power in external dealings that few other underdeveloped ex-colonies possessed. Yet smaller countries such as Tanzania also avoided some of the worst features of neo-colonialism by seeking aid and expertise from several countries (Armstrong, 1987).

These developments had implications for the international planning influence of Western countries which had not been formal colonial powers. Here was one of the principal ways in which the international planning influence of the United States grew (Cody, 1998). Yet less dominant affluent countries such as Canada, Australia, the Scandinavian countries and Western Germany, not lately major colonial powers, similarly exported their own conceptions of planning from the 1960s. Countries from the communist bloc sometimes used comparable methods to increase their influence in parts of Africa and Asia.

More recently there has been a growing tendency for international bodies such as the United Nations Centre for Human Settlements (Hàbitat) and the World Bank to play important roles (Okpala, 1990). These have purveyed generalized Western-determined planning and development solutions, premised increasingly on economic liberalization. The disappearance in the 1980s of a communist alternative and the wider effects of global economic change have strengthened this latest variant of imposition. Although at the technical level, the export of foreign planning aid is now being undertaken more sensitively than ever before, with growing emphasis on indigenous expertise, the wider sense of imposition remains very strong. The scope for negotiation, apparently so great in the bright confident morning of independence, has narrowed.

Contested Imposition

Countries where planning has been externally imposed often, though not invariably, have underdeveloped civil societies. This, with the absence of both elective democratic government and indigenous reformist movements, has been a key part of the colonial experience. Yet such formidable obstacles, although they seriously weakened the possibilities of any formal negotiation of what was proposed by colonial powers, did not condemn the recipient population to absolute passivity. A more typical situation within long established colonial empires was indigenous obstruction of externally imposed planning projects. Measures that were particularly repugnant to local interests and sensitivities might well provoke rioting or other forms of protest. More typically, indigenous populations might simply abuse or superimpose their own meanings or customary uses on external planning forms.

The case of colonial Singapore, which has been meticulously documented (Yeoh, 1996), provides a particularly good example of this. A British colony, its highly urbanized character made it an early target for British sanitary and planning ideas. From 1913, when municipal elections were abolished, authority was vested in a nominated body which proved more amenable to the 'progressive' principles of British-style municipal management (undertaken by British professionals). Yet this apparent authoritarianism was actually rather more subtle in operation. Nominations included a growing number of the indigenous population. This approach gave influence to those Europeanized Singaporeans who could be expected broadly to support the British town planning model. At the same time they also had to mediate between the indigenous population as a whole and colonial authority. In effect, this usually meant trying to contain opposition.

Reality, however, was more complex. Wholesale zoning powers sought for the Singapore Improvement Trust founded in 1927 were compromised by property interests of all races. However, there was strong and persistent Asian opposition by both owners and occupiers to the more modest proposals to open up what to British eyes were congested districts. Similarly attempts effectively to anglicize public space by limiting street trade proved practically impossible to enforce. Conflicts were particularly strong where planning proposals affected indigenous sacred spaces.

The pattern in French colonies, at least showpieces such as Morocco or Indo-China, was supposed to be different (Wright, 1991). By the time of World War One, the official imperial ideology had become an enlightened approach called 'associationism'. In planning terms, this involved modern colonial built forms, yet planned in styles that were supposed to defer to indigenous culture. Moreover they were developed as new settlements alongside indigenous traditional communities, without any direct intention to replace them. The rigid racial segregation that was typical of British imperial planning was also rejected. The intention was that the indigenous population would gradually realize the superiority of the new settlements, planned by leading French *urbanistes*, and increasingly use and occupy these spaces themselves. It promised, at least, a different social geography to that of the British colonial city, which rested on the separatist concept of the 'dual mandate' (Home, 1997).

Yet the French strategy also acknowledged the potential tensions with the colonized peoples and sought to avoid them, though without actually involving indigenous viewpoints. Despite physical results that were often impressive, the overall outcomes scarcely lived up to the ideals. Invariably the financial benefits of these planned urban developments went overwhelmingly to French interests. Only small numbers of the indigenous elite were able to embrace fully the spirit of 'associationism'. And, though it took different forms, colonial planning was challenged, actively and passively, by the majority of indigenous people. Thus in Indo-China, enlightened *urbanisme* could not tame the rising indigenous challenge to the colonizers in major cities such as Saigon and Hanoi. Around Moroccan cities such as Casablanca, burgeoning indigenous *bidonvilles* (shack communities) were soon challenging the colonial planning process.

As the case of Indo-China shows, the contesting of externally imposed planning was an integral part of a much wider process of challenging imperial dependence. This link with struggles for national self-determination confers a wider resonance on the planning history of these countries. It contains, too, some faint glimmerings of that conscious exercise of critical selectivity that was the hallmark of diffusion in the Western heartlands of planning innovation and their immediate neighbours.

Authoritarian Imposition

The most acute type of imposition has occurred in situations of extreme repression. Characteristic of this type of diffusion would be externally imposed planning proposals and methods of enforcement which grant few if any concessions to established indigenous interests. This can sometimes lead to a curious phenomenon whereby 'purer' expressions of one country's planning approach may appear elsewhere, in lands appropriated as colonies. Invariably, conquering powers are far less compromised in overriding indigenous democratic or property rights than in the imperial homeland.

Perhaps the most extreme example of this phenomenon was the short-lived Nazi replanning of the provinces of Poland incorporated into the German Reich in the early 1940s (Fehl, 1992). Seeking to impose a new regional order, the planners of the SS (amongst them the geographer Walter Christaller) adopted a version of Ebenezer Howard's social city that had been entirely stripped of its original social reformist meanings. In this form it became the basis for a new Germanic ethnic template, to be implemented by seizure of indigenous property, forced depopulation, slave labour, and extermination. Jews alone suffered such wholesale dispossession within Germany proper, where most existing property rights were treated more respectfully.

Another example was the imposition of Japanese notions of planning (in effect, the rather imperfectly assimilated pastiche of Western planning ideas) on its colonies, Taiwan, Korea and Manchuria (Hein, 1998). Again, such planning efforts were frequently far more interventionist than anything undertaken in the imperial homeland. Thus Taiwan had building controls from 1895 and housing laws from 1900, well in advance of comparable developments in Japan. By the 1930s, land readjustment in the Japanese colonies was also being undertaken in a far more draconian fashion, without compensation, than would have been tolerated in Japan itself.

There were comparable episodes of planning in other colonial settings. Thus the early planning of Algeria, though skilfully undertaken by French military engineers, was a heavy handed exercise of imperial power, without concession to indigenous society or culture (Malverti and Picard, 1991). Similar charges have been laid against the British, especially in the most grandiose exercises in imperial planning such as New Delhi (Irving, 1981). Yet extreme authoritarianism, without reference to indigenous sentiments, has actually been quite rare in twentieth century colonial planning. As we have seen, indigenous populations were not usually meekly accepting of these alien forms of planning, imposed through imperial power.

CONCLUSIONS AND SPECULATIONS

Amongst the impositional forms of diffusion, context – the power relationship between the 'exporter' and the 'importer' of planning – has clearly assumed the central role in shaping the diffusion experience. The relationship was absolute in authoritarian imposition but increasingly modified by other factors as we ascend the categories in table 3.1. Effectively, the influence of context would tend to increase as the power relationship between the originating and receiving countries became more uneven. Where the power relationship was more even or favoured the receiving country, however, indigenous reformist milieux could be expected to play a more important and autonomous role, often adapting what was imported. Further down table 3.1, however, the likelihood of adaptation was much lower. There was instead a stronger likelihood that purer versions of the exported model might appear than had been found in its country of origin.

The role of individuals as independent variables in the diffusion process remains less amenable to generalization, however. Key individuals could become significant if not primary determinants in all diffusion types. Clearly, though, the way they could exert influence would vary according to context. The more authoritarian nature of colonial power probably gave the individuals in whom that power was vested the greatest scope to shape outcomes. Where indigenous reformism was more established, the extent of the individual's role would depend on the persuasive appeal of his/her proposals, particularly within reformist and professional milieux.

A more human way of expressing this explanatory problem is to go back to the story in the introduction. If Cerdà *had* sold his work to Haussmann, or at least made greater efforts to promote his pioneering *Teoría* outside Spain, perhaps the course of international planning history might have been different. Barcelona might have become a mecca of late nineteenth century planning, alongside Paris, Frankfurt, Birmingham and Chicago. On the other hand, it is doubtful whether one individual can ever surmount the limits imposed by context. Spain's terminal decline as a world power in the late nineteenth century would almost certainly have prejudiced reformers in other countries against adopting any Spanish ideas, whatever their intrinsic merits. It certainly ruled out colonial demonstrations of the kind that played such a key part in the international spread of British and French planning during the twentieth century.

Today, paradoxically, Barcelona's planning and other lessons are being widely studied, borrowed and, to varying degrees, adapted in both the post-industrial and Hispanic developing worlds (Borja, 1996). The context has now shifted to remarkable global economic success, underpinned by progressive reformism and dazzling professional expertise. Cerdà's modern equivalent has been the city's charismatic and visionary recent Mayor, Pasqual Maragall. Unlike Cerdà, however, Maragall has played on the world stage, importing and adapting external planning models (for example, from Baltimore) and, even more, promoting the international spread of the Barcelona model.

Now, of course, we accept globalization as a reality of everyday life. The jet airliner, satellite telecommunications, and the internet have accelerated an internationalization of information that was originally made possible by the steamship, the railway, the mechanized printing press, the postal service, and the telegraph. Throughout the world the lessons of Barcelona (or indeed any other admired planning model) can today be examined more conveniently than ever before. Even past, unrecognized lessons can finally be diffused – Cerdà would doubtless be astonished to learn that it is now possible to buy video cassettes with commentaries in several languages, explaining his great plan for the *Eixample.*

Despite all this, the likelihood is that, in most respects, the diffusion of planning will continue as before. Modern communications certainly allow borrowing to be more rapid, more comprehensive, and less spatially bounded. Yet the process is being driven (as it always was to some extent) by economic imperatives. Throughout the world, cities are now exposed to the full rigours of global market forces. Their leaders seek planning models from successful cities everywhere in the continual battle to win or retain highly mobile international capital. In Beirut, for example, now rebuilding itself after a destructive civil war to regain its role as the Middle East's main international centre, planners have quite deliberately drawn on the widest possible range of Western planning expertise and models (Gavin and Maluf, 1996). Despite occasional echoes of French colonial links, this borrowing process is, however, largely orchestrated by Lebanese interests.

More generally, the effective ending of all but the final vestiges of formal colonialism in the last years of the century may perhaps reduce the extent of impositional diffusion. We may, at least, see a shift to more negotiative forms than have been typical for much of the twentieth century. Yet colonialism continues to cast a long shadow of dependence over the poorest parts of the world, especially in Africa. For many countries, saddled with huge external debt burdens and lacking sufficient indigenous reformist and professional resources, diffusion will necessarily continue to be an externally-determined process. Nor is it certain even that the more authoritarian forms of imposition have entirely gone. Thus the chronic instability of post-imperial or post-communist nationalism in disputed regions of the Balkans and Middle East is bringing a reordering of settlement, enforced by military power.

Yet, while such trends are regrettable, there is also an emergent type of impositional diffusion by consent that can be welcomed. The European Union is the clearest example, where powerful affluent countries have lately begun to defer (rhetorically, at least) to mutually agreed models for environmental management and planning that transcend the nation state. Such initiatives recall the spirit of internationalism that characterized many European planning movements at the beginning of the twentieth century. There are much weaker signs that the same spirit has also found global expression in the recent Earth Summits. If (and this is a very big 'if') tangible achievement follows, then one of the promises of twentieth century planning may finally be fulfilled. Whether or not this occurs, however, there is much about how planning diffusion occurs that will not change. Fundamentally, it will continue to be shaped by the endlessly fascinating mix of context, reformist and professional milieux, and individual action that largely determined its course during the twentieth century.

ACKNOWLEDGEMENT

My thanks to my colleague Roger Zetter for advice on literature on aid-related planning.

REFERENCES

Albers, G. (1997) *Zur Enwicklung der Stadtplanung in Europa: Begegnungen, Einflüsse, Verflechtungen.* Wiesbaden: Vieweg.
Armstrong, A. (1987) Tanzania's expert-led planning: An assessment. *Public Administration and Development*, 7, pp. 261-271.
Barker, J.M. (ed.) (1997) *Old Institutions – New Images.* Proceedings of the International Conference, John Curtin International Institute, Perth: Curtin University.
Bédarida, M. (1990) La 'renaissance des cités' et la mission de Geo B. Ford, in Gaudin, J. P. (ed.) *Villes Réfléchies: Histoire et Actualité des Cultures Professionelles dans l'Urbanisme.* Dossiers des Seminaires, Techniques, Territoires et Societes, no. 11/12, Paris: Délégation à la Recherche et à l'Innovation, Ministère de l'Equipement, du Logement, des Transports et de la Mer, pp. 33-42.
Borja, J. (ed.) (1996) *Barcelona: An Urban Transformation Model 1980-1995.* Urban Management Series Volume 8. Quito: Urban Management Programme.

Bosma, K. and Hellinga, H. (eds.) (1997) *Mastering the City 1: North-European City Planning 1900-2000*. Rotterdam: NAI Publishers/EFL Publications.

Breen, A and Rigby, D. (1996) *The New Waterfront: A Worldwide Success Story*. London: Thames and Hudson.

Buder, S. (1991) *Visionaries and Planners: The Garden City Movement and the Modern Community*. New York: Oxford University Press.

Claude, V. (1989) Sanitary engineering as a path to town planning: The singular role of the *Association générale des hygiénistes et techniciens municipaux* in France and the French-speaking countries, 1900-1920. *Planning Perspectives*, **4**, pp. 153-66.

Cody, J. (1998) Private Hands and Public Gloves: Options for globalizing US planners, 1945-1975, in Freestone (ed.), pp. 95-100.

Collins, G.R. and Collins, C.C. (1965) *Camillo Sitte and the Birth of Modern City Planning*. London: Phaidon.

Estapé, F. (1996) Ildefons Cerdà i Sunyer, in Palà, M. and Subirós, O. (eds.) *1856-1999 Contemporary Barcelona Contemporánea*. Centre de Cultura Contemporània de Barcelona: Barcelona, pp. 53-55.

Evenson, N. (1989) *The Indian Metropolis: A View Toward the West*. New Haven: Yale University Press.

Fehl, G. (1992) The Nazi Garden City, in Ward, S.V. (ed.) *The Garden City: Past, Present and Future*. London: E & FN Spon, pp. 88-106.

Freestone, R. (1989) *Model Communities: The Garden City Movement in Australia*. Melbourne: Nelson.

Freestone, R. (1997) The British connection: Convergence, divergence and cultural identity in Australian urban planning history, in Barker (ed.), pp. 61-70.

Freestone, R. (ed.) (1998) *The Twentieth Century Urban Planning Experience: Proceedings of the 8th International Planning History Society Conference and 4th Australian Planning/Urban History Conference*. Sydney: University of New South Wales.

Gavin, A. and Maluf, R. (1996) *Beirut Reborn: The Restoration and Development of the Central District*. London: Academy Editions.

Gold, J.R. (1997) *The Experience of Modernism: Modern Architects and the Future City 1928-1953*. London: E & FN Spon.

Hall, P. (1996) *Cities of Tomorrow: An Intellectual History of Urban Planning and Design in the Twentieth Century*. Updated edition. Oxford: Blackwell.

Hall, T. (ed.) (1991) *Planning and Urban Growth in the Nordic Countries*. London: E & FN Spon.

Hall, T. (1997) *Planning Europe's Capital Cities: Aspects of Europe's Nineteenth Century Urban Development*. London: E & FN Spon.

Hardy, D. (1991) *From Garden Cities to New Towns: Campaigning for Town and Country Planning , 1899-1946*. London: E & FN Spon.

Hass-Klau, C. (1992) *The Pedestrian and City Traffic*. London: Belhaven.

Hein, C. (1998) Japan and the transformation of planning ideas: Some examples of colonial plans, in Freestone (ed.), pp. 352-357.

Hein, C. and Ishida, Y. (1998) Japanische Stadtplanung und ihre deutsche Wurzeln. *Die Alte Stadt*. **3**, pp. 189-211.

Home, R. (1997) *Of Planting and Planning: The Making of British Colonial Cities*. London: E & FN Spon.

Irving, R.G. (1981) *Indian Summer: Lutyens, Baker and Imperial Delhi*. New Haven: Yale University Press.

Ishida, Y. (1988) Some Failures in the Transference of Western Planning Systems to Japan, in TIPHC, pp. 543-555.

King, A.D. (1976) *Colonial Urban Development: Culture, Social Power and Environment*. London: Routledge.

King, A.D. (1990) *Urbanism, Colonialism and the World-Economy: Cultural and Spatial Foundations of the World Economic System*. London: Routledge.

Lock, M. (1947) *Reconstruction in the Netherlands: An Account of a Visit to Post-War Holland by Members of the Town Planning Institute*. London: Jason.

Lorange, E. and Myhre, E. (1991) Urban Planning in Norway, in Hall, T. (ed.), pp. 116-166.

Malverti, X. and Picard, A. (1991) Algeria: Military genius and civic design. *Planning Perspectives*, **6**, pp. 207-236.

MLCERG (Max Lock Centre Exhibition Research Group) (1996) *Max Lock 1909-1988: People and Planning. An Exhibition of His Life and Work*. London: University of Westminster.

Okpala, D.C.I. (1990) The roles and influences of external assistance in the planning, development and management of African human settlements systems. *Third World Planning Review*, **12**, pp. 205-229.

Parsons, K.C. (1992) American influence on Stockholm's post World War II suburban expansion. *Planning History*, **14**(1), pp. 3-14.

Perry, M., Kong. L. and Yeoh, B. (1997) *Singapore: A Developmental City State*. Chichester: John Wiley.

Sanyal, B. (1990) Knowledge transfer from poor to rich cities: A new turn of events. *Cities*, **7**, pp. 31-36.

Schubert, D. (1995) Origins of the neighbourhood unit idea in Great Britain and Germany: Examples from London and Hamburg. *Planning History*, **17**(3), pp. 32-40.

Schubert, D. (1997) *Stadterneuerung in London und Hamburg: Eine Stadtebaugeschichte zwischen Modernisieriung und Disziplinierung*. Wiesbaden: Vieweg.

Sidenbladh, G. (1964) Planning Problems in Stockholm, in Planning Commission of the City of Stockholm, *Stockholm Regional and City Planning*. Stockholm: Planning Commission of the City of Stockholm, pp. 55-64.

Simpson, M.A. (1983) *Thomas Adams and the Modern Planning Movement: Britain, Canada and the United States, 1920-1940*. London: Mansell.

Smets, M. (1977) *L'Avènement de la Cité-Jardin en Belgique: Histoire de l'Habitat Social en Belgique de 1830 à 1930*. Bruxelles: Pierre Mardaga.

Sutcliffe, A. (1981) *Towards the Planned City: Germany, Britain, the United States and France, 1780-1914*. Oxford: Blackwell.

Tetlow, J.D. (1959) Sources of the neighbourhood idea. *Journal of the Town Planning Institute*, **45,** pp. 113-5.

TIPHC (Third International Planning History Conference) (1988) *The History of International Exchange of Planning Systems*. Tokyo: City Planning Institute of Japan/ Planning History Group.

TMG (Tokyo Metropolitan Government) (1994) *A Hundred Years of Tokyo City Planning*. TMG Municipal Library no 28. Tokyo: TMG.

van der Heiden, C.N. (1988) Foreign influence on Dutch planning doctrine, in TIPHC, pp. 89-112.

Ward, S.V. (1997) A paradoxical persistence? British influences on Canadian and Australian urban planning, in Barker (ed.), pp. 51-60.

Ward, S.V. (1999) The international diffusion of planning: A review and a Canadian case study. *International Planning Studies*, **4**, pp. 53-77.

Watanabe, S.J. (1980) Garden City Japanese style: The case of Den-en Toshi Company Ltd, 1918-1928, in Cherry, G.E. (ed.), *Shaping an Urban World*. London: Mansell, pp. 129-143.

60   Urban Planning in a Changing World

Watanabe, S.J. (1988) Japanese vs Western urban images: Western influences on the Japanese architectural profession, 1910-1920s, in TIPHC, pp. 568-84.

Watanabe S.J. (1992) The Japanese Garden City, in Ward (ed.), pp. 69-87.

Williams, R.H. (1996) *European Union Spatial Policy and Planning*. London: Paul Chapman.

Winston, D. (1957) *Sydney's Great Experiment*. Sydney: Angus and Robertson.

Wright, G. (1991) *The Politics of Design in French Colonial Urbanism*. Chicago: Chicago University Press.

Wynn, M. (ed.) (1984) *Planning and Urban Growth in Southern Europe*. London: Mansell.

Yeoh, B.S.A. (1996) *Contesting Space: Power Relations and the Urban Built Environment in Colonial Singapore*. Kuala Lumpur: Oxford University Press.

Yerolympos, A. (1996) *Urban Transformations in the Balkans (1920-1920): Aspects of Balkan Town Planning and the Making of Thessaloniki*. Thessaloniki: University Studio Press.

Name Index